The SAGE
Handbook of

International
Marketing

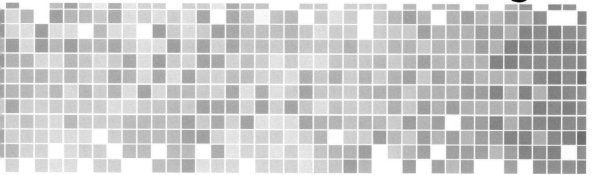

The SAGE
Handbook of

International
Marketing

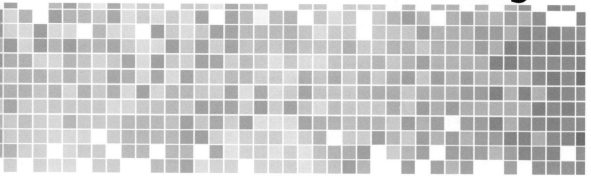

Edited by

Maasaki Kotabe
and Kristiaan Helsen

Los Angeles • London • New Delhi • Singapore • Washington DC

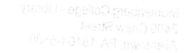

First published 2009

SAGE Publications Ltd
1 Oliver's Yard
55 City Road
London EC1Y 1SP

SAGE Publications Inc.
2455 Teller Road
Thousand Oaks, California 91320

SAGE Publications India Pvt Ltd
B1/I 1, Mohan Cooperative Industrial Area
Mathura Road
New Delhi 110 044

SAGE Publications Asia-Pacific Pte Ltd
33 Pekin Street # 02-01
Far East Square, Singapore 048763

Library of Congress Control Number: 2008925349

British Library Cataloguing in Publication data

A catalogue record for this book is available from the British Library

ISBN 978-1-4129-3428-2

Typeset by CEPHA Imaging Pvt. Ltd., Bangalore, India
Printed in Great Britain by The Cromwell Press, Trowbridge, Wiltshire
Printed on paper from sustainable resources

Contents

About the Contributors

Preet S. Aulakh is the Pierre Lassonde Chair in International Business and Director of the PhD Program at the Schulich School of Business, York University, Toronto, Canada. He received his PhD from the University of Texas at Austin. His research focuses on structuring and managing international alliances and partnerships, international technology licensing, and internationalization of firms from emerging economies. His research has been published in journals such as *Academy of Management Journal*, *Journal of International Business Studies*, *Journal of Marketing*, *Organization Science*, among others.

Gary Bamossy is a Professor in the Marketing Group at the McDonough School of Business, Georgetown University. He was Professor of Marketing at the Vrije Universiteit in Amsterdam from 1985 to 1999 and Director of the Global Business Program at the University of Utah prior to coming to Georgetown in 2005. His research looks at the global diffusion of material culture, and he is co-author of *Consumer Behaviour: A European Perspective*, 4th edn., 2009 (Pearson/Prentice-Hall).

Daniel C. Bello (PhD, Michigan State University) is the Marketing Roundtable Research Professor in the Department of Marketing at Georgia State University. Previously, he was on the faculty at the University of Notre Dame and held management positions in the Product Development Group at Ford Motor Company. His research interests include distribution strategy in domestic and international channel systems. He has published widely in professional journals such as *Journal of Marketing*, *Journal of the Academy of Marketing Science*, *Journal of International Business Studies* and *Journal of Business Research*, among others. Currently, he serves as Marketing Editor (2007–2010) of the *Journal of International Business Studies*. Previously, he served as Editor-in-Chief (2003–2007) of the *Journal of International Marketing*. He also has served, or serves, on the Editorial Review Boards of the *Journal of Marketing*, *Journal of the Academy of Marketing Science*, *Journal of International Marketing* and *Journal of Business Research*.

Robert Bird is an Assistant Professor of Legal Studies at the University of Connecticut. Robert received his JD and MBA from Boston University. Before joining academia full-time, Robert practiced civil litigation and legal research in Connecticut. He has served as a clerk for the Connecticut Appellate Court, the US Bankruptcy Court, and the Massachusetts Superior Court. His research interests include employment law and international intellectual property law, including compulsory licensing and foreign direct investment. Guest lectures include presentations at Indiana University, University of Texas, New York University, and the United Nations. In 2003, he received the Junior Faculty of the Year award from the Academy of Legal Studies in Business. He has published research articles in the *American Business Law Journal*, *Boston University International Law Journal*, *Cincinnati Law Review*, *Kentucky Law Journal*, and the *Trademark Reporter*.

Thomas Brashear-Alejandro (PhD, Georgia State University) is an Associate Professor of Marketing at the University of Massachusetts Amherst. His work focuses on international marketing, sales management, business to business marketing and strategic marketing. Tom has published his work in the *Journal of the Academy of Marketing Science, Journal of Business Research, European Journal of Marketing, Journal of Business and Industrial Marketing* and the *Journal of Personal Selling and Sales Management*. He is on the Editorial Board of the *Journal of Business Research* and served as guest editor for the *Journal of Business and Industrial Marketing* and for a special edition of *Journal of Personal Selling and Sales Management* on international sales management. Tom has served as a visiting professor at the Universidade Pontificia Catolica in Rio de Janeiro and Fundacão Dom Cabral in Belo Horizonte, Brazil.

Forrest Briggs is an Atlanta native and a doctoral student at Georgia State University. His research interests include marketing to consumers at the bottom of the pyramid as well as personal selling and sales management. He is an academic member of the American Marketing Association and other professional associations.

Keith D. Brouthers is Professor of Business Strategy at King's College London, University of London. He is ranked among the world's leading scholars in international entry mode, international management, and Central and Eastern European research. Keith's research has been published in leading academic journals including *Strategic Management Journal, Journal of Management, Journal of International Business Studies, Journal of Management Studies, Management International Review, International Business Review, Thunderbird International Business Review, Long Range Planning, Journal of Business Research,* and *Entrepreneurship Theory and Practice.*

Lance Eliot Brouthers is Professor of Western Hemispheric Trade at The University of Texas at El Paso. He has published over 80 authored articles, proceedings and book chapters on international business strategy, the international business environment and international entrepreneurship.

Julien Cayla is a Lecturer in Marketing at the Australian School of Business. His research program is an attempt to integrate anthropological theories and methodologies to the study of marketing in the global marketplace. Julien received his PhD in 2003 from the University of Colorado. His thesis examined the way companies learn about culture in the context of their work with ad agencies. This work received the prestigious Alden Clayton Prize from the Marketing Science Institute as well as the Sheth Foundation Best Doctoral Dissertation Prize. His most recent work on Asian brands is forthcoming in the *Journal of Consumer Research.*

Yi Chen Cathy is Assistant Professor of Marketing at the Lee Kong Chian School of Business at Singapore Management University. She received a PhD in marketing from Anderson School of Management, University of California, Los Angeles. She holds a BA from Huazhong University of Science and Technology and an MA from University of International Business and Economics, Beijing. Her research areas include Nation Equity, Emotions in Consumer Decision-making, Promotion, Reference Price and Culture. She has previously published in *Journal of Consumer Research.* Before joining academia, she worked in the telecommunications industry in China in international marketing.

Raveendra Chittoor is an Associate Professor in the strategic management group at the Indian Institute of Management Calcutta, India. His research focuses primarily on issues related to entrepreneurship, emerging economies and internationalization of firms from India and has been published or accepted for publication by international journals such as *Organization Science, Family Business Review* and *Journal of International Management.* He regularly presents his research at annual meetings of Academy of Management and Academy of International Business.

Terry Clark is Professor and Chair in the Marketing Department at Southern Illinois University, Carbondale, where he teaches Marketing Strategy and Global Marketing in the undergraduate, MBA and PhD programs. Prior to joining SIU, he was on the faculty of the Goizueta Business School of Emory University (1993–1999), and the College of Business at the University of Notre Dame (1986–1993). He is also Director of Barking Dawg Productions, the Marketing/Advertising arm of Southern Illinois University, Carbondale, in which capacity he has responsibility for building, crafting, and general stewardship of 'Brand SIU'.

Paul D'Angelo is Assistant Director of Elderhostel International and Study Abroad in the School of Social Work at SIU. In those capacities, he is involved with social development and social policy issues related to poverty alleviation, HIV-AIDS, multicultural aspects of health care, international adoption and the application of information communication technologies in addressing social problems, around the world. His interests include global health policy, law, and gerontology.

Marnik G. Dekimpe (PhD, University of California, Los Angeles) is Research Professor of Marketing at Tilburg University (The Netherlands) and Professor of Marketing at the Catholic University Leuven (Belgium). He is also an Academic Trustee with the Marketing Science Institute. His work has been published in *Marketing Science, Management Science,* the *Journal of Marketing Research,* the *Journal of Marketing,* the *International Journal of Research in Marketing* and the *Journal of Econometrics,* among others. His current research interests deal with understanding the hard-discounter phenomenon, the impact of product-harm crises, the drivers of private-label success, the internationalization of retail firms, and the measurement of long-run marketing effects.

Desislava Dikova is an Assistant Professor at the University of Groningen, the Netherlands. In her doctoral dissertation, she examined foreign direct investment modes in the transitional economies of Central and Eastern Europe, and focused on their performance implications. Her current research interests include international market entry and establishment modes, pre-acquisition processes, and strategic fit models. Prior to embarking on an academic career, Dr. Dikova worked briefly for the Bulgarian Ministry of Agriculture and Forestry (in Sofia) and the European Commission's Directorate General for Regional Policy (in Brussels).

Jonathan Doh is Herbert Rammrath Chair in International Business, founding Director of the Center for Global Leadership, and Associate Professor of Management at the Villanova School of Business. His research centers on international strategy and corporate responsibility. He has authored more than 35 refereed articles, 20 chapters in scholarly edited volumes, and 50 conference papers on topics such as strategy for emerging markets, global corporate responsibility, and corporate–NGO relations. He is co-author or editor of five books, including *Multinationals and Development* (with A. Rugman, 2008, Yale University Press). He received his PhD from George Washington University in strategic and international management.

Mark Elsner is a Visiting Research Scholar at Leeds School of Business, University of Colorado and Doctoral Candidate at the Department of Marketing, University of Mainz.

He studied economics and communication science in Mainz and Madrid and worked in consulting before becoming a scientic fellow in Mainz. He is a lecturer for several masters' degree courses in marketing strategy and an advisor for diploma theses. His research interest lies in the investigation of the impact of consumer generated content in the Internet, electronic word of mouth, and the influence of the Internet on global competitive interplay and price wars.

Georges Enderle is John T. Ryan Jr. Professor of International Business Ethics at the Mendoza College of Business, University of Notre Dame, and a former President of the International Society of Business, Economics, and Ethics (2001–2004). Educated in Philosophy (Munich), Theology (Lyon), Economics (Fribourg), and Business Ethics (St. Gallen), he has extensive research and teaching experiences in Europe, the United States, and China and is the author or editor of 18 books, including *Developing Business Ethics in China* (2006), *Business Students Focus on Ethics* (2000), *International Business Ethics* (1999), *Handlungsorientierte Wirtschaftsethik* (Action-oriented Business Ethics 1993), *and Lexikon der Wirtschaftsethik* (German Encyclopedia of Business Ethics 1993).

Katrijn Gielens (PhD, Catholic University Leuven, Belgium) is Associate Professor of Marketing at the University of North Carolina at Chapel Hill. Her work has been published in the *Journal of Marketing Research,* the *Journal of Marketing*, the *Journal of Consumer Research*, and the *International Journal of Research in Marketing*. Her current research interests deal with private-label tiers, the introduction of new products, the internationalization of retail firms, and price promotion effects.

Michael Grund is Professor for Marketing and Head of the Center for Marketing at the University of Applied Sciences (HWZ) in Zürich. After obtaining a degree in Marketing, Logistics and Psychology at the University in Mannheim (Germany), Michael started work as doctoral student and research fellow at the European Business School (Germany) and the University of Basel (Switzerland). After obtaining his PhD in Marketing, he spent several years in the telecommunications industry in Switzerland before joining HWZ in 2006. His research focuses on globalization, global competition, international competition and quality competition. He is currently working on a series of cross-national and -continental comparisions of competitive conduct and focus.

Terrence Guay is Clinical Associate Professor of International Business at Pennsylvania State University's Smeal College of Business. His research focuses on the competition between governments, international organizations, NGOs, and other non-state actors to shape business behavior and the international business environment. He has published two books and several articles and book chapters on the effects of government policies on the global defense industry; cooperation and competition in transatlantic economic relations; the impact of economic sanctions on international business; NGOs and corporate codes of conduct; corporate social responsibility; and corporate political strategy. He received his PhD from Syracuse University.

Oliver Heil is the Chaired Professor of Marketing at Mainz. He studied economics at Bonn, econometrics at University of Pennsylvania and marketing at the Wharton School. He taught at Indiana University's Kelly School, at UCLA's AGSM and at HKUST. He researches signaling, global competition, price wars, over-acting, antitrust, luxuries, crises, reputation, and Internet competition. He has served and will serve as co-editor (Special Issue on Competition) for *International Journal of Research in Marketing,* as Editorial Board member/reviewer for Journals such as *JMR, JM, IJRM, Marketing Science*, and *Management Science*. His papers have appeared in leading academic and professional journals. He has received awards from MSI, EMAC, Schmalenbach, DFG, IRA, DAAD, and has won a best research paper award. He also serves as a trustee at MSI. Oliver's latest book is on competitive crisis management.

Kristiaan Helsen is an associate professor of marketing at the Hong Kong University of Science and Technology. He holds a PhD in marketing from the University of Pennsylvania. His research has appeared in the *Journal of Marketing Research*, the *Journal of Marketing*, *Marketing Science*, and the *Journal of the Academy of Marketing Science*, among others. He is also co-author (with Masaaki Kotabe) of *Global Marketing Management*, a textbook on international marketing. He is a member of the editorial board of the *International Journal of Research in Marketing*. Research interests include duration modeling, product harm crises, international marketing, and product diffusion.

Monica A. Hodis is a doctoral candidate in Marketing at Southern Illinois University, Carbondale. She has a BS in Economics (Management) from the West University of Timisoara, Romania, and an MBA from Southern Illinois University, Carbondale. Her research interests include dysfunctional consumer behavior, vicarious learning in online environments, IM and social networking, and the role of emotions in advertising. Her research has appeared in the *Journal of International Management*.

Andrew Inkpen is the Seward Chair in Global Strategy at Thunderbird. His research addresses various aspects of international management and strategy, including the management of joint ventures and alliances, international knowledge transfer, and interfirm trust. His research has been published in various journals, including *Strategic Management Journal*, *Academy of Management Review*, *Organizational Science*, *California Management Review* and *Journal of International Business Studies*.

Subhash C. Jain is a Professor of International Business, Director of the Center for International Business Education and Research (CIBER), and the Director of the GE Global Learning Center, at the School of Business, University of Connecticut. He is the author of more than 100 publications, including nine books. He holds a PhD and an MBA from the University of Oregon; and a B.Com and M.Com from the University of Rajasthan (India). He has presented seminars both in the United States and abroad on various topics including global marketing strategy, export strategy and global business negotiations. He serves as a consultant to different companies and governments worldwide.

Johny K. Johansson is the McCrane/Shaker Professor of International Business and Marketing, McDonough School of Business, Georgetown University, where he specializes in international marketing strategy. He is a graduate of the Stockholm School of Economics and University of California at Berkeley. He has conducted seminars at institutions worldwide including Stanford, INSEAD and Hitotsubashi, and executive seminars for multinational companies, including General Electric, Honda and Beiersdorff. He is the author of *Global Marketing* (4th edn), and co-author of *Relentless: The Japanese Way of Marketing*. His most recent book is *In Your Face: How American Marketing Excess Fuels Anti-Americanism*, (Financial Times/Prentice-Hall, 2004).

Constantine S. Katsikeas is the Arnold Ziff Research Chair in Marketing and International Management and the Marketing Department Chair at Leeds University Business School. His main research interests focus on international marketing and purchasing, competitive strategy, and collaborative exchange relationships. He has published widely in these fields and articles of his have appeared in *Journal of Marketing, Organization Sciences, Strategic Management Journal, Journal of the Academy of Marketing Science, Decision Sciences, Journal of International Business Studies, Journal of International Marketing* and other journals.

Sonia Ketkar is Assistant Professor of International Business in the College of Business and Economics at Towson University. Prior to joining Towson in 2006, she received her PhD in Business Administration (International Business) from Temple University. She teaches courses in international trade, investment and multinational strategy. She has worked on research papers on outsourcing, foreign entry, foreign exit, subsidiary strategy and divestiture decisions. She has also presented her research at leading management and international business conferences.

Gary A. Knight (PhD, Michigan State University) is Associate Professor and Director of International Business at Florida State University. He has authored numerous articles in the *Journal of International Business Studies, Journal of World Business, Management International Review* and elsewhere. He has co-authored three books, including *International Business*, (1st edn), published by Prentice-Hall. He has extensive experience in international business in the private sector. He has won several awards for research and teaching, including best teacher in the MBA program and the Hans Thorelli 5-Year Award for his article 'Entrepreneurship and Strategy: The SME Under Globalization'.

Masaaki 'Mike' Kotabe holds the Washburn Chair Professorship in International Business and Marketing at the Fox School of Business and Management at Temple University. He received his PhD from Michigan State University. Prior to joining Temple University in 1998, he was Ambassador Edward Clark Centennial Endowed Fellow and Professor of Marketing and International Business at the University of Texas at Austin. Dr. Kotabe served as the Vice President of the Academy of International Business in 1997–98. In 1998, he was elected a Fellow of the Academy of International Business for his significant contribution to international business research and education. Dr. Kotabe has written more than 100 scholarly publications, including the following books: *Global Sourcing Strategy: R&D, Manufacturing, Marketing Interfaces* (1992), *Anticompetitive Practices in Japan* (1996), *Global Supply Chain Management* (2006), and *Global Marketing Management*, 4th edn (2007).

Trichy V. Krishnan is a marketing faculty at the NUS Business School, NUS, Singapore. His research interests are in new product diffusion, retailing and other channel issues, and licensing.

His papers have appeared in all leading marketing journals including *Marketing science, Journal of Marketing research, Management Science, International Journal of Reseach in Marketing*. He reqularly reviews for all leading marketing journals and is a member of the editorial board of *International Journal of Research in Marketing*. Having lived in India, Europe, the USA and Singapore for extended periods, topics related to international matters, various cultural differences are always of special interest for him. Recently he used this knowledge to help an international market research company develop online ad spend forecasts for many countries where no data were available.

V. Kumar (VK) has been recognized with numerous teaching and research excellence awards and two lifetime achievement awards for his contributions to Marketing Strategy and B2B marketing. He has published over 100 articles in many scholarly journals in marketing, including the *Harvard Business Review, Journal of Marketing, Journal of Marketing, Marketing Science* *and Operations Research.* His current research focuses on retailing, international diffusion models, customer relationship management, forecasting, international marketing research and strategy, resource allocation, sales promotion and interaction orientation. He was recently listed as one of the top five ranked scholars in marketing worldwide. He has consulted for many Global Fortune 500 firms. He received his PhD from the University of Texas at Austin.

Leonidas C. Leonidou is Professor of Marketing at the School of Economics and Management of the University of Cyprus. He has research interests in international marketing, relationship marketing, strategic marketing, and marketing in emerging economies. He has published extensively in these fields and his articles have appeared in various journals, including *European Journal of Marketing*, *Industrial Marketing Management*, *International Marketing Review*, *Journal of Business Research*, *Journal of International Business Studies*, *Journal of International Marketing*, *Journal of the Academy of Marketing Science*, *Journal of World Business*, and *Management International Review*.

Durairaj Maheswaran (Mahesh) is the Paganelli-Bull Professor of Marketing and International Business at the Stern School of Business, New York University. He received a PhD in marketing from Kellogg School of Management, Northwestern University. He has a Bachelor degree in Engineering from University of Madras and a MBA from Indian Institute of Management, Calcutta. He has six years of industry experience in advertising and marketing research. He has published widely in leading publications, including the *Journal of Marketing Research*, *Journal of Consumer Research*, *Journal of Personality and Social Psychology* and *Journal of Consumer Psychology*. He is the Editor of the *Journal of Consumer Psychology* and was an Associate Editor with the *Journal of Consumer Research*. He is a Past President of the Society of Consumer Psychology.

Jason Patrick McNicol is currently enrolled in the International Business Doctoral Program at the University of Texas at El Paso. He has a Bachelor's degree in Business from Texas Tech University and a Master's degree from the University of Texas at El Paso. His areas of interest include international entrepreneurship and strategy.

Jeffrey Meyer is a PhD student at Texas A&M University. His main research interest is in the area of hybrid innovation, with an emphasis on the pricing, bundling, and diffusion aspects. Other research interests include the broad areas of services marketing and customer satisfaction. He holds a MS degree in Marketing Research from the University of Texas at Arlington and a BS in Statistics from Iowa State University. Previously, he worked for several years as a senior marketing research consultant for the Principal Financial Group, conducting numerous research projects involving topics such as customer satisfaction, retention, and segmentation, among others.

Michael J. Mol is a senior lecturer in Strategic Management at the University of Reading, and Visiting Researcher of London Business School's M-Lab. He researches strategic management in large firms, with particular interests in sourcing strategy and management innovation. His publications have appeared, or are due to appear, in – among others – *Academy of Management Review*, *Research Policy*, *Sloan Management Review*, and *Strategic Organization*. He has also (co-)authored four books, including the recent *Outsourcing: Design, Process and Performance* (Cambridge University Press) and *Giant Steps in Management* (FT/Prentice-Hall). Michael holds a PhD from RSM Erasmus University.

Janet Y. Murray is E. Desmond Lee Professor for Developing Women Leaders and Entrepreneurs in International Business at the University of Missouri–St. Louis. Her research focuses on global sourcing and international marketing strategies. She has published in *Journal of Marketing, Strategic Management Journal, Journal of International Business Studies*, and other journals. She is a recipient of four Best Paper Awards. In October 2005, Michigan State University CIBER identified Professor Murray as the 21st most prolific IB researcher (among a total of 1,908 authors) in 1996–2005. She serves on the editorial review boards of *Journal of International Business Studies, Journal of International Management, Journal of International Marketing*, and *Strategic Outsourcing*.

Patrick E. Murphy is the C.R. Smith Co-Director of the Institute for Ethical Business Worldwide and Professor of Marketing in the Mendoza College of Business at the University of Notre Dame. His work has appeared in leading journals and he has written or edited several books on marketing ethics. He has served as a journal editor and on multiple editorial review boards. Murphy won teaching awards at Notre Dame in 2005 and 2006. Currently, he is an Academic Advisor of the Business Roundtable Institute for Corporate Ethics. He holds a BBA from Notre Dame, an MBA from Bradley, and a PhD from Houston.

Miguel Rivera-Santos is an Assistant Professor of strategy and international business at Babson College. His research focuses on strategic alliances and inter-organizational collaboration, and, more specifically, on how organizations can use alliances to pursue their own strategic goals. His current research interests include the organizational specificities of cross-sector alliances, such as firm–NGO and firm–government alliances, the structure of cross-sector networks, and the impact of cross-sector collaboration on poverty in the context of Base-of-the-Pyramid initiatives. His research has been published in academic books and journals. He is also the author of several case studies on alliances and on strategies in BOP environments.

John Roberts holds a joint appointment as Scientia Professor at the University of New South Wales and Professor of Marketing at the London Business School. His research interests revolve around the intersection of evidence-based marketing and management practice. John has won the American Marketing Association's John Howard Award, its William O'Dell Award, and its Advanced Research Techniques Forum Best Paper Award. He has been a finalist in the John Little Award three times and was a finalist in the ISMS inaugural Marketing Practice Award. John sits on the Editorial Boards of *Marketing Science, Journal of Marketing Research, Journal of Forecasting*, and *International Journal of Research in Marketing*. He is an Academic Trustee of the Marketing Science Institute.

Saeed Samiee is the Collins Professor of Marketing and International Business at The University of Tulsa. He has served as a visiting Professor and has lectured at business schools in over a dozen countries. Prior to joining TU as the Director of the International Management Center, he was a member of the faculty at the University of South Carolina. He received his PhD from The Ohio State University. Professor Samiee has contributed to scholarly journals in marketing and international business as an author and a member of editorial review boards, including the *Journal of Marketing, Journal of the Academy of Marketing Science*, and *Journal of International Business Studies*. He currently serves on 10 editorial review boards, including *Journal of International Business Studies*.

Bernd Schmitt is the Robert D. Calkins Professor of International Business School in New York and the Executive Director of the Center on Global Brand Leadership. His research focuses on language, global branding and customer experience. For further information, please visit www.meetschmitt.com.

Venkatesh (Venky) Shankar is Professor and Coleman Chair in Marketing and PhD Director at the Mays Business School, Texas A&M University. He has a marketing PhD from Kellogg School, Northwestern University. His research has been published in *Journal of Marketing Research, Marketing Science, Management Science, Strategic Management Journal,* and *Journal of Marketing.* He is a winner of the Clarke Award for Outstanding Direct Marketing Educator, the IBM Faculty Partnership Award, the Green Award for the Best Article in *Journal of Marketing Research,* and the Lehmann Award for the Best Dissertation-based Article in an AMA journal. He is co-editor of *Journal of Interactive Marketing,* Academic Trustee, MSI and President of Marketing Strategy SIG, AMA. He has been a visiting faculty at MIT, INSEAD, Singapore Management University, SDA Bocconi, Indian School of Business, and Chinese European International Business School.

Nader Tavassoli is Chair of the Marketing Faculty at London Business School and non-executive chairman of The Brand Inside (www.thebrandinside.com). His research focuses on brand strategy, internal branding, marketing communications, and consumer psychology, with a special emphasis on cross-cultural differences in behavior.

Marios Theodosiou is an Assistant Professor of Marketing at the Department of Public and Business Administration, University of Cyprus. He received his doctorate in international marketing from Cardiff Business School, United Kingdom. His current research interests include: standardization versus adaptation of marketing strategies in international markets, export marketing strategy, and export sales management. He published articles in several international journals, including the *Journal of the Academy of Marketing Science, Strategic Management Journal, Journal of Business Research, Journal of International Marketing, Journal of World Business, International Business Review* and the *European Journal of Marketing.* He currently serves on the Editorial Review Board of *Industrial Marketing Management.*

Suman Ann Thomas is a Doctoral Candidate in the Department of Marketing at NUS Business School, National University of Singapore. She is an engineer with an MBA from Indian Institute of Management, Ahmedabad and worked for ICICIBank, India and has an overall corporate experience of four years before pursuing an academic career. Her research interests are in Consumer Search and Choice Behavior, Customer Targeting, Consumer New Product Adoption and Growth, Structural Modeling, Learning Models and Strategic Interactions of Firms in Marketing.

Preface

Research in international marketing has evolved over the years, and has always reflected the climate of the time. Three major changes that have taken place in the last decade or so should be noted. *First*, the landscape of the global economy changed drastically in the last decade or so. The Asian and Latin American financial crises, the further expansion of the European Union (EU), the economic recovery of Japan from its decade-long recession, and the emergence of BRIC (Brazil, Russia, India and China) as economic powerhouses, have occurred during the this period. For example, up until mid-1990s, we were pretty certain that the Asian economy would grow at a fairly fast pace as it had done in the previous 40 years. However, to everyone's surprise, the Asian economic miracle was brought to a screeching halt by the region's financial crisis toward the end of 1998. The ramifications of the Asian financial crisis are not limited to Asian countries and their trading partners. Another epoch-making event was the introduction of a common European currency, known as the euro, on January 1, 1999. China's role as the world's factory is well established; India's increased role in information technology development is obvious. At the time of this writing in 2008, Brazil and Russia, among other resource-rich nations, are benefiting from skyrocketing prices of oil and other resources, shifting enormous amounts of wealth from resource-poor to resource-rich countries.

Second, the explosive growth of information technology tools, including the Internet and electronic commerce (e-commerce), has had a significant effect on the way we do business internationally. This is a relatively new phenomenon that we need to have a careful look at. On one hand, everyone seems to agree that business transactions will be faster and more global early on. And it is very true. As a result, marketing management techniques such as customer relationship management and global account management have become increasingly feasible. However, on the other hand, the more deeply we have examined this issue, the more convinced we have become that certain things would not change, or could even become more local as a result of globalization that the Internet and e-commerce bestow on us.

Third, it is an underlying human tendency to desire to be different when there are economic and political forces of convergence (often referred to as globalization). When the globalization argument (and movement) became fashionable in the 1980s and 1990s, many of us believed that globalization would make global marketing easier. Marketing beyond national borders, indeed, has become easier, but it does not necessarily mean that customers want the same products in countries around the world. For example, many more peoples around the world try to emphasize cultural and ethnic differences as well as accept those differences than ever before. Just think about many new countries being born around the world as well as regional unifications taking place at the same time. Another example is that while e-commerce promotion on the Internet goes global, product delivery may need to be fairly local in order to address local competition and exchange rate fluctuations as well as the complexities (export declarations, tariffs, and non-tariff barriers) and increased costs (due primarily to higher oil prices and security needs) of international physical distribution. From a supply-side point of view, globalization has brought us more products from all corners of the world. However, from a demand-side (marketing-side) point of view, customers have a much broader set of goods and services to *choose from*. In other words, marketers now face all the more divergent customers with divergent preferences – far from a homogeneous group of customers.

Indeed, these environmental changes we have observed in the last decade or so are more than extraordinary. As a result, researchers in international marketing are facing enormous challenges to address those changes in their theory development and empirical studies.

We have decided to compile the SAGE Handbook of International Marketing not just to stockpile, reflect, and critique on past research but more importantly to address where the discipline is heading. Of course, such an endeavor requires enormous intellectual power. We recruited truly world-class researchers who have been conducting cutting-edge research and are recognized as thought leaders in their respective research areas. These researchers are so highly coveted around the world that they are truly jet-setters. Despite their busy schedules, they were kind enough to take up on a task of developing thought-provoking chapters with their critical review of the existing literature and their vision of future directions for further theory development across a wide range of research areas in international marketing.

We hope that this comprehensive Handbook not only provides an in-depth authoritative review of the literature but also helps define the direction of research in international marketing for years to come. Researchers, including those pursuing research careers in international marketing, find it useful to consult with this Handbook as the first step to understanding the nature and scope of research in various areas of research collectively constituting the discipline. We sincerely hope that this Handbook will help junior researchers develop the discipline further and even influence the direction of research in related disciplines such as management and strategy.

Before closing, we would like to acknowledge many people involved in this Handbook project. First and utmost, we would like to thank the chapter authors for taking the time to share their state-of-the-art thinking on their research areas. Second, we would like to acknowledge the Advisory Board members for their critical review of the chapter manuscripts for further improvement. Third, we should recognize our two brilliant editors, Delia Martinez Alfonso and Clare Wells, at SAGE Publications, who have given us encouragements and directions throughout the project.

Overview

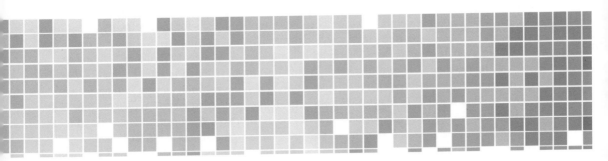

1

Theoretical Paradigms, Issues, and Debates

Masaaki Kotabe and Kristiaan Helsen

Marketing is essentially a creative corporate activity involving the planning and execution of the conception, pricing, promotion, and distribution of ideas, products, and services in an exchange that not only satisfies customers' current needs but also anticipates and creates their future needs at a profit.[1] Marketing is not only much broader than selling; it also encompasses the entire company's market orientation toward customer satisfaction in a competitive environment. In other words, marketing strategy requires close attention to both customers and competitors. Quite often marketers have focused excessively on satisfying customer needs while ignoring competitors. In the process, competitors have outmaneuvered them in the marketplace with better, less-expensive products. The same logic applies to research in international marketing. Research focus on both customers and competitors is equally important.

Companies generally develop different marketing strategies depending on the degree of experience and the nature of operations in international markets. Companies tend to evolve over time, accumulating international business experience and learning the advantages and disadvantages associated with complexities of manufacturing and marketing around the world. As a result, many researchers have adopted an evolutionary perspective on internationalization of the company just like the evolution of species over time. In the following pages we will formally define and explain five stages that characterize the evolution of international marketing. Of course, not all companies go through the complete evolution from a purely domestic marketing stage to a purely global marketing stage. An actual evolution depends also on the economic, cultural, political, and legal environments of various national markets in which the company operates, as well as on the nature of the company's offerings. A key point here is that many companies are constantly under competitive pressure to move forward both reactively (responding to the changes in the market and competitive environments) and proactively (anticipating the change).

Marketing products and services around the world, transcending national and political boundaries, is a fascinating phenomenon. The phenomenon, however, is not entirely new. Products have been traded across borders throughout recorded civilization, extending back beyond the Silk Road that once connected East with West from Xian to Rome on land and the recently excavated sea-trade route between the Roman Empire and India that existed 2,000 years ago. However, since the end of World War II, the world economy has experienced a spectacular growth rate never witnessed before in human history, largely led by big US companies in the 1950s and 1960s, then by European and Japanese companies in the 1970s and 1980s, and most recently joined by new emerging market firms, such as Lenovo, Mittal Steel, and Cemex. In particular, competition coming recently from the so-called BRIC countries[2] has given the notion of global competition a touch of extra urgency and significance.

On a political map, country borders are as clear as ever. But on a competitive map, financial, trading, and industrial activities across national boundaries have rendered those political borders increasingly irrelevant. Of all the forces chipping away at those boundaries, perhaps the most important are the emergence of regional trading blocs (e.g., NAFTA, the European Union), technology developments (particularly in the IT area) and the flow of information. Today people can see for themselves what tastes and preferences are like in other countries. For instance, people in India watching CNN and Star TV now know instantaneously what is happening in the rest of the world. A farmer in a remote village in Rajasthan in India might ask the local vendor for Surf (the detergent manufactured by Unilever) because he has seen a commercial on TV. More than 10 million Japanese traveling abroad every year are exposed to larger-size homes and much lower consumer prices abroad. Such information access creates demand that would not have existed before.

The availability and explosion of information technology such as telecommunications has forever changed the nature of global competition. Geographical boundaries and distance have become less of a constraint in designing strategies for the global market.

The other side of the coin is that not only firms that compete internationally, but also those whose primary market is home-based, will be significantly affected by competition from around the world.

We often hear terms such as global markets, global competition, global technology, and global competitiveness. In the past, we heard similar words with 'international' or 'multinational' instead of global attached to them. What has happened since the 1980s? Are these terms just fashionable concepts of the time without some deep meanings? Or has something inherently changed in our society?

EVOLUTION OF MARKETING ACROSS NATIONAL BOUNDARIES

There are five identifiable stages in the evolution of marketing across national boundaries. Therefore, knowing the dynamics of the evolutionary development of international marketing involvement is important for two reasons. First, it helps in the understanding of how companies learn and acquire international experience and how they use it for gaining competitive advantage over time. This may help an executive to be better prepared for the likely change needed in the company's marketing strategy. Second, with this knowledge, a company may be able to compete more effectively by predicting its competitors' likely marketing strategy in advance.

Domestic marketing

The first stage is domestic marketing. Before entry into international markets, many companies focus solely on their domestic market. Their marketing strategy is developed based on information about domestic customer needs and wants, industry trends, economic, technological, and political environments at home. When those companies consider competition, they essentially look at domestic competition. Today, it is highly conceivable that competition in a company's home market is made up of both domestic competitors and foreign competitors marketing their products in the home market.

Domestic marketers tend to be ethnocentric and pay little attention to changes taking place in the global marketplace, such as changing lifestyles and market segments, emerging competition, and better products that have yet to arrive in their domestic market. Ethnocentrism is defined here as a predisposition of a firm to be predominantly concerned with its worldwide viability and legitimacy only in its home country – that is, where all strategic actions of a company are tailored to domestic responses under similar situations. As a result, they may be vulnerable to the sudden changes forced on them by foreign competition. US automobile and consumer electronics manufacturers suffered from this ethnocentrism in the 1960s and 1970s as a result of their neglect of imminent competition from Japanese low-cost manufacturers.

Export marketing

The second stage is export marketing. Usually, initial export marketing begins with unsolicited orders from foreign customers. When a company receives an order from abroad, it may reluctantly fill it initially, but it gradually learns the benefit of marketing overseas. In general, in the early stage of export marketing involvement, the internationalization process is a consequence of incremental adjustments to the changing conditions of the company and its environment, rather than a result of its deliberate strategy. Such a pattern is due to the consequence of greater uncertainty in international business, higher costs of information, and the lack of technical knowledge about international marketing activities. At this early export marketing stage, exporters tend to engage in indirect exporting by relying on export management companies or trading companies to handle their export business.

Some companies progress to a more involved stage of internationalization by direct exporting, once three internal conditions are satisfied. First, the management of the company develops favorable expectations of the attractiveness of exporting based on its earlier experience. Second, the company has access to key resources necessary for undertaking additional export-related tasks. Such availability of physical, financial, and managerial resources is closely associated with firm size. Particularly, small companies may have few trained managers and little time for long-term planning as they are preoccupied with day-to-day operational problems, and consequently find it difficult to become involved in exporting. Third, management is willing to commit adequate resources to export activities. The company's long-term commitment to export marketing depends on how successful management is in overcoming various barriers encountered in international marketing activities. An experienced export marketer has to deal with difficulties in maintaining and expanding export involvement. These difficulties include import/export restrictions, cost and availability of shipping, exchange rate fluctuations, collection of money, and development of distribution channels, among others. Overall, favorable experience appears to be a key component in getting companies involved in managing exports directly without relying on specialized outside export handlers. To a large degree an appropriate measure of favorableness for many companies consists of profits. An increase in profits due to a certain activity is likely to increase the company's interest in such activity.

External pressures also encourage companies into export marketing activities. Saturated domestic markets may make it difficult for a company to maintain sales volume in an increasingly competitive domestic market; it will become much more serious when foreign competitors begin marketing products in the domestic market.

Export marketers begin paying attention to technological and other changes in the global marketplace that domestic marketers tend to ignore. However, export marketers still tend to take an ethnocentric approach to foreign markets as being an extension of their domestic market and export products developed primarily for home country customers with limited adaptation to foreign customers' needs.

International marketing

Once export marketing becomes an integral part of the company's marketing activity, it will begin to seek new directions for growth and expansion. This stage is called international marketing. A unique feature of international marketing is its polycentric orientation, with emphasis on product and promotional adaptation in foreign markets whenever necessary. Polycentric orientation refers to a predisposition of a firm to the existence of significant local cultural differences across markets, necessitating the operation in each country being viewed independently (i.e., all strategic decisions are thus tailored to suit the cultures of the concerned country). As the company's market share in a number of countries reaches a certain point, it becomes important for the company to defend its position through local competition. Because of local competitors' proximity to, and familiarity with, local customers, they tend to have an inherent 'insider' advantage over foreign competition. To strengthen its competitive position, the international marketer could adapt its strategy, if necessary, to meet the needs and wants of local customers in two alternative ways. First, the company may allocate a certain portion of its manufacturing capacity to its export business. Second, because of transportation costs, tariffs, and other regulations, and availability of human and capital resources in the foreign markets, the company may even begin manufacturing locally.

If international marketing is taken to the extreme, a company may establish an independent foreign subsidiary in each and every

foreign market and have each of the subsidiaries operate independently of each other without any measurable headquarters control. This special case of international marketing is known as multidomestic marketing. Product development, manufacturing, and marketing are all executed by each subsidiary for its own local market. As a result, different product lines, product positioning, and pricing may be observed across those subsidiaries. Few economies of scale benefits can be obtained. However, multidomestic marketing is useful when customer needs are so different across different national markets that no common product or promotional strategy can be developed.

Multinational marketing

In this stage the company markets its products in many countries around the world. Management of the company comes to realize the benefit of economies of scale in product development, manufacturing, and marketing by consolidating some of its activities on a regional basis. This regiocentric approach suggests that product planning may be standardized within a region (e.g., a group of contiguous and similar countries), such as Western Europe, but not across regions. Products may be manufactured regionally as well. Similarly, advertising, promotional, and distribution costs may also be shared by subsidiaries in the region. In order for the company to develop its regional image in the marketplace, it may develop and acquire new regional brands to increase up its regional operations. Even when having difficulty occupying a market, a firm may think out of the box regarding an alliance or a partnership that can lead it into the market.

Global marketing

The international (country-by-country) or multinational (region-by-region) orientation, while enabling the consolidation of operations within countries or regions, tends to result in market fragmentation worldwide, nonetheless. Operational fragmentation leads to higher costs. As many Japanese companies entered the world markets as low-cost manufacturers of reliable products in the 1970s, well-established US and European multinational companies were made acutely aware of the vulnerability of being high-cost manufacturers. Levitt (1983), an ardent globalization proponent, argues:

Gone are accustomed differences in national or regional preference. Gone are the days when a company could sell last year's models – or lesser versions of advanced products – in the less developed world .... The multinational and the global corporation are not the same thing. The multinational corporation operates in a number of countries, and adjusts its products and practices in each – at high relative costs. The global corporation operates with resolute constancy – at low relative cost – as if the entire world (or major regions of it) were a single entity; it sells the same things in the same way everywhere.

Global marketing refers to marketing activities by companies that emphasize the following:

1 *Standardization efforts* – standardizing marketing programs across different countries particularly with respect to product offering, promotional mix, price, and channel structure. Such efforts increase opportunities for the transfer of products, brands, and other ideas across subsidiaries and help address the emergence of global customers.
2 *Coordination across markets* – reducing cost inefficiencies and duplication of efforts among their national and regional subsidiaries.
3 *Global Integration* – participating in many major world markets to gain competitive leverage and effective integration of the firm's competitive campaigns across these markets by being able to subsidize operations in some markets with resources generated in others and responding to competitive attacks in one market by counter-attacking in others (Zou and Cavusgil 2002).

Although Levitt's view is somewhat extreme, many researchers agree that global marketing does not necessarily mean standardization of products, promotion, pricing, and distribution worldwide, but rather it is a company's proactive willingness to adopt a global perspective, instead of country-by-country or region-by-region perspective, in developing a marketing strategy. Clearly, not all companies adopt global marketing. Yet, an increasing number of companies are proactively trying to find commonalities in their marketing strategy among national subsidiaries.

Although this evolutionary perspective holds true, it by no means suggests that all companies develop their marketing strategies along a unidirectional evolutionary trajectory. As the reader can see below, marketing strategies reflect the climate of the time as well as executives' belief systems. In this book, the term international marketing, unless otherwise specified, will refer to marketing across national boundaries, whether the firm's orientation is multidomestic or global.

THE CLIMATE OF THE TIME

International marketing has undergone fundamental changes in the last two decades. Global political and economic liberalization trends and the explosive growth of information technology have created tremendous business opportunities and challenges for international marketers. The opening up of new markets in Eastern Europe and a tendency toward economic liberalization in the emerging markets around the world have spawned new business opportunities. In particular, China and India, two leading emerging economic powers, stand out in the crowd with an annual growth rate of 7–10 per cent and 4–7 per cent, respectively, since the dawn of the twenty-first century. Similarly, the emergence of regional trading blocs in the form of the EU (European Union), the NAFTA (North American Free Trade Agreement), and MERCOSUR (Mercado Común del Sur) have necessitated reorganization in the production and marketing strategies of firms. Advances in information technology, including obviously the Internet, have further added immediacy and permeability to the effect of these developments. The changes in strategy include serving different markets from one production source or the shifting of production facilities for greater efficiency.

At the same time, the Asian financial crisis in the latter half of the 1990s also provided a significant reality check on the wisdom of globally integrated strategy development. Wildly fluctuating exchange rates make it difficult for multinational companies to manage globally integrated but geographically scattered activities. Indeed, many companies are scurrying to speed steps toward making their procurement, manufacturing, and marketing operations in Asian countries more local. Japanese companies seem to be one step ahead of US and European competitors in this localization strategy. Since the yen's sharp appreciation in the mid-1980s, Japanese manufacturers have moved to build an international production system less vulnerable to currency fluctuations by investing in local procurement and local marketing (Kotabe 2002).

TWO COUNTERACTING FORCES AT WORK

Over the years, two fundamental counteracting forces have shaped the nature of marketing in the international arena. The same counteracting forces have been revisited by many authors in such terms as 'standardization vs. adaptation' (1970s), 'globalization vs. localization' (1980s), 'global integration vs. local responsiveness' (1990s and beyond).

During the 1960s and 1970s, being aware of economic and cultural diversities around the world, marketers in general believed that adapting marketing activities to local markets was of utmost importance. In the 1980s and 1990s, however, being swayed by the seemingly converging and intertwined market economies around the world, marketers gave a high priority to developing globally integrated marketing strategy in pursuit of economic efficiency. Most recently, we have come a full circle to realize that it is not an either/or issue (e.g., Ghemawat 2007). Terms may have changed, but the quintessence of the strategic dilemma that multinational companies face today has not changed and will probably remain unchanged for years to come.

Markets are neither as homogeneous nor as dominated by the traditional Triad Powers of the world – the United States, Western Europe, and Japan – as believed in the 1980s–1990s. The dawn of this new century has already shown that emerging economies are increasingly important drivers of global economic development. As a result, forward-looking, proactive firms seriously have to possess the willingness and develop the ability to pursue the benefit of operational integration for economic efficiency and sensitivity to local markets simultaneously.

RESEARCH IN INTERNATIONAL MARKETING

In a way, the climate of the time is reflected in the research streams in international marketing. The market trends mentioned earlier have imparted added importance to research in international marketing. Past reviews of international marketing research (Douglas and Craig 1992; Aulakh and Kotabe 1993; Pieters *et al.* 1999; Kotabe 2003) highlighted deficiencies of the discipline in two aspects – that international marketing research was fragmentary and exploratory without a strong theoretical framework, and that it lacked the methodological rigor compared to most other areas of academic marketing research. One symptom of the latter phenomenon is the fairly small number of publications of international marketing related research in two of marketing's most prestigious journals: the *Journal of Marketing* and the *Journal of Marketing Research* (see Table 1.1). While the first deficiency in international marketing research was attributed to the opportunistic nature (Albaum and Peterson 1984) and lack of synthesis

Table 1.1 Number of articles labeled as 'International Marketing' in the *Journal of Marketing* and the *Journal of Marketing Research*

Year	Number of articles in Journal of Marketing	Year	Number of Articles in Journal of Marketing Research
1991–95	14 (230)	1992–96	0
1996	0 (77)	1997	0
1997	3 (72)	1998	0
1998	3 (89)	1999	1
1999	5 (137)	2000	1
2000	1 (78)	2001	1
2001	3 (81)	2002	1
2002	1 (90)	2003	0
2003	1 (91)	2004	0
2004	1 (119)	2005	0
2005	0 (140)	2006	0
2006	2 (126)	2007	0
2007	2 (147)		

*As classified in each volume's final issue; the number between parentheses is the total number of articles classified (some articles have multiple classifications).

(Bradley 1987) of international marketing research, the latter was attributed to the inherent difficulties encountered in research involving more than one country (Aulakh and Kotabe 1993). Difficulties stemmed from financial constraints in data collection, problems of data comparability in cross-cultural research and the implementation of methodological techniques in foreign markets. There have been various attempts to address the problems encountered in international marketing research (e.g., Craig and Douglas 2000).

Our objective is to organize and highlight the development of various research streams in international marketing. This handbook, consisting of 26 chapters written by authorities in their respective areas, promises to make a mark in the state-of-the-art development of the research streams in international marketing.

First, this handbook provides a fairly broad timeframe for the reader to probe any significant changes in the field, both in terms of the substance of research and methodologies used. Second, it helps the reader see to what extent these two fundamental concerns raised in the 1980s have been addressed. Third, it addresses new and/or neglected areas of research that will gain in importance.

An overview

The micro-context of research in international marketing constitutes the bulk of research conducted in the field. Although there is no single best way to arrange various topics, they are arranged as follows. Section 1 surveys research in key market environmental factors that affect international marketing strategy; namely, globalization issues, political and institutional environment, and legal environment. Section 2 examines research in consumer behavior as it represents the initial interfaces between firms and customers. In particular, the effect of country of origin in consumer behavior has received a significant amount of research attention over the years. Section 3 details research in various modes of entry and exit strategies and their performance implications.

Section 4 addresses various issues related to global competitive strategy, encompassing research issues related to competitive strategy, marketing standardization, and global sourcing. These chapters provide theoretical, managerial, and empirical insights into the workings of global marketing strategy. Marketing strategy is a subset of competitive strategy. As such, the literature on competitive strategy has had a profound impact on the development of global marketing literature.

With these issues in the background, Section 5 focuses on the development of global marketing strategy, covering product development and diffusion, global branding, pricing, communication, distribution, retailing, and sales management. Section 6 focuses on emerging issues, including the role and effect of the Internet, marketing strategies for emerging markets, small multinational enterprises, and marketing ethics.

CLOSING REMARKS

International marketing as an academic discipline has come a long way. The compilation of research work represented in this handbook was a daunting task as chapter authors as well as reviewers are all world-class researchers and are busy people. They were kind enough to allocate a good amount of their precious time in developing these thoughtful and insightful chapters. This handbook is comprehensive. Researchers, including those pursuing research careers in international marketing, will find it useful to consult with this handbook as the first step to understanding the nature and scope of research in the various areas of research that collectively constitute the discipline. We sincerely hope that this handbook will help junior researchers to develop the discipline further and even influence the direction of research in related disciplines such as management and strategy. As stated earlier, international marketing researchers complement management and strategy researchers in subjecting supply-side theories to demand-side considerations.

NOTES

1 This definition is modified from the American Marketing Association's definition of marketing, and is strongly influenced by Drucker's conception of two entrepreneurial functions – marketing and innovation – that constitute business. Contemporary thinking about marketing also suggests the task of the marketer is not only to satisfy the current needs and wants of customers, but also to innovate products and services, anticipating their future needs and wants. See Peter F. Drucker, *The Practice of Management* (New York: Harper & Brothers, 1954), pp. 37–39; and also Frederick E. Webster, Jr., 'The Changing Role of Marketing in the Corporation,' *Journal of Marketing*, 56 (October 1992), pp. 1–16.

2 Brazil, Russia, India, and China.

REFERENCES

Albaum, G. and Peterson, R. A. (1984) 'Empirical research in international marketing', *Journal of International Business Studies*, 15 (Spring/Summer): 161–173.

Aulakh, P. S. and Kotabe, M. (1993) 'An Assessment of theoretical and methodological development in international marketing: 1980–1990', *Journal of International Marketing*, 1(2): 5–28.

Bradley, M. F. (1987), 'Nature and significance of international marketing: A review', *Journal of Business Research*, 15: 205–219.

Craig, C. S. and Douglas, S. P. (2000) *International Marketing Research*, 2nd edn. New York: Wiley.

Douglas, S. P. and Craig. C. S. (1992) 'Advances in international marketing', *International Journal of Research in Marketing*, 9(4): 291–318.

Drucker, P. F. (1954) *The Practice of Management*. New York: Harper & Brothers.

Ghemawat, P. (2007) *Redefining Global Strategy: Crossing Borders in a World Where Differences Still Matter*. Boston: MA: Harvard Business School Press.

Kotabe, M. (2002) 'To Kill Two Birds with One Stone: Revisiting the Integration-Responsiveness Framework', in M. Hitt and J. Cheng (eds), *Managing Transnational Firms*. New York: Elsevier, 59–69.

Kotabe, M. (2003) 'State-of-the-Art Review of Research in International Marketing Management', Chapter 1, in S. C. Jain (ed.), *Handbook of Research in International Marketing*. Northampton, MA: Edward Elgar Publishing, 3–41.

Levitt, T. (1983) 'The globalization of markets', *Harvard Business Review*, 61(3): 92–102.

Pieters, R., Baumgartner, H., Vermunt, J. and Bijmolt, T. (1999) 'Importance and similarity in the evolving citation network of the International Journal of Research in Marketing', *International Journal of Research in Marketing*, 16 (June): 113–127.

Webster, F. E., Jr. (1992) 'The changing role of marketing in the corporation', *Journal of Marketing*, 56 (October): 1–16.

Zou, S. and Cavusgil, S. T. (2002) 'The GMS: A broad conceptualization of global marketing strategy and its effect on firm performance', *Journal of Marketing*, 66 (October): 40–56.

Changing Market Environments

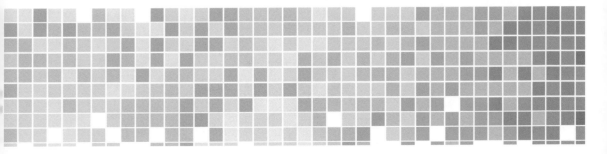

The Ancient Road: An Overview of Globalization

Terry Clark, Monica Hodis, and Paul D' Angelo

INTRODUCTION[1]

The world entered a period of accelerating change in the decades following World War II (WWII). One aspect of this change was the rise and spread of Western Multinational Corporations (MNCs). Primarily in pursuit of markets and profits, MNCs incidentally took production, finance, management and marketing know-how to almost every country on earth. In more recent decades, the invention and worldwide diffusion of electronic media and communication technologies have accelerated the adoption of what had been local or national (mainly Western) tastes in music, food, fashion, and movies across the entire world. Today, nuanced teenage fashion innovations in New York or London spread quickly to Rio and Delhi via MTV. Similarly, the Internet now makes it possible for a professor from Orissa, India, teaching in Saskatoon, Canada, to keep up with the daily news in Bhubaneshwar (capital of Orissa), in her mother tongue (Oriya), by visiting *The Samaja* online (http://www.thesamaja.com/).

A single word points to theses and a host of related changes: globalization. Although there is much disagreement about what globalization is and what exactly it is doing, paradoxically, a statement such as 'globalization is reshaping the lives of the peoples of the world' seems beyond dispute. Over the past 30 years, 'globalization' has gone from being an ethereal 'pie-in-the-sky' concept, to a hotly debated idea, which some people believed had no referent in the real world, to the current widely accepted view that it is something that is revolutionizing and reshaping human life around the world. Today, globalization is accepted by all but a few academic curmudgeons (e.g., 'The evidence is in and it shows that globalization is a myth'[2] (Rugman 2003, p. 409)) as an incontestable reality. Yet, globalization is a reality we know little about – or rather, one we are only beginning to fathom and to understand.

Before the mid-1980s there was little serious discussion of globalization *per se* in the mainstream academy (notable exceptions include Marx and Engels 1848; McLuhan 1964; Wallerstein 1975). Virtually all of the now burgeoning literature on the subject was published after 1985. One reason for this is that globalization was 'discovered' simultaneously and independently across a variety of unrelated disciplines. Contact between these disciplines was infrequent and fragmentary. The result has been that theories of globalization developed in isolation. For example, distinct perspectives on globalization emerged in: philosophy (e.g., Collins 2000); literature (e.g., Brennan 1997; Landow 2006); engineering (Reader 2006); sociology (e.g., Sklair 1991); geography (e.g., Herod, O Tuathail and Roberts 1998); meteorology (e.g., Eddy, Ceschger and Oeschger 1993); labor relations (e.g., Munck 2002); ecology (e.g., Karliner 1997); anthropology (e.g., Lewellen 2002; Edelman 1999); media studies (e.g., Albarran and Chan-Olmsted 1998; Rantanen 2004); music (e.g., Taylor 1997; Baumann and Fujie 2000); psychology (e.g., Sampson 1989; Lewis and Araya 2002); public health (e.g., Barnett and Whiteside 2006; Murray and Lopez 2002), criminology and law enforcement (e.g., Friman and Andreas 1999; Hagedorn 2007); feminism and women's studies (e.g., Eschle 2001); ethics (e.g., Kung 1998); linguistics (e.g., Crystal 1997); education (Burbules 2000; Monkman and Stromquist 2000); higher education (e.g., Currie and Newson 1998); and law (e.g., Shapiro and Brilmayer 1999).

Despite what is now an immense literature, the exact meaning (and even significance) of globalization continues to be the subject of intense debate. A full assessment has been hindered by the fact that dialogue between the various disciplines has been limited, in part because jargons and methodologies differ, but also because scholars naturally tend to focus on those aspects of globalization which are of immediate relevance to their traditional foci. Today, it is increasingly clear that the fragmented views are all pointing to the same phenomenon (Clark and Knowles 2003): globalization. The purpose of this essay is to survey the concept, and specifically to try to understand what it means for International Business (IB) scholars and practitioners. In order to make discussion intelligible, we begin by developing a definition for globalization.

DEFINITION

No consistent, generally accepted or satisfying definition for globalization has emerged from IB. This problem is not limited to IB. In part, the definitional void stems from the fact that the word 'global' has been used in a variety of often contradictory ways (see Clark and Knowles 2003), leading to confusion about the topic and about what any particular author is saying. Indeed, in IB, there has been considerable resistance to embracing a view of globalization that is not strictly trade and/or economics-centric (typical of this perspective are the views of leading IB scholar Alan Rugman (e.g., 2001 and 2003)). The definitional void has been worsened by disciplinary isolation. Scholars naturally want focus on aspects of globalization that have immediate relevance to their own disciplinary interests. However, in doing so, they miss the important fact that globalization is a hugely complex phenomena, with a domain possibly encompassing, or at least touching, all other disciplinary domains.

We begin with the truism that globalization is a phenomena affecting the whole world. In that context, Wallerstein (1975) develops the concept of 'world-system' as a sort of historically evolving planet-wide social system. He offers two examples of such systems – world-empires, and world-economies. For Wallerstein, globalization is simply the dénouement of historical processes, animated primarily by trade, political and military powers. Globalization is what the world-system has evolved into in the modern world. Implicit in Wallerstein's world-system is the idea of 'world sub-systems'. A world sub-system is a component of the world-system, relating to a specific and limited set of phenomena, having planet-wide extension. Emerging and/or existing world sub-systems include such things as inflation/interest rates; business cycles; fashion/pop music; technical/professional standards; consumption behaviors; diseases; and media.

Perusal of definitions suggests three common factors in most conceptualizations of globalization: (1) integration of national/regional phenomena into world sub-systems; (2) the process(es) by which this integration occurs; and (3) mechanisms that facilitate integration, by transmitting influence from one location to another. Building on these points, developed by Clark and Knowles (2003), we extend the definition as follows:

The process by which economic, political, cultural, social, and other systems of nations are integrating into world sub-systems is called *Globalization*:

- A *world sub-system* is a planet-wide complex of channels capable of transmitting stimuli simultaneously to many locations at wide geographic distances;
- The extent to which the economic, political, cultural, social, and other relevant systems of nations are actually integrated into world sub-systems is called the *degree of globalization*;
- The *degree of globalization* of the various economic, political, cultural, social, and other relevant systems of nations varies considerably.

Although this definition is general, it is not limiting. It embodies the central idea many have been struggling to articulate and model in their own disciplinary contexts, using their own metrics, models, and theories. The definition also conceptualizes globalization as a dynamic process, proceeding in different ways and in varying degrees with different phenomena, and allows for the possibility of having no affect at all. Furthermore, the definition posits two meta-categories of phenomena: world sub-systems and the world system – the presumed dénouement of the globalizing process. This dénouement is, in all probability, hypothetical, occurring if at all, at some indeterminate point in the future. However, the phase plane leading towards that dénouement (partial world and sub-world

systems) is of great and tangible interest. Assuming metrics appropriate for a given situation (economic, cultural, social, etc.), the definition also provides a framework for capturing the rate at which globalization is proceeding in particular contexts.

The definition is illustrated in Figures 2.1a, 2.1b and 2.1c. Figure 2.1a represents a stylized autarkic world of impermeable (vertical) boundaries, in which nation-states have absolutely no interactions with each other. In it, all cultural, political, technological, economic, disease systems, etc., are contained strictly within the national system and develop

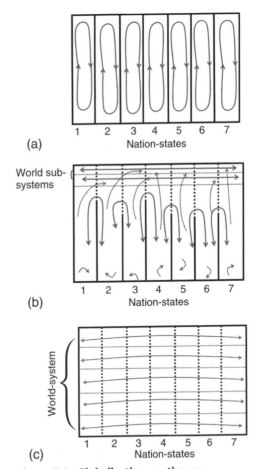

Figure 2.1. Globalization continuum
Source: Based on Gellner (1983), p. 9. Figure reprinted with permission. From Gellner, E. (1983) *Nations & Nationalism*, Blackwell Publishing.

idiosyncratically without reference to or benefit from the systems of other nation-states. This represents one end of the globalization continuum.

In Figure 2.1b, boundaries between nation-states now have some degree of permeability (indicated by the dotted portions of the vertical boundaries), allowing the systems within nation-states to influence those of other nations. This influence could be in the way of trade, travel, technology transfer, communication, etc. Such influences may be planned (e.g., technology transfer), or unplanned (e.g., a radio station's footprint extending beyond its intended market, into another country). Note also the emergence of world sub-systems (represented by horizontal dotted lines). These sub-systems represent what happens when national systems interact more broadly and openly, and so meld to become a new and emergent system, common to all nations (e.g., fashion, professional standards, language, etc.). This represents a midpoint in the globalization continuum.

In Figure 2.1c, all boundaries between nation-states are fully permeable, at all levels, allowing for unfettered intermingling of national systems. Note the dominance (over national systems) of the many world sub-systems and the emergence of a true world-system. This represents the other end of the globalization continuum.

HISTORY OF AN IDEA

How new is globalization? Answers to this question will be dependent upon how one defines the term. If globalization is defined strictly in terms of trade and economics (e.g., post-WWII international institutions and the rise and spread of Multinational Corporations (MNCs) (Vernon 1973; Rugman 2001)), etc., then the answer is clearly that it is a recent phenomenon. However, nothing could be further from the truth. Indeed, many scholars understand globalization to have its origins in

the fifteenth and sixteenth centuries, others argue it is of more ancient lineage, and that it has been operating in different ways, and to different degrees in every age (see, for example, Wallerstein 1975; Braudel 1984; Chanda 2007). This possibility is reflected in the definition developed above, which characterized globalization, neither in terms of technology nor MNC activities (the main drivers of globalization according to some), but rather in terms of processes, which may be ancient and/or modern, that are integrating world sub-systems into world sub-systems. Given that technology *per se* is not the central issue driving globalization (although, it may certainly accelerate it), we are free to seek globalization's roots prior to the twentieth century, and indeed, prior to the industrial revolution.

Our views of globalization are often weighted heavily by events subsequent to WWII. For example, the justly influential *Sovereignty at Bay* (Vernon, 1973), paints a picture of the rise and seemingly inexorable spread of US MNCs throughout the world, and of the often unintended changes they brought with them. In this way, it is tempting to see globalization as beginning in 1945 and co-evolving with rising US economic power. However, this view is historically myopic, and simply inaccurate. Even if globalization has accelerated since WWII (which it surely has), it has been developing for a very long time. There is much evidence to support this view. For example, Chanda (2007) explains globalization in terms of the ancient (and modern) activities of business people (traders); religious missionaries (preachers); explorers (adventurers); and soldiers (warriors). His argument is that these four classes of human beings/human activities unwittingly became agents in the grand historical process of world integration – globalization. Chanda's chronology provides some compelling illustrations. For example:

- 'Ancestors walk out of Africa ... reach India ... Reach Malaysia ... Reach Australia ... Reach China ...' (p. 322) ~50,000–28,000 BC.
- 'Traders travel to Çatal Höyük to buy obsidian for use as scythes' (ibid.) 8th millennium BC.

- 'Buddhist council dispatches missionaries' (p. 323) ~3rd century BC.
- 'Indian king sends mission to Rome' (ibid.) 1st century BC.
- 'Jesus says: "Go then, and make disciples of all nations": Christianity reaches India' (p. 324) ~30 AD.
- 'Spreading Buddhist faith promotes silk trade in Central Asia' (ibid.) 4th century AD.
- 'Muhammad leads Muslim army to capture infidel lands ... Caliph Monsoor builds new capital in Baghdad; Arab armies capture Spain from North Africa' (p. 325) ~7th–8th centuries AD.
- 'Al-Biruni's account of India in Arabic opens door to West; Leif Erikson sails to Vinland' (p. 325) ~11th century AD.
- 'African slaves are sold in China' 12th century AD (p. 326).
- 'Marco Polo returns to Venice after trip through Asia' (ibid.) 13th century AD.
- 'Chinese navigator Zheng He explores Indian Ocean: Portuguese bring back first African slaves' (ibid.) 15th century AD.
- 'Gujarati Muslim traders spread in Southeast Asia; Chinese porcelain shops open in Lisbon' (p. 327) 16th century AD.
- 'Jesuit missionary creates national language by romanizing Vietnamese ... Englishman William Congreve learns rocketry from India's Tipu sultan (knowledge originated with Mongols and Persians)' (p. 327) 18th century AD.
- '... stock news, delivered by homing pigeon of Reuters, is upgraded with introduction of telegraph ... with steamships, largest migration in history begins' (p. 328) ~19th century AD.

We can extend Chanda's point by considering how, from ancient times, migration, cartography, linguistic trends, religion and economics have all either reflected, or been agents in the ancient globalizing trend:

- Many observers specifically link the massive transnational migrations, currently underway in the world,[3] to globalization (e.g., Koslowski 2005; Papastergiadis 2000). The argument goes (in line with our definition, above) that when large groups of human beings move, they take their cultures, their religions, their technologies, etc. with them. In so doing, they have an integrating effect on the places to which they migrate. It is interesting to note that if human migration is

indeed a significant factor in globalization, then *de facto* (as per Chanda, above), globalization must be an ancient phenomenon, since human migration is ancient. For example, when the Celts migrated from the area around the Caspian Sea to the British Isles around 1,000 BC, did they not have an integrating effect in transmitting their culture, language, technologies, etc. along the way? How else can this be understood other than an early example of globalization?

- Ptolemy's famous map of the world, from around 150AD, clearly reveals an effort to project a sphere onto a flat surface. From this, it can be inferred that emerging views of a global geographic perspective existed in the second century, and that the earth was understood to be a single sphere on which all humanity lived.
- Regarding religion, it is interesting to note that all of the great world religions have, since ancient times, had a comprehensive belief in the unity of humanity and the unity of the planet (granted, most have acted contrary to their belief on this point from time to time, but the beliefs constitute truly global perspectives).
- Recent discussion on the rise of English as the first global language (Crystal 1997) should be placed in the historical perspective of the integrating power of Akkadian, Sanskrit, Turkic, Greek, Latin, Arabic, and other transnational languages of the ancient world. Ostler (2006) makes a good case that the influence of these older languages was, in their heyday, similar to that of English today.
- The efforts of Mitchell (1927), Schumpeter (1939), and others to understand the nature, causes and extent of business cycles, and particularly of the Great Depression of the 1930s, were based on the assumption that economic phenomena are somehow linked transnationally (although it took until the mid-1980s for economists such as McKibbin and Sachs (1991) and Dornbusch (1980) to model these linkages).

To sum up the discussion in this section, we conclude that globalization is clearly not a recent phenomenon. To ignore this fact would perpetuate IB's disciplinary isolation, and encourage an idiosyncratic view of the subject. Acknowledgment of globalization's ancient lineage makes richer, wider, and deeper theorizing possible. Moreover, it throws open a wide door for data gathering, and for the examination of the forces behind the process. Readers interested in a fuller discussion of this point should peruse the classic works by Wallerstein (2001) and Polanyi (1947), the enlightening essays by Kysucan (2001) and Holub (2001), and Chanda's (2007) interesting book.

HISTORY OF A WORD

Although, as we have shown, the process of globalization is ancient, our awareness of it is not. Indeed, the term 'globalization' itself is of relatively recent origin. In this section, we provide a brief background on the use of this humble word which is now used to characterize our age.

Human beings seem always to have had an appetite for labeling times – those past, and those in which they live, – 'stone age', 'age of discovery', 'age of reason', 'silver age', the 'enlightenment', etc. More recently, the 1950s were dubbed the 'atomic age', the 1960s the 'industrial society', the 1970s 'late capitalism', the 1980s the 'risk society', and the 1990s the 'postmodern society'. The grand successor to these (and all such) epithets is the term 'globalization'. Whatever meaning is implied by this word 'globalization', and whatever controversy surrounds it, it has become the label *nonpareil* for the world in which we live today.

'Globalization' derives from 'globe' and 'global', geometric terms used to describe spheres. Use of 'global' to refer specifically to the earth is over 400 years old (Waters 1995). By extension, and in common usage, the term was also used in reference to things related to, influencing, or covering the world, taken as a whole (Elden 2005). However, the term was not used in reference to travel until the 1890s, and in reference to trade until the 1950s. Probably the first use of the term in English, in the way it is used today, was in a 1959 *Economist* article reporting an increase in Italy's 'globalized quota' for imports of cars (Waters 1995). Shortly afterwards, the 1961 Merriam-Webster dictionary included definitions of 'globalism' and 'globalization' (ibid.). The entry traced uses of 'global' back to 1640, and 'globalization' to 1951. The Oxford English Dictionary's first example of the word's use, from the October 1962 *Spectator*, notes that: 'Globalisation[4] is, indeed, a staggering concept'.

But the word (or at least the thing it was to represent) was not limited to English. Similar concepts also emerged outside the English-speaking world. In the German-speaking world the term 'weltanschauung',[5] introduced as a neologism by Kant in the eighteenth century, gradually evolved into the notion of an all-encompassing idea of the universe and of man's relation to it. More recently, around the time of their appearance in English language publications, the French words 'mondialization' and 'globalization', were used in *Le Monde* (Worthington 2001). The term 'mondialisation' was explicitly and extensively discussed in the French journal *Arguments* in the 1950s (Elden 2006). Although 'mondialization' and 'globalization' are clearly related, they are not identical. For example, as Axelos explains:

> … *globalization* is a kind of mondialization without the world … *Globalization* names a process which universalizes technology, economy, culture. But it remains empty. The world as an *opening* is missing. The world is not the physical and historical totality, it is not the more or less empirical ensemble of theoretical and practical ensembles. It deploys itself. (Kostas Axelos in Elden 2005, p. 3)[6]

Abstract and vague though it is, this discussion clearly argues for the adoption of a world-embracing gestalt, because humanity was entering a planetary (global) era. Viewed from the vantage point of 2007, the discussion certainly reflects, at the least, a kind of proto-globalization and presages the notion of a global society and of globalization, as we understand the terms today.

Marshal McLuhan was the first to articulate the modern idea of globalization in his discussions of a 'global village', opening the way to the current usage of the terms global and globalization:'... we have extended our central nervous system itself in a global embrace, abolishing both space and time as far as our planet is concerned' (McLuhan 1964, p. 3).

McLuhan's insight was almost prophetic of things to come – of the time (through which we are now living) when technology and communications were to revolutionize human life on the planet. Long before the Internet, McLuhan understood that media was in some sense integrating the humanity, creating a global community not unlike a small village. Interestingly, he saw communication, not trade nor technology *per se* as the key driver.

Although McLuhan articulated the concept with uncanny clarity in the 1960s, globalization was not to become academically significant until around the mid-1980s (Robertson 1992). Despite a slow start, the globalization literature has, by some accounts, emerged at a faster rate than the process itself! (Guillen 2001).

'Globalization' entered the vocabulary of business practitioners and academics via Levitt's classic 1983 *HBR* article 'Globalization of Markets'. This article sets out with manifesto-like cadence to articulate the world Levitt saw emerging. And, although Marx and Engels used quite different vocabularies, the similarities between the worlds envisaged by the *Communist Manifesto* and Ted Levitt are startling. Levitt argued that:

> 'A powerful force drives the world towards a converging commonality ... a new commercial reality – the emergence of global markets for standardized consumer Products ... Gone are accustomed differences in national or regional preferences' (p. 92)

Because consumer preferences were being homogenized, global corporations were encouraged to bring standardized products at lower prices to markets worldwide. Cosmopolitanism was becoming '... the property and defining characteristics of all sectors everywhere in the world' (Levitt 1983, p. 101); different cultural preferences, national tastes, standards, and business institutions were seen now as vestiges of a past that was being falsely perpetuated by misguided corporations that erroneously customized their international offering.

Levitt uses the words 'globe', 'global', and 'globalization' over 50 times throughout his account. While his views on globalization are now viewed as somewhat crude, and have either been discredited or modified considerably, his 1983 account remains seminal, both for what he tried to describe, and for the vocabulary he brought to the task, and into the lives of IB practitioners and scholars.

MEASURING GLOBALIZATION

Any idea that purports to be as extensive, as all-encompassing and as (potentially) world-changing as globalization, could never hope to remain a 'mere' concept for very long. The stakes are simply too high. While the academic pioneers of globalization theory struggled to give empirical expression to what they were describing, they also felt the need for tangible ammunition on the polemical front. Similarly, national and international policy advocates, feeling an obligation to respond to what they believed was a momentous historical phenomena, needed something more than narrative arguments to convince skeptics. Hence, there have been numerous attempts to develop quantitative measures of globalization. Interestingly, none of these efforts to quantify globalization does so *in toto*. Rather, they all quantify globalization at either level of the nation-state or at the level of the organization (MNC). We briefly describe and evaluate two measures that take a nation-state perspective, and one that takes an MNC-perspective.

The Swiss Institute for Business Cycle Research (the Konjunkturforschungsstelle, der ETH Zürich, or more simply KOF), developed a globalization index based on an assessment of cross-border economic, social and political activities in 122 countries. Their longitudinal data set covers the period

1970–2005, and attempts to capture economic flows and restrictions, information flows and personal contacts across national boundaries, as well as cultural proximity between countries. The index is developed by applying a series of nested weightings (determined using principle components analysis), to the various data sets. For example, economic activities are weighted 36%, social activities 38%, and political activities 26%. Each of these general categories is broken down into sub-areas, each of which receives a weighting within the category. For example, 'social activities' is broken down into 'data on personal contact' (29%), 'data on information flows', (35%) and 'data on cultural proximity' (37%). Finally, these subcategories are broken down into specific, weighted and measurable items. For example, 'data on cultural proximity' is broken down into the number of McDonald's restaurants per capita (40%), the number of IKEA stores per capita (40%), and trade in books as a percentage of GDP (20%). All in all, the index uses 25 specific empirical measures. These are combined using the weights (as shown above), into a single globalization index for each country. A sampling of these is shown in Table 2.1.

Management consultancy firm A.T. Kearney, in collaboration with *Foreign Policy* magazine, also developed a widely influential metric of globalization. The A.T. Kearny/ *Foreign Policy* globalization index (hereafter the ATK/FP index) is quite similar to the KOF index in that it identifies conceptual

areas of global integration, and breaks them down in various ways to arrive at specific empirical measures. These measures are weighted and combined to build up the numerical indices for the general categories. The four components of globalization the ATK/FP envisages are: (1) Economic integration (unbundled into trade and FDI inflows and outflows); (2) Cross-border personal contacts (unbundled into cross-border travel and tourism, telephone traffic, remittances and personal transfers; (3) Technological connectivity (unbundled into the number of Internet users, Internet hosts, and secure servers); and (4) Political engagement (unbundled into the country's membership in representative international organizations, contributions to UN peacekeeping, ratification of certain multilateral treaties, and governmental transfer payments and receipts). Unlike the KOF index, which assigns weights to the components using a statistical technique, the ATK/FP index assigns component weightings somewhat arbitrarily (e.g., triple weighting on FDI and double weighting). However, in other respects, the ATK/FP index is more sophisticated in that the index is normalized, adjusted for country/economy size, and more amenable for longitudinal comparisons. A sampling of the ATK/FP index is shown in Table 2.2.

An alternative perspective to measuring globalization from the perspective of nation-states can be found in UNCTAD's

Table 2.1   2007 KOF Globalization Index

Country	GI	Country	EG	Country	SG	Country	PG
1. Belgium	92.09	1. Singapore	95.90	1. Switzerland	95.38	1. France	98.64
2. Austria	91.38	2. Luxembourg	95.14	2. Austria	92.49	2. USA	96.67
3. Sweden	90.02	3. Belgium	91.94	3. Singapore	92.26	3. Russia	96.04
4. Switzerland	88.60	4. Malta	91.39	4. Belgium	90.82	4. Italy	95.62
5. Denmark	88.42	5. Estonia	90.76	5. Netherlands	89.41	5. UK	95.52

GI = Globalization Index
EG = Economic Globalization
SG = Social Globalization
PG = Political Globalization

Source: http://globalization.kof.ethz.ch/static/pdf/rankings_2008.pdf

Table 2.2   2006 A.T. Kearny/*Foreign Policy* Globalization Index

2006 GI Rankings	Dimensions				Economic integration		Personal contact			Technological connectivity			Political engagement			
	Economic	Personal	Technological	Political	Trade	FDI	Telephone	Travel	Remittances and Personal Transfers	Internet Users	Internet Hosts	Secure Servers	International Organizations	U.N. Peacekeeping	Treaties	Government Transfers
1. Singapore	1	3	12	29	1	1	1	4	49	10	12	13	33	10	42	47
2. Switzerland	9	1	7	23	17	7	2	6	2	17	15	5	33	9	42	10
3. United States	58	40	1	41	62	36	18	33	52	6	1	1	1	25	58	38
4. Ireland	4	2	14	7	4	5	3	3	9	26	20	8	11	1	31	23
5. Denmark	8	8	5	6	20	6	6	16	16	12	3	7	11	13	6	8

Source: http://www.atkearney.com/shared_res/pdf/Globalization-Index_FP_Nov-Dec-06_S.pdf

'Transnationality Index' (TNI). Although ostensibly a measure of how international-ized MNCs are, the TNI can also be con-strued as reflecting organizational responses to globalization (or, perhaps, reflecting the degree to which MNCs are driving globaliza-tion). As such, it represents an interesting supplement to the KOF and ATK/FP global-ization indices. TNI is calculated by averaging a firm's ratios of: (1) foreign assets to total assets; (2) foreign sales to total sales; and (3) foreign employment to total employment (UNCTAD 2005). The resulting index reflects each firm's degree of engagement in world trade. Put another way, it suggests the extent of the firm's response to glob-alization. As such, it provides insight lack-ing in the more general indices described above. A sampling of the TNI is shown in Table 2.3.

Alternatively, the TNI may be interpreted as providing insight into one of the vehicles of globalization. For example, by aggregat-ing firms by industry, it is possible to identify

Table 2.3   UNCTAD's 2005 Transnationality Index

TNI Rank	Firm	Assets			Sales			Employment		
		Foreign*	Total*	Ratio	Foreign**	Total**	Ratio	Foreign***	Total***	Ratio
2	Asia Food	3.3	3.5	0.94	1.2	1.3	0.97	34.3	41.8	0.82
3	News Corp.	50.8	55.3	0.92	17.8	19.1	0.93	35.6	38.5	0.92
7	Vodafone	243.8	262.6	0.93	50.1	59.9	0.84	47.5	60.1	0.79
10	BP	141.6	117.6	0.80	192.9	232.6	0.83	86.7	103.7	0.84
21	Honda	53.1	77.8	0.68	54.2	70.4	0.77	93.0	131.6	0.71
42	Chevron/Texaco	50.8	81.5	0.62	72.3	120.0	0.60	33.8	61.5	0.55
53	VW Group	57.9	150.5	0.38	71.2	98.4	0.72	160.3	334.9	0.48
77	Generia Motors	258.0	674.5	0.38	54.1	134.2	0.40	150.0	305.0	0.49

* In billions of $US
** In billions of $US
*** In thousands

Source: http://goingglobal2006.vtt.fi/pdf/wir05overview_full.pdf

Table 2.4 Industry Transnationality Index

Industry	# Firms	TNI
Chemicals	7	61
Beverage, food, tobacco	9	54.24
Petroleum, petroleum refining	11	46.78
Electronics, electrical engineering	17	43.76
Metals	7	41.77
Motor vehicles and parts	13	37.62
Trading	7	29.33

Source: Ietto-Gillies and Seccombe-Hett (1997)

which sectors of the world economy are the most integrated, or most globalized (Ietto-Grillies and Seccombe-Hett 1997). Table 2.4 provides a sampling of industry TNIs.

One of the problems with many definitions of globalization is that while they help us to imagine, classify and describe a large-scale phenomena, which many believe is transforming the world, they are so general that they don't easily lend themselves to empirical examination. On the other hand, the quantitative indices that have been developed (including those mentioned above), leave one wondering what to do with statements such as 'Belgium has a globalization index of 92.09, while Burundi has a globalization index of 22.41' (KOF 2008 Globalization Index). All economic indices are abstractions of 'life on the ground', of what real people are doing in and with their lives. As such, perhaps, at the margin, viewed collectively, the measures of globalization outlined above may be interpreted as connective nerves into the living heart of globalization. However, our views of what globalization is might well change, suggesting that what we believe is indicative that globalization will change too. Moreover, the technologies driving communication, travel, etc. today could change in unimaginable ways (as they have in the past), shifting the dynamic, speed, content, and even the locus of globalization. Thus, a strong caveat is suggested in the use of all current quantitative globalization indices: none of them measures globalization *per se*. What they do measure are variables and vectors, believed to be significantly indicative of

the historic process we call globalization, as it is progressing at the present time, in the context of present political, cultural technological regimes. Globalization indices (those above, and others) are used in three ways: (1) in the popular press, to illustrate stories on globalization (e.g., Chen 2007); (2) by NGOs as polemical ammunition in a variety of policy debates (e.g., Gutierrez 2007); and (3) by economic and business academic researchers in combination with other quantitative variables in pursuit of a variety of research questions (e.g., Baily and Solow 2001).

A less grandiose and perhaps more useful and tractable approach to gaining empirical insight into globalization is suggested by Clark and Knowles (2003), in the form of four questions: 'What are the pertinent integrating mechanisms [of globalization]?'; 'In which direction is [globalization's integrating] influence flowing?'; 'What is the strength of the [various integrating mechanisms'] influence?'; 'Which factors inhibit globalization?' (p. 367). These questions suggest a way out of the 'grand-index' trap. They also open up novel ways of thinking about globalization. Perhaps more importantly, they imply a multidisciplinary agenda for globalization studies in IB.

PARADOXES OF GLOBALIZATION

A paradox is a statement or proposition, contrary to received opinion, or seemingly opposed to common sense: yet it is true. In this context, there are many unexamined beliefs surrounding globalization, which when unbundled and considered in the cold light of reason, are in fact not true. Put another way, there are several globalization paradoxes which are worth examining. In this section, we look at five of these: the philosophical, the logical, the economic, the Americanization, and the emotional paradoxes.

Philosophical paradox

For many, globalization is seen as the invention of Western corporations and of American Business Schools: MBAs are its evangelists. Anti-globalization protests in Madrid in 1994, in London, Seattle and elsewhere in 1999, and at the G-8 meeting in Genoa in 2001, were fueled in large measure by a somewhat misguided and popularized understanding of anti-globalization thinkers John Zerzan and Arundhati Roy. This perspective understands globalization to be a new and dangerous idea, foisted on the world by multinational corporations in pursuit of profit. The scenario goes further to pit grass-roots and local interests against 'evil' global corporations.

The paradox is that Karl Marx and Friedrich Engels were the first to describe globalization – and they did so in 1848! It should be noted that while Marx, the economist, and Marx, the political scientist, have largely been discredited, Marx, the sociologist, remains relevant (e.g., Tushman and Nelson 1990; Clegg, Hardy, Lawrence and Nord 2006). It is in this context that the remarkable picture of globalization painted by Marx should be seen. Moreover, as mentioned above, the Communist Manifesto bears some striking resemblances to Levitt's 1983 description of globalization. Consider the following excerpts (arcane words such as *bourgeoisie, proletarian,* etc. have been replaced by more modern terms, to highlight the remarkable picture Marx and Engels paint:

> Modern industry has established the world market ... This market has given an immense [boost to the] development [of] ... communication ... [which] ... in turn ... [further emphasizes] the extension of [Western corporate] industry ... From http://www.anu.edu.au/polsci/marx/classics/manifesto.html
>   The need of a constantly expanding market for its products [pushes corporations] ... over the entire surface of the globe ... [they] ... must nestle everywhere, settle everywhere, establish connections everywhere (ibid.)
>   [Multinational Corporations have] ... through ... [their] exploitation of the world market, given

> a cosmopolitan character to production and consumption in every country ... old-established national industries have been destroyed or are daily being destroyed. They are dislodged by new [global] industries ... [which draw] ... raw material ... from the remotest [parts of the earth] ... whose products are consumed ... in every [part] ... of the globe. In place of the old wants ... we find new wants, requiring for their satisfaction the products of distant lands ... (ibid.)
>   National differences and antagonism ... are daily ... vanishing, owing to the development of ... [a world business class] ... to free ... [trade] ... to the world market, to uniformity in the [methods] ... of production and in the conditions of life ... (ibid.)

Note in particular how similar this last quote is to Levitt (1983):

> A powerful force drives the world towards a converging commonality ... a new commercial reality – the emergence of global markets for standardized consumer products ... Gone are accustomed differences in national or regional preferences (p. 92).

At the very least, we can say that as an exercise in descriptive imagination, the *Communist Manifesto* is remarkable. Re-reading it today, one is struck by an amazing portrayal of the world we recognize around us, circa 2009, and of what we now call globalization.

Logical paradox

A second paradox has to do with what we expect from globalization. A central tenet of virtually all globalization literature is that world markets, cultures and governmental institutions are increasingly becoming integrated. Indeed, this thought is central to the definition developed in this article. A naïve interpretation of this fact is that nations are becoming less important as globalization proceeds. One version of this naïve view, sometimes referred to as 'hyperglobalization' (Held *et al.* 1999), is captured exquisitely in the titles of Kenichi Ohmae's two highly influential books – *Borderless World* (1990), and *The End of the Nation State* (1996). These (and many other) books make the argument that nations and their associated structures, are being trumped and transcended by the advance of multinational enterprise and economic globalization.

The paradox is that, if anything, the opposite is happening. At the very time when globalization is moving, full steam ahead, nationalism and related phenomena are increasing. There are many indicators of this. For example, the 'mere' fact that the number of nation-states has increased sharply since WWII, rising from around 104 in 1945 to over 214 today, is not insignificant. Far from the world becoming more and more borderless, it is, at least in this very practical way, becoming encumbered with more and more borders, more and more nation-states. Moreover, nationalism is also stronger throughout the world today than at any time since the 1930s. Reflecting on this, prominent globalization scholar Castells (1998) observes that the '… age of globalization … [is] also the age of nationalist resurgence …' (p. 27). Paradoxically, at the very time the hyper-globalizationalists are anticipating a one world economy, the number of aspirant 'nationalist' movements (e.g., for the Kurds and in Scotland, East Timor, and Chechnya, etc.) pushing for an independent existence is increasing alarmingly, leading political scientist Ernest Gelner to argue that the '… number … of potential nations is probably much, *much* larger than that of possible viable states' (Gellner 1983, p. 2).

Economic paradox

Leading pro-globalization arguments make a strong case that globalization is simply the industrial revolution, going out to the rest of the world – a growth- and wealth-engendering mechanism that rationalizes economic activity everywhere. One result is that infrastructural blank spots around the globe – roads, communications, human capital, etc. are filling in, leading to vastly increased industrial efficiency everywhere. In light of these arguments, one might be forgiven for assuming that the gap between the haves and the have-nots in the world is closing.

The paradox is that, in many cases, the gap between the rich and the poor is increasingly widening. Consider the following samples of remarks:

> [Globalization] … has generated anxieties about inequality … [and] shifting power … (World Bank 2002, p. 1).
>
> One of the most disturbing global trends of the past two decades is that countries with around 2 billion people are in danger of becoming marginal to the world economy. Incomes in [certain developing] … countries are falling, poverty has been rising, and they participate less in trade today than they did 20 years ago (ibid., p. x).
>
> The process that has come to be called 'globalization' is exposing a deep fault line between groups who have the skills and mobility to flourish in global markets and those who either don't have these advantages or perceive the expansion of unregulated markets as inimical to social stability and deeply held norms (Rodrik 1997, p. 2).
>
> … the inequality trends which globalization produced prior to WWI were at least partly responsible for the interwar retreat from globalization … (Williamson 1996, p. i).
>
> [in the context of globalization] … in both the most advanced and the least advanced countries the rich have gotten richer and the poor have gotten poorer. This is a great paradox … (Luttwak 1999, p. 61).

This widening gap is as perplexing as it is disturbing. While economic theory suggests, and in fact persuades, that such gaps should be short-lived, their emergence is alarming, and may in fact be fuelling anti-globalization arguments. While such views are myopic, the economic paradox is disturbing.

Americanization paradox

Ritzer (2004) developed an interesting theory explaining why globalization is so often taken to be an American phenomenon thrust upon the world. According to Ritzer, globalization's primary drivers are the market and consumption activities of capitalism. With capitalism as the main driver Ritzer goes on to argue that McDonaldization is the effective means for globalization's spread. Ritzer defines McDonaldization as '… the process by which the principles of the fast-food restaurant are ... [dominating] more and more sectors of ... the world' (p. 1). McDonalization is not primarily about the fast food industry. Rather, it reflects a particular type of economic rationalization that has swept all sectors of the US economy, and is now proceeding to do the same thing all over the world – in other words, globalization.

Implied in Ritzer's argument is the notion that globalization has taken a particular form and tone. To understand this better, imagine that a capitalist Fiji, or India, or Chile, and not the USA had been the dominant economy in the modern world. Given an energetic and expansive capitalism, the resulting globalization would surely have had a distinctively Fijian, Indian or Chilean character to it. However, it is the USA, and not these other nations, that has enjoyed economic and cultural hegemony since WWII. As a result, globalization has, thus far, had a distinctly American character. Indeed, since WWII, American media, firms, their products and symbols have gained a ubiquitous presence across the globe – hence, globalization is sometimes referred to as the Americanization of the world. This is mistaking the first mover for the process itself. The paradox is that American media, firms, their products and symbols are getting stiff competition from all over the world.

The explanation is that US firms, products, symbols, etc. enjoyed a first mover's advantage after WWII. That is, they had the first opportunity to give post-WWII globalization its complexion. However, as globalization proceeds and more and more nations climb aboard the global bandwagon, that advantage is simply not sustainable. How could it be otherwise when globalization is taking modern methods of organization, production and communication to every corner of the planet? For example, many US industries, including highly influential cultural industries are experiencing increasing competition. Europeans are turning away from American TV programming in favor of European programming. Movies produced in Britain, Hong Kong, and elsewhere are increasingly hitting a global nerve. When the Mumbai movie industry turns its attention to producing films for global markets – watch out Americanization! This is globalization's Americanization paradox.

Emotional paradox

Clark and Knowles (2003) argue that globalization makes a strange bedfellow, in the sense that it polarizes people into those who are *for*, and those who are *against* it, and that it does so in paradoxical ways. In the IB literature, globalization is usually portrayed as generally beneficial. However, serious and sophisticated critiques of globalization do exist. In the context of a wider consideration of all views, an examination of the political distribution of arguments, pro- and con-globalization, is very enlightening. One might be forgiven for assuming that those who are for or against globalization come from the same political perspective. Yet, not all who are against globalization are anti-business or politically left of center, nor are all those who are for globalization pro-business or politically right of center. There are groups on both the right and left who are pro-globalization *and* groups on the right and left who are contra-globalization (the entire argument here derives from Clark and Knowles 2003).

A closer look reveals that globalization makes for some strange bedfellows. Not surprisingly, most MNCs and most IB literature is implicitly right of center and pro-globalization. More surprising however is where Marxists fall – pro-globalization. Indeed, Marxists were among the first to hold positive views of globalization (re-read *sans* political content, the *Communist Manifesto*, and Bukharin's (1973) *Imperialism and the World Economy*, both of which portray a remarkable modern view of globalization). Compare this with the moderate left-of-center pro-globalization views held by such institutions as the World Bank.

However, those with anti-globalization views also form an unexpectedly mixed group.

For example, right-of-center nationalists such as Ross Perot (in the USA), Sir James Goldsmith (in the UK), and Jean-Marie Le Pen (in France), shared an anti-globalization stance with left-of-center union organizers and ecologists.

Clearly, opinions on globalization are not as simple as they may appear at first glance: important, relevant and complex counter-perspectives exist on all sides of the issue. Clark and Knowles (2003) sum up the matter of globalization's emotional paradox in this way:

> The dominant opinion in IB is only one *opinion* on the subject. Such an opinion is held on the basis of values, political conviction, and taste, rather than on an indisputable analysis of incontrovertible facts ... IB scholars do not have to agree with the counter-perspectives to benefit from some of the serious scholarship they provide. Even if one disagrees with all counter-perspectives, the fact that important decision makers hold those views and develop policy consistent with them suggests, at the very least, that there will be variables of interest to IB scholars emanating from them (p. 364).

THE FUTURE OF GLOBALIZATION

Globalization is the process by which economic, political, cultural, social, and other relevant systems of nations are integrating into world sub-systems. It is a complex process that has been at work, in various ways, and to different degrees, since ancient times. Oddly, it is also a phenomenon that has gone largely unnoticed (and unnamed) until fairly recently. Reflecting this fact, a number of accounts of globalization begin with the rise and spread of American MNCs immediately after WWII. Only in the past two decades (or so) has globalization *per se* become of interest to the IB, or any academic community.

Much of the literature implicitly assumes globalization represents a sort of perpetual revolution. Serious reflection suggests that is improbable. We are in what might be called globalization's 'phase plane'. The changes wrought in this phase plane have been so consuming to contemporary observers that little effort has gone into looking beyond what we are presently going through, into imagining what the steady-state outcomes might look like. However, we may now be within shouting distance of globalization's climax, its dénouement. At least, if we have defined our subject adequately, it is now possible to imagine what its end-state might look like.

Like all transitions, globalization's phase plain implies a 'from what', and a 'to what'. The 'from what' is history, and, since WWII, we have increasingly characterized that history in terms of the globalizing process – at a minimum, the commercial/economic/social/cultural integration the world has experienced since 1945. The 'to what' (25 years out and beyond) is, as yet, unknown. In this final section, we explore the likely end-state of the ancient historical process we call globalization. Our speculations are based on four heroic assumptions: (1) no worldwide conflict (WWIII) occurs; (2) no new and devastating diseases emerge; (3) the *tendency* towards democracy continues around the world; and (4) technology continues evolving along the current trajectory (electronics, communication, etc.). These are heroic assumptions, because they have never held over long periods in the past, and it is improbable they will hold in the future.

Nevertheless, in the short- to mid-range time horizon (~25 years), they may hold up well enough for us to support some reasonable speculations. We foresee three likely 'steady-state' features of the world after globalization: (1) the re-emergence of the political as the world's key organizing principle; (2) the reversal of some cultural flows; and (3) a middle class world.

RE-EMERGENCE OF THE POLITICAL AS THE KEY ORGANIZING PRINCIPLE

The *Communist Manifesto* describes a world increasingly dominated by economic, and decreasingly influenced by political interests. Less ideological characterizations of the world Marx and Engels imagined would simply argue the virtues of markets. Ted Levitt, probably put it best, in his seminal 1983 article (eerily reminiscent of the *Communist Manifesto*), when he argued that:

> A powerful force drives the world towards a converging commonality … a new commercial reality – the emergence of global markets for standardized consumer products … Gone are accustomed differences in national or regional preferences (p. 92).

All sides of the current globalization debate seem to concede, gladly or unhappily, that free trade, markets, marketing, the pursuit of profit, etc., have been major factors in reshaping the world (i.e., globalization) since 1945. Those who endorse the changes (e.g., Bhagwati 2003) see the economic side of globalization as taking the industrial revolution (i.e., higher standards of living, etc.) to the rest of the world. Those who are unhappy with globalization (e.g., Klein 2002, 2007; Danaher 1997; Danaher and Burbach 2000), [7] see it essentially as toxic, devastating to human lives, and fundamentally lacking in democratic consent.

In the 1960s, MNCs were often portrayed as exploiters of developing nations (e.g., Baran 1973). By the 1980s, the wealth and job creation power of MNCs began to be apparent (Bauer 1984), and a sort of bidding war began as national (and regional) governments attempted to attract and/or keep MNCs in their territory. For their part, some MNCs were able to extract concessions in exchange for their job-creating presence (Narula and Dunning 2000). In the process, the relative strength of governments declined vis-à-vis the MNCs.[8] The situation has been facilitated by the integration of the world economy in the technical sense – trade arrangements, currencies, inflation, interest rates, etc. Such technical integration has made it necessary for governments to coordinate economic policy. The result was a *de facto* erosion of national governmental power, and the growth of corporate influence and power.

The current hegemonic dominance of MNCs and global markets is untenable in the long run. It is untenable, not because globalization's more radical critics are correct, but because global firms are ill-equipped to address some of the larger common issues facing humanity – global pollution, intellectual property protection, disease, and warming, use of the high seas, Antarctica, etc. As Kuttner (1997) puts it, society is logically prior to markets. Without a counterbalancing civil/political force, global markets would likely produce global company towns. However, in a converging world, in which there are differing views of the place of the market in society, the hegemonic dominance of global markets and global companies will not likely continue as it has, because they cannot, independently, provide the stability (laws, property rights) needed for their own existence. Only governments can do that. Just as early articulations of environmentalists' concerns seemed at first radical (e.g., Carson 1962), only to be made mainstream by the 1990s (recall George Bush senior's campaign pledge to become the environmentalist president), so current radical anti-globalization arguments will become domesticated, non-controversial, and main stream over the next decade or so, as globalization brings more and more nations into its sweep [this seems to be exactly the point Kagan (2008) is making]. Thus, we expect the emergence of international, national, regional and other significant governance regimes to emerge to counterbalance the current dominance of global markets.

REVERSAL OF CULTURE FLOWS

Since the end of WWII, the USA has enjoyed a significant economic, cultural, technological and military hegemony over the rest of the world. One reason for this dominance was the USA's first mover advantage after WWII – the USA was the only significant economy not materially devastated by the war.

At the war's end, America's productive capacity, geared up to make tanks, ships and airplanes, simply switched over to produce autos, washing machines and toasters. In 1945, when the fighting stopped, there was a world of burgeoning demand, and only one country ready to meet it – the USA. For a generation, US MNCs went out into the world, with virtually no foreign competition (Vernon 1973). One unintended consequence of this was that US culture went along with the MNCs. The result was an effective cultural hegemony in American expressive products (movies, books, TV shows, music, etc.). We referred to this as the 'Americanization Paradox' above. A generation came to maturity under the influence of this US cultural dominance.

However, the world did recover from WWII, and by the early 1970s, US commercial hegemony began to erode as serious competitors entered the fray (particularly, but not limited to, German and Japanese auto manufacturers). One interpretation of this is that after a hiatus caused by WWII, the process we call globalization kicked back into life. In short order, France, Italy, Britain, the Netherlands, Korea, etc. followed, and began vying for market share in an increasingly open trade environment. By the early 1990s, India, China, Brazil, and many other nations made a showing in global markets, first simply as attractive manufacturing locations, then as legitimate competitors in world trade.

Although the USA is likely to continue as an economic and cultural leader, it is unlikely it can continue the dominance it enjoyed 1945–1975. In a globalizing world, in which free trade is the order of the day, it is inevitable that other nations vie for, and win, a share of global markets. Just as US cultural hegemony was an unintended consequence of its emergence as a first mover after WWII, so an unintended consequence of China, India and other nations becoming serious players in global markets, is that US cultural hegemony will be eroded as the expressive products of those other nations become available. Although the USA may have invented the modern movie and music industries, globalization has spread industry savvy worldwide. Diffusion of such savvy can only reasonably lead to many reversals of culture flows:

> Over the next century, disruptive innovations won't be coming from countries like the United States. They'll also be emerging from dynamic, hungry, rising economies that offer plenty of room for risk taking, flights of fancy and cross border synthesis (Caryl 2007, p. 45)

Moreover, since the current dominant global language is English, there will be an advantage to countries outside of the West that employ English as their working language. India, for example, has a domestic market of over a billion people. Indian film makers churn out more film products each year than does Hollywood. Moreover, Indian film makers are as sophisticated and as technically astute as their Hollywood colleagues, in every way. When Bollywood turns its immense resources more fully toward larger world markets, two consequences will emerge: (1) they will begin to produce film products suitably tailored to wider tastes; and (2) they will produce products with distinctly Indian values embedded in them. Multiply this sort of change across the developing world, wherever and whenever local expressive products can be suitably refocused toward world markets, and we begin to understand the potential for unusual and historically unprecedented patterns of cultural influence.

MIDDLE CLASS WORLD

Perhaps the most amazing outcome of globalization to emerge over the next 25 years will be a substantially middle class world. By 'substantially middle class world', we mean that most people on the planet will have left the drudgery of subsistence living behind them to become discerning consumers, with appetites for the same commercial accoutrements and life of ease and satiability enjoyed by most in the West. If our heroic assumptions hold, that outcome is certain.

Globalization, that great and ancient integration of the world, means, among other things, that technological know-how travels, eventually, to the ends of the earth. This dispersion of know-how has accelerated since the end of WWII, when free trade emerged as the regime of choice around the world. That openness meant, of course, the availability of every type of Western consumer product, with a consequent impact on tastes around the world. It also meant the grandstanding of Western wealth-producing capital goods, technological savvy and managerial know-how, everywhere on the planet. This potent combination of taste for Western goods, and the ability to make them, is transforming production and consumption everywhere. Idiosyncratic, inefficient, local capital goods and methods are being swept away in favor of global best practices. Increasingly, tastes, and expectations of what one may hope for in life, are molded, everywhere in the world, in the same way, by the same influences.

The largest growth rates for most industries are no longer found in the West. Rather, they are found in the developing world. The emergent demand for consumer goods in India, China, and elsewhere is gigantic. As tastes for the good life mature, and as global firms compete to supply that good life – urban and rural infrastructure (electricity, water, power, roads, sewers, etc.), TVs, DVDs, Internet, mobile phones, automobiles, fashionable clothes, magazines, music and food snacks – a middle class existence will begin to take shape everywhere on earth. Signs of the middle class explosion are already evident in India, where '... since 1985, more than 400m ... have risen out of relative poverty ... and another 300m will

follow over the next two decades if the economy continues to grow ...' (Ram-Prasad 2007). In 2003, China's middle class had risen to around 1.9% of China's 1.3 billion people (i.e., 250 million). The proportion of middle class is expected to rise to 40% by 2020.[9]

CONCLUSION

Too much energy has been wasted in debate over whether or not globalization exists, on when it started, and on whether we should foster it or stop it. Globalization is not a human invention; rather, it is an unintended consequence of human life and human behavior here on earth. It cannot be stopped – at least not by any deliberate human effort. Certainly unintentional human actions – wars, depressions, disease, etc. might do that. The reality seems to be, that no matter what we call it, globalization is simply part of the natural evolution of humanity. At the margin, we may be able to influence and manage some of its effects. The re-emergence of the political, outlined above, reflects one way this will occur. However, it is unlikely we will be able to eliminate all negative consequences of the process. No change comes without trade-offs. And, arguably, never in the history of mankind has there been such a sweeping all-pervasive change as the phase of globalization we are currently moving through.

As an historically complex phenomenon, a fuller understanding of globalization will emerge only from multiple perspectives, across multiple disciplines. There is, perhaps, no discipline better positioned to lead this intellectual expedition than IB. Yet, because of a pervasive intellectual myopia (see Clark and Knowles 2003; Clark, Knowles and Hodis 2004) there is perhaps no discipline currently more ill-suited for the task. Let us hope we do not cede ownership of such an important topic to others.

NOTES

1 Much of the material in this section is an adaptation and extension of Clark and Knowles (2003) and Clark, Knowles and Hodis (2004).

2 In answer to Rugman, and others with similar views, Chanda has written '... the economic definition [of globalization] leaves other questions unanswered. How, for example, did the coffee bean, grown first in Ethiopia, end up in our cups after a journey through Java and Columbia? How did the name of Bodhisattva *Avalokiteswar*, translated into Chinese as *Guanyin* and into Japanese as *Kwanon*, inspire the Japanese brand name for a camera?' (2007, p. xi).

3 About 200 million people (3% of the world's population) were international migrants in 2005. Between 1995 and 2000, around 2.5 million migrants per year moved from less to more developed nations (Population Reference Bureau 2007).

4 *Globalisation* is the British variant of the word *globalization*.

5 Note related words *weltwirtschaft* (global economy) and *weltethos* (global ethic).

6 In translation from *Des Demons – Atelier en directe de la Pensee d'Edgar Morin*, August 2000, Sao Paulo.

7 Suggestively titled *Corporations Are Gonna Get Your Mama* (1997) and *Globalize This!* (2000).

8 The suggestively titled *Sovereignty at Bay* (Vernon 1973) and *Twilight of Sovereignty* (Wriston 1992), are representative of the literature taking this view.

9 A widely reported figure coming from a report of the Chinese Academy of Social Sciences (see http://www.chinadaily.com.cn/english/doc/2004–03/30/content_319105.htm)

REFERENCES

Albarran, Alan B. and Chan-Olmsted, Sylvia M. (1998) *Global Media Economics: Commercialization, Concentration and Integration of World Media Markets*. Ames: Iowa State University Press.

Baily, M. N. and Solow, R. M. (2001) 'International productivity comparisons built from the firm level', *Journal of Economic Perspective*, 15(3) (Summer): 151–172.

Baran, Paul A. (1973) *The Political Economy of Growth*. London: Penguin Books.

Barnett, T. and Whiteside, A. (2006) *AIDS in the Twenty-First Century: Disease and Globalization*. New York: Palgrave Macmillan.

Bauer, Peter. T. (1984) *Reality and Rhetoric: Studies in the Economics of Development*. Cambridge: Harvard University Press.

Baumann, M. P. and Fujie, L. (2000) 'Local musical traditions in the globalization process', *The World of Music*, 42(3): 121–144.

Bhagwati, J. (2003) *In Defense of Globalization*. New York: Oxford University Press.

Braudel, F. (1984) *The Perspective of the World*. New York: Harper and Row.

Brennan, T. (1997) *At Home in the World: Cosmopolitanism Now*. Cambridge: Harvard University Press.

Burbules, N. (2000) *Globalization and Education*. London: Routledge Falmer.

Burkharin, N. (1973) *Imperialism and World Economy*, Monthly Review Press New york.

Carson, R. (1962) *Silent Spring*. Boston: Houghton Mifflin.

Caryl, C. (2007) 'Why Apple Isn't Japanese', *Newsweek*, 10 December, 42–45.

Castells, M. (1998) *End of the Millennium*. London: Blackwell.

Chanda, N. (2007) *Bound Together*. New Haven: Yale University Press.

Chen, Louis (2007), 'In creativity, size doesn't matter', *Taipei Times*, 26 Aug, p. 8.

Clark, T., and Knowles, L. (2003) 'Global myopia: globalization theory in international business', *Journal of International Management*, 9(4): 361–372.

Clark, T., Knowles, L. and Hodis, M. (2004) 'Global dialogue: a response to the responders in the special globalization issue of JIM', 19(4): 511–514.

Clegg, S., Hardy, C., Lawrence, T. and Nord, W. R. (eds) (2006), *SAGE Handbook of Organization Studies*. London: Sage Publications.

Collins, R. (2000) *The Sociology of Philosophies: A Global Theory of Intellectual Change*. Cambridge: The Belknap Press of Harvard University Press.

Crystal, David (1997) *English As A Global Language*. Cambridge: Cambridge University Press.

Currie, J. and Newson, J. (eds) (1998) *Universities and Globalization: Critical Perspectives*. London: Sage Publications.

Danaher, K. (ed.) (1997) *Corporations Are Gonna Get Your Mama: Globalization and the Downsizing of the American Dream*. Monroe: Common Courage Press.

_____and Burbach, R. (eds) (2000) *Globalize This! The Battle Against the World Trade Organization and Corporate Rule*. Monroe: Common Courage Press.

Dornbusch, R. (1980) *Open Economy Macro-economics*. New York: Basic Books.

Eddy, J. A., Ceschger, H. and Oeschger, H. (eds) (1993) *Global Changes in the Perspective of the Past, the Dahlem Workshop on Global Changes in the Perspective of the Past*. Hoboken: John Wiley & Son Ltd.

Edelman, Mark (1999) *Peasants Against Globalization: Rural Social Movements in Costa Rica*. Stanford: Stanford University Press.

Elden, S. (2005a) 'Mondialisation without the world: interview with Kostas Axelos', *Radical Philosophy*, 130: 25–28.

Elden, S. (2005b) 'Missing the point: Globalization, deterritorialization and the space of the World', *Transactions of the Institute of British Geographers*, 30(1): 8–19.

Elden, S. (2006) Introducing Kostas Axelos and "the World", *Environment and Planning D: Society and Space*, 24(5): 639–642.

Eschle, C. (2001) *Global Democracy, Social Movements and Feminism*. Boulder: Westview Press.

Friman, R. H. and Andreas, P. (1999) *Illicit Global Economy and State Power*. Boulder: Rowan & Littlefield Publishers.

Gellner, E. (1983) *Nations and Nationalism*. Oxford: Blackwell.

Guillen, M. F. (2001) 'Is globalization civilizing, destructive or feeble? A critique of six key debates in the social-science literature', *Annual Review of Sociology*, 27(1): 235–260.

Gutierrez, L. T. (ed) (2007) *Solidarity, Sustainability and Non-Violence* (E-Newsletter), Vol. 3, No. 6 (June).

Hagedorn, John M. (2007) *Gangs in the Global City*. Champaign: University of Illinois Press.

Held, D., McGrew, A., Goldblatt, D. and Perraton, J. (1999) *Global Transformations: Politics, Economics, and Culture*. Stanford: Stanford University Press.

Herod, A., O Tuathail, G. and Roberts, S. M. (1998) *An Unruly World? Globalization, Governance, and Geography*. New York: Routledge.

Holub, Margaret (2001) *Globalization and the Maccabees*. (http://www.mcjc.org/mjoldart/MJAMH039.htm)

Ietto-Grillies, G. and Seccombe-Hett, T. (1997) 'What so internationalization indices measure?' *Research Working Papers in International Business*. Centre for International Business Studies, London: South Bank University, 6–97. (http://www.lsbu.ac.uk/cibs/pdf/6-97.pdf)

Karliner, J. (1997) *The Corporate Planet: Ecology and Politics in the Age of Globalization*. San Francisco: Sierra Club Books.

Kagan, R. (2008), *The Return of History*, Alfred A. Knopf.

Klein, N. (2002) *No Logo*. New York: Picador.

_____ (2007) *The Shock Doctrine: The Rise of Disaster Capitalism*. New York: Metropolitan Books.

Koslowski, R. (2005) *International Migration and the Globalization of Domestic Politics*. New York: Routledge.

Kung, H. (1998) *A Global Ethic for Global Politics and Economics*. New York: Oxford University Press.

Kuttner, R. (1999) *Everything For Sale*: University of Chicago Press.

Landow, G. P. (2006) *Hypertext 3.0: Critical Theory and New Media in an Era of Globalization*. Baltimore: The Johns Hopkins University Press.

Levitt, T. (1983) 'The globalization of markets', *Harvard Business Review*, 61(3): 92–102.

Lewellen, Ted C. (2002) *Anthropology of Globalization*. Westport: Greenwood Publishing Group.

Lewis, G. and Araya, R. (2002) 'Globalization and Mental Health', in N. Sartorius, W. Gaebel, J. J. Lopez-Ibor, and M. Maj (eds), *Psychiatry in Society*. Chichester: Wiley, pp. 57–78.

Lopez, A., Mathers C., Ezzati, M., Jamison, D. and C. Murray (Editors) (2006), *Global Burden of Disease and Risk Factors*, Oxford University Press, NY.

Luttwak, E. (1999) *Turbo-Capitalism: Winners and Losers in the Global Economy*. New York: HarperCollins Publishers Inc.

Marx, K. and Engel, F. (1848) *The Manifesto of The Communist Party*. (http://www.gutenberg.org/etext/61)

McKibbin, W. and Sachs, J. (1991) *Global Linkages: Macroeconomic Interdependence and Cooperation in the World Economy*. Washington, DC: The Brookings Institution.

McLuhan, M. (1964) *Understanding Media: The Extensions of Man*. New York: McGraw-Hill.

Mitchell, W. C. (1927) *Business Cycles the Problem and Its Setting*. New York: National Bureau of Economic Research.

Michael L. and Richard R. Nelson (1990), "Introduction: Technology, Organizations, and Innovation" *Administrative Science Quarterly*, Vol. 35, No. 1, Special Issue: Technology, Organizations, and Innovation: March, pp. 1–8.

Monkman, N. P. and Stromquist, K. (2000) *Globalization and Education*. Lanham: Rowman & Littlefield Publishers.

Munck, R. (2002) 'Globalization and democracy: A new "great transformation"?', *Annals of the American Academy of Political and Social Science*, 581(1): 10–21.

Murray, C. J. L. and Lopez, A. D. (eds) (1996) *The Global Burden of Disease*. Cambridge: Harvard University Press.

_____ (2000) 'Industrial development, globalization and multinational enterprises: New realities for developing countries', *Oxford Development Studies*, 28(2): 141–167.

Narula, R. and Dunning, J. H. (1990) *Borderless World*. New York: Harper Collins Publishers.

Ohmae, K. (1996) *The End of the Nation State: The Rise of Regional Economies*. New York: Free Press Paperbacks.

Ostler, N. (2006) *Empires of the Word: A Language History of the World*. New York: Harper Perennial.

Papastergiadis, N. (2000) *The Turbulence of Migration: Globalization, Deterritorialization and Hybridity*. Cambridge: Polity Press.

Polanyi, K. (1947) *The Great Transformation*. Boston: Beacon Press.

Population Reference Bureau (2007) *Population Bulletin*. Vol 62, No. 3 (September).

Ram-Prasad, C. (2007) 'India's middle class failure', *Prospect Magazine*, 138 (September) http://www.prospect-magazine.co.uk/pdfarticle.php?id=9776

Rantanen, T. (2004) *The Media and Globalization*. London: Sage Publications.

Reader, J. (2006) *Globalization, Engineering and Creativity*. San Francisco: Morgan and Claypool Publishers.

Ritzer, G. (2004) *The Globalization of Nothing*. Thousand Oaks: Pine Forge.

Robertson, R. (1992) *Globalization: Social Theory and Global Culture*. London: Sage Publications.

Rodrik, D. (1997) *Has Globalization Gone too Far?* Washington, DC: Institute for International Economics.

Rugman, A. M. (2001) *The End of Globalization*. New York: AMACOM/American Management Association.

_____ (2003) 'Regional strategy and the demise of globalization', *Journal of International Management*, 9(4): 409–417.

Sampson, E. E. (1989) 'The challenge of globalization for psychology: Globalization and psychology's theory of the person', *American Psychologist*, 44(6): 914–921.

Schumpeter, J. A. (1939) *Business Cycles: A Theoretical, Historical, and Statistical Analysis of the Capitalist Process*. New York: McGraw-Hill.

Shapiro, I. and Brilmayer, L. (1999) *Global Justice*. New York: New York University Press.

Sklair, L. (1991) *Sociology of the Global System*. Baltimore: Johns Hopkins University Press.

Taylor, P. M. (1997) *Global Communications, International Affairs and the Media Since 1945*. London: Routledge.

UNCTAD (2005) *World Investment Report: Transnational Corporations and the Internationalization of R&D*. New York: United Nations.

Vernon, R. (1973) *Sovereignty at Bay: The Multinational Spread of U.S. Enterprises*. London: Penguin Books.

Wallertsein, I. M. (1975) *Modern World-System I: Capitalist Agriculture and the Origins of European World-Economy in the 16th Century*. Burlington: Academic Press.

_____ (2001) 'America and the World: The Twin Towers as Metaphor', *Social Science Research Council*, http://www.ssrc.org/sept11/essays/wallerstein.htm

Waters, M. (1995) *Globalization*. London: Routledge.

Williamson, J. (1996) 'Globalization and inequality then and now: the late 19th and late 20th centuries compared', *National Bureau of Economic Research*, Working Paper Series No. 5491, March.

Worthington, G. (2001). 'Globalisation: perceptions and threats to national governmentin Australia', *Politics and Public*

Administration Group, Parliamentary Library of the Parliament of Australia, Research Paper 27. (http://www.aph.gov.au/library/pubs/rp/2000-01/01rp27.htm)

World Bank, Washington, DC (2002) *Globalization Growth, and Poverty, Building an Inclusive World Economy*. New York: Oxford University Press (http://goingglobal2006.vtt.fi/pdf/wir05overview_full.pdf)

Wriston, W. B. (1992) *Twilight of Sovereignty*. New York: Scribner Book Company.

3

The Changing Global Political and Institutional Environment

Jonathan Doh and Terrence Guay

INTRODUCTION: THE CHANGING GLOBAL POLITICAL AND INSTITUTIONAL ENVIRONMENT

International marketing – and international business more broadly – does not operate in a vacuum. A range of actors, each of whom has particular interests and values, and often approaches international business from a different perspective, works with and sometimes against companies to shape this environment. Until fairly recently, companies seeking to expand markets abroad were required to navigate the domestic political environments of those countries. This required, for example, complying with different health, workplace, environmental and other regulations, or working with government officials to obtain necessary import or export licenses or approval for constructing a factory. Companies also needed to stay abreast of the local economic and social situation, political rivalries, and relations that the country had with its neighbors. Being aware of such 'political risk' was an important factor when deciding whether to export to another market, invest in that country, or avoid it entirely (Bremmer 2005). No company wants to see its investments nationalized (or taken over) by the local government, or have rebel groups sabotage its facilities or kidnap employees. Consequently, understanding the political environment of other countries was a prudent thing for managers to do.

Although the necessity of timely and accurate information regarding the political and institutional environment remains critical, the emergence of new actors and important new global trends has changed the way companies must view these environments. Companies entering the international arena now must contend with international organizations (IGOs) like the World Trade Organization (WTO), which sets and enforces global trade rules, and the European Union (EU), which regulates much of the business activity in Europe. In addition, companies must interact with relatively new entities on the world stage, known as non-governmental organizations (NGOs). NGOs are non-profit, issue-oriented groups that are interested in the effects that economic activities have on the environment, workers, urbanization, human rights, and other concerns. It is not unusual for companies to develop strategies for interacting with all of these actors – foreign governments, IGOs, and NGOs – and successful companies do so (Baron 1995).

As the actors have changed, so have the political issues that affect international business. With the end of the Cold War, most countries have abandoned 'do-it-yourself' economic development strategies, and embraced many market-oriented policies, including privatizing formerly state-owned businesses, encouraging foreign investment, and removing non-tariff barriers. As discussed in Chapter 2, globalization has eliminated many of the barriers to international business. But these changes also have produced a different set of problems that countries and companies face in the early years of the twenty-first century (Bosworth and Gordon 2001). For example, the scientific evidence seems to confirm that increased human economic activity is affecting the world's climate. Also, greater economic interdependence among countries has provided more opportunities for 'good' business, but also has made it easier for 'bad' business (e.g., smuggling, human trafficking, drugs trade, and money laundering) to thrive (Naím, 2005). These two examples – and there are many more – illustrate the complexity of the problems that political leaders face today. Also, many of these leaders are turning to business, NGOs, and IGOs to help solve them. As companies are drawn into these forums, they need to understand the political dynamics of the issues and the actors if mutually agreeable solutions are to be found.

In this chapter we provide a deeper explanation of the themes described above. It begins by discussing the overall institutional environment for international business and the increasing interest in the quality and stability of institutions for growth, development and international economic integration around the world. We continue by exploring the decline of the bilateral business – government bargaining process that characterized multinational interactions with host governments in earlier periods, and discuss the emergence of new actors and institutions that now are

directly involved in defining the terms of international business and marketing. We then describe the rise and importance of international and regional organizations, and why international-oriented businesses need to pay attention to them. The rise of NGOs is the focus of the fourth section. We discuss the reasons for their increased prominence in international affairs, and the kinds of international business issues that are important to them. The next section describes how the nature of political issues has changed in recent years, and how the variety of actors have interacted to address some of them. The chapter concludes by suggesting new avenues of research that will help scholars better understand the interrelationships between politics, institutions, and international business.

THE CHALLENGE OF INSTITUTIONS AND INTERNATIONAL MARKETING

The importance of institutions in the organization of modern economic life is reflected in the extensive managerial research on institutional theory and its applications. North (1986, 1993) argues that institutional stability, fairness, and the like are critical for economic growth. Such institutional environments are demonstrated by a well-specified legal system, a clearly defined and impartial third (judicial) party of government to enforce property rights, and a set of attitudes towards contracting and trading that encourage people to engage in transactions at low costs (North 1986, 1993).

North notes that the absence of a 'stable structure facilitating interactions' (North 1990), such as rule of law and a good quality bureaucracy in government (Schleifer and Vishny 1993), results in significantly higher transaction costs. In particular, institutional deficiencies stemming from inconsistent enforcement of rules, ineffective legal frameworks (LaPorta et al. 1998) and corruption in governments (Doh et al. 2004) have been

Table 3.1   Governance indicators for selected countries, 2005[a]

	Voice and accountability	Political stability	Government effectiveness	Regulatory quality	Rule of law	Control of corruption
Australia	95	74	95	96	95	95
Austria	90	82	92	94	97	97
Belgium	93	67	94	87	91	91
Chile	83	76	86	91	87	90
China	6	39	52	45	41	31
Colombia	37	4	53	54	32	53
Denmark	100	78	99	98	99	98
Egypt	18	21	43	34	55	43
Equatorial Guinea	5	52	5	8	7	0
Finland	100	98	99	99	98	100
Ghana	59	50	54	50	48	45
Haiti	10	4	5	12	2	1
Iraq	9	0	1	6	0	5
Malaysia	34	62	80	67	66	65
Nigeria	30	5	20	15	6	6
North Korea	0	41	0	0	10	3
Singapore	38	84	100	100	96	99
Somalia	2	0	0	0	0	0
USA	89	49	92	93	92	92

Source: Kaufmann, D., Kraay, A. and Mastruzzi, M. (2006), *Governance Matters V: Governance Indicators for 1996–2005*, World Bank Policy Research Working Paper 4012 and 'A Decade of Measuring the Quality of Governance', September 2006

[a] Data indicates percentile rank

sources of instability which, in turn, impede growth and innovation. Overall, weak legal and regulatory institutions (North 1986, 1993) that fail to provide for basic public goods, property rights and other protections (Levy and Spiller 1996) result in poor economic performance and instability (Henisz and Williamson 1999).

Drawing from North's (1990, 1993) new institutional economics, researchers have focused on hazards associated with the makeup and distribution of political systems (Henisz 2000) and have called attention to the risks associated with institutional voids – environments characterized by the absence of formal, functional institutional mechanisms (Khanna and Krishna 1997, 2000; Khanna *et al.* 2005). Another approach to measuring institutional quality focuses on 'governance infrastructure', aspects of host country environments that reflect the complex and interrelated dimensions of the institutional apparatus for overseeing private sector development and property protection (Kaufmann and Kraay 2002; Kaufmann *et al.* 1999).

There are several approaches to measuring the quality and reliability of institutional governance. The World Bank has maintained updated aggregate governance research indicators for 213 countries for 1996–2005, for six dimensions of governance: Voice and Accountability; Political Stability and Absence of Violence; Government Effectiveness; Regulatory Quality; Rule of Law; and Control of Corruption. The methodological approach and validity of these measures are discussed in Kaufmann, Kraay and Mastruzzi (2006). Table 3.1 reports these indicators for a selection of developed and developing countries for 2006. The nexus between the quality of institutional governance and growth and development is readily apparent, as is the close correlation between and among several of these indicators.

Obviously, the quality and consistency of institutions has direct bearing on the overall environment for international marketing and the specific marketing strategies that are suitable to different institutional contexts.

In the next section we explore a more specific literature on the interactions between multinationals and host government institutions and the emergence of new actors in that institutional dynamic.

THE END OF BILATERAL BUSINESS–GOVERNMENT BARGAINING AND THE EMERGENCE OF NEW INSTITUTIONAL ACTORS

Scholars have long been interested in the interactions among multinational enterprises (MNEs) and the host governments in which they do business. IB scholarship dealing with the MNE interactions with political actors and institutions can be divided into two related streams. Dahan, Doh and Guay (2006) summarize the various streams of this literature and some of the critiques and shortcomings associated with it.

The political risk stream, as represented by the work of Robock (1971), Kobrin (1979), Simon (1984), and others, views the MNEs' political environment as mostly a given; firms must react by either complying with or exiting the host country (Boddewyn 1988). The bargaining model as proposed by Vernon (1971) and further explicated by Kobrin (1987) proposes that MNEs typically face more favorable terms early in the investment process but that their bargaining power erodes as their investment commitment increases. The model has served as a powerful perspective for understanding the dynamics of multinational–host country relations, is prominent in the IB literature and has enjoyed many extensions. It offers a more dynamic view of the MNE as a political player involved in bargaining with the host country (Fagre and Wells 1982; Vernon 1971). Although significant theoretical enhancements have extended the scope of this approach over the past three decades (Moran 1985), there is growing skepticism about the efficacy of the bargaining model (Boddewyn 1988; Boddewyn and Brewer 1994).

Dahan, Doh and Guay (2006) identify four principal shortcomings of these models: (1) they are centered on the national level (i.e., MNEs interact with states, overlooking other types of public authorities and political levels); (2) they consider primarily dyadic relationships (MNEs–states) while MNEs increasingly develop relationships with a multiplicity of public and private actors, (3) they deal with the MNE as the focal organization (with no consideration for collective actions undertaken by MNEs within groupings such as clubs, associations, fora, etc); and (4) they restrict their analysis to the political environment of MNEs, that is, cover hard power in the forms of compulsory regulations, formal public policies and court rulings, thus missing 'soft power' aspects such as spreading ideas, shaping cognitive frames through discursive strategies and symbolic actions, and participating in the promotion of certain social norms and values.

Vernon (1971) proposed a specific application of these models of MNE–host country relations in the obsolescing bargain model (OBM). He argued that the changing dynamic of bargaining relations between MNEs and host governments is a function of goals, resources and constraints on both parties (Vernon, 1971). Under this scenario, the desire of the host government to attract investment results in the initial bargain favoring the MNE. However, the relative bargaining power shifts to the host country government as the MNE commitment becomes more substantial and more difficult to reverse. Once this bargaining power shifts, the host government imposes additional conditions on the MNE, ranging from higher taxes to contract renegotiation to complete expropriation of MNE assets.

Kobrin's (1987) early insight that FDI in manufacturing industries and export-oriented investment was less vulnerable to host country intervention demonstrated that these models are subject to important conditions and constraints. These conditions and constraints have come to suggest that the bargaining model is outdated and in need of reconsideration.

Indeed, the model was largely repudiated in the late 1980s and 1990s (Stopford and Strange 1991), reflecting, in part, evidence that outright expropriations in developing countries had declined precipitously through the period. Doh and Ramamurti (2003, p. 342), however, observed that 'creeping' expropriations were replacing outright takings, noting that 'beneath these generally favorable statistics lies a troubling pattern: governments continue to engage in a pervasive practice of selective and disruptive recontracting ...'.

Recent contributions have sought to extend or revise the political risk and bargaining models (Ramamurti 2001) rather than proposing alternative conceptualizations. Ramamurti (2001) contended that the emergence of multilateral organizations and other state–state trade and investment agreements severely constrained intervention by host governments. Teegen, Doh and Vachani (2004) added the rise of NGOs to this mix (which we discuss below), suggesting at least a trilateral, as opposed to a bilateral, set of relationships. These extensions, however, do not completely undermine the relevance of the model, as most recently evidenced by the actions of developing country governments, especially those in Latin America (e.g., Venezuela, Bolivia, Ecuador, Peru).

The institutions created by a society to govern social, economic and legal transactions have a critical role to play in the ability of firms to enter and operate in foreign markets. The nature of bargaining and negotiation among MNE, host country and other stakeholders over the terms of investment constitutes an important dynamic in this process. These interactions have evolved significantly over the past decades, such that host governments have somewhat less influence over the terms of investment and instead compete for those investments, while other institutions such as international organizations and NGOs are more involved and engaged.

In the next section, we discuss how the emerging of the WTO and regional trading arrangements – especially the EU – have affected the political and institutional environment for international marketing. We subsequently address the emergence of nongovernmental organizations (NGOs) as important players in this mix.

THE EMERGENCE AND DEVELOPMENT OF MULTILATERAL AND REGIONAL INSTITUTIONS

As discussed in Chapter 1, globalization affects international business and international marketing in multiple ways. Globalization is often perceived as a unifying force that serves to homogenize rules, decision-making, and markets. However, scholars have identified significant variations on this theme. On the one hand, a need has developed for global organizations to construct rules to govern international business (Barnett and Finnemore 1999; Maggi 1999). The number of international organizations has increased dramatically over the past two decades. While most of these organizations are of the non-governmental variety (discussed further below), international inter-governmental organizations (IGOs) have expanded as well. The Union of International Associations estimates that there are over 7,000 IGOs. They include prominent organizations like the United Nations, which has a tremendous impact on international business. For example, the World Health Organization (WHO) is the directing and coordinating authority for health within the UN system and has, among other initiatives, campaigned for a ban on tobacco advertising. The World Bank, also a part of the UN, provides financial assistance to developing countries, and multinational corporations often participate in programs that support economic developing, such as building infrastructure. The UN also has sponsored initiatives with the private sector such as the Global Compact, which promotes good corporate citizenship in the areas of human rights, labor, the environment, and anti-corruption. There are numerous IGOs that are not affiliated with the UN, which cover a range of areas, such as the Organization for Economic Cooperation and Development (OECD), whose members consist of 30 of the world's richest countries, the Organization of the Petroleum Exporting Countries (OPEC), which coordinates the petroleum policies of its 13 members, and INTERPOL, which facilitates international police cooperation.

While it is beyond the scope of this chapter to examine a wide range of IGOs, it is instructive to focus on two prominent ones to emphasize the extent to which IGOs impact international business and international marketing: the World Trade Organization (WTO) and the European Union (EU). The WTO came into being in 1995, but its predecessor organization, the General Agreement on Tariffs and Trade (GATT), dates back to 1947. The mission of both organizations has been to reduce barriers to trade. Focus initially was on tariffs, but has now shifted to non-tariff barriers, since the tariffs on most tradable goods have been cut considerably over the course of negotiations and agreements (known as 'rounds' in international trade parlance).

The WTO consists of 151 member countries, about two-thirds of whom are developing countries. This creates challenges for the organization, since the needs of developing and developed countries are quite diverse. Developing countries receive special provisions, such as extra time to fulfill their commitments. But there remain considerable disagreements between developed and developing countries, particularly in the two main areas where developed countries make it difficult for developing countries to enter their market – agriculture and textiles. The most recent round of trade negotiations, known as the Doha round, began in November 2001. However, disagreements over how far developed countries should reduce subsidies and import tariffs brought negotiations to a standstill.

While its economic objective is clear, the WTO is controversial. Critics argue that it is not democratic, preferences economics over labor and environmental issues, and reduces the power of national governments (Atik 2001; Conca 2000; Wallach and Naim 2000). The WTO's defenders, including Bhagwati (2004, 2005), counter that trade liberalization has done more good than harm, and that it is unfair to apply developed country norms of labor and environmental concerns to less developed countries. The debate is both utilitarian (i.e., is the world as a whole better off economically with an organization that regulates international trade, even if it means that national governments find their policy options circumscribed?) and normative (i.e., is the WTO gaining too much power at the expense of national governments?). However, states create IGOs like the WTO for a variety of reasons (Keohane 1982). IGOs serve as a source of information for participants; they reduce the transaction costs of (in the case of trade-oriented IGOs) beginning anew every time countries seek to negotiate trade agreements; and they often create a demand for additional IGOs that promote greater independence among participants. For business, IGOs can provide both opportunities and threats. Globally competitive firms benefit from the market-opening dimension of IGOs, but less competitive industries often resist trade agreements. As a result, national governments often find themselves playing 'two-level games', that is negotiating with domestic interest groups as well as other countries (Putnam 1988).

While the WTO represents the 'internationalizing' of trade, numerous smaller organizations signify the 'regionalizing' of trade and economic patterns. These include: NAFTA, the North American Free Trade Area that includes the USA, Canada, and Mexico; MERCOSUR, or Southern Common Market founded by Argentina, Brazil, Paraguay, and Uruguay; and the 21 Pacific Rim countries that comprise the Asia-Pacific Economic Cooperation (APEC). According to the WTO, 205 regional agreements were in force in July 2007. The WTO expects this figure to reach close to 400 by 2010. However, the regional groups vary considerably in terms of membership, extent of interconnected economies, breadth of agreements, and trade reduction commitments. While regionalism has grown dramatically, some fear that it has come at the expense of lower trade barriers at the global level (Bhagwati, Greenaway and Panagariya 1998). The result is a 'spaghetti bowl' affect, whereby numerous overlapping agreements complicate and distort the patterns of trade. Thus, one debate is whether regionalism detracts from, or contributes to, international trade (Frankel 1998; Srinnivasen 1998). None of these trading and investment agreements has developed the supranational institutional apparatus that now characterizes the EU, however, some are beginning to establish administrative architecture that will increasingly influence international business and marketing within their respective regions of coverage. Here we focus on the EU as it is an archetype for other regional arrangements and potentially a harbinger of how regionalism may evolve in other contexts in the future.

The most well-known and most sophisticated of the regional groups is the EU. The EU's origins date to the creation by Belgium, France, Germany, Italy, Luxembourg, and the Netherlands of the European Economic Community (EEC) in 1957. The organization expanded multiple times and now includes 27 countries from Ireland to Cyprus and from Finland to Portugal and most countries in between. While the EEC's original purpose was to achieve security in Europe through the expansion of economic interdependencies, specifically through the reduction of trade barriers, the organization underwent name changes and numerous policy expansions, such that the EU of today is far more than an economic club. At the economic level, internal tariffs have been eliminated, and one of the organization's primary economic goals since the 1986 Single European Act (SEA) has been the gradual removal of non-tariff barriers. In fact, the SEA's objective is to remove all of the barriers to the movement of goods, services, capital, and people throughout the EU.

The formation of a truly single economic market would represent, by itself, a regional organization far more integrated than any other. But the EU is more than that. The pressures for economic integration have 'spilled over' into political integration, the result being cooperation in justice and police matters, as well as the development of common foreign, security, and defense policies. Even the euro, the common currency used by 13 countries, represents more than an economic achievement, since countries have relinquished their ability to set national monetary policy (i.e., controlling interest rates through a national central bank) and have agreed to constraints on fiscal policy. The EU is empowered to vet large-scale mergers (including companies domiciled outside Europe, like General Electric–Honeywell and Boeing–McDonnell Douglas) and investigate and punish allegations of anti-competitive practices. The EU came down hard on Microsoft for the company's anti-competitive business practices, resulting in a fine of about $700 million.

The multifaceted power of the EU has pushed scholars to examine the organization's decision-making processes and regulatory impact (Rosamond 2000). The multi-level governance (MLG) literature (Marks et al. 1996; Wessels 1997) accepts that both the EU and national governments have roles to play in terms of policy-making and regulatory functions, that these functions often overlap specific policy areas, and that a range of actors (including companies, various interest groups, European Commission officials, and national-level politicians and bureaucrats) are active simultaneously across both layers. Others view the EU as a 'regulatory state', which 'may be less of a state in the traditional sense than a web of networks of national and supranational regulatory institutions held together by shared values and objectives, and by a common style of policy-making' (Majone 1996, p. 276). A third characterization of the EU is based on institutionalist literature. The three general strands of institutionalism tend to focus on how interest groups, transaction costs, or the EU's own preference-shaping capabilities mould the organization's development (Pierson 1996; Pollack 1996). Such diverse perspectives result in a focus on different levels of analysis (e.g., the international, European, and national environments), as well as different actors (e.g., domestic interest groups, bureaucratic politics, national governments, etc.).

One consequence of the EU's growing influence is the expansion of the lobbying efforts from businesses and other parties affected by the organization's policies. While numbers vary, the EU estimates that about 15 000 professional lobbyists operate in Brussels today. Another estimate of the European lobbying landscape by Guéguen (2002), counts over 1,000 EU trade associations, around 750 NGOs, European representative bodies from around 500 major companies, 130 regional offices (since each European region has its own representative organization in Brussels), 130 specialist law firms, and an unspecified number of consultants, all of which total around 3,000 lobbying structures in Brussels. With about four-fifths of all economic and labor market legislation in national parliaments originating from the EU, it is obvious why so many lobbyists have established themselves in that city.

Scholars studying the relationship between lobbying groups and EU decision-making focus on policy networks (Peterson 1995; Richardson 1996). A policy networks approach is mainly interested in the actors involved in developing and implementing specific policies and the dynamics of their interactions. At this level, scholars are interested in such questions as: Which groups are providing advice? Who appears to be most influential? How do policymakers use the information they are given? What happens to these networks once a policy decision has been made? How does feedback impact subsequent policy development? Such questions allow us to understand which actors and stakeholders are important in the day-to-day activities of the organization. A policy network approach to understanding the EU may be viewed as a corollary to MLG, since it emphasizes the dispersion of power and authority across multiple political layers in Europe.

Finally, it is important to note that EU laws, regulations, and policies are more than just a European issue. Increasingly, European rules are becoming international ones (Buck 2007). Companies realize that, if they want to sell to 480 million consumers within the EU, they must comply with EU rules concerning product safety, financial regulation, consumer rights, and other regulations that are typically more stringent than those in other countries. But companies that can meet EU standards are almost assured of meeting those of any other country, since governments around the world often copy the EU's rules. One consequence is that European companies, such as those in the mobile phone industry, often benefit from a first-mover advantage. Some scholars argue that such measures can increase the international competitiveness of a country's or regional organization's companies (Porter 1990).

To summarize, IGOs like the WTO and EU have become formidable, if controversial players, in the twenty-first century business environment. Research questions oriented around international trade likely will center on the suitability of the WTO to resolve disputes among members whose positions in the global economy range from highly-skilled service economies to low-cost manufacturing hubs to agrarian-focused economies, as well as the competition between business groups and other societal actors to shape national trade policies. With respect to the EU, attention will continue to be devoted to understanding decision-making within the organization, and the relative influence of economic and non-economic actors. More broadly, scholars will be interested in the tensions between increasing economic competitiveness and the necessary reforms that many European countries will need to make to their socioeconomic models to adapt to greater international competition.

THE RISE OF NGOs AND OTHER NON-STATE ACTORS

The emergence of nongovernmental organizations (NGOs) and other non-state actors has had an important impact on the political and institutional environment for international marketing. On the one hand, criticisms of globalization and MNEs by many NGOs have created friction and pressure on MNEs to be more responsive to the range of stakeholders they encounter in their global activities. On the other hand, many MNEs and NGOs are forging new partnerships in which they jointly advance initiatives designed to promote sustainable development in global regions.

Civil society, also referred to as the 'third sector' or the 'non-profit' sector, is used to broadly describe all aspects of society that extend beyond the realm of the public sector and the private sector (Teegen, Doh and Vachani 2004). Although the term NGO is relatively recent, associations among 'like-minded individuals' have been part of ancient and modern history. Unlike state-based membership inherent in citizenship, association in civil society is voluntary and is characterized by individuals coalescing around common ideas, needs, or causes to promote collective gain. It can be said that once these individuals come together in an organized or semi-organized fashion, they are taking collective action (Olson 1971).

When individuals or groups within civil society work together to advance a broad common set of interests, and these interests become a significant force in shaping the direction of society, the outcomes of this process are often called social movements (Teegen, Doh and Vachani 2004). Social movements can be thought of as broad societal initiatives organized around a particular issue, trend, or priority (Teegen, Doh and Vachani 2004). Modern examples include the environmental movement and the women's/ feminist movement. When civil society groups come together to form more organized relationships, the entities that emerge are often referred to as nongovernmental organizations or NGOs. NGO is a broad term and is used somewhat loosely to refer to all organizations that are neither an official part of government (at any level) nor private, for-profit enterprise.

Teegen, Doh and Vachani (2004, p. 466) define *social purpose* NGOs as 'private, not-for-profit organizations that aim to serve particular societal interests by focusing advocacy and/or operational efforts on social, political and economic goals, including equity, education, health, environmental protection and human rights'. Teegen, Doh and Vachani (2004) further differentiate among various functions of NGOs. *Advocacy* NGOs work on behalf of others who lack the voice or access to promote their interests. They engage in lobbying; serve as representatives and advisory experts to decision-makers; conduct research; hold conferences; stage citizen tribunals; monitor and expose actions (and inactions) of others; disseminate information to key constituencies; set/define agendas; develop and promote codes of conduct; and organize boycotts or investor actions. In these ways, NGOs give voice and provide access to institutions to promote social gain and/or mitigate negative spillovers from other economic activity. *Operational* (may also be termed programmatic or service-oriented) NGOs provide critical goods and services to clients with unmet needs. NGOs have long stepped in to serve as critical 'safety nets', where politically challenged, indebted, or corrupt states are unable or unwilling to provide for unmet needs, and where global problems defy traditional nation-state responsibilities. Examples of such operational activities include relief efforts provided by the Red Cross/Red Crescent, natural resources monitoring by the World Wide Fund for Nature, and the distribution of medicinal drugs by Doctors Without Borders.

Although some NGOs focus primarily on advocacy or operational service delivery, many others pursue both sets of activities simultaneously, or evolve from one to the other.

For example, Oxfam, the global development and poverty relief organization, advocates for changes in public policy that would provide greater support to its efforts, while also contributing directly to health, education and food security in the developing countries in which it operates.

NGOs have assumed a significant and influential role in global affairs. According to Lindenberg (1999), fiscal crises, ideological shifts, and privatization have all led to a decline in the scope and capacity of the state. In response, a growing global not-for-profit sector has emerged that, in part, has begun to fill the humanitarian vacuum left by the corporate sector and the nation-state. The number of NGOs in the world has increased in recent decades (Spar and La Mure 2003). A number of global events have led to this increase. One impetus in the recent resurgence in civil society is the political failure of centrally planned economies, such as the former Soviet Union and Central and Eastern Europe. Globalization is another important force in NGO history. While many NGOs have criticized globalization and its impact (Stiglitz 2002), globalization has facilitated the growth and development of NGOs.

The modern era of NGO activism can be traced to 1984, when a range of NGOs, including church and community groups, human rights organizations, and other anti-apartheid activists, built strong networks and pressured US cities and states to divest their public pension funds of companies from doing business in South Africa. The Comprehensive Anti-Apartheid Act banned new US investment in South Africa, export sales to the police and military, and new bank loans, except to support trade. The combination of domestic unrest, international governmental pressure, and capital flight posed a direct, sustained, and ultimately successful challenge to the white minority rule, resulting in the collapse of apartheid (Doh and Guay 2004).

NGOs have also pushed to have greater access to the trade policy and other international governmental agreements and processes, systems that have historically been limited to governments acting as agents of their domestic constituencies. NGOs have expressed a great deal of interest in the trade policy dispute settlement mechanism under the General Agreement on Tariffs and Trade (GATT) and its successor agreement, the World Trade Organization (WTO). In addition to individual corporate–NGO interactions, NGOs have also been very active in collective efforts to develop, implement and enforce industry-wide standards, codes of conduct, and agreements.

Examples of intergovernmental agreements that have been shaped and influenced by NGOs include those multilateral and regional trade agreements discussed above, such as the WTO, the North American Free Trade Agreement (NAFTA), the UN Global Compact, the International Labor Organization Declaration of Principles concerning Multinational Enterprises and Social Policy, and the Organization for Economic Cooperation Guidelines for MNEs. Examples of international codes sponsored directly by not-for-profit NGOs include the Social Accountability International SA8000 standard, Rugmark, a standard that certifies rugs and carpets as meeting basic standards for labor and human rights, and the Forest Stewardship Council (FSC) standard that certifies lumber as consistent with sustainable practices (Doh and Guay 2004).

The NGO sector, in both developed and developing countries, has experienced exponential growth since the mid-1970s. In terms of international development, it is now estimated that over 15 percent of total overseas development aid is channeled through NGOs. Indeed, a report published by the United Nations and the NGO Sustainability notes that the global non-profit sector, with its more than $1 trillion turnover, could rank as the world's eighth largest economy. For the United States, in the 1970s, approximately 70 percent of resource flows to the developing world were from official development assistance and 30 percent were private. In 2003, just 15 percent of $102.5 billion in resource flows were comprised of direct government assistance, with 85 percent coming from nongovernmental resources, of which 45 percent was private capital flows, 15 percent NGO assistance, and 25 percent personal remittances (USAID 2006). Teegen, Doh and Vachani (2004) propose that the emergence of civil society in general, and the activism of civil society NGOs in particular, have broad implications for the role, scope and definition of corporations in the global economy, and therefore for international management as a research field. Doh and Teegen (2003) point out that the emergence of NGOs has, in some cases, supplanted the role of host governments in the historic business–government bargaining relationship, such that NGOs yield significant power over the MNEs' right to operate in developing countries.

In addition, NGOs are facing criticism and pressure over the perception that they are often less accountable for their actions than their government and business counterparts. Specifically, the corporate governance scandals in the United States and around the world have resulted in increasing attention to the role of boards, interlocking board directorates, and the overlapping board membership among corporations and nonprofit NGOs. The American Enterprise Institute (AEI), in cooperation with the Federalist Society for Law and Public Policy Studies, has launched a program initiative called 'NGO Watch' whose mission is to highlight 'issues of transparency and accountability in the operations of non-governmental organizations (NGOs) and international organization (IOs)' (AEI 2006).

Increasingly, NGOs are engaging in both collaborative and combative relationships with MNEs in the areas of development. Lindenberg and Dobel (1999, p. 12) summarize the dilemma for NGOs of closer ties to MNEs: 'The NGOs face a continuing agenda of how to maintain their mission integrity and autonomy even as they seek these funds. At the same time they need to protect their own legitimacy in the eyes of funders and recipients and not be used by

states or corporations for their own purposes.' In response, many NGOs are no longer willing to adopt an either/or approach to their interactions with companies. Rather, they have assumed an increasingly sophisticated and multifaceted relationship with business firms. In moving into this more complex role, they must ask, 'when does it make sense to cooperate with the corporate sector and when might it be necessary to provide contravening pressure?' (Lindenberg and Dobel 1999, p. 12).

By the same token, companies are now more strategically evaluating their decisions to engage in collaboration with NGOs. Starbucks' relationship with NGOs has been the subject of a number of cases and research efforts. Lindenberg (1999), for example, documents Starbucks' long-standing relationship with CARE (USA). Beginning in 1991, one of CARE's managers in the northwest region approached a Starbucks staff member regarding CARE programs and development seminars. Starbucks had already carved out a strong social responsibility position, and given that Starbucks sourced coffee from regions where CARE was active, some kind of relationship seemed logical and appropriate (Lindenberg 1999). Thus, the relationship began as a philanthropic one in which CARE received $2 from the sale of coffee samplers. Subsequently, reports Lindenberg, the relationship became more transactional with Starbucks donating resources directly to CARE projects. By the late 1990s, 'the relationship moved from the transactional to more integrative stage in which CARE staff members were offered opportunities for training and sabbaticals in Starbucks corporate units, such as human resources and marketing. Starbucks staff members participated more frequently' (Lindenberg 1999, p. 605). Ultimately, Starbucks began to consult CARE on issues related to codes of conduct and standards regarding its overseas business practices, including Starbucks' decision to move into the sale of 'fair trade' coffee. By 2001, Starbucks had contributed more than $1.8 million to CARE (Argenti 2004).

On the NGO side, Oxfam has been the subject of a number of analyses of its relationship with corporations. Oxfam's approach to these relationships could generally be characterized as 'engagement' as opposed to close partnerships. Lindenberg (1999) reports that Oxfam Great Britain has pursued an evolving, comprehensive strategy that is complex, dynamic and involves multiple corporate relationships.

> Oxfam's corporate engagement strategy includes three dimensions: funding and cooperation, policy dialogue with joint standard setting and monitoring, and pressure tactics. Oxfam GB's president defines funding and cooperative relationships as ones in which Oxfam and its corporate partners have similar long-term values and goals about the development process, not unlike the decade-long relationship between CARE and Starbucks. Oxfam has such relationships with Northern Foods and the Cooperative Bank, two UK corporations. When Oxfam engages in policy dialogue, the second dimension of its strategy, neither Oxfam nor the corporations involved are under any illusions that their values or basic objectives are highly compatible. Rather, their commitment is to engage in civil discussion about issues of common concern (Lindenberg 1999, p. 605).

Nonetheless, Oxfam has recently worked more closely with corporations in areas that include its 'Making Trade Fair' campaign and related initiatives regarding 'fair trade' certified coffee. According to Oxfam America's President, 'The most innovative international NGOs of the future will have moved from the hands-on operational style of the 1960s to a highly complex and diverse set of institutional partnerships, joint ventures, and networking relationships' (Offenheiser, Holcombe and Hopkins 1999, p. 137).

Beyond NGOs, there are other categories of non-state actors that have dramatically altered the political and institutional environment for international marketing. In particular, different types of terrorist groups have emerged that are exerting substantial influence on how MNEs engage in international marketing around the world. We address the issue of terrorism in the next section.

TWENTY-FIRST CENTURY ISSUES

Thus far, we have concentrated our discussion of the impact of political issues on international business and marketing on organizations (international, regional, and non-governmental). It should be clear that the rise of such actors is changing dramatically the traditional concept of business–government dynamics. However, the nature of international politics also is changing, in terms of the issues that have reached increased prominence in recent years. As discussed earlier, traditional political topics for international business used to revolve around market entry, foreign investment, and terms-of-trade issues. With the evolution of international organizations, and the standardized rules that they set for members, these former political issues have become institutionalized and more technical in nature. Today, the political issues are less economically narrow, yet still can have a major impact on a global company's success.

The new issues include the environment; working conditions; data privacy; terrorism; development; transparency; and (broadly) corporate social responsibility (see Chapter 26). While it is beyond the space constraints here to describe each of these (and others) in much detail, we sketch some of the main controversies that have been raised in the scholarly and mainstream literature.

Perhaps the most dominant of these issues in recent years is that of the global environment. From rivers to oceans and deserts to the atmosphere, there is a growing awareness that economic development can be detrimental to the environment, various species, and human health (United Nations Development Programme 2007). Climate change has received considerable attention, and many countries, businesses, and international organizations have begun to address it. The 1997 Kyoto Protocol requires certain countries to reduce their greenhouse gas emissions by five percent below their 1990 levels by 2008–2012. Consequently, companies operating within these countries are bound by the initiatives governments have implemented to meet their goals. The politics of Kyoto are significant, since a handful of prominent countries (including the United States and Australia) did not adopt the agreement and have faced considerable pressure from those countries that did, as well as from international organizations and NGOs (Lisowski 2002). Going forward, new economic powers like China and India will face pressure to pursue economic development in more environmentally friendly ways.

The area of labor represents another and fairly new source of controversy. The concern here is that increased global competition is forcing companies to search for ever cheaper means of production. Countries like China and, to a lesser extent, India are viewed as the primary beneficiaries of this process, since these countries have hundreds of millions of workers eager to participate in globalization. Some critics argue that globalization is straining the ability of richer countries to provide the social programs necessary to sustain popular support for market-opening policies (Rodrik 1997). In both the labor and environmental controversies, there is a debate as to whether competition among companies – and countries to attract the foreign investment that global firms provide – is leading to a 'race to the bottom' or 'race to the top' in terms of environmental and labor regulations (Adnett 1995; Bhagwati 1997; Lee 1997). Consequently, companies in the manufacturing, footwear, and apparel industries have been forced by critics – NGOs as well as rich country governments – to respond to labor abuse allegations.

There are also international disputes over health, science, and food safety. Genetically-modified organisms (GMOs) are at the core of these issues, with consumers in certain parts of the world (particularly Europe) skeptical about the safety of such products, and protective of locally-grown crops and their farmers (Prakash and Kollman 2003; Soule 2003). The biotechnology industry was forced to respond with a multi-pronged strategy: persuade European consumers that

GMOs were safe; lobby the EU to change its regulatory processes; and encourage the US government to negotiate with EU officials to provide greater market access to GMOs. Efforts by international organizations like the WTO to resolve such disagreements have led to inconclusive results (McKinney 2006).

The debate over GMOs is representative of a larger debate about how to resolve disputes over local values and norms of behavior in an international marketplace. National governments traditionally have sought to protect and promote the interests of their citizens within the international environment. But when companies seek to sell their products and services in new markets (as in the GMO case), or utilize different business practices, attempts by home and host country governments to resolve such disputes can be fraught with controversy. This was the case with data privacy concerns (Long and Quek 2002). The business practice for many US companies is to collect a variety of information about their customers, which is then refined to market other products from affiliated companies. Citizens in Europe and other countries, however, have much stricter regulations concerning the kind of information companies can collect, how they can use it, and how long they can keep it. For global companies seeking to cross-market their services and products, different regulations complicate the ability to do business in other countries. In the case of data privacy, different regulations also make it more difficult to operate globally, since even information like employee office phone numbers is protected under EU rules (Scheer 2003). This is far from being simply a US–EU dispute, since Canada, Australia, New Zealand, South American, and parts of Asia have adopted similar privacy standards. While a resolution to the US–EU disagreement over personal information was reached, with US companies agreeing to provide higher levels of protection for information related to European customers and employees, disagreements over other regulatory and values differences are likely to expand and intensify in the coming years as other countries (particularly in Asia and Africa) become more integrated in the global economy.

Terrorism has emerged as a major issue in the risk and security faced by MNEs around the world. Prior to 9/11, terrorism was not a principal concern to most MNEs, with perhaps the exception of those involved in resource extraction, or those operating in the most politically volatile regions of the world. Since 9/11, however, the emergence of global networks of terrorist cells, the emergence of terrorism in seemingly 'safe' countries, and the interaction between terrorism, failed states and broader violent conflict has exacerbated MNEs concerns about security and safety, not to mention overall market access and operation. A survey of 154 MNEs conducted by the Economist Intelligence Unit (EIU) (2007) found that 36 percent of the respondents regarded 'terrorist attacks by individuals/groups outside our home market', as presenting the highest risk to their company's operations over the next five years – an increase of 8 percentage points over the previous five years.

As a result, companies will need to develop strategies that address these issues. While some of these issues are more relevant to certain sectors, practically all global companies will need to respond. For example, the oil and automobile industries are among the most affected by climate change, and companies have developed different strategies in response (Levy and Kolk 2002; Mikler 2007). The strategies are due partly to differences in home country environments, as well as attempts to reposition within the industry and to be viewed as leaders in the climate change controversy. But concerns about climate change are shaping corporate strategies in a wide swathe of industries, including energy, tourism, airline, forestry, packaging, construction, and agriculture – to name just a few. Similarly, incidents of sweatshop conditions in developing countries at the same time as workers in rich countries express growing insecurity about their jobs and standard of living, places global companies in virtually every industry

in an awkward position (German Marshall Fund 2006). Labor-intensive and manufacturing industries feel the most political heat, but so do information technology, financial services, and pharmaceutical companies who outsource and offshore software design, computer programming, business processing, and research and development work. While there is no obvious solution to these 'twenty-first century issues' that have economic, political, and social roots and consequences, there are some innovative strategies that companies and their stakeholders have developed together.

FUTURE DIRECTIONS

Companies, governments, and (increasingly) IGOs and NGOs are tied inextricably into resolving contentious new issues such as those discussed in the previous section. The modes and intensity of interactions will change over time and by issue, as will the actors involved. Thus, research in the coming years will focus on these structures, assessing the relative influence of the various actors and measuring the ability of these arrangements to provide mutually satisfying solutions to challenging global problems.

Some promising research in these areas has begun. For example, scholars have started to investigate the use of corporate codes of conduct (Kearney 1999; Williams 2000). These codes are voluntary agreements by companies to address concerns such as labor and environmental practices. These codes often are the result of interactions between companies, NGOs, IGOs, and governments. Doh and Guay (2004) found that NGOs have the greatest impact on codes of conduct when they intervene early in the code development process; when they forge transnational coalitions with other organizations, including other NGOs, companies, and governments; when codes are devised outside of IGOs (since constituent governments are often more influential); and when the structure of codes explicitly provides for involvement by non-business and non-state actors (e.g., NGOs are tasked with monitoring company compliance).

More broadly, the concept of 'global governance' has become an increasingly popular theme in the international business and social science literature. The term is an acknowledgement that national governments cannot, on their own, solve transnational issues, and that other private and civil society actors, as well as IGOs, can play constructive roles in such matters (Hall and Biersteker 2003; Karns and Mingst 2004; Ottaway 2001). However, the structure of global governance can take on a variety of forms, depending on the issue area and the power of relevant actors. For example, Haufler (2001) argues that industry self-regulation (through codes of conduct, trade association standards-setting, and self-policing) has allowed certain industries to avoid more stringent government regulations while moving policy-making outside of the public realm. And, as noted above, NGOs have become increasingly important actors in brokering solutions to transnational problems. Even in those circumstances in which, whereby companies have responded to NGO pressure in the hopes of averting more restrictive government regulations, the complex dynamics of global governance are being played out.

Understandably, these changing dynamics between actors and the issues they are addressing are not without controversy (Esty 1998; Murphy 2000; Woods 2001). Critics contend that these evolving forms of governance undermine national sovereignty, and weaken the ability of governments to control what happens within their borders. Further, the increasing ability of IGOs and NGOs to shape global rules and norms of behavior implies a lack of accountability (i.e., it is much more difficult to know who to blame or punish if decisions produce bad outcomes), as well as a lack of inclusiveness (i.e., not all stakeholders may have an equal seat at the table – if they have a seat at all). These concerns are not alleviated by the presence of one of the newest categories of actors to enter

the global governance dynamic – privately funded, high profile foundations, sometimes led by celebrities, that have become major catalysts for developments assistance and social innovation. The Bill and Melinda Gates Foundation is a quintessential illustration of this new category of actor. The Gates Foundation, with more than $33 billion in assets, is increasingly directing its investments to NGOs – both global and local. One program supports a World Health Organization venture with an Indian vaccine maker to sell a meningitis vaccine in Africa for far less than existing vaccines. Other foundations, such as Skoll, Schwab, and Google's in-house private philanthropic investment are also taking these innovative approaches to social and environmental development around the world. Celebrities such as the rock singer Bono, and his DATA foundation (Debt, AIDS, Trade, Africa) are having a major impact in drawing attention to global issues and marshalling public, private and non-profit actors to work toward solutions.

IGOs, too, have an important place in future research. As mentioned above, the EU's regulations and standards are rapidly becoming global standards. But the rise of new economic powers, particularly China and India, may present alternative models of rules-setting, thereby placing other national regulatory bodies and multinational corporations in a quandary over whose rules to follow. Consequently, the extent to which business-related regulations change, how they change, and the actors involved will be an important avenue of research. The proliferation of regional trade organizations continues to raise questions about their 'value-added' to economic growth, and their discriminatory impact on companies domiciled outside member countries (Lee and Park 2005). Finally, while the WTO likely will remain the most important international trade organization over the next few decades, it also will be criticized by less influential member countries, as well as NGOs and civil society groups who feel excluded from the organization's decision-making (Esty 1998).

It is very likely that the WTO and other IGOs will respond to these pressures, and important research contributions will assess how and why these organizations open their decision-making processes to neglected groups.

Lastly, the increasing importance of the BRIC (Brazil, Russia, India, and China) countries and other rapidly developing countries will change the nature of political issues pertinent to global business. Issues of market access and trade barriers, as mentioned previously, are less important today for most companies than they were a quarter century ago. More pressing issues for many companies include violations of intellectual property rights (which affect the consumer goods, media, and pharmaceutical industries, among others), the impact of terrorism, energy, and the global impact of health matters (from AIDS to avian flu). It is very likely that new economic actors will treat these issues differently, or at least prioritize them in other ways, than OECD countries (i.e., the roughly 30 richest countries of the world that are members of the Organization for Economic Cooperation and Development). Scholars already have noted that institutional differences exist in Europe and the United States that shape different corporate responses to public policy issues and relations with NGOs (Doh and Guay 2006). Clearly, there is much more to learn about how institutions in the BRIC and other non-OECD countries structure the influence of companies, NGOs, and other actors.

Recent and rapid developments in the global political economy are changing the relationship between international business, politics and the overall institutional environment. This chapter has sketched only a few of these changes, but they are ones that are likely to have a significant impact on international business and marketing in the coming years. Scholars are in the early stages of assessing the influence of new actors like NGOs and IGOs, as well as new issues like the environment and science and technology, on companies' market and political strategies. The field is ripe for multidisciplinary research on these key issues for many years to come.

REFERENCES

Adnett, N. (1995) 'Social dumping and European economic integration', *Journal of European Social Policy*, 5(1): 1–12.

American Enterprise Institute (2006) NGO watch. http://www.ngowatch.org/

Argenti, P. (2004). 'Collaborating with activists: How Starbucks works with NGOs', *California Management Review*, 47:91–116.

Atik, J. (2001) 'Democratizing the WTO', *George Washington International Law Review*, 33: 451–472.

Barnett, M. N. and Finnemore, M. (1999) 'The politics, power, and pathologies of inter-national organizations', *International Organization*, 53(4): 699–732.

Baron, D. P. (1995) 'Integrated strategy: Market and non-market components,' *California Management Review*, 37(2): 47–64.

Bhagwati, J. (1997) 'Trade liberalization and "fair trade" demands: Addressing the environmental and labour standards issues', in *Writings on International Economics*. Oxford: Oxford University Press.

Bhagwati, J. (2004) *In Defense of Globalization*. Oxford: Oxford University Press.

Bhagwati, J. (2005) 'From Seattle to Hong Kong', *Foreign Affairs*, 84(7), http://www.foreignaffairs.org/2005/7.html.

Bhagwati, J., Greenaway, D. and Panagariya, A. (1998) 'Trading preferentially: Theory and policy', *The Economic Journal*, 108: 1128–1148.

Boddewyn, J. J. (1988) 'Political aspects of MNE theory', *Journal of International Business Studies*, 19: 341–363.

Boddewyn, J. J. and Brewer, T. L. (1994) 'International business political behavior: New theoretical directions', *Academy of Management Review*, 19(1): 119–143.

Bosworth, B. and Gordon, P. H. (2001) 'Managing a globalizing world', *Brookings Review*, 19(4): 3–5.

Bremmer, I. (2005) 'Managing risk in an unstable world', *Harvard Business Review*, 83(6): 51–60.

Buck, T. (2007) 'Standard bearer: How the European Union exports its laws', *Financial Times*, 10 July.

Conca, K. (2000) 'The WTO and the undermining of global environmental governance', *Review of International Political Economy*, 7(3): 484–494.

Dahan, N., Doh, J. P. and Guay, T. R. (2006) 'The role of multinational corporations in transnational institutional building: a policy-network perspective', *Human Relations*, 59(11): 1571–1600.

Doh, J. P. and Guay, T. R. (2004) 'Globalization and corporate social responsibility: How nongovernmental organizations influence labor and environmental codes of conduct', *Management International Review*, 44(2): 7–29.

Doh, J. P. and Guay, T. R. (2006) 'Corporate social responsibility, public policy, and NGO activism in Europe and the United States: An institutional-stakeholder perspective', *Journal of Management Studies*, 43(1): 47–73.

Doh, J. P. and Ramamurti, R. (2003) 'Reassessing risk in developing country infrastructure', *Long Range Planning*, 36(4): 337–353.

Doh, J. P., Rodriguez, P., Uhlenbruck, K., Collins, J. and Eden, L. (2003) 'Coping with corruption in foreign markets', *Academy of Management Executive*, 17(3): 114–127.

Economist Intelligence Unit (2007) *Under Attack: Global Business and the Threat of Political Violence*, http://www.lloyds.com/NR/rdonlyres/0926E705-A16C-4432-B607-A4925A9EFEAB/0/360terrorismreport.pdf

Esty, D. C. (1998) 'Non-governmental organizations at the World Trade Organization: Cooperation, competition, or exclusion', *Journal of International Economic Law*, 1(1): 123–148.

Fagre, N. and Wells, L. T. (1982) 'Bargaining power of multinationals and host governments', *Journal of International Business Studies*, 13: 9–23.

Fawcett, L. and Hurrell, A. (1995) *Regionalism in World Politics*. Oxford: Oxford University Press.

Frankel, J. A. (1998) *The Regionalisation of the World Economy*. Chicago: University of Chicago Press.

German Marshall Fund (2006) *Perspectives on Trade and Poverty Reduction: A survey of Public Opinion*. Washington, DC.

Guéguen, D. (2002) 'Governance and the role of associations in economic management: A response from an EU public affairs practitioner', in J. Greenwood (ed.), *The Effectiveness of EU Business Associations*. Basingstoke: Palgrave, pp. 46–52.

Hall, R. B. and Biersteker, T. (eds) (2003) *The Emergence of Private Authority in Global Governance*. Cambridge: Cambridge University Press.

Haufler, Virginia (2001) *A Public Role for the Private Sector: Industry Self-Regulation in a Global Economy*. Washington: Carnegie Endowment for International Peace.

Henisz, W. J. (2000) 'The institutional environment for economic growth', *Economics and Politics,* 12(1): 1–31.

Henisz, W. J. and Williamson, O. E. (1999) 'Comparative economic organization – within and between countries', *Business and Politics,* 1: 261–277.

Karns, M. P. and Mingst, K. A. (2004) *International Organizations: The Politics and Processes of Governance*. Boulder, CO: Lynne Reienner Press.

Kaufmann, D. and Kraay, A. (2002) *Governance Matters II: Update Indicators for 2000/2001*. World Bank Policy Research Working Paper 2772. Washington, DC: The World Bank.

Kaufmann, D., Kraay, A. and Mastruzzi, M. (2006) *Governance Matters V: Governance Indicators for 1996–2005*. World Bank Policy Research Working Paper 4012. Washington, DC: The World Bank.

Kaufmann, D., Kraay, A. and Zoido-Lobaton, P. (1999) *Governance Matters. Policy Research Working Paper 2196*. Washington, DC: The World Bank.

Kearney, N. (1999) 'Corporate codes of conduct: The privatized application of labour standards', in S. Picciotto, and R. Mayne, (eds) *Regulating International Business: Beyond Liberalization*. Basingstoke: Macmillan, pp. 205–234.

Keck, M. E. and Sikkink, K. (1998) *Activists Beyond Borders: Advocacy Networks in International Politics*. Ithaca, NY: Cornell University Press.

Keohane, R. O. (1982) 'The demand for international regimes', *International Organization*, 36(2): 325–355.

Keohane, R. O. and Nye, J. S. (2000) *Power and Interdependence*, 3rd edn. New York: Longman.

Khanna, T. and Krishna, P. (1997) 'Why focused strategies may be wrong for emerging markets', *Harvard Business Review*, 75(4) (July–August): 41–51.

Khanna, T. and Krishna P. (2000) 'The future of business groups in emerging markets: long-run evidence from Chile', *Academy of Management Journal*, 43: 268–285.

Khanna, T., Krishna, P. and Jayant, S. (2005) 'Strategies to fit emerging markets', *Harvard Business Review*, 83: 63–74.

Kobrin, S. J. (1979) 'Political risk: a review and reconsideration', *Journal of International Business Studies*, 10(1) (Spring/Summer): 67–80.

Kobrin, S. J. (1987) 'Testing the bargaining hypothesis in the manufacturing sector in developing countries', *International Organization*, 41: 609–638.

La Porta, R., Lopez-de-Silanes, F. Shleifer, A. and Vishny, R. (1998) 'Law and finance', *Journal of Political Economy,* 106: 1113–1155.

Lee, E. (1997) 'Globalization and labour standards: A review of issues', *International Labour Review*, 136(2): 173–189.

Lee, J.-W. and Park, I. (2005) 'Free trade areas in East Asia: Discriminatory or non-discriminatory?', *The World Economy*, 28(1): 21–48.

Levy, B. and P. Spiller (1994). 'The Institutional Foundations of Regulatory Commitment: A Comparative Analysis of Telecommunications Regulation', *Journal of law, Economics and Organization*, 10(1): 201–246

Levy, D. L. and Kolk, A. (2002) 'Strategic responses to global climate change: conflicting pressures on multinationals in the oil industry', *Business and Politics*, 4(3): 275–300.

Lindenberg, M. (1999) 'Declining state capacity, voluntarism, and the globalization of the not-for-profit sector', *Nonprofit and Voluntary Sector Quarterly*, 28: 147–167.

Lindenberg, M. and Dobel, J. P. (1999) 'The challenges of globalization for Northern international relief and development NGOs', *Nonprofit and Voluntary Sector Quarterly*, 28: 4–24.

Lisowski, M. (2002) 'Playing the two-level game: US president Bush's decision to repudiate the Kyoto protocol', *Review of International Political Economy*, 11(4): 101–119.

Litvin, D. (2003) *Empires of Profit: Commerce, Conquest and Corporate Responsibility*. New York: Textere.

Long, W. J. and Quek, M. P. (2002) 'Personal data privacy protection in an age of globalization: The US–EU safe harbor compromise', *Journal of European Public Policy*, 9(3): 325–344.

Maggi, G. (1999) 'The role of multilateral institutions in international trade cooperation', *American Economic Review*, 89(1): 190–214.

Majone, G. (1996) 'A European regulatory state?', in J. Richardson (ed.), *European Union: Power and Policy-making*. London: Routledge.

Marks, G., Scharpf, F., Schmitter, P. C. and Streeck, W. (1996) *Governance in the European Union*. London: Sage.

McKinney, J. A. (2006) 'United States–European Union trade dispute over biotechnology agricultural products', *EUSA Review*, 19(4): 12–15.

Mikler, J. J. (2007) 'Varieties of capitalism and the auto industry's environmental initiatives: National institutional explanations for firms' motivations', *Business and Politics*, 9(1), Article 4.

Moran, T. H. (1985) 'Risk assessment, corporate planning and strategies', in T. H. Moran (ed.), *Multinational Corporations: The Political Economy of Foreign Direct Investment*. Lexington, VA: Lexington Books, pp. 107–117.

Murphy, C. (2000) 'Global governance: poorly done and poorly understood', *International Affairs*, 76(4): 789–803.

Naím, M. (2005) *Illicit: How Smugglers, Traffickers, and Copycats are Hijacking the Global Economy*. New York: Doubleday.

North, Douglass C. (1986) 'The new institutional economics', *Journal of Institutional and Theoretical Economics,* 142: 230–237.

North, D. C. (1990) *Institutions, Institutional Change, and Economic Performance*. New York: Cambridge University Press:

North, D. C. (1993) 'Institutions and credible commitment', *Journal of Institutional and Theoretical Economics*, 149: 11–23.

Offenheiser, R., Holcombe, S. and Hopkins, N. (1999) 'Grappling with globalization, partnership, and learning: a look inside Oxfam America', *Nonprofit and Voluntary Sector Quarterly*, 28(4):121–139.

Olson, M. (1971) *The Logic of Collective Action: Public Goods and the Theory Of Groups*. Cambridge, MA: Harvard University Press.

Ottaway, M. (2001) 'Corporatism goes global: International organizations, nongovernmental organization networks, and transnational business, *Global Governance*, 7(3): 265–292.

Peterson, J. (1995) 'Decision-Making in the European Union: Towards a framework for analysis', *Journal of European Public Policy*, 2(1): 69–93.

Pierson, P. (1996) 'The path to European integration: A historical institutionalist analysis', *Comparative Political Studies*, 29(2): 123–163.

Pollack, M. A. (1996) 'The new institutionalism and EC governance: The promise and limits of institutional analysis', *Governance*, 9(4): 429–458.

Porter, M. (1990) 'The competitive advantage of nations', *Harvard Business Review*, 90(2): 73–93.

Prakash, A. and Kollman, K. I. (2003) 'Biopolitics in the EU and the U.S.: A race to the bottom or convergence to the Top?', *International Studies Quarterly*, 47(4): 617–641.

Putnam, R. (1988) 'Diplomacy and domestic politics: The logic of two-level games', *International Organization*, 42(3): 427–460.

Ramamurti, R. (2001) 'The obsolescing 'bargain model'? MNC-host developing countries relations revisited', *Journal of International Business Studies*, 32(1): 23–39.

Richardson, J. (1996) 'Policy-making in the EU: Interests, ideas and garbage cans of primeval soup', in J. Richardson (ed.), *European Union: Power and Policy-Making*. London: Routledge, pp. 3–30.

Robock, S. H. (1971) 'Political risk identification and assessment', *Columbia Journal of World Business*, 7: 6–20.

Rodrik, D. (1997) *Has Globalization Gone Too Far?* Washington, DC: Institute for International Economics.

Rosamond, B. (2000) *Theories of European Integration*. Houndmills, Hampshire: Palgrave.

Scheer, D. (2003) 'Europe's new high-tech role: Playing privacy cop to World', *Wall Street Journal*, 10 October.

Schleifer, A, Vichny, R (1993). "Corruption." *Quarterly Journal of Economics*, 58(3): 599–617.

Simon, J. D. (1982) 'Political risk assessment: past trends and future prospects', *Columbia Journal of World Business*, 17(3): 62–71.

Soule, E. (2003). 'Corporate strategy, government regulatory policy and NGO activism: The case of genetically modified crops', in J. P. Doh, and H. Teegen (eds), *Globalization and NGOs: Transforming Business,* *Government, and Society*. Westport, CT: Praeger.

Spar, D. L. and La Mure, L. T. (2003) 'The power of activism: assessing the impact of NGOs on global business', *California Management Review*, 45: 78–101.

Srinnivasen, T. N. (1998) 'Regionalism and the WTO: Is nondiscrimination passé?', in A. Krueger, Anne O. (ed.), *The WTO as an International Organization*. Chicago: University of Chicago Press, pp. 329–352.

Stiglitz, J. E. (2002) *Globalization and its Discontents*. New York: Norton.

Stopford, J. M. and Strange, S. (1991) *Rival states, Rival Firms: Competition for World Market Share*. Cambridge: Cambridge University Press.

Teegen, H. and Doh, J. P. (eds) (2003) *Globalization and NGOs: Transforming Business, Governments, and Society*. New York: Praeger.

Teegen, H., Doh, J. P. and Vachani, S. (2004) 'The importance of nongovernmental organizations (NGOs) in global governance and value creation: an international business research agenda', *Journal of International Business Studies,* 35(6): 463–483.

United Nations Development Programme. (2007) *UNEP 2007 Annual Report*.

Wallach, L. and Naím, M. (2000) 'The FP interview: Lori's war', *Foreign Policy*, 118: 28–55.

United States. Agency for International Development (2006) *The Global Development Alliance: Public–Private Alliances For Transformational Development*. Washington, DC: USAID Office of Global Development Alliances.

Vernon, R. (1971) *Sovereignty at Bay: The Multinational Spread of U.S. Enterprises*. New York, NY: Basic Books.

Wessels, W. (1997) 'An ever closer fusion: A dynamic macropolitical view on integration processes', *Journal of Common Market Studies*, 35(2): 267–299.

Williams, O. F. (2000) *Global Codes of Conduct: An Idea Whose Time Has Come*. Notre Dame, IN: University of Notre Dame Press.

Woods, N. (2001) 'Making the IMF and the World Bank more accountable', *International Affairs*, 77(1): 83–100.

4

Marketing and the Global Legal Environment

Subhash Jain and Robert Bird

INTRODUCTION

Companies active in overseas markets must cope with widely differing laws. A company has to consider not only the laws of its home country wherever it does business, but it must also be responsive to the host country's laws. For example, without requiring proof that certain marketing practices, such as horizontal price-fixing among competitors, and price discrimination, have adversely affected competition, US law nonetheless makes them illegal. Even though such practices may be common in a foreign country, corporations cannot engage in them. Simultaneously, host country laws must be adhered to even if they forbid practices that are allowed in the firm's nation of origin.

From the marketing standpoint, a firm should be especially careful in obeying laws pertaining to competition, price setting (such as price discrimination and resale price maintenance), distribution arrangements (such as exclusive dealership), product quality (such as wholesomeness, packaging, warranty and service patents and trademarks), personal selling (such as white-collar employment/labor laws), and advertising (such as media usage, information provision).

In addition, there are international laws that are of particular relevance to the marketer. Agreements under institutions such as the World Trade Organization (WTO) the International Monetary Fund (IMF) and the World Bank compose international laws of sorts that influence business in different ways. The WTO's regulations are particularly relevant for marketers since they deal with trade restrictions and barriers that affect market potential. The TRIPS agreement presents a cohesive set of standards for intellectual property protection.

The material in this chapter is organized into four sections. Section one deals with home country laws. Host country laws are examined in section two. The third section is devoted to international laws and the final section concludes the chapter.

HOME COUNTRY LAWS

Corporations located in a home country and their home-based officers remain liable to laws in the home country even if substantial operations are abroad. For instance, individuals must comply with US Internal Revenue

Service (IRS) laws, and corporations are bound by US antitrust laws. One application of the US antitrust laws to an American company overseas is the Gillette Company case. Many years ago, the Justice Department sought an injunction against Gillette for its acquisition of shares in Braun AG of Germany. The Justice Department held that Gillette's acquisition of Braun would restrict competition in shaving devices in the USA, given the fact that Braun makes electric razors and that Braun had previously relinquished to a third company its rights to sell in the US market until 1976 (Brumley 1988, p. 3). (For readers' interest, Gillette acquired Braun AG in the late 1980s.)

Some laws, however, have been specially enacted to direct multinational marketing activities, such as the Foreign Corrupt Practices Act (FCPA) of 1977, discussed in more detail later in this chapter. Basically, the intention of these laws is to protect American economic interests, ensure national security, maintain recognized standards of ethics, and promote fair competition.

Laws affecting foreign trade

The USA, relative to other nations, has a liberal attitude toward exports and imports. Nevertheless, there are many regulations that a US exporter must be aware of in the conduct of business. First of all, the government prohibits trading with some nations, for example, Iran, Cuba, North Korea and, until recently, Vietnam. Also, exportation of several products, among them defense-related equipment, must be cleared with the US Department of Commerce by obtaining a license permitting shipment.

The US government imposes some restrictions, via the IRS, on pricing for intra-company foreign transactions. The IRS ensures that prices are not underestimated to save US taxes. For example, a US corporation may export certain goods to its subsidiary, say, in Germany, at a very low price. This would reduce the corporation's US taxes.

It is for this reason that the IRS is authorized to review pricing and demand change, if necessary, in such company-to-company overseas transfers.

In regard to imports, the US markets traditionally are open to all nations with few restrictions. For health and safety reasons, food products from many developing countries are usually the subject of those restrictions. For example, several years ago the Food and Drug Administration detained Sri Lankan tea imports for special testing following terrorist threats to contaminate that nation's black tea with cyanide. Sri Lanka provides about 11 percent of US tea imports, or about 21 million pounds of black tea annually. Similarly, in 2004, Mexican tomatoes and other fruits were prohibited from entering the USA, since some of these products had been reportedly poisoned.

Although the federal government basically subscribes to free trade and has supported through GATT (now the WTO) the worldwide effort toward this goal, various legislative and non-legislative measures have been adopted to protect domestic US industry. Protectionism increased in the 1970s when more and more US companies showed signs of crumbling, often from an inability to compete in the world market. The textile, tire, and auto industries cut production or closed down entire factories, largely because US consumers purchased imports. Consequently, workers and industries applied continuing pressure for tougher tariffs and trade quotas. Thus, for some products, like automobiles, import duties were increased. For other products, like textiles, quotas were imposed on imports from various countries. For steel, the government set minimum prices on imports to make domestic steel competitive.

Antitrust laws

As noted earlier, the US antitrust laws apply to US corporations in their international dealings as well as in their domestic transactions. More specifically, US businesses must carefully ascertain if antitrust laws would be violated in any way in the following situations:

- When a US firm *acquires* a foreign firm.
- When a US firm *engages in a joint venture* abroad with another American company or a foreign firm.
- When a US firm *enters into a marketing agreement* with a foreign-based firm. The Justice Department has become very strict in the application of US antitrust laws on foreign operations of US corporations. The enforcement takes several forms:
  - In 1980 the Justice Department initiated criminal grand jury probes into allegations that US and foreign competitors illegally set the prices of uranium, phosphate, and ocean shipping rates.
  - In 1985 it reviewed the overseas licensing agreements of some two dozen multinationals to see whether their prices or territorial arrangements unreasonably prevented overseas producers from selling in the USA.
  - In 1990 it investigated oil company reactions to the new two-tier pricing system for foreign crude oil along with other aspects of their relations with oil-producing countries.
  - In 1997 it examined the 'marketing' merger between Texaco and Shell Oil and its impact on US gasoline prices.

The antitrust laws are being legislated outside the USA as well, especially in EU countries. In 1999 Italy's competition authority nailed Coca-Cola for its anti-competitive practices. It has been claimed that Coca-Cola and CCBI, its affiliated bottler, along with six other local bottlers, not only dominate the Italian market, but have also abused this power to damage their competitors. One prong of Coke's strategy targets wholesalers. They are bound in by a complicated system of exclusivity bonuses and discounts, which are designed less to boost sales of Coke than to oust Pepsi from the market. To illustrate, a Roman wholesaler was lured into a 4 percent extra discount for exclusively carrying Coke by ousting Pepsi (*The Economist*, 1999), The matter was settled after the Italian court exonerated Coca-Cola of any wrongdoing. Similarly, Europe's leading brewers, including Heineken, Carlsberg, Peroni, and Interbrew

have been charged with price-fixing and market division. EU authorities have cracked down on cartels in the shipping, automobile, steel-pipe, and cement industries (*Business Week*, 2000).

Foreign corrupt practices act (FCPA) and corruption

The FCPA, passed by Congress in 1977, has stringent antibribery provisions prohibiting all US companies on file with the Securities and Exchange Commission (SEC) from making any unauthorized payments. These payments include those made to foreign officials, political parties, or candidates. The law prescribes a $1 million penalty to a corporation for violation of the law. Corporate officers connected with illegal payments may be fined $10,000 or be subjected to a five-year imprisonment term, or both.

How FCPA can create hindrances is illustrated by the Coca-Cola Company's deal with the former Soviet Union. In 1986 Coca-Cola signed a $30 million six-year agreement to expand its business in the USSR. Until then, Coca-Cola was sold only in Moscow shops for tourists, and the company's Fanta orange soda was available in only a few other cities. Published reports indicated that the Coca-Cola Company paid bribes to people in the Soviet Union to crack the Soviet market. Subsequently, a federal grand jury initiated an investigation to determine if the allegations of wrongdoing were correct. Although the company was finally proved innocent, it had to endure subpoenas of its documents and other inconveniences to prove its innocence (*The Wall Street Journal*, 1988). For over ten years, Diagnostic Products Corp.'s (a US company) employees in China had been bribing doctors to buy laboratory testing kits. US authorities fined the company for violating US anti-bribery laws (Wonacott 2005).

In part, the FCPA is an effort to extend American moral standards to other countries. The act also seeks to enlist US MNCs as instruments of US foreign policy. The FCPA, therefore, marks a major attempt by the US government to enforce a series of noneconomic foreign policy objectives through private enterprise, which has traditionally been considered to have only economic purposes. The FCPA places American corporations doing business abroad in an awkward position. On the one hand, they must comply with the US law, and on the other, they have to compete with other foreign companies whose governments do not prohibit such payments. In some nations where American business is conducted, bribery is commonplace; the FCPA could weaken the competitive position of US corporations in such countries.

In addition to the fact that the FCPA adversely affects US trade, critics of the act argue that the USA should not try to force its moral principles and concepts of right and wrong on the whole world. Questionable practices such as bribery will continue in certain countries whether US corporations participate or not. The best that can be hoped is that, in the future, international bribery perhaps might be controlled through an international agreement effected through the WTO.

The Omnibus Trade and Competitiveness Act of 1988 was passed to limit the scope of the FCPA. The primary change concerned the FCPA's prohibition against payments to third parties by a US firm 'knowing or having reason to know' that the third party would use the payment for prohibited purposes. Under the new law, the US firm must have actual knowledge of or willful blindness to the prohibited use of the payment. The act also clarifies the types of payments that are permissible and would not be considered bribery (*The Wall Street Journal*, 1999). For example, under the FCPA as originally enacted, payments to low-level officials who exercise only 'ministerial' or 'clerical' functions were exempt. Unfortunately, this provision provided little guidance to companies in determining whether a given foreign official exercised discretionary authority: special problems arose in countries in the Middle East and Africa, where foreign officials can be employed part-time. Overall, the trade act provides a US business with better guidance by specifying the types of payments that are permissible rather than which individuals can receive them. The act specifies that a payment for a routine government action such as processing papers, stamping visas, or scheduling inspections, may be made without criminal liability. These changes to the FCPA make it easier for US companies to do business in foreign countries by removing concerns about inadvertent violations. They have become more blatant at currying favor with developing countries, especially the large emerging markets. For example, Goldman Sachs agreed to make a $62 million donation to help a troubled Chinese brokerage in order to get approval for an investment banking venture (*Financial Times*, 2005).

Another international legal topic important to marketing managers is the global regulation of corruption. Since its foundation about ten years ago, Transparency International (TI) has done much to raise awareness of corruption around the world. Yet the problem has not moved any closer to a solution. Corruption is rampant both in governments as well as in the private sector. However, new technology has so improved flows of information that the media and the public are increasingly calling businesses and politicians to account (*Financial Times*, 2003).

Increased global trade has had an associated impact on contract with foreign public officials. In the past, firm representatives would bribe government officials in order to secure a competitive advantage over international rivals. Bribery as a marketing strategy was perceived to be just another way of doing business in nations with government corruption (Scott *et al.* 2002).

Today, international law prohibits bribery of government officials. The OECD Convention on Combating Bribery of Foreign Public Officials in International Business Transactions (OECD Convention), effective as of February, 1999, requires signatories to enact anti-bribery domestic legislation and harmonize that legislation with the OECD

Convention provisions. Each nation's anti-bribery legislation must make bribery a criminal offense. Both individuals and corporations must be held liable when appropriate and the proceeds of the bribery must be subject to seizure and confiscation (Pacini *et al.* 2002). Given the rise of anti-bribery laws, global firms must reconsider their marketing strategy. This involves more than simply halting bribes, but finding creative ways to market products in countries where focus on personal loyalties rather than collective rules are the norm. Firms must also creatively traverse a political environment with a dominance of a ruling elite or a government with questionable legitimacy without running foul of international laws (Scott *et al.* 2002).

Anti-boycott laws

From time to time nations attempt to put pressure on each other through programs of economic boycott. The early 1980s Arab boycott of companies doing business with Israel is an example of such a tactic. Most Arab states did not recognize Israel and hoped that an economic boycott would contribute to Israel's collapse. The oil fortunes of these Arab countries gave them significant economic clout to implement the boycott. Companies that dealt with Israel were blacklisted with the intention of squeezing Israel from all directions and forcing the country into economic isolation.

The US government adopted various measures to prevent US companies from complying with the Arab boycott. For example, the Tax Reform Act of 1976 included a measure that denied foreign income tax benefits to companies that subscribed to the boycott. The law pre-empts any state or local regulations dealing with boycotts fostered or imposed by foreign countries (Huszagh 1981).

The Arab boycott crumbled toward the end of the 1980s, making it easier for US companies to continue their operations in Israel and at the same time seek out business in Arab states. For example, the Coca-Cola Company began making inroads into the Gulf, Lebanon, Jordan, and Saudi Arabia as the boycott became ineffective (*The Economist* 1994).

Laws to protect domestic industry

The US government has legislated many laws to protect domestic industry. From time to time, the government sets quotas on imports. For a number of years the sugar import quotas were set so as to preserve about half the market for US producers. Often quotas are split among several countries interested in exporting to the USA. Such allocation is partly influenced by political considerations. Thus, a certain proportion of a quota may be assigned to a developing country even though its price is higher than that of other exporters. For a few years early in the 1980s, the US government had imposed quotas on Japanese car imports. Recently, a debate has been going on in the federal government about limiting steel exports to the USA by establishing quotas for different categories of steel and distributing it among the exporting nations.

Quotas usually provide only temporary relief to domestic industry. In the long run, a domestic industry must stand on its own. If it is inherently inefficient, quotas amount to a support of inefficiency. However, sometimes quotas are appropriately and productively used to buy time so an infant industry can mature and compete effectively.

Laws to eliminate tax loopholes

Many federal laws are designed to eliminate tax loopholes. A prominent example is legislation against tax havens, countries that provide out-of-the-ordinary privileges to multinationals in order to attract them to their lands. Tax havens make it more profitable for companies to locate there than in the USA (*Business Week* 2000b). Stanley Works, a Connecticut company, decided to reincorporate in tax-friendlier Bermuda and save $30 million in taxes. (Stanley withdrew its plans to relocate under political duress from state officials.) US-based multinationals are taxed at up to 35 percent of their corporate income, the fifth highest rate among OECD nations. And the tax applies to income earned anywhere, not just within the USA. By contrast, European countries don't tax foreign-sourced income (*The Wall Street Journal* 2002). This puts US multinationals at a competitive disadvantage both at home and abroad. There are four types of tax havens:

1 Countries with no taxes at all, such as the Bahamas, Bermuda, and the Cayman Islands.
2 Countries with taxes at low rates, such as the British Virgin Islands.
3 Countries that tax income from domestic sources but exempt income from foreign sources, such as Hong Kong, and Panama.
4 Countries that allow special privileges, which generally are suitable as tax havens only for limited purposes.

Tax havens offer corporations a legal way to save on taxes. However, a country must offer more than tax benefits to be a good market. Political stability, availability of adequate means of communication and transportation, economic freedom for currency conversion, and availability of professional services are important criteria for evaluating a tax haven.

Tax treaties

Tax treaties are arrangements between nations that prevent corporate and individual income from being double-taxed. The USA has tax treaties with over 70 nations. Thus, foreigners who own securities in US corporations and who are from countries with which there is a tax treaty pay a withholding tax of about 15 percent, while those from non-tax treaty countries pay a 28 percent tax.

The tax treaties are meant to provide a fair deal to individuals and corporations from friendly countries and thus encourage mutually beneficial economic activity. Usually, under a tax treaty, the country where the primary business activity takes place is provided the right to be the principal receiver of tax revenue. A small proportion of the tax may accrue to the other nation. Take, for example, the case of a Thai exporter with a business in the USA. Since there is a tax treaty between the USA and Thailand, the income of the Thai businessman, as far as his US operations are concerned, would be taxable under the US IRS rules. However, he would pay only a negligible tax in Thailand.

Businesses, particularly the MNCs, use tax treaties in various ways to seek maximum benefits. Consider the following situations:

• A tax treaty between the USA and England requires a 15 percent withholding tax on dividends.
• A tax treaty between the USA and the Netherlands specifies a 5 percent withholding tax.
• A tax treaty between the Netherlands and Great Britain calls for a 5 percent withholding tax. Additionally, dividends from foreign sources are not taxed in the Netherlands.

According to these arrangements, a US company could establish a holding company in the Netherlands that might receive dividend income from a British subsidiary. The holding company, in turn, remits the dividends could be remitted to the parent company in the USA. The combined tax in the whole process would amount to 10 percent rather than 15 percent.

Tax treaties between the USA and different countries are reviewed from time to time. This permits periodic changes in treaty agreements to accommodate changes in the country's monetary and fiscal policies. Usually, a treaty spells out the procedure for consultation and negotiation between officials of the two countries, should disagreements occur.

HOST COUNTRY LAWS

The breadth and scope of domestic legal protection relevant to marketing managers varies widely. Domestic legal systems range from largely transparent to predominantly corrupt and efficient. Domestic legal systems may also have overlapping complexities not present in Western countries. Ghana, for example, has two legal systems – one based on traditional law and the other on common law inherited from the United Kingdom. Kenya has three separate legal systems, a common law, a civil law, and an Islamic law system, operating at the same time (Koku 2005).

Marketing managers must be able to assess the functionality of a nation's legal system and then make market entry decisions based in part on that functionality. In some countries, contract disputes can languish in court for years before the judicial process is completed and a final decision is reached (Bird 2006b; Koku 2005). Corruption in the judicial system may produce an adverse decision even when the law clearly favors the foreign firm. The presence or absence of a functioning, transparent, and speedy legal system can and should influence a marketing manager's national entry strategy.

For example the target nation's legal system impacts the firm's international channel relationships. While in developed legal systems legal contracts can deter opportunism by distributors, such contracts provide fewer disincentives in developing nations. Contracts should be developed along with mutual trust between the global firm and the distributor (Cavusgil *et al.* 2004). Development of trust matures the supplier–global firm affiliation from a merely transactional exchange to a relational contact. Whereas parties to a transactional exchange seek to maximize benefit in each transaction, parties to a relational contract maximize their benefit over the entire relationship. Parties in such relationships may even make sub-optimal decisions to preserve harmonious long-term exchanges. Trust and relationships and not formal contracts may be most effective in managing channel relationships abroad.

Domestic intellectual property rights

Intellectual property rights also raise issues of domestic law. Piracy of patents, and the failure to control that piracy by certain governments, reduces a firm's interest in innovation because it will recoup less on its investment, particularly when concerning pharmaceutical drugs. The failure of a firm to control piracy injures the very consumers interested in firm's product. Consumers interested in purchasing expensive handbags, for example, become financial victims of the pirates when purchasing the knock-off product. In other cases, such as food or medicines, pirated goods can harm or even kill consumers of the fake merchandise (Shultz and Nill 2002). Trademark infringements can confuse consumers as to the source of the goods. Buyers of the original and more expensive brand might feel betrayed by the manufacturer because the presence of knock-offs denigrates the prestige and importance of the once-exclusive product (Jain 1996). Infringement of even unrelated trademarks by a competitor or pirate can dilute the ability of a product's trademark to serve as mental trigger for a product attribute or a product category (Morrin and Jacoby 2000).

The failure to enforce intellectual property laws is prevalent even in the most advanced developing countries. For example, Brazilian government enforcement against illegal copying of academic books and other materials is virtually non-existent. Piracy of compact disc recordings represents over half of all Brazilian sales. In Russia, the majority of audio and video disks sold are pirated. In India, illegal booksellers operate openly and the strong majority of entertainment software sold is pirated. In China, over eighty manufacturing plants produce illegal goods for sale around the world. Firms lose billions of revenue each year by the failure of governments to protect domestic and foreign intellectual property around the world (Bird 2006b).

Savvy marketing strategies, however, can successfully circumvent even rampant piracy.

When a major foreign telecommunications company successfully penetrated the Chinese market, the market quickly became saturated with cheap imitations of their products. Instead of threatening to withdraw from the Chinese market, the firm advertised that it would invest all profits back into China, donate funds to charities popular with government officials, and develop a pool of local suppliers. In essence, the firm re-branded itself from just another short-term American investor to an enterprise committed to the development of the Chinese economy. After the firm implemented these measures, previously lax Chinese enforcement of intellectual property became more aggressive and piracy of the firm's products significantly decreased (Donaldson and Weiner 1999).

In another example, Heinz faced rampant copying of its baby food products, with pirates even brazenly copying uniforms and delivery trucks to deliver the pirated product. An obvious intellectual property disaster, Heinz remarketed the problem and a consumer protection issue. Heinz recruited reporters to observe the pirates' shoddy manufacturing and sanitary condition and emphasized the public health issue present for Chinese infants. As one executive reported, '[o]nce people saw what was going into the pirate's product, stuff that could make their baby quite ill, it became pretty clear who the "bad guy" was' (Donaldson and Weiner 1999, p. 426). Well-publicized raids soon followed, with reporters on-scene whose travel expenses were paid for by Heinz. Afterwards the company experienced no further serious piracy problems (Donaldson and Weiner 1999).

Franchising

Issues can also arise from the arrangements global firms make with local domestic concerns. Franchising, an agreement where the owner of a license permits the licensee to sell goods under the licensor's trademark, has become an increasingly popular sales channel.

Franchising can be marketed through three kinds of agreements. A Direct Franchise Agreement gives the franchisee the right to open one franchise with all training, publicity, and advertising provided by the franchisor. Suitable for culturally and linguistically similar markets, this agreement allows the franchisor to maintain great control over the franchise but with significant costs. Other options include a Master Franchise Agreement, which gives a single franchisee rights to an entire country and is most useful for a establishing a long-term arrangement in a foreign market. Finally, a Joint Venture gives the maximum control to the franchisor but also creates increased exposure to local tax and labor laws (LaFranchi 2001).

Franchise agreements must be carefully tailored by licensors to retain desired control over their brand while giving franchisees enough discretion to utilize the brand in the local market successfully. Agreements should address issues such as quality standards, royalty level, length of agreement, and right of use to the licensor's trademarks. An agreement that grants a licensee an excessively large exclusive geographic area could tie the hands of the licensor for using its own intellectual property. An agreement that fails to address sub-franchises could give a foreign franchisee the undesirable discretion to further sub-franchise the licensor's trademark. Local counsel is essential for navigating the frequently labyrinthine requirements of domestic franchising law (LaFranchi 2001).

Brand oversight is essential, as one poor franchise can impact the brand value of all other franchises, and controlling one's brand may be doubly difficult in an international setting. For example, in the early 1970s a McDonald's Corp. entered into an agreement with Raymond Dayan, a French franchisee, to develop and operate McDonald's restaurants in Paris. According to one McDonald's executive, the only observable likeness to a McDonald's restaurant was the sign. In spite of years of good faith assistance by McDonald's, Dayan's restaurants completely ignored the company's strict food control standards. Grease dripped from vents collected in a cup hung from the ceiling, insecticide was blended with chicken breading, dogs defecated near stored food, and food was held on for so long and served so cold that McDonald's managers inspecting the franchise found Dayan's products nearly inedible. Only after years of litigation was McDonald's able to terminate Dayan's license and rehabilitate its brand (Shaw and LaFontaine 2005; Dayan v. McDonald's Corp 1984). Today, at least 1,000 McDonald's franchises exist throughout France, generating $3 billion in annual revenue (Super-Sized Empire 2005).

Gray market goods

A related problem to intellectual property is the marketing manager's control of gray market goods. Gray market goods are genuinely branded merchandise that is distributed to certain markets through channels unauthorized by the brand owner (Bucklin 1993). Sales of gray market goods have been estimated at $60 to $80 billion annually in the United States alone (Goodale 2000). In the United States, gray market imports have been generally allowed, especially in cases where there is little possibility of confusion. In the past, the Supreme Court has allowed the entry of gray market imports where the domestic trademark owner and the foreign manufacturer are subject to common control. Under the 'first sale' doctrine the right of a producer to control distribution of a trademarked product does not extend beyond the first sale of that product (Nester 2003). The European Union has shown signals that it might be more restrictive. In a 1999 European Court of Justice Decision, the court permitted re-importation from one country to another, but forbade importation from countries outside European Union borders. The rationale behind this 'regional trademark exhaustion' principle was to promote open access in intra-European markets

while protecting the integrity of that market from outsiders (Schaffer *et al.* 2005).

Marketing managers should avail themselves of any legal opportunities available to curtail gray market goods. These goods compete directly with those imported and sold by the authorized distributor and reap the benefits of web sites and technical support that the legitimate importer may be paying for (Fornaro 2003). Gray market goods could cause high price conscious consumers to select these goods at a lower price. The lower price may lead consumers to believe that the product is of lower quality. Consumers might also perceive gray market goods as more risky and perhaps even illegal (Huang *et al.* 2004). If the gray market goods are electronic, they may not be manufactured to domestic standards or be incompatible with a nation's electrical voltage system (Fornaro 2003).

Advertising

While some international legal topics have moved stridently toward globalization, advertising law and regulation has not been so aggressive. The outlook for future harmonization does not appear promising as considerable disparities still exist between various domestic legal systems (Petty 1994). While United States regulations allow relatively broad claims by advertisers, nations such as Germany and Japan have exacting standards for accuracy. For example, when a German snack food company sued a competitor who claimed that its chips contained '40 percent less fat', the court interpreted that statement as an assertion comparable to any existing brand. As the chips were not 40 percent less fat than all brands, the court enjoined the advertising program. Similarly, a Fair Trade Committee in Japan prevented Pepsi from advertising its cola as the 'choice of the neXt generation', as it does in the United States, because in Japan Pepsi was second in popularity to Coca-Cola and thus it could not make that claim (Schaffer *et al.* 2005).

There is also wide variance in comparative advertising rules. For example, in 1997 the European Union issued a directive prohibiting comparative advertising that, among other things, creates confusion between two products, presents products as imitations or replicas bearing a protected name, or takes unfair advantage of the reputation of a trademark. Yet, European countries vary in their level of enforcement and firms are taking advantage of the differences. For example, when competitors of Dyson Appliances sued over Dyson's comparative advertising pertaining to a bag-free vacuum cleaner, the competitors deliberately chose to sue in Belgium because of that nation's strong advertising law (Wright and Morgan 2002).

Global marketing strategy must also take into account the unique difficulties of marketing dangerous or controversial products. In the United States, plaintiffs may readily file a legal action based upon product liability or negligence. In Japan, by contrast, numerous barriers keep many plaintiffs out of the Japanese court system. The litigious nature of a society, a proactive governmental role in compensation, and the presence of procedural barriers, and a cultural value on social harmony, make lawsuits based upon injury from products relatively rare. Similarly, in Europe, plaintiffs shoulder additional risk in filing actions because a losing plaintiff must pay the defendant's legal fees if the plaintiff does not prevail at trial. European social programs also more generously compensate injures when compared to US counterparts. The presence or absence of such incentives can influence whether or how to market dangerous products within a given legal system (Delpo 1999).

Particularly controversial products might be subject to unusual regulation. For example, while almost all countries restrict the advertising of tobacco and alcohol products, some nations take more aggressive measures. In 1993, France banned most liquor advertising and all tobacco advertising with one notable exception – French wine. Bulgaria's restrictions on tobacco include a total ban outside tobacco shops. The United Kingdom, by contrast, only requires regulation by self-imposed and subjected industry guidelines. In 1995, Iran's spiritual leader banned Coca-Cola and Pepsi-Cola because purchasing them would advance Zionism and the 'World Arrogance', also known as the United States (Schaffer *et al.* 2005; News on Iran 1995).

Agency law

Marketing managers must also decide whether to use agents or other authorized representatives to distribute products. In many countries, personal relationships based upon local ties are often an effective method to enter the market. An agent can provide the necessary contacts that a foreign enterprise lacks. With adopting a foreign agent, however, comes legal risks. For example, some countries have laws in place that specifically protect local agents from arbitrary discharge by their multinational employers. These laws can even supersede written contracts signed by the agent and the foreign firm. For example, Paraguayan law prohibits terminating Paraguayan agents working for foreign firms without just cause unless a very large payment is made to the representative when doing so. In the European Union, Council Directive 86/653 allows parties to agree to a fixed term contract. However, if the relationship continues past that fixed term it becomes an evergreen contract, which allows the principal to terminate the agent only by a three-month written notice for any relationship lasting over three years.

The directive also provides for an 'economic conditions alarm,' which requires the principal to notify the agent if it expects that the agent's business volume will fall significantly below what the agent normally expects. Such laws may seem unduly burdensome to marketers in the United States, but are perceived as necessary in some countries to equalize what is perceived to be an imbalance of bargaining power (Schaffer *et al.* 2005). In addition, the choice between using an independent agent (a representative legally and economically independent from the principal) or a dependent agent (a representative with a close or near-exclusive relationship with the principal) can impact tax treatment under the agent's and principal's tax laws (Libin and Gillis 2003).

INTERNATIONAL LAWS

International intellectual property law

One of the most important aspects of international law to marketers is the enactment and protection of intellectual property rights abroad. Intellectual property, the notion that an entity can receive a limited monopoly on the use or sale of a creative idea, offers numerous advantages to the savvy marketer. Firms may exploit intellectual property rights to sustain a competitive advantage by licensing a new technology or generating revenue from a useful patent. Intellectual property rights also protect brand equity through the restricted use of a firm's tag-lines and symbols. Marketing managers with intellectual property right at hand can also implement vertical and horizontal product differentiation, convey information more strategically, raise entry barriers to competitors, and create power with suppliers who want to associate with a successful brand (Reitzig 2004).

Three types of intellectual property dominate the international intellectual property landscape and concern the marketing manager most: (1) copyrights, which prohibit unauthorized reproduction of artistic works such as books, photos, music, or paintings; (2) patents, which grant inventors of mechanical or other devices exclusive use of that invention; and (3) trademarks, which prohibit duplication of a tag-line, symbol, design, or catchphrase that firm's use to aid and simplify brand recall of a product or service (Shultz and Nill 2002).

The most relevant intellectual property treaty is the Trade Related Aspects of Intellectual Property Rights (TRIPS) agreement of 1994. Prior to TRIPS, countries offered widely differing levels of intellectual property protection based upon unique cultural, economic, historical and other factors. The TRIPS agreement now binds over 120 signatories to follow previous conventions, such as the Berne Convention and the Paris Convention, and requires significant protections for each kind of intellectual property right. These protections impact patent, copyright, and trademark laws. TRIPS requires signatories to provide patent protection to almost any invention or process regardless of the field of technology. Developing countries that once offered exceptions for food products, medicines, and agriculture are no longer able to do so. TRIPS harmonizes the length of patent terms by requiring that nations protect patents for at least 20 years (Harris 2004).

Regarding trademarks, firms must be able to register trademarks that must be protected for at least seven years and renewable indefinitely (WTO 2006a). TRIPS members must recognize as a trademark any sign that could be capable of distinguishing the goods or service of one producer from another. Members can require that the mark has been used and has commercial distinctiveness as conditions for registration. Nations cannot cancel marks for non-use until a minimum of three-years of continuous non-use has passed. TRIPS also augments the Paris Convention by requiring members to prohibit the use of marks that could create confusion to an already established famous mark. This requirement applies to both trademarks and service marks (Sanjeev 2001).

Signatories of TRIPS must now provide copyright protection under the Berne Convention and extend that protection to source and object code of computer programs. National laws must also protect data compilations. Authors and their successors must have the ability to authorize or prohibit the commercial rental of their works to the public. The term of protection for copyright must be for the life of the author, or 50 years from publication or creation of the work (WTO 2006b).

In short, signatories must treat foreign intellectual property rights holders the same as domestic ones. Furthermore, nations must have systems in place to enforce intellectual property rights and prevent export of infringing goods. TRIPS may be enforced by the WTO and includes a settlement mechanism for resolving disputes (WTO 2006a).

Other more focused treaties apply to specific types of intellectual property. For example, the Patent Cooperation Treaty (PCT) presents a unified method for filing patent applications on an international basis (WIPO 2006a). While not granting an 'international patent', the PCT system allows for a single filing and search with procedures maintained by relevant national authorities. Similarly, the Madrid Protocol allows a trademark owner to file a single application that could potentially protect the mark in multiple countries more expeditiously and cheaply than individual national filings (WIPO 2006b). Numerous bilateral and unilateral treaties protect intellectual property rights on a country-by-country basis.

Marketing managers selling products with geographic designations, such as Dijon Mustard or Idaho Potatoes, face special challenges. Such products might run afoul of geographic indications provisions in TRIPS that prevent the misleading use of a geographic origin in a trademark. For example, Anheuser-Bush, manufacturer of Budweiser beer, has been in a protracted and global dispute with a Czech brewery, who claims that the term 'Budweiser' is a geographic designation referring to beer from a region in what is now the Czech Republic (Bird 2006a).

Intellectual property laws may be perceived as suppressing global human rights. The aggressive protection of patents and brand equity may result in reducing poor countries access to food, healthcare, and agricultural products. Local suppliers may fail to compete, thus providing little incentive to a foreign producer to reduce prices. The result may be a backlash, especially in developing countries,

against Western products, entertainment, and culture. Intellectual property rights may encourage the practice that most multinationals follow – few take much effort to localize their marketing mix, which only further enhances the marketing problems that firms face when selling on a global scale (Witkowski 2005).

Privacy

Another issue pertinent to marketing legal environment is the management and transfer of personal data. In 1995, the European Union issued a directive that required member states to establish laws protecting data privacy involving use of personal data that has an extraterritorial impact. European Union firms are thus severely restricted in what personal data may be transferred to nations that do not provide an 'adequate level of protection.' (EU Directive 1995 art. 25.4).

Initially, the 1995 Directive posed significant problems to United States firms wishing to collect European personal data and export that data to the United States. That problem was at least partially resolved by a 'Safe Harbor Principles' agreement in 2000 which allows United States firms to satisfy European Union requirements by self-certifying and declaring that it will follow the guidelines of the Safe Harbor Principles agreement. This does not resolve all problems with management of European data, however. As American firms and others increasingly outsource marketing functions to third parties in developing countries, the data privacy rules in those countries are implicated. For example, India has been a significant target for outsourcing by developed country firms, but lacks any legislative enactments or regulations relevant to data privacy protection (Gaut and George 2006). Therefore, a United States firm obtaining personal data from the European Union may be restricted in outsourcing that data to other countries for marketing and analysis. As the European Union and other entities increasingly strengthen data privacy protection, the requirements for the maintenance, security, and transfer of data will become increasingly rigorous to satisfy national and supra-national legislative requirements.

Conflict resolution

Although international relationships can be profitable, managers should expect to 'hope for the best but prepare for the worst' in global business. At the root of many potential conflicts lies a difference in culture. Whereas certain Western negotiators may take an aggressive negotiating stance, certain Asian negotiators might go to greater lengths to achieve an amicable settlement. Americans might view the formation of a written agreement as a mere necessary step to be completed and then put aside. Other cultures in Asia and Latin American might see the negotiating process as an opportunity to build long-lasting relationships that grow and change over time. The written contract may not be perceived as a final statement of the terms, but a living document whose demands change as the parties needs change. Such different expectations can be the source of unnecessary disputes between global businesspeople.

If disputes do arise, they may be resolved through methods of Alternative Dispute Resolution (ADR). ADR requires a voluntary submission to the process and can take various forms. For example, mediation is a voluntary and non-binding tool, whereby the parties agree upon an impartial mediator to facilitate a solution. Arbitration, by contrast, is more formal, more adversarial, and involves a neutral arbitrator who may issue a decision that binds the parties. Most developed nations have arbitration laws on their books that permit arbitration to occur and specify the effects of arbitral awards. These include the British Arbitration Act, the Arbitration Law of the People's Republic of China, and the US Federal Arbitration Act. The 1985 UNCITRAL Model Law on International Commercial Arbitration has provided a template that China, Mexico, Russia, and Canada have followed.

A challenge of international arbitration is enforcement of arbitration awards. Promulgated in 1958, the New York Convention requires signatories to the convention to enforce arbitration awards from other signatories unless the arbitrator acted outside her authority or other limited exceptions apply. The New York Convention currently has over 140 signatories and has significantly increased predictability in the transaction of global business (Steele 2007).

Companies can control the location of any dispute resolution procedure by inserting a forum selection clause into the contract. A forum selection clause is a term that establishes in advance where any disputes will be litigated or arbitrated. Forum selection clauses are often enforceable by foreign courts as long as the forum selected has some relation to the parties. In 2005, members of the Hague Conference on Private International Law approved the Convention of Choice of Court Agreements. This Convention establishes uniform rules for the treatment of forum selection clauses and the recognition of judgments that arise from them (Anonymous 2006).

CONCLUSION

International marketing law is continually changing. Domestic legislatures are constantly updating their laws to adapt to new social and political trends. Supra-national organizations such as the European Union have promulgated continent-wide regulations. Multinational enterprises are increasingly forming long-term joint ventures and partnerships with local firms in developing countries, where new markets have sprung up and are experiencing rapid growth. Even the smallest concern can conduct business online, potentially reaching consumers around the world and involving Internet-based agreements and sales.

These trends demand a close understanding of the laws and regulations that influence marketing practice, and it is essential to understand the legal philosophy of the country. Countries may follow common law or code law. Common law is based on precedents and practices; England, for example, is a common-law country. Code law is based on detailed rules; Mexico is a code-law country. The legal basis of a country can affect marketing decisions in multifaceted ways.

~~Corporations from the United States~~ involved in international marketing should comply not only with US laws but also with host country laws. Worldwide, different countries follow different sets of laws. An international marketer should be particularly familiar with host country laws pertaining to competition, price setting, distribution arrangements, product liability, patents and trademarks, and advertising.

Another important legal environment aspect is the jurisdiction of laws. The question of which laws will apply in which particular matters must be understood. In some instances, those of the country where the agreement was made apply; in others, those of the country where the business was conducted apply. It is desirable to have a jurisdictional clause in agreements. If there is none, when a conflict of interest occurs, it may either be settled through litigation or be referred for arbitration.

In addition to heeding both US and host country laws, international marketers must be aware of treaties and international conventions. By and large, the relevant laws of the host country would be those concerning tariffs, dumping, export/import licensing, foreign investment, foreign investment incentives (provided by the government to attract foreign business), and restrictions on trading activities. The relevant US laws would be those affecting foreign trade, antitrust laws, antiboycott laws, laws to protect domestic industry, laws to prevent loopholes in the existing tax laws (tax haven laws), tax treaties, and laws that pertain to US government support of US business abroad.

Some international treaties and conventions are concerned with the protection of property such as patents, trademarks, models, and the like, in foreign countries. Some international laws have provisions for the encouragement of both worldwide economic cooperation and prosperity and standardization of international products and processes.

REFERENCES

Anonymous (2006) 'Private International Law – Civil Procedure – Hague Conference Approves Uniform Rules of Enforcement For International Forum Selection Clauses – Convention on Choice of Court Agreements, Concluded June 30, 2005,' *Harvard Law Review*, 119 (January): 931–938.

Bird, R. C. (2006a) 'This Bud's for you: understanding intellectual property Law through the ongoing dispute over the Budweiser trademark', *Journal of Legal Studies Education*, 23(1): 53–85.

Bird, R. C. (2006b) 'Defending intellectual property rights in the BRIC economies', *American Business Law Journal*, 43(2): 317–363.

Brumley, R. H. (1988) 'How Antitrust Law affects international joint ventures,' *Business America*, 26 (November 21): 2–4.

Bucklin, L. P. (1993) 'Modeling the international gray market for public policy decisions', *International Journal of Research in Marketing*, 10(4): 387–405.

Bucklin, L. P. (2000a) 'Invasion of the cartel cops', *Business Week*, (May 8): 130.

Bucklin, L. P. (2000b) 'Taxing times for tax havens', *Business Week*, (October 30): 96.

Cavusgil, S., Tamer, S. D. and Zhang, C. (2004) 'Curbing foreign distributor opportunism: an examination of trust, contracts, and the legal environment in international channel relationships', *Journal of International Marketing*, 12(2): 7–21.

Dayan v. McDonald's Corp. (1984), 466 N.E.2d 958 (Ill. App.).

Delpo, M. C. (1999) 'Tobacco abroad: legal and ethical implications of marketing dangerous United States products overseas', *Business and Society Review*, 104(2): 147–162.

Donaldson, J. and Weiner, R. (1999) 'Swashbuckling the pirates: a communications-based approach to IPR protection in China', published in *Chinese Intellectual Property Law and Practice*. New York: Aspen Publishers.

Donaldson, J. and Weiner, R. (1994). 'A red line in the sand', *The Economist*, (1 October): 86.

Donaldson, J. and Weiner, R. (1999).'Going for Coke', *The Economist*, (14 August): 51.

EU Directive (1995) Directive 95/46/EC Protection of Individuals with Regard to the Processing of Personal Data on the Free Movement of Such Data, 1995 O.J. (L281) 31. http://www.cdt.org/privacy/eudirective/EU_Directive_.html#HD_ NM_42.

Fornaro, M. (2003) 'A parallel problem: grey market goods and the Internet', *Journal of Technology Law and Policy*, 8 (June): 69–91.

Fornaro, M. (2003). 'Battling against bribery is hard craft', *Financial Times*, (23 January): 10.

Fornaro, M. (2005). *Financial Times*. (19 May): 6.

Gaut, D. R. and George, B. C. (2006) 'Offshore Outsourcing to India by US and E.U. Companies: Legal and Cross-Cultural Issues that Affect Data Privacy Regulation in Business', *U.C. Davis Business Law Journal*, 6(2): 13–48.

Goodale, G. M. (2000) 'The new customs gray market regulations: boon or bust for US trademark owners?', *AIPLA Quarterly Journal*, 28 (Fall): 335–359.

Harris, D. P. (2004) 'TRIPS' rebound: an historical analysis of how the TRIPS Agreement can ricochet back against the United States', *Northwestern Journal of International Law and Business*, 25(1): 99–164.

Huang, J.-H., Lee, B. C. Y. and Ho, S. H. (2004) 'Consumer attitude toward gray market goods', *International Marketing Review*, 21(6): 598–614.

Huszagh, S. R. (1981) 'Exporter perceptions of the US regulatory environment,' *Columbia Journal of World Business*, (Fall): 22–31.

Jain, S. C. (1996) 'Problems in international protection of intellectual property rights', *Journal of International Marketing*, 4(1): 9–32.

Koku, P. S. (2005) 'Towards an integrated marketing strategy for developing markets', *Journal of Marketing Theory and Practice*, 13(4): 8–21.

LaFranchi, J. W. (2001) 'International franchising: legal structures and issues', http://www.strasburger.com/calendar/articles/intl/jwl_intl01.pdf.

Libin, J. B. and T. H. Gillis (2003) 'It's a small world after all: the intersection of tax jurisdiction at international, national, and subnational levels', *Georgia Law Review*, 38 (Fall): 197–298.

Morrin, M. and Jacoby, J. (2000) 'Trademark dilution: empirical measures for an elusive concept', *Journal of Public Policy and Marketing*, 19(2): 265–276.

Nester, L. A. (2003) 'Keywords, trademarks, and the gray market: why the use is not fair', *Marquette Intellectual Property Law Review*, 7: 235–258.

News on Iran (1995) National Council of Resistance on Iran – Foreign Affairs Committee, No. 24, www.iran-e-azad.org/english/noi/noi-24.pdf.

Pacini, C., Swingen, J. A. and Rogers, H. (2002) 'The role of OECD and EU conventions in combating bribery of foreign public officials', *Journal of Business Ethics*, 37(4): 385–405.

Petty, R. D. (1994) 'Advertising law and social issues: the global perspective', *Suffolk Transnational Law Review*, 17 (Spring): 309–349.

Reitzig, M. (2004) 'Strategic management of intellectual property,' *Sloan Management Review*, 45(3): 35–40.

Sanjeev, D. (2001) 'TRIPS: international trademark law that promotes global trade', *Journal of Contemporary Legal Issues*, 12: 458–463.

Schaffer, Richard, Earle, B. and Augusti, F. (2005) *International Business Law and its Environment* (6th edn.). Mason, OH: Thomson Corporation.

Scott, J., Gillard, D. and Scott, R. (2002) 'Eliminating bribery as a transnational marketing strategy,' *International Journal of Commerce and Management*, 12(1): 1–17.

Shaw, K. and LaFontaine, F. (2005) Franchisers protect valuable brands through higher company ownership, http://www.gsb.stanford.edu/news/research/econ_shaw_franchising.shtml

Shultz, C. J. and Nill, A. (2002) 'The societal conundrum of intellectual property rights: a game-theoretical approach to the equitable management and protection of IPR', *European Journal of Marketing*, 36(5/6): 667–688.

Steele, B. L. (2007), 'Enforcing international commercial mediation agreements as arbitral awards under the New York Convention', *UCLA Law Review*, 54 (June): 1385–1412.

Super-Sized Empire (2005) *The Orange County Register*, http://www.ocregister.com/ocr/2005/05/16/sections/news/beyond_the_news/article_521162.php

Super-Sized Empire (1988). 'Coke said to face inquiry over sales in Soviet Union', *The Wall Street Journal*, (12 June): A22.

Super-Sized Empire (1999). 'Doing business abroad with few restraints', *The Wall Street Journal*, (June 5): B1.

Super-Sized Empire (2002). 'Stanley worked over', *The Wall Street Journal*, (5 August): A10.

Witkowski, T. (2005) 'Antiglobal challenges to marketing in developing countries: exploring the ideological divide', *Journal of Public Policy and Marketing*, 24(1): 7–23.

WIPO (World Intellectual Property Organisation) (2006a) International Protection of Industrial Property: Patent Cooperation Treaty, http://www.wipo.int/pct/en/treaty/about.htm

WIPO (World Intellectual Property Organisation) (2006b) Madrid System for the International Registration of Marks, http://www.wipo.int/madrid/en/

Wonacott, P. (2005) 'Medical Companies See Troubling Side of Chinese Market,' *The Wall Street Journal*, (1 October): A1.

Wright, L. B. and Morgan, F. W. (2002) 'Comparative advertising in the European Union and the United States: legal and managerial issues', *Journal of Euro-Marketing*, 11(3): 7–30.

WTO (2006a) Understanding the WTO: intellectual property: protection and enforcement, http://www.wto.org/english/thewto_e/whatis_e/tif_e/agrm7_e.htm

WTO (2006b) TRIPS Agreement on trade-related aspects of intellectual property rights: Part II – Standards concerning the availability, scope and use of intellectual property, http://www.wto.org/english/tratop_e/trips_e/t_agm3_e.htm

Wall Street Journal (2002) 'Stanley worked over', *The Wall Street Journal*, (5 August): A10.

Consumer Behavior Research

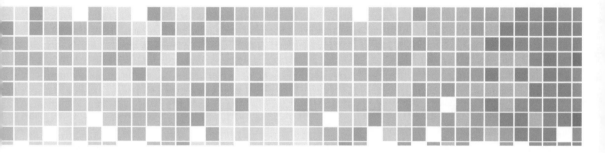

5

Consumer Cognition Across Cultures

Bernd H. Schmitt and Nader T. Tavassoli

INTRODUCTION

Do consumers in different cultures evoke different mental structures and processes when they process commercial information? How can we describe these differences? Do these differences affect behavior?

These questions, which form the core of research on consumer cognition across cultures, have been barely addressed. Rather than being cross-cultural or comparative in its approach, most research on consumer cognition has been culture-bound. This reality is reflected also in consumer cognition's core discipline of psychology where 'culture' was a keyword in only 1.2 percent of articles in the major cognitive and experimental psychology journals between 1994 and 2002 (Hansen 2005). Even when cultural factors are considered in psychological or consumer behavior research, data are most often collected on convenience samples of middle-to-upper class students. Students, however, may constitute a biased sample, and student cognitions may not be representative of the culturally determined cognitions of the broader population: Students are likely to be more analytical in their thinking than the general population, and perhaps more

critical of, if not rebellious toward, cultural values. This may result in temporary frames of thinking and thought processes, and pose a major limitation to our understanding of general cognitive differences across cultures.

As a result, research on consumer cognition across cultures is 'still in its infancy' (Maheswaran and Shavitt 2000, p. 59). Our review therefore cannot provide a broad-based review of an established field. We must be selective and will focus on relatively developed streams of cross-cultural research on consumer cognition. In doing so, we will provide a critical reflection of the field rather than discussing the findings of books and articles in detail.

We will make reference to relevant fields outside consumer cognition (such as social psychology, sociology, anthropology and ethnography) only in passing. Moreover, our focus will be consumer research that uses experimentation and other empirical methods rather than interpretive research. There is a long tradition in sociology and ethnography, going back to Emile Durkheim and Bronislaw Malinowski, which views cognition as a collective phenomenon. This research provides case-based 'thick descriptions' rather than empirical generalizations (Geertz 1973).

In consumer research, this approach has been applied in interpretive research on migration, subcultures, gift giving, or studies on interpersonal behavior. This research has been reviewed (Luna and Gupta 2001) and will not be discussed here.

We have grouped the research that we are going to review into three categories: cognitive maps (e.g., individualism–collectivism), cognitive styles (e.g., analytic-holistic), and cognitive skills (e.g., writing systems). For each category of research, we provide a broad-based context, going back to the historic and philosophic roots – the ontological foundations – of the particular research domain. We then examine the current status of consumer and marketing research in this category and, if necessary, point out limitations and gaps in understanding. Before we begin, we briefly define three key terms: 'cognition', 'across', and 'culture'.

Cognition

The term 'cognition' covers the domains of perception, memory and knowledge representation, language processing, reasoning and problem-solving, as well as domains of 'social cognition' such as attitude formation and change, judgment, and decision making. The fundamental unit of analysis in the marketing literature has overwhelmingly been the individual, and not the collective (Brewer and Chen 2007) or culture. Cognitions here are thus treated as being embedded exclusively in the minds of individuals, rather than as distributed cognitions that emerge from complex interactions among persons that may be specific to cultural contexts (e.g., Atran, Medin and Ross 2005).

Across

We review research that looks 'across' cultures and that is comparative in nature. This limits the review to *etic* research and excludes indigenous *emic* research (see Luna

and Gupta 2001). Etic research relies on the assumption of cognitive universals. Indeed, psychological systems are, if only tacitly, assumed to be universal if not innate (Norenzayan and Heine 2005), an unstated assumption of 'psychic unity' (e.g., Murdock 1945). Psychology's biological roots (Benjamin 1988), the computer analogy in cognitive science (Block 1995), and the concept of a universal grammar in linguistics (Pinker 1994) underpin this view. Following this view, everybody has the same 'hardware'. What differs is the 'software' (for example, the schemata) or ecological'inputs' that vary across cultures.[1]

An etic approach thus requires that researchers identify commonalities in consumer cognition and then examine how ecology and other cultural factors mediate and moderate its differentiated development and expression. We recognize, however, that cultural constructs are often an oversimplification; not being a manipulated variable, they are often confounded. Therefore, we include studies of biculturals (e.g., Benet-Martínez *et al.* 2002; Hong *et al.* 2000; LaFromboise, Coleman and Gerton 1993) and bilinguals that provide one method of controlling for this confound. Moreover, many countries are becoming increasingly multicultural and there are often distinctive subcultures within national boundaries where individuals differ substantially in the degree to which they identify with, adhere to, and practice cultural norms (Cleveland and Laroche 2007; Douglas and Craig 1997). We therefore include several within-country comparisons that allow for a cross-cultural comparison.

Cultures

The term 'culture' has been variously defined throughout history and, by an earlier count, there were over 200 definitions in the social science literature alone (Lonner 1994). Broadly speaking, Wikipedia, the online encyclopedia, defines culture as 'patterns of human activity and the symbolic structures that give such activities significance and importance'. However, within this broad definition, we are witnessing a diversification of more specific conceptualizations of culture and a broad list of cultural factors and influences in the literature. The focus of the cognitive approach to culture tends to be on symbolic cultural structures and processes affecting individual thought. Such symbolic structures may include frames of thinking (or what we will call 'cognitive maps'), specific thought processes (or 'cognitive styles') as well as competencies in particular task domains (or 'cognitive skills'). The ultimate outcome of individual cognitive processes is actual consumer behavior – for example, awareness of certain brands, attaching meaning to such brands, and embellishing them with commercial symbolism. Culturally affected consumer cognition thus in turn becomes a contributor to symbolic cultural structures.

The most popular operationalization of culture has been that of national culture, such as described by Hofstede's (1980) and Schwartz (1992) (for a review, see Steenkamp 2001). National boundaries are a convenient and practical delineator for data collection as well as for the deployment of marketing activities by multinational firms. Several studies have established meaningful commonalities within nations and significant differences between nations. However, some have presented strong arguments that caution against the use of the conventional method of using nations as the cultural unit of analysis (Steenkamp 2001; Douglas and Craig 1997).

One argument against using national cultural norms to explain individual cognition is that population-level parameters do not exist as such (i.e., in the heads of consumers) but are only the statistical output of a sample of the population. It is, therefore, not obvious how they might relate to individual cognition and the case has to be carefully made. For example, if one examines the correlation between caloric consumption and GDP between countries, this correlation is positive (Parker and Tavassoli 2000). People in richer countries consume, on average, more calories. On the other hand, the correlation between personal income and caloric consumption among the population of a single country is often negative. This highlights the dangers of blindly using descriptive characteristics of national culture to make inferences about individual consumer behavior. We must, therefore, be careful not to confuse dimensions of culture (e.g., values or institutions) with those of an individual (norms or schemas).

In the remainder of the chapter, we review the three core categories in which research on consumer cognition across cultures has been conducted: cognitive maps, cognitive styles and cognitive skills. As mentioned earlier, we view cognitive maps as broad-based, culturally acquired frames of thinking such as materialism and individualism–collectivism. Cognitive styles include more specific consumer thought processes that may differ across cultures, such as cue sensitivity to central versus peripheral message cues and attention to particular types of information. Finally, cognitive skills include competencies in a particular domain, for example, language or spatial processing.

COGNITIVE MAPS

Cognitive maps are general frames of thinking that reduce uncertainties which individuals have about the environment. Cognitive maps represent, in the individual mind, past environmental challenges faced by a culture and how a functionally oriented society might respond to them (László and Masulli 1993). At the individual level, cultural cognitive maps manifest themselves as memory traces. Neurologically, these traces may be viewed as transient patterns of neuronal excitations which are shaped by sensory inputs throughout life, starting at birth. Early learning and socialization has profound effects on the development of cultural cognitive maps and shape future inputs and thought, thus establishing rules of conduct and roles in society.

In the consumer literature, two types of cognitive maps have been extensively researched: materialism and individualism–collectivism. Materialism is relevant and closely related to consumer behavior because of its inherent link to commercialism and consumption decisions about economic goods. Individualism–collectivism is relevant because it reflects the tension between individual goal fulfillment and the social nature (transactional or otherwise) of commercial contexts.

Materialism

Materialism, in its broadest sense, has been a central topic of cultural debate for a long time and cross-cultural comparisons find that materialism varies across countries (Eastman *et al.* 1997; Kilbourne, Grünhagen and Foley 2005). One measure of the materialism in culture may be the degree to which materialistic messages appear in marketing communications. As a case in point, in the late 1980s within Chinese culture, adverts in the People's Republic of China were found to be mostly utilitarian – possibly reflecting its anti-materialistic society – and mostly hedonistic in Hong Kong, with Taiwan falling in between but moving in the direction of Hong Kong (Tse, Belk and Zhou 1989). Marketing activity, however, is not only a reflection of a culture's materialism but also plays an important role in propagating materialism itself via the content shown in advertising, thus affecting the importance and centrality that materialism has for an individual.

One major source of transfer of materialistic values is religion (O'Guinn and Belk 1989), which has been shown to affect consumer behavior in general as well (Cornwell *et al.* 2005; Sood and Nasu 1995). As Max Weber argued in his classic *The Protestant Ethic and the Spirit of Capitalism*, Martin Luther gave moral justification to worldly pursuits and Calvinism suggests that material wealth reflects one's value as a person, a pursuit that is at best morally neutral in Catholicism. Similarly, William James (1890) linked the sense of self to possessions – financial assets, clothing and housing. Other religions are antithetical to goals such as acquisition, achievement and affluence. For example, in Hinduism and Buddhism (e.g., in the *Four Noble Truths*) the focus is on the elimination of desires for possessions and selfish enjoyment, a theme echoed by early Greek philosophers, such as Pythagoras, who required the foregoing of individual possessions before a follower could become his student.

This suggests that a cultures-level of materialism should be correlated with wealth. However, a study across 13 countries (Ger and Belk 1996a) did not find a simple relationship between affluence and materialism. A similar conclusion was reached by Feather (1998) in a study across Australia, Canada and the United States.

In consumer research, materialism has been characterized both as a personality trait characterizing the importance a consumer attaches to worldly (i.e., secular, or non-spiritual) possessions (Belk 1985), and as a cultural orientation representing an individual's attitude toward the role of possessions in life, such as the importance of acquisitions, and their effect on happiness and possession-defined success (Richins and Dawson 1992). Specifically, Hunt, Kernan and Mitchell (1996) have described how this value orientation 'can be viewed as maps for the retrieval of social information as well as structures that enable subsequent evaluations and problem solving activity' (p. 69). At the individual level, materialism thus serves to influence the perception (e.g., making things more salient), encoding (e.g., what is important), representation (e.g., person–possession links) and subsequent retrieval of information from memory; goal-setting, problem-solving and planning behaviors. Materialism can provide a frame for interpreting and evaluating events in consumers' environments (Hunt, Kernan and Mitchell 1996). As such, materialism may affect consumption behaviors such as luxury purchasing (Wong and Ahuvia 1998), compulsive buying, personal savings and consumer debt, charitable contributions, gift giving, as well as the relation between possessions and the self, and the signaling to others via possessions.

Moreover, materialism has been described as a value: a belief about desirable end-states and modes of conduct that guide evaluations and choices. However, values are seen to transcend specific situations and the measurement of materialism is context specific (e.g., Richins and Dawson 1992) and at the individual level may, therefore, be seen more as an attitude structure that is underpinned by value systems that individuals hold (Kilbourne, Grünhagen and Foley 2005). Indeed, materialism across countries has been found to be positively correlated with Schwartz's (1992) self-enhancement values and negatively correlated with self-transcendence (Kilbourne, Grünhagen and Foley 2005). Schwartz's (1992) value scales have been validated across the world, and this suggests that materialism and its consequences offer a rich opportunity for further analysis.

Materialism is often regarded by researchers as something negative and misguided and consumers interviewed in the USA, Turkey, Romania, and Western Europe overwhelmingly shared this impression (Ger and Belk 1999). One reason is that it is seen as widening the gap between the consumption of the rich and the poor. Another is sacrificing 'necessities' like food and healthcare with 'luxuries' such as televisions and refrigerators (e.g., Ger and Belk 1996b).

It is difficult to interpret cross-country differences in a meaningful way because materialism seems to manifest itself in very different ways in different cultures. Moreover, it is not clear whether an etic measure of materialism that can be globally applied exists. For example, research in the USA, Singapore, Thailand, Japan, and Korea has questioned the measurement equivalence and construct validity of the material values scale (Richins and Dawson 1992) due to its inclusion of reverse-worded items (Wong, Rindfleisch and Burroughs 2003). On the other hand, materialism – when measured by a subset of 9 items from Richins and Dawson (1992) – was found to be invariant and thus valid across Canada, Germany, and the USA (Kilbourne, Grünhagen and Foley 2005).

Individualism and collectivism

The individualism–collectivism dimension is the most widely used cultural dimension in cross-cultural marketing research. Consumer research on individualism–collectivism was particularly prominent in the 1990s, following a similar focus in psychology in the 1980s. Individualism represents the degree to which people prefer to act as individuals. Individuals display self-reliance, in contrast to collectivists that view themselves as members of an integrated group. Individualistic societies have an 'I' orientation; collectivistic societies have a 'we' orientation (Hofstede 1980). Moreover, in individualist societies, people tend to think of others as individuals, whereas group membership (in-group versus out-group) is more important in collectivist societies (Triandis 1995).

It has been argued (and debated) that the individualism–collectivism dimension is a cognitive map that helps people to adapt to the environment, such as climate and terrain via its limiting and motivating influence on economic activity (e.g., the ability to farm) (e.g., Hofstede 1980; Triandis 1995). For example, agriculture and livestock rearing foster complementary, cooperative activities, and community culture – factors which promote a more collectivistic culture. Marketing plays an active role in replicating cognitive maps such as individualism, for example, through consumption symbols such as brands (Aaker and Schmitt 2001; Benet-Martínez et al. 2002).

A culture's level of individualism–collectivism has been associated with various aspects of consumer decision-making: studies have examined the extent to which it influences advertising appeals (Han and Shavitt 1994; Alden, Hoyer and Lee 1993), the persuasive process (Aaker and Williams 1998; Aaker and Maheswaran 1997), country of origin effects (Gürhan-Canli and Maheswaran 2000a), word-of-mouth referral behavior (Money, Gilly and Graham 1998), impulsive buying behavior (Kacen and Lee 2002), stated preferences for consumption symbols (Aaker and Schmitt 2001), and preference for web sites (Steenkamp and Geyskens 2006). For example, on the latter topic, individualistic consumers gave more weight to privacy/security protection and to customization in their perceived value judgments (Steenkamp and Geyskens 2006).

Several studies have examined the preference for various advertising appeals. Alden, Hoyer and Lee (1993) concluded that humorous advertisements in collectivist and individualist cultures share universal cognitive structures but the content differs along the individualism–collectivism dimension. It has generally been found that people from individualistic countries respond more favorably to individualistic appeals while the reverse applies for individuals from collectivist countries (Gregory and Munch 1997; Han and Shavitt 1994; Wang et al. 2000; Zhang and Gelb 1996). This effect was moderated by product category and was more pronounced for publicly consumed products than for products purchased and consumed privately (Zhang and Gelb 1996). An exception to these findings are two studies by Aaker and Williams (1998) who reported ego-focused emotional appeals (pride, happiness) to be more persuasive for members of a collectivist culture, while other-focused appeals (empathy, peacefulness) led to more favorable attitudes for people living in individualist nations. The authors argue that the novelty of the claim induced more elaboration.

Research on biculturals shows that individuals can access both types of cognitive maps based on the situation (e.g., priming) (e.g., Benet-Martínez et al. 2002; Hong et al. 2000; LaFromboise, Coleman and Gerton 1993). Studies of Hong Kong bicultural individuals found that language manipulation (Cantonese vs. English) increases tendencies to choose compromise options in a product decision task, endorse associated decision guidelines that advocate moderation as opposed to extreme paths, defer decision-making in problems where it can be postponed, and endorse decision guidelines that advocate caution rather than decisive action (Briley, Morris and Simonson 2005). A more complex view demonstrates that East Asian-Western biculturals who compartmentalize individualism–collectivism react less favorably to advertising appeals that contain both an individual and interpersonal focus than biculturals who have integrated the two cognitive maps (Lau-Gesk 2003).

Limitations and future directions The majority of articles have used Hofstede's (1980) research to select individualist and collectivist countries in which they conducted their studies without measuring respondents' actual orientation. Hofstede's data were collected over 35 years ago among IBM managers and are likely to be unrepresentative of today's populations, especially when it comes to urban students who make up the majority of respondents. Industrial urban settings dominated by technology should promote an individualistic culture with a greater focus on personal achievement (and a decline in nepotism) and the focus shifted from kinship-based solidarity to individualism (Griswold 1994). Moreover, in countries such as China, student respondents were the beneficiaries of a one-child policy rather than a politically charged collective based on agriculture. Indeed, Fernandez et al. (1997) collected data in nine countries on four continents and concluded that significant shifts in value classifications have occurred since 1980 and modernization has been found to increase individualism in Korea (Cha 1994) and, anecdotally, in Japan (Triandis 1995).

A different limitation has already been discussed earlier, namely that cultural analysis has been based on some estimation of population parameters for the cultural norms in question, typically ones that were collected at the level of a nation. The leap from statistical regularity in a sub-sample of population to a population as a whole is faulty in the same way that a leap from a US sample to a world sample is. A leap across generations may be even more problematic. On the positive side, there has been corroborating evidence on individual level traits in the USA – where idiocentrism refers to person-level individualism (independent self) and allocentrism refers to person-level collectivism (interdependent self) – that cross-cultural level theoretical conclusions are analogous at the individual level (Dutta-Bergman and Wells 2002). Lee (2000) also investigated allocentrism and idiocentrism and found a tendency toward allocentrism in collectivist countries and idiocentrism in individualist countries, but also a high degree of variance within cultures.

Other cognitive maps

Several studies have examined multiple cultural maps and their interplay, such as the horizontal (valuing equality) versus vertical (valuing hierarchy) dimension (Shavitt et al. 2006) or the effect of having versus not having power and its influence on the self concept and cognition (Oyserman 2006). For example, it was found that US consumers evaluated their home-country product more (less) favorably when it was superior (inferior) in quality to a product made in Japan (Gürhan-Canli and Maheswaran 2000a). US consumers' vertical/individualist orientation was suggested to promote the desire to be superior to others in their social group (Triandis and Gelfand 1998) such that they would hold favorable attitudes about a higher-quality product regardless of its country of origin (Gürhan-Canli and Maheswaran 2000a). In other words, the vertical/individualist value of 'being the best' is more important than home-country group membership.

Roth (1995) has examined how power distance and individualism affect brand image strategies for functional, social and sensory products. Nakata and Sivakumar (1996) examined how links between the five dimensions of national culture – individualism; power distance; masculinity; uncertainty avoidance; and the Confucian dynamic – impact the implementation stages of new product development. Others have shown that credible brands reinforce group identity and are more valued in collectivist countries, whereas they provide more value to high-uncertainty-avoidance consumers because they have lower perceived risk and information costs (Erdem, Swait and Valenzuela 2006). While these studies introduce alternative cognitive maps, the dominance of the individualism–collectivism research tradition remains since Maheswaran and Shavitt (2000) highlighted the need to focus on less explored cultural dimensions.

COGNITIVE STYLES

While cognitive maps focus on cultural content, cognitive styles relate to qualitative differences in thought processes. Unfortunately, in comparison with research on cognitive maps, there is less research on this topic in marketing and consumer research, and, as we will show, the research has been less paradigmatic in nature. Therefore we suggest that the interested reader consult, for example, the literature on cognitive styles in psychology, including research on holistic versus analytical cognition (Nisbett et al. 2001); field-dependent versus field-independent perceptual skills (Berry 1976); and psychological differentiation (Witkin et al. 1962). Interestingly, these literatures also offer striking parallels to the collectivism–individualism construct. For example, the concept of a field–independent cognitive style (Witkin et al. 1962) includes that of an individualistic society's interdependent self (Markus and Kitayama 1991). And a field–dependent cognitive style (Witkin *et al.* 1962) reflects a collectivistic society's interdependent self (Markus and Kitayama 1991). In other words, some cultural differences attributed to cultural content (cognitive maps) may be confounded by differences in cognitive styles, and vice versa.

Comparative consumer research on cognitive styles has been conducted as part of persuasion, attitude and decision research. This research has been relatively ad hoc in nature, demonstrating isolated empirical effect and lacking at this point a unifying theme – similar to individualism–collectivism. For example, Aaker and Maheswaran (1997) found that dual-process models of persuasion such as the ELM (e.g., Petty, Cacioppo and Schumann 1983) are cross-culturally generalizable, but that certain cues are considered central by one culture and peripheral by another. Similarly, Lee and Green (1991) found that the Fishbein behavioral intentions model can be applied to collectivistic cultures, but that the societal norms component has a higher relative weight than in individualistic cultures.

Moreover, when faced with information incongruity, North Americans tend to rely solely on diagnostic information (attenuation strategy) while people in an East Asian culture tend to follow an additive strategy in which both pieces of information are combined to jointly influence evaluations (Aaker and Sengupta 2000). North Americans are persuaded more by promotion-focused information, and Chinese people are persuaded more by prevention-focused information, but only when initial, automatic reactions to messages are given. Corrections to these default judgments occur when processing is thoughtful (Briley and Aaker 2006b). Westerners are relatively less patient and therefore discount the future to a greater degree than do Easterners, and thus Westerners value immediate consumption relatively more. Furthermore, when Easterners are faced with the threat of a delay in receiving a product

(i.e., a prevention loss), they are more impatient, whereas when Westerners are faced with a promotion loss, their impatience increases (Chen, Ng and Rao 2005).

Finally, through its impact on motivations and goals, culture can influence decision inputs, types of options preferred, and the timing of decisions (Briley and Aaker 2006a). A widely researched concept of these motivations in consumer behavior is ethnocentrism (Balbanis *et al.* 2001; Batra *et al.* 2000; Klein and Ettenson 1999; Shimp and Sharma 1987). Ethnocentrism is the desire of the consumer to prefer domestic products based on patriotic considerations and can result in various motivations, including defense effects. Research on country-of-origin effects is relevant to this topic (Gürhan-Canli and Maheswaran 2000a, 2000b). Speaking to the motivational nature of this effect, when consumers' mortality was made salient to them – triggering defensive mechanisms – foreign brands were evaluated as less desirable (Nelson *et al.* 1997).

Limitations and future directions   Additional research on cognitive styles is desperately needed. As we noted, most research is ad hoc rather than theory guided. Research in this area requires a systematic approach to cognitive styles that specifies which cognitive style is likely to affect which task domain (for example, information search, evaluation, decision-making, or choice). Moreover, the relation between maps and styles should be examined more closely. For example, it may be worthwhile exploring whether there is a relation between materialism and ethnocentrism, or between individualism–collectivism and promotion versus prevention focus.

COGNITIVE SKILLS

It has been suggested that the human intellect cannot be separated from the technologies invented to extend cognitive processes (Olson 1976). Consider language. Literacy relates to cognitive skills through specific practices involved in the use of language. Different forms of written script (e.g., alphabetic, phonemic, and with or without word division) promote specific cognitive skills related to their use (Scribner and Cole 1981).

Comparative consumer research on cognitive skills had focused primarily on language – on grammar, writing systems and the attention to auditory versus visual information resulting from it – and in that regard, a broad-based theory (based on the so-called Whorfian Hypothesis) has been evoked. In the following we review such linguistic consumer research as well as related work on order and spatial processing.

Language is one of the most visible aspects of culture. On the one hand, language is a core medium through which members of a culture are educated about reality (ecology), symbols to communicate norms and navigate the social maze. On the other hand, there has long been the idea that language influences thought itself. In the West, this idea was extensively debated by eighteenth-century philosophers such as Vico, Condillac, Maupertius, Mondboddo, and Reid, and Herder and Leibnitz, who considered language to be connected to the 'spirit' of a people, as an embodiment of the Volksgeist (Jahoda and Krewer 1997). More formal theories (e.g., by von Humboldt ([1836] 1988) gained notoriety in the United States through Whorf's linguistic relativity hypothesis ([1940] 1956). Most debates on the Whorfian Hypothesis have centered on the idea that the semantic structures of different languages are incommensurable, with the consequence that speakers of specific languages might think and act differently. Several early empirical tests of this hypothesis have been called into question, however, and it has been argued that natural languages may be too ambiguous and schematic to be functional as a mental code and that we share a universal 'mentalese' (Pinker 1994). This position implies that language does not affect thought; that we learn and evaluate verbal information using similar mental processes across languages.

More recently, the Whorfian Hypothesis has been reconceptualized in terms of how linguistic forms are represented, how they operate in the mind and how they affect the concepts and categories that denote objects and relations in the world (Hunt and Agnoli 1991). One of the basic premises of this idea is that 'different languages pose different challenges for cognition and provide differential support for cognition' (p. 387). Research in marketing is compatible with those of Hunt and Agnoli (1991) who argue that language may not alter perception but that it can affect classification and linguistically based records of events. Language is also a cognitive skill that brings with it 'computational' ease that favors some thought processes over others. Writing systems thereby influence unconscious habitual thought rather than limiting thought potential, based on memory processes routinely invoked in the processing and retrieval of written language, even for bilinguals.

Comparing English with Chinese communications

Most of the marketing literature has compared stimuli and communications written in the alphabetic English writing system to the use of Chinese logographs that are read by one-quarter of the world's population in China, Japan and Korea. Alphabetic letters that are used in the Latin alphabet (e.g., English, German, and Spanish), Arabic, Hebrew, and Cyrillic writing systems (e.g., Russian), are inherently meaningless. They represent sounds. And with 26 letters matched to over 3,500 syllables available, English is a sound-rich but visually poor language. In contrast, the over 10,000 Chinese logographs represent meaning and each corresponds to a single spoken syllable. With only about 450 syllables available in Mandarin Chinese, for example, spoken Mandarin is relatively sound-starved. This results in an abundance of homophones: words that mean different things but are pronounced in the same way, such as 'dear' and 'deer' in English. In contrast, logographs are visually rich, each consisting of a unique stroke combination. Originally, logographs' meanings were represented as pictorial abstractions. However, even though pictures are still used as a learning device for logographs, a Chinese reader will not experience reading a sentence as a string of pictures. Indeed, most words contain multiple logographs, many of which, or parts of which (i.e., radicals) indicate the word's pronunciation without any reference to its meaning.

The meanings of words Nevertheless, Western marketers still need to be aware of logographs' meanings when trying to create a Chinese version of a brand name. Supposedly, the logographs originally used for the Chinese version of Coca-Cola sounded similar to the English original but resulted in the rather surreal sequence of 'bite the wax tadpole' in terms of their meaning. Today, Coca-Cola's logographs have the more fortunate meaning of 'brings happiness to your mouth'. These meanings matter: even when consumers do not try to actively make sense of the meaning inherent in a brand name's Chinese logographs, they appear to influence consumer memory and evaluation. For example, if a brand name contains logographs that correspond in meaning to the product or service offered – as in the case of Coca-Cola – this can improve memory for the brand name and the brand's target claim (Lee and Ang 2003). A brand name that is translated both in terms of sound and category meaning is also evaluated more favorably by proficient bilinguals than one translated either based on sound or meaning alone (Zhang and Schmitt 2004).

The situation is more complicated in practice, however, as Western brands in China commonly use a dual naming strategy with both the original alphabetic name and the adapted Chinese name appearing with equal or different prominence on the packaging. For example, when a translated Chinese name matches only the original's sound but not meaning, it is evaluated more positively by bilinguals when the emphasis is on the original English brand name rather than Chinese translation (i.e., the original name is printed in a larger font). This is presumably because this type of emphasis pre-activates expectations about the Chinese translation's pronunciation (Zhang and Schmitt 2001).

Grammar There is an additional layer of meaning inherent in Chinese and that is its grammar. Chinese is a classifier language, with the mandatory use of elements such as collective nouns, e.g., 'a school of fish' that are rare in English. These classifiers often depict perceptual properties of objects such as shape, size, thickness, and length, and conceptual properties such as bendable, elastic and graspable. Classifiers have been found to affect consumer memory and choice (Schmitt and Zhang 1998; Zhang and Schmitt 1998). For example the classifier *zhang* is used for flat, extended objects such as table or paper. These commonalities create associations, even when product categories are written without them. As a result, Chinese speakers were more likely to place objects with common classifiers into categories, to remember these in clusters defined by shared classifiers, and to evaluate objects with shared classifiers as closer substitutes in consumer choice than do English speakers for the same objects (Schmitt and Zhang 1998). Classifiers also affect consumer evaluations of advertisements (Zhang and Schmitt 1998).

Auditory and visual attention The meaning inherent or lacking from symbols of writing only represents one linguistic difference. Writing systems are also processed with a different emphasis and reading alphabetic words involves sound-based mental processes to a greater degree, whereas reading logographs involves visual processes to a greater degree. For example, English speakers were able to recall more (nonsensical) words when they spoke them, whereas

Chinese speakers remembered more when they wrote them. It appears that it is easier to retrieve the stored 'sounds' represented by the alphabet that contains only a few visual symbols but many syllables, whereas it is easier to access the visual store for the large inventory of logographs that are matched by relatively few syllables (Schmitt, Pan and Tavassoli 1994).

Heightened visual attention in reading logographs also appears to raise the significance of visual features, such as the font used in marketing communications (Pan and Schmitt 1996). For example, attitude ratings provided by Chinese consumers were more sensitive than those of American consumers to the match between the femininity or masculinity of fonts used for brand names of feminine (e.g., lipstick) and masculine products (e.g., motorcycles). While the font of alphabetic brand names did not affect brand evaluations, Chinese consumers more favorably evaluated feminine (masculine) products written in fonts that had been rated as more feminine (masculine).

Chinese consumers also appear to pay more attention, possibly subconsciously, to a brand name's color such as the UPS brown (Tavassoli 2001). Color is an important brand-recognition cue, to the extent that about half copy the colors of a national brand, presumably in an attempt to confuse consumers. The greater reliance on visual short-term memory makes this copycat strategy more effective with readers of Chinese logographs than of alphabetic English words. When print colors had been covertly associated with poor- versus high-quality brands, Chinese but not English readers evaluated a new brand more positively when it was printed in the high-quality color than in the poor-quality color (Tavassoli 2001).

Memory retrieval   Advertisers use a variety of non-linguistic auditory and visual elements to capture and hold consumers' attention and to serve as retrieval cues for later recall, for example, when reinstated as part of an integrated marketing campaign. Visual elements

such as logos (Nike's swoosh) and images (the Michelin baby) appear to be more potent retrieval cues for Chinese than English ad copy (Tavassoli and Han 2001, 2002; Tavassoli and Lee 2003). In contrast, auditory elements such as music (Chevrolet's 'Like a Rock'), sound effects (the MGM lion's roar), and brand identifiers (e.g., Intel's trademarked 'tune') were more potent retrieval cues for English than Chinese ad copy (Tavassoli and Han 2001, 2002; Tavassoli and Lee 2003). This cross-linguistic difference is also an important consideration for advertising tracking studies that try to use the most sensitive memory cues to test advertising effectiveness.

Nonverbal distractions   Auditory and visual elements are not only potent memory retrieval cues for words, but they can have the unintended negative effect of interfering with the concurrent processing of the verbal ad copy during encoding. Stimulating music was found to be more detrimental to message reception and the generation of message-related thoughts for alphabetic ads, whereas engaging visual graphics were relatively more detrimental for logographic ads (Tavassoli and Han 2001, 2002; Tavassoli and Lee 2003). In other words, based on the overlap in mental processing, there is a trade-off between interference and integration between linguistic and non-linguistic stimuli for effective advertisement design.

Order processing   The above framework on interference and integration is based on short-term memory storage. In addition to storage, short-term memory also includes a rehearsal component. Phonological short-term memory rehearses information by re-circulating it in a serial manner, much like one would try to remember a telephone number. Rehearsing alphabetic words appears to rely more on the phonological loop than does rehearsing logographs and consumers were better at reconstructing the presentation order of alphabetic words than of logographs (Tavassoli 1999; also Tavassoli and Han 2001). This has important implications for attitudes and product choice because memory for order affects what information is remembered initially and thus anchors memory-based judgments, as well as affecting measures of top-of-mind awareness. Indeed, compared to Chinese, judgments in English were found to be more sensitive to the order in which verbal information was presented (Tavassoli and Lee 2004).

Spatial processing   In contrast to primarily relying on the phonological loop for rehearsing verbal information, rehearsing logographs involves to a greater degree visual short-term memory, which rehearses information as if viewing a scene that contains the imagined objects and retains physical relations among objects. It was found that people remembered better the spatial location of logographs that had been presented scattered on a single page than of alphabetic words (Tavassoli 2002; also Tavassoli and Han 2001). Chinese consumers may, therefore, be more sensitive to spatial changes to the brand identity such as the reconfiguration of a website.

Limitations and future directions   Most research has been on written language and written responses presented in static ways. Moreover, only lip service has been paid to the processing of sentences or entire paragraphs; much of the research focuses on the processing of individual words, and not on verbal information that extends over time. Such research strips away a lot of the realism of actual consumer situations. Most marketing communications and commercial messages that reach consumers are multi-sensory – they use text, images and auditory information – and they do so in dynamic ways extended over time.

CONCLUSION

We have divided our review of research on consumer cognition across cultures into three broad research categories: cognitive maps, cognitive styles, and cognitive skills. Research on cognitive maps – broad-based cultural frames that individuals use – has been focused around two key themes: materialism and individualism–collectivism. Despite some limitations that require future research, research on individualism–collectivism, in particular, can be described as relatively 'mature': there has been significant progress in understanding how individualistic and collectivistic maps emerge out of the physical and cultural environment and what consequences they have in decision-making and in responding to advertising messages. In contrast, research on cognitive styles lacks a unifying theoretical theme, although several interesting empirical insights have been offered. Finally, consumer research on cognitive skills has focused on one domain in particular – language. This language research has examined cultural and linguistic influences on consumer behavior in quite some detail. However, language processing is more than processing individual words, presented in various modes or writing systems, and needs to be expanded beyond the (written) word level, just as research on cognitive skills needs to be expanded beyond language competencies. The three levels of consumer cognition – cognitive maps, styles and skills – also share commonalities. Whereas traditional approaches to understanding them dissected them apart and settled them within the boundaries of paradigms, future research needs to address them in an integrated manner.

Within each section of this review, we attempted to discuss the historic and philosophical roots and thus enlighten the ontological status of each construct. This part of our review revealed that consumer researchers today often struggle with issues that are decades, if not centuries, old. Current research is rich in data and in demonstrating various isolated effects. However, except for individualism–collectivism and language, current research is weak in developing major theoretical paradigms that enrich the broad-based philosophical conceptions that have been developed about consumer cognition many years ago.

Methodologically, we recommend that future research be more interdisciplinary and multi-paradigmatic in nature. Current research on consumer cognition largely follows an information processing paradigm and does not make contact with anthropological or ethnographic research, and vice versa. If we view, as we have done in the beginning of this chapter, individual consumer cognition as culture-bound – that is, as being affected by the symbolic structures of a culture, and as contributing via its commercial output to culture – then interdisciplinary research that follows various paradigms and combines empirical work with 'thick descriptions' should be most welcome.

Finally, future research could benefit from more specifically focusing on consumers: individuals that make consumption decisions about economic goods. Consumption-related situations share characteristics with but also differ substantially from situations considered in other fields, much in the same way that behaviors at a funeral will differ from those at a bachelor party (e.g., Cole 1996; cf. Vygotsky 1978). One might, therefore, expect an approach to cross-cultural analysis that highlights consumer settings in which more general psychological tendencies have been found to not directly apply to choice behaviors. Unfortunately, the lack of situational analysis is a major shortcoming of much of the literature we reviewed.

NOTES

1 The political climate makes even the contemplation of a different view suspiciously racist. On the one hand, selection pressures that result in genetic group-level differences are likely to be related to traits such as thermal fitness rather than to traits relevant to consumer cognition (Cavalli-Sforza and Cavalli-Sforza 1995). However, even if the relevant genetic makeup is the same across

cultures, there are biocultural influences on developmental plasticity that could result in 'hardware' differences between cultures (Li 2003). Given the level of analysis in most consumer and marketing research, this is not a topic that we explore, but it is a one that scholars may be interested in and one that may shape future theorizing.

REFERENCES

Aaker, J. L., Benet-Martínez, V. and Garolera, J. (2001) 'Consumption symbols as carriers of culture: A study of Japanese and Spanish brand personality constructs', *Journal of Personality and Social Psychology*, 81(3): 492–508.

Aaker, J. L. and Maheswaran, D. (1997) 'The effect of cultural orientation on persuasion', *Journal of Consumer Research*, 24(3): 315–328.

Aaker, J. L. and Schmitt, B. H. (2001) 'Culture-dependent assimilation and differentiation of the self', *Journal of Cross Cultural Psychology*, 32(5): 561–576.

Aaker, J. L. and Sengupta, J. (2000) 'Additivity versus attenuation: the role of culture in the resolution of information incongruity', *Journal of Consumer Psychology*, 9(2): 67–82.

Aaker, J. L. and Williams, P. (1998) 'Empathy versus pride: the influence of emotional appeals across cultures', *Journal of Consumer Research*, 25(3): 241–261.

Alden, D. L., Hoyer, W. D. and Lee, C. (1993) 'Identifying global and culture-specific dimensions of humor in advertising: a multinational analysis', *Journal of Marketing*, 57(2): 64–75.

Atran, S., Medin, D. L. and Ross, N.O. (2005) 'The cultural mind: environmental decision making and cultural modeling within and across populations', *Psychological Review*, 12(4): 744–776.

Balbanis, G. Diamantopuolos, A., Mueller, R. and Melewar, T. (2001) 'The impact of nationalism, patriotism, and internationalism on consumer ethnocentric tendencies', *Journal of International Business Studies*, 32 (1): 157–175.

Batra, R., Ramaswamy, V., Alden, D. L., Steenkamp, J.-B. E. M. and Ramachander, S.

(2000) 'Effects of brand local and non-local origin on consumer attitudes', *Journal of Consumer Psychology*, 9(2): 83–95.

Belk, R. W. (1985) 'Materialism: trait aspects of living in the material world', *Journal of Consumer Research*, 12(3): 265–280.

Benet-Martínez, V., Leu, J., Lee, F. and Morris, M. W. (2002) 'Negotiating biculturalism', *Journal of Cross-Cultural Psychology*, 33(5): 492–516.

Benjamin, L. T. (1988) *A History of Psychology: Original Sources and Contemporary Research*. New York: McGraw-Hill.

Berry, John W. (1976) *Human Ecology and Cognitive Style: Comparative Studies in Cultural and Psychological Adaptation*. New York: Sage.

Block N. (1995) 'The mind as the software of the brain', in E. E. Smith and D. N. Osherson (eds), *Thinking*. Vol. 3, 2nd edn. Cambridge, MA: MIT Press, pp. 377–425.

Brewer, M. B. and Chen, Y-R. (2007) 'Where (who) are collectives in collectivism? Toward conceptual clarification of individualism and collectivism', *Psychological Review*, 114(1): 133–151.

Briley, D. A. and Aaker, J. L. (2006a) 'Bridging the culture chasm: ensuring that consumers are healthy, wealthy, and wise', *Journal of Public Policy & Marketing*, 25(1): 53–66.

Briley, D. A. and Aaker, J. L. (2006b) 'When does culture matter? Effects of cultural and personal knowledge on the anchoring and adjustment of judgments', *Journal of Marketing Research*, 43(3): 395–408.

Briley, D. A., Morris M. W. and Simonson, I. (2000) 'Reasons as carrier of culture: Dynamic versus dispositional models of cultural influence on decision making', *Journal of Consumer Research*, 27(2): 157–178.

Briley, D. A., Morris, M. W. and Simonson, I. (2005) 'Cultural chameleons: Biculturals, conformity motives, and decision making', *Journal of Consumer Psychology*, 15(4): 351–362.

Cavalli-Sforza, Luigi. L. and Cavalli-Sforza, Francesco (1995) *The Great Human Diasporas: The History of Diversity and Evolution*. Reading, MA: Perseus Books.

Cha, H. (1994) 'Aspects of individualism and collectivism in Korea', in U. Kim, H. C. Triandis, C. Kagitcibasi, S.-C. Choi, and G. Yoon (eds), *Individualism and Collectivism: Theory,*

Methods and Applications. Thousand Oaks, CA: Sage, pp. 137–156.

Chen, H. A., Ng, S. and Rao, A. R. (2005) 'Cultural differences in consumer impatience', *Journal of Marketing Research*, 42(3): 291–301.

Cleveland, M. and Laroche, M. (2007) 'Acculturaton to the global consumer culture: scale development and research paradigm', *Journal of Business Research*, 60(3): 249–259.

Cole, Michael (1996) *Cultural Psychology: A Once and Future Discipline*. Cambridge, MA: Belknap Press.

Cornwell, B., Chi Cui C., Mitchell V., Schlegelmilch, B., Dzulkiflee, A. and Chan, J. (2005) 'A cross-cultural study of the role of religion in consumers' ethical positions', *International Marketing Review*, 22(5): 531–546.

Douglas, S. P. and Craig, C. S. (1997) 'The changing dynamic of consumer behavior: implications for cross-cultural research', *International Journal of Research in Marketing*, 14(4): 379–395.

Dutta-Bergman, M. J. and Wells, W. D. (2002) 'The values and lifestyles of idiocentrics and allocentrics in an individual culture: a descriptive approach', *Journal of Consumer Psychology*, 12(3): 231–242.

Eastman, J. K., Fredenberger, B., Campbell, D. and Calvert, S. (1997) 'The relationship between status consumption and materialism: a cross-cultural comparison of Chinese, Mexican and American students', *Journal of Marketing Theory and Practice*, 5(1).

Erdem, T., Swait, J. and Valenzuela, A. (2006) 'Brands as signals: a cross-country validation Study,' *Journal of Marketing*, 70(1): 34–49.

Feather, N. T. (1998) 'Attitudes toward high achievers, self-esteem, and value priorities for Australian, American, and Canadian students', *Journal of Cross-Cultural Psychology*, 29(6): 749–760.

Fernandez, D., Carlson, D. S., Stepina, L. P. and Nicholson, J. D. (1997) 'Hofstede's country classification 25 years later', *Journal of Social Psychology*, 137: 43–54.

Geertz, C. (1973) *The Interpretation of Cultures: Selected Essays*. New York: Basic Books.

Ger, G. and Belk, R. W. (1996a) 'Cross-cultural differences in materialism,' *Journal of Economic Psychology*, 17(1): 55–77.

Ger, G. and Belk, R. W. (1996b) 'I'd like to buy the world a Coke: consumptionscapes in a less affluent world', *Journal of Consumer Policy*, 19(3): 271–304.

Ger, G. and Belk, R. W. (1999) 'Accounting for materialism in four cultures', *Journal of Material Culture*, 4(2): 183–204.

Gregory, G. D. and Munch, J. M. (1997) 'Cultural values in international advertising: an examination of familial norms and roles in Mexico', *Psychology and Marketing*, 14(2): 99–119.

Griswold, W. (1994) *Cultures and Societies in a Changing World*. Thousand Oaks, CA: Pine Forge Press.

Gürhan-Canli, Z. and Maheswaran, D. (2000a) 'Cultural variations in country of origin effects', *Journal of Marketing Research*, 37(3): 309–317.

Gürhan-Canli, Z. and Maheswaran, D. (2000b) 'Determinants of country-of-origin evaluations', *Journal of Consumer Research*, 27(1): 96–108.

Han, S-P. and Shavitt, S. (1994) 'Persuasion and culture: advertising appeals in individualistic and collectivistic societies', *Journal of Experimental Social Psychology*, 30(4): 326–350.

Hansen, I. G. (2005) 'The psychological confluence and divergence of religion and culture and the implications for tolerance', *Unpublished Manuscript*, University of British Columbia.

Hofstede, G. (1980) *Culture's Consequences: International Differences in Work-related Values*. Beverly Hills, CA: Sage.

Hong, Y-y, Morris, M. W., Chiu, C-y. and Benet-Martínez, V. (2000) 'Multicultural minds: a dynamic constructivist approach to culture and cognition', *American Psychologist*, 55(7): 709–720.

Hunt, E. and Agnoli, F. (1991) 'The Whorfian hypothesis: a cognitive psychology perspective', *Psychological Review*, 98(3): 377–389.

Hunt, J. M., Kernan, J. B. and Mitchell, D. J. (1996) 'Materialism as social cognition: people, possessions, and perception', *Journal of Consumer Psychology*, 5(1): 65–83.

James, W. (1890) *The Principles of Psychology*. New York: H. Holt and Company.

Jahoda, G. and Krewer B. (1997) 'History of cross-cultural and cultural psychology', in J. W. Berry, Y. Poortinga, and J. Pandey (eds.), *Handbook of Cross-Cultural Psychology*, Vol. 1, *Theory and Method*, 2nd edn. Needham Heights, MA: Allyn & Bacon, pp. 1–42.

Kacen, J. J. and Lee, J. A. (2002) 'The influence of culture on consumer impulsive buying behavior', *Journal of Consumer Psychology*, 12: 163–176.

Kilbourne, W., Grünhagen M. and Foley, J. (2005) 'A cross-cultural examination of the relationship between materialism and individual values', *Journal of Economic Psychology*, 26(5): 624–641.

Klein, J. and Ettenson, R. (1999) 'Consumer animosity and consumer ethnocentrism: an analysis of unique antecedents', *Journal of International Consumer Marketing*, 11: 5–25.

LaFromboise, T., Coleman, H. L. K. and Gerton, J. (1993) 'Psychological impact of biculturalism: Evidence and theory', *Psychological Bulletin*, 114(3): 395–412.

László, E. and Masulli, I. (1993) *The Evolution of Cognitive Maps: New Paradigms for the Twenty-first Century*. Philadelphia, PA: Gordon and Breach.

Lau-Gesk, L. (2003) 'Activating culture through persuasion appeals', *Journal of Consumer Psychology*, 13(3): 301–315.

Lee, C. (1992) 'On cognitive theories and causation in human behavior', *Journal of Behavior Therapy and Experimental Psychiatry*, 23(4): 257–268.

Lee, J. A. (2000) 'Adapting Triandis's model of subjective culture and social behavior relations to consumer behavior', *Journal of Consumer Psychology*, 9: 117–126.

Lee, Y. H. and Ang, K. S. (2003) 'Brand name suggestiveness: a Chinese language perspective', *International Journal of Research in Marketing*, 20(4): 323–336.

Lee, C. and Green, R. T. (1991) 'Cross-cultural examination of the Fishbein behavioral intentions model', *Journal of International Business Studies*, 22(2): 289–305.

Li, S-C. (2003) 'Biocultural orchestration of developmental plasticity across levels: the interplay of biology and culture in shaping the mind and behavior across the life span', *Psychological Bulletin*, 129(2): 171–194.

Lonner, W. J. (1994) 'Reflections on 25 years of JCCP', *Journal of Cross-Cultural Psychology*, 25(1): 8–24.

Luna, D. and Gupta, S. F. (2001) 'An integrative framework for cross-cultural consumer behavior', *International Marketing Review*, 18(1): 377–386.

Maheswaran, D. and Shavitt, S. (2000) 'Issues and new directions in global consumer psychology', *Journal of Consumer Psychology*, 9(2): 59–66.

Markus, H. and Kitayama, S. (1991) 'Culture and self: Implications for cognition, emotion and motivation', *Psychological Review*, 98(2): 224–253.

Money, R. B., Gilly, M. C. and Graham, J. L. (1998) 'Explorations of national culture and word-of-mouth referral behavior in the purchase of industrial services in the United States and Japan', *Journal of Marketing*, 62: 76–87.

Murdock, G. P. (1945) 'The common denominator of cultures,' in R. Linton (ed.), *The Science of Man in the World Crisis*. New York: Columbia University Press, pp. 123–142.

Nakata, C. and Sivakumar, K. (1996) 'National culture and new product development: an integrative review', *Journal of Marketing*, 60(1): 61–72.

Nelson, L. J., Moore, D. L., Olivetti, J. and Scott, T. (1997) 'General and personal mortality salience and nationalistic bias', *Personality and Social Psychology Bulletin*, 23: 884–892.

Nisbett, R. E., Peng, K., Choi, I. and Norenzayan, A. (2001) 'Culture and systems of thought: holistic versus analytic cognition', *Psychological Review*, 108(2): 291–310.

Norenzayan, A. and Heine, S. J. (2005) 'Psychological universals: What are they and how can we know?', *Psychological Bulletin*, 131(5): 763–784.

O'Guinn, T. C. and Belk, R. W. (1989) 'Heaven on earth: consumption at Heritage Village, USA', *Journal of Consumer Research*, 16(2): 227–238.

Oyserman, D. (2006) 'High power, low power, and equality: culture beyond individualism and collectivism', *Journal of Consumer Psychology*, 16(4): 352–356.

Pan, Y. and Schmitt, B. H. (1996), Language and brand attitudes: The impact of script and sound matching in Chinese and English. Journal of Consumer Psychology, 5(3): 263–277.

Parker, P. M. and Tavassoli, N. T. (2000) 'Homeostasis and consumer behavior across countries', *International Journal of Research in Marketing*, 17(1): 33–53.

Petty, R. E., Cacioppo, T. and Schumann, D. (1983) 'Central and peripheral routes to advertising effectiveness: the moderating role of involvement', *Journal of Consumer Research*, 10(2): 135–146.

Pinker, S. (1994) *The Language Instinct*. New York: Harper Perennial.

Richins, M. L. and Dawson, S. (1992) 'A consumer values orientation for materialism and its measurement: scale development and validation', *Journal of Consumer Research*, 19(3): 303–316.

Roth, M. S. (1995) 'The Effects of culture and socioeconomics on the performance of global brand image strategies', *Journal of Marketing Research*, 32: 163–175.

Schmitt, B. H., Pan, Y. and Tavassoli, N. T. (1994) 'Language and consumer memory: the impact of linguistic differences between Chinese and English', *Journal of Consumer Research*, 21(3): 419–431.

Schmitt, B. H., and Zhang, S. (1998) 'Language structure and categorization: the role of classifiers in consumer cognition, judgement and choice', *Journal of Consumer Research*, 25(2): 108–122.

Schwartz, S. H. (1992), 'Universals in the content and structure of values: theoretical advances and empirical tests in 20 countries', in M. Zanna (ed.), *Advances in Experimental Social Psychology*. Orlando, FL: Academic Press, pp. 1–65.

Scribner, S. and Cole, M. (1981) *The Psychology of Literacy*. Cambridge, MA: Harvard University Press.

Sharma, S., Shimp, T. A. and Shin, J. (1995) 'Consumer ethnocentrism: a test of antecedents and moderators', *Journal of the Academy of Marketing Science*, 23(1): 26–37.

Shavitt, S., Ashok K., Lalwani, J. Z. and Torelli, C. J. (2006) 'The horizontal/vertical distinction in cross-cultural consumer research', *Journal of Consumer Psychology*, 16(4): 325–351.

Shimp, T. and Sharma, S. (1987) 'Consumer ethnocentrism: construction and validation of the CETSCALE', *Journal of Marketing Research*, 24(3): 280–289.

Sood, J. and Nasu, Y. (1995) 'Religiosity and nationality: an exploratory study of their effect on consumer behavior in Japan and the United States', *Journal of Business Research*, 34: 1–9.

Steenkamp, J-B. E. M. (2001) 'The role of national culture in international marketing research', *International Marketing Review*, 18(1): 30–44.

Steenkamp, J-B. and Geyskens, I. (2006) 'How country characteristics affect the perceived value of web sites', *Journal of Marketing*, 70(3): 136–450.

Tavassoli, N. T. (1999) 'Temporal and associative memory in Chinese and English', *Journal of Consumer Research*, 26(2): 170–181.

Tavassoli, N. T. (2001) 'Color memory and evaluations for alphabetic and logographic brand names', *Journal of Experimental Psychology: Applied*, 7(2): 104–111.

Tavassoli, N. T. (2002) 'Spatial memory for Chinese and English', *Journal of Cross-Cultural Psychology*, 33(4): 415–430.

Tavassoli, N. T. and Han, J. K. (2001), 'Scripted thought: processing Korean Hancha and Hangul in a multimedia context', *Journal of Consumer Research*, 28(3): 482–493.

Tavassoli, N. T,. and Han, J. K. (2002) 'Auditory and visual brand identifiers in Chinese and English', *Journal of International Marketing*, 10(2): 13–28.

Tavassoli, N. T. and Lee, Y. H. (2003) 'The differential interaction of auditory and visual advertising elements with Chinese and English', *Journal of Marketing Research*, 40(4): 268–280.

Tavassoli, N. T. and Lee, Y. H. (2004) 'The effect of attribute order on judgment in Chinese and English', *Journal of Experimental Psychology: Applied*, 10(4): 258–266.

Triandis, H. C. (1995) *Individualism and Collectivism*. Boulder, CO: Westview Press.

Triandis, H. C. and Gelfand, M. (1998) 'Converging measurement of horizontal and vertical individualism and collectivism', *Personality and Social Psychology Bulletin*, 74: 118–128.

Tsai, J. L., Ying, Y.-W. and Lee, P. A. (2000) 'The meaning of "being Chinese" and "being American"', *Journal of Cross-Cultural Psychology*, 31(3): 302–332.

Tse, D. K., Belk, R. W. and Zhou, N. (1989) 'Becoming a consumer society: a longitudinal and cross-cultural content analysis of print ads from Hong Kong, The People's Republic of China, and Taiwan', *Journal of Consumer Research*, 15(4): 457–472.

Tse, D. K., Lee, K-H., Vertinsky, I. and Wehrung, D. A. (1988) 'Does culture matter? A cross-cultural study of executives' choice, decisiveness and risk adjustment in international marketing', *Journal of Marketing*, 52(4): 81–95.

von Humboldt, W. (1836/1988). On language: The diversity of human language-structure and its influence of the mental development of mankind (P. Heath, Trans.). Cambridge, UK: Cambridge University Press.

Vygotsky, L. S. (1978) *Mind in Society: The Development of Higher Psychological Processes*. Cambridge, MA: Harvard University Press.

Wang, C. L, Bristol, T., Mowen, J. C. and Chakraborty, G. (2000) 'Dimensions of connectedness–separateness and advertising appeals to the cultural and gender-specific self', *Journal of Consumer Psychology*, 9(2): 107–115.

Whiting, J. W (1960) 'Resource mediation and learning by identification,' in I. Iscoe and H. W. Stevenson (eds.), *Personality Development in Children*. Austin, TX: University of Texas Press, pp. 113–125.

Whorf, B. L. ([1940] 1956), *Language, Thought and Reality: Selected Writings of Benjamin Lee Whorf*, John B. Carroll (ed.). Cambridge, MA: The MIT Press.

Witkin, H. A., Dyk, R. B., Faterson, H. F., Goodenough, D. R. and Karp, S. A. (1962) *Psychological Differentiation*. New York: Wiley.

Wong, N. Y. and Ahuvia, A. C. (1998) 'Personal taste and family face: luxury consumption in Confucian and western societies', *Psychology and Marketing*, 15(5): 423–441.

Wong, N., Rindfleisch, A. and Burroughs, J. E. (2003) 'Do reverse-worded items confound measures in cross-cultural consumer research? The case of the Material Values Scale', *Journal of Consumer Research*, 30(1): 72–91.

Zhang, S. and Schmitt, B. H. (1998) 'Language-dependent classification: the role of classifiers in consumer cognition, judgment and CHOICE', *Journal of Experimental Psychology: Applied*, 4(4): 375–385.

Zhang, S. and Schmitt, B. H. (2001) 'Creating local brands in multilingual international Markets', *Journal of Marketing Research*, 38(3): 313–325.

Zhang, S. and Schmitt, B. H. (2004) 'Activating sound and meaning: the role of language proficiency in bilingual consumer environments', *Journal of Consumer Research*, 31(1): 220–228.

Zhang, Y. and Gelb, B. D. (1996) 'Matching advertising appeals to culture: the influence of products' use conditions', *Journal of Advertising*, 25(3): 29–46.

Zhou, N. and Belk, R. W. (2004) 'Chinese consumer readings of global and local advertising', *Journal of Advertising*, 33(3): 63–77.

6

Nation Equity: Country-of-Origin Effects and Globalization

Durairaj Maheswaran and Cathy Yi Chen

INTRODUCTION

Country-of-origin effects have a long and well-established history in the field of international business. In his book, *The Description of the World*, Marco Polo wrote about silk from China and spices from India (Marco Polo 1298). In the academic domain, extensive research has documented that consumers evaluate the efficacy of a product based on its country of origin. Favorable country-of-origin perceptions are often reflected in correspondingly favorable product evaluations (Maheswaran 1994).

With the advent of globalization, the decrease of trade barriers, and the digitization of the world economy, consumers now have access to products from around the world. As consumers evaluate the assortment of products available to them, the country of origin of a product will have an increasingly important role in their decision-making. For example, Champagne from France or electronics from Japan have always enjoyed a premium image in the minds of consumers. Gruma, one of Mexico's leading flour producers, has successfully leveraged its positive country image as tortilla chips manufacturers and marketed its tortilla chips in the global market (*BusinessWeek* 2007).

In general, favorable or unfavorable country associations develop over time as a function of the superior or inferior performance history of the products that originate in that country. As the reputation of a country begins to evolve, based on the quality of the existing products, these perceptions of superiority or inferiority are also transferred to new products that originate in that country. While most academic research in the domain of country of origin has focused on the perceptions of a country based on the performance of its products, there is evidence to suggest that consumers' perceptions of the country may go beyond inferences based on product performance alone. For example, the historical animosity between some Eastern Asian countries and Japan may affect the purchase of Japanese products in these countries, despite universally favorable beliefs towards the reliable performance of its products. In accord, recent studies have shown that a product's country of origin has implications for the product's evaluations that extend beyond product attributes. Specifically, consumers may form positive or negative feelings towards a country based on cultural, political, historical or economic factors. These feelings, though unrelated to the product performance, may influence consumers' evaluations and purchase intentions of the products originating in the target countries (Hong and Kang 2006; Klein, Ettenson and Morris 1998; Maheswaran and Chen 2006). Thus, current research findings suggest that country of origin is a multidimensional construct that incorporates perceptions based on both product performance-related and product-unrelated aspects. Hence, a framework that integrates the various facets of country perceptions is needed to systematically examine the effects of country of origin in the context of globalization.

In this chapter, we propose the concept of 'Nation Equity' as the integrating framework to capture the traditional performance-based country of origin effect and the normative effect of product-unrelated country perceptions on consumer and business decision making. Nation Equity is defined as 'equity or goodwill associated with a country'. These associations often go beyond company or product performance-related perceptions, and may be positive or negative as a function of culture, politics, economic development, religion and other macro-factors. Unlike brand or corporate equity that is primarily based on company activities on, nation equity associations are induced by factors that are external to the company or the product, yet, they have impact on the company and its products. For example, when a Danish newspaper, Jyllands-Posten, published cartoons that offended the religious sentiments of Islamic countries, it led to a boycott of the products from Denmark's largest dairy producer, Arla, in the Middle East, costing the company about US$ 50 million in 2006 (BBC News 2006). Thus, a company and its products may be vulnerable to emotions arising from events that are beyond the immediate purview of a company.

These incidental emotions, though not directly related to the actions of the company, may affect its business because of the negative associations to the country of origin. Similarly, political events such as the Iraq conflict may evoke several types of emotional responses to the United States and, to the extent that these emotions influence the perceptions of the United States, they are likely to have a corresponding effect on perceptions and acceptance of products from American companies. Research has shown that emotional responses, in general, could differ both in their valence (negative or positive) and in their focus on the decision criterion (e.g., country of origin or other product information) for evaluating the product (Lerner and Keltner 2000; Maheswaran and Chen 2006). Thus, the impact of incidental events such as military conflicts on the consumers will depend on the type of emotion (e.g., anger or sadness) invoked and whether the consumers focus on the country of origin in their decisions. For example, American Express, by virtue of its brand name association with the United States, may be unfavorably evaluated if the United States has negative associations for consumers in the Middle East and if those consumers use the 'country of origin' as a decision criterion. Alternately, if the United States is seen as a champion of democracy, it may induce positive emotions and the enhanced perceptions of United States would favor American Express.

Thus, broadening the performance-based view of country-of-origin effects and viewing countries as having equity associated with them, would enable companies to gain a better understanding of the impact of country of origin on their operations, as well as facilitating a more comprehensive study of country of origin in the academic domain. In this chapter, we first review past research on country-of-origin effects that focus on product performance; examine the theoretical frameworks that form the basis of these effects; and discuss emerging issues in this domain. Subsequently, we elaborate the concept of nation equity, summarize recent research examining non-performance related or normative country of origin effects and highlight the importance and future research directions in the area of nation equity. To be consistent with previous research, the term 'country-of-origin effects' is used in this review to refer to the traditional performance-based country of origin effects. Nation equity will refer to the generalized effects of country of origin that includes both performance and normative dimensions.

TRADITIONAL COUNTRY-OF-ORIGIN EFFECTS: QUALITY/PERFORMANCE-BASED

Country of origin can influence consumers' perceptions of a product's quality, performance, design, quality, prestige, price, as well as consumers' product evaluations and purchase decisions. The effect of country of origin has been interpreted as a type of halo effect, where consumers rely on their general impressions of a country to form some beliefs about a product's attributes or performance. Early research on the country-of-origin effect focused on its role as an information cue (Bilkey and Nes 1982, for a review). That is, consumers may form general impressions of countries or hold idiosyncratic beliefs about a country based on their direct or indirect product experiences. These impressions or beliefs about a country may, in turn, work as decision cues that provide consumer information to infer beliefs regarding attributes, such as the quality of similar products originating in the target country (Steenkamp 1990). For example, consumers may believe that there are more trained and educated workforces as well as more stringent quality control systems in countries that are economically more developed. Therefore, the products made in such countries tend to be perceived as having higher quality and evaluated more favorably (Schooler 1971). Alternatively, consumers may have accumulated direct, positive experiences with cars or electronics made in Japan and gradually updated their impressions of

Japan, which in turn, lead to more favorable evaluations for the products made in Japan relative to the counterparts made in other countries.

Roth and Romeo (1992) investigated the relationship between consumer preferences for a country's products and perceptions of a country's economy. They argue that the effect of country of origin on product evaluations is based on the fit between the country's image and the product characteristics. If there is a match between the perceived 'strength' of a country and the skills that are needed to design and manufacture the product, the country of origin would have a positive effect on product evaluations. For example, consumers prefer cars that are made in Germany because of the general association of Germany with superior engineering and workmanship, as well as being technologically advanced. Similarly, France is associated with a positive image for design and fashion, which are important features for handbags (apparel, shoes) but unimportant for beer. In this case, the country-of-origin information (i.e., Made in France) should positively influence consumers' willingness to purchase handbags but not beer. Likewise, consumers may have unfavorable country image towards a certain country (e.g., Hungary) in terms of innovation and workmanship, which are important features for automobiles but not for beer. In this case, the country of origin information should negatively influence consumers' willingness to purchase automobiles but not beer made in Hungary.

Consistent with the halo effect mechanism, previous research finds that country of origin influences consumers' beliefs of attributes and only has an indirect effect on product evaluations (Erickson, Johansson and Chao 1984). Based on the Fishbein and Ajzen's multi-attribute model (1975), Erickson and colleagues conducted simultaneous equation regressions to estimate a model that incorporated two-way influences between attitudes and beliefs, the impact of image variables (country of origin) on both beliefs and attitudes, as well as the impact of familiarity on attitudes. The data suggests that the image variable, country of origin, appears to have only direct effects on beliefs but not on attitudes.

Han (1989) extended the findings from Erickson, Johansson and Chao (1984) by identifying conditions under which the country of origin only influences beliefs (i.e., halo effect) or has a direct effect on product evaluations. Specifically, Han (1989) implicates consumer knowledge or familiarity with the product as moderators of the halo effect. Two processes are documented through which country of origin can influence product evaluations: halo effect and summary construct. When consumers are not familiar with the product made in a certain country, they would infer the product attributes using the general perceptions of quality for product made in such country. For example, US consumers are relatively less familiar with Korean-made cars. When asked to evaluate, consumers may infer the technology or workmanship involved in the car based on a general image of Korean-made products and thus rate it more, or less, favorably. When consumers get more familiar with the product made in a certain country, however, the country of origin would work as a summary construct that directly affects the product evaluations. In other words, the country-of-origin perception that is summarized, based on previous experience or specific knowledge, directly influences product evaluations of new products.

As noted earlier, the halo effect focuses on the situations when the country-of-origin image is a perception based on previous experience or knowledge of products originating in such a country. However, country images may have strong emotional and affective aspects that are formed in direct experiences during holidays or encounters with foreigners, or in indirect experiences with countries and their citizens through art, education or mass media (Verlegh and Steenkamp 1999). As noted earlier, even though the emotional aspects of a country's image tend to be independent of the products, they may still influence the evaluations consumers have towards products originating in the country. For example, Schooler (1965) found that Guatemalan students gave lower evaluations to products from El Salvador and Costa Rica than to domestic and Mexican products because of a general negative attitude toward people from El Salvador and Guatemala. The general country of origin image may also influence consumers' inference on other product attributes other than quality. For example, the image of France is related to hedonic characteristics that include aesthetic sensitivity, refined taste and sensory pleasure (Peabody 1985). As a result, French-sounding brand names make a product sound more 'hedonic' (vs. utilitarian), and thus have a positive impact on the evaluations of 'hedonic' products like perfumes and wines (Leclerc, Schmitt and Dubé 1994). These effects will be discussed further in the section 'Normative Country of Origin Effects'.

Process

While a majority of past studies examines the effect of country of origin on consumer evaluations, there has been relatively little research on the process underlying the use of country of origin in consumer evaluations (Samiee 1994). Hong and Wyer (1989) propose four hypotheses concerning the cognitive processes underlying the effects of country-of-origin and specific attribute information on product evaluation: country of origin as another attribute; country of origin as a heuristic cue; country of origin as a factor that biases the information encoding; and country of origin as a curiosity-eliciting factor that increases attribute elaboration. More recently, Maheswaran (1994) proposes a theoretical framework based on the Dual Process Models of Persuasion. This framework suggests that stereotypical beliefs of country of origin are used as heuristics in consumer decision making.

Dual Process Model The heuristic-systematic model (Chaiken 1980, 1987; Chaiken and Eagly 1983) and the elaboration likelihood model (Petty and Cacioppo 1981, 1986) distinguish between two concurrent modes of information processing: systematic (or central) processing and heuristic (or peripheral) processing. Systematic processing is conceptualized as a comprehensive, analytic orientation to information processing in which perceivers access and scrutinize all informational input for its relevance to their judgment task. Heuristic processing is a more limited mode of information processing that both requires less effort and is less capacity-demanding than systematic processing. It focuses on a subset of available information that enables the perceivers to use heuristics or simple decision rules to formulate their judgments quickly and efficiently. Applied to product evaluations, systematic processing implies that people form or update their attitudes by actively attending to cognitively elaborating product attributes. In contrast, heuristic processing implies that people form or update their evaluations by invoking heuristics or stereotypes such as 'Japanese cars are reliable'. The country-of-origin based stereotypes may often be biased and represent a less accurate knowledge structure that is based on limited observations or context-dependent situations. Yet, they can play a constructive role of providing simplicity and predictability in complex decision settings (Maheswaran 1994; Taylor 1981).

Country of Origin as a Stereotype The country of origin of a product represents a knowledge structure similar to the stereotype of a person, which links a stimulus or set of stimuli to highly probable features. The stereotype of a country may reflect 'the overall perception consumers form of products from such a country, based on their prior perceptions of the country's production and

marketing strengths and weakness' (Roth and Romeo 1992). As noted earlier, stereotypical beliefs or images of the manufacturing nation are used as heuristics and have a substantial impact on the quality judgments of its products (Han 1990; Hong and Wyer 1990; Maheswaran 1994).

Consumers may acquire such stereotypes based on a few observations of the target products from a particular country. The observations may be context-dependent and are likely to vary across situations. For example, consumers may form stereotypes such as 'French clothing is fashionable' based on a recent fashion show they watched on TV, or 'Kraft food products are superior' because of a comparison of Kraft with a local store brand. In some cases, the stereotype may even be based on inferences rather than on any observation of the target product. For example, on the basis of stereotype for Japan as a nation that manufactures reliable electronic products, consumers may infer that electronic components made in Japan (e.g., alarm clocks) are technologically more advanced and of high quality.

Among various theoretical frameworks that address the mechanisms underlying nation equity effects. The Heuristic-Systematic Model seems to provide a more comprehensive conceptualization of how nation equity influences consumers' evaluations. The research based on the Heuristic-Systematic Model has also identified both cognitive and affective factors that may moderate the use of nation equity in decision making.

Factors influencing the country-of-origin effect

Based on the dual process models, recent research examines the effect of various factors, such as expertise, emotion, and culture on the use of country of origin in evaluations.

Expertise Maheswaran (1994) differentiates experts and novices who use country of origin differently during attribute processing and product evaluations, and demonstrates that country of origin serves as a stereotype heuristic that may have direct as well as indirect effect on product evaluations; the effect is moderated by consumers' ability and argument ambiguity.

Novices are found to rely on country of origin as a useful heuristic, and use such information in their evaluations regardless of whether the attributes are ambiguous or unambiguous. When the attributes are unambiguous, country of origin directly influences the novices' product evaluations. When the attribute information is ambiguous, however, country of origin biases the interpretation of attributes and indirectly influences the evaluations. For example, strong and neutral attributes are rated more positively when the country of origin is favorable (vs. unfavorable). In contrast, although experts can use both country-of-origin information and attributes information in product evaluations, country of origin is found to have very little influence on the product evaluations when the attributes are unambiguous and diagnostic. When the attributes are ambiguous, even experts may be unable to resolve the ambiguity and they will be guided by the country-of-origin beliefs to engage in selective processing of attributes.

Emotion Maheswaran and Chen (2006) show that incidental emotions that consumers experience before their product evaluations influence the use of country-of-origin information in the information processing. Previous research has demonstrated that specific emotions with the same valence may have different effects on subsequent judgments. For example, anger is more likely to lead to heuristic processing, whereas sadness is more likely to lead to systematic processing in a subsequent decision (Bodenhausen *et al.* 1994). Consistently, Maheswaran and Chen (2006) find that angry consumers are more likely to use country-of-origin information in product evaluations than sad consumers. In addition, they identify agency

control associated with the emotion as the underlying dimension that determines whether and how the country of origin is used in product evaluations.

Emotions vary on the dimension of agency control, namely human control or situation control (Smith and Ellsworth 1985; Tiedens and Linton 2001). For example, anger is strongly associated with human control. Thus, people who are angry tend to believe that other people can influence or should be responsible for the situation. In contrast, sadness is strongly associated with situation control. Therefore, sad people tend to believe that the event is beyond human control and are more prone to attribute the negative consequences to the situational characteristics. The agency attribution related to an incidental emotion influences the weight given to the country of origin information in a subsequent product evaluation task. Specifically, country of origin has a strong effect on product evaluations only when the incidental emotions are associated with strong human control.

Culture Gürhan-Canli and Maheswaran (2000a) find that the country-of-origin effect differs across countries. In Japan, the country of origin influences consumers' product evaluation such that the product originating in the home country (versus foreign country) is always evaluated more favorably, regardless of whether the product attributes are superior or inferior to competition. In the United States, however, the product originating in the home country is evaluated more favorably only when the product is superior to competition. The vertical dimension of individualism and collectivism is found to explain the difference between the two countries. Specifically, if the home product is superior to competition, consumers are likely to evaluate it favorably because it enhances people's competitive goals of possessing a superior product and the group membership is beneficial to individuals. However, if a foreign product has superior attributes, group membership and country of origin do not benefit individuals and their importance in evaluations is likely to be minimized. The preference for a superior product, regardless of its origin, is consistent with the characteristics of vertical individualism, in which people are competitive and attempt to achieve individual goals at the expense of group goals. In contrast, consumer's preference for the home product, regardless of its superiority, is mediated by people's willingness to sacrifice for the collective goals. This is consistent with the characteristics of vertical collectivitstic culture, which expect people to sacrifice their personal preferences and make evaluations to enhance the group interest.

Similarly, Swaminathan, Page and Gürhan-Canli (2007) also find that the country-of-origin information has a larger impact on product evaluations when consumers are primed with an interdependent self-construal. Self-construal reflects the extent to which individuals view themselves either as an individuated entity or in relation to others. People with independent self-construal consider themselves as unique and value characteristics that distinguish them from other members of the group. People with interdependent self-construal see themselves as part of a group and define themselves with respect to other group members. Individualistic cultures tend to reward independence and frequently activate the independent self, making it chronically accessible. In contrast, collectivistic cultures frequently promote the interdependent self, making it chronically accessible. Thus, the interdependent (vs. independent) self-construal captures the extent to which consumers have a collectivistic (vs. individualistic) cultural orientation.

Specifically, Swaminathan, Page and Gürhan-Canli (2007) examine the impact of negative information in the context of a failed line extension in both electronics and sports shoes using real brand names. When consumers are primed with an interdependent self-construal, negative information about the product extension leads to lower evaluations only for the brand of foreign origin and not for the brand of local origin. Consumers with a salient interdependent self-construal tend to generate more counter-arguments that are based on the brand's country of origin. For example, they may argue that Dell is a reliable American brand and thus the ratings, showing that the new line of Dell TV is not doing as well as its competitors, are not trustworthy. When consumers are primed with an independent self-construal, however, the country of origin of the brand (foreign or local) does not seem to moderate the effect of negative information on evaluations. Instead, consumers have lower evaluations when they are presented with low ratings of the line extension if they don't feel a strong connection to the brand. When consumers believe the brand is important in expressing their self-identities, they are more buffered against negative information by generating more self-concept-related counter-arguments.

Emerging trends in globalization

The globalization of world economies and the resulting changes in manufacturing and marketing practices have both promoted and reduced the use of country-of-origin information in consumer decision-making. Consumers now have access to products and brands from many different countries. Given that products from different countries do vary in terms of quality and other aspects, country-of-origin information may become more relevant in consumer decision-making. However, the definition of country of origin may be undergoing a transformation. Many companies have established production units in countries and areas with low cost and labor. It is common to observe products with multiple countries involved in the design and product process, or brands that are commonly associated with one country but now are manufactured in many different countries. For example, the Japanese auto makers now have plants in the United States that produce automobiles carrying Japanese brand names. Given the trend in multiple country associations to brands, the use of country of origin may involve some interesting complications. We discuss three important issues below. First, do consumers use the combination of the countries in evaluating the product? Second, how do consumers weigh the country-of-origin information relative to other extrinsic cues? Third, would the complexity of country associations make consumers less confident about the exact country of origin of a particular product and thus, less concerned about this information? How these questions influence the magnitude of country of origin in the current world is worth further investigation.

Multiple countries of origin While the traditional country-of-origin research paradigm has assumed that a product can be specifically tied to a country in which it is made, an emerging trend is a proliferation of 'hybrid products' that are associated with multiple countries (Chao 1993; Han and Terpstra 1988; Johansson and Nebenzahl 1986). It is a common practice that different specialized tasks in the production process, such as production of parts, product design and final assembly, are assigned to different countries. 'Country of origin' should no longer be treated as synonymous with the 'Made in ...' or 'Assembled in ... .' concept but should be extended to incorporate concepts such as 'Designed in ...', 'Engineered in ...' or even 'Parts supplied by ...' To examine the country-of-origin effect in a bi-national or multinational context has become increasingly important since (1) manufacturing has been largely moved to developing countries because of the low cost of labor and raw materials there, (2) strategic alliance as a form of inter-firm collaboration has become a dominant business form, and (3) consumers nowadays are more likely to encounter products with multiple country associations.

Han and Terpstra (1988) differentiate the country of manufacturing/assembly and the country of the brand. They classify the

products into four categories: foreign-branded/foreign-made (e.g., Korean TV made in Korea), foreign-branded/domestic-made (e.g., Honda Civic made in the USA), domestic-branded/foreign-made (e.g., GE TV made in Korea), and domestic-branded/domestic-made (e.g., Ford Escort made in the USA). Pair-wise comparisons of the perceived quality of a product are made between any two of the four categories. For example, the differences between foreign-branded/foreign-made and domestic-branded/foreign-made show the effect of foreign brand names (e.g., whether a Korean TV manufacturer should consider selling through a US seller and replacing with a US brand name such as GE). The differences between foreign-branded/foreign-made and foreign-branded/domestic-made will show the effect of foreign production (e.g., whether the Korean TV manufacturer should manufacture locally). Han and Terpstra conducted interviews that cover two categories (automobiles and television) associated with four countries (USA, Japan, Germany and Korea). The data reveal that both the country of manufacturing (i.e., traditional country of origin) and the country of the brand affect consumer perceptions of product quality. Notably, however, the country of manufacturing has more powerful effects on consumer evaluations of product quality than the country of the brand, given the levels of stimuli.

Similarly, Chao (1993) also made a distinction between hybrid and non-hybrid products, but specifically compared the effect of the country of design (COD) and the country of assembly (COA). For example, Honda Civic is designed in Japan but can be manufactured in the USA. Chao (1993) examined a television set that was assembled in Taiwan, Thailand or Mexico and designed in the USA, Japan or Taiwan. It is found that consumers infer higher quality only for TV sets designed in Japan. For TV sets designed in Taiwan or the USA, however, the inferred quality is influenced by the price. Interestingly, Chao (1993) does not find an interaction between the country of design and the country of assembly. This may suggest that a poorly perceived product quality associated with a particular country of assembly could not be compensated for by having the product designed in a country with a positive design stereotype. However, such an implication needs to be dealt with caution and it is necessary to conduct further research to compare the countries of assembly with positive or negative stereotypes.

Since it has become more difficult for consumers to identify the target country with which a product can be associated, the ambiguity in the perceptions of a specific country of origin may possess a challenge for the consumers. Interestingly, the use of multiple country-of-origin information has not been found to dampen the impact of country of origin. For example, Verlegh and Steenkamp's (1999) meta-analysis report that there are no significant differences between the effect sizes for hybrid and non-hybrid products.

Country of origin and other cues In real life situations, the country of origin is often one of several decision cues available to the consumers. In early studies on the country-of-origin effect, only a single cue (i.e., the country of origin) is involved. That is, the country of origin is the only information supplied to respondents on which to base their evaluations. While these single cue studies provide some insights on consumer behavior when country of origin is salient, it is also important to examine the effect of country of origin when other intrinsic (quality, design etc.) and extrinsic cues (brand name etc.) are available (Bilkey and Nes 1982; Johansson, Douglas and Nonaka 1985).

Johansson, Douglas and Nonaka (1985) suggest that the impact of country of origin may be considerably more complex than is typically assumed in the presence of other cues. Johansson and colleagues adopt a multi-cue approach to investigate the impact of country of origin on product evaluations (Erickson, Johansson and Chao 1984;

Johansson, Douglas and Nonaka 1985). Using a multi-attribute attitudinal model, they examine the effect of product attributes as well as country of origin on overall evaluations and the reciprocal effect of overall evaluations on consumer beliefs of specific attributes. US and Japanese subjects evaluated several models of cars made in the United States, Japan and Germany in terms of overall evaluations, familiarities, attributes and importance of each attribute. Their findings revealed a persistent halo effect and suggest that the country-of-origin effect may occur predominantly in relation to evaluations of specific attributes rather than overall evaluations.

Similarly, Chao (1993, 1995) reports the interaction of country-of-origin cues with price information and their subsequent effects on product quality perceptions. The findings show that when consumers have confidence in the high quality of a country of origin (e.g., Japan), the price-quality heuristic is less likely to be used to infer product quality. However, when consumers' confidence in a country of origin is low (e.g., Taiwan), higher price tends to be used to suggest higher quality.

As the distinctiveness of the country-of-origin information becomes diminished because of multiple country associations or as manufacturing tends to relocate to various countries, it is likely that brand names may become a marketing focus and thus have a stronger impact on evaluations than the country of origin. For example, Nike products are being manufactured in many developing countries like Indonesia and yet the brand continues to enjoy a dominant position in the market. This observation suggests that consumers may focus on the brand name and discount the country of origin. Alternately, if Brut Champagne were to be brewed from vineyards outside of France, consumers may not necessarily focus on the brand name and discount the country information. An interaction between brand names and country-of-origin effect has been documented in previous literature

(Cordell 1992). The country-of-origin effect is stronger for an unfamiliar brand than for a familiar brand. In addition, for products with high performance risk, the country-of-origin effect is stronger and consumers tend to derogate the products manufactured in less developed countries.

Leclerc, Schmitt and Dubé (1994) also examine the interaction of the country of origin and brand name on product evaluations. Specifically, they compare the effect of the two cues on consumer perceptions and product evaluations when they are congruent or incongruent to each other. For example, French-sounding brand names and 'Made in France' labels are congruently associated with hedonic perceptions and should influence the product evaluations favorably. However, French-sounding brand names with 'Made in US' labels would be incongruent and should lead to less cohesive brand image and influence the product evaluations negatively.

Interestingly, Leclerc *et al.* (1994) find that, although either a French-sounding brand name or a 'Made in France' label alone can increase the hedonic perception, incongruent brand names and country of origin do not significantly decrease the perceived perception relative to the situation when the two cues are both available and congruent. It is argued that congruent extrinsic cues like French-sounding brand names and 'Made in France' labels may be considered redundant and do not enhance product perceptions.

In addition, Leclerc *et al.* (1994) find that country of origin has less effect on product evaluations than brand names, which contrasts with Han and Terpstra (1988)'s finding that the country of manufacturing has more powerful effects than the brand name on consumer evaluations of bi-national products. There may be several reasons for such difference. First, since the survey data is collected using a within-subject design in Han and Terpstra (1988), respondents may be more sensitive to the comparison of country of manufacturing than the country of brand, since the former is more related to

the domestic employment and economy, whereas the latter is related to corporate strategy. Second, it is becoming increasingly common that the country of manufacturing is different from the country of brand. As consumers become more brand-conscious and the product quality difference among various manufacturing countries has greatly diminished, the effect of brand names may have increased relative to the effect of country of origin. The inconsistencies emphasize the need to understand what is driving the weights assigned to one cue versus another on product perceptions. The relative influence of country of origin versus brand name may be moderated by several factors that are both internal and external to the product and identifying these factors would be of interest.

Country-of-origin effects: To be or not to be? To investigate the generalizability of the country-of-origin effect, several meta-analyses have been conducted. For example, Peterson and Jolibert (1995) have examined 52 articles and computed an omega-squared to assess the effect sizes of the country of origin in these studies. They find that the effect size of country of origin is a function of whether the dependent variable is a quality/reliability perception or a purchase intention. The average effect size for quality/reliability perception is 0.30, whereas the average effect size for purchase intention is 0.19. Relative to the quality/reliability perceptions, the country-of-origin effect sizes involving purchase intentions are also more sensitive to the influence of the study characteristics. In addition, they find that, on average, large samples produce greater effect sizes than small samples, single-cue studies produce larger effect sizes than multiple-cue studies, and the effect size may be inflated by utilizing verbal product descriptions than actually presenting the physical product. Contrary to the original belief, however, only marginally different effect sizes are found between within-subjects designs and between-subjects designs.

Verlegh and Steenkamp's (1999) meta-analysis finds that the country-of-origin effect is larger when subjects are asked to compare products from more developed countries (MDCs) with products from less developed countries (LDCs), instead of products from only MDCs or only LDCs. Consistent with Peterson and Jolibert (1995), the effect sizes for multi-cue country-of-origin studies are smaller than those for single-cue studies. However, they find that between-subjects designs yield smaller effect sizes than within-subjects designs. Whether student samples or representative consumer samples are used does not seem to influence the magnitude of the country-of-origin effect. Thus, extant research establishes that country-of-origin effect is robust and its magnitude is moderated by the presence of other extrinsic cues or economic factors. These studies and the meta-analyses reinforce the need to examine country-of-origin effects along with other product-related information.

However, some recent research findings suggest the possibility that the country of origin of a product is less of a concern for most consumers. Samiee, Shimp and Sharma (2005), demonstrate that there is a lack of knowledge about the origin of a brand among American consumers. They conducted a national survey to measure the Brand Origin Recognition Accuracy (BORA) of 84 brands (40 from the USA and 44 from foreign countries) representing different product categories. Brand origin is defined as the country a brand is associated with, or the headquarters of where the brand's owner is perceived to be located, regardless of where it is manufactured. The survey shows that the average BORA score for all 84 brands is 35 per cent, whereas the correct recognition for US brands is significantly higher (49 per cent) than the recognition for foreign brands (22.3 per cent). Samiee *et al.* (2005) argue that if the origin of a brand plays a salient role in consumers' everyday judgments and decision-making processes, it would be expected that consumers would

possess reasonably accurate abilities to recognize a brand's country of origin. Since the national survey suggests that consumers' brand origin recognition is modest at best, the role of country of origin in brand choice would also be nominal under natural conditions. These findings appear to point out the diminishing importance of country-of-origin information in consumer decision-making. A similar proposition is also advanced in another recent survey examining the recognition and recall of country-of-origin information among young consumers. This study from Anderson Analytics finds that most college students are unsure where their favorite products come from – and may not even care. The diminishing attention to country of origin among the Internet-oriented youth may be related to the way their world has been defined. 'Being online transcends geography. … Point of origin is becoming less relevant.' said Ted Morris, senior VP, global alliances at BrandIntel (Bulik 2007).

While these studies raise the possibility that country of origin is not spontaneously used by consumers in evaluating products, they also suggest that when country of origin is salient, they may influence evaluations. For example, according to the study from Anderson Analytics, although young consumers do not care about where their cell phones are made, the origins of luxury goods definitely influence the consumer perceptions and the expected price. In this study, when consumers are aware of the country of origin of a brand, their brand evaluations are higher when its origin country has a favorable image in that product category (Bulik 2007). For example, Hermès scored 23 per cent higher with college students who correctly identified it as a French brand rather than as a UK brand. Similarly, Lexus got 13 per cent higher ratings from students who knew it was a Japanese brand than it did from those who thought it was a US brand. Similarly, the findings of Samiee *et al.* (2005) suggest that consumers are heterogeneous in terms of how much they care about the country of origin. Their study documents that the brand origin recognition accuracy is moderated by consumers' product familiarity, socioeconomic class, international travel experience, gender and consumer ethnocentrism. For example, higher social economic class increases the recognition accuracy for both domestic and foreign brands. More interesting, in the Anderson Analytics study even though the young consumers may not have perfect knowledge as to the origin of some products, they have very clear ideas about which countries produce the highest-quality goods overall: Japan was first at 81.8 per cent, followed by the USA at 78.5 per cent, Germany at 77.1 per cent. Samiee *et al.* (2005) also demonstrate that consumers have very high brand origin recognition accuracy for products made in Japan. Thus, the emerging findings suggest that given the complexity of the global environment, country of origin may be becoming less salient during the decision-making process. However, when the country associations are made salient during the purchase process by increased marketing efforts such as advertising and other priming mechanisms, they are actively used in decision-making.

The country of origin of a brand can become temporarily salient for various reasons. For example, there were a few product recalls and consumer complaints about products 'Made in China' in 2007. This involved the toy giant Mattel's withdrawal of 'Made in China' toys from the global market three times within a month because of these toys containing 'impermissible levels of lead' in their paint and potentially lethal loose magnets. There were also investigations involving pet food imported from China on reports of a chemical additive in the product that may have caused the death of some pets. Toxic ingredients were also found in Chinese fish and toothpaste exports, while the deaths of patients in Panama were blamed on improperly labeled Chinese chemicals mixed into cough syrup. The series of incidents have generated global

concern about the safety of Chinese products and may have temporarily increased consumer sensitivity to the origin of some inexpensive consumer packaged goods that are commonly made in China. The country of origin of a brand can also be made salient because of non-product related factors. As reviewed earlier, consumers in the Middle East become aversive to products from Denmark after a Danish newspaper published cartoons that offended the religious sentiments of Islamic countries. Chinese and Korean consumers tend to boycott products from Japan after their Prime Minister visited the Yasukuni Shrine to Japan's war heroes.

In sum, the globalization of world economies and the increase of world trade has set three major trends in motion. These emerging trends are (1) the traditional definition of country of origin is changing and now the final product is a combination of several countries; (2) brand names are used as proxies for country of origin; and (3) the spontaneous association of the country of origin may be diluted due to the digitalizing of the economies. While these trends have raised concerns about the importance of studying the country-of-origin effects, given consumers' limited knowledge of such effects, there has been unequivocal evidence showing the intertwining effect of country of origin with other extrinsic cues, especially the effect of non-product based country image on consumers' willingness to purchase products from such a country. As one top executive at a Japanese automaker sensibly worried, after several anti-Japanese protests in China 'if the bad feelings between the two countries linger, that could shape consumer decision later, particularly for young people' (Beech 2005). These observations strongly endorse the importance of nation equity that goes beyond simple product-based associations and highlight the significance of building nation equity. It is obvious from the vast literature on country-of-origin effects that when country image is evoked either because of product or non-product related events and becomes salient, it is clearly diagnostic and influences subsequent product evaluations.

NORMATIVE COUNTRY-OF-ORIGIN EFFECTS

Relative to the extensive literature on country-of-origin effects that are based on product performance, the normative effect of country of origin based on non-product or non performance related perceptions are not well understood. In the next section, we will review three normative effects of the country of origin that are independent of product performance and characterize the multidimensional nature of 'Nation Equity'. Specifically, we identify and explore three major effects: foreignness effect, ethnocentrism effect and animosity effect.

Foreignness effect

A preference for foreign-made (or non-local) products has been documented in past research on country of origin. Specifically, a positive relationship between product evaluations and the degree of economic development is reported (Schooler 1971), especially in many developing countries, such as the People's Republic of China (Sklair 1994), Vietnam (Schultz, Pecotich and Le 1994), Nigeria (Arnould 1989), the Democratic Republic of Congo (Friedman 1990), Zimbabwe (Burke 1996), Romania and Turkey (Bar-Haim 1987; Ger, Belk and Lascu 1993) and Ethiopia and Peru (Belk 1988). The foreignness effect is distinct from a specific product performance-based favorable evaluation as a function of congruence with a favorable country image. It refers to a general preference for foreign products regardless of product category or performance.

To examine the underlying mechanism that guides the preferences for foreign products,

Batra *et al.* (2000) collected data in two large cities in India (Bombay and Delhi) and found that consumers have more favorable attitudes towards brands perceived as having a non-local country of origin than brands seen as local. Furthermore, such attitudinal enhancement is stronger for consumers who are highly susceptible to normative influences and for product categories that are high in social signaling value, suggesting reasons beyond the brand quality assessment. Additional mediating analyses reveal that the effect of country of origin on brand attitudes is mediated by consumer's admiration of the lifestyles of economically developed countries. That is, in addition to suggesting overall quality, a non-local country of origin can also increase a brand's desirability for symbolic, status-enhancing reasons (Batra *et al.* 2000). Interestingly, consumer ethnocentrism is not found to moderate the foreignness effect. It is possible that a brand seen as generally non-local, instead of coming from one specific country, may simply not evoke as much hostility from ethnocentric consumers.

While economic factors may explain the foreignness effect in developing countries, foreignness effect is also observed in some economically developed countries such as Japan and Singapore. In Japan, some product categories are dominated by local products whereas others are dominated by foreign products. For example, in the cosmetics market, the skincare segment has leading brands which are mainly local ones. In contrast, the foreign brands are the market leaders in the beauty care segment. It would be useful to understand the differentiating factors that lead to either ethnocentrism or foreignness effect in countries where both phenomena are observed.

In addition to economic factors, there might be other psychological reasons that may lead to the foreignness effect. One such factor would be self-esteem. Consumers may achieve self-enhancement by using products from foreign countries, or signal their belonging to a certain elite group that is associated with desirable foreign products and thus acquire a collective reflected glory (Chen, Brockner and Katz 1998).

Ethnocentrism effect

Contrary to foreignness effect, previous research has also documented an aversion to foreign products because of protective instincts towards local brands. While country of origin has often been examined in the context of evaluating products from a foreign country, consumers can also use country-of-origin information in their evaluations of home country products. Several corporations around the world advertise their home country affiliations to gain a competitive advantage in their respective domestic markets. For example, consumer products from the Kao Corporation in Japan and from Singha Beer of Thailand often use ethnocentric appeals to promote their products in their local markets. In the latest of its four advertising themes in the last five years, Saturn is also taking the ethnocentric route and uses an advertising slogan that focuses on the fact that it is 'American Made'. The Saturn brand is marketed by General Motors Corp. and is targeted at consumers in the United States who are potential buyers of imported brands. The brand campaign launched in 2007 on television, in print, online and out of home, asks the consumers to 'Rethink American' and attempts to direct the consumers' attention to its 'Made in USA' claim (Halliday 2007).

Consumers may have different feelings towards products manufactured in their home country versus foreign countries. Also, consumers' feeling towards products from their home countries are driven by considerations that may be unrelated to the product efficacy or performance or its competitive position. Consumers' preferences for products made in their home countries have been found to be correlated with personality variables like level of dogmatism and conservatism (Bilkey and Nes 1982). Gürhan-Canli

and Maheswaran (2000b) examined consumers' attitudes towards home country products in two countries, the United States and Japan. Their findings show that Japanese consumers buy home country products regardless of whether they are superior or inferior to competition. In contrast, American consumers are not persuaded by home country labels alone, but require that the product be superior to competition before evaluating them favorably. These findings seem to suggest differences in ethnocentrism effects across countries. Ethnocentrism towards home country products is more likely to occur in collectivist countries like Japan,. In individualistic countries like the United States, however, ethnocentrism may only be selectively used in product evaluations.

While the preference for home country products is one of the aspects, ethnocentrism has also been conceptualized to specifically describe consumers' attitude towards foreign products and their beliefs about the appropriateness or even the morality of buying foreign-made products (Shimp and Sharma 1987). From the perspective of ethnocentric consumers, purchasing imported products is wrong because it hurts the domestic economy, causes loss of jobs and is unpatriotic. To non-ethnocentric consumers, however, foreign products should be evaluated on their own merits without the consideration for where they are made. To measure consumers' ethnocentric tendencies, Shimp and Sharma (1987) developed a 17-item CETSCALE and tested its reliability and validity of the scale in four cities across the United States. With the increasing globalization of business, foreign brands are available in more parts of the world and the competition between domestic and multinational firms is increasing in virtually all countries. In light of this situation, consumer ethnocentrism was further examined at a cross-national level and the CETSCALE has been validated across four different countries (the USA, France, Japan and West Germany) (Netemeyer, Durvasula and Lichtenstein 1991).

Consumer ethnocentrism may often be confused with patriotism, nationalism or internationalism since they are all centered on general attitudes towards one's country and on attitudes towards other countries. However, patriotism is a commitment and describes a readiness to sacrifice for the nation, while nationalism is commitment plus exclusion of others and describes a readiness to sacrifice bolstered by hostility towards others. Internationalism, on the other hand, reflects positive feelings for other nations and their people (Druckman 1994). Balabanis *et al.* (2001) examine the relationship between consumer ethnocentrism and patriotism, nationalism and internationalism in Turkey and in the Czech Republic. Although the data of both countries confirms that the three concepts do collectively have an impact on consumer ethnocentrism, the specific antecedent of consumer ethnocentrism in each country is not necessarily consistent. In some countries (e.g., Turkey), consumers are ethnocentric from pure love and attachment to their country (i.e., patriotism is the major antecedent), while in other countries (e.g., the Czech Republic), they are out of feelings of economic superiority and national dominance (i.e., nationalism is the major antecedent).

Thus, extant research on ethnocentrism indicates that preference for home country products may manifest itself in many different ways. One possibility is to have a preference for home country products regardless of quality; the other conceptualization is to reject foreign products based on their potential to harm domestic products or industry. In addition, several other related concepts like patriotism, internationalism, and nationalism may also stem from the consideration of domestic country origin of the product.

Animosity effect

In addition to the moral and economic aspects of buying home country products or rejecting foreign products, there may also be other emotional reasons associated with boycotting the products from a target country. As noted earlier, the boycott of Arla foods in the Middle East is one example of animosity effect. Similarly, the renaming of French Fries as Freedom Fries in the United States to express the displeasure with the French in the beginning of the Iraq Conflict is yet another variation of animosity effects.

Animosity is defined as the remnants of antipathy related to previous or ongoing military, political or economic events (Klein, Ettenson and Morris 1998). It is different from consumer ethnocentrism in two aspects mainly. First, consumer ethnocentrism measures beliefs about the appropriateness and morality of purchasing foreign products in general, whereas animosity is a country-specific construct. Consumer ethnocentrism predicts consumers' purchase behavior when the choice is between a domestic brand and a foreign brand, whereas animosity is more predictive when the choice is between two foreign brands, provided that consumers hold hostility towards one of the countries (Klein 2002). Thus, a consumer's score on CETSCALE may be misleading when animosity is involved and should be considered with caution, since those who find it perfectly acceptable to buy foreign products in general may refuse to buy any product from a specific country if they have negative attitudes towards the target country.

Second, consumer ethnocentrism is correlated with quality judgment in the sense that those who score high in CETSCALE also believe that the products made in their own country have better quality. Animosity, however, may be independent from quality judgment and is only predictive of behavior. A consumer with animosity towards a certain country may refuse to buy the product originating in the target country without derogating the quality of the products. Such behavior can be found throughout the world. For example, Jewish consumers boycott German products because of the holocaust during WWII and Australian consumers refuse to purchase French products because of French nuclear tests in the Pacific. Similarly, during WWII, the atrocities committed by the Japanese army against the civilians in Nanjing during the occupation, known as the 'Nanjing Massacre', have also resulted in implications for the purchase of Japanese products. Klein *et al.*'s survey (1998) in Nanjing demonstrates that, similar to other parts of the world, Japanese products are viewed quite positively by Chinese consumers in terms of quality judgment. However, those consumers with high animosity are more reluctant to purchase Japanese products. The pattern of the findings is invariant even when consumer ethnocentrism is held constant.

While some animosity effects such as the Arla Foods and Freedom Fries have short-term implications for the purchase of products, yet others seem to have a continued impact on the conduct of business. The animosity between China and Japan provides an interesting case in point with an ongoing series of incidents that seem to go beyond the response warranted by the conflict situation. For example, in April 2005, Japan's Education Ministry approved textbooks that minimized the extreme nature of the country's wartime involvement in China. This resulted in a strong reaction from the Chinese people that evolved from peaceful demonstrations at the beginning, to the destructive vandalizing of Japanese restaurants and a series of boycotts of Japanese cars and electronics in major cities, resulting in major financial setbacks for Japanese companies. These incidents suggest the possibility that the enduring and transient nature of animosity may be moderated by several factors and that the extremity of the emotional response may also vary as a function of either historic or economic factors.

Distinct from the traditional country-of-origin research, which focuses on its role as an information cue that affects judgments of product quality, the animosity model suggests a very different process. As an emotion that is unrelated or incidental to the product evaluations, consumer animosity does not influence product attribute judgments or quality perceptions, but has a direct negative effect on consumers' purchase behavior. Consistently, Maheswaran and Chen (2006) examine how negative incidental emotions influence the country-of-origin effect in the subsequent product evaluations. Their findings suggest that animosity towards a country, based on historical, military or economic reasons, may influence consumers' reactions towards products from the target countries if the event that generates the animosity is attributed to the country instead of to chances or uncontrollable factors.

Hong and Kang (2006) examine a situation when consumers may have, in general, positive country-of-origin stereotypes based on functional aspects, but negative emotions (e.g., animosity) towards the country, as a result of its political or social policies. For example, consumers may have positive impression of German-made products in general but have negative emotions towards Germany because of the nature of their military actions during WWII. They find that opposing effects may occur depending on which subset of country-of-origin related knowledge is activated and accessible during evaluations. The country of origin has a positive effect on product evaluations when a favorable subset of the stereotype is activated, but a negative effect when an unfavorable subset is activated. However, such an effect would occur only when the product is atypical and not strongly associated with the functional aspects of the country of origin stereotypes (e.g., dress shoes made in Japan).

Thus, the above findings examining animosity effects suggest that animosity is a distinct construct from ethnocentrism and evokes asymmetric patterns of response from consumers. The antecedents of animosity are also quite different from ethnocentrism. In addition, animosity effects seem to have both transient and enduring effects on consumer response to conflict situations. The emotional nature of the animosity response to conflict appears to vary in degree across situations. These findings and the lack of specific insights that would explain the variations in animosity effects across various situations suggest that several issues related to the animosity effects need further examination.

Thus, the above review clearly identifies distinct effects that are associated with the use of country-of-origin information in product evaluations: performance-based effect, foreignness effect, ethnocentrism effect and animosity effect. These effects stem from both product performances related and unrelated factors. It is interesting to note that consumers have different sets of responses to foreign brands and local brands and these responses are both favorable and unfavorable. In addition to performance-based evaluations, consumers also exhibit emotional responses that vary both in intensity and in the content across situations. More important, while extant research answers some questions, it also identifies several areas that need further investigation. The diversity of effects strongly underscores the need for an integrated framework to examine the multidimensional nation equity in multiple domains.

BUILDING NATION EQUITY: IMPORTANCE AND IMPLICATIONS

Extant research has mostly examined how nation equity influences the evaluation of brands originating in the target country. It is clear that favorable nation equity is beneficial to companies and countries. Yet, very little is being done by either the companies or the countries to build positive perceptions and diminish negative associations. The implications of enhancing nation equity are strategic and can transcend the product domain.

Nation equity can play a key role in promoting international trade, tourism and economic development. An interesting example of the importance of nation equity in international trade domain is the recently concluded Free Trade Agreement (2007) between the United States and Korea that provides an opportunity to increase bilateral trade. While the expectation at the negotiation level is that both countries will equally benefit by this agreement, it is likely that the relative favorableness of the nation equity between American and Korean consumers may benefit one country over the other. In general, American products enjoy a favorable image in Korea; however, it is not clear that many Korean products are similarly viewed in America, with the exception of specific industries like Consumer Electronics and Automobiles. For example, LG, Samsung and Hyundai are well known and accepted among American consumers. Nonetheless, the success of these individual firms has not translated in to enhancing the nation equity of Korea as a country. Hyundai has achieved a leadership position in the US mid-size sedan market, yet its success has been confined only to this segment. Its continued efforts at launching a new brand in the luxury sedan market have not been successful. In order for Korea to benefit from the FTA, they need to improve the overall image of Korean-made products and, perhaps, leverage the success of brands like Samsung and Hyundai by possibly highlighting the collective origin of the successful Korean brands and strengthening the positive stereotypical beliefs of Korean-made automobiles and electronic products. In addition to strengthening their key industries, the positive image in the few industries should be leveraged to benefit related industries like Steel, where companies such as Posco have an excellent performance record, but limited equity.

Nation Equity plays a major role in the political domain, an area that has received very little attention in terms of academic research. There have been many instances that suggest negative equity associated with a country and based on political perceptions has influenced business. For example, when China National Offshore Oil Corporation (CNOOC) made the offer to acquire the American oil producer Unocal, the political elite was not very enthusiastic about Chinese corporations controlling strategic natural resources. Despite the offer being competitive from a business perspective, Chevron Corporation, a US company, was chosen to be the merger partner. The differences in political philosophy between the United States and China have created a negative equity for China and have led to negative perceptions of Chinese corporations. Yet another example of the impact of nation equity in the political domain is the case of Dubai Ports. When Dubai Ports was a leading contender for the acquisition of the operations of some key ports in the United States, there was considerable political opposition to the control of entry point to the country by corporations based in an Islamic country. As in the case of CNOOC, the offer made business sense, yet, it was not encouraged because of the negative equity associated with Islamic countries in the United States. These examples endorse the view that countries need to be concerned about their equities and make efforts to build and maintain positive equity and actively combat negative equity.

In a related domain where the concept of nation equity has enormous implications is the geopolitical context. When governments implement decisions that have global implications such as economic sanctions or military actions, they will induce responses that may have implications that resonate in the business domain. For example, the involvement of the United States in the Iraq conflict has generated a lot of debate about its potential impact on the operations of US businesses in the Middle East as well as globally. The question 'Is the Iraq conflict bad for American business?' has been foremost in the minds of both business and political leaders. While a lot of anecdotal evidence supporting both 'yes' and 'no' outcomes have been discussed, this issue has neither been examined nor fully understood. Based on the nation equity framework we would advance the premise that government actions (e.g., the Iraq conflict), may evoke powerful emotions among consumers; these emotions may influence consumers' perceptions of the country, and to the extent that the perceptions become negative, they will subsequently impact consumer willingness to buy products from corporations that originate from the United States. Despite this possibility, neither government nor corporations have proactively addressed the potential outcomes. While it may be argued that some of the implications may be transient, the loss of revenues is real and could be minimized by specific intervention strategies.

In addition to political and historical perceptions leading to the formation of negative equity, social and cultural images that are broad, consensually shared beliefs and judgments related to a country, its citizens, and their culture, may also lead to a negative equity (Leclerc *et al.* 1994). For example, news on issues such as child exploitation and prostitution could generate negative perceptions of Thailand, which influence business decisions like whether to set up regional operations in Thailand or whether business travelers are willing to have a vacation with their families in Thailand. Despite the abundant natural resources, friendly people, and low cost of living, the negative equity associated with social and cultural issues in Thailand is reducing its ability to compete effectively in the lucrative business and corporate travel market.

While negative images can be detrimental to business operations, countries with no prior well-defined perceptions may also be at a disadvantage. For example, Norway is the world leader in the shipbuilding industry and has a major oil industry. Yet most people know Norway only for its natural scenery and salmon. A recent study shows that because many consumers may not have a very clear image associated with Norway, the 'Made in Norway' information may lead to more unfavorable evaluations than the cases when no country-of-origin information is released. In other words, a lack of equity may hurt rather than be neutral when competing in the global market (Chen and Maheswaran 2007).

While distinct positive and negative equity associations may have obvious impact, the impact of nation equity for countries with both favorable and unfavorable associations is less understood. For example, Japan enjoys positive images because of its superior product performance. However, in some countries like China and Korea, Japan also has a negative image due to the invasion during WWII. As Hong and Kang (2006) demonstrate, when nation equity contains both favorable and unfavorable information, the country of origin may have either a positive effect or a negative effect on product decisions depending on what subset of the perceptions is activated. However, yet another possibility is when the valence of nation equity is ambiguous, the business and products originating in that country become vulnerable to government policies or political disputes. For example, in recent years, almost every visit of Japan's Prime Minister to the Yasukuni Shrine, where the Japanese war heroes are honored, is followed by a wave of boycotts of Japanese merchandise in China and Korea. Although Chinese consumers still associate Japanese products with quality, they also tend to have negative perceptions based on historical animosity. Because of the negative equity, Chinese consumers are also less tolerable to the failures of Japanese products. For example, on September 14 2006, the General Administration of Quality Supervision, Inspection and Quarantine (GAQSIQ) announced that nine products released by SK-II, a Japanese cosmetics company, contained the banned heavy metals chromium and neodymium. During the crisis, SK-II

admitted that the products they sell in China have some 'delicate differences' from those sold in Japan. Although these 'delicate differences' are not well defined, the Chinese consumers felt discriminated against and reacted drastically. In the end, the nationwide request for return of SK-II products led to the temporary withdrawal of SK-II from the Chinese market. It is likely that the extreme reaction of Chinese consumers is a reflection of the sensitive Sino-Japanese relations and the long-existing animosity Chinese consumers have for Japan. Thus, lack of clear positive equity appears to make a country and its products vulnerable to unfavorable and incidental outcomes.

SUMMARY AND CONCLUSIONS

In this chapter, we have reviewed past research that demonstrates the traditional product performance-based country of origin effect, and recent research that examines the effect of non product-based factors such as politics, history, economics and culture on consumers' perceptions of countries and their subsequent willingness to purchase products originating from that target country. We propose the concept of 'Nation Equity' to incorporate the complex, multidimensional country-of-origin effect in the era of globalization. We have also reviewed some theoretical models (e.g., Dual Process Model, Stereotyping Model), that have examined country-of-origin effects. These models not only help us to understand the mechanism through which the nation equity influences product evaluations, but also provide a framework to manage nation equity. Future research should examine the potential strategies based on these models to build, maintain and modify nation equity.

We have identified a strong emotional content to the perceptions of countries and their subsequent implications for product decisions. Future research should also examine the different types of emotions and their implications as well as develop a typology of positive (e.g., happiness) and negative (e.g., anger, sadness, etc,) emotions that will lead to a focus on country of origin. Previous research has mainly focused on the negative emotions and their effect on product evaluations. The conditions under which positive incidental emotions (e.g., positive feelings generated from travel experiences or from cultural products such as movies and books) influence consumers' acceptance of products from the related country should also be examined. For example, the developmental aid provided by the United States may have induced favorable emotions in the Southeast Asian countries. It is important to understand whether these positive emotions and associations would generate any impact on consumers' evaluation and purchase of products from the United States.

In terms of the interface between government and business, additional investigation should outline intervention strategies that government agencies (e.g., State and Commerce departments) and corporations could use to manage effectively any potential negative impact of geopolitical conflicts on business operations. These strategies should involve the efforts of all parties to inhibit negative emotions, combat any negative impact and minimize the focus on the country in decision-making. Government agencies and corporations could implement intervention strategies (e.g., advertising) that are targeted at generating positive emotions and associations to the country as well as promoting decision contexts where country of origin is critical. These important issues await further investigation.

Another important domain that could benefit from more inquiry is the role of nation equity in generating profits and revenue for the economy as a whole. Research should explore and understand how varying dimensions of nation equity influence a country's tourism revenue, the potential to expand export, and the ability to attract foreign investment and businesses. In general,

expanding the purview of country-of-origin effects to include the impact of micro- and macro-perceptions of countries under the nation equity framework would provide considerable synergies in understanding this powerful concept. Thus, the nation equity research has broader implications.

Several contributions are envisaged for consumer behavior, government agencies and multinational corporations. First, nation equity research will provide a structured framework based on which government and corporations could design and evaluate strategies to minimize the negative emotional impact of extraneous geopolitical events on business operations. Second, it will provide a better understanding of the defining role of country perceptions and emotion-based decision-making from a consumer perspective and in the context of a globalization. Third, for multinational corporations, it would provide insights on how country image interacts with marketing activities such as advertising to affect the market share of their products. It will also reinforce the need to extend their advertising beyond immediate corporate objectives and to examine more macro-level strategies like nation advertising. Finally, it would create greater awareness of the impact of macro factors in the global context that may appear unrelated to the business domain, but may still have significant business and consumer related implications, and thus lead to better consumer, corporate and government interface in the global context.

REFERENCES

Arnould, E. J. (1989) 'Toward a broadened theory of preference formation and the diffusion of innovations: cases from Zinder Province, Niger Republic', *Journal of Consumer Research*, 16(2): 239–267.

Balabanis, G., Diamantopoulos, A., Mueller, R. D. and Melewar, T. C. (2001) 'The impact of nationalism, patriotism and internationalism on consumer ethnocentric tendencies',

Journal of International Business Studies, 32(1): 157–175.

Bar-Haim, G. (1987) 'The meaning of Western commercial artifacts for Eastern European youth', *Journal of Contemporary Ethnography,* 16: 205–226.

Batra, R., Ramaswamy, V., Alden, D. L., Jan-Benedict, E., M. Steenkammp, M., Ramachander, S. (2000) 'Effects of brand local and nonlocal origin on consumer attitudes in developing countries', *Journal of Consumer Psychology*, 9(2): 83–95.

BBC News, (2006) 'Arla predicts £37m boycott cost'. 2 March, 2006.

Beech, H. (2005) 'When push comes to shove: after anti-Japanese protests in China, how can relations between the two powers get back on track?' *Time.*

Belk, R. W. (1988) 'Third world consumer culture', in E. Kumcu and A. F. Firat (eds), *Research in marketing: Supplement 4. Marketing and development: Toward broader dimensions.* Greenwich, CT: JAI, pp. 103–127.

Bilkey, W. J. and Nes, E. (1982) 'Country-of-origin effects on product evaluation', *Journal of International Business Studies*, 13(1): 89–99.

Bodenhausen *et al.* (1994) 'Negative affect and social judgment: the differential impact of anger and sadness', *European Journal of Social Psychology, Special Issue: Affect in Social Judgments and Cognition,* 24(1): 45–62.

Bulik, B. S. (2007) 'Ditch the flags; kids don't care where you come from; Internet-oriented youth don't know, or bother, about country of origin', *Advertising Age*, 78(23): 1–59.

Burke, T. (1996) *Lifebuoy Men, Lux Women.* Durham, NC: Duke University Press.

BusinessWeek 2007. 'Wrapping the Globe in Tortillas'.

Chaiken, S. (1980) 'Heuristic Versus Systematic Information Processing and the Use of Source Versus Message Cues in Persuasion', *Journal of Personality and Social Psychology,* 39: 752–766.

Chaiken, S. (1987) 'The Heuristic Model of Persuasion', in M. P. Zanna, J. M. Olson and C. P. Herman (eds), *Social Influence: The Ontario Symposium.* Vol. 5, pp. 3–39. Hillsdale, NJ: Lawrence Erlbaum Associates, Inc.

Chaiken, S. and Eagly, A. (1983) 'Communication modality as a determinant of persuasion: the role of communicator salience, *Journal of Personality and Social Psychology*, 45: 241–256.

Chao, P. (1993) 'Partitioning country of origin effects: consumer evaluations of a hybrid product', *Journal of International Business Studies*, 24(2): 291–306.

Chao, P. (1995) 'Product-country images: impact and role in international marketing', *Journal of Marketing*, 59(2): 115.

Chen, C. Y. and Maheswaran, D. (2007) *'Further Investigaton of Nation Equity: The Effects of Country Related Emotions on Country of Origin Effects,* Working Paper presented at 2007 informs Marketing Science Conference, Singapore Management University, Singapore.

Chen, Ya-Ru, Brockner, J. and Katz, T. (1998) 'Toward an explanation of cultural differences in in-group favoritism: the role of individual versus collective primacy', *Journal of Personality and Social Psychology*, 75(6): 1490–1502.

Cordell, V. V. (1992) 'Effects of consumer preferences for foreign sourced products', *Journal of International Business Studies*, 23(2): 251–269.

Druckman, D. (1994) 'Tools for discovery: experimenting with simulations', *Simulation & Gaming,* 25(4): 446–455, 536–544.

Erickson, G. M., Johansson, J. K. and Chao, P. (1984) 'Image variables in multi-attribute product evaluations: country-of-origin effects', *Journal of Consumer Research,* 11(2): 694–699.

Fishbein, M. and Ajzen, I. (1975) 'A Bayesian analysis of attribution processes', *Psychological Bulletin,* 82(2): 261–277.

Friedman, J. (1990) 'Being in the world: globalization and localization', *Theory, Culture & Society,* 7: 311–328.

Ger, G., Belk, R. W. and Lascu, D. N. (1993) 'The development of consumer desire in marketing and developing economies: the cases of Romania and Turkey', in L. McAlister and M. L. Rothschild (eds), *Advances in Consumer Research,* Vol. 20, pp. 102–107. Provo, UT: Association for Consumer Research.

Gürhan-Canli, Z. and Maheswaran, D. (2000a) 'Cultural variations in country of origin effects', *Journal of Marketing Research*, 37(3): 309–317.

Gürhan-Canli, Z. and Maheswaran, D. (2000b) 'Determinants of country-of-origin evaluations', *Journal of Consumer Research*, 27(1): 96–108.

Halliday, J. (2007) 'Saturn lets domestic roots show in "Rethink American" Effort', *Advertising Age,* 16 May.

Han, C. Min (1989) 'Country image: halo or summary construct?', *Journal of Marketing Research*, 26(2): 222–229.

Han, C. Min and Terpstra, V. (1988) 'Country-of-origin effects for uni-national and bi-national', *Journal of International Business Studies*, 19(2): 235–255.

Hong, Sung-Tai and Kang, Dong Kyoon (2006) 'Country-of-origin influences on product evaluations: the impact of animosity and perceptions of industriousness on judgments of typical and atypical products, *Journal of Consumer Psychology*, 16(3): 232–239.

Hong, Sung-Tai and Wyer, R. S. Jr. (1989) 'Effects of country-of-origin and product-attribute information on product evaluation: an information processing perspective', *Journal of Consumer Research*, 16(2): 175–187.

Hong, Sung-Tai and Wyer, R. S. Jr. (1990) 'Determinants of product evaluation: effects of the time interval between knowledge of a product's country of origin and information about its specific attributes', *Journal of Consumer Research*, 17(3): 277–288.

Johansson, J. K., Douglas, S. P. and Nonoka, I. (1985) 'Assessing the impact of country of origin on product evaluations: a new methodological perspective', *Journal of Marketing Research*, 22(4): 388–396.

Johansson, J. K. and Nebenzahl, I. D. (1986) 'Multinational Production: effect on Brand Value', *Journal of International Business Studies*, 17(3): 101–126.

Keller, K. L. (1993) 'Conceptualizing, measuring, and managing customer-based brand equity', *Journal of Marketing*, 57(1): 1.

Klein, J. G. (2002) 'Us versus them, or us versus everyone? Delineating consumer aversion to foreign goods', *Journal of International Business Studies*, 33(2): 345–363.

Klein, J. G., Ettenson, R. and Morris, M. D. (1998) 'The animosity model of foreign product purchase: an empirical test in the People's Republic of China', *Journal of Marketing*, 62(1): 89–100.

Leclerc, F., Schmitt, B. H. and Dubé, L. (1994) 'Foreign branding and its effects on product perceptions and attitudes', *Journal of Marketing Research,* 31(2): 263–270.

Lerner, J. S. and Keltner, D. (2000) 'Beyond valence: toward a model of emotion-specific influences on judgment and choice' *Cognition & Emotion. Special Issue: Emotion, Cognition, and Decision Making*, 14(4): 473–493.

Maheswaran, D. (1994) 'Country of origin as a stereotype: effects of consumer expertise and attribute strength on product evaluations', *Journal of Consumer Research*, 21(2): 354–365.

Maheswaran, D. and Chen, C. Y. (2006) 'Nation equity: incidental emotions in country-of-origin effects', *Journal of Consumer Research*, 33(3): 370–376.

Netemeyer, R. G., Durvasula, S. and Lichtenstein, D. R. (1991) 'A cross-national assessment of the reliability and validity', *Journal of Marketing Research*, 28(3): 320–327.

Peabody, D. (1985), *National Characteristics*. Cambridge: Cambridge University Press.

Peterson, R. A. and Jolibert, A. J. P. (1995) 'A Meta-Analysis of Country-of-Origin Effects', *Journal of International Business Studies*, 26(4): 883–900.

Petty, R. E. and Cacioppo, J. T. (1981) *Attitudes and Persuasion: Classic and Contemporary Approaches*. Dubuque, IA: Wm. C. Brown.

Petty, R. E. and Cacioppo, J. T. (1986) 'The Elaboration Likelihood Model of Persuasion', in *Advances in Experimental Social Psychology,* 19, L. Berkowitz, (ed.), New York: Academic Press, pp. 123–205.

Polo, Marco (1298/1976). *The Description of the World*. New York: AMS Press, 1976.

Roth, M. S. and Romeo, J. B. (1992) 'Matching product category and country image perceptions: a framework for managing country-of-origin effects', *Journal of International Business Studies*, 23(3): 477–497.

Samiee, S. (1994) 'Customer evaluation of products in a global market', *Journal of International Business Studies*, 25(3): 579.

Samiee, S., Shimp, T. A. and Sharma, S. (2005) 'Brand origin recognition accuracy: its antecedents and consumers' cognitive limitations', *Journal of International Business Studies*, 36(4): 379–397.

Schooler, R. D. (1965) 'Product bias in the Central American Common Market', *Journal of Marketing Research*, (November): 394–397.

Schooler, R. D. (1971) 'Bias phenomena attendant to the marketing of foreign goods in the US', *Journal of International Business Studies*, (Spring): 71–80.

Schultz, C. J., II, Pecotich, A. and Le, K. (1994) 'Changes in marketing activity and consumption in the Socialist Republic of Vietnam', in C. J. Schultz II, R. W. Belk and G. Ger (eds), *Research in Consumer Behavior*, Vol. 7, pp. 225–257. Greenwich, CT: JAI.

Shimp, T. A. and Sharma, S. (1987) 'Consumer ethnocentrism: construction and validation of the CETSCALE', *Journal of Marketing Research*, 24(3): 280–289.

Sklair, L. (1994) 'The culture-ideology of consumerism in urban China: some findings from a survey in Shanghai, in C. J. Schultz, II, R. W. Belk and G. Ger (eds), *Research in Consumer Behavior*, Vol. 7, pp. 259–292. Greenwich, CT: JAI.

Smith, C. A. and Ellsworth, P. C. (1985) 'Patterns of Cognitive Appraisal in Emotion', *Journal of Personality and Social Psychology*, 48(4): 813–838.

Steenkamp, J.-B. E. (1990) 'Conceptual model of the quality perception process', *Journal of Business Research*, (December): 309–333.

Swaminathan, V., Page, K. L. and Gürhan-Canli, S. (2007) "My" brand or "our" brand: the effects of brand relationship dimensions and self-construal on brand evaluations', *Journal of Consumer Research*, 34(2): 248–259.

Taylor, S. E. (1981) 'A Categorization Approach to Stereotyping', in D. L. Hamilton (ed.), *Cognitive Processes in Stereotyping and Intergroup Behavior*. Hillsdale, NJ: Erlbaum, pp. 83–114.

Tiedens, L. Z. and Linton, S. (2001) 'Judgment under emotional certainty and uncertainty: the effects of specific emotions on information processing', *Journal of Personality and Social Psychology*, 81(6): 973–988.

Verlegh, P. W. J. and Steenkamp, J.-B. E. (1999) 'A review and meta-analysis of country-of-origin research', *Journal of Economic Psychology*, 20: 521–546.

7

Researching International Markets: Philosophical and Methodological Issues

V. Kumar

INTRODUCTION

A market researcher approached a Saudi, a Russian, a North Korean, and a New Yorker and asked, 'Excuse me, what is your opinion on the meat shortage?'. To which, the Saudi says, 'What's a shortage?'; the Russian says, 'What's meat?'; the Korean says 'What's an opinion?'; and the New Yorker says 'Excuse me? What's excuse me?' (India Herald 1998). This humorous example demonstrates the most important problem faced by international marketing researchers – differences in perceptions due to cultural and regional idiosyncrasies. The differing opinions stem from the various cultural connotations each country holds, and understanding such differences would go a long way in assisting a researcher to learn about a market and thereby aid decision-making.

As noted by the above example, researchers have to be careful about the various idiosyncrasies that exist in countries while conducting research across cultural borders. For any company to launch operations on a global level, it takes a lot of resources in terms of finance and manpower. This chapter emphasizes the importance of marketing research methodology and the various issues that it poses in international marketing research.

The emphasis on international marketing research has increased with heightened activity in international trade and the emergence of global corporations. This has resulted in increased globalization of business, and has had a major impact on all facets of business, including marketing research. The increase in global competition, coupled with the formation of regional trading blocs, has spurred the growth of global corporations and the need for international marketing research. The need to collect information relating to international markets, and to monitor trends in these markets, as well as to conduct research to determine the appropriate strategies that will be most effective in international markets, is expanding rapidly. The next section defines and discusses the international marketing research process.

WHAT IS INTERNATIONAL MARKETING RESEARCH?

International Marketing Research (IMR) can be defined as 'market research conducted either simultaneously or sequentially to facilitate marketing decisions in more than one country' (Kumar 2000).

The international marketing research process calls for studying the various market characteristics for facilitating marketing decisions that can be taken across countries. The studies deal with tracing the various components that are responsible for marketing of the product. Kumar (2000) discusses the international marketing research process, which provides researchers with a systematic, planned approach to the study, and ensures that all aspects are consistent with each other. The framework of an international research process is illustrated in Figure 7.1.

In the first step of the research process, a decision is taken regarding the reason why the research has to be done. At this stage, the research is poorly defined and only partially understood. Therefore, at this stage it is advisable that the firm and the researcher understand the research purpose thoroughly, before proceeding further. The second step is to define the research problem. Research problems may not always be the same across different countries or cultural contexts. This may be due to differences in socio-economic conditions, levels of economic development, or differences in any of the macro-environmental factors. The researcher should identify such cultural connotations and define the research problem in a precise manner so as to obtain managerially relevant results. If the research problem is not clearly defined, it could lead to project failures. A major reason for the failure of international research projects is the self-reference criterion (SRC) adopted by researchers in a foreign country. SRC assumes that the environmental variables (cultural and others) that are prevalent in the researcher's domestic market are also applicable to the foreign country. Therefore, researchers should take care in avoiding SRC while conducting an international study.

One of the most important aspects of international marketing research is deciding on

the unit of analysis. This is the third step in the international research process. It is essential for the researcher to have a clear idea of the unit of analysis, both at the macro- and micro-level. While macro-level data consists of segments such as countries and cities, the micro-level data consists of firms, customers, and market segments. For instance, while an area that has more than 2,500 inhabitants is considered urban in the USA, localities with more than 10, 000 inhabitants are considered to be urban in Switzerland. Therefore, it is necessary for the researcher to choose the unit of analysis carefully for conducting the study.

Once the unit of analysis has been identified, the next step is to start collecting data for the research. When data for certain variables are not available, the researcher can look towards the secondary sources of data, which comes at a fraction of the cost of primary data. Secondary sources of information are useful in evaluating country or market environments. They are also useful in demand estimation of a target market, and in monitoring environmental change. However, the secondary sources of data suffer from drawbacks such as lack of accuracy and outdated information. All aspects of secondary sources of data are discussed in detail in later sections of this chapter. Secondary data are used to arrive at initial hypotheses about the research project. These tentative conclusions are then used to conduct a cost-benefit analysis, which constitutes the fifth step in the international marketing research process.

If the study proves to be financially viable, the researcher then starts working on the research design. The choice of the research design depends on the nature of research. The types of research can be classified as – (a) exploratory research; (b) descriptive research; and (c) causal research. Section 2 of this chapter explains in detail the different types of research and their applications. This step also includes solving the issues pertaining to primary data collection – namely the issue of equivalence of data, deciding on the qualitative methods to be used (if exploratory

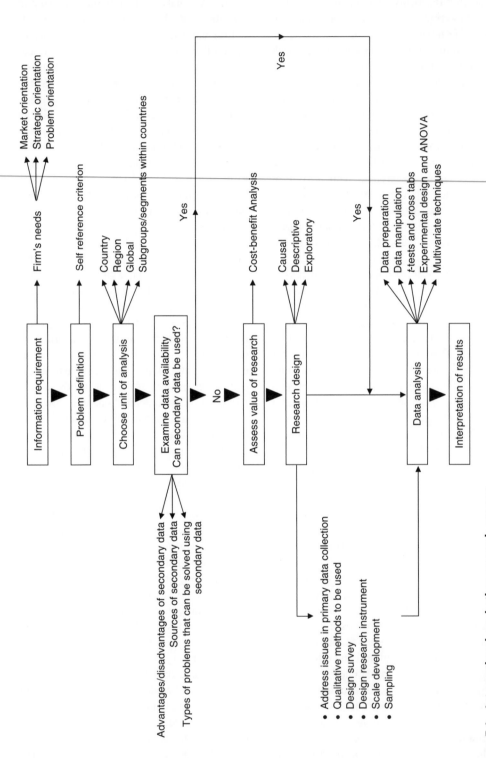

Figure 7.1 International marketing research process

research is undertaken), designing surveys for data collection, designing the research instrument, developing scale for measurement, and determine the sampling characteristics. These concepts are discussed in later sections of this chapter.

Once the research has been conducted, the next step is data analysis, where the data is prepared to be worked on. Preparation of data includes coding, editing, and checking for reliability of data. The researcher then conducts within-country and across-country analysis. For the purpose of analysis, univariate (cross-tabulation, *t*-tests, and analysis of variance) or multivariate (analysis of covariance, regression analysis, discriminant analysis, conjoint analysis, cluster analysis, factor analysis, and multidimensional scaling) techniques are used. The section on data analysis discusses the techniques available for data analysis. The final step in the international research process is to interpret and present the results. Here, the researchers apply their knowledge to use the information obtained during the data collection and analysis stages, and arrive at conclusions that will aid them in the decision-making process.

The process of international marketing research is not totally different from domestic marketing research. The disciplines that apply to domestic research apply to international research also. The major differences between international marketing research and domestic research are that (a) international research involves national differences between countries arising out of political, legal, economic, social and cultural differences, and (b) the problem of comparability of research results arises due to these differences. While differences do exist between domestic and international research, the international marketing research process is much more complicated than the domestic version. It is more complicated because of the necessity to ensure equivalence before any cross-cultural study is conducted. A thorough research of the proposed international market is very important before launching a new product or service. Although it is complex, it can be an extremely beneficial process.

International marketing research involves researchers belonging to one culture or country studying the lifestyles, attitudes, values and beliefs of consumers in another culture. Given the vast differences between countries and between cultures even within one country, there is a very high possibility of the researcher misinterpreting the words and actions of consumers in another country. Therefore, it is important to know the different sources of biases and how to avoid them. While the sources of biases are varied in nature, they can be broadly classified into culture, geography and communication.

Culture is one of the major sources of biases in international marketing research. The SRC, as noted earlier, allows the values, beliefs and attitudes of the researcher to affect the way in which he/she interprets the verbal and non-verbal cues of respondents in a foreign culture. This effect is even more pronounced when the researcher is conducting a study in a culture that is vastly different from his/her own. To illustrate this, consider the case of McDonald's in India, where it sells the Big Mac as 'Maharaja Mac'. They have successfully countered the problem of SRC and have modified the product to include mutton patties, as against beef patties, since most Indians consider cows sacred and do not eat beef (Cateora and Graham 1999).

Another major source of bias is geography. For instance, an American researcher conducting a study in Canada might have a mistaken notion that geographic proximity implies similarity in consumer habits and attitudes. This would be a blunder, as an international marketing research initiative should view each country as unique.

The third source of bias is communication. A lot of vital information is lost in translations and international marketing research is heavily dependent on translations and back translations. An example would be Hindi, the language spoken by many in Northern parts of India. There are many versions of this language, depending on the region that it is spoken in. Most studies use professional translators. Even so, a lot of miscommunication occurs at every stage of the translation process. This contributes significantly to the bias.

Addressing the above mentioned biases requires a lot of effort from the researcher. From the researcher's point of view, it can be achieved philosophically and/or methodologically. Therefore, in this chapter, we look into both the philosophical and methodological issues of countering the problem of bias. Figure 7.2 illustrates the philosophical and methodological issues that arise during an international study.

The following sections talk about these two sets of issues in detail.

PHILOSOPHICAL ISSUES

Philosophical issues are those issues that set the tone of the proposed research. That is, these issues help decide the nature of research, how the research is to be done, the type of data required for the research, and the mode of data collection. In the current international business scenario, it is essential for

marketers to identify the right market and prospect the right customers. In doing so, they face certain issues that tend to put a hold on the marketing research activities. These factors will have to be addressed in order to carry on efficiently with the research. Typically, they include factors such as problem identification, research design, and culture-specifics of the proposed study. Philosophical issues also include probing for personal opinions, beliefs and values and can serve to uncover hidden issues through surveys.

In this section we will look into the ways in which international research can be conducted; the comparability issues; the various forms of research; the methods of data collection; the survey method of data collection; and techniques in designing questionnaires for data collection.

How is research done across countries?

Having defined the concept of international marketing research, we now address the classification of international marketing research. International marketing research includes a range of operations from single-country

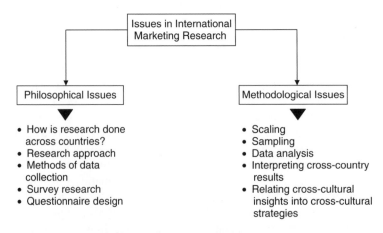

Figure 7.2 Issues in researching international markets

research to the more elaborate multi-country research. A brief description of each mode is provided below.

Single-country research This method of research is carried out when organizations need to conduct research in a single foreign country market. Typically, this need arises when a researcher, based in country A, wants to know whether the marketing strategies that work well in its domestic environment can be translated to a country market B. The single-country research is useful in bringing out the unique characteristics of the foreign market that would require adapting the product to serve the needs of the local consumers better.

Multi-country research This method of research involves research to be conducted in more than one country market. Multi-country research can be further classified into three broad categories:

- Independent multi-country research: Perhaps, the most common form of international marketing research, this type of study is undertaken when subsidiaries of the companies independently conduct research on the same products in a number of countries. In this mode of research, the researcher conceptualizes a research plan for the proposed study. Examples of this type of research are brand awareness/perception of international products or test marketing of new products. The major disadvantages of this type of research are that it often leads to duplication of effort (such as questionnaires, etc.) and since such studies are conducted in isolation, comparisons of results across countries are made difficult. Even though this type of study is carried out independently, it offers a considerable degree of comparability between the findings, provided the researcher encourages a research philosophy and study guidelines that are to be observed by colleagues in other countries.
- Sequential multi-country research: When researching a range of geographical markets, this mode of study is the most preferred. It is attractive as the lessons can be learned in the first one or two markets to be researched and then can be applied to the other countries subsequently involved in the research program.

This procedure is useful in (a) defining the limits of the subject matter to be covered, (b) identifying and avoiding operational snags from occurring elsewhere, and (c) refining the focus areas of the research study in subsequent markets. The sequential approach is typically used when a product or service is the subject of rolling launch across countries.
- Simultaneous multi-country research: Perhaps, the 'purest' form of research, this type of research involves conducting marketing research in multiple country markets simultaneously. It is a test for the researcher capabilities and also creates in its most acute form, the question of comparability.

What is comparability? Comparability refers to the applicability of research results of one country to another. This is one of the most important challenges faced by a researcher, in the case of a multi-country study. Comparability of research results is essential to any study that has been set up to facilitate decision-making. The research study should be structured in such a manner that it provides room for valid comparisons between countries. For instance, consider the case of marriage or being engaged. While in England, getting engaged involves a formal or semi-formal agreement to marry, in Spain or Italy it means no more than to have a boyfriend or girlfriend. Similarly, German women receive a gold band at the time of engagement, which they later transfer to the other hand and use as a wedding ring. Hence, for a jeweler trading in wedding and engagement rings, the precise meaning of engagement and marriage with reference to each country is essential to make sound business decisions.

Since international marketing decisions are made on a multinational basis with diverse strategies, comparability attains vital importance to any researcher. However, comparability should not be confused with standardization. There is a clear distinction between comparability at the data collection stage and comparability at the interpretation stage. While comparability at the interpretation stage is mandatory, replication of data collection techniques may not be practical, owing to cultural differences. In fact, it is the differences between the countries and the necessity to allow for them, that makes international research different from the national research. In other words, research methods in a multi-country study can be considerably different and yet allow comparability on a direct and interpretative level. The researcher's main concern should be the comparability of responses obtained from similar methods rather than equality of the instruments of measurements themselves. Comparability is thus concerned with the end and not the means. Having decided on the mode of international study, and upon completion of the feasibility study of the proposed research, the research approach has to be designed.

Research approach

The research approach for an international study can be classified into one of three broad categories – (a) exploratory, (b) descriptive, and (c) causal. These categories differ significantly in terms of research purpose, research questions, the precision of the hypotheses that are formed, and the data collection methods that are used. An explanation of the three categories is provided below.

Exploratory research Exploratory research is used when insights pertaining to (a) the general nature of a problem, (b) the possible decision alternatives, and (c) relevant variables that need to be considered, are sought. As per this method, the researcher begins without any preconceptions regarding the findings. Also, since there is little prior knowledge, this method is highly flexible, unstructured, and qualitative. The absence of structure permits an in-depth study of interesting ideas and clues about the problem situation. Typically, the exploratory research hypotheses are either ill defined, or they do not exist at all.

Descriptive research Descriptive research pertains to a large proportion of marketing research. It is employed to provide a precise snapshot of some aspect of the market environment. While hypotheses often exist in this mode of study, they may be tentative and speculative. In an international setting, the researcher uses this mode of study to look for similarities and differences that may occur between markets and consumer groups. The goal of this method is to maximize accuracy and minimize systematic error.

Causal research Causal research is used when it is necessary to illustrate that one variable causes or determines the values of other variables. The level of precision of this mode is higher than that of the other types. Since unambiguous conclusions regarding causality must be presented, this research is most demanding in terms of time and financial resources. This type of research is useful only if the research objective is to identify these interrelationships and if this knowledge makes a contribution to the corporate decision-making process.

Once the research approach has been finalized, the next step is to collect data. The type of research approach, to an extent, determines the method of data collection. The following section discusses the various methods of data collection.

What are the methods of data collection?

Data forms the soul of any research study and the data collection process is an important phase in the research study. This is because the method of data collection is seldom easy and many factors are to be considered before starting data collection. The methods of data collection can be broadly viewed as (a) primary data research; (b) secondary data research; and (c) the Internet. Figure 7.3 provides a snapshot of the sources of data collection. We will look into each of these in detail.

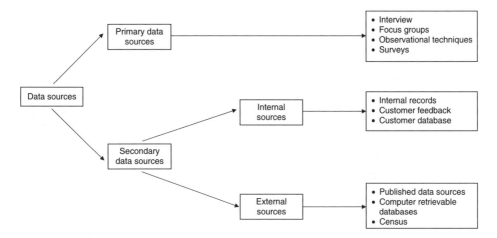

Figure 7.3   Sources of data collection
Source: Adapted from Kumar V., 'International Marketing Research' (Prentice Hall 2000)

Primary data research When a specific research objective is to be addressed, primary data are collected. Primary data are usually collected to aid in a specific project, such as a product launch. A company may choose to collect primary data on a continuous basis also. This may be used to plan its corporate strategy and for future research activities. Despite the accuracy it provides, primary data is not so widespread in international marketing research. This is because of the cost involved in collection of data.

A variety of methods, ranging from qualitative research to surveys to experiments, comprise primary data. It is to be noted that some methods are better suited to one category of research than another. It is also essential for the researchers to note that not all data collection methods work in all countries. This is due to differences in availability of infrastructure, cultural differences, geographic limitations and language barriers. Since the process of primary data collection is a costly affair, researchers should obtain preliminary information on the country of interest before starting the actual data collection process. A description of the sources of primary data and their issues in international

marketing research are covered in this section.

Sources of primary data Primary data is collected by contacting the respondents directly and acquiring relevant information. The process' of contact may be through interviews, focus groups, observational techniques or surveys. In international research, and specifically in a multi-country study, the cost of collecting primary data may be very high. Further, when collecting primary data, the researcher must be very clear about the information that needs to be collected. For instance, if the research is meant for working women, then parts of the country with maximum concentration of working women must be covered. The idea is to collect the maximum amount of relevant information with minimum expense of time and effort. The popular methods of primary data collection are provided here.

Interviews: Interviews are a popular form of collecting primary data. These interviews help researchers to obtain in-depth information about the topic under study. Since interviews are unstructured or semi-structured, there is maximum freedom to respond, within the boundaries of the topic. Such interviews are normally taped (with the permission of the respondent) for future analysis. A one-on-one or telephone interview can always yield good results, provided the right person is being interviewed. While telephone interview offers the advantage of being cost-effective and minimal field staff, a personal interview technique can reduce the error due to non-response. A caveat here is the interviewer bias that researchers should watch out for.

Focus Groups: A focus group discussion is the process of obtaining possible ideas or solutions to a marketing problem from a group of respondents by discussing it. The emphasis in this method is on the results of group interaction when focused on a series of topics a discussion leader introduces. Each participant in a group of five to nine or more persons is encouraged to express views on each topic, and to elaborate on or react to the views of the other participants. The objectives are similar to interviews, but the moderator plays a more passive role than an interviewer does.

A popular method of collecting primary data, focus groups tend to bring out latent issues that are seldom brought out in personal interviews. This is possible because a number of people attend to discuss a common topic. They are an excellent means of acquiring information on perceptions, attitudes and other behavioral attributes. In an international setting, a researcher has to be very careful in using this technique, as many cultural traits would have to be accounted for to get the exact results, with interplay of verbal and non-verbal communication. For instance, non-verbal communication is complicated in Saudi Arabia and most Arabs express themselves using different gestures.

Observational Techniques: In this mode of data collection, the researcher plays the role of a non-participant and observes the activity and behavior of the subjects. This can be conducted by personal means or through mechanical devices and can be either obtrusive or non-obtrusive. However, a non-obtrusive method of observation may yield more normal reactions than obtrusive means. Recently, in October 2003, Procter and Gamble conducted observational studies to redesign its Swiffer mop by visiting homes across the USA. This led to the launch on the Swiffer CarpetFlick in August 2005 that had inputs from the end-users (Ellison 2005). In the international context, this technique is used to observe previously unobserved traits and practices.

Surveys: Surveys are the most widely used technique in collecting primary data. They are usually conducted with the help of questionnaires and are administered personally, through mail or by telephone. In the international context, however, this technique faces problems such as – (i) inability to understand the questionnaire and respond to it; and (ii) inadequate telephone and mail facilities. For instance, Venezuelan homes do not have numbers but have individual names. In such a scenario, finding the right address can be a problem. Similarly, many less developed countries do not have adequate telecommunication networks and hence administering telephone surveys may be difficult.

Issues in collection of primary data While collecting primary data, several issues need to be considered to have error-free data. The issues are discussed here.

Sample size: The problem of appropriate sample size can be an issue for researchers to reckon with. Some common problems encountered are debate over research with large samples versus research with small samples and how to decide on the appropriate number of samples. Another problem could be the lack of research sites to satisfy a project design.

Culture bias: This involves the set of beliefs, values and assumptions that the researcher has, which has influence on the research study. Hence, the researcher should be careful so as to not influence the research results through their culture-centric interpretation as this may yield biased outcomes.

Interpretation of results: At every stage of data collection, a review of data collected should be made by the researcher to ensure completeness and accuracy of data. This is extremely critical in bringing out meaningful insights. Further, such an exercise may uncover areas of further probing and refining the research framework. Another important issue is that with qualitative data involved, the researcher has an added responsibility to write well without any bias creeping in.

Language problems: One of the basic tools in the communication process is language. Since language is an integral part of the culture it originates from, this character is reflected in the origin and variety of words being used. This is why Bedouins have an ample vocabulary for types of sand and Mexicans for types of hot peppers. Language will be one of the most important challenges, among other issues, when entering into international markets. The point to be remembered here is that translation should be given its due share of importance or else it could lead to cultural gaffes.

Confidentiality and trust: Confidentiality refers to keeping the names of the respondents private. This is very important in order for the researcher to gain access to research sources. The researcher should convince the respondents that their names will be kept safe and their personal information will not be disclosed to any third party members. Further, gaining trust entails requesting permission for recording the respondents' statements using a tape recorder, a thank you letter after the interview and follow-up calls for any further clarifications or additional visits.

Resource mobilization: This refers to adhering to time and cost factors. For a researcher time and costs are two invaluable resources through which a research is conducted. Hence, careful and meticulous planning would help the researcher to keep to timelines and to save costs by avoiding delays. Since time eventually translates to expense, careful scheduling of field research has to be efficient. This also encompasses identifying alternate sources of data collection and a well thought-out research design.

Technological requirements: This refers to ensuring the support features, with respect to resources such as telephones, fax machines, mail facilities, and transportation facilities, are available and are maintained in proper functioning order. In the international setting, a researcher might face problems in transportation facilities when working in less developed countries by way of poor roads and improper connectivity. Such logistical and resource needs must be properly ensured and alternatives for them have to be identified. Another problem could be the compatibility issues when using multiple software packages. This has to carefully done so as to avoid any delay in translation process.

In all, while primary data is useful for specified research projects by bringing out accurate and precise information, they have their own issues. For a researcher conducting an international study, the decision to collect primary data must be well thought-out and should be a planned exercise. This will not only bring out the most relevant information but will also economize on the resources being used. However, the case with secondary data collection is totally different.

Secondary data research   Secondary data refers to data that are already available, because they were collected for some purpose other than solving the present problem. The sources of secondary data are: (1) the existing company information system, (2) databanks of other organizations, including government sources such as the US Census Bureau or trade association studies and reports, and (3) syndicated data sources, such as consumer purchase panels, where one organization collects reasonably standardized data for use by client companies.

The most significant benefits of using secondary data are savings in cost and time. Secondary data research involves just identifying the relevant source, extracting the data and reporting them. While secondary sources may be abundant, this should involve very little time, effort, and money compared with primary research. Further, in some cases secondary data can be more accurate than primary data. For instance, if information on a company's sales, profits, and so forth is required, reliable and accurate information can be acquired from government-released sources rather than from the companies themselves.

The biggest limitation of using secondary sources is the problem of fit. Since secondary sources are data collected for some other purpose, it may not be in the format as required for the proposed research study. For instance, if the problem demands income classification in increments of $5,000 ($0–$5,000; $5,001–$10,000, etc.), it does not help if the researcher gets income classification in increments of $7,500 ($0–$7,500; $7,501–$15,000, etc.). Since the researchers may not know how the data was collected, they would have to make assumptions before proceeding with it. This might lead to increased error in the results.

Sources of secondary data Due to the overwhelming amount of information available, researchers should be sure about the source of the information and its authenticity. The secondary sources of information are manifold. For the sake of simplicity, the sources of secondary data can be broadly classified into internal sources and external sources.

Internal Sources: Internal sources refer to the information that can be obtained from the organization. The major advantages in using internal sources of information are – (a) easy availability, (b) reasonable accessibility on a continuous basis, and (c) relevance to the organization's situation. The internal sources of a company's data are threefold. They are: internal records, customer feedback and customer database.

a. Internal records: The internal records of a company are primarily derived from the accounting and control systems, and the databases that store company- and customer-level information. The advantages of using these data are ready availability, easy accessibility, and organization-centric data. With advances in information technology and supply chain management, customers are now more tightly tied to suppliers, thereby improving the timeliness and depth of the sales information available to managers. For instance, American Hospital Supply has supplied hospitals with computers so that hospital order entries go directly to the sales department, where they are stored in a computer and can be immediately accessed and analyzed for trends and transaction details.

b. Customer feedback: This is an important source of data for the company. This can be by way of compilations of product returns, service records, customer correspondence and complaint letters. This type of data offers a wealth of information as to the customer satisfaction levels and the awareness level of the products.

c. Customer database: A customer database is raw information on the customer that can be sorted and enhanced to produce useful information. Records of frequent customers and their transactions are maintained, and the companies use this data to find out what is common among its customers. A direct usage for such databases is in developing and implementing rewards programs. When Harrah's launched its Total Rewards program by tracking the activities of its customers from its customer database and rewarding them appropriately, its share of customers' gaming budgets increased from 36 per cent to 50 per cent (Hoffman 2005). These data can also be used to find out about customers' product preferences, form of payment, and so on. These customer databases are now being used extensively by marketing managers for formulating relationship marketing strategies.

External Sources: External sources of information refer to the information that is obtained from outside of the organization. The external sources of a company's data are: published data sources, computer retrievable databases and censuses.

a. Published data sources: Published data are by far the most popular source of secondary information. Not only are the data readily available, often they are sufficient to answer the research question. However, the researcher is confronted with the problem of matching a specific need for information with a bewildering array of secondary data sources of variable and often indeterminate quality. It is therefore imperative for the researcher to undertake a flexible search procedure that will ensure that no pertinent source is overlooked, and then adhere to some general criteria for evaluating quality of data. The major published sources are the various government publications (federal, state, provincial, and local), periodicals and journals, and publicly available reports from such private groups as foundations, publishers, trade associations, unions, and companies.

b. Computer retrievable databases: Despite the presence of a wide variety of printed bibliographies, directories, and indices, a search can be very time-consuming. Recent advances in computer technology have resulted in more efficient methods of cataloging, storing and retrieving published data. The growth in the number of databases available electronically through computers has been dramatic. It is estimated that over 5,000 on-line databases are available to researchers and analysts working in almost every area of business, science, law, education, and the social sciences. Some of the popular databases are ESOMAR; The Economist; Dun and Bradstreet Identifier; World Bank data; Standard and Poor's database; and Data-Star, among others. Apart from the on-line versions of databases, databases also come in the form of compact disks and floppy disks. These provide the additional feature of data portability.

c. Census: A survey that contacts all members of a population is called a census. In most research studies, it is not practical to conduct a census because of the limitations in terms of resources and time. Nevertheless, government census information offers valuable data for the marketing researcher. A census typically encompasses information on births, deaths, marriages, income tax returns, unemployment records, export declarations, automobile registrations, and so on. An excellent example of a census is *The Statistical Abstract*, published by the United States Census Bureau.

With such a wide variety of information sources available, the usual procedure to obtain secondary information is to start out with the most available, least costly source. With this as a reference point, the researcher can go from one source to another. However, the overall concentration should be on the relevancy of the information required. As with primary data, secondary data also has some issues in its collection.

Issues in collection of secondary data The issues in collection of data can be viewed as follows.

Availability of data: There is a general dearth of information when it comes to availability of secondary data for less developed countries. Even if data are available, they may either be dated information or not authentic. This creates problems for the researcher in the data collection stage of the study.

Interpretation of data: Data interpretation issues are very common when comparing data collected from multiple countries. For instance, in Germany, consumer expenditures are estimated based on tax receipts. However, in the United Kingdom, they are estimated on the basis of a combination of tax receipts, household surveys and production sources. Therefore, the researcher has to be careful in identifying the correct type of data for a given research need.

Data accuracy: The problem with accuracy of data is that different sources often report different values for the same macro-economic factor, such as gross national product, per capita income, or the number of television sets in use. This casts some doubt on the accuracy of the data. This may be due to different definitions followed for each of those statistics in different countries. Typically, data from highly industrialized nations are likely to have a higher level of accuracy than data from developing countries, because of the difference in the sophistication of the procedures adopted.

Comparability of data: Business statistics and income data vary from country to country because different countries have different tax structures and different levels of taxation. Hence, it may not be useful to compare these statistics across countries. Another statistical problem arising is the classification of standard age categories by various countries. Table 7.1 provides an example of such a classification.

Likewise, measurement units are not necessarily equivalent from country to country. For example, in Germany the expense incurred in buying a television would be classified as entertainment expense, whereas in the United States it would be classified as furniture expense. Similarly, while the term 1 billion is numerically represented as 1,000,000,000 in the United States, it is represented as 1,000,000,000,000 in the United Kingdom.

In all, secondary data are key sources of information for conducting international marketing research. This is in partly due to their ready availability, the high cost of collecting primary data versus the relatively low cost of secondary data, and the usefulness of secondary data in assessing whether specific problems need to be investigated, and if so, how. Further, secondary data sources are particularly valuable in assessing opportunities in countries with which management has little familiarity, and in product markets at an early stage of market development. They thus form an integral part of the international marketing research process. A major source of secondary data is the Internet. Owing to its volume and importance in the present day, they require a separate section to be discussed upon. The following section talks about marketing research on the Internet.

Marketing research on the internet   The Internet is an important tool that has added a new dimension to marketing research. With millions of bytes of relevant information available, decision-making has assumed a new perspective. The number of Internet users around the world is constantly growing. *The Computer Industry Almanac* has reported that, by the year 2009, 1.63 billion people around the world will have Internet access. Further, it estimates that, by 2009, Asia Pacific region will have nearly 690 Internet million users, Western Europe will have over 300 million Internet users and North America will be home to nearly 275 million Internet users (*Marketing News* 2005). The Internet will continue to have a tremendous impact on the area of marketing research.

The value of the Internet as a marketing research tool is being debated by some people today. They think that quality information is hard to find and that the Internet connection in many places is too slow. Although there is some truth in these statements, they need some qualification. Like any traditional information resource, the Internet has certain advantages and disadvantages. Some information can be found easily on the Internet while other information sources are not available at all. Besides this, the Internet is characterized by very dynamic technological developments, which in turn influence the information search process. The following section looks at the various sources of data on the Internet.

Sources of data on the internet   Data collection has been greatly benefited by the pervasive presence of the Internet. It is possible to obtain information at firm-level,

Table 7.1   Age classification across four countries

Venezuela	Germany	Spain	Italy
10–14	14–19	15–24	13–20
15–24	20–29	25–34	21–25
15–34	30–39	35–44	26–35

Source: Kumar V., *International Marketing Research*, (Prentice Hall 2000).

industry-level, or at a macro-level. Access to the information can be received directly by using the Internet address (URL) of the website. There are links that provide access to different sites. If the researcher does not have the precise address of the websites, search engines can help obtain the information. This section explains all of these aspects of the Internet. The sources of data from the Internet can be classified as primary and secondary sources, based on the data collection process.

Primary Sources: The Internet is now being used for collecting primary information for use in mainstream marketing, though with caution. The various ways of collecting information are briefly discussed here.

a. E-mail surveys: This is a popular means of conducting research and collecting data on the Internet. This technique uses e-mail for the entire process of receiving, completing, and returning questionnaires. This type of survey technique has a number of advantages:

- Greater speed of delivering and receiving feedback through electronic mail over regular postal mail. Questionnaires are delivered, or redelivered if lost, in a matter of seconds.
- Cost-savings benefits over regular mail surveys.
- No intermediaries – e-mail messages are usually read only by the recipient.
- Asynchronous communication. Unlike telephone surveys, messages can be sent, read, and replied to at the convenience of the user.

However, some of the less desirable properties of e-mail surveys are that the security of electronic mail is low in comparison with traditional media. Also, even though many researchers guarantee anonymity of participants, respondents often may not answer truthfully for fear that their identity might be revealed somehow.

b. Interactive forms: This method is also a useful method of gathering data. According to this technique, primary data is collected through interactive forms which are filled out on the screen. For example, in order to gain specific demographic information and

reading habits about Internet users, one company that provides access to newspapers and magazines ran a contest for those willing to fill out an on-line survey. It is estimated that in 2004, nearly 33 million people out of adult internet users in the USA have rated a product, service, or person using an on-line rating system. These systems, also referred to as 'reputation systems,' are interactive word-of-mouth networks that assist people in making decisions about which users to trust, or to compare their opinions with the opinions expressed by others. Many websites utilize some form of this application, including eBay, Amazon, and Moviefone (Rainee and Hitlin, website).

c. On-line panels: On-line panels are an effective way of conducting Internet research whereby groups of people agree to participate in surveys and exchange their views. Companies such as Harris Interactive and Synovate conduct on-line panels with members from all over the world. The information collected from the members through these panels is used for developing business and marketing solutions. Apart from being cost-effective and fast, on-line panels provide high quality data acquired from willing, interested, and motivated participants. As they provide anonymity and convenience for the panel members, they provide a viable option for marketers to research sensitive topics. Some of the other advantages of on-line panels include the possibility of covering a wide audience, the ability to conduct international research from one place and the viability of electronic monitoring of respondents through log file analyses.

d. On-line focus groups: On-line focus groups are conducted entirely on-line – everything from recruitment and screening (which the recruiter does via e-mail) to moderation of the discussion itself. This method allows researchers to reach target segments more effectively. On-line focus groups, while lacking the dynamics of a face-to-face discussion, provide a unique alternative to the traditional method. An on-line environment allows respondents to interact voluntarily 'behind their computer screens' and therefore encourages them to respond with honest and spontaneous answers. Furthermore, all respondents, extroverted and introverted, get a fair chance to express their views, and 'instant messaging' allows the key focus-group players to interact privately with each other. Although on-line respondents do not 'hear' each others' answers, they can see them. Thanks to 'emoticons' (the use of certain keys, which, typed in combination, look like facial expressions) cyberspace allows on-line focus-group participants, and moderators to express themselves.

An excellent example of conducting marketing research through on-line focus groups is Greenfield On-line. Greenfield On-line is the pioneer of using the Internet for marketing research and is the world's largest Internet-based marketing research panel. Thousands of households participate in its quantitative and qualitative research projects. Many Fortune 500 and smaller cutting-edge companies worldwide rely on its experience, valid research methodologies, and innovative technologies to deliver fast, accurate, and actionable answers to important business questions.

Secondary Sources: The main advantage of using the Internet is probably its usefulness in researching secondary information. As shown in Table 7.2, nearly 73 per cent of on-line adults utilize the Internet for searching or gathering information and another 67 per cent use it for making a purchase.

The Internet competes with several other on-line resources to satisfy the information needs of businesses and consumers. Businesses typically rely on professional databases such as Lexis/Nexis, ABI/Informs or Knight-Ridder. Consumers most often utilize commercial on-line services such as America On-line or CompuServe. Although the latter also provide Internet access, they represent a comprehensive information resource in themselves. Further, the presence of search engines have improved the research capabilities and provided valuable support to researchers. Search engines such as Google, Alta Vista, MSN and Yahoo! vie against each other to provide the most accurate information based on the search words provided. According to a recent forecast by the Kelsey Group, the global on-line local search market, which includes Internet Yellow Pages, local search and wireless, is set to grow to nearly $13 billion by 2010 (Burns, website).

Apart from the normal search sites, the local search engines (applicable to a particular geographical region) have gained immense popularity and use. The sheer number of local search sites operating today is astounding. The reason for the vast number of local search engines is due to consumer search behavior trends and search engines' ability to translate the search query into locally relevant results. Providing local content as a part of search results enables the consumers to make better-informed decisions. An example of this can be found in the case of Expedia.com. Apart from the usual flight schedules and tariffs, the site provides information on local attractions, a vast photo gallery section, and information on local hotels. Such websites are horizontal aggregators of local merchant content and act as vertical aggregators within their horizontal approach. In short, the more content a business has in its profile, the better visibility it will receive inside the search engines (Wool, website).

Table 7.2   Uses of on-line services

Activity	Percentage of on-line adults
E-mail	90
Searches	73
Research for making purchase	67
Information on health, dieting, or fitness	66
Browse news	58
Research on education	45
Job searches	44
On-line chatting	42
On-line games	32
Religious or hobby-related information	30

Source: Pew Internet and American Life Project, 2005.

In all, the main advantages of the Internet at this point are its broad scope, and the cost advantages it provides. These characteristics make it a very appealing medium to use for both consumers and businesses. Also, it is expected that the technical constraints of the Internet, such as low bandwidth, will be gradually resolved in the future, making it less cumbersome to use in terms of downloading times. Despite its wide presence and extended implications for marketing research, the Internet throws up a lot of important issues for the researcher.

Issues with research on the internet With the Internet covering a wide gamut of information, the issues that come with it are important too and need to be considered before venturing onto the Internet for data collection. The issues with research on the Internet are:

Website effectiveness: The world of Internet is home to over 36 million websites, and is still growing. To ensure the success of a website in the web world means more than just achieving a healthy hit rate. Though a healthy hit rate may signify a website's popularity, it does not convey anything about the viewers' time spent at the website or the site's effectiveness. In other words, to know the true effectiveness of a website, one has to look into the finer aspects such as on-line traffic, web experience of viewers, and purpose of the website. This has more important implications for researchers who rely on websites for secondary information. They have the responsibility to ascertain the accuracy and the relevancy of the information published, otherwise they may end up using dated information for their research.

Identity theft: As the Internet grows to reach a wider audience, it brings with it the issue of identity theft. According to the Federal Trade Commission, identity theft occurs when a person obtains personal information of others without permission to commit fraud or other crimes. The type of information prone to theft includes details such as Social Security Number (SSN),

credit card number and driver's license numbers among other pieces of identification. The criminals use this information to impersonate innocent people, usually spending as much money as they can in a short time, before moving on to another victim. The Javelin/Better Business Bureau Report released in January 2005, identifies that in 2004 nearly 9.3 million Americans were victims of identity theft and the cost incurred due to identity theft is estimated at $52.6 billion (Privacyrights, website). Since there is widespread awareness about the issues of data theft, respondents may be concerned about giving out information to interviewers. This is an issue that has to be addressed with care and caution.

Privacy issues: In this digital era, the Internet has become an important part of daily life. An increasing number of everyday activities are now being performed with the help of the Internet. This means that, given the amount of data being exchanged every minute and the dearth of federal laws in the USA governing disclosure of information to website visitors, the issue of on-line privacy is assuming great significance (Frost 2003). This affects individuals, companies and societies as a whole. People would want to maintain their privacy by controlling the information received about them by others. According to a survey conducted in Ireland in 2003, approximately 56 per cent of Irish adults agreed with the statement, 'if you use the Internet your privacy is threatened'; up from 37 per cent in 1997. To better address this issue, it is essential for researchers to account for this issue when collecting data through the Internet.

Speed: While the Internet may be a promising place to be able to collect data, the issue of speed still lingers on despite the importance being given to improve the bandwidth. In many developing and less developed countries, the Internet is still a luxury and researchers are forced to rely on traditional data collection methods such as mail surveys and interviews. Hence researchers will have to be careful in depending on the Internet for data collection as the speed of data transmissions varies drastically from one country to the other.

The Internet is a worldwide network of computers originally designed by the US government to provide an alternative communications network. Today, the Internet is a network of home and business users, libraries, universities, organizations, and others. The Internet can level the playing field for marketing to potential customers through efficient use of the medium. Both commercial and academic ventures have explored the characteristics of users of the Internet as well as uses for the Internet. With respect to international marketing research, the Internet is a goldmine of information. The challenge lies in extracting the required information for the research purpose.

With the aid of the above discussed methods of data collection, the researcher can obtain information for the proposed study. However, survey research being one of the most prominent methods of data collection, the following section deliberates on the survey research technique in international marketing research.

Survey research

Survey research is one of the most popular means of collecting primary data. There are a number of ways in which surveys can be conducted. With technological advancements propelling the world, many new survey methods have developed. Fax and e-mail are two important techniques of survey research that have evolved over the years. In international marketing research, the choice of survey method may be difficult owing to the difference in technological advancements in different countries. This is further made complicated by the various idiosyncrasies present in the countries. Table 7.3 lists some of the idiosyncrasies of select regions.

Data collection through surveys   In international marketing research, the choice of

a specific research instrument is a difficult one because of the difference in technological advancements in different countries. This section provides the three most popular forms of survey research – personal interviews, telephone interviews and mail surveys – and discusses the usefulness of each of the methods in various international settings.

Personal interviews   The different methods of conducting interviews can be classified based on the respondents to be contacted and on the means of contacting them. In this section the different types of personal interview methods are discussed.

Door-to-door interviewing: In this type, consumers are interviewed in person in their homes, and this method has been considered the best survey method. This is because: (a) it is a personal, face-to-face interview with advantages like feedback from the respondent, (b) it offers the ability to explain complicated tasks, use special questionnaire techniques, and show the respondent product concepts and other stimuli for evaluation, and (c) the consumer is seen as being at ease in a familiar, comfortable, secure environment.

Typically, personal interviews tend to be the preferred mode of data collection outside the United States and Canada (Monk 1987). This is because of lower wage costs than in the United States. Interviewers in Latin countries, and particularly in the Middle East, draw suspicion among the respondents. This is because, tax evasions being prevalent in Latin American countries, interviewers are often suspected of being tax inspectors. In the Middle East, where interviewers are invariably male, interviews with housewives often have to be conducted in the evenings when husbands are at home.

Executive interviewing: The industrial equivalent of door-to-door interviewing, this type of survey involves interviewing business people at their offices concerning industrial products or services. This type of interviewing is very expensive because: (a) individuals involved in the purchase decision for the

Table 7.3 Idiosyncrasies of select regions

Asia	Europe	Latin America	Middle East
The Chinese have a habit of telling a person whatever they believe he or she wants to hear, whether or not it is true. This plays an important role while conducting surveys.	Given the excellent telecommunication network, it is normal for a Swede not to reciprocate calls.	Most Argentines maintain little physical distance between speakers and tend to broach personal issues pertaining to family. They are frank in voicing their opinions, but take extreme care in being diplomatic.	In the Middle East, direct eye contact for too long is considered offensive. Likewise, private conversations and whispering while in a group are considered rude.
Surveys in China, when approved by authorities lead to higher response rates, implying a strong presence of bureaucracy.	The French value their personal time at home, are often unreceptive to questions being posed, and are proven to resist innovations of any kind.	Most Latin Americans are uncomfortable talking over the telephone or responding to mail and prefer one-to-one interviews. They prefer the respondent fees in kind rather than in cash.	In a recent AMER World Research survey, the new generation of Arab respondents were found to be conservative in their clothing styles, considered family and marriage to be strong institutions and believed that while women should get more prominence, the family takes precedence.
Chinese respondents are cooperative and eager to try new products. They are also more patient when compared to their Hong Kong counterparts.	In Germany, it is important that the dealings are made specific either in writing or verbally. Germans are intensely private and tend to keep their opinions to themselves.	Latin Americans have great difficulty in saying 'no' as an answer. Likewise, asking favors is common in Latin America. It is advisable to say that 'I shall try' rather than a firm 'no'.	Women in the Middle East do not have as much freedom as women in the Western world and hence the moderator must take special interest in introductions if the discussion is to be truly open and candid.
The Chinese get uncomfortable when questioned on family and financial aspects. They prefer the use of title and first names to be avoided and are an extremely group-oriented and community-based people.	While the Germans prefer one-to-one talk to telephonic conversations, the British are more amenable to telephone calls than to direct marketing programs.		
The Japanese hesitate to criticize new product ideas.			

product in question must be identified and located, (b) after they are located, that person should agree to be interviewed and a time for the interview has to be finalized, and (c) an interviewer must go to the particular place at the appointed time, with long waits and cancellations being a common occurrence.

Mall-intercept surveys: Mall-intercept or shopping-center interviews are a popular solution when funds are limited and the respondent must see, feel, or taste something. In this mode of research, interviewers stationed at entrances or selected locations in a mall randomly approach respondents and question them, either at that location or invite them to be interviewed at a special facility in the mall. These facilities have equipment that is adaptable to virtually any demonstration requirement. Since interviewers do not travel and respondents are plentiful, this proves to be a cost-effective method of interviewing. However, shopping center users, who are not representative of the general population, visit the center with different frequencies, and shop at different stores within the center. These problems can be minimized with the special sampling procedures. Mall Intercept Surveys are very popular in the United States and Canada, though not commonly used either in the European countries or in developing countries.

Self-administered questionnaires: As the name suggests, this method does not involve interviewers. Even though this reduces the cost of the interview process, a major disadvantage of this technique is that no one is present to explain things to the respondent and clarify responses to open-ended questions. This sometimes results in useless responses to open-ended questions. However, the absence of an interviewer results in the elimination of interviewer bias.

Omnibus surveys: These are regularly scheduled (weekly, monthly, or quarterly) personal interview surveys with questions provided by a number of separate clients. The questionnaires, based on which the interviews are conducted, will contain sequences of questions on different topics. Each sequence

of questions is provided by one client, and the whole questionnaire is made up of such sequences of questions, on diverse topics, from different clients. A major advantage of this technique is that the total costs are minimized, since the rates are based on the number of questions asked and tabulated, and the cost of the survey is shared by the clients. Further, the results are available quickly, because all the steps are standardized and scheduled in advance.

Telephone interviews   With improvements in the telecom sector, telephone interviewing has gained much popularity among researchers. This technique is useful when a large sample is involved. Apart from keeping the costs down, a telephone interview offers the flexibility to be scheduled when the respondents are not available for a personal interview. While the process of conducting a telephone interview is similar to that of a personal interview, the difference lies in selecting the sample.

There are three basic approaches to obtaining telephone numbers when selecting study participants for telephone interviews – pre-specified lists, directories, or random dialing procedure. Pre-specified lists, such as membership rosters, customer lists, or lists purchased from commercial suppliers of telephone numbers, are sometimes used for selected groups of people. This use, however, is not widespread in marketing research. The use of a directory is a traditional one, where the directory is provided by either a telephone company or a commercial firm. However, a directory may be inadequate for obtaining a representative sample of consumers or households, since some people of the desired sample size might not be listed.

A random-digit dialing is a non-directory procedure for selecting all the telephone number digits at random. Although this approach gives all households with telephones an approximately equal chance of being called, it has severe limitations. It is costly to implement, both in time and resources, since not all possible telephone numbers are in service, and therefore many telephoning attempts are to non-existent numbers. Additionally, completely random-digit dialing does not discriminate between telephone numbers in which a researcher is interested and those of no interest. A variation of this technique is systematic random-digit dialing. In this technique, a researcher specifies those telephone area codes and exchanges, or prefixes, from which numbers are to be selected. Thus, numbers not of interest are avoided.

With respect to the international context, telephone interviews face a great many challenges. In countries such as India, which is predominantly rural, the telephone penetration is only 1 per cent, and hence telephone surveys may not be the ideal method to adopt (Sopariwala 1987). Even in relatively affluent societies such as Great Britain, telephone penetration is only 80 per cent, and telephone interviewing is not widely used because many practitioners are still skeptical about it. In Britain and France, there are substantial declines in telephone response rates in large cities. The Eastern European countries and countries in the newly formed Commonwealth of Independent States have a poor telecommunication system. In such countries, conducting telephone surveys may not be a good idea.

Mail surveys: In mail surveys, questionnaires are mailed to potential study participants, who complete and return them by mail. The major advantages of this technique are that they cover a broader respondent base; they do not require any field staff, and are free from interviewer bias. This technique is ideally suited for industrial surveys where the respondents are highly knowledgeable and the topic of the survey is relevant.

One of the biggest disadvantages in using mail surveys is non-response rates. Even though the cost of mailing questionnaires is relatively low, because of poor response rates, the cost-per-survey may be very high. Another problem in this technique is that the researcher has no control over the questionnaire after it has been mailed out. The researcher cannot: (a) clear any doubts the respondent may have, (b) control selective answering of the questions, and (c) avoid misinterpretation of the questions by the respondent.

Other common problems in international marketing research include loss of questionnaires in the mail, incorrect addresses and lack of formal address. For instance, mail surveys are ineffective in countries such as Brazil, where it has been reckoned that 30 per cent of the domestic mail is never delivered; or Nicaragua, where all the mail has to be delivered to the post office. In places such as Hong Kong, people live on houseboats and have no formal address. This can create confusion in delivery of mail and can result in non-response. Researchers need to be aware of all these problems before deciding on a mail survey for international marketing research.

There are as many survey methods as there are different forms of communication technology. As the technology for communication progresses, the number of survey methods also proliferates. Recent advances in fax technology and in electronic mail have introduced many new possibilities for conducting error-free surveys. Therefore, a researcher has to know the mechanics of each method clearly, and also how it performs compared with the other methods. The choice among different survey methods is never an easy one. In all, surveys will continue to dominate as a method of data collection for marketing research, at least for the next few decades. Rapid advancement in technology is changing the very nature of data collection and survey methods. However, while conducting surveys for international research, a number of issues have to be taken into account.

Issues with survey research The techniques of survey research are not without issues, especially when it involves research in international markets. An explanation of the various issues is provided here.

Usage characteristics Each of the three survey techniques discussed above have their own uses and limitations. While mail surveys may be ideally suited for industrial studies, telephone interviews will be successful depending on the telecommunication network. An option available to increase response rates in mail surveys is an approach with incentives. However, some cultures may take offense at such obligations and in some cultures mail thefts are said to have taken place because of incentives included in them. In all, the economic stature of each country decides the most appropriate technique to be used. The most cost-effective technique is the one that accounts for the maximum reach and the response rate that it achieves in each country.

Data requirements The researcher conducting the survey should have three basic requirements: (1) thorough knowledge about the project, (2) information about the industry, and (3) cultural sensitivity. Industry information and knowledge about the project is likely to help the researcher to design the survey better. These two requirements are also important when the survey respondents are professionals and experts in that field. Cultural sensitivity goes a long way in assisting the researcher in conducting a meaningful research. This includes knowledge of the culture, the traditions and the local language to be able to better interact with the respondents.

Cultural influences Each culture dictates the way in which the survey methods take place. For instance, personal interviews in the United States do not last more than 20 or 25 minutes. However, in France, Germany and Italy they last longer as the interviewer tends to explain every detail of the question. Respondents in Germany are very particular when it comes to duration of the surveys, and they strictly adhere to the agreed time limits. However, the French and Italians are more flexible with their time. Further, the refusal rate for interviews is higher in the above-mentioned European countries as people there are subjected to many interviews.

Similarly, the Japanese consider it impolite if they are surveyed over the telephone, and in Hong Kong researchers are not allowed inside people's residences. Hence researchers will have to bear all of this in mind before deciding on the survey technique and launching one.

Language Language is likely to pose a big problem to the researchers while conducting surveys, especially in counties where multiple dialects are spoken. For instance, India has 22 national languages recognized by its Constitution and an estimated 844 different dialects prevalent across the country (Know India, website). Research studies have shown that only 28 per cent of the entire European population can read English with the percentages being even lower in South America and Asia. This means that for effective international marketing, communicating effectively in the regional languages is vital. According to the US State Department, US companies stand to lose $50 billion in potential sales from poor translations. Companies can get into trouble with translations that are inaccurate or culturally inappropriate. Professional translations on the other hand will convey a high-quality image of products or services and leverage the marketing message (Visionarymarketing, website). Therefore, it is essential that market researchers be aware of the need for a delicate balance between language specifics and cultural implications.

The choice of a data collection method involves a series of compromises in matching the often conflicting requirements of the situation with the strengths and limitations of the available methods. Part of the skill of research design is in adapting a basic data collection method, whether personal or telephone interview or mail survey, to those constraints. This process of adaptation means exploiting the advantages as well as blunting the limitations, which to some extent makes generalizations suspect. The greatest potential for effective adaptation of method to situation lies with combinations of methods, or specialized variants of basic methods.

In all, survey research is bound to be the most dominant data collection method in the future. With technology growing at such a tremendous pace, newer and better methods to conduct surveys are becoming more common. With the dawn of the age of multimedia computing, e-mail surveys are also likely to become more prevalent. This introduces a number of challenges to the researcher, who has to contend with language, cultural, and a host of other problems. This challenge is prominently felt in designing the questionnaire, the most popular tool for data collection

Designing the questionnaire

Survey research plays a vital role in today's dynamic and information-critical world. Survey results are an important tool on which managers around the world base their decisions. Hence, it is imperative that surveys be conducted in an accurate and unbiased manner. An important component for the survey is the questionnaire. A good questionnaire is therefore necessary in accomplishing the research objectives. Surveys have to be customized according to the research specification and the questionnaires are much more than a collection of questions. This involves a series of activities that are undertaken to ensure the questionnaire yields accurate and desired information.

First, the researcher should be clear as to what is being measured and should decide on the required variables. This involves having a check on the research problem and the data collected. The next step is to design and structure the content of the questionnaire. Then the questionnaire should be properly worded and checked for logical continuity. The final step is to pre-test the questionnaire for any problems and rectify them. While designing a questionnaire, the researcher should ensure the following factors are incorporated:

- the questionnaire should be easily understood by the respondents, which includes language, context and topic being researched;

- the respondent should have adequate knowledge in answering the questions;
- the respondent should be able to participate in the research willingly and not be subjected to any pressure, as this might lead to biased responses

A good questionnaire accomplishes the research's objectives. Surveys must be custom-built to the specification of given research purposes, and they are much more than a collection of unambiguous questions. A number of constraints are imposed on the development of an appropriate questionnaire.

Questionnaire development

While developing questionnaires across countries in a multi-country study, it is essential to focus on equivalence of information collected and not on equivalence of the instrument used to collect the information. In other words, the questionnaires do not have to be identical in a multi-country study. Instead, the questionnaire should convey the purpose of the research to the respondent and draw responses that will be useful for the study. For instance, for a study on attitudes of women, the questionnaire design and survey method will be different for women in the United States and women in the Middle East. This is because, in many Middle Eastern countries, women are predominantly homemakers and are not involved in decision-making, unlike women in the United States who are career-oriented and have an important role in decision-making.

In terms of format, content and wording questions can be categorized under the following types – open-ended versus closed-ended questions; direct versus indirect questions; and verbal versus non-verbal questions.

Open-ended versus closed-ended questions

Open-ended questions are the type of questions that give respondents the freedom to provide their own responses, while closed-ended questions offer a set of choices from which the respondent chooses the most applicable choice.

An open-ended question is typically used when the researcher wants to elicit information from the respondent. This type of question does not impose any restriction on the respondent and therefore eliminates bias. An advantage of using this type of question is that the researcher does not have to be familiar with the entire range of responses that can be obtained from a specific question. However, the limitation of this type of questioning is that the questions cannot be pre-coded and that they may be lacking in terms of clarity. The problem with the clarity and depth of responses depends to a great extent on: (1) the articulateness of the respondent in an interview situation, and (2) the researcher's ability to summarize accurately. Open-ended questions are also time-consuming, both during the interview and during tabulation. Classifications must be established to summarize the responses, and each answer must be assigned to one or more categories. This involves subjective judgments that are prone to error.

A closed-ended question has the advantage of being easily understood and provides room for coding and analysis on the computer. There is less potential error due to differences in the way questions are asked and responses recorded. Typically, a closed-response question takes less time than an equivalent open-ended question. Perhaps the most significant advantage of these questions in large-scale surveys is that the answers are directly comparable from respondent to respondent, assuming each interprets the words the same way. However, a major drawback of this type of questioning is that a thorough research has to be done and all possible options have to be identified for the response set. This becomes very difficult in international marketing research as certain cultures may view the choices very differently. Further, some cultures tend to be neutral when they are offered choices. This tends to cause significant bias in the survey.

Direct versus indirect questions Direct questions are those questions which are unambiguous with respect to the question content and meaning. On the other hand, indirect questions probe the respondent by asking them to list choices of their friends rather than their own. Direct questions are used when the topic is not controversial or something that would make the respondent uncomfortable. For sensitive topics, however, indirect questions are the best option available. In the international marketing research the researcher will have to spend some time finding out what is sensitive to the people and what they consider controversial. For instance, Latin American respondents are extremely suspicious when questioned about their income and taxes, as tax evasions are a common occurrence in that part of the world. Similarly, Asians are very uncomfortable talking about their sexual preferences while people in the United States are more liberal to such topics of discussion. Hence, a thorough knowledge about cultures is crucial for designing direct and indirect questions in international marketing research.

Verbal versus non-verbal questions When designing questionnaires, the questions are framed in such a manner that the questions can be read out to the respondents (interviews) or the respondent can read the questions (in mail surveys). However, when children or people with low literacy levels are involved, it may be necessary for researchers to use non-verbal cues, picture cards or other visual aids. In international marketing research, the researchers have to be careful in using non-verbal cues as they might differ between cultures. For instance, a side-to-side facial movement is considered as an agreement in Asian countries, but considered as a disagreement in many Western countries. Therefore, researchers will have to apply caution while using such cues during the interview process.

The issue of question format is an important one when constructing a questionnaire for cross-national research (Hunt, Sparkman and Wilcox 1982). The researcher may lack experience with purchasing behavior or relevant determinants of response in another country or cultural context. Use of open-ended questions may thus be desirable in a number of situations. Since they do not impose any structure or response categories, open-ended questions avoid the imposition of cultural bias by the researcher. However, open-ended questions will have to be used with care in cross-national research, in order to ensure that bias does not occur as a result of differences in levels of education. Another consideration is whether direct or indirect questions should be utilized. Direct questions avoid any ambiguity concerning question content and meaning. On the other hand, respondents may be reluctant to answer certain types of questions. An additional consideration in instrument design is the extent to which non-verbal, as opposed to verbal, stimuli are utilized in order to facilitate respondent comprehension. Particularly where research is conducted in countries or cultures with high levels of illiteracy, as, for example, in Africa and the Far East, it is often desirable to use non-verbal stimuli such as show cards. In short, whatever be the format of questioning, the main focus must be on their use in surveys in order to ensure that respondents understand verbal questions, relevant products, and product concepts. In doing so, researchers often come across the issue of establishing equivalence.

What is construct equivalence?

Construct equivalence deals with the function of the product or service that is being researched and not the method used in collecting information. Countries that are being researched must have the same perception or use for the product being studied. If not, the comparison of data becomes meaningless. For instance, while studying the bicycle market researchers need to understand that bicycles fall under the category of recreational sports in the United States, whereas in India and China they are considered as basic means of transportation. This understanding is vital in drawing conclusions and results based on the research. Construct equivalence consists of three parts – functional equivalence, conceptual equivalence and category equivalence – as illustrated in Figure 7.4.

Functional equivalence Functional equivalence involves establishing that a given concept or behavior serves the same purpose or function from country to country. For instance, in the United Kingdom, Germany and Scandinavia beer is considered as an alcoholic beverage, whereas in countries such as Spain, Greece and Italy it is treated as a soft drink. Similarly, grocery shopping may be a chore for people in the United States, but in many countries it is considered as a social activity with close interactions between the customer and the grocer. Hence, the researcher should establish the functional equivalence and researchers have to ensure that they ask the right question to the right set of people.

Conceptual equivalence Conceptual equivalence deals with individual interpretation of

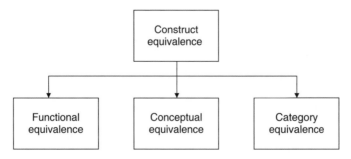

Figure 7.4 Construct equivalence
Source: Adapted from Kumar V., International Marketing Research (Prentice Hall 2000)

objects and stimuli. This type of equivalence focuses on individual variations in attitudes and behavior rather than societal norms and behavior. In establishing this equivalence, researchers are more concerned about personality traits, social interactions and practices, as they vary vastly among people from different cultures. For instance, while an engagement in the United Kingdom means a commitment to marry, in Italy or Spain it merely refers to having a boyfriend or girlfriend. Therefore, the researchers have to understand the differences in socio-cultural patterns in establishing conceptual equivalence.

Category equivalence Category equivalence relates to the category in which relevant objects or stimuli are placed. For instance, many cultures have sweets as part of the meal, but in China they are not considered to be so. Similarly, many countries differ in the way they classify alcoholic drinks, soft drinks and carbonate sodas. Hence, researchers have to be careful in ascertaining which category a particular product appears in each country and accommodate that into the research survey.

A questionnaire that does not establish these equivalences will not capture the real picture. Further, designing the questionnaire and establishing equivalence is only solving half the problem. Identifying and interpreting the various response styles of respondents to questionnaires is the other major component. Therefore, it is preferable to include researchers who are familiar with the foreign country or culture in the questionnaire development phase.

Response styles in questionnaires

When filling out a questionnaire, it is generally believed that the answers provided by the respondent are based on the substantive meaning of items to which they respond. However, it is well known that responses to questionnaires are often influenced by

content-irrelevant factors called response styles (Baumgartner and Steenkamp 2001). A response style can be defined as a tendency to respond systematically to questionnaire items on some basis other than what the items were specifically designed to measure (Paulhus 1991). Baumgartner and Steenkamp (2001) list seven important types of response styles. They are:

1 Acquiescence Response Style (ARS) – ARS refers to the tendency to agree with the item, regardless of content. This type is also called agreement tendency, yea-saying, or positivity.
2 Disacquiescence Response Style (DARS) – DARS refers to the tendency to disagree with the item, regardless of content. This type is also called disagreement tendency, nay-saying, or negativity.
3 Net Acquiescence Response Style (NARS) – This type refers to the tendency to show greater acquiescence than disacquiescence. This type is also referred to as directional bias.
4 Extreme Response Style (ERS) – This type refers to the tendency to endorse the most extreme response, regardless of the content.
5 Response Range (RR) – This type refers to the tendency to use a narrow or wide range of response categories around the mean response.
6 Midpoint Responding (MPR) – This refers to the use of middle scale category, regardless of the content.
7 Non-Contingent Responding (NCR) – This type refers to the tendency to items carelessly, randomly or without any purpose.

Each of these response styles has important implications in cross-national research. The country-specific variations in these response styles may easily be misinterpreted as substantive differences in the marketing constructs examined, which could have adverse effects on the decisions made by international marketers. Therefore, response styles are an important threat to the validity of both domestic and cross-national survey-based marketing research.

There have been many research studies on response styles. In a recent research study, the extreme response style in cross-national research has been investigated through the Item-Response Theory (IRT) model (De Jong, Steenkamp, Fox and Baumgartner, forthcoming). To investigate the effect of culture on ERS, they employed Hofstede's (2001) framework of cultural dimensions and the classification of countries based on the classification. From Hofstede's index, they considered four factors – individualism; masculinity; uncertainty avoidance; and power distance. They found that the socio-demographic variables such as age, gender, and education have a minor influence on ERS, but culture exerts a strong and predictable effect on ERS. They observed that women tend to score higher on ERS than men, and that both younger and older respondents are prone to respond extremely.

Further, with respect to the four factors, they found that ERS is positively related to individualism, masculinity, and uncertainty avoidance. In other words, countries that are low on individualism, masculinity, and uncertainty avoidance have relatively low ERS scores. While this result may seem contradictory to the finding on women having higher ERS scores than men, it should be noted that masculine and feminine characters refers to the historical gender role patterns in a society and not to fundamental personality traits. Therefore, it would be inappropriate to equate masculine/feminine characters with contemporary gender roles. Also, they found that ERS scores are not related to power distance.

This study shows that, cross-nationally, people differ in their tendency to use the extremes of the rating scale, and items also differ in the extent to which they elicit extreme responses. In all, culture plays an important role in explaining cross-national differences in ERS, and has definite implications for international marketing research. However, even with careful designing of the questionnaire and identification of response styles, there are bound to be some issues with the questionnaire design.

Issues in questionnaire design

In designing a questionnaire, especially in the international setting, researchers may come across issues that need to be considered while conducting the survey. An explanation of the issues is provided here.

Questionnaire wording The wording of questions can have a large impact on how a respondent interprets them. Even small changes in wording can shift respondents' answers, but it is difficult to know in advance whether or not a wording change will have such an effect. The researcher may not be aware of the purchasing behavior or relevant determinants of response in another country or cultural context. In such a scenario, use of open-ended questions may avoid problems of misinterpretation of question and ensure relevant answers. Furthermore, they do not require familiarity with all the respondents' possible responses. Some of the issues that the researchers should be aware of while wording the questions are: simplicity of the vocabulary; avoiding words with vague or ambiguous meanings; avoiding leading questions, as they may lead to biased answers; applicability of questions to the respondents; and avoiding verbose question structure.

Layout of the questionnaire Sequencing and logical layout of the questionnaire is essential for the easy administering of the survey. If the questions are not logically flowing, then the possibility of prior questions influencing answers to subsequent questions may arise, also known as order bias. Some pointers that will help researchers develop an easy flowing questionnaire are: (1) open with an easy and non-threatening question to instil and gain respondents' confidence, (2) avoid sudden shifts in topics of questioning, (3) it is advisable to proceed from broad or general questions to specific questions and, (4) avoid sensitive or controversial questions at the beginning of the questionnaire. The physical layout of the questionnaire also will influence whether the questionnaire is interesting and easy to administer. For self-administered questionnaires, the quality of the paper, the clarity of reproduction, and the appearance of crowding are important variables.

Cultural factors   Even if the questionnaire is appropriately worded and logically sequenced, there is still bound to be some bias in the responses because of cultural responses. While drafting a questionnaire, an in-depth knowledge of the social, psychological and cultural aspects of the society is, thus, crucial. This also includes the word selection and usage. For instance, the Japanese do not have an exact equivalent for the word 'husband'. Similarly, research has found that there were no direct translations of concepts related to 'trust' in Japanese. Therefore, marketing researchers have to take care in expressing themselves bearing in mind the various cultural significances of each society.

Translation   Translation is a major problem that researchers face in international marketing research. In order to get effective translations, it is always advisable to take professional help as it is critical to relate to the native speakers and the on-line translation options may not be adequate in that regard. The need for effective translations is highlighted by the following example. A US toothpaste manufacturer promised its customers that they would be more 'interesting' if they used the firm's toothpaste. However, in Latin American Countries 'interesting' is another euphemism for 'pregnant'. So, accurate translations would help companies to avoid cultural gaffes.

In order to get effective translations, the translators have to be identified with proper planning. A few tips to identify the right translators are: (1) ensure that the service provider works with translators who are native speakers of the language, (2) apart from translation expertise, the translators should also have market and industry information, and (3) the file formats used by the researcher and the service provider should be the same, so as to avoid extra work.

While sufficient time should be allotted for the translation work, the researcher must ensure that the source material is well written. Providing as much background material as possible would help translators to understand the product-specific needs and hence result in a much closer translation.

The philosophical issues that were discussed in this section help the researcher to set the tone for the research and start the research study. These issues covered topics such as types of international research, designing the research approach, looking out for data collection, incorporating the survey method of data collection, and how to design a questionnaire for research. They help the researcher to pave the way for the actual research study and ultimately link to the interpretation of results and conclusion of the study. While these issues may seem like initial hurdles, failure to acknowledge and account for them may prove costly for the researcher. The failure to do so might produce erroneous results or may even lead to the research project not continuing. The next section talks about methodological issues that are quite different from philosophical issues in principle and definition.

METHODOLOGICAL ISSUES

Methodological issues are those issues that concern data evaluation and analysis. They concern how the research is conducted and how the results are interpreted. While the philosophical issues may deal with the initial hurdles at the start of a research project, this set of issues deals with the actual research and the issues that arise thereof. These issues can hamper any cross-cultural study and have to be addressed with care and caution. By addressing such issues, consumer inputs can be gathered in a multiplicity of different ways, interpreted and analyzed to arrive at a range of business insights. This would give rise to the formulation of creative solutions for research issues and would pave the way for new strategic directions forward.

This section covers: the scaling techniques involved in questionnaire analysis; the concept of cross-cultural response bias; the various sampling techniques involved; dealing with sampling equivalence; data analysis; the interpretation of cross-country results; and relating cross-cultural insights into cross-cultural strategies. Each of the issues mentioned is discussed in the following sections.

Scaling

Scaling is the process of creating a continuum on which objects are located according to the amount of the measured characteristic they possess (Aaker, Kumar and Day 2006). An example of a scale is the dichotomous scale for sex. The object with male (or female) characteristics is assigned the number 1 and the object with the opposite characteristics is assigned the number 0.

Measurement of scales Since the scales are used for measuring attitudes, they are also known as attitude measurement scales. The assignment of numbers is made according to rules that should correspond to the properties of whatever is being measured. It is therefore very important to understand the differences among the types of scales and to be able to identify them in practice. The various measurement scales are explained here.

Nominal scale: In a nominal scale, objects are assigned to mutually exclusive, labeled categories. That is, if one entity is assigned the same number as another, then the two entities are identical with respect to a nominal variable. Otherwise, they are just different. Sex, geographic location, and marital status are examples of nominally scaled variables. The only arithmetic operation that can be performed on such a scale is a count of each category.

Ordinal scale: In an ordinal scale, objects are ranked and arranged in a particular order with regard to some common variable. This scale provides information as to which object has more of a characteristic and which has less of it. Since the difference between the ranks is not known, a mean cannot be drawn based on this scale. However, median and mode can be computed on such a scale.

Interval scale: In an interval scale, the numbers that are used to rank the objects also represent equal increments of the attribute being measured. This implies that ordinal scales give room for comparing differences. For example, Fahrenheit and Celsius temperatures are measured with different interval scales and have different zero points. In this type of scale, the entire range of statistical operations can be employed to analyze the resulting number, including addition and subtraction. Consequently, it is possible to compute an arithmetic mean from interval-scale measures, apart from median and mode.

Ratio scale: Ratio scale is a modified interval scale with a meaningful zero point. With this scale, it is possible to say how much greater or lesser one object is than another. This scale also gives the opportunity to compare absolute comparisons of magnitude.

Having looked at the different measurement scales, let us now look at the types of scales available for questionnaire design.

Types of scales A scale can have many dimensions depending on the attribute it is trying to measure and how the construct is defined. Scales can be broadly classified into single-item, multiple-item and continuous scales. Figure 7.5 illustrates the classification of scales used in marketing research.

Single-item scales Single-item scales are those scales that have only one item to measure a construct. The types of single-item scales are discussed in this section.

Itemized category scales: This is the most commonly used scale in marketing research. This scale gives the respondents options to indicate their opinions about the object being measured. For instance, the respondents may be asked to rate their satisfaction level on a scale of +2 to −2, with +2 being 'very satisfied' and −2 being 'very dissatisfied'. Another example of this scale is to ask the respondents to compare their satisfaction level with that of the product's competitors. A few examples of itemized category scales are provided in Figure 7.6.

Comparative scales: A variant of the itemized category scale, this type of scale includes an explicit comparison in the question statement. For instance, respondents can be asked to compare one product/service with another. An example of this is as follows:

As compared to *Wal-Mart*, how would you rate your local grocer?

_____ Excellent   _____ Very good
_____ Average   _____ Poor

Rank order scales: This type of scale requires the respondents to arrange the objects in ascending or descending order with regard to some criterion. Such a ranking method is commonly used in international surveys. Since this ranking type requires considerable mental effort on the part of the respondents, it is advisable to limit the number of objects to five or six in order to obtain meaningful ranks. In cases where the number of objects is more than six, the ranking can be done in two stages. In the first stage, the respondents can be asked to rank the objects into two or three classes. In the second stage, objects in each class can then be individually ranked.

Q-sort scaling: When the ranking is difficult even in two stages, a Q-sort scaling can be done. In this method, the respondents are asked to sort the various characteristics or objects that are being compared into various groups, such that the distribution of the number of objects or characteristics in each

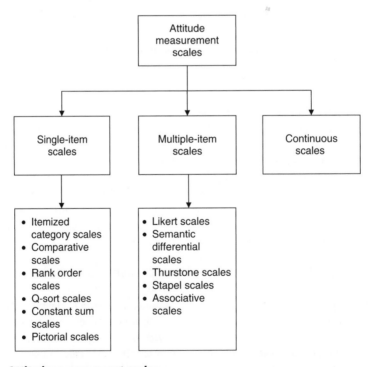

Figure 7.5 Attitude measurement scales
Source: Adapted from Kumar V., International Marketing Research, (Prentice Hall 2000)

(a) Give us your opinion about the local transport system

☐ Very satisfied   ☐ Quite satisfied   ☐ Somewhat satisfied   ☐ Not satisfied

(b) Give us your opinion about the local transport system

Very satisfied				Very dissatisfied
+2	+1	0	−1	−2

(c) Give us your opinion about the news channels you see regularly

	Excellent	Very good	Average	Below average
HNN News	_____	_____	_____	_____
News Now	_____	_____	_____	_____
News Cast	_____	_____	_____	_____

Figure 7.6   Itemized category scales

group follows a normal distribution. In Q-sort scaling, a relatively large number of groups or piles should be used (10 or more), as this increases the reliability or precision of the results.

Constant-sum scales: This type of scale asks the respondents to allocate a fixed number of points (usually 100) among different categories such that the division of points reflects their relative references. An example of this type is provided below.

Allocate 100 points among these factors so that the points indicate how important each of these factors is in your choice of a news channel.

Reliability of the news	_____
Variety of news	_____
Coverage of local news	_____
Coverage of national and international news	_____
Total	100

Pictorial scales: In pictorial scales the various categories of the scale are depicted pictorially. The respondents are shown a concept or read an attitudinal statement and are asked to indicate their degree of agreement or interest by indicating the corresponding position on the pictorial scale. In an international setting, it is of prime importance to design one that the respondent will comprehend and which will enable him or her to respond accurately. Commonly used pictorial scales are the 'thermometer scale' and the 'funny faces scale'. Pictorial scales are used mainly when the respondents are young children or other people who are illiterate.

Multiple-item scales   When it is not possible for the researcher to capture the entire range of attitudes of the respondent through a single-item scale, multiple-item scales are used. These scales obtain information about the respondent's attitude along different aspects of the object and then combine all these to form an average score indicative of the overall attitude of the respondent toward the object. The types of multiple-item scales are described below.

Likert scales: This type of scale requires a respondent to indicate the degree of agreement or disagreement with a number of statements related to the characteristics of the object. They are also called summated scales, because the scores on the individual items are summed to produce a total score for the respondent. A Likert scale usually consists of two parts, the item part and the evaluative part. The item part is essentially a statement about a certain product, event, or attitude. The evaluative part is a list of response categories ranging from 'strongly agree' to 'strongly disagree'.

Semantic differential scales: This type of scale is widely used in international marketing research to reflect the set of beliefs or attitudes that the respondent has about an object. In this scale, respondents are asked to rate each attitude on a number of five- or seven-point scale, bounded at each end by polar adjectives or phrases. Care should be taken to ascertain that the adjectives used are relevant in the country where the survey is administered and the respondents understand the implications of the category. An example of this scale is provided below.

Give us your opinion about two news channels – *News Now* and *News Cast.*					
Good local coverage ___	___	___	___	___	Bad local coverage
Reliable ___	___	___	___	___	Unreliable
Good global coverage ___	___	___	___	___	Bad global coverage

Thurstone scales: This type of scale provides researchers with a uni-dimensional scale with interval properties and hence is also referred to as method of equal-appearing intervals. The procedure for administering a Thurstone scale is a two-stage process. In the first stage, researchers generate a number of adjectives (usually 100), that reflects all degree of favorableness towards the object. A group of judges than classifies these according to their degree of favorableness or unfavorableness. The intervals between the categories are treated as equal and the scale value for each category is the median value assigned by the judges. This results in a scale consisting of 10 to 20 categories indicating various degrees of favorableness. In the second stage, respondents rate different aspects of the object on different categories in this scale. Owing to its two-stage procedure, this scale is both time-consuming and expensive to construct. However, the scale is easy to administer and requires a minimum of instructions. Further, it is possible that the scale categories could depend on the judges selected for the process.

Stapel scales: This type of scale is a simplified version of the semantic differential scales, where the categories have only one pole. Respondents provide a score to the category depending on their preference and a higher positive score implies higher preference.

Associative scaling: This type of scale overcomes the limitations of semantic differential scales, where the respondent needs to be familiar with all of the objects to respond usefully. In associative scaling, the respondent is asked to associate one alternative with each question. For example, if the proximity of a grocery store is to be considered, the respondents are asked to make their choice of the store that satisfies them the most in this criterion from a list of stores. This technique is best suited for market tracking studies, where the emphasis is on understanding shifts in relative competitive positions.

Continuous scales Also referred to as graphical scales, continuous-rating scales require the respondents to rate objects by placing a mark at the appropriate position on a line that runs from one extreme of the criterion variable to the other (Narayana 1977). While this technique is easy to construct, scoring is cumbersome and unreliable. Further, these scales do not provide much new information. Hence, continuous-rating scales are not widely used in marketing research.

Therefore, based on the type of research and the attribute that is being measured, the type of scale can be used accordingly. Ultimately, the researcher's choice will be shaped by: (1) the specific information that is required to satisfy the research objectives, (2) the adaptability of the scale to the data collection method and budget constraints, and (3) the compatibility of the scale with the structure of the respondent's attitude. While in domestic marketing research the issues with respect to scales may not be high, in international marketing research, researchers have to face an important issue – the issue of equivalence. Specifically, this issue arises when there is a need to compare results across countries. The following section briefly describes the issue of equivalence in scales and the ways of measuring them.

Measuring equivalence In international marketing research, the very meaning of a scale may change because of cultural influences. Consequently, international marketing research calls for appropriate equivalence and comparability checks. It is important for the researcher to be able to compare data across countries and, hence, it is essential to examine the various aspects of data collection process and establish their equivalence. This is illustrated by the following example of a survey conducted in Europe (Min-Han and Ro 1994). In a survey regarding the number of baths women take, it was observed that Belgian women take a greater number of baths that any other nationality. However, a closer look at the data revealed that the time period was not comparable. In Belgium the women were asked if they had taken a bath in the last seven days. In all other countries the question had been 'Have you had a bath in the last three days?'.

Measurement equivalence relates to establishing equivalence in terms of procedures used to measure concepts or attitudes (Crimp and Wright 1995). Three aspects will have to be considered in order to establish measurement equivalence. They are: (1) calibration equivalence, (2) translation equivalence, and (3) metric equivalence.

Calibration equivalence Calibration equivalence refers to the calibration system used in the measurement. This would include monetary units, measures of weight, distance and volume and perceptual cues such as color, shape or form. In international marketing research, this issue has to be taken care of, since various countries around the world follow different units of weights and measures. For instance, Americans are used to weighing things by the pound or ton while the British and most of the Commonwealth countries use the gram and kilogram.

Similarly, this holds true for currencies. For instance, one billion in the United States may not mean the same amount in the United Kingdom. Researchers should also take care to establish equivalence in terms of interpretation of perceptual cues. Even in the case of colors, several cultures hold varied perceptions for them. White, for example, is considered a symbol of purity and peace in the Western world but, a color of mourning for the Japanese (Jacobs, Keown, Worthley and Ghymn 1991). In the People's Republic of China, notes written using red ink suggest that the writer will die soon and the number four should be avoided at all costs as this, too, signifies death.

Translation equivalence Translation is essential for a research study that involves respondents from multiple countries. The translation should be able to convey the same meaning to the respondents in their local language. This process can get complicated when the researcher has to interpret and translate non-verbal clues. It should be noted that verbatim translation of questionnaire into another language may not be possible, due to lack of equivalent words. For instance, there is no equivalent term for 'husband' in Japanese. The researcher should thus, focus on conveying the intent of the question to the respondent and obtain an answer that can be comparable across countries.

Metric equivalence Metric equivalence refers to the score or scale equivalence. In international marketing research, equivalence has to be established in terms of the responses to a given measure in different countries. The scales used in different countries may vary depending on the culture and education level of the respondents. For instance, in the United States researchers typically use a five- or seven-point scale; however, there are countries where scales can have as many as 20 categories. Another culture-specific decision is to determine whether the scale should be unipolar or bipolar and, whether there should be a neutral point on the scale. For instance, Japanese people tend to remain neutral if given a choice. Hence, researchers studying the Japanese market should design scales with no neutral point, in order to obtain meaningful results.

Thus, establishing equivalence for an international marketing research study is an important task and requires judgmental decisions on the part of the researcher. The researcher will have to decide on the methodology that will work in the respective country. Another country specific aspect is the issue of cross-cultural response bias. This arises when researchers study multiple countries and are influenced by the results. The next section provides ways of dealing with cross-cultural response bias.

Dealing with cross-cultural response bias

Cross-cultural researchers conducting studies across different cultural groups need to consider whether the scores obtained are comparable. In order to achieve meaningful cross-cultural comparisons, the issues of equivalence and response bias have to be addressed. Response bias refers to the respondents' desire to give socially acceptable answers. The cultural tendencies belonging to different cultural groups are likely to change the responses of participants and make them impossible to compare across cultural groups and therefore resulting in a bias (Fischer 2004). Hofstede (1980) was among the first to advocate the use of standardization as an adjustment of raw

scores in cross-cultural research to correct for such response tendencies.

Techniques such as Structural Equation Modeling (Cheung and Rensvold 2000; Little 1997, 2000) and Item Response Theory (Butcher, Lim and Nezami 1998; Huang, Church and Katigbak 1997) can be used to identify whether different response strategies were used by participants in different samples. Researchers can then decide whether they want to standardize their data or not. There are four major groups of standardization procedures. These four groups are: (1) adjustment of means, (2) adjustment for dispersion (e.g., using standard deviation), (3) adjustments using means and dispersions, and (4) covariate analysis. These groups can be classified into within-subject, within-group, and within-culture categories, based on the statistical information they use for standardization.

The within-subject standardization procedure refers to the adjustments of scores for each individual using the mean for that individual across all variables. The average of a subset or all variables for that particular individual is subtracted from each individual's raw score. Hence, the resulting score is the relative position of the individual on a variable in relation to the other scores. The mean across variables for this individual will average to zero. This procedure is also called ipsatization (Hicks 1970).

The within-subject standardization procedure has several variants. The most common form is the computation of z scores, whereby the group mean is subtracted from the variable raw score and then divided by the standard deviation (Howell 1997). Hence, the resulting score is the relative position of one specific individual on one variable relative to the position of other individuals in that group. The mean across individuals is zero and, assuming a normal distribution of responses, the resulting standard deviation will be 1. An adjustment procedure, commonly referred to as 'centering', is also available, wherein only the mean across individuals is used (Aiken and West 1991).

In the within-culture standardization, instead of using the group mean across one item (as in z transformation), the mean across all items and all individuals (the grand mean) is used (Bond 1988; Leung and Bond 1989). It is possible to adjust this deviation score by dividing it by the standard deviation across items and individuals.

A combination of within-subject and within-culture, called double standardization, can also be used. Initially, the scores are adjusted within the individual (within-subject standardization), and then the resulting scores are adjusted within the group (within-culture standardization). Thus, the means for each individual across variables and the mean for each variable across individuals will be zero. Assuming normality of the raw data, the adjustment using the standard deviation should yield standard deviations of 1 for both individuals across variables and variables across individuals.

It is important to note that these standard procedures can be done both at item level and at construct level. One may standardize individual items using the relevant mean across either items or individuals or one may standardize the mean for one specific construct using the relevant mean across items, constructs, or individuals.

With variations in the type of scale to be used according to the construct to be measured, scaling techniques are an important function in the international research roadmap. As a result, many issues arise when scaling techniques are involved. The following section deliberates on the issues in designing scales.

Issues in designing scales Designing scales are a crucial factor to obtaining meaningful insights from marketing research. In international marketing research, this poses a challenge as culture and local perceptions decide the responses and, researchers may come across issues that need to be considered while designing the scales. An explanation of the issues is provided here.

Pan-cultural scales: An important issue in the area of international marketing is whether the same scales can be used to respondents all over the world, or does a pan-cultural or global scale exist. From the research that has been conducted to find out a pan-cultural or global scale, the semantic-differential scale seems to come closest to being a truly pan-cultural scale. It consistently gives similar results in terms of concepts or dimensions that are used to evaluate stimuli, and also accounts for a major portion of the variation in response when it is administered in different countries. It is also true that literacy, educational levels and culture influence the response formats of the scales employed and may induce some cultural biases.

Response formats: Another issue that is important in international research is whether response formats, particularly their calibration, need to be adapted for specific countries and cultures. For example, in France a 20-point scale is commonly used to rate performance in primary and secondary schools. Consequently, it has been suggested that 20-point scales should also be used in marketing research. In general, verbal scales are more effective among less educated respondents, but a more appropriate procedure for illiterate respondents would be scales with pictorial stimuli.

Communication: Communication is determined by the cultural background of a country. This factor has a major part in designing scales in international marketing research. For instance, while the Swiss talk very literally, the Japanese are not precise in their communication. Similarly, spoken and written words have multiple meanings in Japanese and the meaning depends on the context the words are being used in (Usunier 1996). Therefore, in certain countries comparisons and scale ideas have to be conveyed explicitly and with clarity. This becomes a very important issue in deciding on the type of scale to be used.

Education: The educational system of a country reflects the culture and heritage of the country significantly. Education and child-rearing practices have been proven to be one of the most efficient ways of studying national character. It also decides the receptiveness of people towards foreign products and concepts. This not only concerns the researchers undertaking the study, but also the companies who wish to transcend national boundaries with their products. In order to design scales, it is essential for researchers to know the education level of the target population, as this will help researchers decide on the type of scale to be used.

Thus, designing scales is a crucial step in obtaining research results from a study. This has to factor in various issues such as education, literacy, and culture to decide on the appropriate scales that have to be used. While the problems discussed above are significant considerations, the researcher has to bear in mind that all techniques are not equally suitable for all purposes. Like scales, sampling is also another important methodological issue that concerns international marketing research. The next section talks about sampling techniques and its various issues in detail.

Sampling

International marketing research aims to study the characteristics and preferences of a population. Population is defined as the set of all objects that possess some common set of characteristics with respect to marketing research problems. A survey that contacts all members of the population is called a census. Since census is not a practical option in most research studies, researchers choose a subset of elements from the population and from this subset obtain a sample. They then make an inference about the population, based on the relevant information obtained from the sample. The key here is to make sure that the sample selected is representative of the population so as to achieve meaningful and unbiased results. For this, a thorough understanding of the process of sampling is essential.

Process of sampling When a decision is made to use a sample, a number of factors must be taken into consideration. The various steps involved in the sampling process are given in Figure 7.7.

The first step in the sampling process is to determine the target population. This has to be defined clearly and precisely, as, the narrower the definition is, the better the results from the sample obtained will be. In international marketing research, this attains more importance due to differences in decision-making processes among various countries. A good knowledge about the market will aid the researcher in deciding the target population and sample size. Before proceeding to the second stage, the differences pertaining to population and sampling frame have to be addressed.

The next step is to decide the sampling frame. The sampling frame is a list of population members used to obtain a sample. In international marketing research, this can create problems as documented information sources are found wanting. Also, the decision-making process may vary among countries. For instance, in Japan decisions are still made by the consensus of every family member (Leslie 1992). A list of members belonging to the sampling frame should then be obtained. While in developed countries this information can be easily obtained from professional organizations and database marketing companies, in developing countries, where marketing research is still in its infancy, finding a reliable source may pose a problem for the researchers.

The third step involves selecting a sampling procedure. There are many ways of obtaining a sample and many decisions associated with generating a sample. A researcher should first choose between using a Bayesian procedure and a traditional sampling procedure. Next, a decision is made to sample with or without replacement. Most marketing research projects employ a traditional sampling method without replacement, because a respondent is not contacted twice to obtain the same information. Among traditional

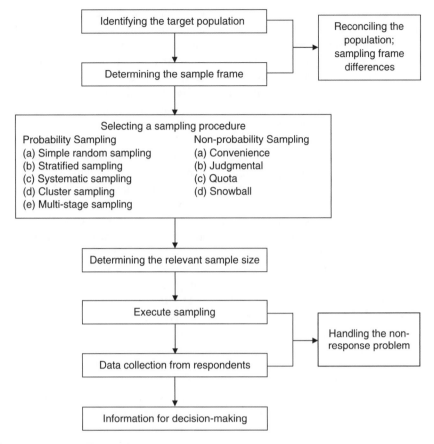

Figure 7.7 The sampling process

sampling procedures, some are informal or even casual. In most cases, however, the situation is more complex. It is then necessary to obtain a representative sample of the population consisting of more than a handful of units. The preferred approach is to use probability sampling to obtain a representative sample. The next section will discuss probability and non-probability sampling in detail.

In the fourth step, the sample size is determined. The size of a sample can be determined by using statistical techniques or through some ad hoc methods. Ad hoc methods are used when a person knows from experience what sample size to adopt or when there are some constraints that determine the sample size. The rule of thumb and comparable studies are some ways in which

sample size can be determined through ad hoc methods. Determination of sample size depends on four factors. They are: (1) the number of groups and subgroups that will be analyzed, (2) the value of information in the study, (3) the cost of the sample, and (4) the variability of the population.

In the fifth and sixth steps, the sampling is executed and, using the sampling design, data is collected from the respondents. The object of sampling is to obtain a body of data that are representative of the population. Unfortunately, some sample members become non-respondents because they: (1) refuse to respond, (2) lack the ability to respond, or (3) are inaccessible.

Non-response can be a serious problem. It means that the sample size has to be large enough to allow for non-response. Further, it also indicates the possibility that those who respond differ from non-respondents in a meaningful way, thereby creating biases. The seriousness of non-response bias depends on the extent of the non-response. If the percentage involved is small, the bias is small. A way to correct the response bias is to replace each non-respondent with a 'matched' member of the sample. Three more approaches are: (1) to improve the research design to reduce the number of non-responses, (2) to repeat the contact in order to reduce non-responses, and (3) to attempt to estimate the non-response bias. Therefore, the non-response problem has to be handled before proceeding to the decision-making stage.

Owing to uncertainties regarding the definition of population and sampling frame, selecting a sampling procedure is very crucial in international marketing research. The roadmap provided in this section would help the researcher to understand the sampling process and use appropriate sampling techniques. The types of sampling are described in the following section.

Types of sampling

Due to differences in population and sampling frame, selecting a sampling procedure is very crucial in international marketing research. The sampling methods available can be broadly classified into: (a) probability sampling, and (b) non-probability sampling. This section provides in detail the various types of sampling.

Probability sampling

In probability sampling, each member of the population has a known probability of being selected. In most probability sampling procedures, a sampling frame is needed and information on objects/sampling units is necessary prior to employing the sampling process. Probability sampling involves four considerations. First, the target population must be specified. Second, the method for selecting the sample needs to be developed. Third, the sample size must be determined. The sample size will depend on the accuracy needs, the variation within the population, and the cost. Finally, the non-response problem must be addressed. The various types of probability sampling are discussed below.

Simple random sampling: Simple random sampling is an approach in which each population member, and thus each possible sample, has an equal probability of being selected. This method is used when the population from which the sample is to be chosen is homogenous. An easy way to perform this sampling type is to write names from the sample on small sheets of paper, mix them in a bowl, and randomly draw the desired number of sheets. Another way of picking out a random sample is to use computer generated random numbers.

Stratified random sampling: Also referred to as proportional sampling, this is a two-step process which improves the accuracy and efficiency when compared to simple random sampling. In the first step the population is divided into clear-cut groups or strata based on certain factors. This means that each of these groups will contain members of the population who are homogenous to a great extent. In the second stage, the simple random sampling procedure can be employed for each of these groups. This type of sampling ensures that the sample will be representative of the population and further guarantees that each subgroup in a given population is well represented, no matter how small the subgroup may be. This sampling method is used frequently in international marketing research.

Systematic random sampling: This technique is used where the respondent knows that the list of population members to be sampled is in some order: random, cyclical, or monotonic. Thus, if the population contains 1,000 $(= N)$ people and a sample size of 100 $(= n)$ is desired, every tenth $(= I$, sampling interval) person is selected for the sample. A starting point could be randomly chosen between the first name and the Ith name initially, and then every I^{th} name is chosen. However, this technique is used most frequently in telephone interviews, where surveys are done in a particular area.

Geographic coverage is a major drawback of using simple random sampling, stratified random sampling, and systematic random sampling techniques. If the population is spread over a large area, it becomes difficult to obtain a representative sample. This problem is overcome by cluster sampling.

Cluster sampling: Cluster sampling is a technique where the entire population is divided into similar groups, or clusters that are very similar, and each cluster represents a mini-population. A random sample of these clusters is then drawn. Unlike the stratified random sampling technique, here clusters are selected for sampling, and all members in these clusters are surveyed. In international marketing research, owing to lack of information and high cost of research, most researchers opt for multi-stage sampling.

Multi-stage sampling: As the name suggests, this type of sampling is done in many stages. Consider, for instance, a soft drink manufacturer who intends to conduct a study to find out the brand awareness of the beverage they manufacture. All countries where the brand awareness is to be studied are first divided into regions that are similar on a predetermined set of variables, such as per capita income or annual sales of the beverage. These regions are broken down into countries and further into cities. Clusters of residential areas are identified in each of these cities. Researchers then draw a random sample of a certain number of clusters depending on the sample size they need. All members in these clusters are surveyed. The results obtained can be extrapolated to get the awareness figure of the entire area. Depending on the complexity of the information, this type of sampling can involve three or four stages.

Non-probability sampling

In non-probability sampling, researchers do not develop a sampling frame. Therefore, efficiency and precision are affected. However, this mode of sampling is used in exploratory research, pre-testing questionnaires, and surveying homogenous population. In many international marketing research studies, this type of sampling is used frequently because of the costs and the troubles of developing a sampling frame are saved. However, they are used legitimately and effectively. The various types of non-probability sampling are discussed below.

Judgmental sampling: Judgmental sampling is adopted when the researcher knows the market well enough to choose a sample using expert judgment. This method is used when the researcher needs quick results. It can be used with reasonable accuracy when the sample size is very small, as in an exploratory research or a questionnaire pretest. Common forms of judgmental sampling can be found in mall-intercept surveys, and when probability sampling is not feasible or prohibitively expensive. In international marketing research, the researcher may not always know the market very well. In such a case, incorporating such a sampling technique might introduce bias in the research study.

Snowball sampling: Snowball sampling is used when the population consists of individuals in specialized areas. The interviewer starts out with one individual and asks the individual to identify similar individuals who meet the population characteristics. This method is effective in sampling highly specialized population segments. This design can be used to reach small populations, such as deep-sea divers, people confined to wheelchairs, families with triplets, among others.

Convenience sampling: Convenience sampling is used when information has to be obtained quickly and inexpensively. The procedure is simply to contact sampling units that are convenient – a church activity group, a classroom of students, women at a shopping center on a particular day, the first 50 recipients of mail questionnaires, or a few friends and neighbors. This method is not very accurate and can be used only in exploratory research.

Quota sampling: Quota sampling is judgmental sampling with the constraint that the sample includes a minimum number from each specified subgroup in the population. Suppose that a 500-person sample of a city is desired and it is known how the population of the city is distributed geographically. The interviewers might be asked to obtain 100 interviews on the east side, 150 on the west side, and so on. However, in a haste to meet quotas, researchers may sometimes ignore the statistical issues. Therefore care should be taken when implementing this method of sampling.

Sampling in the international context requires certain special care and is seldom an easy task. The major problems here are the absence of information on sampling frames in other countries, and one of sampling equivalence. Sampling equivalence is discussed in the following section.

Sampling equivalence In international marketing research, it is essential to ensure that the samples drawn from different countries are comparable. As mentioned earlier, the emphasis is not on the method used, but on the equivalence of the information collected from the sample. In order to ensure sampling equivalence, two steps are to be followed.

The first step is to decide who should be contacted for the survey and whether the study needs single or multiple respondents from a single household. For instance, if the purchasing behavior regarding toys is being studied, researchers need to understand that, while in the United States children get to select their toys, in other countries parents may make the purchase decisions. Hence, while collecting information on toys, in the United States children will have to be interviewed and in other countries parents will have to be interviewed.

The second issue deals with the extent to which the sample is representative of the population. For instance, researchers in developing countries may not have access to databases regarding information on markets due to unavailability, and this would render the designing of sampling frame difficult. In such cases, the researcher will have to resort to other methods to obtain representative samples. In such situations, judgment or snowball sampling may be effective.

Sampling in international research poses some special problems. The absence of reliable sampling lists and small sample sizes brings a number of concerns into the study. Moreover, adopting the same sampling method in different countries may not yield the best results. Even if one adopts the same sampling procedure across all countries, sampling equivalence will not necessarily be achieved. Therefore, researchers will have to take care to ensure such issues do not hinder their study. The following section describes ways of conducting market research with a small sample size.

How to conduct market research with small sample size? In international marketing research, often researchers may have to encounter a small sample size. This, apart from hindering the study, may also affect the subsequent analyses that follow the sampling stage. In such a scenario, a country pooling technique would help the researchers solve the problem. This technique requires that countries with *similar* characteristics be pooled to get a sufficiently large sample, in order to carry on a 'normal' research study. However, care should be taken in selecting the countries for pooling, as incorrect pooling may lead to biased and unusable research results. The pooling can be done according to three factors. They are:

Economic status: Economic status is perhaps an easy way to pool countries. Accordingly, countries can be pooled based on economic wealth; market potential index; Gross National Product (GNP); population; inflation; price levels; unemployment rate; and interest rates among other categories. Countries can be clubbed together on the basis of economic conditions. Such a pooling would provide the researchers a larger sample to work with. Typically, such a pooling technique would be helpful in studies involving effects of prices on sales and marketing mix models.

Geographical proximity: As the name suggests, countries within close proximity are to be pooled. Factors such as size of the country, neighbors, common climatic conditions and demographic indicators, among others, can be considered for this pooling technique. However, neighboring countries need not warrant a geographical pooling technique. For instance, even though the Canadian market may be similar to the United States market, because of their geographical proximity, both countries should be addressed as two distinct cultures. Typically, segmentation studies use this type of pooling.

Cultural setting: Pooling based on cultural factors is probably the most challenging among the three pooling techniques. Cultural factors such as measures of high/low context culture; attitudes of people; differences in lifestyle; religion; language; literacy; values; work ethics; and family and gender roles can be considered for this type of pooling. A useful tool in such a technique would be the Hofstede's classification of countries based on Individualism vs. Collectivism, Power Distance, Uncertainty Avoidance, and Masculinity vs. Femininity and Strategic Orientation (short term vs. long term).

The challenge of this technique lies in the frame of reference used to pool a set of countries. The frame of reference is an important factor in determining or modifying a marketer's reaction to situation. For instance, Belgium is neatly divided in half, between Flanders in the north and Wallonia in the south. However, while the Flemish people use margarine, the Walloons use butter (Sager 1997). Therefore, within a single country, a researcher could encounter many cultures and this factor has to be considered while adopting a culture pooling technique. Typically, product positioning and product acceptance studies would use this type of pooling.

Thus, pooling based on economic, geographical or cultural factors provides researchers a way out of the small sample size problem. A caveat here is that the nature of the study should be considered when deciding on the appropriate pooling technique. This would ensure that the study, apart from producing significant results, would also aid in developing effective strategies.

Thus, with the sampling techniques discussed here, the required data can be collected by the researcher using appropriate methods. However, in order to develop effective strategies, analysis of data collected is crucial. The next section discusses at length the data analytics involved in international marketing research.

Data analysis

Once the required data is collected, the next stage is to analyze the collected information to develop meaningful strategies. Data analysis is a means of converting the collected information into actionable sets of conclusions and reports. Data analysis is crucial to any study as it helps the researcher to quantify the findings. However, the accuracy of the study depends on the research design, and data analysis cannot be called upon to rescue a poorly designed study.

An understanding of the principles of data analysis is useful for several reasons. First, it can lead the researcher to information and insights that otherwise would not be available. Second, it can help avoid erroneous judgments and conclusions. Third, it can provide a background to help interpret and understand analysis conducted by others. Finally, knowledge of the power of data analysis techniques can constructively influence research objectives and research design. With the collected data, appropriate data analysis methods have to be used. The type of data analysis required will be unique to each study. However, nearly all studies involving data analysis will require the editing and coding of data, will use one or more data analysis techniques, and will have to be concerned with presenting the results effectively.

The raw data obtained from the questionnaires must undergo preliminary preparation before they can be analyzed using statistical techniques. The quality of the results obtained from the statistical techniques and their subsequent interpretation depend to a great degree on how well the data were prepared and converted into a form suitable for analysis. The major data preparation techniques include: (1) data editing, (2) coding, and (3) statistically adjusting the data (if required).

Data editing Data editing is done to identify omissions, ambiguities, and errors in responses. These errors can result because of: (a) interviewer error, (b) inconsistencies in questionnaire filling, (c) lack of cooperation, and (d) ineligible respondents. While the preferred way to correct such errors may be to contact the respondent again, the prohibitively high costs in international marketing research may not allow the researcher to do so. The next best alternative in such a scenario is to discard the questionnaire as unusable. A less extreme alternative would be to discard only those questions with problems and retain the other questions. For those questions with illegible or missing answers, the researcher can group such answers into a 'no opinion' or 'don't know' category. Another alternative available for such responses is the use of mean profile values, wherein for any respondent the researcher can input missing values or infer the values matching the respondent's profile to that of another similar respondent.

Data coding Once the data has been edited for inconsistencies, the data must be coded for easy use and retrieval of information for further analysis. Coding the questionnaire involves identifying the respondents and the variables used in the survey. It is essential that every research project has a coding sheet that describes the data and where it is located. Typically, such a coding sheet would contain information such as: (a) name of the variable, (b) what the variable represents in the project, (c) the format of the variable, (d) the units used to describe the variable, (e) the location of the variable in the database, and (f) any other comments.

In data coding, coding closed-ended questions is fairly straightforward as compared with open-ended questions. In the case of open-ended questions, the researcher has to generate a list of all possible responses that can be expected for that question. If the responses do not match, the researcher has to exercise judgment and place the responses in one of the listed categories. In an international research study, generating such a list can become complicated owing to differences in cultural and product usage characteristics.

Another aspect related to data coding is the harmonization of coding patterns. In an international study, it is crucial to code patterns across countries so that different categories are harmonized. This is made possible by deciding the guidelines for coding in a centralized location and having local agencies implement equivalent versions of the same in individual countries. The central office has to verify the coding sheet before using it for analysis. Once the response sheet has been coded, data can be fed into the computer for further analysis.

Data adjustment After the data is edited and coded, the data may require some adjustments to be made in certain cases. These may be due to: (a) non-responses or missing values to certain questions, (b) clubbing of certain categories in the case of insufficient number of responses and altering the data accordingly, (c) ensuring uniformity of scales so that the least preferred and most preferred values are represented in the same manner, and (d) checking for reliability of data to ensure that the data is acceptable to a specific country or culture. Some of the data adjustment methods are provided here.

Weighting: Weighting is a procedure by which each response in the database is assigned a number according to some pre-specified rule. Most often, weighting is done to make the sample data more representative of a target population on specific characteristics. Categories under-represented in the sample are given higher weights, while over-represented categories are given lower weights. Weighting also is done to increase or decrease the number of cases in the sample that possess certain characteristics. Weighting may also be used for adjusting the sample so that greater importance is attached to respondents with certain characteristics. Weighting should be applied with caution, and the weighting procedure should be documented and made a part of the project report.

Variable respecification: This is a procedure in which the existing data are modified to create new variables, or in which a large number of variables are collapsed into fewer variables. The purpose of this procedure is to create variables that are consistent with the study's objectives. For instance, suppose the original variable represented the reasons for purchasing a house, with eight response categories. These might be collapsed into four categories: price, location, amenities, and neighborhood. Respecification also includes taking the ratio of two variables to create a new variable, taking square root and log transformations, and using dummy variables.

Scale transformation: Scale transformation involves the manipulation of scale values to ensure comparability with other scales. In the same study, different scales may be employed for measuring different variables. Therefore, it would not be meaningful to make comparisons across the measurement scales for any respondent. Some respondents may consistently use the lower end of a rating scale, whereas others may consistently use the upper end. These differences can be corrected by appropriately transforming the data.

Standardization, a common scale transformation procedure, allows the researcher to compare variables that have been measured using different types of scales. For example, if sales are measured in actual dollars, and prices in cents, then the actual value of the variance for the sales variable will be higher compared with price, because of the units of measurement. To compare the variances, both variables can be brought down to a common unit of measurement. This can be achieved by forcing the variables, by standardization, to have a mean of zero and a standard deviation of one. Mathematically, this is done by first subtracting the mean $\bar{X}$ from each score and then dividing by the standard deviation s_x. However, standardization can be done only on interval- or ratio-scaled data.

Having edited, coded, and statistically adjusted the data the next step is to devise strategies for the actual data analysis. The next section discusses such strategies available to researchers.

Strategy for data analysis Typically, the first step in data analysis is to identify each variable independent of other variables. This is achieved by tabulation of data. Tabulation helps the researcher understand the distribution of variables and calculate some key descriptive statistics. Descriptive statistics are statistics normally associated with a frequency distribution that helps summarize the information presented in the frequency table. These include: (1) measures of central tendency (mean, median, and mode); (2) measures of dispersion (range, standard deviation, and coefficient of variation); and (3) measures of shape (skewness and kurtosis). Descriptive statistics are useful in summarizing large sets of data. However, there is loss of information as one single number is used to communicate all of the information related to an entire data set. These statistics are used extensively for nominally scaled variables. When relations among and between nominally scaled variables are of interest, cross-tabulations are used.

In cross-tabulation, the sample is divided into subgroups in order to learn how the dependent variable varies from subgroup to subgroup. Cross-tabulation tables require fewer assumptions to construct, and they serve as the basis of several statistical techniques such as χ-square and log-linear analysis. Percentages are computed on each cell basis or by rows or columns. When the computations are by rows or columns, cross-tabulation tables usually are referred to as contingency tables, because the percentages are basically contingent on the row or column totals. Having looked at the strategy for conducting data analysis, let us look into the statistical techniques available for conducting data analysis.

Data analysis is not an end in itself. Its purpose is to produce information that will help address the problem at hand. There are several techniques that will aid the researchers in doing so. They are outlined in the following section.

Techniques for data analysis Based on the nature of the problem, the statistical techniques can be classified into univariate or multivariate. Univariate techniques are appropriate when there is a single measurement of each of the n sample objects, or when there are several measurements of each of the n observations but each variable is analyzed in isolation. On the other hand, multivariate techniques are appropriate for analyzing data when there are two or more measurements of each observation and the variables are to be analyzed simultaneously. An illustration of the statistical techniques is provided in Figure 7.8.

A brief explanation of the univariate and multivariate techniques of data collection follows.

Univariate techniques: These techniques are of two types – non-metric and metric. While non-metric data are measured on a nominal or ordinal scale, metric data are measured on an interval or ratio scale. Nonparametric statistical tests can be used to analyze non-metric data and parametric statistical tests are used to analyze metric data. Nonparametric tests do not require any assumptions regarding the distribution of data. For both non-metric and metric data, the next level of classification involves

determining whether a single sample or multiple samples are involved. Further, in the case of multiple samples, the appropriate statistical test depends on whether the samples are independent or dependent.

For non-metric data, with a single sample, chi-square, Kolmogorov-Smirnov (K-S), and RUNS tests can be used. For two or more independent samples, chi-square, rank sum tests, K-S, and ANOVA (Kruskal-Wallis ANOVA) should be used. For two or more dependent samples, sign test, Wilcoxon test, McNemar, and Cochran Q-tests can be used. For metric data, t-tests and z-tests can be used for one or two samples. For more than two samples, the analysis of variance (ANOVA) is used.

Multivariate techniques: Multivariate statistical techniques can be broadly defined as 'a collection of procedures for analyzing the association between two or more sets of measurements that were made on each object in one or more samples of objects'. Based on the ability to partition the data into dependent and independent variable sets, these techniques can be classified into dependence and interdependence techniques. In the case of interdependence techniques, classification is done on the basis of principal focus of analysis, i.e., whether the focus is on the object or on variables.

Dependence techniques are appropriate when one or more variables can be identified as dependent variables and the remaining as independent variables. The appropriate choice of dependence techniques further depends on whether there are one or more dependent variables involved in the analysis. In interdependence techniques, the variables are not classified as dependent or independent; rather, the whole set of interdependent relationships is examined. The interdependence techniques can be further classified as focusing on variables or objects, i.e., as variable interdependence or inter-object similarity techniques.

Based on the data collected, appropriate techniques can be used to conduct data analysis. The data analysis enables the

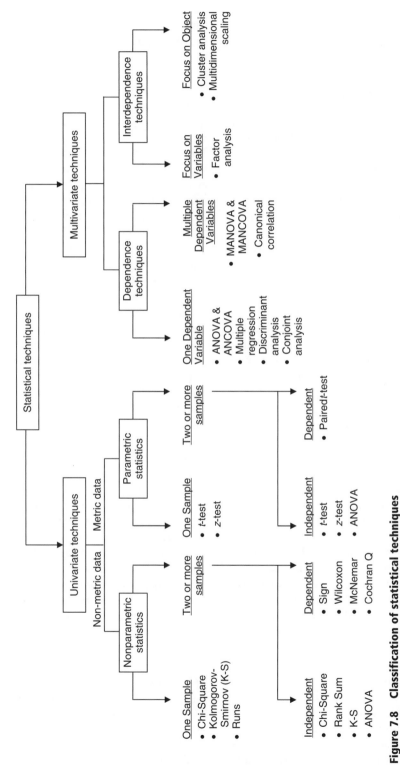

Figure 7.8 Classification of statistical techniques
Source: Adapted from Kumar V., *International Marketing Research* (Prentice Hall 2000)

researcher to interpret the results and eventually develop some conclusions. The following section talks about interpreting the results of an international study.

Interpreting cross-country results

After concluding an international research study, the next stage is to interpret the results. This step is crucial in qualitative and observational techniques, and is entirely dependent on the researcher. In interpreting results, the major cause of concern is SRC. SRC, as noted earlier on in this chapter, is an unconscious tendency to one's own cultural values, experiences, and knowledge as the basis of decisions. It impedes the ability of a researcher to define the problem in its true light. For instance, products packaged in aluminum containers instead of plastic containers are very common in developing countries. This provides the user with the option of reusability of the container. However, an American researcher should not attribute efficient recycling as the motive for such a purchase.

In certain cases, researchers find it easier to develop research instruments specific to one country and then coordinate and compare across countries. Here, both researchers who are familiar with the country and those who are not, examine the instruments and the data and draw conclusions. An alternative method is to consider one country and then compare the results across other countries. Though this method is time-consuming, it is preferred by researchers. This method also poses a number of intersection problems, as researchers from different cultural backgrounds have to be in constant touch with one another.

Therefore, while interpreting the data collected in an international study, researchers must take care in considering the country-specific implications that can impact the results of the study. The researchers have to understand that the results derived on the study will vary across countries and have to

consider it while making business decisions. The next section discusses relating the results learnt in a cross-cultural study to the culture-specific strategies that aid in decision making.

Relating cross-cultural research insights to cross-cultural strategies

The true reward of any international research study is how well the research insights materialize into strategies that can be implemented effectively. Consider, for example, the case of brand positioning in different cultures. Insights from international marketing research are essential to position a product/brand accordingly. Alden, Steenkamp and Batra (1999), based on the concept of globally shared meanings, have put forth a brand positioning strategy to assist international marketing managers.

Accordingly, the global consumer culture positioning (GCCP) strategy is defined as one that identifies the brand as a symbol of a given global culture. Here, signs such as language, aesthetics and themes that reflect the cultural orientation are used for the brands. Examples of brands that have used such strategies include Sony ('My First Sony'), which positioned one of its products as appropriate for young people around the world; Philips ('Let's Make Things Better'), whose advertisements explicitly feature people from different countries; and Benetton ('The United Colors of Benetton'), whose slogan emphasizes the unity of humankind.

Similarly, a local consumer culture positioning (LCCP) strategy is also adhered to sometimes. This strategy is defined as one that associates the brand with local cultural meanings, reflects the local culture's norms and identities, is portrayed as consumed by local people in the national culture, and/or is depicted as locally produced for local people. Examples of brands that have utilized this strategy include Chevy Trucks and Dr Pepper soft drinks. They have been positioned in the USA as part of the 'American' way of life.

The third type of consumer culture positioning is the foreign consumer culture positioning (FCCP) strategy. It is defined as a strategy that positions the brand as symbolic of a specific foreign consumer culture. In other words, where a brand's personality, use occasion, and/or user group is associated with a foreign culture. An example of this can be found in the use of 'Singapore Girl' of Singapore Airlines. Since language, English in particular, provides modernism and internationalism to the consumers, one way of effective GCCP communication is to use English words, written and/or spoken, in its communications. Similarly, a brand manager incorporating LCCP would want to highlight the local language, and a brand manager intending to highlight FCCP may use spoken and written words from the foreign culture in its advertising and/or brand name.

Apart from the three culture positioning strategies, an alternative consumer positioning strategy may include the esthetic construction and display of brand logos. For instance, certain logos such as AT&T (abstract globe), Nike (swoosh), Royal Dutch/Shell (shell), and Mercedes-Benz (three-pointed star) signify that the brands are less related to their specific cultures in terms of their appearance. Therefore, it is crucial for managers to ascertain the country, consumer segment, and product category factors in order to come up with a suitable strategy that would convey their brand(s) effectively to the targeted audience.

SUMMARY

International marketing research, therefore, links the organization with its future markets. The basic activities of such an exercise include specification of the research problem, data collection, data analysis, interpretation of results, and developing effective cross-cultural strategies. This will help the management understand a particular market, identify the market-specific problems and opportunities, and develop the future course of marketing action. International marketing research has grown in popularity and need over the last two decades. However, over the last few years, it has had a major leap forward and has a promising future. This is due to the increasing privatization of world economy; an array of innovations that have invaded the marketplace; more companies looking at the world market to export and import products and services; and the technological advancements that continue to drive the Internet. These are bound to drive very many research projects that cut across diverse cultures and markets. This includes the developing world that is fast becoming an attractive business prospect for corporations.

In their recently published book, Mahajan and Banga (2005) have argued that most global corporations focus on selling their products and services to the richest 14 per cent of the world's population, who reside in the developed world, while the opportunities provided by the remaining 86 per cent – the developing economies – have not been capitalized on enough. When entering developing economies, their complex and distinctive characteristics pose a major challenge to the companies. These developing economies are characterized by emigrations to developed economies; fragmented markets; weak distribution networks; underdeveloped technology; and a sizeable youth population. Despite these issues, these markets provide a major business opportunity to corporations. For instance, while selling shampoo and detergent for a nickel may seem like a distraction from the high-priced items of developed markets, these sachets account for more than $1bn in annual sales in India for Hindustan Lever (subsidiary of Unilever) alone.

In a similar approach it was proposed that companies take cognizance of the bottom of the economic pyramid, as doing business with the world's 4 billion poorest people – two-thirds of the world's population – will require radical innovations in technology and business models (Prahalad 2006).

The economic pyramid captures the distribution of wealth and the capacity to generate incomes in the world. At the top of the pyramid are the wealthy, with numerous opportunities for generating high levels of income. More than 4 billion people live at the bottom of the pyramid (BOP) on less than $2 per day. This approach proposes that corporations can successfully create markets at the BOP that can also help to eradicate poverty. The reason for pursuing this BOP is two-fold. Firstly, the poor represent a 'latent market' for goods and services. Engaging private enterprises at the BOP is a critical element in creating inclusive capitalism, as private sector competition for this market will foster attention to the poor as consumers. Secondly, the BOP, as a market, provides a new growth opportunity for the private sector and a forum for innovations. For instance, Bangladeshi women entrepreneurs do a brisk business by renting out their cell phones by the minute to other villagers. It is estimated that the poor in Bangladesh spend as much as 7 per cent of their income on means of communications.

With such exciting options opening up for furthering business activities across national boundaries, researching developing markets will be a challenge as they have to be studied in a whole new light. Therefore, the key takeaway point from a researcher's viewpoint is to take cognizance of the fact that these markets are constantly growing and transforming. In order to have a successful presence in such economies, a thorough understanding of the local economy and an appropriate research structure and design of the study is critical.

This chapter has discussed the various issues that would come in the way of international marketing research, and the ways in which the issues can be sorted out. The philosophical and methodological issues discussed in this chapter are intrinsic to any international research study, and the researcher will have to solve the issues so that the research study can yield a marketing strategy that will be both applicable and successful.

ACKNOWLEDGMENT

The author wishes to thank Bharath Rajan and Sarang Sunder for their assistance in the preparation of this chapter. The author owes additional thanks to Renu for copyediting this manuscript.

REFERENCES

Aaker, D. A., Kumar, V. and Day, G. S. (2006) *Marketing Research*, 9th edn. Hoboken, NJ: John Wiley & Sons, Inc.

Aiken, L. S. and West, S. G. (1991) *Multiple Regression: Testing and Interpreting Interactions*. Newbury Park, CA: Sage.

Alden, D. L., Steenkamp, J.-B. E.M. and Batra, R. (1999) 'Brand positioning through advertising in Asia, North America and Europe: the role of global consumer culture', *Journal of Marketing*, 63: 75–87.

Baumgartner, H. and Steenkamp, J.-B.E.M. (2001) 'Response styles in marketing research: a cross-national investigation', *Journal of Marketing Research*, 38: 143–156.

Bond, M. H. (1988) 'Finding universal dimensions of individual variation in multicultural studies of values: the Rokeach and Chinese values surveys', *Journal of Personality and Social Psychology*, 55: 1009–1015.

Burns, E. (website). 'Local search to hit $13B by 2010,' Retrieved June 5, 2007, from http://www.clickz.com/showPage.html?page=3585511

Butcher, J. N., Lim, J. and Nezami, E. (1998). 'Objective study of abnormal personality in cross-cultural settings: the Minnesota Multiphasic Personality Inventory (MMPI-2)', *Journal of Cross-Cultural Psychology*, 29: 189–211.

Cateora, P. R. and Graham, J. L. (1999) *International Marketing*, 10th edn. Boston, MA: Irwin Mcgraw Hill.

Cheung, G. W. and Rensvold, R. B. (2000) 'Assessing extreme and acquiescence response sets in cross-cultural research using structural equations modeling', *Journal of Cross-Cultural Psychology*, 31: 160–186.

Crimp, M. and Wright, L. T. (1995) *The Marketing Research Process*, 4th edn. Herefordshire: Prentice Hall.

De Jong, M. G., Steenkamp, J.-B. E. M., Fox, J.-P. and Baumgartner, H. (forthcoming). 'Using item response theory to measure extreme response style in marketing research: A global investigation', *Journal of Marketing Research*.

Ellison, S. (2005, July 14) 'Studying messy habits to sweep up a market,' *Wall Street Journal*. pp. B–1.

Fischer, R. (2004) 'Standardization to account for cross-cultural response bias', *Journal of Cross-Cultural Psychology*, 35: 263–282.

Frost, R. (September 22, 2003) 'Who is securing your identity on-line?' http://www.brandchannel.com/features_effect.asp?pf_id=177

Hicks, L. E. (1970) 'Some properties of ipsative, normative and forced-choice normative measures', *Psychological Bulletin*, 74: 167–184.

Hoffman, T. (2005, 27 June) 'Harrah's bets on loyalty program in Caesars deal', *ComputerWorld*. pp. 10.

Hofstede, G. (1980) *Culture's Consequences: International Differences in Work Related Values*. Beverly Hills, CA: Sage.

Hofstede, G. (2001) *Culture's Consequences: Comparing Values, Behaviors, Institutions, and Organizations Across Nations*, 2nd edn. Thousand Oaks, CA: Sage.

Howell, D. C. (1997) *Statistical Methods for Psychology*. Belmont, CA: Duxbury Press.

Huang, C. D., Church, A. T. and Katigbak, M. S. (1997). 'Identifying cultural differences in items and traits: differential item functioning in the NEO personality inventory', *Journal of Cross-Cultural Psychology*, 28: 192–218.

Hunt, S., Sparkman, R. D. and Wilcox, J. B. (1982) 'The pretest in survey research: Issues and preliminary findings', *Journal of Marketing Research*, (May), 19(2): 269–273.

India Herald (1998) Adapted from India Herald 22 May 1998, p. 27.

Jacobs, L., Keown, C., Worthley, R. and Ghymn, K.I. (1991) 'Cross-cultural comparisons: global marketers beware', *International Marketing Review*, 8(3): 21–30.

Know India (website). 'India at a glance', Retrieved June 5, 2007, from http://india.gov.in/knowindia/india_at_a_glance.php

Kumar, V. (2000) *International Marketing Research*. Upper Saddle River, NJ: Prentice Hall.

Leslie, E. (1992) 'Some observations on doing business in Japan', *Business America*, 113(3), 2–4.

Leung, K. and Bond, M. H. (1989) 'On the empirical identification of dimensions for cross-cultural comparisons', *Journal of Cross-Cultural Psychology*, 20: 133–151.

Little, T. D. (1997) 'Mean and covariance structures (MACS) analysis of cross-cultural data: practical and theoretical issues', *Multivariate Behavioral Research*, 32: 53–76.

Little, T. D. (2000) 'On the comparability of constructs in cross-cultural research: a critique of Cheung and Rensvold', *Journal of Cross-Cultural Psychology*, 31: 213–219.

Mahajan, V. and Banga, K. (2005) *The 86% Solution: How to Succeed in the Biggest Market Opportunity of the 21st Century*. New Jersey, Wharton School Publishing.

Marketing News (2005) 'World's on-line population estimates', *Marketing News*, 15 July, 2005, p. 28.

Min-Han, Lee and Ro (1994) 'The choice of survey mode in country image studies', *Journal of Business Research*, 29(2) 151–162.

Monk D. (1987) 'Marketing research in Canada', *European Research*, 271-274.

Narayana, C. L. (1977) 'Graphic positioning scale: An economical instrument for surveys', *Journal of Marketing Research*, 14: 118–122. Also see S. I. Lampert (1979). 'The attitude pollimeter: A new attitude scaling device', *Journal of Marketing Research*, 578–582.

Paulhus, D. L. (1991) 'Measurement and control of response bias', in J. P. Robinson, P. R. Shaver and L. S. Wright (eds.), *Measures of Personality and Social Psychological Attitudes*. San Diego, CA: Academic Press, pp. 17–59.

Prahalad, C. K. (2006) *The Fortune at the Bottom of the Pyramid: Eradicating Poverty Through Profits*. New Jersey, NJ: Wharton School Publishing.

Privacyrights (website) 'How many identity theft victims are there?', Retrieved 5 June, 2007, from http://www.privacyrights.org/ar/idtheftsurveys.htm

Rainee, L. and Hitlin, P. (website). 'The use of on-line reputation and rating systems', Retrieved 5 June, 2007, from http://www.pewinternet.org/PPF/r/140/report_display.asp

Sager, I. (1997, 2 June) 'The stealth computer – Annual design awards', *Business Week*, 103.

Sopariwala, D. (1987) 'India: Election polling in the world's largest democracy', *European Research*, 174–177.

Usunier, J.-C. (1996) *Marketing Across Cultures*, 2nd edn. Herefordshire: Prentice Hall.

Visionarymarketing (website) 'Lost in translation', Retrieved 5 June, 2007, from http://www.visionarymarketing.com/articles/lostin translation

Wool, B. (website). 'Local content is king', Retrieved 5 June, 2007, from http://www.clickz.com/showPage.html?page=3625234

Changing Market Environments

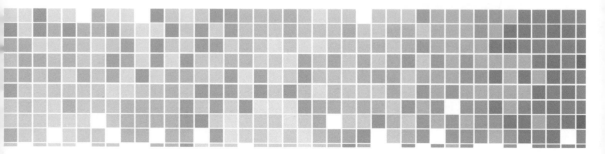

Capturing Market
Requirements

8

Research into Exporting: Theoretical, Methodological, and Empirical Insights

Constantine S. Katsikeas, Leonidas C. Leonidou, and Saeed Samiee

INTRODUCTION

Exporting is the foreign market entry mode most commonly adopted by business organizations aiming to grow and develop in international markets and operations. As opposed to foreign direct investment methods (e.g., licensing, joint venturing, and wholly owned production) export engagement requires lower fixed and operating costs, involves fewer resource commitments, and exposes the firm to lower business risks. Exporting is a highly desirable business activity as it can assist companies (especially small- to medium-sized ones) in: (1) improving their financial position through more sales revenues and profits; (2) accumulating valuable marketing experience by operating in difficult and multifarious markets; (3) transferring innovative technologies and know-how from more advanced and sophisticated environments; and (4) exploiting idle operating capacity and improving production efficiency (Czinkota and Ronkainen 2006). Furthermore, increased emphasis on globalization demands

that firms rationalize their international production and supply markets through exporting. Automobile manufacturers provide an excellent example in this regard. German car manufacturers, Mercedes Benz and BMW, for example, manufacture several globally popular models only in the USA and supply all other markets through exporting. These beneficial outcomes can in turn help firms strengthen their competitive edge and achieve sustainable growth.

However, firms engage in exporting for a variety of reasons and a number of theories have attempted to explain this activity. There is a consensus, however, among experts that firms, particularly small- and medium-sized ones, often engage in exporting reactively rather than pursuing a proactive and conscious strategic thrust intended to make them international (Leonidou, Katsikeas, Palihawadana and Spyropoulou 2007). The reasons frequently cited by firms for initially engaging in exporting include receiving an unsolicited order from abroad, manufacturing overcapacity and/or excess inventory, domestic economic downturns, intense domestic competition (especially from foreign firms) and request/demand by an important domestic customer who is moving abroad. It is thus not surprising that exporting is the oldest and virtually indispensable mode of internationalization.

The theoretical roots of exporting and the question 'Why does exporting exist?' were first addressed by economists, with the pioneering work on absolute advantage by Smith (1776), and the subsequent theories of comparative advantage by Richardo (1817), factor endowments by Ohlin (1933) and Hechesckler (1950), factor prices by Samuelson (1948), demand similarity by Linder (1961), and international product life cycle by Vernon (1966). Although these theories introduced useful knowledge in explaining trade activities between nations, their focus was mainly macro-economic, providing little insight into the way in which

managers operate and the attitudes and behavior of individual business organizations in performing their export activities. As a result, the early 1960s saw the emergence of a new stream of research, which began to examine the exporting phenomenon from a more business-oriented perspective.[1]

During the early years, dozens of exporting studies appeared in various books, academic journals, and business magazines, with their number experiencing an exponential growth over time (see Figure 8.1). Although early studies on exporting (and international marketing) were described as too sporadic, simplistic, and fragmented to yield meaningful and reliable insights into firms' international behavior (Albaum and Peterson 1984), subsequent research has increasingly improved in terms of conceptual thinking and methodological robustness (Cavusgil, Deligonul and Yaprak 2005). These developments were responsible for gradually moving this body

Figure 8.1　Evolution of exporting research (1967–2007)

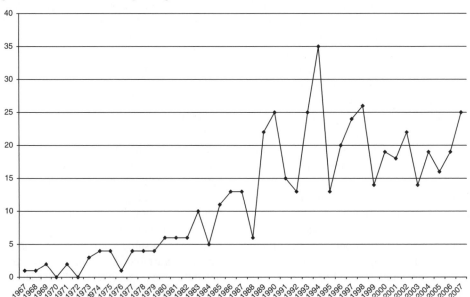

Source: Based on a number of export-related articles published in the *Journal of International Business Studies, Management International Review, Journal of World Business, International Marketing Review, Journal of International Marketing, International Business Review, Journal of Global Marketing*, and *Advances in International Marketing*

of knowledge from an early phase of identification and exploration toward a more advanced stage characterized by maturity and sophistication. While some researchers (e.g., Kamath, Rosson, Patton and Brooks 1987) believe that research on exporting issues has been 'exhausted' (or 'dried-out') in terms of new ideas, thoughts and directions, others (e.g., Leonidou and Katsikeas 2006) argue that exporting research is undergoing a period of 'consolidation' and 'readjustment', in view of new theoretical advancements and practical developments.

In light of this controversy, and taking into consideration the enormous amount of research accumulated on exporting, this chapter aims to shed light on three major areas: (1) to identify the possible theoretical underpinnings of exporting research and suggest possible ways of how theory on the subject can be further advanced in the future; (2) to assess the research methodologies adopted by exporting studies and identify areas that require attention; and (3) to assimilate empirical knowledge of exporting research into well-defined categories and indicate avenues of future investigation. Each of these three objectives will be analyzed separately in the next three sections, while the chapter will end with a set of conclusions and implications.

THEORETICAL UNDERPINNINGS

Much of the exporting research, particularly relatively early work, has often been described as atheoretic, lacking solid theories and conceptual frameworks that could effectively guide researchers (Katsikeas, Leonidou and Morgan 2000). However, there is consensus among various assessments of the empirical literature that the relevance and rigor of exporting research has improved significantly over time (Zou and Stan 1998; Leonidou, Katsikeas and Samiee 2002). A holistic examination of exporting research identifies several paradigms that have played and/or have the potential to play an influential

role in the development of the pertinent literature. These refer to the following: neoclassical economic, transaction cost, resource-based view, industrial organization, political economy, relational, and internationalization (see Table 8.1).

The paradigm that implicitly or explicitly governed many exporting studies is the '*neoclassical micro-economic*'. This paradigm considers the structure of relative prices, market equilibrium, and income distribution as the outcome of the maximizing behavior of individual business organizations (Bucklin 1970; Carman 1980). It also attempts to explain the way in which various business functions are allocated across different institutions, using the achievement of maximum economic efficiency as a fundamental criterion. Although this paradigm is well advanced in terms of scientific rigor, it suffers from a number of shortcomings: (1) strict adherence to logical empiricism, where exporting is examined from a hypothetic-deductive perspective; (2) establishment of association between independent and dependent variables, without any linkage to a wider body of knowledge; and (3) insufficient understanding of various inter-organizational issues (e.g., exchange processes) in export markets (Kamath *et al.* 1987).

The *transaction-cost paradigm* emphasizes the efficiency implications of exporting, which is the result of handling three major dimensions: (a) transaction-specific investments, that is, physical or human resources assigned to a specific export arrangement, necessitating the existence of safeguarding mechanisms that would reduce the risk of subsequent opportunistic exploitation; (b) external uncertainty, that is, the decision environment within which exporter–importer exchanges take place, giving rise to the problem of adapting to unpredictable contingencies; and (c) internal performance ambiguity, that is, ambiguity about the level of performance achieved from exporting, demanding an evaluation to ascertain compliance with the contractual agreement (Williamson 1975; Casson 2005). This paradigm has been used

Table 8.1   Summary of paradigms used in exporting research

Paradigm	Theoretical context	Examples of application areas
Neoclassical micro-economic	Organizations seek to attain maximum economic efficiency by engaging in exporting, through a manipulation of relative prices, market equilibrium, and income distribution, as well as the allocation of various functions across different institutions.	Export initiation Motives and barriers to export Process of export development Adaptation/standardization of export marketing mix and its drivers
Transaction cost	Emphasis on the efficiency implications of exporting, which is the outcome of handling properly transaction-specific investments, external uncertainty of the decision environment, and internal performance ambiguity.	Behavioral aspects of export distribution channels: • Trust • Commitment • Conflict • Satisfaction • Relationship performance
Resource-based view	Stressing the role of the firm's resources and capabilities which are transformed into value offerings. These help create a competitive advantage which in turn will lead to enhanced export performance.	Links between sources of advantage and positional advantages achieved Relationships of competitive advantages and performance outcomes in export ventures
Industrial organization	Export performance is determined essentially by industry structure in the export market and the effective implementation of the export strategy chosen by the firm.	Antecedents and consequences of export marketing strategy: • Relationships of internal and external factors with export marketing program components • Link(s) between export marketing strategy and performance
Political economy	The exporting firm is a social system comprising sets of internal and external forces of an economic and socio-political nature, which affect the collective behavior and performance of the parties involved.	Behavioral aspects of export distribution channels
Relational	Exporting firms are engaged not only in economic transactions, but also in behavioral exchanges. Both exporters and their overseas buyers are equal partners, depending on each other on resources, knowledge, and expertise.	Export initiation Development of export operations Exporter–importer relationships
Internationalization	Exporting is an evolutionary and sequential process, comprising a series of incremental decisions. These decisions are based on an interplay between foreign experiential knowledge and increasing resource commitment.	Pre-export behavior Export development process Foreign market selection Foreign market expansion

particularly in examining the relationships between exporters and their overseas distributors, especially regarding various behavioral dimensions, such as opportunism, uncertainty, and relational investments.

The *resource-based view* stresses the importance of the firm's resources and capabilities as a key to understanding business performance (e.g., Pieffer and Salancik 1978; Amit and Shoemaker 1993; Peteraf 1993). In this framework, theoretical work on dynamic capabilities distinguishes between capabilities and other resources available to the firm (Teece, Pisano and Shuen 1997). In the context of exporting, resources are the firm-specific asset stocks that constitute the raw materials available to the export business venture of the firm, whereas capabilities are the processes by which resources are developed, combined, and transformed into value offerings for the export market (Morgan, Kaleka and Katsikeas 2004). This paradigm suggests that firms are idiosyncratic bundles of resources and capabilities that are possessed or are available for deployment by the firm (Conner 1991; Grant 1991). The deployment of superior resources and superior capabilities should lead to the achievement of competitive advantage in the market in which the firm has chosen to operate, and this in turn should enhance performance (Barney 1991). This paradigm was particularly applied by researchers focusing on the export strategy-performance link (e.g., Rodriguez and Rodriguez 2005).

The *industrial organization* paradigm suggests two fundamental sets of factors that drive the export performance of the firm. The first concerns the structural characteristics of the export market (in which the firm has chosen to operate) that determine the degree of competitive intensity experienced by the firm. The second driver refers to the ability of the firm to achieve and sustain an advantage position and superior performance in export market activities through the effective implementation of planned export strategy (Porter 1985; Scherer and Ross 1990). Choice of export strategy is influenced by foreign market imperatives, competitive advantage is derived from implementing this strategy effectively, and superior performance outcomes result from the achievement of positional advantage in the export target market (Collis 1991). This paradigm has been used to examine relationships of external factors with export marketing program elements and export performance and also in association with the resource-based view in order to study antecedents and consequences of export marketing strategy (see, for example, Morgan *et al.* 2004).

The *political economy* paradigm views the firm as a social system comprising interacting sets of major economic and sociopolitical forces which affect the collective behavior and performance of the parties involved (Stern and Reve 1980). In this context, there are four major groups of variables which are likely to influence an exporting situation: internal economy (e.g., the economic structure and processes); internal polity (e.g., the sociopolitical structure and processes); external economy (e.g., the prevailing and prospective economic environment); and external polity (e.g., the external sociopolitical system). Although this paradigm has the potential to explain various aspects of firms' export behavior, it has been used mainly within the domain of export distribution channels (Peng and York 2001).

Another theoretical effort is the *relational paradigm* (Håkansson 1982; Johanson and Mattson 1987; Dyer and Singh 1998), which views exporting as comprising not only economic transactions, which are expressed in terms of exchanging products and money, but also numerous behavioral interactions between the parties which involve information, social, and other intangible elements. According to this paradigm, exporters and their overseas customers are regarded as equal partners who perform various tasks that share great similarities (Cunningham 1980). The trading parties also depend on each other for resources, knowledge, expertise, and other elements important to the establishment and development of the exporter–importer working relationship and, thus, their performance will largely depend on how this relationship is managed (Styles and Ambler 1994).

A final approach refers to *internationalization theory*, which was first expressed by the Uppsala model (Johanson and Vahlne 1977). The roots of this model lie mainly in behavioral theory (Cyert and March 1963) and the theory of the growth of the firm (Penrose 1995). According to this theory the firm's involvement in export activities is seen as an evolutionary and sequential process, which is based on a series of incremental decisions. This is largely attributed to the interplay between the development of experiential knowledge of foreign markets and operations, on the one hand, and the increasing commitment of organizational resources, on the other (Johanson and Vahlne 1977). This conceptualization has served as a platform for long-standing contributions on pre-export behavior, export motivations, choice of export markets, foreign market entry, and other aspects of company internationalization.

RESEARCH METHODOLOGIES

The bulk of exporting research has been mainly of an empirical nature, denoting a tendency among researchers to acquire more 'hands-on', experiential knowledge about export-related issues. This can be mainly attributed to the existence of limited theoretical knowledge on the subject, and the subsequent need to explore the applicability of ideas and concepts developed in more advanced disciplines. In the sections that follow, an attempt is made to evaluate the methodologies adopted by empirical studies on exporting in five broad areas: scope of research, sampling frames, constructs and research tools, data collection, and analytical methods (see Table 8.2).

Scope of research

Research into exporting was mainly rooted in the United States, as a reflection of the leading role that this country began to play in international trade soon after the end of the Second World War, along with the availability

Table 8.2   Methodological developments of exporting research

Methodological aspects	Early exporting research	Late exporting research
Scope of research	Main focus on North America – Emphasis on single country settings (and even regions within country) – Coverage of both consumer and industrial goods – Use of multiple industry settings – Emphasis on small-to- medium sized firms	Gradual shift of research to European and other countries – Small increase in multi-country studies – Emphasis on both consumer and industrial products – Increasing coverage of many industries – In addition to smaller firms, some attention to larger firms
Sampling frames	Focus mainly on exporters (and to a lesser extent on non-exporters) – In many cases the sampling method was not disclosed – Mainly small samples (<99 units)	Greater attention to the export venture as the unit of analysis – Greater use of probabilistic methods – Emphasis on mid-sized samples (100–500 units)
Constructs and research tools	Mainly studies of an exploratory nature – Arbitrary selection of constructs and weak operationalizations – Using mainly dichotomous scales – Extensive use of open-ended questions – Limited evidence for questionnaire pre-testing	Mainly studies adopting a formalized approach – More robust operationalization of constructs – Using mainly interval and ratio scales – Extensive use of pre-coded questions – Greater attention to questionnaire pre-testing
Data collection	Data were collected using mainly mail surveys – Response rates were relatively low – Lack of testing for non-response bias – CEO/president was the most common source for obtaining data	Mail surveys still have a dominant role in data collection – Improvement in response rates – Tendency to check for non-response bias – Export executives/marketing managers and owners are the most common key informants
Analytical methods	Minimal attention to the reliability and validity of the measures used – Extensive use of descriptive statistics and simple statistical analyses	Increasing reporting of the reliability of the scales used, and attention to measure validation – Use of multivariate statistical methods and structural equation modeling

of researchers with an interest in studying the subject.[2] However, there was a gradual shift in this research to European countries (especially the UK) and more recently to other regions (e.g., South East Asia, Oceania, and South America). Hence, today there is universal concern about export-related issues, which is consistent with the globalization trends in the world economy. Irrespective of the geographic region, the bulk of exporting research was conducted in single-country settings, although there has been a growing tendency for more multi-country studies. In terms of product focus, the majority of studies covered multiple industries, involving both consumer and industrial goods. Only a few studies have examined firms' exporting behavior by industry type, thereby minimizing the effects of industry- and product-specific factors. Surprisingly, the exporting of services, although experiencing serious growth in international business in the last few decades, was virtually neglected by researchers in the field. Small- to medium-sized manufacturers provided the focus of exporting research, mainly because governments around the globe have instituted a variety of programs to encourage export-inactive firms to consider exporting as an attractive growth alternative. These comprehensive programs often provide the means to conduct export-relevant research aimed at assisting these firms. Additionally, smaller firms' limited financial, human, and allied resources make exporting a more attractive approach to entering foreign markets, as compared with other more costly methods (e.g., foreign production) available to larger firms.

Sampling frames

The nature of exporting research is such that the unit of analysis in the overwhelming majority of cases has been the exporting firm and, to a lesser extent, strategic business units comprising large corporations. Recently some researchers (e.g., Cavusgil and Zou 1994; Morgan *et al.* 2004) have concentrated on a specific export venture (that is, a specific product or line exported to a particular foreign market), in order to avoid problems in the analysis caused by the diversity of foreign market environments and different products that a firm might export. Firms selling their goods solely in the domestic market provided the focus of a few studies, usually aiming to examine pre-export behavior issues. In the majority of studies, research samples were extracted using probabilistic methods (mainly stratified random), while non-probability samples (mainly judgemental) were less frequently employed. In some studies, the small size of the target population permitted the contacting of all firms in the target group. Sample sizes rarely exceeded the 500 mark, and in the majority of cases these were within the 150–300 range. This in part reflects relatively low response rates in some research. It would also be the result of the difficulty associated with obtaining an adequate sample of firms engaged in exporting, which is particularly problematic in less developed and emerging markets where accurate and up-to-date directories are less common. On the other hand, the use of relatively small sample sizes may question the external validity of the study findings, especially in the case of countries with a large population of exporters (e.g., the USA, the UK, and Germany) and industrial sectors incorporating a large number of firms (e.g., foodstuffs, wearing apparel, and electronics). The problem of having representative samples is even more acute, taking into consideration the fact that most studies adopted a local (e.g., a specific state or region), rather than a nationwide, perspective in drawing their samples.

Constructs and research tools

Initial studies on exporting were mainly of an exploratory nature, aiming to capture certain aspects of this business phenomenon. As such, these studies were characterized by an arbitrary selection of constructs which were inadequately operationalized. With the accumulation of more knowledge on the subject, however, studies increasingly adopted a more formalized approach and tried to use and augment constructs introduced by previous research efforts. For instance, while early studies used 5–8 items to capture export stimulation, more recent studies employed as many as 30 items. However, there are still several constructs in the exporting literature (e.g., psychic distance, export involvement, and export performance) that lack relative uniformity and convergence in operationalization. These developments in construct definition and operationalization were inevitably reflected in the design of the questionnaires used, which have also shown a constant improvement over time. For example, there has been a gradual shift from dichotomous to ordinal scales, from open-ended to pre-coded questions, and from few to many measures of firm characteristics.

Data collection

The principal method for collecting data in exporting research has been through mail surveys. This was followed by personal interviews, which were more frequently used in the case of studies using quite lengthy semi-structured questionnaires or adopting a case study research approach. Drop-in questionnaires were utilized on a less frequent basis and telephone interviews were the least employed, probably due to the difficulties involved in first asking and then recording the answers to questions concerning complicated exporting issues. Notably, some recent studies used electronic surveys for data collection purposes, and it seems that this contact method has the potential to gain momentum in the future due to its lower cost, wider reach, and faster response. The average response rates in exporting studies could be described as less than ideal (which has to

exceed 50 per cent (Mangione 1995)), this being mainly attributable to the use of mail surveys as the dominant form of data collection. Not surprisingly, higher response rates were observed in the case of face-to-face interviews as opposed to mail surveys. Notably, only a few studies, especially the most recent ones, have undertaken tests for non-response bias, usually following the procedure recommended by Armstrong and Overton (1977). This finding, coupled with the low response rates mentioned earlier, casts some doubt as to the representative status of the samples used in many studies. Key informants were mainly the CEO or the owner of the company, which can be attributed to the comparatively small size of the firms under study. Export officers and marketing managers provided two other types of informants on exporting issues. With few exceptions, assessment of key informant competency was virtually neglected in export studies.

Analytical methods

Due to simple operationalizations of the constructs used in the early phases of exporting research, little attention was devoted to examining aspects of reliability and validity of the measures. However, recent studies have increasingly followed rigorous measure validation procedures, helping in this way the development of scales that could be useful for subsequent research efforts in the field. With regard to the analytical methods used, early research was characterized by the extensive use of descriptive statistics (e.g., percentage frequencies, mean scores, and cross-tabulations) and simple statistical analyses (e.g., Chi-square, Pearson correlations, and Student-t). More recent work has deployed multivariate analytical methods (e.g., factor analysis, multiple regression, and MANOVA) and structural equation modeling (using LISREL, EQS, or AMOS). Obviously, this reflects a change in research designs from more exploratory and descriptive studies toward more formalized and causal approaches.

EMPIRICAL KNOWLEDGE

Empirical knowledge on exporting has increased considerably over time, both in terms of breadth and depth. Three major factors were responsible for this: (1) the transfer of ideas, concepts, and techniques developed within other business and non-business disciplines; (2) the execution of review studies that consolidated exporting knowledge and allowed researchers to build on earlier findings; and (3) the emergence of new publication outlets, especially since the early 1980s, specializing in international business or marketing. This section provides an overview of the evolution of exporting knowledge over time. A distinction is pursued among the early, intermediate, and late phases of exporting research (see Table 8.3).

Early phases of exporting research (mid-1960s to early 1980s)

Early research on exporting took three major directions. The first direction tried to analyze exporting from the perspective of firms located in a specific country or groups of countries. For instance, some studies (e.g.,

Table 8.3   Evolution of exporting knowledge

Phases	Thematic areas	Specific issues
Initial	○ Analysis of exports at country level	Exports from Japan Exports from LDCs and NICs Agricultural exports
	○ Export promotion/assistance	Awareness/usage/effectiveness Export promotion organizations
	○ Why, how, or where firms export	Export intention/propensity Attitudes toward exports Export stimulation Barriers to exporting Export development models
Intermediate	○ Determinants of export behavior	Environmental forces Organizational factors Managerial characteristics
	○ Export information/research	Information needs Information sources Information use
	○ Export strategy	Adaptation versus standardization NPD, branding, product elimination Pricing approaches, financing methods Channels, middlemen, freight forwarding Promotion mix, media habits, salesforce
	○ Exporter-importer relationships	Trust, opportunism, commitment Control, communication, satisfaction
Late	○ Export performance	Performance measurement Drivers of performance
	○ Export competitive advantage	Resources and capabilities Competitive strategy Performance outcomes
	○ Contemporary exporting aspects	Organizational learning Export market orientation Internet exporting Interfunctional interactions

Sarathy 1986) focused on the growing success of Japanese firms in international markets, while others (e.g., Wortzel and Wortzel 1981) examined exporting from developing and newly industrialized countries. There were also studies focusing on agricultural exports (e.g., Ayal and Hirsch 1982), mainly due to the fact that, in the 1960s, this was the economic sector that played a key role in the prosperity of many countries. To some extent, this line of research could best be described as an application of international trade issues within a micro-business domain.

The second direction examined the offering of export promotion programs in assisting indigenous manufacturers to initiate exports and/or develop successful operations in export markets. This is due to the fact that exporting is highly regarded as a crucial economic activity by many public policy-makers, because it is a serious source of foreign exchange, provides many employment opportunities, encourages backward and forward linkages, and releases resources to support other economic activities. Export promotion research was particularly centered on the awareness, usage, and effectiveness of various export promotion programs, as well as the ability of various governmental and other agencies to successfully design and deliver these programs (e.g., Czinkota and Ricks 1981).

The third stream tried to answer questions regarding why, how, or where business firms export. In this context, studies addressed one or more of the following research issues/areas:

- Export intention/propensity: Here the emphasis was mainly on the pre-export activity of firms, as well as on the preconditions for engaging in export operations. Concepts like previous extra-regional expansion (e.g., Wiederscheim-Paul, Olson and Welch 1978), future export intention (e.g., Simpson and Kujawa 1974), and the consideration of exporting as an innovative activity (e.g., Lee and Brasch 1978), were among those employed to help understand why some firms avoid exporting, while others are more inclined to sell abroad.
- Attitudes toward export: Many researchers (e.g., Cavusgil, Bilkey and Tesar 1979) also tried to

investigate specific attitudes toward export, including risk, costs, and profits, and how these discriminate between domestic versus exporting firms, as well as between various groups of exporters, such as passive versus aggressive, sporadic versus regular, and neophyte versus experienced.
- Export stimulation: Factors stimulating firms to initiate and subsequently develop exports were widely studied (for a review, see Leonidou 1995a). Depending on their location these were grouped into internal (e.g., managerial interest) and external (e.g., unsolicited orders), while based on their responsiveness they were classified into proactive (e.g., possession of a unique product) and reactive (e.g., competitive pressures).
- Barriers to exporting: This is one of the most commonly researched areas, focusing on the identification of the obstacles encountered by firms when performing their exporting activities (e.g., for a review, see Leonidou 1995b). These barriers can be internal (e.g., limited financial resources) or external (e.g., fierce competition), and found in the domestic (e.g., unfavorable home rules and regulations) or foreign (e.g., high tariffs/non-tariffs) environment of the firm.
- Export development models: A number of models attempted to provide a comprehensive approach to explain how firms engage, grow, and develop in exporting (for a review, see Leonidou and Katsikeas 1996). Researchers commonly offered a stage-wise explanation, viewing export development as a progressive interaction between the acquisition of experiential knowledge and commitment of resources to foreign markets and operations. They also emphasized the firm's gradual entrance into psychologically more distant markets, as well as the greater adaptation to and control over export marketing programs.

Intermediate phases of exporting research (mid-1980s to mid-1990s)

The focus of exporting research gradually shifted emphasis to other issues, which can be broadly defined as drivers of export behavior. One stream of research examined the influential role of environmental, organizational, and managerial factors. The environment comprises forces that can have a broad (e.g., sociocultural) or close (e.g., competition) effect on various aspects of the firm's export activities (e.g., Rao, Erramilli and Ganesh 1990). Environmental effects on exporting include, *inter alia*, domestic economic recession, the inhibiting role of regulatory forces, and the political risk in foreign markets. Organizational factors were among the most widely researched influences on firms' export behavior (for a review, see Leonidou 1998). These consist of four major groups, namely company characteristics (e.g., firm size), operating elements (e.g., product characteristics), enterprise resources (e.g., financial means), and business objectives (e.g., growth objective). Of these, the most widely researched is company size, revealing mixed findings regarding its impact on various facets of exporting. Managerial determinants of exporting also constituted a major area of research, as demonstrated by the dozens of studies that have been conducted on the subject (for a review, see Leonidou, Katsikeas and Piercy 1998). These referred to either objective (e.g. age) or subjective (e.g., risk perception) characteristics of the decision-maker, as well as to managerial traits that can have either a specific (e.g., foreign language ability) or general (e.g., quality and dynamism) association with exporting.

Export information/marketing research provided the second systematic area of research, although the issue of information has been peripherally tackled in earlier studies on exporting (for a review, see Leonidou and Theodosiou 2004). The emphasis was on export information needs (relating to the broad environment, task environment, the foreign market, and the marketing mix), export information sources (e.g., company efforts, other firms/individuals, commercial associations, service organizations, information providers, and government outlets), and export information use (e.g., instrumental, conceptual, or symbolic). Export information was repeatedly stressed to provide the basis for effectively targeting foreign markets, an area of research which also grew during this phase.

In particular, the emphasis was on identifying and evaluating the attractiveness of prospective foreign markets.

Another research area which experienced significant growth during this phase relates to export strategy, with particular reference to the elements of the export marketing program. The issue that attracted focal attention is the degree of standardizing (i.e., offering the same marketing program across export markets as that used in the domestic market) or adapting (i.e., customizing marketing program elements to the particular requirements of overseas markets) the export marketing strategy (e.g., Cavusgil and Naidu 1993). Other issues that have been researched concern elements of the export marketing program, including: (a) new product development, branding strategy, and product elimination (e.g., Atuahene-Gima 1995); (b) pricing approaches and methods of export financing (e.g., Thach and Axinn 1991); (c) types of export channels, selection of export middlemen, and freight forwarding (e.g., Ramasesham and Patton 1994); and (d) promotion mix, media habits, and sales organization effectiveness (e.g., Cavusgil, Zou and Naidu 1993). Of all dimensions of export marketing strategy, distribution was the most widely studied, while the least attention was given to promotion (probably due to the limited promotional activity undertaken by smaller companies in export markets).

A final stream of research examined behavioral aspects of buyer–seller relationships in foreign markets, focusing on a variety of dimensions including trust, opportunism, commitment, communication, satisfaction, and power (e.g., Raven, Tansuihaj and McCullough 1993). These aspects were particularly examined within the context of the working relationship between the exporting manufacturers and their overseas distributors. Empirical studies on cross-border exchange relations have been influenced by concepts and general knowledge advanced within the well-developed domain of interorganizational relationships in the domestic market.

Late phases of exporting research (mid-1990s to the present)

The dominant topic of the most recent research effort on exporting is the *export performance*, which is viewed as the outcome of five major sets of influential factors, namely, managerial (e.g., personal, experiential, attitudinal, and behavioral), organizational (e.g., size, operations, resources, and objectives), environmental (e.g., task and macro-environment), target marketing (e.g., market identification and selection), and marketing program (e.g., product, price, distribution, and promotion) (for a review, see Zou and Stan 1998). An interesting aspect of this line of research is the identification of factors that are conducive to superior export performance, as well as the way in which performance has been operationalized (Madsen 1997; Shoham 1998; Lages and Lages 2004). Katsikeas *et al.*' s (2000) review identified 42 different performance indicators that were used in exporting research, of which 23 were of an economic nature (e.g., sales-related, profit-related, market share-related), 14 were non-economic measures (e.g., product-related, market-related, miscellaneous), and the remaining five were general in nature (e.g., perceived success, achievement of objectives, performance satisfaction). Despite this wide array of measures, most of the studies neither employ multidimensional measures of performance, nor conceptualize performance within the right frame of reference, stakeholder perspective, and time horizon.

An issue that has recently attracted considerable empirical attention concerns the achievement and sustainability of competitive advantage in export markets. Drawing primarily from the strategy literature, different types of resources and capabilities have been identified that play an important role in the achievement of a competitive advantage position and superior performance in export ventures. To create and sustain competitive advantage, export venture resources and capabilities must have four important attributes: they must be valuable, rare, inimitable, and non-substitutable (e.g., Barney 1991; Collis 1991; Zou, Fang and Zhao 2003). In this context, most studies have examined the relationships of certain types of resources and/or capabilities with specific types of export positional advantages and individual export performance dimensions. Interestingly, drawing from the resource-based view of the firm and industrial organization theory, Morgan *et al.* (2004) developed and tested an integrated model of drivers and performance outcomes of export competitive advantage at a high level of abstraction (theoretical level).

Other areas of exporting research have recently emerged that draw mainly from knowledge developed in the mainstream management and marketing literature. One stream of research focuses on the role of *organizational learning* in influencing firms' export behavior and performance. Export growth and development is viewed as a process of learning and knowledge accumulation, which in turn affects performance in export markets and operations (Yeoh 2004). Drivers of organizational learning in exporting have been identified and consistent support for a positive association of organizational learning with export venture performance provided.

Another group of studies examines the role of antecedents and consequences of *export market orientation*. Cadogan and associates (2001, 2002) suggest several important factors (e.g., export coordination, export leadership, export systems and structures, and exporting experience) in influencing the development of export market-oriented behavior. Such behavior, in turn, have been found to influence different aspects of export performance.

A distinct group of studies investigates the significance of *Internet exporting*, with emphasis on the factors that determine success in adopting the Internet as a channel to export markets. Evidence suggests that commitment to the Internet facilitates successful exporting (Andersen 2005). Integration of such technology into export marketing activities leverages the influence of a firm's export orientation on its marketing competences and this, in turn, positively impacts export performance (Prasad, Ramamurthy and Naidu 2001).

Research has also been conducted on *interfunctional interactions* between the export department and other functional areas, with attention to connectedness and conflict issues (Cadogan *et al.* 2005). Export commitment, organizational training and reward systems, relative functional identification, centralization, and employee job satisfaction and commitment have been found to be key drivers of successful interfunctional interactions. Conditions have also been identified under which connectedness and conflict influence firms' export performance.

Finally, some researchers (e.g., Moen 2002) have tried to explain the issue of 'born globals' (or 'instant internationals'), that is newly established firms with a significant involvement in exporting. This phenomenon has been facilitated recently by various trends, such as the increasing importance of niche markets in various countries, the opportunities associated with the rapid advances in communication technology, and the increasing role of global networks and alliances (Knight and Cavusgil 1996). The issue of 'born globals' has been examined from a number of perspectives, with particular attention being given to entrepreneurial-related factors (McAuley 1999).

CONCLUSIONS AND IMPLICATIONS

Almost 40 years after its inception, exporting literature has managed to reach a level of maturity and sophistication, allowing it to stand on its own as a discipline within the overall sphere of international marketing/business. This has helped shed light on many aspects of this important foreign market entry and expansion mode, which have been useful to business practitioners (especially those managing firms of smaller size), public policymakers (particularly those

responsible for designing and implementing export promotion programs), and academic researchers (interested mainly in marketing, management, and international business). Despite these developments, the exporting field still has room for proliferation on theoretical, methodological, and empirical grounds.

From the *theoretical* perspective, the exporting literature has gradually changed its atheoretic status to one characterized by an increasing employment of theoretical paradigms originating mainly in the strategic management and marketing fields. Despite this paradigmatic diversity, the exporting area still lacks clear mid-level theories that would help raise its level of conceptual advancement. A number of measures could be taken toward this end: (1) establishing a central academic body or institute with the goal of fostering academic thought on exporting and, importantly, assisting in the development of universal definitions, terms, and concepts; (2) encouraging future research to adopt more causal and theoretically anchored research designs that would link concepts which are currently fragmented and scattered into an integrated theoretical framework; (3) conducting studies with a more qualitative orientation, focusing on in-depth interviews with managers, focus group discussions, and other methods (e.g., case studies) that will help bring to the surface issues that are often not transparent in quantitative research; and (4) cultivating an approach among researchers which builds on the findings of previous research and makes use of the various review assessments of exporting research taking place at regular intervals.

From the *methodological* standpoint, exporting research has made great strides as studies with simplistic and scientifically indefensible methodologies have gradually given way to studies with more sophisticated designs, robustness, and detail. Indeed, current research on exporting employs methodologies which are on a par with those used in studies conducted in more developed fields in marketing and management. However, there is still much room for improvement and attention to the following issues should be high priority for scholars wishing to conduct exporting research: (1) the international nature of exporting necessitates the design of studies that should involve multi-country settings to obtain a cross-cultural validation of findings; (2) research samples for quantitative studies need to become more representative, by increasing, whenever possible, sample sizes to reasonable levels and providing a nationwide coverage of the target countries; (3) scale development for key exporting research constructs has to become more systematic and transparent, and one way to achieve this is through publishing validated construct operationalizations at regular intervals; (4) data collection can now be conducted using electronic means, which would allow faster and higher response from managers irrespective of location; and (5) the recent tendency toward employing rigorous analytical methods, like structural equation modeling, should continue in order to obtain more robust and insightful results in future investigations.

From the *empirical* point of view, research on exporting has taken many diverse directions, with new streams of research developing over time. As a result, 40 years of research has produced a wealth of exporting knowledge which has helped establish its crucial status within the international marketing/business discipline. However, there are a number of research avenues that warrant particular attention: (1) pre-export behavior: the emphasis here should be on the transformation of export intention into actual involvement in exporting, as well as understanding the antecedents and future strategic consequences of this intention; (2) export development: exporting is a developmental process over time and, as such, longitudinal studies are sorely needed to develop a better understanding of, not only the process, but also the profile of firms that tend to make more rapid progress as committed and successful exporters; (3) export business relationships: it is important to realize that both exporters and importers are equally active in interna-

tional business exchanges, and, as such, research should equally focus on both parties and identify the factors that are conducive to superior relationship performance; as such, there is an acute need for dyadic studies that incorporate the conditions, views, and strategies of both exporters and importers; (4) export marketing strategy: although export strategy has been extensively covered in prior studies, future research should focus on the co-alignment or fit between the export marketing program and the environmental context in which it is implemented in order to achieve enhanced export performance outcomes; (5) export performance: multidimensional conceptualizations and operationalizations should be used to assess the complex phenomenon of export performance, which might be viewed as the outcome of a step-wise dynamic process (i.e., sources of advantage → positional advantage → performance).

Exporting is an area of inquiry which has grown rapidly and experienced a phenomenal development over time. It can be safely suggested that it has rightly acquired its own status within the wider international marketing/business domain. However, contrary to some claims that the exporting field has already been exhausted, our view is that there is still much room for development. This can be achieved through a consolidation of knowledge accumulated on the subject, an infusion of ideas, concepts, and theories from other disciplines, and a more systematic assessment of current exporting practice. The usefulness of the results of these efforts could be verified and augmented through input received from scholars specializing in the field, as well as managers involved in export marketing activities. All these will subsequently lead to theory development and practical advancement in this important area of business.

NOTES

1. Since the 1950s, economists have extensively studied exporting from both a macro-economic and a micro-economic perspective, producing a sizeable

number of articles published mainly in economics journals. However, the evaluation of this stream of research is beyond the scope of this chapter which focuses on studies conducted at the business level and published in business journals.

2. A considerable amount of early research on exporting was also conducted in Scandinavian countries by researchers, including Carlson, Johanson, Vahlne and Wiedersheim-Paul, although most of this work was not published in English. A review of Nordic contributions to international business is provided by Björkman and Forsgren (1997).

REFERENCES

Albaum, G. and Peterson, R. A. (1984) 'Empirical research in international marketing: 1976–1982', *Journal of International Business Studies*, Spring/Summer: 161–173.

Amit, R. and Shoemaker, P. J. H. (1993) 'Strategic assets and organizational rents', *Strategic Management Journal*, 14(1): 33–46.

Armstrong, J. S. and Overton, T. S. (1977) 'Estimating non-response bias in mail surveys', *Journal of Marketing Research*, 29(1): 18–34.

Atuahene-Gima, K. (1995) 'The influence of new product factors on export propensity and performance: An empirical analysis', *Journal of International Marketing*, 3(2): 11–28.

Ayal, I. and Hirsch, S. (1982) 'Marketing factors in small country manufactured exports: Are market share and market growth really important?', *Journal of International Business Studies*, Fall: 73–85.

Barney, J. B. (1991) 'Firm resources and sustained competitive advantage', *Journal of Management*, 17(1): 99–120.

Björkman, I. and Forsgren M. (1997) 'Nordic contributions to international business research', in I. Björkman and M. Forsgren (eds), *The Nature of the International Firm*. Copenhagen: Handelshøjkolens Forlag, 11–29.

Bucklin, L. (1970) *Vertical Marketing Systems*. Glenview, IL: Scott Foresman.

Cadogan, J. W., Paul, N. J., Salminen, R. T., Puumalainen, K. and Sundqvist, S. (2001) 'Key antecedents to "export" oriented behaviors: A cross-cultural empirical examination', *International Journal of Research in Marketing*, 18: 261–282.

Cadogan, J. W., Sundqvist, S, Salminen, R. T. and Puumalainen, K. (2002) 'Market-oriented behavior comparing service with product exporters', *European Journal of Marketing*, 36 (9/10): 1076–1102.

Cadogan, J. W., Paul, N. J., Salminen, R. T., Puumalainen, K. and Sundqvist, S. (2005) 'Export marketing, interfunctional interactions, and performance consequences', *Journal of the Academy of Marketing Science*, 33(4): 520–535.

Carman, J. M. (1980) 'Paradigms for marketing theory', in J. N. Sheth, (ed.), *Research in Marketing*, 3. Greenwich, CT: JAI, pp. 1–36.

Casson, M. (2005) Visions of international business', in P. J. Buckley (ed.), *What is International Business?* Palgrave, pp. 30–31.

Cavusgil, S. T. and Zou, S. (1994). 'Marketing strategy-performance relationship: An investigation of the empirical link in export market ventures, *Journal of Marketing*, 58(1): 1–21.

Cavusgil, S. T., Bilkey, W. J. and Tesar, G. (1979) 'A note on the export behavior of firms: exporter profiles', *Journal of International Business Studies*, 10(2): 91–97.

Cavusgil, S. T., Zou, S. and Naidu, G. M. (1993) 'Product and promotion adaptation in export ventures: an empirical investigation', *Journal of International Business Studies*, 24(3): 479–506.

Cavusgil, S. T, Deligonul, S. and Yaprak, A. (2005) 'International marketing as a field of study: a critical assessment of earlier development and a look forward', *Journal of International Marketing*, 13(4): 1–27.

Collis, D. J. (1991) 'A resource-based analysis of global competition: The case of the bearings industry', *Strategic Management Journal*, 12: 49–68.

Conner, K. R. (1991) 'A historical comparison of resource-based theory and five schools of thought within industrial organization economies: do we have a new theory of the firm?', *Journal of Management*, 17(1): 121–154.

Cunningham, M. T. (1980) 'International marketing and purchasing of industrial goods – features of a European research project', *European Journal of Marketing*, 14(5/6): 332–339.

Cyert, R. M. and March, J. G. (1963) *A Behavioral Theory of the Firm*. Englewood Cliffs, NJ, USA: Prentice Hall.

Czinkota, M. R. and Ricks, D. A. (1981) 'Export assistance: Are we supporting the best programs?', *Journal of World Business*, Summer: 73–78.

Czinkota, M. R. and Ronkainen, I. R. (2006) *International Marketing*. USA: Harcourt, Inc.

Dyer, J. H. and Singh, H. (1998) 'The relational view: cooperative strategy and sources of Inter-organizational competitive advantage', *Academy of Management Review*, 23(4): 660–679.

Grant, R. M. (1991) 'The resource-based theory of competitive advantage: Implications for strategy formulation', *California Management Review*, 33(Spring): 114–135.

Håkansson, H. (1982), *International Marketing and Purchasing of Industrial Goods*. Chichester: John Wiley and Sons.

Heckesckler, E. (1950) 'The effects of foreign trade on distribution and income', in H. S. Ellis and L. A. Metzler (eds), *Readings in the Theory of International Trade*. London: Allen and Unwin.

Johanson, J. and Mattson, L. G. (1987) 'Inter-organizational relations in industrial systems: a network approach compared with transaction-cost approach', *International Studies of Management and Organization*, 17(1): 387–393.

Johanson, J. and Vahlne, J. E. (1977) 'The internationalization process of the firm: A model of knowledge development and increasing foreign commitment', *Journal of International Business Studies*, Spring/Summer: 23–32.

Kamath, S., Rosson, P. J., Patton, D. and Brooks, M. (1987) 'Research on success in exporting: Past, present, and future', in P. J. Rosson and S. D. Reid (eds), *Managing Export Entry and Expansion*. New York: Praeger, pp. 398–421.

Katsikeas. C. S., Leonidou, L. C. and Morgan, N. A. (2000) 'Firm-level export performance assessment: review, evaluation, and development', *Journal of the Academy of Marketing Science*, 28(4): 493–511.

Knight, G. A. and Cavusgil, S. T. (1996) 'The born global firm: a challenge to traditional internationalization theory', *Advances in International Marketing*, 8: 11–26.

Lages, L-F. and Lages, C. R. (2004) 'The STEP scale – a measure of short-term export performance improvement', *Journal of International Marketing*, 12(1): 36–56.

Lee, W. Y. and Brasch, J. J. (1978) 'The adoption of export as an innovative strategy', *Journal of International Business Studies*, 9(1): 85–93.

Leonidou, L. C. (1995a) 'Export stimulation research: review, evaluation, and integration', *International Business Review*, 4(2): 133–156.

Leonidou, L. C. (1995b), 'Empirical research on export barriers. Review, assessment, and synthesis', *Journal of International Marketing*, 3(1): 29–43.

Leonidou, L.C. (1998), 'Organizational determinants of exporting', *Management International Review*, 38(1): 7–52.

Leonidou, L. C. and C. S. Katsikeas (1996) 'The export development process: an integrative review of empirical models, *Journal of International Business Studies*, 27(3): 517–531.

Leonidou, L. C. and Theodosiou, M. (2004) 'The export marketing information system: an integration of the extant knowledge', *Journal of World Business*, 39: 12–36.

Leonidou, L. C. and Katsikeas, C. S. (2006) 'Research in export marketing: Evaluation, trends, and future directions', Paper presented at the 35th EMAC Conference, Athens.

Leonidou, L. C., Katsikeas, C. S. and Piercy, N. F. (1998) 'Identifying managerial influences on exporting: past research and future directions', *Journal of International Marketing*, 6(2): 74–102.

Leonidou, L. C., Katsikeas, C. S. and Samiee, S. (2002) 'Marketing strategy determinants of export performance: a meta-analysis', *Journal of Business Research*, 55(1): 51–67.

Leonidou, L. C., Katsikeas, C. S., Palihawadana, D. and Spyropoulou, S. (2007) 'An analytical review of the factors stimulating smaller firms to export: Implications for policy-makers, *International Marketing Review*, 24(6): 735–770.

Linder, S. B. (1961) *An Essay on Trade and Transformation*. New York: Wiley.

McAuley, A. (1999) 'Entrepreneurial instant exporters in the Scottish arts and crafts sector', *Journal of International Marketing*, 7(4): 67–82.

Madsen, T. K. (1987) 'Empirical export performance studies: A review of conceptualizations and findings', *Advances in International Marketing*, 12: 177–198.

Mangione, T. W. (1995) *Mail Surveys: Improving the Quality of Social Research Methods*. Thousand Oaks, CA: Sage Publications.

Moen, Q. (2002) 'The born globals: a new generation of small European exporters', *International Marketing Review*, 19(2): 156–175.

Morgan, N. A., Kaleka, A. and Katsikeas, C. S. (2004) 'Antecedents of export venture performance: a theoretical model and empirical assessment', *Journal of Marketing*, 68(1): 90–108.

Ohlin, B. (1933) *Interregional and International Trade*. Oxford: The University Press.

Peng, M. W. and York, A. S. (2001) 'Behind intermediary performance in export trade: Transactions, agents, and resources', *Journal of International Business Studies*, 32(2): 327–346.

Penrose, E. T. (1995) *The Theory of the Growth of the Firm*, 3rd edn. Oxford: Oxford University Press.

Peteraf, M. (1993) 'The cornerstones of competitive advantage: a resource-based view', *Strategic Management Journal*, 14(3): 179–1991.

Pieffer, J. and Salancik, G. R. (1978) *The External Control of Organizations: a Resource Dependence Perspective*. New York: Harper and Row.

Porter, M. (1985) *Competitive Advantage*. New York: The Free Press.

Prasad, V. K., Ramamurthy, K. and Naidu, G. M. (2001) 'The influence of Internet-marketing integration on marketing competencies and export performance', *Journal of International Marketing*, 9(4): 82–110.

Ramaseshan, B. and Patton, M. A. (1994) 'Factors influencing international channel choice of small business exporters', *International Marketing Review*, 11(4): 19–34.

Rao, C. P., Erramilli, M. K. and Ganesh, G. K. (1990) 'Impact of domestic recession on export marketing behavior', *International Marketing Review*, 7(2): 54–65.

Raven, P., Tansuihaj, P. and J. McCullough, J. (1993) 'Effects of power in export channels', *Journal of Global Marketing*, 7(2): 97–116

Richardo, D. (1817) (reprint 1981) *The Principles of Political Economy and Taxation*. Cambridge: Cambridge University Press.

Rodriguez, J-L. and Rodriguez, R. M. (2005) 'Technology and export behavior: a resource-based view approach', *International Business Review*, 14: 539–557.

Sarathy, R. (1986) 'Is exporting worthwhile? Exploratory evidence from Japan', *Management International Review*, 25(4): 22–32.

Samuelson, P. (1948) 'International trade and the equalization of factor prices', *Economic Journal*, 58: 163–184.

Scherer, F. M. and Ross, D. (1990) *Industrial Market Structure and Economic Performance*. Boston: Houghton Mifflin.

Shoham, A. (1998) 'Export performance: a conceptualization and empirical assessment', *Journal of International Marketing*, 6(3): 59–81.

Simpson, C. L. and Kujawa, D. (1974) 'The export decision process: an empirical inquiry', *Journal of International Business Studies*, Spring: 107–117.

Smith, A. (1776) (reprint 1963) *An Enquiry into the Nature and Causes of the Wealth of Nations*. Homewood, IL: Irwin.

Stern, L. W. and Reve, T. (1980) 'Distribution channels as political economies: a framework for comparative analysis', *Journal of Marketing*, 44(3): 52–64.

Styles, C. and Ambler, T. (1994) 'Successful export practice: The U.K. experience', *International Marketing Review*, 11(6): 23–47.

Teece, D. J., Pisano, G. and Shuen, A. (1997) 'Dynamic capabilities and strategic management', *Strategic Management Journal*, 18(7): 509–535.

Thach, S. V. and Axinn, C. N. (1991) Pricing and financing practices of industrial exporting firms', *International Marketing Review*, 8(1): 32–46.

Vernon, R. (1966) International investment and international trade in the product life cycle, *Quarterly Journal of Economics*, 80(2): 190–207.

Wiedersheim-Paul, F., Olson, H. C. and Welch, L. S. (1978) 'Pre-export activity: the first step to internationalization', *Journal of International Business Studies*, Spring/Summer: 47–58.

Williamson, O.E. (1975) *Markets and Hierarchies: Analysis and Antitrust Implications*. New York: Free Press.

Wortzel, L. H. and Wortzel, H. V. (1981) 'Export marketing strategies for NIC and LDC-based firms', *Columbia Journal of World Business*, Spring: 51–60.

Yeoh, P-Y. (2004) 'International learning: Antecedents and performance implications among newly internationalizing companies in an exporting context', *International Marketing Review*, 21(4/5): 511–535.

Zou, S. and Stan, S. (1998) 'The determinants of export performance: A review of the empirical literature between 1987 and 1997', *International Marketing Review*, 15(5): 333–356.

Zou, S., Fang, E. and Zhao, S. (2003) 'The effect of export marketing capabilities on export performance: An investigation of Chinese exporters', *Journal of International Marketing*, 11(4): 32–55.

9

International Franchising and Licensing

Lance Eliot Brouthers and Jason Patrick McNicol

INTRODUCTION

International franchising and international licensing are relatively new topics in international business. Both are types of entry modes. International franchising is an equity shared mode of entry, such as joint ventures, while international licensing is a non-equity mode of entry, such as exporting. The size of franchise and licensing activity is immense. For instance, the franchising sector generates over 18 million jobs in the United States alone and yields $1.53 trillion in economic output.

Like joint ventures, franchising is considered a less risky investment decision than a wholly owned subsidiary. It provides entrepreneurs a low-risk opportunity to co-own a business with a proven format for success. In addition, franchising provides opportunities to capture economies of scale while empowering the entrepreneur (Elango and Fried 1997).

In contrast to international franchising, international licensing is considered a non-equity independent mode of entry because it does not require an investment on the part of those selling or buying the license (Rasheed 2005). Generally licensees pay a percentage of their sales (called a royalty) in exchange

for being granted the license (Feldman et al. 2002).

Franchising/licensing has been viewed differently by economists, marketers, strategic managers and legal scholars (Elango and Fried 1997). From the perspective of economists, franchising/licensing represent options that allow economies to grow (Lapan 2000; Hagan 1962). Strategy scholarship views franchising/licensing as organizational forms that allow for firm expansion (Combs and Ketchen 1999; Combs and Michael 2004). Legal scholars have examined how the contractual agreements in a franchise/license system affect the parties involved (Lafontaine 1992). Lastly, from a marketing perspective, franchising/licensing is viewed as distribution channels that capture economies of scale and aid firm growth and development (Kaufmann and Rangan 1990).

DEFINITIONS OF FRANCHISING AND LICENSING

Franchise/license agreements typically involve contractual arrangements. These contracts represent relational exchanges; this means that benefits and burdens are shared in the relationship (Grünhagen and Dorsch 2003). Before we understand the relationships involved, we need to understand who the party members are.

In a franchise system, one firm (the franchisor) sells the right to a second firm (the franchisee) to market goods or services under the franchisor's brand name and use business practices developed by the franchisor (Combs and Michael 2004). Put differently, it is the rental of an intangible proprietary asset and the operation of a decentralized production or distribution process. Typically, the franchisee acquires rights from the franchisor to conduct business in a geographically specified market (Cavusgil 1998).

In exchange for these rights, the franchisee typically must follow the strategic business model provided from the franchisor with respect to product mix, operating procedures and quality. In return the franchisor provides managerial expertise, training, advertising assistance, operating procedures and site selection (Shane 1996). In contrast, in licensing agreements, one firm (the licensor) rents proprietary knowledge (i.e., know-how, trademarks and/or copyrights) to a second firm (the licensee) for use in the development and sale of products in the host country market (Cavusgil 1998). Where franchising requires the franchisee to follow strict business practices, licensing does not. Licensing allows an entrepreneur to obtain proprietary knowledge without having to follow business practices and/or other requirements of the licensor (Fosfuri 2006).

Franchising

From an entrepreneur's perspective, franchising is an important means of doing business because of the perceived benefits it offers in certain external environments. Typically, franchising exists in markets where competition is high, customer tastes change quickly and highly localized market segments

exist (Martin 1988; Elango and Fried 1997) Examples of markets where intense competition exists and franchising is used widely include the food industry (e.g., Subway, McDonald's, Sonic), convenience stores (e.g., 7-Eleven, Circle K) and tax preparation (Jackson Hewitt Tax Service, Liberty Tax Service) to name a few. Franchises are less likely to appear in markets where higher wages and higher market risks exist (Michael 1996); higher wages are commonly considered to be either a proxy for higher levels of technical skills (e.g., accounting, computer, etc.) and/or more segmented local markets (e.g., investment locations) either of which undermine the standardization benefits provided by franchising (Combs and Michael 2004).

Typically, franchisors require an upfront payment for rights to the franchise. This payment is a flat fee and may or may not be adjusted based on the franchisee's potential. One purpose of the upfront payment is to 'make' the franchisee examine his/her entrepreneurial ability in order to determine whether s/he will be able to run a successful business; the franchisor imposes a self-selection process to determine the best candidates for franchising. The potential franchisee determines whether the upfront payment is less than the potential profits generated from the franchise (Caves and Murphy 1976). The franchisor benefits from successful franchisees because the franchisor earns royalties based on performance; royalties account for a big portion of the profits for the franchisor (Azoulay and Shane 2001). If a poor franchisee is selected, then royalties are lower. Hence, the upfront payment paid to the franchisor is thought to help to select high quality franchisees that provide high royalties to the franchisor.

Depending on the environment, the franchisor can opt for any of five franchising as illustrated in the strategies shown in Table 9.1. First, a sole venture strategy can be pursued when the franchisor wishes to use a pilot franchise to aggressively promote the franchise trademark, do market research, modify

Table 9.1 Five franchising strategies

Strategy	Description
Sole venture	Franchisor wishes to use a pilot franchise to aggressively promote the franchise trademark, do market research, modify products and/or adapt services to the local market.
Multi-unit	Franchisor allows a franchisee to own multiple franchise outlets - divided into incremental and master franchising. *Incremental franchising* occurs when the franchisor allows a successful franchisee to operate additional franchise units. *Master franchising* is where the franchisor agrees to let the franchisee own several franchisees in a specific geographic location from the time the contract is formed.
Conversion franchising	Expansion of franchise units by employing independent business owners or competitor franchisees.
Product and trade name	Franchisee adopts most business operations from the franchisor in order to sell goods produced by the franchisor.
Business format	Constant relationship between franchisor and franchisee that provides the franchisee with the entire concept of the business (includes product, service, and trademark).

products and/or adapt services to the local market (Alon and Banai 2000).

Second, multi-unit franchising is quite different from sole venture franchising. In this situation, the franchisor allows a franchisee to own multiple franchise outlets (Kaufmann and Dant 1996). Multi-unit franchising can be divided into incremental and master franchising. Incremental franchising occurs when the franchisor allows a successful franchisee to operate additional franchise units. Master franchising is where the franchisor agrees to let the franchisee own several franchisees in a specific geographic location from the time the contract is formed (Garg and Rasheed 2003; Frazer and Winzar 2005). In summary, incremental franchising is based on current performance whereas master franchising is based on contract formation.

Third, a franchisor could expand the franchise by conversion franchising, which is the expansion of franchise units by employing independent business owners or competitor franchisees (Hoffman and Preble 2003). Fourth, a product and trade name franchise is where a franchisee adopts most business operations from the franchisor in order to sell goods produced by the franchisor (Combs and Castrogiovanni 1994). In this situation, the dealer agrees to take part identity of the supplier to become a preferred seller of the goods produced (Elango and Fried 1997). An example of this would be an automobile dealer such as Ford. Ford (the franchisor) manufactures automobiles, but leaves the selling of automobiles to the local dealership (the franchisee).

The fifth and final type of franchising is business format franchising. This is an ongoing relationship between the franchisor and franchisee that, in addition to product, service, and trademark, provides the franchisee with the entire concept of the business (Curran and Stanworth 1983; Elango and Fried 1997; Tracey and Jarvis 2007).

Licensing

Licensing is a market-based alternative that permits firm innovations to be profitable (Fosfuri 2006). Typically, research and development ideas, inventions, formulas, technological know-how, services, brands, art, music, designs and trademarks are what are licensed by a firm (Glazer 1991; Mottner and Johnson 2000). In exchange for these assets, the licensee typically provides the licensor with a lump-sum payment, and/or a royalty fee per unit, and a commitment to follow the licensing contract (Hill *et al.* 1990). Firms lacking production and marketing capabilities are the most prone to engage in granting licenses (Fosfuri 2006). Hence, licensing is a wealth enhancing strategic decision for both sides because licensees are familiar with the application of licensed assets but avoid the costs (managerial, financial, and technical) associated with developing such assets (Gleason, Mathur and Singh 2000) while licensors are able to profit from markets in which they cannot or will not invest (Kulatilaka and Lin 2006).

Franchising vs. licensing

However similar franchising and licensing are, they are still quite different. Franchising has two key characteristics. First, franchising typically occurs when there is a notable service component that must occur proximate to customers. For example, restaurant chains are heavily franchised because there is a large customer service component. Second, franchising allows the franchisor to allocate responsibilities, decision rights and profits to the franchisee while upholding a predetermined level of performance standards among franchisees, managing the brand image and coordinating activities to capture economies

of scale (Caves and Murphy 1976). With regard to information, decisions such as pricing, wages, and (in many systems) location, that require local information and human capital are delegated to the franchisee, who is more knowledgeable about local demand, labor markets, and real estate (Michael 1996). The franchisee is responsible for maintaining the franchise outlet while the franchisor develops the system's trademark and builds operating procedures to develop standardized products. By partitioning decisions and aligning with other franchisees, the franchise system achieves efficiencies in information, in supervision, and in scale (Michael 1996).

Where franchising basically sells the entire business, licensing only sells proprietary knowledge. If an entrepreneur wishes to own a business without franchising, s/he could still license a company trademark, patent, or operating system in the development of the business. While these components are incorporated into the franchise model, an entrepreneur could use only the proprietary knowledge to save on costs while starting a business.

One key difference between franchising and licensing is that of management. In a

Table 9.2   Franchising vs. Licensing

	Franchising	Licensing
Structure	Notable service component	Only sells proprietary knowledge
	Franchisor allocates responsibilities, decision rights, and profits to franchisee – must maintain predetermined level of quality among brand name and performance	Management is 'hands off' – licensee does not have to meet predetermined levels of quality
	Franchisee is responsible for setting prices, wages, and determining location	Licensee is responsible for setting prices, wages, and determining location
	Franchisor develops system's trademark and standardized products	May license a trademark, patent, or operating system without having to develop a standardized business
Benefits	System creates efficiencies in information, supervision, and scale	Saves developmental costs
	Franchisees receive services (i.e., training, production processes, blueprints, etc.)	Expertise, capital resources, and local knowledge are not needed to grow the brand – lowers Licensor risk
	Growth of brand name allows firm to capture economies of scale quicker	Licensee uses strong brand name to attract customers
	Franchising enhances likelihood of firm survival and growth	
	Creates brand name equity (franchise reputation)	

franchise system, the franchisees establish local outlets, set local policy (i.e., price, hours, staffing) and manage day-to-day operations, but are required to meet certain standards set by the franchisor (Combs and Michael 2004). In contrast, in a licensing agreement, the licensee is solely responsible for establishing local outlets, setting local policy (i.e., price, hours, staffing) and managing day-to-day operations (Hill, Hwang and Kim 1990).

Benefits of franchising

Franchising provides unique benefits to entrepreneurs. From the franchisee perspective, franchisees are provided services (i.e., training, production processes, blueprints, etc.) to get the franchise up and running. In addition, the franchisor makes periodic visits to the new unit to insure operating procedures are being followed, trademarks are being used properly, and to provide marketing services (Michael 1996).

From the franchisor perspective, franchising allows the entrepreneur to expand the trademark more quickly to capture economies of scale (Caves and Murphy 1976). Newer entrepreneurs tend to be at a competitive disadvantage because initial costs of production can be very expensive and a minimal point of efficiency needs to be reached (Martin and Justis 1993; Caves and Murphy 1976). Through franchising a franchisor can typically reach the minimal point more rapidly, allowing the venture to become cost effective (Martin and Justis 1993).

More importantly, franchising enhances the likelihood of firm survival and growth (Shane 1996). Typically, capital is expensive which hinders firm growth. An entrepreneur may not be able to grow quickly because the entrepreneur cannot afford the capital needed to maintain the high growth. Franchising represents one way for the entrepreneur to gain capital quickly and inexpensively in order to grow quickly, which in turn increases the size and economic prowess of the firm promoting its likelihood of survival.

Lastly, franchising may lead to brand name equity (Garg and Rasheed 2003). Brand name equity is also referred to as franchise reputation. As a franchise brand name builds brand name equity, customers begin to see each franchise unit as being the same and providing the same level of quality. Also, brand name quality may reduce the ability of customers to distinguish service differences between franchise units. By building the brand name, the franchisor is able to build a consistent level of service that attracts customers.

The aforementioned benefits let us know the potential that franchising has to offer. However, to understand the franchise phenomenon more closely, two key theories have been applied, agency theory and resource scarcity theory. Each theory provides a unique perspective of the franchise framework.

AGENCY THEORY AND FRANCHISING

Agency theory examines the exchanges that take place between a principal (the franchisor) and an agent (the franchisee) (Sharma 1997). Usually, principals delegate authority to the agent (Eisenhardt 1989). A critical assumption is that the interests of the principal and agent diverge (Eisenhardt 1989; Jensen and Meckling 1976); the goals of the franchisee may not be the same as the franchisor. This results in the likelihood that agents may misrepresent information and effort (Jensen and Meckling 1976) in order to achieve personal goals rather than franchisor goals. In order to avoid these goal misalignment problems, the principal has to expend resources to keep agent goals aligned with principal goals.

Franchising is a means to reduce agency problems. High upfront fees exist either because there is high brand name equity (such as McDonald's) or the franchisor does not have confidence in the value of the product or service. Upfront fees typically include land and building costs, equipment, and initial stock of items (Business Link 2008).

Due to the high upfront payment fee made by franchisees, monitoring outlet managers is minimal because the franchisee has already made a huge investment in the outlet (Norton 1988). Put simply, the franchisee should already have a high level of motivation to be successful and run the franchise unit properly if s/he is to recoup the high investment cost. If s/he is able to maintain high motivation, then s/he should be able to have a continuous profit stream (Combs and Ketchen 2003; Klein 1995).

When examining franchising from the agency perspective, there exist two types of agency problems, vertical agency and horizontal agency problems. Vertical agency problems occur when there is conflict between a franchisee and outlet managers (Combs and Michael 2004). Franchisees provide full effort when operating franchise units because their incomes are linked directly to their effort. However, the unit (outlet) managers tend not to give full effort (shirk) because they do not have strong ownership incentives (Rubin 1978). As a result, outlet managers need to be monitored more closely, but monitoring is expensive (Bradach 1997). In order to reduce shirking by outlet managers, franchising may provide residual claims (profits after expenses) to the franchisee and manager (Fama and Jensen 1983).

Even though franchising may reduce monitoring costs, vertical agency problems may still occur. Franchisors are just as likely to seek opportunistic behavior as much as franchisees. According to Storholm and Scheuing (1994), franchisors may put franchise outlets too close together; close a franchise just to reopen it as a franchisor owned outlet; force franchisees to purchase inputs from the franchisor; embezzle advertising royalties; and write contracts that favor franchisors when disputes arise (Combs and Michael 2004). Franchisees may release proprietary knowledge, fail to pay royalties, and not follow proper standards (Combs and Michael 2004; Storholm and Scheuing 1994).

In order to align franchisors and franchisees vertically, Klein (1995) proposed the concept of quasi-rents. According to Klein, the franchise brand name creates pricing power that allows the franchisor to pay franchisees a payment that is greater than the opportunity costs of acting opportunistically. This payment is termed quasi-rent, which is an efficient means to reduce opportunism and thus aligns franchisees with franchisors. If the franchisor terminates the franchisee contract because the franchisee has not upheld quality standards or has released proprietary knowledge, then the franchisee loses the quasi-rent. However, if the franchisor puts franchise units too close together or embezzles advertising royalties, then the franchisee is still entitled to the quasi-rent. Hence, this quasi-rent helps prevent opportunist behavior by franchisors and franchisees.

Horizontal agency problems occur when franchisees free-ride on other outlets. Franchise outlets operate under the same brand name, allowing customers to transfer their same perceptions across all outlets, causing spillover effects to other franchisees (Combs and Michael 2004). While some franchisees invest heavily to uphold standards, others may not be so willing, leading to under-investment. Moreover, customer mobility enhances horizontal agency problems. Imagine that a franchise is in a location that mainly serves one time customers, such as a fast food chain located on a freeway. This franchise unit may be less willing to uphold quality standards because the likelihood of a repeat customer is low. Again, the franchisor could expend additional costs to monitor franchisees, but this undermines one of the key advantages of franchising, reduced monitoring costs. To avoid additional costs, when horizontal agency problems may occur, the franchisor may own the outlet itself. Hence, franchisors have to be concerned with monitoring costs (vertical agency) and customer mobility (horizontal agency) when establishing franchise units (Combs and Michael 2004).

RESOURCE SCARCITY

Franchising is a tool used by entrepreneurs to acquire capital and establish distribution networks as quickly as possible. When a firm is in the early stages of firm growth, franchising provides a way for young firms to avoid industry-related problems (Martin and Justis 1993). However, young firms may be constrained by capital availability because of asymmetric information flows (Evans and Jovanovic 1989); firms may not have access to capital because the information they obtained is not equal to what is in the market.

Oxenfeldt and Kelly (1969) proposed a model to explain the inability of young firms to acquire capital – the resource scarcity theory. From this perspective, young firms franchise in order to gain access to scarce resources, especially financial and managerial resources (Combs and Michael 2004). As mentioned before, young firms lack the ability to quickly gain capital in order to gain efficiencies to be competitive with the market (Combs and Ketchen 2003). In addition, young firms lack the managerial experience needed to make proper decisions regarding growth and survivability. Franchising then allows the firm to gain proper capital and managerial experience to expand at a rate to make the firm competitive. Consistent with this perspective, Castrogiovanni, Combs and Justis (2006) suggest that as franchisers mature and grow their proportion of franchises shrink.

CONTRIBUTIONS OF AGENCY AND RESOURCE SCARCITY THEORY

A topic of considerable debate is resource scarcity (Combs and Ketchen 1999). The problem centering on resource scarcity is capital (Combs and Ketchen 2003); if some entrepreneurs have access to capital, why do they still franchise? According to some researchers (Norton 1995; Rubin 1990), franchising is a costly source of capital; this

means it is inefficient to obtain capital via franchising. However, this perception relies on the assumption that debt and equity markets are perfect, which does not appear to be the case (Combs and Ketchen 1999); asymmetry of information is constant in capital markets. It has also been argued that the agency theory model is very robust (Norton 1995; Shane 1998). The reason agency theory is more robust is because it is able to incorporate risk; franchisees have to provide their own capital, meaning they are at risk if the franchise unit fails.

Despite the current debates regarding resource scarcity and agency theory perspectives, some studies suggest both perspectives are necessary to understand the franchise perspective (Castrogiovanni *et al.* 2006; Carney and Gedajlovic 1991; Combs and Castrogiovanni 1994; Lafontaine 1992). For example, Martin and Justis (1993) found that franchising is more likely to occur in immature systems; this means there could be immediate benefits to entrepreneurs, suggesting that, in addition to the agency based perspective, entrepreneurs may wish to franchise to capture short-run benefits. Overall, studies found that firms that lacked resources appeared to franchise, in addition to the agency-based incentives (Martin and Justis 1993). However, these studies used age and size as a proxy for capital; by not finding direct measures of capital, these studies have not been able to accurately examine the resource scarcity perspective. Moreover, resource scarcity studies have failed to examine experience as a managerial resource (Combs and Ketchen 1999). Despite the criticisms against resource scarcity, it appears that this perspective has not been adequately tested and therefore may be a legitimate way to explain franchising.

Even though capital has been difficult to measure, there are studies that support both perspectives. In one of the first studies to examine resource scarcity, Hunt (1973) found support for the resource scarcity perspective. In a later study by Combs and Castrogiovanni (1994), franchising mostly occurred in larger firms, but not in older firms. Older firms were more likely to engage in franchising for agency theory reasons while younger firms were more likely to franchise for resource scarcity reasons (Castrogiovanni *et al.* 2006). Moreover, large, slow-growing companies were found to be more likely to franchise (Alon 2001) because of the need to expand rapidly to capture economies of scale. Lastly, Combs and Ketchen (2003) did a meta-analysis that examined prior franchising studies. They concluded that agency theory appeared to be a good predictor of franchising, whereas resource scarcity perspectives did not. In order to properly study the franchising phenomenon, Combs and Ketchen (2003) suggested that future research focuses more strongly on the research design, specifically stating that construct validity has been weak in prior research and may be improved through the use of agency theory.

Some studies have looked at franchising from a non-theoretical perspective (Elango and Fried 1997). Knight (1986) found that entrepreneurs were likely to franchise because of a known brand name and the ability to start a business more easily. In addition, franchising provides access to managerial help, a 'proven' business plan and name, and greater probability of survival (Baron and Schmidt 1991). From the franchisor perspective, franchising was used to reduce risk. A firm could expand via franchising in order to test the potential of a new market (Fladmoe-Lindquist 1996); a franchisor could determine market potential without using company-owned assets, thereby reducing overall firm risk (Martin 1988).

Licensing theory

Transaction cost economics (TCE) represent to date the dominant theoretical approach to examining licensing. From this theoretical perspective, licensing is most likely to occur where environments protect intellectual property and firms can profit from an intellectual asset (Fosfuri 2006). Put simply, when large

environmental uncertainty is present, the TCE model predicts that transactions will be internalized (Shane 1994), meaning a firm is less likely to license its intellectual assets. TCE theory is discussed in more detail in the international licensing section.

INTERNATIONAL FRANCHISING

The majority of franchising literature has centered on domestic markets (i.e., the United States) (Shane 1996; Martin 1988; Hunt 1973). Theories of resource scarcity and agency problems have been extended to the international franchising literature only in a very limited manner.

Both theoretical perspectives could be used to examine international franchising. For instance, firms wishing to expand into new markets may lack the necessary resources to do so. By franchising, the firm allows the entrepreneur to bear some risk in a foreign market while the franchisor expands their business into a new market. Or a franchisor could decide to expand to a new international market via an agency theory based perspective because the franchisor needs a cost-efficient way to monitor foreign managers while the firm expands.

International franchising appears to occur in two settings. First, firms are likely to franchise in countries where high per capita income and developed retail markets exist (Elango and Fried 1997). Second, international franchising tends to occur where there is great diversity in culture, income, and political systems (Elango and Fried 1997; Welch 1989).

According to Fladmoe-Lindquist (1996), there are four types of international franchisors. First, there is the constrained franchisor, a firm that is unlikely to expand internationally because of limitations in international managerial capabilities and learning capacities. This type of franchisor is likely to expand to a nearby market but is unlikely to expand beyond this point because the franchisor lacks the necessary capabilities to sustain growth and view other potential opportunities. Second, integrated franchisors have great learning capabilities stemming from prior experiences, but do not have many international capabilities. The learning capabilities of these franchisors allow them to recognize international opportunities more easily and expand more quickly, but they are limited by their international capabilities (i.e., administrative efficiency and risk management). Third, conventional franchisors possess some international expansion capabilities but are limited in developing global expansion capabilities. This type of franchisor has administrative efficiency, but is unable to examine host country risk properly; this may lead the franchisor to enter markets that do not have great potential. Lastly, worldwide franchisors have quite a bit of international experience, stemming from dynamic capabilities in management and risk assessment, allowing them to operate in many markets and use different ownership structures. These franchisors have developed substantial international franchising capabilities.

Skills needed to internationalize may be different from the skills needed to expand domestically (Shane 1996). International franchising requires franchisors to use internal and external variables to develop perceptions of benefits and risks (Eroglu 1992). Financial risk affects a firm's survivability (Eroglu 1992); if financial risk is high, then the odds of failure increase, making it difficult for the franchisor to expand. However, international franchising is considered a less risky investment decision when compared with foreign direct investment (Eroglu 1992) because the need for large amounts of financial and physical capital is minimal. In addition, franchising is less affected by economic and political risks because (Aydin and Kacker 1990) franchising requires minimal resource commitments by the franchisor, shifting the responsibility for market volatility to the franchisee.

Host countries typically view franchising positively and tend to be more receptive to franchising than to other means of foreign entry, such as exporting or foreign direct investment (Aydin and Kacker 1990). Commonly, franchising is a less regulated industry because it is more beneficial to the local environment (Eroglu 1992). While foreign direct investment (FDI) requires large initial amounts of foreign capital with the expectation of eventual domestic outflow (i.e., profits, resources, etc.), franchising requires a local entrepreneur to make the initial investment, i.e., local capital. The initial investment pays for managerial training, business practices, and a proven name. In addition, the local entrepreneur hires locals to run the business thus employing more people. Through franchising, the local entrepreneur enhances the likelihood of survival and improves economic welfare in the local market because profits stay in the market along with capital and human resources.

Other factors also may influence a decision to franchise internationally. For instance, some industries (like some services) are not easily exportable, so franchising may be used instead (Aydin and Kicker 1990). A firm's age or experience may influence the decision to franchise internationally; firms with more experience are more likely to franchise internationally (Alon and Mckee 1999) because franchising provides a stable governance structure that allows firms to expand internationally (Fladmoe-Lindquist 1996) while maintaining a constant ownership structure (Alon and McKee 1999). Finally, because franchising allows the characteristics of the business to stay the same regardless of the location (Alon and McKee 1999), it represents an alternative method of FDI in host countries where large distances in geography, culture and time impede information flows and create greater risks (Fladmoe-Lindquist and Jacque 1995).

However, there are reasons why firms have not franchised internationally. First, the lack of managerial expertise and legal barriers hinder international franchising (Elango and Fried 1997). Second, the size and opportunities located within the domestic market may be sufficient; firms may prefer to exploit local markets prior to engaging in what they perceive as being more risky international ventures (Aydin and Kacker 1989). Lastly, the lack of international experience, limited financial resources, and higher foreign market risk may also hinder international expansion activities (Aydin and Kacker 1989; Eroglu 1992).

INTERNATIONAL LICENSING

According to Kotabe, Sahay and Aulakh (1996), licensing has been neglected as an entry mode option in the strategic product planning literature. However, a few prior studies have examined international licensing as a foreign market entry strategy (Calvet 1981; Porter 1986). International licensing provides opportunities for firms that are reluctant to enter foreign markets; licensing allows such firms to use their mobile assets to expand internationally without bearing risks commonly associated with FDI (Mottner and Johnson 2000). Thus, licensing is a low-involvement/low-control entry mode option where: (1) substantial control is granted to the licensee and (2) equity is not required in order to expand internationally (Aulakh, Cavusgil and Sarkar 1998).

Low-involvement entry modes are typically desired when the market risk is high (Chan and Hwang 1992) or perhaps when the market is too small to justify a substantial investment of time and/or resources. In the case of international licensing, much of the risk is shifted to the licensee. Licensees bear the costs of serving the local market and own all assets associated with the business (Hill *et al.*, 1990). In risky markets, limited resource commitments allow the licensor to gain a foothold in the market without having to make large resource investment commitments.

International licensing provides benefits to firms other than minimizing risk. For instance, licensing requires minimal capital outlay. Second, licensing lowers transportation and tariff costs. Third, foreign governments are more receptive to licensing because technology is being brought into the country (Weinrauch and Langlois 1983). Lastly, licensing provides support for production, marketing, and after sales service (Cavusgil 1998).

Risks associated with international licensing include limited returns and lack of control over the licensee (Cavusgil 1998). These risks and benefits are analyzed with other key components to determine whether a firm should license internationally. One key factor affecting the internationalization decision is management's experience and knowledge; prior experience and knowledge affect the propensity to license (Aulakh *et al.* 1998). In addition, industry structure, technology intensity, and resource-based factors affect the decision to internationalize (Kotabe *et al.* 1996). If the cost of learning is high in a foreign market, then the likelihood of licensing is increased (Buckley and Casson 1998).

From a TCE perspective, a critical factor that affects the decision to license internationally is opportunism. One type of risk commonly associated with licensing is the potential for opportunistic behavior (Hill *et al.* 1990). Licensors need to be selective in selecting licensees because a future competitor could be created if the licensee acts opportunistically. If the threat of opportunism is high, then costs associated with monitoring increase (Hill *et al.* 1990). For instance, when considering licensing intellectual property overseas, a firm considers the level of enforcement protecting intellectual property rights in the host country market; lower levels of enforcement increase risks, substantially increasing the risks associated with licensing in that market, reducing the likelihood of an agreement being reached.

FUTURE RESEARCH

The franchising and licensing literatures have drawn upon a few key theories in developing their research streams, but many questions/theories have been so far unexamined. For instance, what influences top managers to pursue international licensing or franchising agreements? According to upper echelon theory, personal characteristics of managers (i.e., personality, age), education and prior experiences influence management decisions (Combs and Michael 2004; Hambrick and Mason 1984). Do they influence international licensing or franchising decisions? Future studies may wish to apply upper echelon theory to franchising/licensing decision making.

A second theory that may help to explain international licensing or franchising decisions is real options theory. Real options theory deals with the notion of staged strategic investments (Reuer 2002; Folta 1998; Bowman and Hurry 1993) under conditions of greater uncertainty (Reuer and Leiblein 2000; Folta 1998; Chi and McGuire 1996; Dixit and Pindyck 1994) where a firm wants to keep its initial investment low while maintaining the option to invest more in the future (Kogut 1991; Dixit and Pindyck 1994; Buckley and Tse 1996; Buckley, Casson and Gulamhussen 2002). By purchasing an option or by using an 'option investment mode' such as licensing, a firm decreases their downside risk while providing an opportunity for future investment once the investment's value becomes more predictable (Folta 1998; McGrath 1997; Dixit and Pindyck 1994; Sanchez 1993). 'Real options' theory has never been applied to the international licensing decision, although it has been applied to technology sourcing methods (Folta 1998; McGrath 1997; Folta and Leiblein 1994).

Third, institutional theory could be applied to international licensing/franchising. Institutional theory examines how organizational decision-making is influenced by social influence; firm behavior is guided by rules, norms, values and taken-for-granted assumptions (Oliver 1997). Only one study has pursued an institutional theory framework when looking at franchising. Shane and

Foo (1999) found that the rate of survival increases with a franchisor's age, size and media certification. Put simply, as a franchise gains more legitimacy it increases its chance of survival. No study has applied institutional theory to international licensing.

The theories discussed here have focused primarily on the franchisor/licensor. Future research may wish to explore how these and other theories affect the international decision-making of the franchisee/licensee. For instance, why would an entrepreneur rather internationally license/franchise than create a new business?

Other unexplored avenues of research exist. For instance, do international franchising and licensing aid in foreign market penetration? Under what conditions may one be preferred to the other? A firm's strategies, goals, and current operations have been shown to influence its decision making process. Do they also influence international franchising/ licensing decisions? Do variables like national culture influence the decision to franchise and/or license? Future research may wish to explore which types of firms or industries are more prone to opt for international licensing and/or which types of firms/industries choose franchising and/or how local laws and/or financing influence licensing/franchising decisions. Last, the relationship between international licensing and/or franchising research to international law and/or international financing has seen scant research. This appears to be fertile ground for new research efforts.

As this chapter points out, we actually know very little about international franchising or licensing. With only a few studies examining international franchising/licensing issues, much more conceptual, theoretical and empirical work is needed. As it stands now, scholars can offer scant advice to those firms wishing to expand their franchising/licensing activities internationally. Neither can scholars provide much useful information to those thinking about purchasing international franchises/ licenses. Given the rapid expansion of international licensing/franchising activities in recent years, there appears to be an urgent need to know more about these activities. Thus, there is much scholarly work to do. We encourage scholars to begin to engage in meaningful research in these very important but under-examined areas.

REFERENCES

Alon, I. (2001) 'The use of franchising by US-based retailers', *Journal of Small Business Management*, 39(2): 111–122.

Alon, I. and Banai, M. (2000) 'Executive insights: Franchising opportunities and threats in Russia', *Journal of International Marketing*, 8(3): 104–119.

Alon, I. and McKee, D. (1999) 'Towards a macro environmental model of international franchising', *Multinational Business Review*, 7(1): 76–82.

Arora, A. and Ceccagnoli, M. (2006) 'Patent protection, complementary assets, and firms' incentives for technology licensing', *Management Science*, 52(2): 293–308.

Aulakh, P. S., Cavusgil, S. T. and Sarkar, M. B. (1998) 'Compensation in international licensing agreements', *Journal of International Business Studies*, 29(2): 409–419.

Aydin, N. and Kacker, M. (1990) 'International outlook of US-based franchisers', *International Marketing Review*, 7(2): 43–53.

Azoulay, P. and Shane, S. (2001) 'Entrepreneurs, contracts, and the failure of young firms', *Management Science*, 47(3): 337–358.

Baron, S. and Schmidt, R. A. (1991) 'Operational aspects of retail franchisees', *International Journal of Retail and Distribution Management*, 19(2): 13–19.

Bowman, E. H. and Hurry, D. (1993) 'Strategy through the option lens: An integrated view of resource investments and the incremental choice process', *Academy of Management Review*, 18(4): 750–782.

Bradach, J. L. (1997) 'Using the plural form in management of restaurant chains', *Administrative Science Quarterly*, 2-42(2): 276–303.

Buckley, P. J. and Casson, M. C. (1998) 'Analyzing foreign market entry strategies: Extending the internalization approach', *Journal of International Business Studies*, 29(3): 539–561.

Buckley, A. and Tse, K. (1996) 'Real operating options and foreign direct investment: a synthetic approach', *European Management Journal*, 14(3): 304–314.

Buckley, P. J., Casson, M. and Gulamhussen, M. A. (2002) 'Internationalization – Real options, knowledge management and the Uppsala approach', in V. Havila, M. Forsgen, and H. Hakansson (eds), *Critical Perspectives on Internationalization*. Oxford: Elsevier Science Ltd. 54-82

Business Link, 2008, buy a franchise, accessed 2/18/08 http://www.businesslink.gov.uk/bdotg/action/detail?type=RESOURCES&itemld=1073791403

Calvet, A. L. (1981) 'A synthesis of foreign direct investment theories and theories of the multinational firm', *Journal of International Business Studies*, 12(1): 43–59.

Castrogiovanni, G. J., Combs, J. G. and Justis, R. T. (2006) 'Shifting imperatives: An integrative view of resource scarcity and agency reasons for franchising', *Entrepreneurship: Theory & Practice*, 30(1): 23–40.

Caves, R. E. and Murphy II, W. F. (1976) 'Franchising: Firms, markets, and intangible assets', *Southern Economic Journal*, 42(4): 572–566.

Cavusgil, S. T. (1998) 'Executive insights: International partnering – A systematic framework for collaborating with foreign business partners', *Journal of International Marketing*, 6(1): 91–107.

Chan, K. W. and Hwang, P. (1992) 'Global strategy and multinationals' entry mode choice', *Journal of International Business Studies*, 23(1): 29–53.

Chi, T. and McGuire, D. J. (1996) 'Collaborative ventures and value of learning: integrating the transaction cost and strategic option perspectives on the choice of market entry modes', *Journal of International Business Studies*, 27(2): 285–307.

Combs, J. G. and Castrogiovanni, G. J. (1994) 'Franchisor strategy: A proposed model and empirical test of franchise versus company ownership', *Journal of Small Business Management*, 32(2): 37–48.

Combs, J. G. and Ketchen Jr., D. J. (2003) 'Why do firms use franchising as an entrepreneurial strategy?: A meta-analysis', *Journal of Management*, 29(3): 443–465.

Combs, J. G. and Ketchen Jr., D. J. (1999) 'Can capital scarcity help agency theory explain franchising? Revisiting the capital scarcity hypothesis', *Academy of Management Journal*, 42(2): 196–207.

Combs, J. G. and Michael, S. C. (2004) 'Franchising: a review and avenues to greater theoretical diversity', *Journal of Management*, 30(6): 907–931.

Contractor, F. J. and Kundu, S. K. (1998) 'Modal choice in a world of alliances: analyzing organizational forms in the international hotel sector', *Journal of International Business Studies*, 29(2): 325–357.

Curran, J. and Stanworth, J. (1983) 'Franchising in the modern economy: towards a theoretical understanding'. *International Small Business Journal*, 1-2(1): 8–6.

Dixit, A. K. and Pindyck, R. S. (1994) *Investment under Uncertainty*. Princeton, NJ: Princeton University Press.

Eisenhardt, K. (1989) 'Agency theory: An assessment and review', *Academy of Management Review*, 14: 57–74.

Elango, B. and Fried, V. H. (1997) 'Franchising research: a literature review and synthesis', *Journal of Small Business Management*, 35(3): 68–81.

Eroglu, S. (1992) 'The internationalization process of franchise systems: a conceptual framework', *International Marketing Review*, 9(5/6): 19–30.

Evans, D. S. and Jovanovic, B. (1989) 'An estimated model of entrepreneurial choice under liquidity constraints', *Journal of Political Economy*, 97(4): 808–827.

Fama, E. F. and Jensen, M. C. (1983) 'Separation of ownership and control', *Journal of Law and Economics*, 26: 301–325.

Feldman, M., Feller, I., Bercovitz, J. and Burton, R. (2002) 'Equity and the technology transfer strategies of American universities', *Management Science*, 48(1): 105–121.

Fladmoe-Lindquist, K. (1996) 'International franchising: capabilities and development', *Journal of Business Venturing*, 11(5): 419–438.

Fladmoe-Lindquist, K. and Jacque, L. (1995) 'Control modes in international service operations: The propensity to franchise', *Management Science*, 41(7): 1238–1249.

Folta, T. B. (1998) 'Governance and uncertainty: the trade-off between administrative control and commitment', *Strategic Management Journal*, 19(11): 1007–1028.

Folta, T. B. and Leiblein, M. J. (1994) 'Technology acquisition and the choice of governance by established firms: Insights from option theory in a multinomial logit model', *Academy of Management Proceedings*. Dallas, Texas.

Fosfuri, A. (2004) 'Determinants of international activity: evidence from the chemical processing industry', *Research Policy*, 33(10): 1599–1614.

Fosfuri, A. (2006) 'The licensing dilemma: understanding the determinants of the rate of technology licensing', *Strategic Management Journal*, 27(12): 1141–1158.

Frazer, L. and Winzar, H. (2005) 'Exits and expectations: why disappointed franchisees leave', *Journal of Business Research*, 58(11): 1534–1542.

Garg, V. and Rasheed, A. A. (2003) 'International multi-unit franchising: an agency theoretic explanation', *International Business Review*, 12(3): 329–348.

Glazer, R. (1991) 'Marketing in an information-intensive environment: strategic implications of knowledge as an asset', *Journal of Marketing*, 55 (October): 1–19.

Gleason, K. C., Mathur, I. and Singh, M. (2000) 'Operational characteristics and performance gains associated with international licensing agreements: The US evidence', *International Business Review*, 9(4): 431–452.

Grünhagen, M. and Dorsch, M. J. (2003) 'Does the franchisor provide value to franchisees? Past, current, and future value assessments of two franchisee types', *Journal of Small Business Management*, 41(4): 366–384.

Grünhagen, M. and Mittelstaedt, R. A. (2005) 'Entrepreneurs or investors: Do multi-unit franchisees have different philosophical orientations?', *Journal of Small Business Management*, 43(3): 207–225.

Hackett, D. W. (1976) 'The international expansion of US franchise systems: Status and strategies', *Journal of International Business Studies*, 7(1): 65–75.

Hagen, E. E. (1962) *On the Theory of Social Change*. Low economic growth begins Homewood, IL: Dorsey Press.

Hambrick, D. C. and Mason, P. A. (1984) 'Upper echelons: the organization as a reflection of its top managers', *Academy of Management Review*, 9(2): 193–206.

Hill, C. W. L., Hwang, P. and Kim, W. C. (1990) 'An eclectic theory of the choice of international entry mode', *Strategic Management Journal*, 11(2): 117–128.

Hoffman, R. C. and Preble, J. F. (2003) 'Convert to compete: competitive advantage through conversion franchising', *Journal of Small Business Management*, 41(2): 187–204.

Hunt, S. D. (1973) 'The trend toward company-operated units in franchise chains', *Journal of Retailing*, 49(2): 3–12.

Huszagh, S. M., Huszagh, F. W. and McIntyre, F. S. (1992) 'International franchising in the context of competitive strategy and the theory of the firm', *International Marketing Review*, 9(5/6): 5–18.

Jensen, M. and Meckling, W. (1976) 'Theory of the firm: managerial behavior, agency costs, and ownership structure', *Journal of Financial Economics*, 3(4): 305–360.

Kaufmann, P. J. and Dant, R. P. (1999) 'Franchising and the domain of entrepreneurship research', *Journal of Business Venturing*, 14(1): 5–16.

Kaufmann, P. and Rangan, V. (1990) 'A model for managing system conflict during franchise expansion', *Journal of Retailing*, 66(2): 155–173.

Klein, B. (1995) 'The economics of franchise contracts', *Journal of Corporate Finance*, 2(1/2): 9–37.

Knight, R. M. (1986) 'Franchising from the franchisor and franchisee points of view', *Journal of Small Business Management*, 24(3): 8–15.

Kogut, B. (1991) 'Joint ventures and the option to expand and acquire', *Management Science,* 37(1): 19–33.

Kotabe, M., Sahay, A. and Aulakh, P. S. (1996) 'Emerging role of technology licensing in the development of global product strategy: conceptual framework and research propositions', *Journal of Marketing,* 60(1): 73–88.

Kulatilaka, N. and Lin, L. (2006) 'Impact of licensing on investment and financing of technology development', *Management Science*, 52(12): 1824–1837.

Lafontaine, F. (1992) 'Agency theory and franchising: some empirical results', *RAND Journal of Economics*, 23(2): 263–283.

Lapan, H. E. (2000) 'Incomplete adoption of a superior innovation', *Economica*, 67(268): 525–542.

Malhotra, N. K., Ulgado, F. M. and Agarwal, J. (2003) 'Internationalization and entry modes: A multitheoretical framework and research propositions', *Journal of International Marketing*, 11(4): 1–31.

Martin, R. E. (1988) 'Franchising and risk management', *American Economic Review*, 78(5): 954–968.

Martin, R. E. and Justis, R. T. (1993) 'Franchising, liquidity constraints and entry', *Applied Economics*, 25(9): 1269–1277.

McGrath, R. G. (1997) 'A real options logic for initiating technology positioning investments', *Academy of Management Review*, 22(4): 974–996.

McIntyre, F. S. and Huszagh, S. M. (1995) 'Internationalization of franchise systems', *Journal of International Marketing*, 3(4): 39–56.

Michael, S. C. (1996) 'To franchise or not to franchise: an analysis of decision rights and organizational form shares', *Journal of Business Venturing*, 11(1): 57–71.

Mottner, S. and Johnson, J.P. (2000) 'Motivations and risks in international licensing: a review and implications for licensing to transitional and emerging economies', *Journal of World Business*, 35(2): 171–188.

Norton, S. W. (1988) 'Franchising, brand name capital, and the entrepreneurial capacity problem', *Strategic Management Journal*, 9(1): 105–114.

Norton, S. W. (1995) 'Is franchising a capital structure issue?', *Journal of Corporate Finance*, 2(1/2); 75–101.

Oliver, C. (1997) 'Sustainable competitive advantage: Combining institutional and resource-based views', *Strategic Management Journal*, 18(9): 697–13.

Oxenfeldt, A. R. and Kelly, A. O. (1969) 'Will successful franchise systems ultimately become wholly-owned chains?', *Journal of Retailing*, 44(4): 69–83.

Porter, M. E. (1986) *Competition in Global Industries*. Boston. MA: Harvard Business School Press.

Preble, J. F. and Hoffman, R. C. (1995) 'Franchising systems around the globe: a status report', *Journal of Small Business Management*, 33(2): 80–88.

Rasheed, H. S. (2005) 'Foreign entry mode and performance: the moderating effects of environment', *Journal of Small Business Management*, 43(1): 41–54.

Reuer, J. J. (2002) 'How real are real options? The case of international joint ventures', in M. A. Hitt, R. Amit, C. Lucier and R. Nixon (eds), *Creating Value: Winners in the*

New Business Environment. Oxford: Blackwell.

Reuer, J. J. and Leiblein, M. J. (2000) 'Downside risk implications of multinationality and international joint ventures', *Academy of Management Journal*, 43(2): 203–214.

Rubin, P. H. (1978) 'The theory of the firm and the structure of the franchise contract', *Journal of Law and Economics*, 21: 223–233.

Rubin, P. H. (1990) *Managing Business Transactions*. New York: Free Press.

Sanchez, R. (1993) 'Strategic flexibility, firm organization and managerial work in dynamic markets', in P. Shrivastava, A. Huff and J. Dutton (eds), *Advances in Strategic Management*, Vol. 9. JAI Press. Greenwich, CT.

Shane, S. (1994) 'The effect of national culture on the choice between licensing and direct foreign investment', *Strategic Management Journal*, 15(8): 627–642.

Shane, S. (1996) 'Hybrid organization arrangements and their implications for firm growth and survival: a study of new franchisors', *Academy of Management Journal*, 39(1): 216–234.

Shane, S. (1998) 'Making new franchise systems work', *Strategic Management Journal*, 19(7): 697–707.

Shane, S. and Foo, M. (1999) 'New firm survival: institutional explanations for new franchisor mortality', *Management Science*, 45(2): 142–159.

Sharma, A. (1997) 'Professional as agent: Knowledge asymmetry in agency exchange', *Academy of Management Review*, 22(3): 758–798.

Storholm, G. and Scheuing, E. E. (1994) 'Ethical implications of business format franchising', *Journal of Business Ethics*, 13(3): 181–188.

Tracey, P. and Jarvis, O. (2007) 'Toward a theory of social venture franchising', *Entrepreneurship: Theory & Practice*, 31(5): 667–685.

Weinrauch, D. and Langlois, A. (1983) 'Guidelines for starting and operating an international licensing program for small business', *Journal of Small Business Management*, 21(4): 24–30.

Welch, L. S. (1989) 'Diffusion of franchise system use in international operations', *International Marketing Review*, 6(5): 7–19.

Zahra, S. A., Matherne, B. P. and Carleton, J. M. (2003) 'Technological resource leveraging and the internationalization of new ventures', *Journal of International Entrepreneurship*, 1(2): 163–186.

10

Joint Ventures and Alliances

Miguel Rivera-Santos and Andrew C. Inkpen

INTRODUCTION

Over the last few decades, joint ventures and alliances have become so prevalent, both internationally and domestically (Terpstra and Simonin 1993), that some authors have argued we are entering an age of 'alliance capitalism', characterized by an 'increasing porosity of the boundaries of firms, countries and markets' (Dunning 1995). As a result, much attention has been devoted to this phenomenon in academia, giving birth to prolific research streams in virtually all the disciplines dealing with business organizations. Ongoing research streams on joint ventures and alliances can thus be found in marketing, strategic management, international business, organizational behavior, human resource management, entrepreneurship, economics, operations management, information systems, finance, accounting, law, organization theory, and sociology. In fact, over 500 empirical papers on joint ventures and alliances were published in the major journals of these disciplines between 1980 and 2006. Many of these papers have focused on the specific case of international alliances.

One of the challenges in studying the alliance field is the variety of organizational forms of inter-organizational cooperation and the many terms used, including strategic alliance, partnership, and joint venture. Alliances may be created by competitors, such as Autolatina, the distribution alliance between Ford and Volkswagen in South America (Rauschenbach 1988); between suppliers and manufacturers, such as Toyota's supplier network in Japan (Dyer and Nobeoka 2000); between manufacturers and distributors, such as the partnerships in wholesale distribution (Anderson and Narus 1990); across industries, such as alliances between industry and educational institutions (Motohashi 2005); and even across private and public sectors, such as alliances between, government, their agencies and private firms in industrial parks (Inkpen and Pien 2006). Similarly, alliances may involve complex activities, such as research and development (Oxley and Sampson 2004) or focus on a narrow set of joint activities, such as branding and advertising (Simonin and Ruth 1998) or co-promotions (Son, Hahn and Kang 2006). Alliances may be formalized, with the creation of a separate, jointly owned entity or informal and non-equity in structure.

There are several characteristics that distinguish alliances from arms-length contractual relationships: (1) the partners are interested in both their own outcomes and the outcomes of their partners; (2) the alliance structure is more than a price-driven financial relationship; (3) there is a mutual hostage dynamic in the alliance relationship, which means that each partner has some ability to control the destiny of the other partner(s); (4) there is some sharing of knowledge and information between the partners, which has the effect of creating the possibility of opportunism; and (5), there will be some uncertainty and ambiguity in the relationship. Given uncertainty and ambiguity, an alliance contract rarely can identify all of the contingencies, which makes trust between partners' managers a key element in alliance management.

Many alliances are marketing-oriented or have implications for the marketing function in a firm, which explains why the study of alliances represents an important thread in marketing research. Firms may use alliances to improve the effectiveness of their branding. This may take the form of brand alliances, in which several firms put their brand or logo together on the same product (Bluemelhuber, Carter and Lambe 2007; Simonin and Ruth 1998), or promotion alliances, in which the advertising effort of several firms is combined (Son *et al.* 2006). With the increasing importance of corporate social responsibility initiatives, cause-marketing alliances that bring together firms and organizations, such as NGOs, foundations, or government agencies, are also becoming popular, especially in international contexts (Dickinson and Barker 2007; Gourville and Rangan 2004; Lafferty 2007). Firms may bundle their products through an alliance, with important implications not only for the firm's ability to specialize in sub-elements of the bundle but also for the firm's pricing and overall marketing strategies (Simonin and Ruth 1995). Many buyer–supplier relationships have taken on characteristics of alliances, such as shared risk and extensive knowledge-sharing between the partners. Alliances are often found in distribution agreements, especially in international expansion strategies, for which foreign firms may prefer to use an existing distribution network rather than to

create a new one (Brown, Dev and Zhou 2003), as well as in customer relationships (Beckett-Camarata, Camarata and Barker 1998). Finally, firms may also use alliances to learn marketing know-how or, more generally, knowledge about specific markets from a partner (Reich and Mankin 1986; Simonin 1999b).

This chapter presents an overarching view of the literature on inter-organizational cooperation, which we define as any agreement between two (or more) organizations to jointly carry out a task involving more interactions than a one-time arm's-length contract. We use the terms 'inter-organizational cooperation' and 'alliances' interchangeably. We will restrict our use of the term 'joint venture' to describe an alliance involving the creation of a jointly owned separate entity by the partners. Our focus is international cooperation embedded within the broader literature on inter-organizational cooperation. Although international alliances have specific features such as amplified cultural differences between partners and multiple institutional environments (Aguilera 2007), the managerial issues found in international cooperation are essentially the same as those found in domestic cooperation. Similarly, our disciplinary focus is marketing, but the cross-disciplinary nature of research on inter-organizational collaboration (i.e., authors grounded in marketing also publish in strategy and international business journals) leads us to refer to advances made in a variety of disciplines, including international business, strategic management, and economics.

This chapter is organized around three main questions. The first question, 'Why do alliances exist?', situates the phenomenon of inter-organizational cooperation within the theories of the firm and explores the various attempts at explaining this phenomenon from a conceptual standpoint. The second question, 'Why use an alliance for international expansion?', explores the situations in which cooperation is preferred over alternative growth vehicles and the determinants of its success and failure. The third question, 'After 25 years of research, what is left to explore?', identifies gaps in the literature and discusses potential avenues for future research.

WHY DO ALLIANCES EXIST?

Cooperation and the theories of the firm

Inter-organizational cooperation has been studied in a variety of academic disciplines with different theoretical approaches used. Each theory sheds light on a specific dimension but none is sufficient to explain the entire phenomenon (Child, Faulkner and Tallman 2005). Industrial organization (IO) (Porter 1980), transaction cost economics (TCE) (Williamson 1975), and the resource-based view of the firm (RBV) (Barney 1991) focus on the motives for cooperation, while agency theory (Jensen and Meckling 1976) and social exchange theory (Kelley and Thibaut 1978) explore the dynamics within an alliance. Network theory (Gulati 1998) places the firm within a network of alliances. Some theories are used across disciplinary boundaries, while others are applied primarily in specific disciplines, such as information processing theory (Miller 1956) in information systems and operations research. Rather than providing an exhaustive and detailed list of theoretical orientations, this chapter discusses IO, TCE, RBV and institutional theories because they have been used extensively in international cooperation literature across academic disciplines (Brouthers and Hennart 2007).

Industrial organization: Cooperation and market power

For IO or mainstream economics scholars, the firm is a locus of production. Because industry structures are not homogenous, firms pursue strategies allowing them to find or defend an attractive position, i.e., a position within the underlying structure of the industry in which higher profitability can be expected (Porter 1980). In this approach, inter-organizational cooperation is one of the moves available to a firm to enhance its competitive advantage or decrease a competitors' advantage. This move may be offensive, when the firm's goal is to expand its power in an industry, or defensive, when the firm's goal is to defend a threatened position (Hymer 1976). In this view, cooperation is an alternative (or a complement) to other competitive moves, the goal of which is ultimately to either increase revenue (or decrease a competitor's revenue) or decrease costs (or increase a competitor's costs).

Alliances may increase a firm's revenue in a number of ways. They can help firms shape the industry, thus improving their market power and competitive positions (Glaister and Buckley 1996). A firm may form alliances to increase its power over its suppliers by increasing the level of concentration in its industry, or to reduce its competitors' power by forming an alliance with the competitors' suppliers (Porter and Fuller 1986). Similarly, a firm may form an alliance with a customer, locking the customer into a long-term relationship and thus preventing competitors from tapping into the related revenue stream. Firms targeting government contracts increasingly form alliances with the government agency for which they provide a service, using a specific form of alliance called public–private partnership (Goldsmith 1997). In some cases, firms may also collude, which is an extreme form of cooperation (Hinloopen and Martin 2006). Besides agreements that are clearly illegal, such as joint decisions on price-setting or production, much of the economics literature on alliances explores the competitive consequences of inter-organizational cooperation to determine if some alliances, such as those for basic research and development, are acceptable from an anti-trust standpoint (Hinloopen and Martin 2006).

In addition to increasing a firm's revenue (or decreasing a competitor's revenue), alliances are also a means by which firms can decrease their costs (or increase a competitor's costs). Firms may directly reduce costs by sharing production or research facilities, thus tapping into economies of scale that would not be achievable by a firm on its own (Hennart 1988). Similarly, firms may reduce their overall costs by forming alliances with a firm possessing a competitive advantage in a complementary activity of the value chain (Child *et al.* 2005; Porter and Fuller 1986), such as distribution. Finally, in the case of highly uncertain activities, such as R&D and standard setting, firms may reduce overall development costs by sharing the related risk with partners (Glaister and Buckley 1996; Porter and Fuller 1986).

In summary, for IO scholars alliances constitute an alternative to other strategic moves. This approach provides valuable insights on how inter-organizational cooperation may be used by firms to improve their global competitive positioning in an industry. The approach has been particularly useful for understanding the motives leading firms to form international alliances (Glaister and Buckley 1996).

Transaction cost economics: Cooperation and the right way to govern transactions

For TCE scholars, a firm is an accumulation of transactions which are less costly to govern through a hierarchy (a firm) than through a market (Williamson 1975, 1985). The degree of specificity of the assets involved in the transaction, the uncertainty surrounding the transaction, and the frequency of the transaction are the three major elements influencing the cost of a transaction. These elements determine the choice between market and hierarchy (Williamson 1985). Markets are efficient for governing unspecific, certain, and infrequent transactions because they avoid the overhead costs associated with a hierarchy. Hierarchies are efficient to govern specific, uncertain, and frequent transactions because they avoid the monitoring costs

associated with a market. Thus, the characteristics of a transaction determine the relative costs of market-based versus hierarchy-based governance.

Sharing characteristics with hierarchies and markets, alliances are viewed as hybrid governance structures (Oxley 1997; Williamson 1985), although some authors argue that, because alliances often involve equity, they should be viewed as a form of hierarchy rather than a distinct hybrid governance structure (Brouthers and Hennart 2007; Hennart 1988). In this view, alliances are the appropriate governance structure for transactions that involve assets with moderate specificity, that exhibit a relatively high level of uncertainty, and that are recurrent over time (Child *et al.* 2005; Williamson 1985). Indeed, transactions involving unspecific assets are best governed by a market since there is little risk of opportunism if the assets, being unspecific, are available from multiple sources. At the other extreme of the continuum, transactions involving highly specific assets are best governed by a hierarchy because, even if alliances have specific protection mechanisms, there is still room for potential opportunistic behaviors by the partner. In contrast, transactions involving moderately specific assets and governed by an alliance are better protected from opportunism than in a market and involve fewer overhead costs than in a hierarchy. Similarly, if uncertainty is high, alliances may be a more efficient governance structure than markets because market-based contracts are an inherently imperfect mechanism to monitor uncertain transactions (Williamson 1975) and because alliances are more flexible than hierarchies (Beamish and Banks 1987). Finally, if a transaction is recurrent over time, markets quickly become more costly than alliances or hierarchies because a market would treat each recurrence of the same transaction as a different transaction, increasing the overall cost.

We should note that several authors have argued that, in addition to the dimensions explicitly discussed by Williamson (1985), information asymmetry has an important impact on the cost of a transaction, especially in the case of horizontal transactions (Brouthers and Hennart 2007). Transactions involving high asymmetry are likely to be governed more efficiently by an alliance than by a market, as the cost of monitoring such a transaction would be very high in an arm's-length relationship.

Comparing the IO and TCE approaches, TCE views alliances as an alternative to other governance structures. This approach provides valuable insights on the relative advantages and disadvantages of a green-field investment, a JV, and an acquisition for international expansion and has been extensively used in the literature on modes of entry into foreign markets (Brouthers and Hennart 2007).

The resource-based view of the firm: Cooperation and the search for resources

RBV scholars view the firm as a bundle of resources (Barney 1991). Because firms possess different combinations of resources, different levels of profitability will be observed in an industry. While some resources are commonly available, others that are valuable, rare, inimitable, and non-substitutable can generate organizational rents (Amit and Shoemaker 1993; Barney 1991). Firms develop firm-specific valuable resources (Barney 1991), strategic assets (Amit and Shoemaker 1993), core competences (Prahalad and Hamel 1990), valuable knowledge (Grant 1996) and dynamic capabilities (Eisenhardt and Martin 2000), upon which they build a competitive advantage. A firm's growth strategy is an attempt to update, improve, or adapt its resource set to create, sustain or expand into new businesses or geographic areas.

For RBV scholars, alliances are one of four major vehicles to acquire new resources. The other three are internal development, the acquisition of a resource in a resource market, and mergers and acquisitions (Capron and

Mitchell 2004; Madhok and Tallman 1998). To develop a resource internally, the firm must be capable of absorbing the risk of developing the resource, both in terms of potential failure and in terms of time and other resources needed for development. If a firm's resource set is too different from the needed resource or if the risk of failure is too high, a firm may not be able to pursue internal development. Alternatively, a firm may acquire the needed resource in a resource market. To do so, the firm must have the financial resources that allow it to acquire the needed resource and, most importantly, the resource must be available. As Amit and Shoemaker (1993) suggest, a valuable resource is unlikely to be acquirable on a market since the value of the resource is directly linked to the fact that it is imperfectly tradable. A firm may also acquire another firm possessing the needed resource. To do so, the firm must be willing to acquire an entire resource set in order to get a specific resource, potentially paying a premium and running the risk of not being able to internalize the targeted resource.

The fourth option available to a firm in search of a new resource is acquisition through an alliance (Inkpen 2000). Alliances are typically faster than internal development, less costly than the acquisition of an entire company, and allow the acquisition of imperfectly tradable and tacit resources such as knowledge that can only be acquired through repeated interactions (Nonaka 1994). In addition, if the targeted resource is embedded in knowledgeable employees prone to leaving if their firm is acquired, alliances reduce the risk of losing the resource before acquiring it (Child et al. 2005). Acquiring resources through alliances also comes with specific challenges and risks. Some firms are better at learning through alliances than others, some resources are easier to learn through an alliance than others, and the structure of the alliance influences the ability to learn (Inkpen 2000; Simonin 1999a). A firm's partner may have specific learning goals, leading to leakage risks for the focal firm (Khanna, Gulati and

Nohria 1998), which has led some authors to question whether firms can simultaneously learn and protect their valuable resources in alliances (Kale, Singh and Perlmutter 2000; Rivera-Santos, Dussauge and Mitchell 2005). We should note that some scholars argue that alliances may be a better vehicle for resource combination across boundaries than for learning (Dyer and Singh 1998; Grant and Baden-Fuller 2004).

In general, RBV scholars view alliances as an alternative to other vehicles for resource acquisition. This view provides valuable insights on why firms select specific partners in international expansion (Hitt *et al.* 2000).

Institutional theory: Cooperation and a firm's institutional environment

For Institutional Theory (IT) scholars, a firm is the result of pressures from institutional environment. These pressures lead firms to adopt similar (isomorphic) structures and practices in order to gain legitimacy and to function well in a specific country (Alcantara, Mitsuhashi and Hoshino 2006; Yiu and Makino 2002). Each country, with its own institutional environment, dictates the economic 'rules of the game' and shapes the nature of competition (Scott 2005). In turn, an institutional environment has three major pillars: the regulatory, normative, and cognitive dimensions of the environment (Scott 1995).

In this view, alliances are a firm's response to characteristics and pressures stemming from the institutional environment. From a regulatory point of view, firms may have to form an alliance in order to operate. A firm may have to form an alliance with a government agency in order to become a provider to that government (Goldsmith 1997). Firms entering foreign markets are often required to establish alliances in industries deemed sensitive or prioritized for development by the host government (Gomes-Casseres 1990). An example is automobile manufacturing in China. Even when not required to do so, a firm may decide to partner with a local player in order to diminish its exposure to the liability of foreignness (Zaheer 1995). A firm may form an alliance with a domestic company or with a government-run company or agency to reduce the risks related to doing business in a country with weak institutions (Tang 2003). From a normative point of view, a foreign firm may decide to form an alliance with a local partner in order to better conform to the host country's cultural norms (Yiu and Makino 2002). Several authors have argued that foreign firms active in China benefit from forming an alliance with a domestic partner because that partner can provide access to *guanxi* networks, which are a backbone of the Chinese business system (Tang 2003; Xin and Pearce 1996). From a cognitive point of view, forming an alliance with a partner familiar with the cognitive structure of decision-makers in a given industry or country is a way for a firm to adapt its own cognitive structures to the needs of a new environment (Yiu and Makino 2002).

In summary, IT scholars view alliances as a means to overcome differences in institutional environments. This approach, although less common than the IO, TCE and RBV in the general alliance literature (Yiu and Makino 2002), provides valuable insights into why firms may choose alliances when entering foreign markets.

Many disciplines and many theories

This section introduces the four major theories that have been applied to the study of alliances and explores how each theory explains inter-organizational cooperation. As we mentioned earlier, other theoretical perspectives have brought interesting insights to the study of alliances. In particular, resource dependence theory views alliances as a way to ensure access to and control of resources crucial for the firm. Real options theory views alliances as an option on acquisition that allows firms to reduce information asymmetry before an acquisition

(Kogut 1991; Reuer and Tong 2005). Network theory views cooperation as the building block of networks of firms that allow their members to access resources located throughout the network (Gulati 1998; Uzzi 1996); Game theory provides insights on firms' decisions to cooperate or compete over time (Parkhe 1993; Zhang and Rajagopalan 2002); Agency theory helps understand the relationship between parent companies and their alliances and provides insights on the control and incentives mechanisms that partners may put in place (Reuer and Miller 1997). Social exchange theory helps understand the relational dynamics within an alliance (Steensma and Lyles 2000).

WHY USE ALLIANCES FOR INTERNATIONAL EXPANSION?

Alliances as vehicles for foreign market entry

The empirical literature on international alliances constitutes a major portion of the broader literature on alliances. The amount of empirical papers found in several academic disciplines, which do not always build on each others' advances, the variety of research questions explored, and the many empirical tools used, make it very difficult to present an overall view of empirical findings in this literature. In this section, we organize those findings around the two major dependent variables found in this literature: the choice of an alliance for international expansion and the performance implications of alliances.

What determines the choice of an alliance for international expansion?

As we discussed in the previous section, alliances are one among several organizational form alternatives from which a firm

can choose. Much of the empirical literature on international alliances has focused on why firms enter foreign markets through alliances as opposed to a greenfield investment or the acquisition of an existing company (see Chapter 11), to exporting and to licensing (Chapter 9) and to licensing (Chapter 10). Two major categories of determinants have been identified: characteristics of the firm and characteristics of the firm's internationalization strategies.

A firm's international experience is one of the most important factors to explain the choice of an alliance for a foreign market entry. Zhao, Luo and Suh (2004), in a recent meta-analysis of academic studies on entry-mode choices, found that firms with international experience tend to choose equity-based alliance modes, confirmingj findings from earlier studies (e.g., Aulakh and Kotabe 1997; Contractor and Kundu 1998). Similarly, firms with experience in forming alliances are also more likely to pursue growth through alliances (Anand and Khanna 2000). However, if a firm combines a long experience of alliances and disappointing performance as perceived by managers, the propensity to use further alliances decreases (Lohrke, Kreiser and Weaver 2006).

Several studies further suggest that firms are also influenced by their home country institutional environment (Li, Lam and Qian 2001). Makino and Neupert (2000) found that Japanese firms tend to use fewer JVs in the US than US firms in Japan and Terpstra and Simonin (1993) found that Japanese firms tend to use more contractual agreements than joint ventures. Pan and Tse (1996) found that Japanese companies tend to collaborate more often overall. More generally, firms from feminine, collective, and uncertainty-avoiding societies are more likely to use alliances for foreign market entry (Steensma, Marino and Weaver 2000) and firms from higher power distance cultures tend to prefer equity-based alliances (Tse, Pan and Au 1997). Building on this line of research, recent findings suggest that the occurrence and the success of cross-border brand alliances depend on the fit between country of origin characteristics and brand characteristics (Bluemelhuber *et al.* 2007).

In addition to firm-level characteristics, the international strategy of a firm also has a strong impact on entry-mode choice. A firm with a goal to transfer a valuable resource to other countries (i.e., a market-seeking objective) is likely to choose entry modes allowing both the transfer of and control over its valuable resource, leading to the choice of equity-based alliances (Brouthers and Hennart 2007; Erramilli, Agarwal and Dev 2002). Following a similar logic, firms may re-create their domestic alliances in international contexts (Martin, Mitchell and Swaminathan 1995). In contrast, firms may also need to leverage local resources they do not possess. The access to local complementary resources is another major determinant of international alliance formation (Anand and Delios 1997; Delios and Beamish 1999). Hitt *et al.* (2000) found that firms from developed markets form international JVs (IJVs) to access local market knowledge or unique capabilities possessed by a local partner, while firms from emerging markets emphasize financial assets, technical capabilities, intangible assets, and willingness to share expertise. Similarly, Si and Bruton (1999) found that local knowledge acquisition is a major determinant of IJV formation in China. Generally, the more difficult to attain or the more tacit the resource and the higher the degree of information asymmetry, the higher the propensity for an alliance (Arora 1996; Balakrishnan and Koza 1993; Chen and Hennart 2004; Davidson and McFetridge 1984; Kogut and Zander 1993).

Finally, characteristics of the country to be entered influence entry-mode choice. Firms may be forced to form an alliance with a local partner by the country's regulations (Gomes-Casseres 1989; Micinski 1992). More generally, firms may also use alliances with local organizations to mitigate country-level risk (Contractor and Kundu 1998; Pan and Tse 1996; Wei, Liu and Liu 2005), to increase legitimacy in the host country (Alcantara *et al.* 2006), to reduce uncertainty

about market potential (Chi and McGuire 1996), to overcome high barriers to entry (Chen and Hennart 2002), and to reduce cultural distance (Zhao *et al.* 2004). We should also note that industry-specific factors influence entry-mode choice, which further complicates the overall picture. Tse, Pan and Au (1997) found that the larger the scale of operations, the more probable the choice of an equity-based investment, such as a JV, and Pan and Tse (1996) found that firms in capital-intensive sectors are more likely to cooperate. Several studies suggest that high-tech sectors tend to lead to shorter and more contractual alliances, while more mature sectors tend to lead to JVs (Hagedoorn and Narula 1996; Nordberg, Campbell and Verbeke 2003).

This brief overview of the empirical findings on why firms may choose alliances for foreign-market entry over other organizational firms supports most of the predictions by the four major theories introduced in the previous section. As IO theory suggests, firms form international alliances to expand a competitive advantage internationally. TCE suggests that firms form international alliances when transaction costs are lower through alliances. In the RBV, firms form international alliances to get access to resources they need or to leverage resources they possess. Finally, IT suggests that firms form alliances to respond to differences in institutional environments. We should note, however, that TCE's asset specificity argument is not supported by a majority of studies on international market entry mode choices. This may be due to measurement issues or to an inadequate application of a concept developed for vertical relationships in empirical studies of horizontal relationships (Brouthers and Hennart 2007).

What are the performance implications of international alliances?

A second major portion of the alliance literature on market-entry mechanisms explores the performance implications of alliances. This literature identifies two specific issues. The first is the adequate level of analysis to measure performance. At the alliance level, performance may be measured the way a firm's performance is measured, i.e., through longevity, profitability or market-share measures. Many scholars argue, however, that if alliances are a vehicle through which firms pursue non-financial goals, alliance performance should be measured at the firm level and reflect the fulfillment of the goals set for the alliance. If a firm forms an alliance to acquire knowledge or to develop a new technology, a dissolution of the alliance may be a sign of success, signaling that the firm no longer needs the alliance, rather than a sign of failure (Dussauge, Garrette and Mitchell 2000; Inkpen and Beamish 1997; Khanna *et al.* 1998). The second issue is endogeneity in the empirical tests. Testing whether specific modes of entry lead to higher chances of IJV survival may be misleading, because, as Shaver (1998) argues, the choice of entry mode is determined by firm- and industry-specific characteristics that also influence survival of a venture.

Characteristics of the partner firms

Various characteristics of the partners influence the potential for alliance success. Three characteristics will be examined: partner ability to manage alliances, which is related to partner alliance experience; partner commitment to alliance success; and partner ability to manage cultural distances.

A firm's alliance experience is identified as one of the major determinants of alliance success in the literature. A firm's alliance experience enables it to develop routines based on its prior successes and mistakes, thus improving the performance of subsequent alliances (Emden, Yaprak and Cavusgil 2005). Research suggests that the number of prior alliances has an impact on rates of new product development (Deeds and Hill 1996), on innovation-related growth (Powell, Koput

and Smith-Doerr 1996) and on overall performance (Anand and Khanna 2000). Yet, the number of prior alliances is in itself often insufficient to build experience. As several studies suggest, firms still need to internalize their alliance experiences and transform them into organizational routines to fully benefit from them in their future collaborations (Simonin 1997; Zollo, Reuer and Singh 2002). Finally, some firms are more adept at managing alliances than others and possess what authors have called a 'cooperative competency' (Sivadas and Dwyer 2000) or 'relational capability' (Lorenzoni and Lipparini 1999) that increases the probability of success in subsequent alliances. Some firms further reinforce this specific alliance competence organizationally. Several studies found, for instance, that firms that 'create a dedicated alliance function (with the intent of strategically coordinating alliance activity and capturing/disseminating alliance-related knowledge)' enjoy greater returns from their alliances and improve their learning processes (Kale, Dyer and Singh 2002; Kale and Singh 2007). We should note that, in addition to alliance experience, the literature also suggests that general international experience has a positive impact on subsequent alliance performance (Child and Yan 2003).

A firm's commitment to the alliance is a second determinant of success because it creates flexibility and a willingness to bear the risks specific to an alliance (Inkpen and Li 1999). This commitment is important in various alliance types (Wu and Cavusgil 2006), including buyer–seller relationships (Skarmeas, Katsikeas and Schlegelmilch 2002) and cross-sector alliances (Mora-Valentin, Montoro-Sanchez and Guerras-Martin 2004). That said, commitment is crucial in cross-cultural alliances where the potential level of mistrust is high (Luo 2002a). Indeed, cultural differences between partners have been identified as one of the major antecedents of alliance dissolution (Parkhe 1991), while findings suggest that partners from culturally close countries find it easier to manage an alliance (Li *et al.* 2001). In domestic alliances, the literature suggests that differences in organizational and professional cultures often lead to alliance instability, as the partners find it difficult to 'read' each other (Carson, Madhok, Varman and John 2003) and make inter-partner knowledge transfers more challenging (Lane and Lubatkin 1998). In international alliances, national culture differences are added to organizational culture differences (Parkhe 1991), magnifying the challenges. Sirmon and Lane (2004), in a model including cultural, organizational, and professional differences in international alliances, further argue that the impact of these differences is likely to be stronger if the domain of one of the social groups is close to the core activity of the alliance. We should note that cultural differences are both a determinant of alliance formation, as we discussed in an earlier section, and a cause of alliance instability, suggesting that, while inter-partner cultural differences are challenging in an alliance, firms still find them more manageable with a partner than without. The literature further suggests that both a firm's experience in international alliances (Emden *et al.* 2005) and its experience in dealing with a specific partner (Simonin 1999a) may mitigate these challenges.

Characteristics of the alliance

The characteristics of the alliance itself also have a major impact on its success. These characteristics fall into two major categories: contractual characteristics resulting from inter-partner negotiations, and procedural characteristics resulting from inter-partner interactions.

The contractual determinants of alliance success result from negotiations among partners and reflect agreement on how to structure and manage the alliance. Negotiations will usually cover a wide range of topics before the actual formation of the alliance and may lead to agreements that are more or less complex, although re-negotiations also typically occur during the lifetime of an

alliance (Reuer and Ariño 2007; Reuer and Ariño 2002). Prior research identifies alliance contracts, the degree of equity sharing, and the organizational features of the alliance as important contractual determinants of alliance success.

Much of the literature on alliance contracts focuses on their incompleteness and inherent inability to control the potentially complex interactions that evolve among partners (Dasgupta and Tao 1998). Contracts are inefficient to fully control risks associated with alliances (Nordberg, Campbell and Verbeke 1996), although evidence indicates that alliance contracts do have an influence on alliance success. Lyles and Salk (1996) found that knowledge transfers and performance are positively related to the existence of specific clauses in the IJV contract.

The existence of an equity sharing agreement among alliance partners is another contractual variable that influences alliance success. Because this agreement increases the cost of opportunistically leaving the alliance (Deeds and Hill 1998), it increases the partners' commitment to the success of the alliance. Confirming this argument, most empirical results suggest that equity-based alliances are more stable than non-equity-based alliances. However, the impact of specific levels of equity ownership on the performance of IJVs is less clear. While some authors argue that a majority equity ownership leads to more stability because there is a dominant partner (Killing 1983), others argue that 50-50 IJVs are more stable precisely because of the lack of a dominant partner (Bleeke and Ernst 1991). At the same time, some authors find asymmetric governance structures to have no impact on the stability or the survival of IJVs (Blodgett 1992; Lee, Chen and Kao 2003). Other studies find that IJVs involving small ownership levels for the international partner have very high mortality rates, while those with high ownership levels have mortality rates comparable to that of wholly owned subsidiaries (Dhanaraj and Beamish 2004).

There are several other important alliance contractual and structural features, including the fit between alliance attributes and alliance form (Murray and Kotabe 2005); the co-location of both partners' alliance activities (McKelvey, Alm and Riccaboni 2003; Owen-Smith and Powell 2004); the types of controls in place in the alliance, such as staffing or decision-making rules (Chalos and O'Connor 2004); and the degree of autonomy given to the alliance structure (Newburry and Zeira 1999).

The contractual characteristics of alliances are the backbone of an alliance. Many authors argue that the interactions between the partners is what really determines the success or failure of an alliance (Doz 1996). Procedural determinants of alliance success are those determinants that result from interactions between alliance partners. Procedural determinants are, of course, related to the contractual features of the alliance because those interactions occur as a consequence of inter-partner negotiations. However, procedural determinants are distinct from contractual features because the inherent incompleteness of contracts precludes the possibility for contracts to fully determine *ex ante* the types of interactions that will occur in an alliance. Two key determinants emerge from this literature: trust and the dynamics of interactions between partners.

Inter-partner trust serves as a 'social lubricant' (Carson *et al.* 2003) that facilitates interactions among partners' employees, increasing the probability of alliance overall success (Ariño, De La Torre and Ring 2001; Aulakh, Kotabe and Sahay 1996; Zaheer, McEvily and Perrone 1997). Dyer and Chu (2003) found that trust between a supplier and a manufacturer significantly increases the amount of information sharing in the alliance. Kotabe, Martin and Domoto (2003) concluded that the duration of a supplier–manufacturer alliance relationship leads to higher performance levels. Walter (2003) found that in supplier–customer relationships, trust leads to more involvement which, in turn, leads to a higher level of new product development. Walter argued that the presence of alliance managers that functioned as 'relationship promoters' significantly increases the level of commitment of alliance employees. Recently, Luo (2008) highlighted the role of perceived procedural fairness on the performance of alliances. More generally, Carson, Madhok, Varman and John (2003) argued that 'trust-based governance' is related to the partners' ability to understand each other in the alliance, which improves the chances of alliance success.

A second important procedural characteristic of alliances is that they evolve over time. The industry may evolve, leading to changes in the partners' needs and goals for the alliance and inter-partner interactions within the alliance also make the alliance evolve. As inter-partner knowledge transfers occur, the bargaining positions of the partners may change, potentially leading to instability (Inkpen and Beamish 1997). Similarly, both internal and external events may lead to an evolution of the perceptions of efficiency and equity within the alliance and ultimately lead to failure (Ariño and De La Torre 1998). Most studies in this literature suggest that the partners' ability to recognize internal evolutions in the alliance and their willingness to adapt to these changes are key determinants of alliance success (Doz 1996).

More generally, contractual and procedural characteristics of an alliance influence the trust and control balance that is central to alliance management. While trust can be viewed as an informal governance structure on its own (Madhok 1995, 2006; Svejenova 2006), 'trust, along with partner collaborative objectives, creates the initial climate that shapes partner interactions; in turn, these interactions lead to subsequent decisions about the nature of controls' (Inkpen and Currall 2004). As a result, trust and control are two inseparable determinants of alliance success (Das and Teng 1998).

AFTER 25 YEARS, WHAT IS LEFT TO EXPLORE?

Avenues for further research

The literature reviewed in the previous sections suggests that significant territory in the international alliance area has been covered. However, many aspects of alliances are under-explored. Among these, some are specific to the study of international alliances, but most apply to all alliances. In this concluding section, we focus on four potential avenues for further research: micro-mechanisms within alliances; alliance portfolios; alliances in emerging markets; and non-traditional alliances.

As our literature review indicates, there are many determinants of alliance success and failure. The accumulation of consistent research results over time suggests that the major mechanisms have been identified and tested and several determinants of success are well refined. The argument that experience increases the success of subsequent alliances is extended by research on general vs. partner-specific experience (Hoang and Rothaermel 2005). Similarly, the impact of equity sharing in IJVs is better understood when the differential impact of different levels of equity sharing is explored (Dhanaraj and Beamish 2004). How these different determinants, which are all micro-mechanisms as opposed to macro-concepts, interact with each other is still unclear. Few studies have explored how mechanisms that increase protection in an alliance may interact with mechanisms increasing knowledge transfers. It is unclear whether the mechanisms that a firm puts in place in alliance to acquire knowledge (Inkpen 2002) are similar to those that facilitate access to (as opposed to acquisition of) knowledge (Grant and Baden-Fuller 2004) and whether these two sets of mechanisms are implementable within the same alliance. These questions are particularly relevant in emerging economies, which typically have weaker institutional and legal protections, and in which foreign firms may be concerned that their domestic partners plan to take advantage of them.

Similarly, the idea that firms build alliance portfolios is not new (Koza and Lewin 1998) and the vast literature on networks has provided valuable insights into how firms can benefit from their portfolio of partners (Lazzarini 2007; Lorenzoni and Lipparini 1999; Uzzi 1996). However, the means by which firms structure their network of alliances, using different alliances for different purposes, still form a burgeoning literature (Hoffmann 2007; Kumar 2005; Lavie 2007; Murray and Kotabe 2005; Parise and Casher 2003). Furthermore, how firms use their network of alliances in conjunction with acquisitions and internal development to support their overall strategy is still unclear. This question is particularly relevant to the study of MNEs in global competition (Ramamurti 2004).

The increasing importance of MNEs from emerging countries also provides an exciting new avenue for research on international alliances. Institutional theory suggests that firms are influenced by their institutional environment and there is some evidence that the diversification patterns of MNEs from emerging economies are unique (Khanna, Kogan and Palepu 2006). It is still unclear, however, whether the same is true about their alliance strategies. As we mentioned in our review of the literature, there is evidence that the alliance strategy of Japanese firms is different from that of Western firms. Very few studies have explored the alliance strategies of firms from emerging economies (Khanna and Rivkin 2006; Luo 2002b). Yet, they may differ not only in terms of motivations (the types of resource sought) but also in terms of preferred organizational structures.

Finally, the international alliance literature (and the alliance literature in general) has paid limited attention to non-traditional alliances. Cross-sector alliances have been virtually ignored, except for the very specific case of alliances between firms and public research institutions, such as universities or government-led research consortia (Fontana, Geuna and Matt 2006). Due to the specificities of the partners involved, alliances with NGOs or with government agencies are likely to differ significantly from traditional alliances. Furthermore, the emerging base-of-the-pyramid literature (Ricart *et al.* 2004) suggests that cross-sector alliances may be a key to untapping these new revenue sources. This line of research is becoming increasingly important in the cause-marketing alliance literature, in which scholars have recently been exploring the impact on brand of alliances between firms and NGOs (Dickinson and Barker 2007; Lafferty 2007).

Conclusion

To conclude, after 25 years of research, the study of international alliances remains a vibrant and exciting field, with important implications for marketing theory and practice. As globalization marches relentlessly forward, more and more firms are being thrust into international competition. Alliances can be a vehicle to accomplish a variety of organizational goals in the global arena, such as market entry, knowledge access, learning, risk sharing, and legitimacy. As a result, there are many interesting research opportunities that are both cross-disciplinary and managerially relevant.

REFERENCES

Aguilera, R. V. (2007) 'Translating theoretical logics across borders: organizational characteristics, structural mechanisms and contextual factors in international alliances', *Journal of International Business Studies,* 38(1): 38–46.

Alcantara, L., Mitsuhashi, H. and Hoshino, Y. (2006) 'Legitimacy in international joint ventures: it is still needed', *Journal of International Management,* 12(4): 389–407.

Amit, R. and Shoemaker, P. J. H. (1993) 'Strategic Assets and Organizational Rent', *Strategic Management Journal,* 13(1): 33–46.

Anand, B. N. and Khanna, T. (2000) 'Do firms learn to create value? The case of alliances', *Strategic Management Journal,* 21(3): 295–315.

Anand, J. and Delios, A. (1997) 'Location specificity and the transferability of downstream assets to foreign subsidiaries', *Journal of International Business Studies,* 28(3): 579–604.

Anderson, J. C. and Narus, J. A. (1990) 'A model of distributor firm and manufacturer firm working partnerships', *Journal of Marketing,* 54(1): 42–59.

Ariño, Á. and De La Torre, J. (1998) 'Learning from failure: towards an evolutionary model of collaborative ventures', *Organization Science,* 9(3): 306–326.

Ariño, Á. De La Torre, J. and Ring, P. S. (2001) 'Relational quality: managing trust in corporate alliances', *California Management Review,* 44(1): 109–134.

Arora, A. (1996) 'Contracting for tacit knowledge: the provision of technical services in technology licensing contracts', *Journal of Development Economics,* 50(2): 233–256.

Aulakh, P. S. and Kotabe, M. (1997) 'Antecedents and performance implications of channel integration in foreign markets', *Journal of International Business Studies,* 28(1): 145–175.

Aulakh, P. S., Kotabe, M. and Sahay, A. (1996) 'Trust and performance in cross-border marketing partnerships: a behavioral approach', *Journal of International Business Studies,* 27(5): 1005–1033.

Balakrishnan, S. and Koza, M. P. (1993) 'Information asymmetry, adverse selection and joint-ventures. Theory and evidence', *Journal of Economic Behavior and Organization,* 20(1): 99–118.

Barney, J. B. (1991). Firm Resources and Sustained Competitive Advantage. *Journal of Management,* 17(1): 99–120.

Beamish, P. W. and Banks, J. C. (1987) 'Equity Joint Ventures and the theory of the multinational enterprise', *Journal of International Business Studies,* 18(2): 1–17.

Beckett-Camarata, E. J., Camarata, M. R. and Barker, R. T. (1998) 'Integrating internal and external customer relationships through relationship management: a strategic response to a changing global environment', *Journal of Business Research*, 41(1): 71.

Bleeke, J. and Ernst, D. (1991) 'The way to win in cross border alliances', *Harvard Business Review*, 69(6): 127–135.

Blodgett, L. L. (1992) 'Research notes and communications factors in the instability of International Joint Ventures: an event history analysis', *Strategic Management Journal*, 13(6): 475–481.

Bluemelhuber, C., Carter, L. L. and Lambe, C. J. (2007) 'Extending the view of brand alliance effects', *International Marketing Review*, 24(4): 427.

Brouthers, K. D. and Hennart, J.-F. (2007) 'Boundaries of the firm: insights from international entry mode research', *Journal of Management*, 33(3): 395–425.

Brown, J. R., Dev, C. S. and Zhou, Z. (2003) 'Broadening the foreign market entry mode decision: separating ownership and control', *Journal of International Business Studies*, 34(5): 473–489.

Capron, L. and Mitchell, W. (2004) 'Where firms change: internal development versus external capability sourcing in the global telecommunications industry', *European Management Review*, 1(2): 157–174.

Carson, S. J., Madhok, A., Varman, R. and John, G. (2003) 'Information processing moderators of the effectiveness of trust-based governance in interfirm R&D collaboration', *Organization Science*, 14(1): 45–57.

Chalos, P. and O'Connor, N. G. (2004) 'Determinants of the use of various control mechanisms in US–Chinese joint ventures', *Accounting, Organizations and Society*, 29(7): 591–609.

Chen, S.-F. S. and Hennart, J.-F. (2002) 'Japanese investors' choice of joint ventures versus wholly owned subsidiaries in the US: the role of market barriers and firm capabilities', *Journal of International Business Studies*, 33(1): 1–18.

Chen, S.-F. S. and Hennart, J.-F. (2004) 'A hostage theory of joint ventures: why do Japanese investors choose partial over full acquisitions to enter the United States?', *Journal of Business Research*, 57(10): 1126–1135.

Chi, T. and McGuire, D. J. (1996) 'Collaborative ventures and value of learning: integrating the transaction cost and strategic option perspectives on the choice of market entry modes', *Journal of International Business Studies*, 27(2): 285–308.

Child, J., Faulkner, D. and Tallman, S. (2005) *Cooperative Strategy: Managing Alliances, Networks, and Joint Ventures*, 2nd edn. Oxford: Oxford University Press.

Child, J. and Yan, Y. (2003) 'Predicting the performance of International Joint Ventures: an investigation in China', *Journal of Management Studies*, 40(2): 283–321.

Contractor, F. J. and Kundu, S. K. (1998) 'Modal choice in a world of alliances: analyzing organizational forms in the international hotel sector', *Journal of International Business Studies*, 29(2): 325–357.

Das, T. K. and Teng, B.-S. (1998) 'Between trust and control: developing confidence in partner cooperation in alliances', *Academy of Management Review*, 23(3): 491–512.

Dasgupta, S. and Tao, Z. (1998) 'Contractual incompleteness and the optimality of equity joint ventures', *Journal of Economic Behavior and Organization*, 37(4): 391–206.

Davidson, W. H. and McFetridge, D. G. (1984) 'International technology transactions and the theory of the firm', *Journal of Industrial Economics*, 32(3): 253–264.

Deeds, D. L. and Hill, C. W. L. (1996) 'Strategic alliances and the rate of new product development: an empirical study of entrepreneurial biotechnology firms', *Journal of Business Venturing*, 11(1): 41–56.

Deeds, D. L. and Hill, C. W. L. (1998) 'An examination of opportunistic action within research alliances: evidence from the biotechnology industry', *Journal of Business Venturing*, 14(2): 141–164.

Delios, A. and Beamish, P. W. (1999) 'Ownership strategy of Japanese firms: transactional, institutional, and experience influences', *Strategic Management Journal*, 20(10): 915–933.

Dhanaraj, C. and Beamish, P. W. (2004) 'Effect of equity ownership on the survival of international joint ventures', *Strategic Management Journal*, 25(3): 295–306.

Dickinson, S. and Barker, A. (2007) 'Evaluations of branding alliances between non-profit and commercial brand partners: the transfer of affect', *International Journal of Nonprofit and Voluntary Sector Marketing*, 12(1): 75.

Doz, Y. L. (1996) 'The evolution of cooperation in strategic alliances: initial conditions or learning processes?', *Strategic Management Journal*, 17: 55–83.

Dunning, J. H. (1995) 'Reappraising the eclectic paradigm in an age of alliance capitalism', *Journal of International Business Studies*, 26(3): 461–492.

Dussauge, P., Garrette, B. and Mitchell, W. (2000) 'Learning from competing partners: outcomes and durations of scale and link alliances in Europe, North America, and Asia', *Strategic Management Journal*, 21(2): 99–126.

Dyer, J. H. and Chu, W. (2003) 'The role of trustworthiness in reducing transaction costs and improving performance: Empirical evidence from the United States, Japan, and Korea', *Organization Science*, 14(1): 57–69.

Dyer, J. H. and Nobeoka, K. (2000) 'Creating and managing a high-performance knowledge-sharing network: the Toyota case', *Strategic Management Journal*, 21(3): 345–367.

Dyer, J. H. and Singh, H. (1998) 'The relational view: cooperative strategy and sources of inter-organizational advantage', *Academy of Management Review*, 23(4): 660–680.

Eisenhardt, K. M. and Martin, J. A. (2000) 'Dynamic capabilities: What are they?', *Strategic Management Journal*, 21(10/11): 1105–1121.

Emden, Z., Yaprak, A. and Cavusgil, S. T. (2005) 'Learning from experience in international alliances: antecedents and firm performance implications', *Journal of Business Research*, 58(7): 883–892.

Erramilli, M. K., Agarwal, S. and Dev, C. S. (2002) 'Choice between non-equity entry modes: an organizational capability perspective', *Journal of International Business Studies*, 33(2): 223–243.

Fontana, R., Geuna, A. and Matt, M. (2006) 'Factors affecting university–industry R&D projects: the importance of searching, screening and signalling', *Research Policy*, 35(2): 309–323.

Glaister, K. W. and Buckley, P. J. (1996) 'Strategic motives for international alliance formation', *Journal of Management Studies*, 33(3): 301–333.

Goldsmith, S. (1997). 'Can business really do business with government?', *Harvard Business Review* (May–June): 110–121.

Gomes-Casseres, B. (1989) 'Joint ventures in the face of global competition', *Sloan Management Review*, 30(3): 17–27.

Gomes-Casseres, B. (1990) 'Firm ownership preferences and host government restrictions: an integrated approach', *Journal of International Business Studies*, 21(1): 1–22.

Gourville, J. T. and Rangan, V. K. (2004) 'Valuing the cause marketing relationship', *California Management Review*, 47(1): 38–57.

Grant, R. M. (1996) 'Toward a knowledge-based theory of the firm,' *Strategic Management Journal*, 17 (Winter Special Issue): 109–122.

Grant, R. M. and Baden-Fuller, C. (2004) 'A knowledge accessing theory of strategic alliances', *Journal of Management Studies*, 41(1): 61–85.

Gulati, R. (1998) 'Alliances and networks', *Strategic Management Journal*, 19(4): 293–317.

Hagedoorn, J. and Narula, R. (1996) 'Choosing organizational modes of strategic technology partnering: International and sectoral differences', *Journal of International Business Studies*, 27(2): 265–285.

Hennart, J.-F. (1988) 'A transaction costs theory of equity joint ventures', *Strategic Management Journal*, 9(4): 361–374.

Hinloopen, J. and Martin, S. (2006) 'The economics of cartels, cartel policy, and collusion: Introduction to the special issue', *International Journal of Industrial Organization*, 24(6): 1079–1082.

Hitt, M. A., Dacin, M. T., Levitas, E., Arregle, J.-L. and Borza, A. (2000) 'Partner selection in emerging and developed market contexts: resource-base and organizational learning perspectives', *Academy of Management Journal*, 43(3): 449–467.

Hoang, H. and Rothaermel, F. T. (2005) 'The effect of general and partner-specific alliance experience on joint R&D project performance', *Academy of Management Journal*, 48(2): 332–345.

Hoffmann, W. H. (2007) 'Strategies for managing a portfolio of alliances', *Strategic Management Journal*, 28(8): 827–856.

Hymer, S. H. (1976) *The International Operations of National Firms: A Study of Direct Foreign Investment*. Cambridge, MA: MIT Press.

Inkpen, A. C. (2000) 'Learning through joint ventures: a framework of knowledge acquisition', *Journal of Management Studies,* 37(7): 1019–1043.

Inkpen, A. C. (2002) 'Learning, knowledge management and strategic alliances: So many studies, so many unanswered questions', in F. J. Contractor and P. Lorange (eds), *Cooperative Strategies and Alliances.* London: Pergamon, pp. 267–289.

Inkpen, A. C. and Beamish, P. W. (1997) 'Knowledge, bargaining power, and the instability of international joint ventures', *Academy of Management Review,* 22(1): 177–202.

Inkpen, A. C. and Currall, S. C. (2004) 'The coevolution of trust, control, and learning in joint ventures', *Organization Science,* 15(5): 586–599.

Inkpen, A. C. and Li, K.-Q. (1999) 'Joint venture formation: planning and knowledge-gathering for success', *Organizational Dynamics,* 27(4): 33–48.

Inkpen, A. C. and Pien, W. (2006) 'An examination of collaboration and knowledge transfer: China-Singapore Suzhou Industrial Park', *The Journal of Management Studies,* 43(4): 779–811.

Jensen, M. C. and Meckling, W. H. (1976) 'Theory of the firm: managerial behavior, agency costs, and ownership structure', *Journal of Financial Economics,* 3(4): 305–360.

Kale, P., Dyer, J. H. and Singh, H. (2002) 'Alliance capability, stock market response, and long-term alliance success: the role of the alliance function', *Strategic Management Journal*, 23(8): 747–767.

Kale, P. and Singh, H. (2007) 'Building firm capabilities through learning: the role of the alliance learning process in alliance capability and firm-level alliance success', *Strategic Management Journal*, 28(10): 981–1000.

Kale, P., Singh, H. and Perlmutter, H. (2000) 'Learning and protection of proprietary assets in strategic alliances: building relational capital', *Strategic Management Journal,* 21: 217–237.

Kelley, H. H. and Thibaut, J. (1978) *Interpersonal Relations: A Theory of Interdependence.* New York: Wiley.

Khanna, T., Gulati, R. and Nohria, N. (1998) 'The dynamics of learning alliances: competition, cooperation, and relative scope', *Strategic Management Journal,* 19(3): 193–210.

Khanna, T., Kogan, J. and Palepu, K. (2006) 'Globalization and similarities in corporate governance: a cross-country analysis', *The Review of Economics and Statistics,* 88(1): 69–90.

Khanna, T. and Rivkin, J. W. (2006) 'Inter-organizational ties and business group boundaries: evidence from an emerging economy', *Organization Science,* 17(3): 333.

Killing, J. P. (1983) *Strategies for Joint Venture Success.* New York: Praeger.

Kogut, B. (1991) 'Joint ventures and the option to expand and acquire', *Management Science*, 37(1): 19–33.

Kogut, B. and Zander, U. (1993) 'Knowledge of the firm and the evolutionary theory of the multinational corporation', *Journal of International Business Studies,* 24(4): 625–645.

Kotabe, M., Martin, X. and Domoto, H. (2003) 'Gaining from vertical partnerships: knowledge transfer, relationship duration and supplier performance improvement in the U.S. and Japanese automotive industries', *Strategic Management Journal*, 24(4): 293–317.

Koza, M. P. and Lewin, A. Y. (1998) 'The co-evolution of strategic alliances', *Organization Science*, 9(3): 225–264.

Kumar, M. V. S. (2005) 'The value from acquiring and divesting a joint venture: a real options approach', *Strategic Management Journal,* 26(4): 221–231.

Lafferty, B. A. (2007) 'The relevance of fit in a cause-brand alliance when consumers evaluate corporate credibility', *Journal of Business Research,* 60(5): 447–453.

Lane, P. J., and Lubatkin, M. H. (1998) 'Relative absorptive capacity and inter-organizational learning', *Strategic Management Journal,* 19(5): 461–477.

Lavie, D. (2007) 'Alliance portfolios and firm performance: a study of value creation and appropriation in the U.S. software industry', *Strategic Management Journal,* 28(12): 1187–1212.

Lazzarini, S. (2007) 'The impact of membership in competing alliance constellations: Evidence on the operational performance of global airlines', *Strategic Management Journal*, 28(4): 345–367.

Lee, J.-R., Chen, W.-R. and Kao, C. (2003) 'Determinants and performance impact of asymmetric governance structures in international joint ventures: An empirical investigation', *Journal of Business Research*, 56(10): 815–828.

Li, J., Lam, K. and Qian, G. (2001) 'Does culture affect behavior and performance of firms? The case of joint ventures in China', *Journal of International Business Studies*, 32(1): 115–132.

Lohrke, F. T., Kreiser, P. M. and Weaver, K. M. (2006) 'The influence of current firm performance on future SME alliance formation intentions: a six-country study', *Journal of Business Research*, 59(1): 19–27.

Lorenzoni, G. and Lipparini, A. (1999) 'The leveraging of interfirm relationships as a distinctive organizational capability: a longitudinal study', *Strategic Management Journal*, 20(4): 317–337.

Luo, Y. (2002a) 'Building trust in cross-cultural collaborations: toward a contingency perspective', *Journal of Management*, 28(5): 669–685.

Luo, Y. (2002b) 'Partnering with foreign businesses: perspectives from Chinese firms', *Journal of Business Research*, 55(6): 481–493.

Luo, Y. (2008) 'Procedural fairness and interfirm cooperation in strategic alliances', *Strategic Management Journal*, 29(1): 27–46.

Lyles, M. A. and Salk, J. E. (1996) 'Knowledge acquisition from foreign parents in international joint ventures: an empirical examination in the Hungarian context', *Journal of International Business Studies*, 27(5): 877–904.

Madhok, A. (1995) 'Revisiting multinational firms' tolerance for joint ventures: a trust-based approach', *Journal of International Business Studies*, 26(1): 117–137.

Madhok, A. (2006) 'How much does ownership really matter? Equity and trust relations in joint venture relationships', *Journal of International Business Studies*, 37(1): 4–11.

Madhok, A. and Tallman, S. B. (1998) 'Resources, transactions and rents: Managing value through interfirm collaborative relationships', *Organization Science*, 9(3): 326–339.

Makino, S. and Neupert, K. E. (2000) 'National culture, transaction costs, and the choice between joint venture and wholly owned subsidiary', *Journal of International Business Studies*, 31(4): 705–714.

Martin, X., Mitchell, W. and Swaminathan, A. (1995) 'Recreating and extending Japanese automobile buyer–supplier links in North America', *Strategic Management Journal*, 16(8): 589–619.

McKelvey, M., Alm, H. and Riccaboni, M. (2003) 'Does co-location matter for formal knowledge collaboration in the Swedish biotechnology–pharmaceutical sector?', *Research Policy*, 32(3): 483–502.

Micinski, A. J. (1992) 'Conditions for joint ventures with foreign participation in Poland', *Journal of Business Research*, 24(1): 67–72.

Miller, G. A. (1956) 'The magical number seven, plus or minus two: some limits on our capacity for processing information', *Psychological Review*, 63(2): 81–97.

Mora-Valentin, E. M., Montoro-Sanchez, A. and Guerras-Martin, L. A. (2004) 'Determining factors in the success of R&D cooperative agreements between firms and research organizations', *Research Policy*, 33(1): 17–40.

Motohashi, K. (2005) 'University–industry collaborations in Japan: The role of new technology-based firms in transforming the National Innovation System', *Research Policy*, 34(5): 583–594.

Murray, J. Y. and Kotabe, M. (2005) 'Performance implications of strategic fit between alliance attributes and alliance forms', *Journal of Business Research*, 58(11): 1525–1533.

Newburry, W. and Zeira, Y. (1999) 'Autonomy and effectiveness of equity international joint ventures (EIJV's): an analysis based on EIJVs in Hungary and Britain', *Journal of Management Studies*, 36(2): 263–285.

Nonaka, I. (1994) 'A dynamic theory of organizational knowledge creation', *Organization Science*, 5(1): 14–38.

Nordberg, M., Campbell, A. and Verbeke, A. (2003) 'Using customer relationships to acquire technological innovation: A value-chain analysis of supplier contracts with scientific research institutions', *Journal of Business Research*, 56(9): 711–719.

Nordberg, M., Campbell, A. J. and Verbeke, A. (1996) 'Can market-based contracts substitute for alliances in high technology markets?', *Journal of International Business Studies*, 27(5): 963–980.

Owen-Smith, J. and Powell, W. W. (2004) 'Knowledge networks as channels and conduits: the effects of spillovers in the Boston Biotechnology Community', *Organization Science,* 15(1): 5–22.

Oxley, J. E. (1997) 'Appropriability hazards and governance in strategic alliances: a transaction-cost approach', *Journal of Law, Economics and Organization,* 13(2): 387–409.

Oxley, J. E. and Sampson, R. C. (2004) 'The scope and governance of international R&D alliances', *Strategic Management Journal,* 25(8/9): 723–750.

Pan, Y. and Tse, D. K. (1996) 'Cooperative strategies between foreign firms in an overseas country', *Journal of International Business Studies,* 27(5): 929–947.

Parise, S. and Casher, A. (2003) 'Alliance portfolios: Designing and managing your network of business-partner relationships', *Academy of Management Executive,* 17(4): 25–39.

Parkhe, A. (1991) 'Interfirm diversity, organizational learning, and longevity in global strategic alliances', *Journal of International Business Studies,* 22(4): 579–601.

Parkhe, A. (1993) 'Strategic alliance structuring: a game theoretic and transaction cost examination of interfirm cooperation', *Academy of Management Journal,* 36(4): 794–829.

Porter, M. E. (1980) *Competitive Strategy.* New York: Free Press.

Porter, M. E. and Fuller, M. B. (1986) 'Coalitions and global strategy', in M. E. Porter (ed.), *Competition in Global Industries.* Boston, MA: Harvard Business School.

Powell, W. W., Koput, K. W. and Smith-Doerr, L. (1996) 'Inter-organizational collaboration and the locus of innovation networks of learning in biotechnology', *Administrative Science Quarterly,* 41(1): 116–145.

Prahalad, C. K. and Hamel, G. (1990) 'The core competence of the corporation', *Harvard Business Review,* 68(3): 79–92.

Ramamurti, R. (2004) 'Developing countries and MNEs: extending and enriching the research agenda', *Journal of International Business Studies,* 35(4): 277–283.

Rauschenbach, T. M. (1988) 'Competitiveness and cooperation in a global industry', *International Journal of Technology Management,* 3(3): 345–350.

Reich, R. B. and Mankin, E. D. (1986) 'Joint ventures with Japan give away our future', *Harvard Business Review,* 64(2): 78–87.

Reuer, J. J. and Ariño, Á. (2002) 'Contractual Renegotiations in Strategic Alliances', *Journal of Management,* 28(1): 47–69.

Reuer, J. J. and Ariño, Á. (2007) 'Strategic alliance contracts: dimensions and determinants of contractual complexity', *Strategic Management Journal,* 28(3): 313–330.

Reuer, J. J. and Miller, K. D. (1997) 'Agency costs and the performance implications of international joint venture internalization', *Strategic Management Journal,* 18(6): 425–438.

Reuer, J. J. and Tong, T. W. (2005) 'Real options in international joint ventures', *Journal of Management,* 31(3): 403–424.

Ricart, J. E., Enright, M. J., Ghemawat, P., Hart, S. L. and Khanna, T. (2004) 'New frontiers in international strategy', *Journal of International Business Studies,* 35(3): 175–200.

Rivera-Santos, M., Dussauge, P. and Mitchell, W. (2005) 'The determinants of inter-partner learning in alliances: an empirical study in e-commerce', in A. Capasso, G. B. Dagnino and A. Lanza (eds), *Strategic Capabilities and Knowledge Transfer within and between Organizations – New Perspectives from Acquisitions, Networks, Learning, and Evolution.* Cheltenham / Northampton, MA, USA: Edward Elgar, pp. 275–305.

Scott, W. R. (1995) *Institutions and Organizations.* Thousand Oaks, CA: Sage.

Scott, W. R. (2005) 'Institutional theory: contributing to a theoretical research program', in K. G. Smith and M. A. Hitt (eds), *Great Minds in Management: The Process of Theory Development.* Oxford: Oxford University Press.

Shaver, J. M. (1998) 'Accounting for endogeneity when assessing strategy perform-ance: Does entry mode choice affect FDI survival?', *Management Science,* 44(4): 571–585.

Si, S. X. and Bruton, G. D. (1999) 'Knowledge transfer in international joint ventures in transitional economies: the China experience', *Academy of Management Executive,* 13(1): 83–91.

Simonin, B. L. (1997) 'The importance of collaborative know-how: an empirical test of the learning organization', *Academy of Management Journal,* 40(5): 1150–1174.

Simonin, B. L. (1999a) 'Ambiguity and the process of knowledge transfer in strategic alliances', *Strategic Management Journal,* 20(7): 595–623.

Simonin, B. L. (1999b) 'Transfer of marketing know-how in international strategic alliances: an empirical investigation of the role and antecedent of knowledge ambiguity', *Journal of International Business Studies,* 30(3): 463–490.

Simonin, B. L. and Ruth, J. A. (1995) 'Bundling as a strategy for new product introduction: Effects on consumers' reservation prices for the bundle, the new product, and its tie-in', *Journal of Business Research,* 33(3): 219–230.

Simonin, B. L. and Ruth, J. A. (1998) 'Is a company known by the company it keeps? Assessing the spillover effects of brand alliances on consumer brand attitudes', *Journal of Marketing Research,* 35 (1): 30–42.

Sirmon, D. G. and Lane, P. J. (2004) 'A model of cultural differences and international alliance performance', *Journal of International Business Studies,* 35(4): 306–320.

Sivadas, E. and Dwyer, F. R. (2000) 'An examination of organizational factors influencing new product success in internal and alliance-based processes', *Journal of Marketing,* 64(1): 31–50.

Skarmeas, D., Katsikeas, C. S. and Schlegelmilch, B. B. (2002) 'Drivers of commitment and its impact on performance in cross-cultural buyer–seller relationships: the importer's Perspective', *Journal of International Business Studies,* 33(4): 757–784.

Son, M., Hahn, M. and Kang, H. (2006) 'Why firms do co-promotions in mature markets?', *Journal of Business Research,* 59(9): 1035–1042.

Steensma, H. K. and Lyles, M. A. (2000) 'Explaining IJV survival in a transitional economy through social exchange and knowledge-based perspectives', *Strategic Management Journal,* 21(8): 831–851.

Steensma, H. K., Marino, L. and Weaver, K. M. (2000) 'Attitudes toward cooperative strategies: a cross-cultural analysis of entrepreneurs', *Journal of International Business Studies,* 31(4): 591–610.

Svejenova, S. (2006) 'How much does trust really matter? Some reflections on the significance and implications of Madhok's trust-based approach', *Journal of International Business Studies,* 37(1): 12–20.

Tang, Q. (2003) 'Relationship mapping', *The China Business Review,* 30(4): 28–30.

Terpstra, V. and Simonin, B. L. (1993) 'Strategic alliances in the Triad: An exploratory study', *Journal of International Marketing,* 1(1): 4–25.

Tse, D. K., Pan, Y. and Au, K. Y. (1997) 'How MNCs choose entry modes and form alliances: the China experience', *Journal of International Business Studies,* 28(4): 779–806.

Uzzi, B. (1996) 'The sources and consequences of embeddedness for the economic performance of organizations: the network effect', *American Sociological Review,* 61(4): 674–698.

Walter, A. (2003) 'Relationship-specific factors influencing supplier involvement in customer new product development', *Journal of Business Research,* 56(9): 721–733.

Wei, Y., Liu, B. and Liu, X. (2005) 'Entry modes of foreign direct investment in China: a multinomial logit approach', *Journal of Business Research,* 58(11): 1495–1505.

Williamson, O. E. (1975) *Markets and Hierarchies.* New York: Free Press.

Williamson, O. E. (1985) *The Economic Institutions of Capitalism.* New York: Free Press.

Wu, F. and Cavusgil, S. T. (2006) 'Organizational learning, commitment, and joint value creation in interfirm relationships', *Journal of Business Research,* 59(1): 81–89.

Xin, K. and Pearce, J. L. (1996) 'Guanxi: connections as substitutes for formal institutional support', *Academy of Management Journal,* 39(6): 1641–1659.

Yiu, D. and Makino, S. (2002) 'The choice between joint venture and wholly owned subsidiary: An institutional perspective', *Organization Science,* 13(6): 667–684.

Zaheer, S. (1995) 'Overcoming the liability of foreignness', *Academy of Management Journal,* 38(2): 341–363.

Zaheer, A., McEvily, B. and Perrone, V. (1997) 'Does trust matter? Exploring the effects of inter-organizational and interpersonal trust on performance', *Organization Science,* 9(2): 141–159.

Zhang, Y. and Rajagopalan, N. (2002) 'Inter-partner credible threat in international joint ventures: an infinitely repeated prisoner's dilemma model', *Journal of International Business Studies,* 33(3): 457–479.

Zhao, H., Luo, Y. and Suh, T. (2004) 'Transaction cost determinants and ownership-based entry mode choice: a meta-analytical review',

Journal of International Business Studies, 35(6): 524–544.

Zollo, M., Reuer, J. J. and Singh, H. (2002) 'Inter-organizational routines and performance in strategic alliances', *Organization Science,* 13(6): 701–714.

11

Establishment Mode Choice: Acquisition versus Greenfield Entry

Desislava Dikova and Keith D. Brouthers

INTRODUCTION

Empirical research on foreign investment mode choice falls into three main categories. The first category examines the choice between non-equity (exporting, licensing and franchising) and equity (foreign direct investment) modes of entry (see Chapters 8 and 9). The second category investigates the desired level of ownership in the case of equity entry; for instance, the choice between a wholly owned and partially owned (joint venture) foreign entity (see Chapter 10). The third category also explores equity entry, but is concerned with investors' motives to buy an existing foreign entity or establish a foreign operation from scratch, which is the choice between an acquisition and a greenfield type of investment.[1]

Typically referred to as the establishment or diversification mode choice, the choice of acquisition versus greenfield depends on the investor's competitive advantage. For example, empirical evidence shows that, among other things, MNEs (multinational enterprises) establish greenfield outlets to exploit proprietary technology abroad while acquisitions are preferred as a means of overcoming

technological barriers in R&D-intensive industries or entering new markets quickly (Anand and Delios 2002; Gielens and Dekimpe 2007; Kogut and Singh 1988; Prabhu, Chandy and Ellis 2005).

Yet other factors also influence this choice. For example, although acquisitions offer a speedy establishment of a local presence, they can be accompanied by post-acquisition integration failures, which are often rooted in cross-cultural differences and technological mismatches. In addition, while greenfields offer an opportunity to preserve and replicate valuable corporate advantages abroad, they require both a great deal of time to establish and the creation of mechanisms to transfer knowledge efficiently. Because of this, firms tend to balance the benefits derived through their firm-specific advantages with those available from other firms in the target market, with industry-specific characteristic, and with country-specific environmental contingencies when determining the appropriateness of each establishment mode alternative.

In this chapter we take a close look at the choice between acquisitions and greenfield modes of entry in order to gain a greater understanding of how firms make this decision.

We began by searching for all published articles that deal with this important issue. We identified 29 empirical studies that focus on the establishment mode choice decision (see Table 11.1). We attempted to include all empirical studies dealing with this topic, yet resource and time constraints may have precluded us from identifying all published work in this area. Because of this we offer our apologies to those authors who have made an important contribution but whose studies are not included here.

The chapter is structured as follows. First, we review the main theories used to explain establishment mode choice. Second we examine the primary independent variables included in past studies and the results obtained. These variables tend to fall into three distinct groups: firm-specific variables, industry-specific variables, and country-specific variables. Finally we discuss future research directions and how scholars can extend and expand our understanding of the establishment mode choice decision in international markets.

THEORIES

The dominant theoretical perspective in the literature on establishment modes is transaction cost economics (Brouthers and Brouthers 2000; Caves and Mehra 1986; Cheng 2006; Cho and Padmanabhan 1995; Hennart and Park 1993; Larimo 2003; Rodriguez-Duarte, Sandulli, Minguela-Rata and Lopez-Sanchez 2007; Tsai and Cheng 2004; Zejan 1990). Transaction cost economics (TCE) explains the existence of firms as a means to lessen the opportunistic potential that arises in contract-based organizations ('markets'). This perspective is primarily concerned with the prevention of conditions that create market failure and the establishment of the most efficient form of governance that minimizes firms' transaction costs (Williamson 1975).

When applied to the establishment mode decision TCE is oriented primarily towards the choice of mode that minimizes the transaction costs associated with the exploitation of existing advantages. For instance, firms seeking to exploit their superior technological competence and preserve it from external market imperfections tend to choose greenfield entry and usually impose their managerial practices on the subsidiary (Chang and Rosenzweig 2001). Greenfield investments tend to provide an efficient way to restrict dissemination of firm-specific advantages and to avoid difficulties associated with imposing company know-how on existing local personnel (Brouthers and Brouthers 2000; Hennart and Park 1993).

However, if the planned local operation is critically dependent on product-specific or local knowledge, the probability of acquiring a local company and its knowledge increases. For example, Japanese firms expanding internationally while diversifying their current business activities tend to prefer acquisitions because they satisfy the need for an accumulation of new product-specific knowledge (Hennart and Park 1993). Similarly, technologically weak companies seek to complement their existing resources by acquiring another firm, thereby accessing and incorporating its knowledge base and organizational know-how (Larimo 2003).

In contrast to the transaction cost explanation of establishment mode selection the knowledge-based view (Grant 1996) suggests that the driving force behind establishment mode selection is the management of a firm's capabilities in terms of the development and deployment of its knowledge base (Kogut and Zander 1992). The knowledge-based view conceptualizes the firm as a set of transferable resources that are transformed into capabilities through dynamic and interactive firm-specific processes (Amit and Schoemaker 1993). The accumulation of firm capabilities is regarded as a dynamic process in which the ability of the firm to acquire, evaluate, integrate, diffuse, deploy and exploit knowledge is critical (Madhok 1997). Thus, whereas the transaction cost perspective treats each foreign entry as

Table 11.1 Establishment Mode Studies

Study	Theoretical perspective	Home country	Host country	Method	Dependent variable	Predictors and Findings
1. Wilson (1980)	International acquisition theory	UK, Germany, Japan, USA	UK, Germany, Japan, USA	Regression analysis	Acquisition (1) Greenfield (0)	Firm-level (home): **Acquisition ratio** (dividing the number of acquis. b/n 1900–1976/1971 by the total number of subsidiaries established) **(N.S.)**; **Diversification degree** (number of different SID codes in the system/firm) **(+acq.)**; **Foreign experience** (subtracting the year of the first implantation from the end year of the database) **(–acq.)**; **Parent-nationality dummy** (UK, W. Germany; Japan; USA). Country-level (host): **Location** (ratio of the implantations located in less developed countries to total number of implantations) **(–acq.)**;
2. Yip (1982)	Relatedness and barriers to entry model	North American markets	North American markets	Regression analysis	Greenfield (0) Acquisition (1)	Time dummy (number of implantations before 1960 to total number) **(–acq. effect for pre 1960)** firm-level (host): **Investment intensity** (average of each year's investment divided by revenues of one incumbent) **(–acq.)**; **Advertising intensity** (average annual expenditures on advertising divided by revenues) **(N.S.)**; **Incumbent parent size** (revenue of parent company) **(+acq.)**; **Relative parent size** (ratio of the size of the parent company to that of subs.) **(N.S.)**;
3. Caves and Mehra (1986)	TCT, agency theory, industrial organization	Various	USA	OLS	Acquisition (1) Greenfield (0)	Firm-level (home): **Entrant parent size** (absolute size in revenues) **(N.S.)**; **Parent diversity** (4 degrees of diversification: single business, dominant business; related business & unrelated business) **(+acq.)**; **Diversification mode** (geographic, segment, related, forward vertical integration, backward vertical integration, unrelated) **(unrelated diversification +acq.)**; **Shared activities and customers** (shared manufacturing, R&D, distribution, sales, advertising, immediate customers, end-users) **(N.S.)**; **Entrant competitiveness** (relative to incumbents) **(–acq.)**; **Entry motivation** (market profitability, market growth, share costs, offense, defense, generate cash, use cash) **(–acq.)**; Country-level (host): **Market growth rate** (4-year average annual change in market sales) **(–acq.)**; **Market concentration** (4-year average share of 3 leading competitors in the common markets) **(N.S.)**; Year dummy (1972–1979) **(N.S.)** Firm-level (home): **Relative size of subsidiary** (employment in the subsidiary divided by total employment (+acq.)**; **Multinationality degree** (number of countries in which parent firm has subsidiaries) **(+acq.)**; **Horizontal investment** (dummy=1 if subsidiary's principal product is one made abroad by its parent, 0 if else); **Level of diversification** (number of 2-digit industries in which the parent operates worldwide) **(+acq.)**; **First-mover** (dummy=1 if the parent was the first from its country to invest in the subsidiary's 4-digit industry) **(+acq.)**; **Oligopoly** (percentage increase 1974–78 in the number of MNEs based in the parent's home country & 2-digit industry) **(+acq.)**; **Joint venture (N.S.)**; Country-level (host): **Available targets** (number of firms within its 4-digit industry) **(N.S.)**; **Industry capacity** (size of the subsidiary divided by the total production workers in the 4-digit industry) **(N.S.)**; **R&D investments** (as a fraction of industry sales) **(N.S.)**; **Advertising investments** (as a fraction of industry sales) **(N.S.)**; **Durable good dummy (N.S.)**.

Study	Theory	Home country	Host country	Method	Dependent variable	Variables
4. Zejan (1990)	TCT	Sweden	Various	Regression analysis	Acquisition (1) Greenfield (0)	**Firm-level (home): International experience** (time in years of foreign operations)**(N.S.); Degree of diversification** (relative shares of the parent's sales in different 6-digit industries in 1978) **(+acq.); Dummy for diversification investment** (=1 if entry is diff. from parent's prime product line) **(N.S.);** Country-level (host): **Industry growth** (growth of industrial production) **(+acq.); Host GDP** (The size of the host market) **(N.S.);** Time dummy (1969–1; 1978=0 indicating a rapid increase of acquisitions) **(+acq.)**
5. Hennart and Park (1993)	TCT, M&A theory; Theory of growth of the firm; Capital market imperfections	Japan	USA	Binomial logistic regression	Acquisition (1) Greenfield (0)	**Firm-level (home): R&D investments** (expenditures as % of domestic sales) **(-acq.); Parent's host-market experience** (in years) **(N.S.); Commonality of product** (dummy=1 if any one of the products produced by the affiliate matched those produced by the parent) **(-acq.); Product diversification (N.S.); Advertising intensity** (adv. expenditures to sales of the parent) **(N.S.); Financial leverage** (ratio of long term debt to market value of the parent) **(N.S.), Investors' endowments of human resources (+acq.);Relative size(+acq.); JV dummy (N.S.);** Country-level (host): **Relative value index** (change in dollar value)**(N.S.); Growth deviation** (from annual growth rate of shipments in the 4-digit US industry)**(+acq.); Incentives for followers** (dummy = 1 if the Japanese investor is a follower **(-acq.); Concentration** (50 largest companies for each 4-digit US industry) **(N.S.)**
6. Andersson and Svensson (1994)	Organizational learning	Sweden	Multiple	Logit probability model	Acquisition (1) Greenfield (0)	**Firm-level (home): International experience** (previous number of manufacturing affiliates) **(+acq.); Size** (total turnover) **(+acq.); R&D intensity** (total R&D expenditures divided by total turnover) **(-acq.); Previous investments in host country** (dummy = 1 if the parent had already at least one affiliate) **(+acq.);** Firm-specific dummies (unspecified) Country-level (host):**GDP host country** (level of sophistication of the host economy) **(+acq.); Growth of host economy (N.S.);** Dummy variable for regions Time dummy **(+acq.)**
7. Cho and Padmanabhan (1995)	TCT, bargaining power model	Japan	Various	Binomial logit	Acquisition (1) Greenfield (0)	**Firm-level (home): Firm size** (parent's global assets)**(N.S.); Relative size** (investment relative to total size of parent)**(N.S.); Degree of diversification (N.S.); Relatedness of investment (N.S.); International experience** (years of operating an affiliate abroad) **(N.S.); Host country experience** (years of operating an affiliate in the host country)**(N.S.); R&D intensity** (R&D expenditures to sales)**(-acq.); Parent's market position** (parent's sales to total sales at home in its core products market)**(N.S.);** Country-level (host): **Economic development** (dummy = 1 for developed countries acc. to WB) **(+acq.); Host policy** (dummy = 1 in case prior government approval for acquisition is needed) **(+acq.);** Country-level: **Cultural distance (N.S.);** Time dummy (distinction b/n earlier and more recent investments) **(+acq.)**.

Continued

Table 11.1 Cont'd

Study	Theoretical perspective/framework	Home country	Host country	Method	Dependent variable (reference category)	Predictors and Findings
8. Anand and Delios (1997)	OLI	Japan	Various	Multinomial logistic model	Greenfield (1) Acquisition (0)	firm-level (host): **Subsidiary age (-acq.); Subsidiary size (+acq.)** Industry-level: **Magnitude of downstream measures** (location-specific advantages) **(+acq.); Employment in upstream occupations** (Retail buyers, purchasing agents, budget analysis) **(-acq.); Employment in management occupations** (administrative, general top managers) **(+acq.).** Country-level: **Cultural distance** (-acq.); **region dummies**
9. Barkema and Vermeulen (1998)	Organizational learning	Netherlands	Various	Binomial logit model	Greenfield (1) Acquisition (0)	Firm-level (home): **Multinational diversity** (in number of countries)(-acq.); **Product diversity** (3-digit Standard Industrial codes) (-acq.); **Product diversity squared (+acq.); Product relatedness (N.S.); Ownership dummy** (WO = 1, otherwise = 0) **(N.S.); Return on equity** (proxy for profitability) **(+acq.);** Firm size (log of assets); **Local experience** (entries into the host country) **(+acq.); Multinational diversity X product diversity (+acq.); Multinational diversity X product diversity squared (-acq.);** Country-level (host): **GNP (N.S.); Legal restrictions** (dummy = 1 if any restrictions on foreign ownership) **(-acq.); country risk** (low, medium or high risk of investment) **(medium risk -acq.);** Country-level: **Cultural distance (N.S.)** Time dummy: (T-1 time dummy controls) **(+acq.)**
10. Shaver (1998)	Econometric concerns	Various	USA	Probit estimates	Acquisition (1), Greenfield (0) Performance (survival-dummy = 1 if the investment stays with the parent 5 years after entry)	Firm-level (home): **Number of subsidiaries** the parent has in the USA**(+acq.); Diversification entry** (dummy = 1 if the firm has operations in the same US 2-digit SIC)**(N.S.); Firm size** (log of parent firm revenues in 1986)**(-acq.); R&D intensity** (R&D expenditures to parent revenue in 1986)**(N.S.)** Country-level (host): **Industry growth prior to entry (-acq.); Industry concentration** (4 item-concentration ratio) **(-acq.)** Performance model: Firm-level (home): **Acquisition entry** (dummy = 1)**(-effect on survival); Self selection** (dummy) **(-effect on survival for acquisition entries); R&D intensity (N.S.); Firm size (N.S.); Host country experience** (former subsidiaries in the US) **(+effect on survival but insignificant when self-selection is corrected for); Related entry (+effect on survival);** Country-level (host): **Industry growth (-effect on survival only when self-selection is corrected for); Industry concentration (N.S.); Industries with many US firms with international operations (+effect on survival)**
11. Padmanabhan and Cho (1999)	Experimental learning	Japan	Various	Logistic regression	Aquisitions (1) Greenfield (0)	Firm-level (home): **International business experience** (in years)(-acq.); **Host country experience (N.S.); Mode experience** (in years) **(+acq.); Firm size** (parent's global assets) **(N.S.); Relative size of foreign operation (N.S.); Relatedness of investment (N.S.); R&D intensity** (R&D expenditures to sales) **(-acq.); Market position** (ration of parent's sales to total industry sales at home in core product market) **(N.S.);** Country-level (host): **Host policy** (dummy = 1 in host countries require governmental approval for acquisition est.)**(+acq.); Economic development** (dummy = 1 for developed market economies); Country-level: **Cultural distance (N.S.)** Time dummy: dummy (= 0 to pre-1986 and 1 for post-1985 FDI) **(+acq.)**

Study	Theoretical perspective	Country (home)	Country (host)	Method	Entry mode coding	Variables (findings)
12. Brouthers and Brouthers (2000)	TCT, institutional and cultural context	Japan	Europe	Logistic regression analysis	Acquisition (0) Greenfield (1)	Firm-level (home): **Relative investment size** (+acq.); **R&D intensity** (R&D expenditures to total sales) (−acq.); **Multinational experience** (export ratio) (−acq.); **Firm diversity** (number of industry codes) (+acq.); **Product relatedness** (+acq.); **R&D intensity X Experience** (−acq.); **Diversity X Experience** (−acq.); Country-level (host): **Market growth** (5-year growth averages) (−acq.); **Uncertainty avoidance** (firms' unwillingness to accept managerial or organizational uncertainty) (−acq.); Country-level: **Cultural distance** (N.S.).
13. Harzing (2002)	International strategy (global) vs. multidomestic)	Multiple	Multiple	Binomial logistic regression	Greenfield (0) Acquisition (1)	Firm-level (home) **Strategy** (multidomestic = 1, global = 0) (+acq.); **R&D intensity** (R&D expenses divided by total sales) (−acq.); **Diversification** (number of different 4-digit SIC codes) (N.S.); **Foreign experience** (log of years) (+acq.); **Relative size of investment** (employees of subsidiary divided by employees at HQ) (+acq.); Country-level: **Cultural distance** (−acq.); Time of investment (+acq.).
14. Anand and Delios (2002)	RBV	Japan, UK, Canada, Germany, France, Netherlands, Switzerland	USA	Grouped probit model	Greenfield (0) Acquisition (1)	Industry-level: **Difference in R&D expenditure intensities** (between host and home countries)(N.S.); **R&D Dummy** (= 1 if R&D intensity in the host country is greater than at home) (+acq.); **R&D intensity of industry** (Sum of R&D intensities in home and host country)(N.S.); **Industry size** (1975–85)(N.S.); **Industry growth rate (N.S.).** Country-level (home): **R&D expenditures** (as % of sales at home) **(N.S.); Home country concentration** (4-firm concentration ratio) (−acq.); Country dummy (Germany-acq.., Japan-acq.); Country-level (host): **Advertising expenses** (% of sales in the host country)(N.S.); **Selling expenses** (and of sales in the host country)(+acq.); **Salesforce employment** (as % of overall employment in the host country)(+acq.); **R&D expenditures** (as % of sales in host country)(N.S.); **US concentration** (4-firm concentration ratio) (N.S.);
15. Larimo (2003)	TCT	Nordic firms	Various	Binomial logistic model	Greenfield (0) Acquisition (1)	Firm-level (home): **Parent size** (global sales)(+acq.); **R&D intensity** (high, medium and low technology industry)(−acq.); **Diversification degree** (number of 4-digit SIC industry)(+acq.); **International experience** (number of foreign manufacturing investments)(N.S.); **Target country experience** (manufacturing experience in the target country)(N.S.); **Dissimilarity of investment**(−acq.); **Ownership dummy** (=1 if entry is via WO unit)(+acq.); Country-level (host): **Economic development** (investments in OECD vs. non-OECD countries) (+acq.); Country-level: **Economic growth** (−acq.); **Cultural distance** (−acq.); Time dummy (after 1985 vs. pre-1986) (+acq.).
16. Elango, and Sambharya (2004)	Industry structure	Various	USA	Multinomial logistic regression	Greenfield (0) Acquisition (1)	Firm-level (home): **Firm size** (number of employees)(N.S.); Industry-level: **Concentration** (at 4-digit SIC level)(−acq.); **Industry import ratio** (total imports at 4-digit SIC level divided by industry shipments)(−acq.); **Plant scale** (total number of employees divided by the number of establishments of the 4-digit SIC industry)(+acq.); **Growth rate in industry shipments** (−acq.); **Demand variation** (absolute variation in the year-to-year shipments of the 4-digit SIC industry over 10-year period)(+acq.); **Industry shipments** (total shipments the year of entry)(−acq.); **Gross profit** (gross profit divided by sales of the 4-digit SIC industry)(+acq.); **R&D intensity** (expenditure at 4-digit SIC industry divided by industry sales)(N.S.); **Advertising intensity** (similar to previous variable)(N.S.)

Continued

Table 11.1 Cont'd

Study	Theoretical perspective	Home country	Host country	Method	Dependent variable	Predictors and Findings
17. Chen and Zeng (2004)	Reputation barriers	Japan	USA	Binomial logistic model	Acquisition (1) Greenfield (0)	Firm-level (home): **Parent's home advertising spending** (N.S.); **Parent's R&D intensity** (−acq.); **Parent's US advertising spending** (−acq.); **Relatedness of US affiliates** (1= if investment is made in related industry) (−acq.) Industry-level (host): **Industry advertising intensity** (total media expenditures)(+acq.); **Industry brand equity** (of all firms at the 2-digit SIC level)(−acq.); **Consumer goods vs. industrial products** (+acq.); **R&D intensity** (of each 4-digit SIC industry)(N.S.); **Industry concentration** (50 largest at 4-digit level) (−acq.); **Industry growth deviation** (difference between the growth of each 4-digit industry)(+acq.)
18. Tsai and Cheng (2004)	TCT, culture	Taiwan	China, South-East Asia and EU	Logistic binomial regression	Greenfield (1) Acquisition (0)	Firm-level (home): **Advertising intensity** (% expenditures to total sales) (−acq.); **R&D intensity** (% expenditures to total sales) (−acq.); **Experience in years** (+acq.); **Experience in scope** (number of countries parents invested in) (+acq.); **Firm size** (total sales) (−acq.); Country-level: **Cultural similarity** (perception measure of similarity of business practices)(+acq.); **Difference in markets for corporate control** (dummy for China, South-East Asia and EU) **(N.S.)**
19. Elango (2005)	Knowledge-based framework	Various	USA	Binomial logistic regression	Greenfield (1) Acquisition (0)	Firm-level (home): measured by Industry level variables: **Physical capital intensity**(−acq.); **Human capital intensity** (Total fixed assets divided by industry value-added of the 4-digit SIC industry)(−acq.); **Human capital intensity** (Total wages divided by value-added of the 4-digit SIC industry)(+acq.); **Value of investment**(+acq.); **R&D intensity**(+acq.); **Nation of origin dummies** (= 1 if home country is Japan or UK, 0 if other)/Japan −acq.; UK +acq.) Industry-level: **Industry size** (−acq.); **Extent of unionization** (% of workers covered under union contracts in the industry) (−acq.); Country-level: **Cultural distance**(−acq.; N.S. if nation of origin dummies added)
20. Somlev and Hoshino (2005)	Bargaining power model	Japan	Europe	Multinomial logistic model	Acquisition (1) Greenfield (0)	Firm-level (home): **International experience** (+acq.); **Subsidiary number** (−acq.); **Subsequent entry** (+acq.) Country-level (home): **Second parent** (dummy for presence of more than one parent (−acq.) Country-level (host): **Labor cost** (employee remuneration)(N.S.); **Market size** (low, medium and high (N.S.); **Host competitiveness** (+acq.); **Industry growth** (−acq.); Time: (**acquisitions preferred between 1987–1992**)
21. Meyer and Nguyen (2005)	Institutional theory	Various	Vietnam	Logit regression	Greenfield (1) JV (acquisition) (0)	Firm-level (home): **Market-oriented strategy** (+acq.); **Host country experience** (previous investments in Vietnam) (+acq.) firm-level (host): **Trend** (subsidiary newness) (−acq.) Country-level (home): **FDI stock** (home-country international business experience) (−acq.) Industry-level (host): **Industry growth** (−acq.) Country-level (host): **Cultural distance** (N.S.); **Real estate available** (+acq.); **SOE/total output** (+acq.); **Market size** (population) (N.S.); **market growth** (GDP growth) (N.S.); **Education** (N.S.); **Transportation infrastructure** (+acq.)

	25. Dikova and van Witteloostuijn (2007)	24. Cheng (2006)	23. Drogendrijk and Slangen (2006)	22. Herrmann and Datta (2006)
	New institutional economics	Industrial competition, TCT, RBV	Culture	Upper echelon theory
	Various	Taiwan	The Netherlands	USA
	Various transition economies	Various	Various	Various
	Logistic regression analysis	Logistic regression	Logistic regression	Multinomial regression analysis
	Greenfield (1) Acquisition (0)	Acquisition (1) Greenfield (0)	Greenfield (1) Acquisition (0)	Acquisition (1) Greenfield (0)

Column 22 — Herrmann and Datta (2006):

Firm-level (home): **CEO age (N.S.); CEO firm experience (N.S.); CEO functional experience** (dummy: throughput experience = 1 output experience = 0)**(+acq.); CEO int. exp.** (in years)**(−acq.); Firm size** (log of employees)**(N.S.); Firm Growth (N.S.); Firm performance** (ROA relative to industry)**(+acq.); Firm greenfield experience (N.S.); Firm acquisition experience (+acq.); Firm JV experience (N.S.); International diversification (N.S.);** Industry-level: **Industry R&D exp. (−acq.); Industry advertising intensity (+acq.)** Country-level (host): **GDP per capita (+acq.); GDP growth (N.S.)**

Column 23 — Drogendrijk and Slangen (2006):

Country-level (host): **Cultural distance (−acq.)** Firm-level (home): **MNE size** (annual sales) **(N.S.); Diversification (N.S.); Host country experience (+acq.); MNE's greenfield experience (−acq.); MNE's acquisition experience (+acq.); MNE type** (dummy = 0 if manufacturing) **(N.S.); R&D to be transferred (−acq.); Unrelated expansion (N.S.); Planned level of subsidiary autonomy (+acq.);** firm-level (host): **Subsidiary size (+acq.); Shared subsidiary ownership (+acq.);** Country-level (host): **Expected demand growth (−acq.); Acquisition restrictions and incentives (N.S.); Lack of acquisition targets (−acq.)** Country-level: **Cultural distance** [(1)Kogut & Singh's index, (2) Schwartz index and (3) Managerial perceptions] **[all −acq.]**

Column 24 — Cheng (2006):

Industry-level: **Industry concentration(+acq.)** Firm-level (home): **Relative firm size (+acq.); Advertising intensity (N.S.), R&D intensity (−acq.); Foreign acquisition experience (+acq.); Training and remuneration intensity (+acq.); Ownership (N.S.)**

Column 25 — Dikova and van Witteloostuijn (2007):

Firm-level (home): **Technological intensity (N.S.) International strategy** (dummy variable: multidomestic = 1, global = 0) **(+acq.); Acquisition experience (+acq.); Greenfield experience (−acq.); Related investment (N.S.); Production subsidiary (−acq.); Relative size of investment (+acq.); Advertising intensity (N.S.); Technological intensity X institutional advancement (+acq.); International strategy X institutional advancement (+acq.);** Industry-level: **Industry dummies** (high tech intensive industries, low tech intensive industries and no tech industries) **(N.S.);** Country-level (host): **Institutional advancement** (civil rights, political stability, government effectiveness, regulatory quality, rule of law, and corruption control) **(+acq.); Host-market concentration (N.S.); Host-market growth (N.S.); Host government investment incentives (N.S.)**

Continued

Table 11.1 Cont'd

Study	Theoretical perspective	Home country	Host country	Method	Dependent variable	Predictors and Findings
26. Rodríguez-Duarte, et al. (2007)	TCT, Knowledge-based theory, strategic theory	Spain	Various	Probit	Greenfield (1) aquisition (0)	Firm-level (home): **Technological intangible asset stock** (number of patents) **(N.S.); Firm size** (Log of average revenues of the firm 1990–1999) **(+acq.); Past performance** (Log of average benefit after taxes for the firm 1990–1999) **(–acq.)** Industry-level: **Average R&D expenditures** (1990–1999) (N.S.); **Concentration ratio** (–acq.)
27. Ruiz-Moreno, et al. (2007)	Two stage decision-making; establishment mode and entry mode	Spain	Various	Logistic regression	Full and Partial Greenfield (0) acquisition (1)	**Difference between R&D of firm and industry** (1990–1999)**(N.S.); Difference between output growth rate of the firm and the industry** (1990–1999) **(–acq.); Difference between average profit of the firm and industry** (1990–1999)**(N.S.)** Firm-level (home): **Firms size** (–acq.); **International experience (N.S.); Host country experience (N.S.)** Industry-level: **R&D intensity (N.S.); advertising intensity (N.S.)** Country-level: **Cultural distance (+acq)** Above results are for wholly and partially owned ventures. Other variations in models that nest establishment mode choice with entry mode (wholly owned versus partially owned) choice
28. Chen, (2008)	RBV	Japan	USA	Probit	Full and Partial Greenfield (0) acquisition (1)	Firm-level (home): **R&D intensity** (–acq.); **Advertising intensity** (–acq.); **Parent's industry knowledge** (dummy=1 if entry is related investment) (–acq.); **Host market experience** (–acq.) Industry-level: **R&D intensity** (+acq.); **Advertising intensity** (+acq.), **Industry growth deviation** (differences in growth rate between industries in the sample)**(+acq.); Industry concentration (N.S.)** Above for wholly owned ventures only. For partially owned subsidiaries only industry growth deviation (+acq.) and industry concentration (–acq.) were significant.
29. Slangen and Hennart (2008)	Cultural distance, Organizational learning	The Netherlands	Various	Logistic regression	Greenfield (1) acquisition (0)	Firm-level (home): **International experience** (+acq.); **Host country experience** (+acq.); **Level of diversification** (+acq.); **Technology transferred to subsidiary** (–acq.); **Relatedness of investment (N.S.); Greenfield experience** (–acq.); **Acquisition experience** (–acq.); **Acquisition experience** (+acq.); **Industry type** (man/serv) **(N.S.)** firm-level (host): **Subsidiary autonomy** (+acq.); **Investment size** (+acq.) Country-level: **Cultural distance** (–acq.); **Cultural distance X International experience (–Acq.); Cultural distance X Greenfield experience** (–Acq.); **Cultural distance X Acquisition experience** (+Acq.); **Cultural distance X Host country experience (N.S.); Cultural distance X Subsidiary autonomy (N.S.)** Country-level (host): **Acquisition restrictions** (–acq.); **Lack of acquisition targets** (–acq.); **Demand growth** (+acq.)

a separate and discrete event and is considered 'static and equilibrium oriented' (Madhok 1997), the knowledge-based view encompasses the dynamics of learning and capability building. The knowledge-based view is the second most preferred theoretical perspective in the field of establishment mode research (Andersson and Svensson 1994; Barkema and Vermeulen 1998; Elango 2005; Padmanabhan and Cho 1999; Slangen and Hennart 2008).

The knowledge-based view, with its roots in the resource-based theory of the firm, postulates that firm resources that are valuable, unique and imperfectly imitable can provide the basis for a firm's competitive advantage (Amit and Schoemaker 1993). To pursue competitive strategies firms employ both tangible and intangible resources, but it is the intangible resources that are most crucial for firms' competitive advantage because intangible resources tend to be rare, socially complex and difficult to imitate (Black and Boal 1994). The knowledge-based view extends resource-based theory in that it considers knowledge to be the most strategically important of the firm's intangible resources (Grant 1996).

Knowledge, especially tacit knowledge, is normally embedded in the firm's human capital (Grant 1996). Because of this, when setting up a new foreign entity, investing companies typically send expatriates to hire and train the local labor force in accordance with the organization's common practices (Barkema and Vermeulen 1998; Hofstede 1991). Therefore, companies prefer greenfield investments to exploit firm-specific advantages that are embedded in the organization's labor force and cannot be separated from the organizational structure (Hennart and Park 1993). In contrast, acquisitions create problems because transferring knowledge across organizational boundaries and imposing beliefs and corporate values on a foreign subsidiary can be very difficult if not impossible (Barkema and Vermeulen 1998; Prabhu et al. 2005) and might not achieve the optimal deployment of the investor's core

competencies (Casson 1995). Consequently, a firm can more effectively transfer superior capabilities to a greenfield subsidiary than in the case of the acquisition of a local firm with diverging practices and routines.

Besides TCE and knowledge-based frameworks discussed above, other theories have been applied to the study of establishment mode choice including: international acquisition theory (Wilson 1980), bargaining power model (Cho and Padmanabhan 1995; Somlev and Hoshino 2005); international strategy (Harzing 2002); resource-based view (Anand and Delios 2002; Anand and Delios 1997; Chen 2008); reputation barriers (Chen and Zeng 2004); upper echelons theory (Herrmann and Datta 2006); and new institutional economics (Dikova and van Witteloostuijn 2007).

Theoretically it appears that establishment mode research has taken a rather traditional view of the mode choice decision, focusing on transaction cost and knowledge-based explanations. Other theoretical perspectives have generated little research interest and multiple theoretical explanations have rarely been explored (for exceptions see Brouthers and Brouthers 2000; Cheng 2006; Rodriguez-Duarte et al. 2007; Slangen and Hennart 2008).

FIRM-SPECIFIC PREDICTORS

A large number of firm-specific variables have been included in previous studies of establishment mode choice (see Table 11.1). Here we discuss the most commonly applied groups of firm-specific variables and explore the theoretical predictions and empirical findings about how they impact the establishment mode decision. These firm-specific variables fall into five groups: measures of diversification; business relatedness; asset specificity; international experience; and relative firm size.

One of the most researched variables in past establishment mode studies has been parent firm's degree or level of diversification.

Diversification refers to the number of products/markets in which the firm does business. As many as 15 studies either examined this variable as a predictor or controlled for its effects on establishment mode choice (Barkema and Vermeulen 1998; Brouthers and Brouthers 2000; Caves and Mehra 1986; Chen and Zeng 2004; Cho and Padmanabhan 1995; Drogendijk and Slangen 2006; Harzing 2002; Hennart and Park 1993; Herrmann and Datta 2006; Larimo 2003; Padmanabhan and Cho 1999; Slangen and Hennart 2008; Wilson 1980; Yip 1982; Zejan 1990).

Most studies argue that highly diversified firms consist of sophisticated management control systems, or management expertise, embedded in senior managers. Such firm-specific intangible assets can be used to acquire subsidiaries, adapt their processes and resources, and operate these entities as quasi-independent subsidiary structures managed by local personnel. For the most part these studies tend to find that highly diversified firms demonstrate a preference for acquisitions rather than greenfield entries (Brouthers and Brouthers 2000; Caves and Mehra 1986; Larimo 2003; Slangen and Hennart 2008; Wilson 1980; Zejan 1990) although Barkema and Vermeulen (1998) report a curvilinear (an inverted U-shape) relationship between a firm's diversity and its establishment mode choice.

Another popular predictor of establishment mode choice is the *relatedness of investment*; an investment made in a related or unrelated business. When a foreign investment is made in a new industry for the parent firm, the investing firm normally lacks the product-specific knowledge required to successfully operate in that particular industry. Because of this lack of knowledge, it is likely that the investor chooses an acquisition entry over a greenfield alternative to obtain the product-specific knowledge needed. According to transaction cost arguments, obtaining such knowledge on the market in disembodied form is difficult if at all possible hence the most efficient alternative

is an acquisition. Empirical support for this variable is mixed (Barkema and Vermeulen 1998) with only five studies finding a significant and positive relationship between unrelated type of investment and the propensity to enter via acquisition (Brouthers and Brouthers 2000; Chen 2008; Chen and Zeng 2004; Larimo 2003; Yip 1982).

Parent firm *asset-specificity*, estimated as technological intensity, is another popular predictor of establishment mode choice. The nature of the firm-specific advantage the investor intends to exploit abroad typically determines whether the establishment mode choice will be a greenfield or an acquisition. Advantages created by advanced technological capabilities are often difficult to combine with an acquired foreign organization as they are tightly-bound to the parent firm. Hence, the most efficient way to exploit such firm-specificities is by 'recreating on foreign soil a clone of the foreign parent' (Hennart and Park 1993, p. 1056). The greenfield establishment mode allows firms to set up a subsidiary that matches closely the organizational culture of the parent, making knowledge sharing more efficient.

Contrary to this, acquisitions are a less efficient way to transfer firm-specific technologies and routines because such technologies and routines are typically developed in a specific corporate and cultural context. In order to be successfully incorporated by the acquired firm, old practices and routines have to be unlearned to make learning of new practices and routines possible (Barkema and Vermeulen 1998) and that process is difficult and time-consuming. Most studies provide empirical support to these arguments (Andersson and Svensson 1994; Brouthers and Brouthers 2000; Chen 2008; Chen and Zeng 2004; Cheng 2006; Cho and Padmanabhan 1995; Drogendijk and Slangen 2006; Harzing 2002; Hennart and Park 1993; Larimo 2003; Padmanabhan and Cho 1999; Tsai and Cheng 2004).

International experience of the parent firm is another predictor widely applied in establishment mode literature. Two separate, but complementary, theoretical arguments have been used in previous research. First, using TCE as a starting point, some scholars maintain that risk is pertinent to international operations and its level usually decreases with experience (Brouthers and Brouthers 2000). This theoretical argument suggests that firms with longer experience in overseas production accumulate knowledge about specific foreign market conditions and are hence more reluctant to pay an acquisition premium which reduces the rate of return on investment (Zejan 1990). Internationally young firms consider acquisition targets as substitutes for experience while mature multinationals are more inclined to establish greenfield ventures. Hence the probability of entry by acquisition is negatively related to the level of accumulated international experience (Caves and Mehra 1986).

Second, the knowledge-based view conceptualizes experience as a primary source of learning in organizations, deeply embodied in organizational memory (Penrose 1959). A firm operating in diverse national markets is exposed to new ideas, practices and consumer demands, which trigger innovations and boost technological and organizational capabilities (Barkema and Vermeulen 1998; Miller and Chen 1996). According to Padmanabhan and Cho (1999), firms' past experiences transform into organizational routines that consequently create a model for future actions and become a source of competitive advantage. These knowledge-based arguments suggest that firms with greater experience have accumulated firm-specific advantages that can be more easily exploited through greenfield ventures, rather than incurring the difficulties of transferring such advantages to acquired organizations.

Despite these theoretical predictions, empirical support is rather weak (Brouthers and Brouthers 2000; Cheng 2008; Ruiz-Moreno, Mas-Ruiz and Nicolau-Gonzalbez 2007; Wilson 1980). Many studies report insignificant results and others report a positive relationship between international experience and the likelihood of an acquisition,

providing opposite results than either theory predicts (Andersson and Svensson 1994; Barkema and Vermeulen 1998; Caves and Mehra 1986; Drogendrijk and Slangen 2006; Harzing 2002; Meyer and Nguyen 2005; Shaver 1998; Slangen and Hennart 2008; Somlev and Hoshino 2005; Tsai and Cheng 2004).

Finally, *relative investment size*, that is the size of the new investment relative to the size of the firm, is another popular firm-level determinant of establishment mode choice. Firms intending to establish a relatively large greenfield subsidiary may experience a shortage of financial and/or managerial resources (Hennart and Park 1993). On the contrary, an acquisition of an existing enterprise provides additional managerial and financial resources and in such a way eases the financial and managerial burden of the parent firm (Brouthers and Brouthers 2000). Most studies examining this issue provide empirical support for the propensity of firms contemplating a large investment to choose an acquisition establishment mode over greenfield venture (Brouthers and Brouthers 2000; Caves and Mehra 1986; Cheng 2006; Dikova and van Witteloostuijn 2007; Harzing 2002; Hennart and Park 1993).

A number of other firm-specific variables have also been examined in one or two studies. Here we summarize those we feel are most important. First, Harzing (2002), and Dikova and van Witteloostuijn (2007) suggest that the international strategy of the firm may influence the choice of establishment mode. They found that firms following a global strategy generally opt for greenfield investments because they strive for a high degree of subsidiary integration. Conversely, firms following a multidomestic strategy typically prefer to acquire indigenous firms to obtain tacit local market knowledge.

Second, Drogendrijk and Slangen (2006) and Slangen and Hennart (2008) observe a relationship between the planned level of subsidiary autonomy and the type of establishment mode. Firms planning to grant little autonomy to their subsidiaries are likely to choose greenfield entry, while those planning on granting much autonomy opt for acquisitions.

Third, Caves and Mehra (1986) found that first-mover advantages and the degree of oligopoly in the MNE's home country (the later an industry-level predictor) exert positive effects on the likelihood of an acquisition entry.

Finally, several studies look at firm level acquisition and/or greenfield experience, suggesting that experience with one establishment mode type would lead to greater use of that mode type (Dikova and van Witteloostuijn 2007; Drogendijk and Slangen 2006; Herrmann and Datta 2006; Padmanabhan and Cho 1999; Slangen and Hennart 2008).

INDUSTRY-SPECIFIC PREDICTORS

While firm-level predictors of establishment mode choice appear in virtually every research study we examined, industry-specific determinants of firms' preference for greenfield or acquisition modes has received far less attention. Only a few studies have included industry-level variables (Table 11.1). Here we present three groups of industry-level variables that research suggests may influence establishment mode choice.

First, industry growth rate can impact the establishment mode decision because of the availability of new customers and the intensity of competition. One fundamental difference between greenfield and acquisition establishment modes is that greenfield ventures increase local supply while the number of firms in an industry is unaffected by acquisition. In industries with relatively low growth rates, the entry of a new firm in the market dilutes the customer base, leading to lower sales and profits for all firms involved (Brouthers and Brouthers 2000; Elango and Sambharya 2004). Because of this, competitors are quick to retaliate when new firms enter the market, hoping to maintain their market share and discouraging expansion of new entrants. Hence, when a firm wants to enter a slow growing market, establishing a new greenfield venture is normally discouraged. Instead entry through acquisition is preferred because acquisition of an existing firm does not increase the number of firms competing in the marketplace (Caves and Mehra 1986; Zejan 1990).

Contrary to this, in fast-growing markets there are many new customers and the addition of a new competitor has far less impact on incumbent firms. Fast-growing markets provide opportunities for niche strategies which means new entrants may not compete directly with existing firms. Furthermore, if markets are growing very rapidly existing firms may have difficulty meeting demand and new entrants simply help reduce waiting times and have no impact on incumbent sales. In these circumstances, establishment mode choice would favor greenfield ventures over acquisitions. Previous scholarship has provided some empirical support for these predictions (Andersson and Svensson 1994; Brouthers and Brouthers 2000; Chen 2008; Drogendijk and Slangen 2006; Elango and Sambharya 2004; Meyer and Nguyen 2005; Rodriguez-Duarte et al. 2007; Shaver 1998; Somlev and Hoshino 2005; Yip 1982; Zejan 1990) although some studies have found a U-shaped relationship (Caves and Mehra 1996; Hennart and Park 1993)

Another industry-level predictor included in past studies is industry concentration. If the industry is highly concentrated, increasing the number of firms competing may provoke a competitive response from incumbent firms which could lead to a drop in prices and decreased profits (Caves and Mehra 1986; Cheng 2006; Hennart and Park 1993; Yip 1982). In a highly competitive industry (that is, less concentrated industry) the supply-increasing characteristics of greenfield establishments are less problematic to the incumbents – as greenfields are less of a threat to incumbents' established level of profit. Hence, in less concentrated industries firms typically prefer greenfield ventures

(Chen and Zeng 2004; Elango and Sambharya 2004). Yet there is little empirical support for the effect of industry concentration on establishment mode choice – only five studies found industry concentration to be related to greenfield ventures (Chen and Zeng 2004; Cheng 2006; Elango and Sambharya 2004; Rodriguez-Duarte *et al.* 2007; Shaver 1998).

The third industry characteristic affecting establishment mode choice is an industry's technological and advertising intensity. Scholars exploring this area have provided several arguments relating to industry-level technical and advertising intensity. Some research suggests that differences in industry technical/advertising intensity reflect differences in technical and market capabilities between countries and hence the applicability of home country resources in target markets. When home country technological intensity is higher than that of the host country in a particular industry, greenfield ventures will be used so that the foreign firm can exploit their advantage. However, if the host or target country has a technological advantage, then acquisition modes will normally be used so that the foreign firm can gain access to this more advanced technology (Anand and Delios 2002; Somlev and Hoshino 2005). Both Anand and Delios (2002) and Somlev and Hoshino, (2005) found support for this proposition.

Other research suggests that total industry technological intensity (not differences) or home/host country technology intensity impacts mode choice (Caves and Mehra 1986; Chen 2008; Herrmann and Datta 2006; Rodriguez-Duarte *et al.*, 2007). Anand and Delios (2002) tested all three factors and found no evidence, Herrmann and Datta (2006) found that a high level of industry technological intensity was related to greenfield modes but Elango (2005) and Chen (2008) found high-level industry technology intensity was related to acquisition modes. Recently Ruiz-Moreno *et al.* (2007) and Rodriguez-Duarte *et al.* (2007) found technological intensity was not a significant predictor of establishment mode choice.

Scholars suggest that industry-level advertising intensity also affects establishment mode choice because it can reflect the level of brand or product awareness in a particular country and hence the ability of a firm to market its products/services. If host country industry advertising intensity is high, foreign firms will prefer acquisition modes of entry. Acquisition modes help foreign firms gain access to new markets through the provision of well-recognized brands and established distribution channels (Anand and Delios 2002; Caves and Mehra 1986). Several studies report a significant positive association between the level of industry advertising intensity and the use of acquisition establishment modes (Anand and Delios 2002; Chen 2008; Chen and Zeng 2004; Herrmann and Datta 2006).

In summary, it appears that despite the small number of studies examining industry-specific variables and establishment mode choice, scholars have identified several industry-level affects that influence this decision. Future research needs to expand our theoretical understanding of these variables and control for their effects when studying establishment mode choices.

Country-level PREDICTORS

The last group of variables discussed here are Country-level predictors of establishment mode choice. Among these Country-level variables are cultural distance, the size, growth and level of development of the target or host country, and host country legal restrictions (Table 11.1).

The most often explored Country-level determinant of establishment mode choice is the cultural distance between the home country of the investing firm and the host country – recipient of the investment (Drogendijk and Slangen 2006; Kogut and Singh 1988). Yet scholars have been unable to reconcile the relationship between cultural distance and establishment mode choice offering two opposing arguments.

The first group of studies suggest that cultural distance makes integration of existing foreign companies difficult (Kogut and Singh 1988) and therefore provides a motivation for investors to establish new ventures from scratch and fully integrate the managerial practices developed at home (Cho and Padmanabhan 1995; Drogendijk and Slangen 2006). These studies tend to find a positive relation between cultural distance and the preference for greenfield investments over acquisitions (Barkema and Vermeulen 1998; Chang and Rosenzweig 2001; Cheng 2006; Drogendijk and Slangen 2006; Elango 2005; Harzing 2002; Herrmann and Datta 2006; Kogut and Singh 1988; Slangen and Hennart 2008; Tsai and Cheng 2004).

The second group of studies maintains that companies establishing subsidiaries in culturally distant countries usually lack knowledge concerning local political, cultural and societal norms which will impact their success. The most efficient way to acquire this country-specific knowledge is by involving a local partner (Anand and Delios 1997; Brouthers and Brouthers 2000; Harzing 2002). Therefore, firms investing in culturally distant countries tend to prefer acquisitions of locally integrated companies, while firms entering culturally similar countries prefer to establish a greenfield subsidiary to exploit firm-specific advantages (Brouthers and Brouthers 2000; Ruiz-Moreno et al. 2007).

A possible explanation for the conflicting evidence about the influence of national culture on investors' mode choice is that cultural distance is not central to transaction cost economics. A full incorporation of the cultural distance perspective in transaction cost theory provides for the possibility of opposing predictions between cultural distance and establishment mode choice (Gatignon and Anderson 1988). Moreover, some authors view cultural distance arguments as 'awkwardly incorporated' in a theory that is predominantly concerned with analyzing the internalization process that results from market failure (Madhok 1997). Other researchers suggest cultural distance findings

may differ because past studies did not consider the moderating influence of international or host country experience, or of planned subsidiary autonomy (Slangen and Hennart 2008).

In addition to cultural distance, the size, growth and level of development of the host country also attracted opposing theories to explain the establishment mode choice, albeit it attracted far less interest (Andersson and Svensson 1994; Cho and Padmanabhan 1995; Elango 2005; Larimo 2003; Meyer and Nguyen 2005; Padmanabhan and Cho 1999; Slangen and Hennart 2008; Zejan 1990). As presented by Zejan (1990), on the one hand the larger the market the smaller the disturbances that an entry via greenfield causes in both existing market share and in the revenue of existing firms (Elango 2005; Somlev and Hoshino 2005). On the other hand, the higher the level of development of the target country, the easier it is to find firms that fit the acquisition requirement of an MNE; hence a positive relationship can be expected between the host country's economic development and the preference for acquisition establishments (Andersson and Svensson 1994; Cho and Padmanabhan 1995; Herrmann and Datta 2006; Larimo 2003; Slangen and Hennart 2008).

Finally, host country restrictive legal policy and a broader regulative institutional environment is the last Country-level variable to receive some attention in establishment mode choice research. Cho and Padmanabhan (1995) and Padmanabhan and Cho (1999) argue that host country policies officially requiring prior governmental approval for the acquisition of local firms may discourage entry via acquisitions. In a similar vein, Barkema and Vermeulen (1998), Meyer and Nguyen (2005) and Slangen and Hennart (2008) suggest that legal restrictions on foreign ownership of local enterprises may affect the choice of establishment mode. Empirical results are mixed, with some studies finding legal restrictions related to the choice of acquisition modes (Cho and Padmanabhan 1995; Meyer and Nguyen 2005) while others find legal restrictions associated with greenfield modes (Barkema and Vermeulen 1998; Slangen and Hennart 2008). Recently Dikova and van Witteloostuijn (2007) found that the level of regulative institutional development was related to acquisition modes of entry, suggesting that more advanced regulative institutional development (in transition economies) facilitates both the process of searching and negotiating for acquisition targets, and of post-acquisition restructuring.

In all, Country-level predictors of establishment mode choice have been shown to have a significant influence on the decision managers make. Future research may expand on this area by reconciling conflicting theories and exploring additional country-specific influences.

FUTURE RESEARCH DIRECTIONS AND CONCLUSION

Despite the growth in acquisition activities over the past two decades and the interest in research on acquisition performance there is little research dealing with the choice firms make between entering new markets through acquisitions or using greenfield, de novo ventures. Our review identified only 29 empirical studies dealing with this choice. As discussed above, existing studies have tended to rely on traditional rational models of mode choice. Below we provide some observations on possible ways to move this line of research forward.

New theories that can be used

Decisions are made by managers and are taken in specific organizational contexts. These restrictions on choice need to be built into future establishment mode decision models. With the exception of Herrmann and Datta (2006), researchers have tended to ignore the human element, taking instead a rational choice perspective. But are management

decisions rational? The literature examining strategic decisions tends to indicate the managers matter; decisions are influenced by managerial (Brouthers, Brouthers and Werner 2000) and management team (Carpenter, Geletkanycz and Sanders 2004) cognitions. Future research on establishment mode choice could make important contributions to both the establishment mode and decision-making literatures by combining insights from rational mode choice models with managerial/cognitive decision-making models.

Other theoretical perspectives also hold promise for advancing our knowledge of establishment mode choice. For example, network theory suggests that firms and managers are embedded in a network of firms and people that can supply information, access to resources, and knowledge (Brass et al. 2004). Since mode choice is dependent, at least in part, on knowledge, resources, and information it might be that network relationships influence the establishment mode choice decision. Some networks might be more useful for establishing greenfield operations while others may provide information needed to make acquisition modes more successful. Taking a network perspective might help future research understand how a firm's position in the larger interrelated world influences the establishment mode decision.

Furthermore, management's attitude toward foreign firms could influence establishment mode choice. Based on the concepts introduced by Perlmutter (1969), managers with ethnocentric views might use greenfield ventures because their organizational culture is based on the concept that domestic ways of doing business are superior and hence acquiring 'inferior' foreign operations would be a waste of resources. Contrary to this, firms with more geocentric organizational cultures may prefer acquisition modes, hoping to benefit from the knowledge and expertise embedded in foreign firms. Future research might want to look at organizational cultural and how this influences the establishment mode choice decision.

Finally, future research may want to combine theoretical perspectives to gain greater insights. Brouthers and Brouthers (2000), for example, combined transaction cost and institutional theories to show how transaction costs are influenced by institutional differences. Yet other theoretical combinations seem to make sense. Combining transaction cost, resource-based and institutional theories would help determine the impact of firm-specific, location-specific and internalization advantages on establishment mode choice. Blending insights from real option theory and transaction cost economics may help us gain a better view of how cost minimization (the focus of transaction cost theory) and value creation (the focus of real option theory) considerations can jointly influence strategic decisions. In general what we suggest is that researchers take a new look at the theory behind the strategic choice of establishment mode structure.

Existing issues that need further exploration

Researchers may also wish to examine several issues that have provided mixed results in past studies; identifying useful theoretical and empirical explanations. For example, researchers have found mixed or weak results for the influence of international experience, cultural or institutional distance, and legal restrictions on establishment mode choice. Are these mixed findings the result of using different measures, not controlling for other confounding variables, or are they a consequence of missing moderating influences? Several studies have begun examining moderating variables (for example Barkema and Vermeulen 1998; Brouthers and Brouthers 2000; Dikova and van Witteloostuijn 2007; Mitra and Golder 2002; Ruiz-Moreno et al., 2007; Slangen and Hennart 2008) yet they do not provide clear results. Hence, future research may wish to delve into these issues to develop a more detailed understanding of why past

results do not seem to match the theoretical predictions.

In addition, the issue of whether establishment mode choice and entry mode choice (the choice between wholly-owned and joint venture modes) are sequential or simultaneous decisions needs much more work, as only one study shows evidence that the ownership decision precedes the establishment mode decision (Ruiz-Moreno et al. 2007). Two types of research may contribute here. First, qualitative research is needed to determine more fully how firms make the establishment mode decision. Is this a first choice (before entry mode), second choice (after entry mode) or are these simultaneous decisions? Second, both theoretical explanations of the choice and empirical testing will be needed and new methodological instruments like structural equation modeling may help.

Finally, decision models are only useful to managers if they lead to normatively superior choices. The establishment mode research we reviewed typically ignored the performance implications of the mode decision. Three studies have begun to explore this important issue. First, Shaver (1998) used factors previously shown to influence the establishment mode choice and examined 5-year survival rates (still controlled by the investing firm). He found that establishment mode itself was not associated with performance (survival) but that, after controlling for self-selection, the selection of the appropriate (variable-driven) mode lead to greater success (longer survival). Likewise, Vermeulen and Barkema (2001), and Tsang and Yip (2007) looked at establishment mode survival (how long existed and still in existence) as a measure of performance. Although they did not examine establishment mode choice, they found that acquisitions tended to have longer survival rates. While these studies provide valuable insights about establishment modes and performance, they do not actually measure subsidiary performance. Hence, future research focusing on objective and perceived measures of establishment mode performance and controlling for the endogeneity of mode choice may help us gain further insights into which theoretical perspectives lead to better performing mode choices.

Methodological issues

Methodologically one key issue that makes comparison of results and development of future research difficult is the lack of clarity in defining greenfield and acquisition modes. For example some studies clearly state that they examine only wholly owned greenfield and acquisition modes (Brouthers and Brouthers 2000). Other studies are less clear about their mode choices. Brouthers and Hennart (2007) suggest that four establishment mode types exist: wholly owned greenfield; wholly owned acquisition; joint venture greenfield; and joint venture acquisition (also called partial acquisition). Researchers need to define and differentiate between these mode types. As Brouthers and Hennart (2007) suggest, researchers are beginning to find that there are significant differences in the factors driving the selection of each of these mode types (Chen 2008; Meyer and Nguyen 2005; Ruiz-Moreno *et al.* 2007).

Finally, Slangen and Hennart (2007) consider the inclusion of multiple home and host countries in many studies' samples the main reason for inconsistencies in findings of the establishment mode literature. They argue that this approach prevents researchers from accurately operationalizing all relevant variables and leads to biases in findings. Hence future research needs to take greater care in making data choices in order to help reduce the influence of extraneous Country-level factors.

CONCLUSIONS

With the boom and subsequent under-performance of acquisitions in the past decade managers and researchers need to think about whether acquisitions are the best way to expand. Establishment mode research focuses directly on this question, attempting to determine when acquisitions are superior to greenfield ventures. Yet much more work needs to be done in this area before a clear picture can be developed. Future research, bringing in theories from other areas, developing more parsimonious models, and using more advanced analytical techniques, can help develop our knowledge about this choice. Making performance an important part of these models will help us to differentiate between more or less successful explanations and will ultimately help managers to make better decisions.

NOTES

1 The term 'acquisition' describes the process of taking an equity stake in an existing foreign enterprise while the term 'greenfield' means developing a new enterprise from the start.

REFERENCES

Amit, R. and Schoemaker, P. J. H. (1993) 'Strategic assets and organizational rent', *Strategic Management Journal*, 14(1): 33–46.

Anand, J. and Delios, A. (1997) 'Location specificity and the transferability of downstream assets to foreign subsidiaries', *Journal of International Business Studies*, 28(3): 579–603.

Anand, J. and Delios, A. (2002) 'Absolute and relative sources determinants of international acquisitions', *Strategic Management Journal*, 23: 119–134.

Andersson, T. and Svensson, R. (1994) 'Entry modes for direct investment determined by the composition of firm-specific skills', *Scandinavian Journal of Economics*, 96(4): 551–560.

Barkema, H. G. and Vermeulen, F. (1998) 'International expansion through start-up or acquisition: a learning perspective', *Academy of Management Journal*, 41(1): 7–26.

Black, J. A. and Boal, K. B. (1994) 'Strategic resources: traits, configurations and paths to sustainable competitive advantage', *Strategic Management Journal*, 15: 131–148.

Brass, D. J., Galaskiewicz, J., Greve, H. R. and Tsai, W. (2004) 'Taking stock of networks and organizations: a multilevel perspective', *Academy of Management Journal*, 47(6): 795–817.

Brouthers, K. D. and Brouthers, L. E. (2000) 'Acquisition or greenfield start-up? Institutional, cultural and transaction cost influence', *Strategic Management Journal*, 21: 89–98.

Brouthers, K. D., Brouthers, L. E. and Werner, S. (2000) 'Influences on strategic decision making in the Dutch financial services industry', *Journal of Management*, 26: 863–883.

Brouthers, K. D. and Hennart, J. F. (2007) 'Boundaries of the firm: insights from international entry mode research', *Journal of Management*, 33: 395–425.

Carpenter, M. A., Geletkanycz, M. A. and Sanders, W. G. (2004) 'Upper echelons research revisited: antecedents, elements and consequences of top management team components', *Journal of Management*, 30: 749–778.

Casson, M. (1995) *The Organization of International Business, Studies in the Economics of Trust*, Vol. 2. Cheltenham: Edward Elgar Publishing.

Caves, R. E. and Mehra, S. K. (1986) 'Entry of foreign multinationals into the US manufacturing industries', in M. E. Porter (ed.), *Competition in Global Industries*. Boston, MA: Harvard Business School Press, pp. 449–481.

Chang, S. J. and Rosenzweig, M. (2001) 'The choice of entry mode in sequential foreign direct investment', *Strategic Management Journal*, 22: 747–776.

Chen, S. F. S (2008) 'The motives for international acquisitions: capability procurements, strategic considerations, and the role of ownership structures', *Journal of International Business Studies*, doi: 10.1057/palgrave.jibs.8400357.

Chen, S. F. S. and Zeng, M. (2004) 'Japanese investors' choice of acquisitions vs. startups in the US: the role of reputation barriers and advertising outlays', *International Journal of Research in Marketing*, 21: 123–136.

Cheng, Y. M. (2006) 'Determinants of FDI mode choice: Acquisition, brownfield, and greenfield entry in foreign markets', *Canadian Journal of Administrative Science*, 23(3): 202–220.

Cho, K. R. and Padmanabhan, P. (1995) 'Acquisition versus new venture: the choice of foreign establishment mode by Japanese firms', *Journal of International Management*, 1: 255–285.

Dikova, D. and van Witteloostuijn, A. (2007) 'Foreign direct investment mode choice: entry and establishment modes in transition economies', *Journal of International Business Studies*, 38(6): 1013–1033.

Drogendijk, R. and Slangen, A. (2006) 'Hofstede, Schwartz, or managerial perceptions? The effects of different cultural distance measures on establishment mode choices by multinational enterprises', *International Business Review*, 15: 361–380.

Elango, B. (2005) 'The influence of plant characteristics on the entry mode choice of overseas firms', *Journal of Operations Management*, 23(1): 65–79.

Elango, B. and Sambharya, R. B. (2004) 'The influence of industry structure on the entry mode choice of overseas entrants in manufacturing industries', *Journal of International Management*, 10: 107–124.

Gatignon, H. and Anderson, E. (1988) 'The multinational corporation's degree of control over foreign subsidiaries: an empirical test of a transaction cost explanation', *Journal of Law, Economics and Organization*, 4: 305–336.

Gielens, K. and Dekimpe, M. G. (2007) 'The entry strategy of retail firms into transition economies', *Journal of Marketing*, 71: 196–212.

Grant, R. M. (1996) 'Toward a knowledge-based theory of the firm', *Strategic Management Journal*, 17: 109–122.

Harzing, A. W. K. (2002) 'Acquisitions vs. greenfield investments: international strategy and management of entry modes', *Strategic Management Journal*, 23: 211–227.

Hennart, J. F. and Park, Y. R. (1993). Greenfield vs. acquisition: the strategy of Japanese investors in the United States', *Management Science*, 39(9): 1054–1070.

Herrmann, P. and Datta, D. K. (2006) 'CEO experience: effects on the choice of FDI entry mode', *Journal of Management Studies*, 43(4): 755–778.

Hofstede, G. (1991) *Cultures and Organizations: Software of the Mind*. Maidenhead, Berkshire: McGraw-Hill.

Kogut, B. and Singh, H. (1988) 'The effect of national culture on the choice of entry mode', *Journal of International Business Studies*, 19(3): 411–432.

Kogut, B. and Zander, U. (1992) 'Knowledge of the firm, combinative capabilities, and the replication of technology', *Organization Science*, 3(3): 502–518.

Larimo, J. (2003) 'Form of investment by Nordic firms in world markets', *Journal of Business Research*, 58(2): 1–13.

Madhok, A. (1997) 'Cost, value and foreign market entry mode: the transaction and the firm', *Strategic Management Journal*, 18(1): 39–61.

Meyer, K. E. and Nguyen, H. V. (2005) 'Foreign investment strategies and sub-national institutions in emerging markets: evidence from Vietnam', *Journal of Management Studies*, 42(1): 63–93.

Miller, D. and Chen, M. J. (1994) 'Sources and consequences of competitive inertia: a study of the U.S. airline industry', *Administrative Science Quarterly*, 39: 1–23.

Mitra, D. and Golder, P. N. (2002) 'Whose culture matters? Near-market knowledge and it impact on foreign market entry timing', *Journal of Marketing Research*, 39(3): 350–367.

Padmanabhan, P. and Cho, K. R. (1999) 'Decision specific experience in foreign ownership and establishment strategies: evidence from Japanese firms', *Journal of International Business Studies*, 30(1): 25–44.

Penrose, E. T. (1959) *The Theory of the Growth of the Firm*. London: Basil Blackwell.

Perlmutter, H. V. (1969) 'The tortuous evolution of the multinational corporation', *Columbia Journal of World Business*, 4 (January–February): 9–18.

Prabhu, J. C., Chandy, R. K. and Ellis, M. E. (2005) 'The impact of acquisitions on innovation: Poison pill, placebo, or tonic?', *Journal of Marketing*, 69: 114–130.

Rodriguez-Duarte, A., Sandilli, F. D., Mingela-Rata, B. and Lopez-Sanchez, J. I. (2007) 'The endogenous relationship between innovation and diversification, and the impact of technological resources on the form of diversification', *Research Policy*, 36: 652–664.

Ruiz-Moreno, F., Mas-Ruiz, F. J. and Nicolau-Gonzalbez, J. L. (2007) 'Two-stage process of FDI: ownership structure and diversification mode', *Journal of Business Research*, 60: 795–805.

Shaver, J. M. (1998) 'Accounting for endogeneity when assessing strategy performance: Does entry mode choice affect FDI survival?', *Management Science*, 44(4): 571–585.

Slangen, A. and Hennart, J. F. (2007) 'Greenfield or acquisition entry: a review of the empirical foreign establishment mode literature', *Journal of International Management*, 13: 403–429.

Slangen, A. and Hennart, J. F. (2008) 'Do multinationals really prefer to enter culturally distant countries through greenfields rather than acquisitions? The role of parent experience and subsidiary autonomy', *Journal of International Business Studies*, doi: 10.1057/palgrave.jibs.8400356.

Somlev, I. P. and Hoshino, Y. (2005) 'Influence of location factors in establishment and ownership of foreign investments: the case of the Japanese manufacturing firms in Europe', *International Business Review*, 14: 577–598.

Tsai, M. T. and Cheng, Y. M. (2004) 'Asset specificity, culture, experience, firm size and entry mode strategy: Taiwanese manufacturing firms in China, South-East Asia and Western Europe', *International Journal of Culture Management*, 14(3&4): 1–27.

Tsang, E. W. K. and Yip, P. S. (2007) 'Economic distance and the survival of foreign direct investments', *Academy of Management Journal*, 50(5): 1156–1168.

Vermeulen, F. and Barkema, H. (2001) 'Learning through acquisitions', *Academy of Management Journal*, 44(3): 457–476.

Williamson, O.E. (1975) *Markets and Hierarchies*. Englewood Cliffs, NJ: Prentice-Hall.

Wilson, B. (1980) 'The propensity of multinational enterprises to expand through acquisitions', *Journal of International Business Studies*, 1: 59–65.

Yip, G. (1982) 'Diversification entry: internal development versus acquisition', *Strategic Management Journal*, 5: 331–345.

Zejan, M. (1990) 'New ventures or acquisitions: The choice of Swedish multinational enterprises', *Journal of Industrial Economics*, 38(3): 349–355.

12

Exit Strategies

Masaaki Kotabe and Sonia Ketkar

INTRODUCTION

The term 'market exit strategy' is considerably broad, especially in the context of international marketing. In international business parlance, a 'market' might refer to geographical space such as a country or national market, regional market, local area market or even product lines or product market. Exit strategies might include various forms of divestitures consisting of complete sale or partial sale of a subsidiary to a domestic or foreign firm, plant closures, spin-offs and the like. In the last three decades, the volume and magnitude of foreign market exits has grown. In spite of this increase in exits, literature seems limited in its exploration of exit strategy in the domestic and particularly in the international context. As a result, 'divestiture continues to lack a research identity that is distinct from other acts of corporate restructuring such as mergers and acquisitions' (Buchholtz, Lubatkin and O'Neill 1999, p. 633).

Perhaps the main reason for the lack of research on market exits is the unavailability of data. As is known to all, researchers rely on either secondary (publicly available data) or primary (survey or interview) data in order to analyze business trends. News information

about foreign market exit often goes undocumented probably because it is not required by law for firms to report a plant closure abroad or a minor sale of foreign assets. As a result, this news often skips attention. Or firms record aggregate figures of foreign divestments, which do not include any specific details due to the sensitive nature of the information about these activities. Firms listed on US stock exchanges are not required by the Securities and Exchange Commission to report activities of individual units if they are organized under one subsidiary.

The issue also lies in how we as managers and researchers choose to define a subsidiary. Managers have also always been extremely secretive about exits and often refuse to disclose even the most basic facts regarding exits for fear that the news might tarnish the firm's image. They maintain strict confidentiality in responding to surveys. This is because (as will be explained later on) traditionally, divestment of a business previously owned or operating in a foreign market was associated with negativity and failure. Also, firms often exit markets by way of sale in order to gain quick liquidity or other such reasons. By doing so, they attempt to show a stronger balance sheet. These reasons may or may not go down well with home-country investors.

This unfavorable view is changing now that managers and shareholders have learned that, in certain cases, market exit is necessary to increase firm value or maintain competitive advantage.

Methodologically, therefore, market exit studies were mostly drawn from case studies. Although studies on market exit are few and far between, nowadays, we see more survey-based studies, possibly due to the change in the outlook on divestments. This change could also be attributed to the way in which we now choose to collect data on exits; by designing our studies as research questions on subsidiary survival rather than exit. Nonetheless, exit studies based on surveys suffer from some amount of non-response bias due to the secrecy surrounding divestments and the dire need for respondents and their firms to remain unidentifiable.

The last three decades have witnessed an exponential increase in mergers and acquisitions (M&A). A press release by PricewaterhouseCoopers Transaction Services suggested that the year 2006 could be a record year for mergers and acquisitions and 2007 could set a record for these activities in the future. A significant portion of this overall increase in M&A consists of global M&A. A growth in the number of M&A almost always includes a growth in the number of divestitures. Firms that buy and sell subsidiaries are said to be active in the market for corporate control, which has been defined as 'the transferring of managerial control to new capital providers through acquisitions, divestitures and other control-transfer mechanisms. Essentially, it is the market for buying and selling businesses or parts thereof' (Hitt, Hoskisson, Johnson and Moesel 1996, p. 1085). The buy side literature that studies mergers and acquisitions from the acquiring firm's perspective is comparatively more evolved than the sell side. As Buchholtz, Lubatkin and O'Neill (1999) put it, 'we know a lot more about the art of buying than we do about the art of selling'. Exit strategies are not always associated with M&A. In fact, exit strategies as part of M&A

entail complete sale by one firm (the seller) to another firm (the buyer). Although complete sales are very common, other exit strategies have been largely ignored in international business inquiries.

Many studies have used the terms, 'exit' and 'divestment', interchangeably because market exits always include some version of divestment. In our discussion in this chapter, we keep up this practice with this compatible terminology. We choose to focus specifically on divestments and not on other forms of market exit that might result from end of contractual agreements such as licensing or export–import contracts and the like. While most people are familiar with the practical definition of divestment, previous literature has defined foreign divestment as 'a reduction of ownership percentage in an active direct foreign investment on a voluntary or involuntary basis through complete or partial sale, liquidation, expropriation and/or nationalization' (Chopra, Boddewyn and Torneden 1978). A multinational company may decide to divest for a variety of reasons, ranging from poor performance, inefficient management, need for liquid resources, restructuring, coordination problems, to minimizing costs, etc. These forms of divestment have been labeled in the literature as 'voluntary divestment'. On the other hand, divestment by a multinational due to nationalization, expropriation or confiscation has been termed as involuntary divestment (Sachdev 1976). It is common for multinationals to involuntarily divest their units in developing countries due to protectionist policies and other governmental stipulations. Thus, involuntary divestments do not stem from the initiative of the multinational but rather that of the host governments or other mandatory factors. Studies in the 1970s proved that involuntary divestments usually represented a very small fraction (between four to eight per cent) of total divestitures (Torneden and Boddewyn 1974). Around that time, international business was not as developed as it is now. MNEs (multinational enterprises) today are more experienced and skilled at bargaining with political parties in host governments. We might therefore expect even fewer involuntary divestments today.

Research on international market exit strategies came to the fore around the 1970s and early 1980s at a time when scholars such as Boddewyn (1973, 1979a, 1979b) and Van Den Bulcke *et al.* (1980) published their findings on the topic (discussed later in this chapter). The following decade of the late 1980s saw a continuation in studies on exit strategies. However, since then, research focused on exit strategies has tapered off to fewer occurrences in scholarly journals. Some scholars might even argue that indeed, exit strategy research has shifted and current research appears to conceptualize exit strategy at the nexus of mergers and acquisitions or as a part of intellectual discussions about foreign subsidiary survival or de-internationalization (Benito and Welch 1997) and restructuring of the multinational organization. There is a stream of literature in international marketing that also investigates the issues of liability of foreignness and liability of newness. Market exits sometimes take place soon after entry into an entirely new culture due to these liabilities. Consequently, since the 1970s–1980s, literature has lacked focus on the exit decision *per se*. On one hand, this understanding of exit strategies reveals a maturity in international business thought, which is now capable of examining a trend in its entirety. On the other hand, it is important to scrutinize exit strategies by themselves before we can apply them to different themes in international business.

Based on previous studies, one could categorize exit strategy research in three phases (Boddewyn 1983). During its first phase in the 1970s and early 1980s, when researchers first began investigating exits by multinational firms, exits by way of divestments were viewed negatively and as a symbol of failure or an inability to deliver profits. They were also considered to be non-strategic (Gilmour 1973) and mere responses to crises or environmental factors (Boddewyn 1983) that were not premeditated. These were motivated by either unpredictable changes in the host country environment or other internal firm-related reasons. Exits were thus almost always considered to be an outcome of financial issues to lower costs for the parent or headquarters. As a result of this unfavorable outlook towards exits, managers were extremely reluctant to discuss these firm events. That is probably why the studies that appeared during this phase were derived from case studies.

Exits in the second phase in the later 1980s were more proactive in nature such that parent firms trimmed down their foreign operations due to over-diversification, which was a strategic reason to concentrate on their core businesses. Thus, the strategic aspect of divestment also became evident in research. During this phase, the market exit issue became more complex in terms of the motivation to divest as well as the changes in corporate strategy. Some firms even indulged in the formation of divestment strategies as part of the strategic management process within the firm. The third or most recent phase of market exit research is more complex and multidimensional. There has been a shift in focus in international marketing studies from headquarters to subsidiary. In this context of market exit, although the parent has the final say in the fate of a foreign subsidiary, subsidiary level research has shown that the subsidiary's position and other subsidiary level factors also affect the divestment decision (Griffin 2003).

In the 1980s, the terms 'crisis' versus 'strategic' divestments (Boddewyn 1983, p. 31) were used to differentiate between different models of foreign exit decision-making although no significant published study has explained these two types of divestment in detail. In 1983, Boddewyn (p. 29) wrote, 'The crisis character surrounding many divestments is likely to hasten and simplify the decision; the need for "impetus" overshadows that for analysis; and the latter may be one-sided with few or no alternatives considered, when it is dominated by "financial" types'. This loaded statement brought out several different aspects of exit decisions.

The author added that sophisticated analysis sometimes took place only when it was time to dispose of the unit whose fate had already been decided – a matter of *ex post facto* rationalization (Boddewyn 1983, p. 29; Gilmour 1973). It is also believed by scholars and practitioners alike that firms necessarily sell an unprofitable subsidiary. Grunberg (1981) justified the lack of literature on international divestments by stating that 'it does not take extensive theoretical or empirical work to establish that companies divest subsidiaries because they have failed in the marketplace'. Despite the parochial attitude toward it, there was a stream of studies on international divestment, (Torneden 1975; Sachdev 1976; Nees 1978; Boddewyn 1979a and 1979b) its determinants, magnitude, consequences, etc. in the 1970s and 1980s when this practice became common.

In this chapter, we discuss existing research literature on international exit strategies. The focal studies are organized under broad themes that appear in such research. Although the basis of this chapter is foreign market exit strategies, we do refer to some studies on domestic exits, the results of which can also be useful to better understand foreign exits. Based on what has been achieved already in this field of study, we recommend avenues for further research.

THEORIES OF MARKET EXIT

Theories of entry and exit: The same?

The theoretical underpinnings for foreign market exits can be traced back to a significant set of studies conducted by Boddewyn and his colleagues in the last few years of the 1970s and early 1980s. There are also some other studies that investigated foreign divestments (Torneden 1975; Sachdev 1976; Nees 1978). The issues covered by all these studies include the magnitude, factors, deterrents and the divestment decision-making process.

Most of these studies assumed and some even attempted to prove (Boddewyn 1983) that foreign divestment or exit was essentially the same as foreign investment or entry such that both phenomena were driven by the same underlying factors. Boddewyn (1981) adapted the eclectic paradigm to support his analysis of the reasons for divestment. He explained that an MNE would divest a unit if the ownership (O), location (L), or internalization (I) conditions set forth in the OLI paradigm ceased to exist. Theoretically, he simply reversed the foreign investment process. In his later paper (Boddewyn 1985), he also suggested that theories of foreign investment and divestment should include a relationship with the host countries of event.

There were a few others, such as Wallender III (1973), who recognized that 'divestment is not the reverse of investment' but his reasoning for the statement was fallacious because he claimed that divestment (or in his case, exit via complete sale of an investment) was final and had no alternatives like investment did. He also claimed that market exit was usually linked with failure. Nevertheless, these studies did provide a solid foundation for market exit research in those years.

The lack of a proper theoretical foundation for early foreign divestments led investment theorists to extend their theories to discuss divestment (Dunning 1988). Doing so again assumes that investment and divestment are simply two sides of the same coin and are determined by the same fundamental factors. Dunning (1988) himself stretched his eclectic theory to include and thereby explain foreign divestments as an attempt to extend his theory to give it more explanatory breadth. It is debatable how much this theoretical extension enables researchers to apply the OLI paradigm successfully to divestment decisions. According to Dunning in a restatement of his theory (1988), divestment is different from investment in two ways, the first being that it requires the absence of only one of either O, L or I variables and the second difference being that some of the barriers to exit might not correspond with the barriers to entry. In the same article, he elaborated on how a firm might lose location advantages due to a change in factor endowments or how it might lose ownership advantages if there is a shift in the balance of advantages, leading to market exit.

The pertinence of the OLI paradigm for explaining exit aside, the application of entry theories to exit decisions was probably realistic of the time or business climate. Investment theories are built on economics of markets and competition and thus do explain divestment also but only up to a limited extent. For example, from the parent's perspective, a seemingly permanent loss of the O, L or I advantages would probably be sufficient incentive to divest. Since then, firms, their management and the environment have changed and become more complex and progress in the research of global issues has led the way for a more in-depth examination of exits.

Strategic view of market exit

Another theoretical explanation for market exit stems from strategy literature, which reflects on the strategic reasons why firms exit geographical or product markets due to lack of strategic fit with the firm's product portfolio or a need to focus on its core competencies (Rumelt 1974). The strategic view was a significant departure from economics-based theories that dominated divestment thought. Whereas financial motives are supposed to be reactive divestments due to poor market share, low profitability and other such performance-based reasons, strategic motives refer to the need to divest due to lack of strategic fit, restructuring and other proactive moves by the multinational firm. Thus, a firm might divest a 'profitable' foreign subsidiary, given a favorable host country environment based on strategic moves. There is no one particular theory that properly elucidates the strategic view of international divestments but several theories and perspectives contribute to understanding such moves

(e.g., portfolio theory, resource-based view, network view of the multinational enterprise, 'MNE'). A simple way to identify strategic reasons for divestment is to refer to Montgomery, Thomas and Kamath's (1984) description. They define a strategic divestiture as 'a divestiture related to corporate or business level strategy'. They continue, 'These divestitures often included decisions to exit an industry or move away from or toward "core" businesses, or to realign a firm's product mix within a given industry.' Thus, strategic motives were made up of two chief related tactics by HQ: (1) to move toward 'core' businesses by getting rid of non-core assets (resource-based view); (2) change in strategy; and (3) realigning the MNE's portfolio (portfolio theory).

The 1970s–1980s was a period of extensive diversification for many multinational firms into both related and unrelated areas and several of them eventually became unmanageable over-diversified corporations. In many of the divestment studies in the more recent past, over-diversification has been the nucleus of the exit argument (Hoskisson, Johnson, and Moesel 1994). When the going got too tough, these firms eventually divested the unrelated businesses and shifted focus back to businesses that held their 'core competencies'. Madura and Rose (1987) defined this process of divestment of non-core businesses in a novel way as RPD or reverse product diversification. According to these authors, RPD possibly led to efficient operations for firms by specialization. This practice was explained by the resource-based *view*.

Pauwels and Matthyssens (2002) reckoned that 'a strategic withdrawal turns out to be a germ of strategic reorientation of the business unit's entire international market portfolio'. The portfolio theory, which applies aptly to US firms in particular, reflects the notion of the multinational firm as a portfolio of units. A multinational firm operates in different multiple countries and in many cases manages different multiple product lines and this array of units is referred to as a portfolio. Portfolio adjustment or restructuring (Hoskisson, *et al.* 1994) refers to changes in the group and type of business units owned and managed by a firm, in our case, a multinational firm. Firms often alter their strategies at all levels of the organization at various times with the intention of restructuring their organization. In keeping with the new strategy, units that no longer have a 'strategic fit' with the organization are often divested. As indicated by Markides (1995), 'in the business press, this practice has had different labels like "de-conglomerating", "de-diversifying", and "getting back to basics"'.

Even strategic reasons are following a different tune today. Nowadays, strategic reasons that dominate the practice include outsourcing (Kotabe and Murray 2004), which is one of the most controversial issues in recent times and often leads to divestment of a vertically integrated unit. Outsourcing could also be the result of a strategic move by the company to focus on its core competencies. Other strategic reasons for exit include inadequate governance or management and inappropriate strategy (Hoskisson, Johnson and Moesel 1994).

Subsidiary evolution and market exit

Past theories that explained exit were primarily headquarters-centric, in that they viewed the exit decision as wholly determined by the parent. The network theory captures the fundamentals of the subsidiary perspective and brings in a notion of heterarchy (Hedlund 1980) in an otherwise hierarchical MNE structure. Based on this view, the subsidiary is more autonomous and capable of defining its own strategy rather than merely conceding to headquarters-assigned role. Subsidiary research has focused on the different roles and strategies for subsidiaries, subsidiary initiatives and subsidiary evolution (evolutionary view, Kogut and Zander 1993). Birkinshaw (1996) explained the notion of

subsidiary mandates or 'any subsidiary responsibility that extends beyond its own market'. He also briefly discussed parent-driven and subsidiary-driven divestment in terms of loss of mandate. Along the same lines, Birkinshaw and Hood (1998) took a developmental view of the subsidiary based on resources and capabilities and showed how subsidiaries could be divested by the parent company due to a shift in 'charter' or the responsibility of the unit in the multinational firm network. According to Griffin (2003), 'the literature has not, in any substantial way, examined subsidiaries' strategic response to divestment'. Thus, at this point in time, foreign subsidiary research stands at a juncture at which we can move on to advance previous studies on subsidiary-driven exits.

ANTECEDENTS TO FOREIGN EXIT STRATEGIES

Before examining exit strategies in detail, it is crucial to understand why firms exit foreign markets. The main difference between involuntary and voluntary exits (described earlier) lies in the factors contributing to such exits. Environmental reasons are primary in causing involuntary exits from foreign markets. In the case of multinational firms, these 'environments' are host countries in which the firm operates. Thus, involuntary divestments were motivated by factors such as political risks, exchange risks, and cultural issues, among others.

Although existing studies have identified and tested the influence of a variety of factors on the voluntary decision to divest, these variables can effectively be captured under two categories – the financial factors and the strategic factors – both of which reflect the phenomenon of market exits from the headquarters perspective. Recent work on subsidiaries, however, has made a case for including a third set of factors that are related to the subsidiary in determining the motivation and mode of exit.

Academically, interest in divestitures abroad peaked when over-diversified multinational corporations started divesting their subsidiaries in foreign markets in the 1970s. Very few previous studies on foreign divestments have focused on the divestment strategy formulation side and instead mainly examined the triggers or motives for divestment and the performance implications of the decision for the parent company. Also, most of the conclusions about foreign exits have been drawn from case studies (Van Den Bulcke *et al.* 1980). When companies first began divesting their foreign units, they were driven by reasons such as prolonged poor performance of the subsidiary, lack of capital (Boddewyn 1979) or other financial difficulties faced by the parent company. In fact, even to this day MNEs being profit-seeking, financial or economic motives are primary in many of the divestment decisions, especially in the case of US MNEs.

As far as implementation of the foreign divestment decision is concerned, there is very limited research in the area. Previous studies suggested that implementation of the decision was influenced by the antecedents and motives (i.e., divestiture context), including whether divestment was being considered by the firm as an outcome of portfolio adjustment, performance decline (the most common reason for US firms), retrenchment, etc. As Boddewyn (1979b, p. 23) suggested, based on product life cycle theorist, Vernon's, work,

> As has often been argued by Raymond Vernon, a portfolio view of foreign subsidiaries is usually inappropriate. Multinationals do not simply rank their subsidiaries and get rid of the bottom ones. This is because the value of a particular foreign investment cannot always be precisely determined if it is linked to other parts of the multinational entity. In other words, maintaining an apparently unprofitable investment in a particular country can be justified if it either reduces the risk to the whole corporate system or increases the yield to any part of it.

Some other reasons for foreign market exits include insufficient resources, poor pre-investment analysis, acquisition gone sour, liability of newness or liability of foreignness

in a new location and other structural or organizational changes (Boddewyn 1979b). Another important factor affecting the exit decision is the size of the business unit (Duhaime and Baird 1987). *Ceteris paribus*, the larger the subsidiary and more related it is to the MNE's core business, the less the likelihood that the firm will exit.

One of the first research questions pursued in the area of foreign market exits was the factors that led to subsidiary exit. Therefore, this theme was primarily explored by early exit studies in the 1970s and 1980s. There onward, researchers moved on to investigate other aspects of the topic. As the focus shifted from a parental or headquarters perspective to the foreign subsidiary, a recent study analyzed the determinants of subsidiary survival and exit. Specifically, the authors concentrated on foreign subsidiaries of Japanese firms that had invested in Canada (Delios and Ensign 2000). They found that exit rates were determined by subsidiary-level variables, including entry mode, size of the unit, expatriates employed and ownership level. Another empirical contribution of the study was that subsidiaries engaged in manufacturing industries and located in Ontario were the least likely to exit. This goes to show that firm sector and geography also go a long way in influencing subsidiary exit.

International exits, like most other business issues, do not rely on a single theory for adequate explanation. As Griffin (2003) put it, triggers for divestment do not 'operate as distinctively as literature implies'. In most cases when a firm undertakes divestment of a subsidiary unit, there are multiple motives involved (Hamilton and Chow 1993). For example, in the 1980s, TRW sold several of its subsidiaries and products that were considered to be low performers with bleak futures. But the publicized aim of the firm in exiting these markets was to concentrate on its core businesses (electronics and automotive) (Waddock 1989). In the global arena, especially, it is not only the factors described above that contribute to the decision to exit. As has been proven time and again, entry strategies and entry modes also have an influence on exit strategies.

FOREIGN MARKET ENTRY, SURVIVAL, AND EXIT

Intimately linked with market exit studies is research on market entry, survival and failure of foreign operations (Li 1995; Delios and Makino 2003; Chung and Beamish 2005). Early knowledge of the foreign exit process was 'macro' in the sense that scholars and managers alike concentrated on understanding divestment (which often led to exits from foreign markets) as compared with foreign investment and the implications of these exits for the parent company and it's multinational operations. As the level of analysis has shifted in recent times to the foreign subsidiary, there has been a spurt of studies on subsidiary survival. One could possibly argue that subsidiary survival and subsidiary exit are essentially two sides of the same coin because a subsidiary non-surviving could lead to exit. Therefore, to obtain a complete picture of the progress in exit research, it is important to acknowledge the contribution of subsidiary survival studies.

Before embarking on a review of the research studies that have made a significant contribution to our understanding of subsidiary exit, it is essential to recognize that two indicators of subsidiary performance, profitability and survival, are strange bedfellows and have different associations with their underlying factors. Barney (1996) suggested that studies should not use subsidiary survival as a measure of performance. Delios and Beamish (2001) illustrated that host country experience has a direct relationship with survival but an indirect one with profitability. Thus, survival does not always provide an exact reflection of profitability of a subsidiary.

In a significant study on the relationship between foreign entry and exit, Li (1995) analyzed a sample of foreign subsidiaries in the US market between 1974 and 1989 and showed that foreign acquisitions and joint ventures had a higher exit rate than other entry modes such as greenfield investments. This finding was confirmed by Barkema, Bell and Pennings (1996). In a follow-up study that further explored this finding, Delios and Beamish (2004) used a large sample of nearly 28 000 foreign subsidiaries worldwide belonging to Japanese firms and, in a longitudinal study, showed that wholly owned subsidiaries and joint ventures had exit comparable exit rates. Li also found a high rate of exit for diversified subsidiaries in unrelated industries. In a similar study of foreign firms in Portugal, Mata and Portugal (2000) found that greenfield modes of foreign entry were more likely to close down than to be divested. Vermeulen and Barkema (2001) took the link between entry mode and survival one step further and upon analyzing post-entry survival rates, found that growth via greenfield mode reduced survival chances of a firm's future ventures. On the other hand, this was not true of joint ventures. Nevertheless, as the authors themselves acknowledged, these findings need to be taken with a pinch of salt, mainly due to the moderating and mediating factors that have not yet been looked at. Entry mode literature has established the important role of cultural, psychic and institutional distance on the survival and performance of subsidiaries. Gaur and Lu (2007) used a sample of Japanese foreign subsidiaries to demonstrate that the greater the institutional distance, the more that subsidiaries that are majority-owned by foreign parents are likely to survive.

Foreign market exit studies have spanned international strategy and marketing literature. Matthyssens and Pauwels conducted a series of studies (Matthyssens and Pauwels 2000; Pauwels and Mathyssens 1999, 2004) that focused on the strategic and marketing aspects of foreign market withdrawal. In these studies on export withdrawal, these authors examined different parts of the entire export withdrawal model from antecedents to the behavioral decision making process and the outcomes of these decisions. They used case studies and showed that withdrawal is not necessarily a sign of failure and might be a conscious firm decision to rearrange its foreign market portfolio. According to these authors, market withdrawal is also an indicator of strategic flexibility by the firm.

It is not only the manner of entry but also timing of entry that has been known to affect subsidiary exit. Delios and Makino (2003) adopted a contingency approach to show that, depending on the ownership advantages, early entrants were more likely to exit than late entrants. In a more recent article, Chung and Beamish (2005) examined survival of foreign subsidiaries before and after the 1997 Asian Financial Crisis and found that after the crisis, foreign entry was more likely to be via wholly owned mode, majority-owned joint ventures or trade contracts. These entries were also more likely to survive under post-crisis circumstances. In a related study, these authors also found that the use of expatriates increased the likelihood of survival for greenfield joint ventures and acquired subsidiaries as compared with greenfield wholly owned subsidiaries. This finding was true for crisis periods but not during stable times. Thus, the link between entry and exit modes has been established in a general manner. The most studied entry mode in this link has been foreign entry through joint ventures. Study of this particular research question has been developed into a very rich stream of research frequented by scholars interested in joint ventures (Barkema and Vermeulen 1997; Pan and Chi 1999; Dhanaraj and Beamish 2004). Decades prior to this intense scrutiny of international joint ventures, Franko (1971) pointed out that multinational firms should look at the potential for success of joint ventures in the long term rather than jumping to conclusions about the short-term viability of the venture.

Much later on, in a study on survival of joint ventures, Barkema and Vermeulen (1997) concluded that cultural differences between partnering firms, specifically in terms of uncertainty avoidance and long-term orientation (as conceptualized by Hofstede 1980),

are more likely to jeopardize joint venture survival. Pan and Chi (1999) found that, in the case of multinational firms in China, equity joint ventures were more likely to survive than cooperative arrangements. There are many such studies, mainly in the context of joint venture performance and success. However, most of these are outside the scope of this chapter.

Due to the boom in M&As in the 1990s, which led to a very great number of cross-border acquisitions, these were followed by an increase in divestments, leading academics to the conclusion that foreign entry by acquisition was more likely to lead to divestment than entry by greenfield modes (Benito 1997). In a theoretical piece investigating another link between multinational strategy and exit, Benito (2005) explained that subsidiaries of transnational firms were most likely to be divested as compared with subsidiaries of firms that follow a multi-domestic or international strategy in the short run and global strategy in the long run.

Just like studies that showed how entry decisions affect exit decisions in foreign markets, a recent study showed that the reverse is also true. Chan, Makino and Isobe (2006) analyzed around 4000 market entry decisions by Japanese firms using a multi-level approach at the host country, industry (global and local) and firm levels. They found that a multinational firm's entry decision was related in an inverted U-shaped curve to entry and exit decisions of other multinational firms, more at the local industry level than at the other levels. Thus, there is a certain amount of interdependent association between entry and exit decisions among rival firms. Studies have shown that foreign subsidiary exits also affect the rate of exit by other firms. Henisz and Delios (2004) found that exits by 'peer' firms increased rate of exit when high levels of political hazards existed. They also showed that a multinational firm's experience with that political governance lowered subsidiary exits when political hazards existed but increased subsidiary exit when the political regime changed.

Once a decision has been made to exit, managers are faced with the execution task – how to exit?

EXIT STRATEGIES AND EXIT MODES

There have been very few studies that have examined implementation of the exit decision and divestment strategies in the international context. From a theoretical standpoint, the term 'exit strategy' could be much broader than the term 'exit mode' in that exit strategy might include the formulation and execution of the plan of action or decision regarding a subsidiary or product line. Nevertheless, exit strategies get implemented via an exit mode unless the firm reverses the decision to exit. Therefore, in this section we use these two terms interchangeably for this very reason. Based on Alford and Berger's study (1999), Frank and Harden (2001) suggest that the 'question of why companies divest is a nested choice model that requires knowledge of how firms choose to structure the divestiture'. In the early 1970s, not too many firms spent time on considering the different alternative exit strategies. Two strategies were popularly used: sell-offs and liquidation. It is only now, and that too mainly in the Triad region, that we observe spin-offs and carve-outs.

Spin-off strategy A 'spin-off strategy' is used by a firm when it lists its subsidiary unit in a foreign country or the home country on a stock exchange. A spin-off thus occurs when a firm distributes to its existing shareholders all of the common stock (usually around 80 per cent and above) it owns in a controlled subsidiary, thereby creating a separate publicly traded company. Depending on the decision of the parent company, spin-offs can grant the parent a very high or low level of control over its operations. However, the very fact that a spin-off is listed as a separate company on a stock exchange gives it more authority over its own operations than it would have had as an operating part of the parent company. In most cases, the spun-off company endeavors to independently manage itself and make its own decisions.

Carve-out strategy A 'carve-out strategy' is adopted by the firm when it offers for sale a minority share in a subsidiary company to the public. It is also known as a partial spin-off due to its very nature. The divested percentage may vary depending on the parent company but is usually much less than 40 per cent of the ownership interest of the parent firm. A carve-out usually has its own board of directors and financial statements but it benefits from the parent's support as well as its resources. Past carve-outs have shown that the divestment activity of the firm does not stop with a carve-out. In many cases, it is followed by a complete spin-off or a buy-back of the divested part. That is why several experts have argued that carve-outs serve as a temporary financial arrangement for firms in some cases.

In the international marketing literature, exit has been almost synonymous with sale, i.e., selling to another firm. In an interesting qualitative study that analyzed in-depth three restructuring decisions, Ghertman (1988) found that in the case of plant closures, the foreign units are responsible for decision-making, whereas in the case of unit sale, the headquarters or parent company make the decision often without consulting subsidiary management. All the same, his study included a very small sample. Also, it would be fascinating to find out if these results hold true for larger samples and twenty years later in today's business world.

In a later study Hennart, Dong-Jae and Ming (1998) delved into understanding why joint ventures as entry modes have a higher probability of exit as compared to wholly owned subsidiaries. Using an example of Japanese subsidiaries in the United States, these authors demonstrated that high exits from joint ventures were more often through sell-offs than liquidation. Mata and Portugal (2000) examined the relationship between entry mode and exit strategies but did not look at exit modes at the subsidiary level. They suggested that a firm had three options to pursue; to continue its operations, to sell off a unit or to close it down. Their study examined the relationship between different entry modes such as acquisitions, joint ventures and greenfield investments and divestment modes. Benito (2005) discussed divestment from the angle of MNEs' international business strategy. His study also dealt with two types of foreign exit strategies, closure and sales in foreign locations. While it is indeed true that these two strategies are probably the ones most commonly employed in divestments in foreign regions, there are other strategies that are increasingly being used by firms to divest foreign operations. For example, in May 2000, Hong Kong based Esprit Holdings Limited unveiled its plans to partially spin-off or carve-out (30 per cent) its European arm in Germany in order to increase the parent company's cash pool. As stated in the press release from the company, implementation of this plan would also benefit the parent by enabling it to raise funds in European capital markets. Nevertheless, spin-offs and carve-outs are more common among domestic operations due to the complexities of implementing these exit modes under different political and legal environments.

Probably one of the more common exit strategies is a closure or 'plant closure' as it is commonly known as, which refers to shutting down the operations of a particular subsidiary or transferring assets to another subsidiary such that it no longer exists. To give a very early example, according to Sony's corporate records, it set up Sony Shannon in 1961 in Ireland, a factory that was a wholly owned subsidiary for the production of transistor radios. But, in 1966, the Shannon plant was closed down on account of numerous debt- and management-related problems (Sony Corporate History, www.sony.net) and Sony exited Ireland at that time. Even nowadays in times of crisis, some firms waste no time in shutting down shop.

For example, some Western firms closed down some of their subsidiaries in South East Asia after the Asian Financial Crisis in 1997. It is important to acknowledge that there is a certain element of local environment determinism that would be likely to affect the choice of exit mode. As Jacques and Lorange (1984) aptly put it,

> Conditions of extreme environmental turbulence such as hyperinflation, however, do exacerbate the intra and inter-periodic volatility in the performance of foreign subsidiaries, as measured in currency terms. This, in turn, might seriously distort the planning process, in that excessive swings in the financial performance of foreign operations may result in shortening the operational planning cycle, myopic decision making, missed investment opportunities or hasty divestments.

Different forces and circumstances underlie the different strategic alternatives (Mata and Portugal 2000). For example, 'dissolution is likely to destroy some of the new capabilities' whereas 'when a business is sold, capabilities are transferred to a new owner and continue to be part of a commercial practice' (Mitchell 1994, p. 577). Thus, different exit modes play various important roles in maintaining competitive advantage for the firm. All the studies mentioned here that shed light on exit modes have indicated that these different strategic alternatives are determined by varying factors and these need to be understood through further inquiry. Divestment decision-making is rarely a very well-organized, systematic process in most firms. But, as more and more companies regularly divest their operations, it is becoming more important for firms to be able to divest their operations with the minimum possible loss, both tangible and intangible.

BARRIERS TO EXIT

In discussing foreign investment scholars never fail to highlight barriers to entry. Similarly, there exist barriers to market exit. Industrial organization theorists in particular emphasize the role of exit barriers. Porter (1976) mentioned two types of barriers to exit, namely, economic or the costs of exit and strategic or the ties between the subsidiary to be divested and the rest of the firm's network. Needless to state, there are high economic costs to market exit. Important among these are 'sunk costs', broadly defined as the investments made by the firm during entry or start of an operation that will not be recovered.

Economic barriers are also linked to the strategic value of the subsidiary. If we conceptualize an MNE as a network of subsidiaries spread out across the globe, we can envision the ties and interdependencies that characterize this network. Severing any of those ties through sale might not lead to disruption in the network and this serves as a barrier to exit. Barriers could also arise from firms' investments in unique or idiosyncratic resources (Dewitt 1998). Other factors that are barriers to foreign market exits could be information asymmetry between headquarters and host country and the differences in identifying success or failure in a market due to different cultural frames of reference or managerial barometers.

An important category of barriers to exit are managerial barriers. Managers sometimes have a strong bias against exit for many reasons, including the resistance-to-change factors and the dearness factor for a manager who invested time and energy to start an operation that now needs to be given up or the stigma associated with exit. There are costs to holding onto a business and managers' reluctance to let go is a barrier to exit.

Literature on barriers to domestic exits is more developed than foreign exits. Harrigan (1981; 1982) has covered the topic of barriers to exit using a sample of domestic firms. Some of these findings could possibly be applied to foreign exits also. Boddewyn (1983), however, suggested that there are lower barriers to exit in case of foreign divestment decisions. In spite of the literature on barriers to exit, some scholars argue that these barriers do not hold force in all types of market exits. As Godar (1997) hypothesized, 'barriers to exit will impact reactive, but not proactive divestment' of foreign subsidiaries because 'it may be less likely to consider barriers in the light of larger strategic changes'. Also, more often than not, firms tend to justify an exit decision after it is made rather than as a precursor to exit (Grunberg 1981).

OUTCOMES OF EXIT STRATEGY

Any discussion on the performance implications of exit strategies finds its roots in the accounting and finance literature. On average, most domestic exit studies that examined the effects of exits by parent firms in domestic operations concluded that exits left the parent in a better post-exit financial situation. This finding is intuitive because the main reason why firms exit is financial, i.e., to improve their balance sheet and remove negative synergies from their portfolio. We can also expect the same to be true in case of foreign exits.

Studies on the performance effects of sell-offs presumed that poor performing units were sold to improve profitability (Duhaime and Baird 1987) and in most cases, that was probably true. Today, even good performers are sold by firms for a variety of reasons. The selection of exit strategy plays an important role in this regard. As acknowledged by some scholars (Frank and Harden 2001), the variables that determine the choice of exit mode influence the 'value of the deal' and thus the performance outcome depends on the strategy selection. One of the few studies that compared the valuation effects of domestic and foreign plant closings, Tsetsekos and Gombola (1992) showed that foreign plants are shut down for plant-specific or country-specific reasons which lower arbitrage opportunities that led to foreign investment in the first place. That is why the negative stock market effects of such announcements are insignificant.

What was common to divestment studies in financial as well as strategic management is the performance implication of divestments (Miles and Rosenfeld 1983; Schipper and Smith 1986) for the headquarters. No significant study so far has examined the performance implications of using a particular exit strategy in the case of international divestments. Firms are ultimately looking to create or obtain value alongside their other motives for divestment. Therefore, from the headquarters perspective one would expect a firm to select a divestment mode that would be valuable for the firm post-divestment. The final decision is reduced to a simple mathematical equation – benefits vs. costs. But these two terms are not purely financial in nature. Costs also include the costs of disposal of specialized assets, breaking contracts and the costs of sacrificing certain customers, among others. However, if businesses were to suitably align or match their strategy to their particular situation, there would not necessarily be any significant differences in post-divestment performance after using any exit strategy. Any strategic orientation is possible provided that there is a fit with the subsidiary context.

CULTURAL DIFFERENCES

It is a well-noted fact in international business research that management styles differ based on the culture of the home country. Back in the 1970s when Western multinational firms dominated global business, scholars noted that there were cultural differences between US and European firms' approaches to market exit (Boddewyn 1979; Nees 1978). There are three ways to organize cultural differences in international exit strategies.

First, most studies noted general differences in approaches related to divestments within the home country itself. For example, they referred to divestment of a unit by a US firm located in the USA and that by a German firm of a unit in Germany. In a study by Hamilton and Chow (1993), who surveyed 98 New Zealand firms that had

engaged in exits in their own market, it was discovered that the primary motives for divestment included the need to gain liquidity or to re-channel funds to core or novel areas. The authors also compared divestors and non-divestors and found that divesting firms in New Zealand are larger and faster-growing than non-divesting ones. In a case of Australian multinational firms, Owen and Yawson (2006) found that larger and more internationalized firms tend to engage in divestments of foreign subsidiaries instead of domestic units. This finding is in line with the basic consensus among exit scholars who agree that, more often than not, foreign subsidiaries are the first to go when faced with pressure for divestiture.

Second, some authors (Li and Guisinger 1991) examined exit strategies and firm failure of foreign multinationals that had invested in one market, e.g., the US market. Using a sample of 85 non-financial foreign firms operating in the US market, they found that the foreign owned firms had lower exit rates overall than domestic US firms in the period from 1978–1988. They also found that firms from culturally dissimilar countries were more likely to fail, providing support for the important role cultural distance plays in delivering exit strategies. Mata and Portugal (2000) used a sample of more than 1000 foreign-controlled firms that either divested or closed down operations in the Portuguese market. They concluded that greenfield forms of entry were more likely to be closed down than divested. The authors also found that firms with ample human capital were less likely to exit. In spite of the interesting findings of such studies, it might be most useful to interpret the findings in their context. Care should be taken when generalizing the results because of the different national environments.

Third, there were other studies that observed comparative patterns of foreign exits by US, European and Japanese multinationals in foreign markets in which they had invested. Boddewyn (1979) reviewed these patterns based on their magnitude and factors.

However, he did not empirically test them. Especially in Europe, exits were seldom publicized and managers were very secretive about these events (Nees 1978). The differences between the exit strategies of US, European and Japanese firms based on past studies are highlighted in Table 12.1.

Traditionally, US firms have engaged in maximum divestiture activity for two obvious reasons, the first being their well-documented emphasis on profitability as a measure of performance and their focus on short-term benefits and the second being their corporate planning methods that involve the portfolio model. Under the portfolio concept, US firms have been known to invest in a multitude of products and product lines and product/market combinations, which they sell when the going gets tough. As a result, they engaged in relatively more acquisition and divestiture activity as compared with European and Japanese MNEs. US firms are also prone to completely selling off their units instead of maintaining even a minority relationship of some sort with their now previous subsidiaries (Ito 1995). Other findings that would support the different patterns of divestment are those by Egelhoff (1984), which state that subsidiaries of US firms submit more performance data to headquarters, US MNEs exercise high levels of output control over their subsidiaries; and also that US firms used fewer home country nationals as managers in the foreign subsidiary than European MNEs did. These factors affect their exit strategies. While US companies are concerned with short-term financial orientation with rewards being related to specific performance indicators, Japanese companies tend to stress on long-term strategic orientation and emphasis on growth rather than merely financial issues. Differences between the divestment strategies of US and Japanese firms can also be attributed to the different structures of the firms. The genealogical structure of Japanese firms implies that they use carve-outs or spin-offs in order to provide for a more flexible organization that leads to benefits through a deliberate separation of core competencies (Ito and Rose 1994).

The 1980s witnessed carve-outs of several subsidiaries of Japanese companies. Their focus being on growth, their divestment strategies enable more efficient management of growth and more opportunity to obtain outside capital. Japanese MNEs are known to partially spin off or carve out their subsidiaries 'under conditions that are unique' (Ito 1995). According to studies by Ito and Rose (1994) and Ito (1995), who have done a significant amount of research on Japanese spin-offs and carve-outs, Japanese firms use spin-offs as a strategy to lower the costs of different governance structures and so that the spin-off can be competitive on its own. 'Hitachi has 650 subsidiaries, most of which are spin-offs' (Ito 1995). The term 'spin-off' has different meanings in US and Japanese management in terms of the purpose of a spin-off as well as the distribution of ownership stake. Japanese firms do not necessarily divest with the intention of getting rid of an unprofitable business. Ito and Rose (1994) explain that some US firms divest their businesses in order to pursue management efficiency by concentrating on their core business. Yet their divestment usually involves selling off the division for profit, instead of maintaining a relationship as in minority equity ownership. In his suggestions for future research in the field, Boddewyn (1983) urged that cultural 'dimensions need to be considered when developing a theory that transcends the U.S. experience'. In a more recent study and using a very large sample of over 26 000 instances of foreign investment by Japanese firms, Makino, Beamish and Zhao (2004) showed that these firms had a lower rate of exit from less developed country markets as compared with more economically advanced markets.

Prior to the turn of the twentieth century, research on foreign divestitures concentrated on firms hailing from the Triad region. These were also the largest multinational firms at that time. Since the year 2000, there has been a growth in multinational firms from

Table 12.1   Selected studies on foreign market exit strategy

Study	Theoretical lens/Literature	Sample	Conclusion comments
Early Studies			
Franko (1971)	Strategy perspective	Foreign manufacturing units of US MNEs	International joint venture survival is related to the choice of multinational strategy. Found that firms that continued to diversify abroad were more likely to use and succeed as joint ventures.
Wallender (1973)	Resource-based perspective	Non-empirical	Highlighted the importance of planning divestments by proper resource allocation, use and management. Firms should develop skills to identify divestible subsidiaries.
Boddewyn and Torneden (1973)	Governments and host country environment	Comparison of 50 largest US trusts with Fortune 500 firms	Divestments in foreign markets are not necessarily and not always associated with hostile governments and related issues. There is a need for firms to plan for seamlessly executing these divestment decisions.
Torneden and Boddewyn (1974)	Report	Select sample of mainly US firms divesting abroad	Provided insights on the foreign divestment decision-making process, mainly the lack of objective analysis.
Torneden (1975)	Report	8 case studies and survey	Disinvestments in majority of the studied cases were due to reversal of previous management mistakes in acquiring unrelated or failing subsidiaries. These subsidiaries were then divested.
Sachdev (1976)	Report	Mainly UK and US multinational firms	At that time, multinational firms in general and UK firms in particular were not adequately prepared for disinvestments. Also pointed out that managerial parochialism during divestment decisions hinder 'learning' from past mistakes.
Chopra, Boddewyn and Torneden (1978)	Non-theoretical report	Fortune 500 firms	The number of divestments was increasing every year. Maximum divestments were by way of sale as compared with liquidation.
Nees (1978)	Decision-making models	Firms in Europe	Highlighted multiple facets of the divestment decision-making process including stimuli, actors and implementation.
Boddewyn (1979)	Financial and strategic perspectives	Non-empirical	Key divestment factors include primarily financial reasons but strategic, organizational and managerial factors also play a role in such decisions. (Article also summarizes findings of previous, related studies).
Boddewyn (1979)	Non-theoretical report	US and European multinationals	There were fewer divestments in Europe due to European firms' greater responsibility toward employees and society. Furthermore, European firms built relationships with the governments and focused less on profits as compared with US firms.
Boddewyn (1983)	Foreign investment theories	Conceptual article	Pointed out several differences and similarities between foreign investment and divestment as well as between domestic and foreign divestment decisions.
Boddewyn (1985)	Foreign investment, industrial organization, economic theory	Conceptual article	Foreign divestment theories should be dynamic and related to the political economy of the countries. Thus, analysis should be both macro- and micro-economic.
Ghertman (1988)	Decision-making models	Case studies of 3 multinational firms from the USA Canada and Europe	Examined roles of parents and foreign subsidiaries in the divestment decision and found that in case of plant closures, the subsidiaries themselves are primarily responsible. However, parents play an active role in sale of units.

Table 12.1   Cont'd

Study	Theoretical lens/Literature	Sample	Conclusion comments
The Other Side of Foreign Investment Theories			
Dunning (1988)	OLI paradigm	Theory development	Loss of any of the OLI (ownership, location, internalization) advantages could lead to divestiture.
Pauwels and Matthyssens (1999)	Internationalization theory, Strategic perspective	Case studies of European firms	Used data from case studies and the internationalization perspective to develop a model of export withdrawal, including the motivators, the behavioral decision-making process and the outcomes of the decision.
Pauwels and Matthyssens (2004)	Internationalization theory, Strategic perspective	Case studies of European firms	Export market withdrawal might be an indication of strategic flexibility by the parent firm. Brings out the details of the withdrawal process that reflects a change in strategy.
Palmer (2004)	Internationalization	Single case study of UK's Tesco	Focuses on international divestment and market withdrawal from in the global retail sector. The Tesco case demonstrates the relationship between investment and divestment. Many firms like Tesco often do not consider the exit pressures when making foreign investments.
Benito (2005)	Integration-responsiveness framework	Conceptual article	Divestment propensities vary based on type of strategy. Transnational subsidiaries will be most likely to be divested. International and multi-domestic units are less likely while global units are least likely to be divested.
Entry Modes and Exit Strategies			
Li (1995)	Organizational learning and experience	Foreign firms in USA	Entry through acquisitions, joint ventures and unrelated diversification has a higher likelihood of exit than entry through wholly owned subsidiaries. Higher experience and learning are associated with subsidiary survival.
Benito (1997)	Host-country environment and strategy	Foreign manufacturing units of Norwegian firms	Related and greenfield subsidiaries are less likely to be divested. Also, economic growth in the host country was inversely associated with divestment of the subsidiary.
Barkema and Vermeulen (1997)	Hofstede's culture dimensions	Dutch MNEs' foreign subsidiaries	Greater cultural distance in terms of uncertainty avoidance and long term orientedness is more likely to lead to exits from joint ventures.
Hennart, Dong-Jae and Ming (1998)	Joint venture literature	Japanese MNEs in USA	Entry by joint ventures is more likely to exit as compared to entry through a wholly owned subsidiary. Furthermore, such exits are more likely to be through sales as compared to liquidations.
Pan and Chi (1999)	Entry mode literature	MNEs in China	Equity joint ventures are more likely to survive than cooperative arrangements.
Mata and Portugal (2000)	Industrial organization, entry mode, internalization	Foreign firms operating in Portugal	Examined different exit modes and found that entry through greenfield operations were more likely to shut down. Ownership and structure affect likelihood of sale but not closure mode.
Delios and Ensign (2000)	Resouces and FDI theory	Japanese MNEs in Canada	Subsidiary size, entry mode, industry sector, geographic location within a country market, ownership and expatriate level affect subsidiary survival and subsidiary exit.

Continued

Table 12.1 Cont'd

Study	Theoretical lens/Literature	Sample	Conclusion comments
Vermeulen and Barkema (2001)	Entry mode, experience	Dutch MNEs' foreign subsidiaries	Internal post-entry growth through greenfields diminished probability of success of future ventures. Acquisitions increase the viability of the firm's future ventures.
Delios and Beamish (2001)	Resources, capabilities and experience	Foreign units of Japanese firms	Found that two indicators of post-entry performance, survival and profitability are determined by different underlying factors. Experience in the host country has a direct effect on subsidiary survival. This effect is moderated by entry mode.
Delios and Makino (2003)	Resources and uncertainty, Contingency approach	Japanese MNEs	Early entrants in a foreign market are more likely to exit than later entrants. This finding was especially true in case of firms that had a technological advantage.
Dhanaraj and Beamish (2004)	Extended transactions cost analysis	Foreign subsidiaries of Japanese firms	Analyzed the impact of equity ownership on survival and found that dissolution rate of international joint ventures lowers with higher level of equity.
Delios and Beamish (2004)	Resources and capabilities	Japanese MNEs' foreign subsidiaries	Foreign subsidiaries that were wholly owned subsidiaries and joint ventures had comparable exit rates.
Chung and Beamish (2005)	Institutional theory	Japanese subsidiaries in Asia	In the post-Asian Financial Crisis environment, firms were more likely to use wholly owned entry modes, majority joint ventures and trade contracts. Subsidiaries that entered via these modes were more likely to survive.
Chung and Beamish (2005)	RBV and dynamic capabilities	Japanese subsidiaries in Asia	In times of crisis but not times of stability, the use of expatriates increased the likelihood of survival for greenfield joint ventures and acquired subsidiaries as compared to greenfield wholly owned subsidiaries.
Chan, Makino and Isobe (2006)	Legitimacy and competition	Japanese MNEs	Firms' foreign market entry decisions are influenced by other MNEs prior entry and exit decisions (inverted U-shaped relationship).

Role of Cultural Distance and Host-country Effects

Study	Theoretical lens/Literature	Sample	Conclusion comments
Li and Guisinger (1991)	Entry mode, ownership and cultural distance	Foreign firms in the US	Foreign firms in the USA failed less often than domestic firms. Newer foreign subsidiaries in the USA had a higher rate of failure than more established ones. Units of culturally distant parents had a higher failure rate.
Tsetsekos and Gombola (1992)	Financial valuation perspective	Foreign and domestic plants of US firms	Analyzed plant closing announcements and showed that foreign plant closings did not significantly affect stock price and did not signify organization wide problems when compared with domestic plant closings.
Makino, Beamish and Zhao (2004)	Investment theory and location	Japanese MNEs	Japanese firms' foreign investment in less developed markets led to lower rate of exit than that in more developed country markets.
Henisz and Delios (2004)	Location factors and politics	Foreign manufacturing units of Japanese firms	Prior exits by 'peer' firms enhance exit rates when political hazards are high. A multinational firm's host country experience with a given host country government moderates the rate of exit in the presence of political hazards but increases exits when the political regime changes.

Table 12.1 Cont'd

Study	Theoretical lens/Literature	Sample	Conclusion comments
Gaur and Lu (2007)	Institutional theory and organizational learning perspective	Japanese foreign subsidiaries	In institutionally distant host countries, chances of subsidiary survival are higher if the unit is majority owned by the foreign parent.
Madura and Rose (1987)	Strategic perspectives	Steel, shipping and motor vehicle industries in 5 countries	Firms were likely to reverse diversify by divesting non-core products. This improved competitive position of the firm through efficiency and specialization but also exposed the firm to greater economic risk.
Culture and Exit Strategy			
Hamilton and Chow (1993)	Multiple perspectives	New Zealand firms	Examined differences between divesting and non-divesting New Zealand firms. Found that larger and rapidly growing firms were more likely to divest units. Primary motive to divest was need for liquidity to focus on core or new areas.
Ito and Rose (1994)	Organizational sociology	Japanese firms	Presented a conceptual framework for the spin-offs structure that is characteristic of large Japanese firms. Spin-offs are implemented differently from US firms.
Ito (1995)	Transactions cost theory	Japanese and US spin-offs	As opposed to US firms, spin-offs by Japanese firms are survival strategies. They are also differently structured by the parent firms.
Griffin (2003)	Strategic perspective	Single, longitudinal case study of CDMI Ireland	Examining the divestment decision from the subsidiary perspective, found that subsidiaries can have control over the triggers and outcomes of such decisions.
Owen and Yawson (2006)	Resources and Diversification	Australian MNEs	Australian multinationals that are highly geographically diversified choose to divest a foreign subsidiary as compared with divesting a domestic unit. Also found that firms divest to exit non-core businesses.

emerging countries. Several examples of this trend can be seen in the popular media.

IMPLICATIONS FOR EXIT STRATEGY RESEARCH IN THE NEW GLOBAL ECONOMY

The idea of divestment in the yesteryears used to be narrower in scope and more financial in nature. Boddewyn (1983) claimed, 'divestment originates in the recognition of a financial aggregate discrepancy'. However, the unsatisfactory performance indicators may actually be a sign of other non-financial problems. Since most of the major multinational firms were also from developed countries, mainly the USA and Western Europe, divestment research was uni-dimensional. With the onslaught of MNEs from emerging economies, international business itself has become more dynamic. Thus, there is a need to study the exit topic further for several reasons. The most important reason is to update existing research, which many would say is outdated. Research issues are a product of their time and in the last decade or so, the international marketing climate has changed drastically. Exit activity used to be concentrated among relatively smaller, newer and unrelated subsidiaries: but now, all types of subsidiaries are regularly divested. Divestment was always assumed to be driven by parental factors but now subsidiary related factors play a very crucial role in determining divestment decisions. Early on, several multinational firms divested their foreign units shortly after entering a new foreign market due to the overbearing liability of newness and foreignness and the costs attached to inexperience. Foreign divestment studies then devoted themselves to addressing this trend. So far divestment studies have been conducted for firms that have divested foreign operations soon after entering the foreign country, as a result of the inadequate experience of the parent (Barkema, Bell and Pennings 1996). Hence, there is great potential to advance our understanding of foreign market exits so that we can move toward better exit strategies.

As MNEs from emerging economies grow larger and new international studies focus on firms from these regions of the world, research questions could address how their unique corporate structures or governance models, such as the South Korean chaebols, family-owned conglomerates (such as Reliance Industries from India) commonly seen in Asia and others influence exit strategies. Having acknowledged the significant role of cultural factors in foreign entry and survival, it is time now to investigate the influence of such factors in exit decisions also.

In a study in 1973, Boddewyn and Torneden found that the foreign divestment decision took on average 15 months from the time a firm considered divestment to the time a commitment was made to the decision. Thereafter, it took around a year to execute the decision. Years later, a study published by Dranikoff, Koller and Schneider in 2002 claimed that due to firms' reluctance to divest, it took several years, sometimes even as many as seven, for firms to commit to the decision. Since then, the nature of global business has changed. The different models of exit decision-making that are applied today could be an interesting avenue for research. In addition, longitudinal studies would probably be able to shed more light on the 'process' of exit decision-making.

Firms and researchers alike are more prone to looking at exits or divestments as purely economic decisions. Nevertheless, the exit decision engages the interests of all stakeholders and these set in motion the 'other' costs of exit. Probably the most audible cost is that of employees. When subsidiaries are sold or closed down, employees feel the brunt of the decision almost immediately. In spite of the attached costs of divesting, there are also costs to holding on to a market for too long. Managers often have a strong desire to hold on to certain businesses for fear that letting go might not only be an acknowledgement of failure but might also entail giving up some advantages that the market contains. These 'other' costs of exits have been neglected and should be explored further.

Some of the important areas that are potential avenues for further research revolve around strategy implementation. These are identified in Figure 12.1. The future research questions or ideas mentioned in the preceding paragraphs and in the figure can be broadly summarized as follows. As compared with headquarters-driven exits, what are the antecedents, moderators and outcomes of subsidiary-driven exits that are either initiated by or managed by the subsidiary? What are the determinants of the 'other' exit modes, such as spin-offs, carve-outs, partial sales and the like in the context of international business? What are the exit practices of multinational firms from emerging economies? There is still no theory that belongs to and adequately explains foreign exits. This leaves a lot of room for theoretical development. Newer theories like the network theory, capabilities perspective and behavioral theories, as applied to management, could probably shed some much-needed light on foreign exits. The majority of the studies that investigated the relationship between entry modes and survival or exit have relied on a sample of Japanese MNEs. Thus, their findings are limited. Replicating these studies with different samples could address the question of generalizability of these findings. Previous studies have hinted

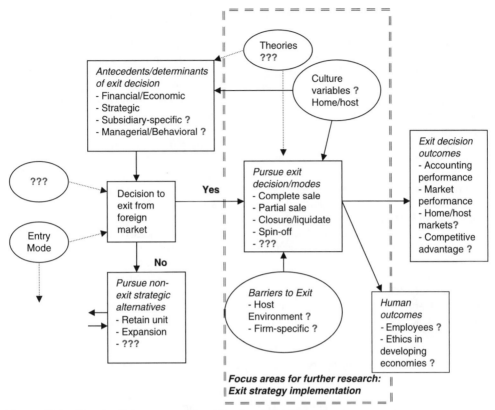

Figure 12.1   Map for future research on foreign exit strategies

that different industries face different pressures for exit. These need to be examined using one industry at a time. Exit strategy literature has been largely economics-driven. As a result, the softer, behavioral perspective is missing, especially in understanding the antecedents and outcomes of exit decisions. In the same vein, the managerial reluctance to let go of a subsidiary and other related issues needs to be studied. International environment has changed once again and the time is now ripe to re-investigate this topic in light of the global business system.

REFERENCES

Alford, A, and Berger, P. (1999), 'The role of taxes, financial reporting, and other market imperfections in structuring divisive reorganizations', Working Paper (University of Pennsylvania).

Barkema, H. G., Bell, J. H. J. and Pennings, J. M. (1996) 'Foreign entry, cultural barriers and learning', *Strategic Management Journal*, 17: 151–166.

Barkema, H. G. and Vermeulen, F. (1997) 'What differences in the cultural backgrounds of partners are detrimental for international joint ventures?', *Journal of International Business Studies*, 28(4): 845–864.

Barney, J. (1996) *'Gaining and Sustaining Competitive Advantage*. Reading', MA: Addison-Wesley.

Benito, G. R. G. (1997) 'Divestment of foreign production operations', *Applied Economics*, 29(10):1365–1378.

Benito, G. R. G. (2005) 'Divestment and international business strategy', *Journal of Economic Geography*, 5(2): 235–251.

Benito, G. R. G and Welch, L. S. (1997) 'De-internationalization', *Management International Review*, 37(2): 7–25.

Birkinshaw, J. (1996) 'How multinational subsidiary mandates are gained and lost', *Journal of International Business Studies*, 3Q: 467–495.

Birkinshaw, J., and Hood, N. (1998) 'Multinational subsidiary evolution: capability and charter change in foreign-owned subsidiary Companies', *Academy of Management Review*, 23(4): 773–795.

Boddewyn, J. J. (1979a) 'Divestment: local vs foreign, and US vs European approaches', *Management International Review*, 19(1): 21–27.

Boddewyn, J. J. (1979b) 'Foreign divestment: magnitude and factors', *Journal of International Business Studies*, 10(1): 21–28.

Boddewyn, J. J. (1983) 'Foreign and domestic divestment and investment decisions: like or unlike?' *Journal of International Business Studies*, 14(3): 23–36.

Boddewyn, J. J. (1985) 'Theories of foreign direct investment and divestment: A Classificatory Note', *Management International Review*, 25(1): 57–65.

Boddewyn, J. J. and Torneden R. L. (1973) 'U.S. foreign divestment: a preliminary survey', *Columbia Journal of World Business*, (8)2: 25–29.

Buchholtz, A. K., Lubatkin, M. and O'Neill, H. M. (1999) 'Seller responsiveness to the need to divest', *Journal of Management* 25(5): 633–652.

Chan, C. M., Makino, S. and Isobe, T. (2006) 'Interdependent behavior in foreign direct investment: the multi-level effects of prior entry and prior exit on foreign market entry', *Journal of International Business Studies*, 37(5): 642–665.

Chopra, J., Boddewyn, J. J. and Torneden, R. L. (1978) 'U.S. foreign divestment: a 1972–1975 updating', *Columbia Journal of World Business*, Spring, 13(1): 16–21

Chung, C. C. and Beamish, P. W. (2005) 'The impact of institutional reforms on characteristics and survival of foreign subsidiaries in emerging economies', *Journal of Management Studies*, 42(1): 35–62

Chung, C. C. and Beamish, P. W. (2005) Investment mode strategy and expatriate strategy during times of economic crisis, *Journal of International Management*, 11(3): 331–355.

Delios, A., and Beamish, P. W. (2001) 'Survival and profitability: the roles of experience and intangible assets in foreign subsidiary performance', *Academy of Management Journal*, 44(5): 1028–1038.

Delios, A., and Beamish, P. W. (2004) 'Joint venture performance revisited: Japanese foreign subsidiaries worldwide', *Management International Review*, 44(1): 69–92.

Delios, A., and Ensign, P. C. (2000) 'A subnational analysis of Japanese direct investment in Canada', *Canadian Journal of Administrative Sciences*, 17(1): 38–52.

Delios, A., and Makino, S. (2003) 'Timing of entry and foreign subsidiary performance of Japanese Firms', *Journal of International Marketing*, 11(3): 83–105

Dewitt, R. (1998) 'Firm, industry and strategy influences on choice of downsizing approach', *Strategic Management Journal*, 19: 50–79.

Dhanaraj, C. and Beamish, P. W. (2004) 'Effect of equity ownership on the survival of international joint ventures', *Strategic Management Journal*, 25(3): 295–305.

Dranikoff, L., Koller, T and Schneider, A. (2002) 'Divestiture: strategy's missing link', *Harvard Business Review*, 80(5): 75–83.

Duhaime, I. M. and Baird, I. S. (1987) 'Divestment decision-making: the role of business unit size', *Journal of Management*, 13(3): 483–498.

Dunning, J. H. (1980) 'Toward an eclectic theory of international production: some empirical tests', *Journal of International Business Studies*, 11(1): 9–30.

Dunning, J. H. (1988) 'The eclectic paradigm of international production: a restatement and some possible explanations', *Journal of International Business Studies*, 19(1): 1–31.

Egelhoff, W. G. (1984) 'Patterns of control in U.S., U.K., and European multinational corporations', *Journal of International Business Studies*, Fall: 73–83.

Frank, K. E. and Harden, J. W. (2001) 'Corporate restructurings: a comparison of equity carve-outs and spin-offs', *Journal of Business Finance and Accounting*, 28(3): 503-529

Franko, L. C. (1971) 'Joint venture divorce in the multinational company', *Columbia Journal of World Business*, 6(3):13–23.

Gaur, A. S. and Lu, J. W. (2007) 'Ownership strategies and survival of foreign subsidiaries: impacts of institutional distance and experience', *Journal of Management*, 33(1): 84–110.

Ghertman, M. (1988) 'Foreign subsidiary and parents' roles during strategic Investment and divestment decisions', *Journal of International Business Studies*, Spring: 47–67.

Gilmour, S. C. (1973) *The Divestment Decision Process*, Unpublished DBA Dissertation, Harvard University, Boston.

Godar, S. H. (1997) *Drivers for the Divestment of Foreign Subsidiaries: An Exploratory Study*, Unpublished dissertation, Temple University, Philadelphia.

Griffin, Ray (2003) 'Subsidiary Divestment: The Case of CDMI Ireland 1970–2002', *Irish Journal of Management*, 24(1): 215.

Grunberg, Leon (1981) '*Failed Multinational Ventures*: The Political Economy of International Divestments' Massachusetts, Toronto: Lexington Books.

Hamilton, R. T. and Chow, Y. K. (1993) 'Why managers divest – evidence from New Zealand's largest companies', *Strategic Management Journal*, 14(6): 479–484.

Harrigan, Kathryn R. (1981) 'Deterrents to divestiture', *Academy of Management Journal*, 24(2): 306–323.

Harrigan, Kathryn R. (1982) 'Exit decisions in mature industries', *Academy of Management Journal*, 25(4): 707–732.

Hedlund, G. (1980) 'The role of foreign subsidiaries in strategic decision-making in Swedish multinational corporations', *Strategic Management Journal*, 1(1): 23–36.

Henisz, W. J., and Delios, A. (2004) 'Information or influence? The benefits of experience for managing political uncertainty', *Strategic Organization*, 2(4): 389–421.

Hennart, J., Dong-Jae, K., and Ming, Z. (1998) 'The impact of joint venture status on the longevity of Japanese stakes in U.S. manufacturing affiliates', *Organization Science*, 9(3): 382–396.

Hoskisson, R. E., Johnson, R. A. and Moesel, D. D. (1994). 'Corporate divestiture intensity in restructuring firms: Effects of governance, strategy and performance', *Academy of Management Journal*, 37(5): 1207–1251.

Hofstede, G. (1980) '*Culture's Consequences: International Differences in Work-related values*'. Beverly Hills, CA: Sage Publications.

Hoskisson, R. E., Johnson, R. A. and Moesel, D. D. (1994) 'Corporate divestiture intensity in restructuring firms: effects of governance,

strategy and performance', *Academy of Management Journal*, 37(5): 1207–1251.

International Divestment: 'A Survey of Corporate Experience', Prepared by Business International SA (Geneva) in collaboration with J. J. Boddewyn, New York.

Ito, K. (1995) 'Japanese spinoffs: unexplored survival strategies', *Strategic Management Journal*, 16: 431–446.

Ito, K., and Rose, E. L. (1994) 'The genealogical structure of Japanese firms: parent–subsidiary relationships', *Strategic Management Journal*, 15: 35–51.

Jacques, L. L. and Lorange, P. (1984) 'The international control conundrum: the case of hyperinflationary subsidiaries', *Journal of International Business Studies*, 15(2): 185–201.

Kogut, B. and Zander, U. (1993) 'Knowledge of the firm and the evolutionary theory of the multinational corporation', *Journal of International Business Studies*, 24(4): 625–645.

Kotabe, M. and Murray, J.Y. (2004) 'Global sourcing strategy and sustainable competitive advantage', *Industrial Marketing Management*, 33(1): 7–14.

Li, J. (1995) 'Foreign entry and survival: effects of strategic choices on performance in international markets', *Strategic Management Journal*, 16(5): 333–351.

Li, J. and Guisinger, S. (1991) 'Comparative business failures of foreign-controlled firms in the United States', *Journal of International Business Studies*, 22(2): 209–224.

Madura, J. and Rose, C. (1987) 'Are product specialization and international diversification strategies compatible?', *Management International Review*, 27(3): 38–44.

Makino, S., Beamish, P. W. and Zhao, N. B. (2004) 'The characteristics and performance of Japanese FDI in less developed and developed countries', *Journal of World Business*, 39(4): 377–392.

Markides, C. C. (1995) '*Diversification, Refocusing and Economic Performance*. Cambridge, MA; London: The MIT Press.

Mata, J. and Portugal, P. (2000) 'Closure and divestiture by foreign entrants: the impact of entry and post-entry strategies', *Strategic Management Journal*, 21(5): 549–562.

Matthyssens, P. and Pauwels, P. (2000) 'Uncovering international market-exit processes: a comparative case study', *Psychology and Marketing*, 17(8): 697–719.

Matthyssens, P. and Pauwels, P. (2002) 'The Dynamics of International Market Withdrawal', *Research Memoranda 048*. Maastricht: METEOR, Maastricht Research School of Economics of Technology and Organization.

Miles, J. A. and Rosenfeld, J. D. (1983) 'The effect of voluntary spin-off announcements on shareholder wealth', *The Journal of Finance*, 38(5): 1597–1606.

Mitchell, W. (1994) 'The dynamics of evolving markets: the effects of business sales and age on dissolutions and divestitures', *Administrative Science Quarterly*, 39: 575–602.

Montgomery, C.A., Thomas, A. R. and Kamath, R. (1984) 'Divestiture, market valuation and strategy', *Academy of Management Journal*, 27(4): 830–840.

Nees, D. (1978) 'The divestment decision process in large and medium-sized diversified companies: a descriptive model based on clinical studies', *International Studies of Management and Organization*, 8(4): 67–95.

Owen, S. and Yawson, A. (2006) 'Domestic or international: divestitures in Australian multinational corporations', *Global Finance Journal*, 17(2): 282–293.

Palmer, M. (2004) 'International retail restructuring and divestment: the experience of Tesco', *Journal of Marketing Management*, 20(9): 1075–1105.

Pan, Y. and Chi, P. S. K. (1999) 'Financial performance and survival of multinational corporations in China', *Strategic Management Journal*, 20(4): 359–385.

Pauwels, P. and Matthyssens, P. (1999) 'A strategy process perspective on export withdrawal', *Journal of International Marketing*, 7(3): 10–37.

Pauwels, P. and Matthyssens, P. (2002) in Subhash Jain's *State of the Art of Research in International Marketing*. Cheltenham, UK: Edward Elgar Publishing.

Pauwels, P. and Matthyssens, P. (2004) 'Strategic flexibility in export expansion: growing through withdrawal', *International Business Review*, 21(4): 496–510.

Porter, M. (1976) 'Please note location of nearest exit: exit barriers and planning', *California Management Review*, 19(2): 21–34.

Price Waterhouse Coopers (2006) 'M and A will set a record in 2007 so long as Goldilocks Economy continues Wednesday December 13', 4:24 pm ET, Source: PricewaterhouseCoopers Transaction Services.

Rumelt, R. P. (1974) *Strategy, Structure and Economic Performance*. Boston MA: Division of Research' Harvard Business School.

Sachdev, J. C. (1976a) 'Disinvestment: a corporate failure or a strategic success', *International Studies of Management and Organization*, 6(1):112–130.

Sachdev, J. C. (1976b) 'Disinvestment: A new problem in multinational corporation host government interface', *Management International Review*, 16(3): 23–35.

Schipper, K. and Smith, A. (1986) 'A comparison of equity carve-outs and seasoned equity offerings', Share price effects and corporate restricting', *Journal of Financial Economics*, 15(1/2): 153–186.

Torneden R. L. (1975) 'Foreign disinvestment by U.S. multinational corporations', *International Executive*, 17(3): 1–3.

Torneden R. L. and Boddewyn, J. J. (1974) 'Foreign divestments: too many mistakes', *Columbia Journal of World Business*, Fall.

Tsetsekos, G. and Gombola, M. (1992) 'Foreign and domestic divestments: evidence on valuation effects of plant closings', *Journal of International Business Studies*, 23(2): 203–224.

Van Den Bulcke, D, Boddewyn, J. J., Martens, B. and Klemmer, P. (1980) *Investment and Divestment Policies of Multinational Corporations in Europe*. New York: Praeger Publishers.

Vermeulen, F. and Barkema, H. (2001) 'Learning through acquisitions', *Academy of Management Journal*, 44(3): 457–476.

Waddock, S. (1989) 'Core strategy: end result of restructuring?' *Business Horizons*, May–June Issue: 49–55.

Wallender III, H.W. (1973) 'A planned approach to divestment', *Columbia Journal of World Business*, 8(1): 33–38.

Wilson, B. D. (1980) *'Disinvestment of Foreign Subsidiaries'*. Ann Arbor, MI: UNI Press.

SECTION 4
Global Strategy

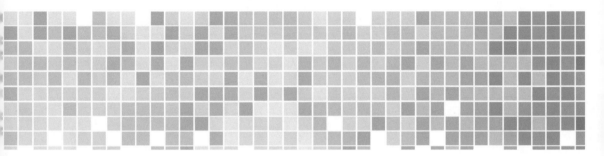

13

Global Competitive Marketing Strategy

Michael Grund, Oliver Heil, and Mark Elsner

INTRODUCTION

There is little doubt that increasingly glob-alized markets have lead to a fundamental rearrangement of the determinants of firms' competitive marketing strategy. Over two bil-lion persons have been added to the world's economies that are largely driven by market structures and, thus, competition. The persons have been added as consumers and competi-tors and, oftentimes, as winners and losers of global competitive interplay. Certainly, global competition has already changed the lives of hundreds of millions of persons.

Not surprisingly, globalization has come to be one of the most controversial discussed issues of our times with a multitude of facets that are frequently misunderstood. As a result, widespread biased perceptions about what world-spanning markets really mean and what they can accomplish for all participants exist. However, it seems safe to state that a global culture based on competitive interplay is on the rise.

Importantly, one has to keep in mind that an emerging global culture will be influenced and formed to a high degree by communica-tion. Here, the technical development of the

past decades – in particular the rapid diffu-sion of the Internet – has obviously paved the way for cultures and societies to become globalized. Consequently, this development forces businesses into rethinking and reassess-ing their competitive advantages. This moti-vated us to discuss the internet explicitly as a catalyst for global competition.

Naturally, the issue of competitive advantage needs to be examined in detail. In particular the competitive advantages of countries or regions have become more and more impor-tant for marketing strategy at firm level, as those developments are about to reshape the environment in which the businesses are playing to a great extent. Thus, to develop a global competitive marketing strategy, several pillars of the market economy need to be examined.

Further, issues of globalization that pertain to global competition need to be identified and translated into meaningful managerial issues. Today's meaning of strategy – e.g., as concepts such as product life cycle (PLC) or established competitive arenas are undergo-ing fundamental change – needs to be clari-fied and contrasted with other strategic and tactical company activities. Consequently, we will examine issues pertaining to competition, globalization at the country, company and consumer levels and link them to a firm's global competitive strategy.

Competition, global competition and global competitive strategy

Competition is viewed as the heart of our market economies. It is the ingenious connection of consumers' and producers' selfishness that makes competition so precise, fast and dynamic. As a result, all stakeholders of society can benefit. More precisely, a producer's selfish desire to maximize profits typically translates into better products as consumers tend to be willing to pay higher prices for such products.[1]

However, today's competition is getting more intense than ever and often arises from rather unlikely sources. It is not a new idea that the utility a product fulfills should be considered as the origin of competition. And the basically identical utility may arise out of very different products. For example, should the airline industry start to look at potential substitutes for business travelers? In some cases this might be sophisticated video-conferencing technology instead of flying to the next meeting in another city.

Additionally, competition is increasingly viewed as the culprit for seemingly undesirable outcomes of the market and marketing process. Among such outcomes are products that are seemingly too cheap, income distributions in Asia that are too heterogeneous, child labor that contradicts beliefs held in Europe and Northern America, wage-limits in Europe that surprise Americans and make Asians wonder, etc. In short, global competition is facing fundamental challenges – and opportunities – resulting in a need to update global strategies.

At the same time global competition is heating up as more and more companies and countries enter the world's markets. While entry by companies is considered 'normal', such entry by countries is somewhat new. For example, China and Russia enter markets largely as 'countries', while their governments are holding the respective companies more or less closely.

At this time of changing competition, perception and attitudes toward global markets and global competition are changing rapidly. Many citizens in Western countries, for example, call for ever more domestic protection, while at the same time they generally enjoy the cheap products made elsewhere, e.g., in Asia. This is especially noteworthy as many European countries are doing very well on the scale of competitive competence and in many studies are seen as the temporary winners of globalization. Notably also, the debate on environmental issues is likely to have much of an effect on global competition and ensuing global strategies. The debate about global warming and global climate issues implies that there is a global responsibility for that one, huge world.

More and more citizens perceive the world as one entity and, thus, one market. As a result, European and American citizens and consumers expect that all countries (especially BRIC, i.e., Brazil, Russia, India and China) respect the globe as a whole and that they are willing to sacrifice 'now' so that things do not worsen 'later'. This is likely to cause tension for various reasons. For example, BRICs request the same rights to develop – and, if necessary, to pollute – as others have done, e.g., Liverpool in England during the industrial revolution. Obviously, major challenges for global competition and global strategies result.

Even though competition develops on a global level, it has also become more and more country-specific. Many European firms seem to run out of competitive advantages that rest in their product's core. Thus, Europeans may be forced to shift competition to new dimensions, for example, heritage. Chinese firms are often perceived as mainly possessing a cost advantage. India may come out ahead due to her ability to include a heritage dimension due to her European 'upbringing', yet being 'hungry'.

One might ask if this leaves US companies a bit 'stuck in the middle'?

By global competitive strategy we mean a consistent and overarching set of objectives, goals and rules that determine a company's decisions and actions around the globe. This implies the necessity to pay close attention to the development of markets on a global scale, anticipating transformation and identifying new competitive advantages. Accordingly, such a strategy determines a company's specification of the marketing mix around the globe. The global competitive strategy will determine how to act, how to react, how to provoke, how to appease, how and when to introduce new products, withdraw old ones, enter or exit markets, etc.

Often, global competitive strategies result from a multi-stage process (e.g., Yip 1992, 1998). Such a process may entail the identification of a company's core competitive advantages and the evaluation of the global potential of the company's competitive advantage. In particular, a global competitive strategy will specify a company's competitive conduct such as its reaction behavior. For example, Porsche maintains a global competitive strategy of not reacting in firm price-cutting, independent of rivals' price-cutting, even if it hurts sales, revenues and profits. The recent persistence during a time when, for example, BMW and Audi cut prices massively attests to this feature of Porsche's global competitive strategy.

NEW DETERMINANTS OF GLOBAL COMPETITION AND GLOBAL STRATEGY

In this section we describe and discuss several new or emerging determinants that are most likely to change the conduct of global competition and the development of global strategy. These determinants include the Internet; new dimensions governing competitive positioning such as humor or heritage; global competitive intelligence; anti-globalization activists and product piracy.

The Internet as a catalyst for global competiton

The worldwide diffusion of the Internet, and associated with it the ongoing digitalization of certain industries, lead to a fundamentally new model for markets and global market competition. Media and entertainment industries, for example, no longer need to reconsider expected sales or worry about a minimum of marketed items, because virtual shelf space is infinite, variable costs are factually non-existent and access to become markets has become fundamentally easier.

In the so-called physical world, this is the main reason for retailers to carry only a limited selection of goods, leading to market structures as we have known them for decades and centuries. In comparison with the above-described 'Internet' economy, those structures conflict with the total fulfillment of individual preferences as only certain ideal types of products are offered, corresponding with the needs and requirements of certain segments. But everyone's preferences are different and even if somewhat sophisticated segments can often be identified, the individual's taste is bound to diverge from that of the 'mainstream' at some point. This is where the unlimited selection of diversified goods of the virtual marketplace – which carries the potential to almost totally fulfill each single consumer's preferences – drastically changes the market structure. The marketing situation is changing from a world of scarcity to a world of abundance leading to 'The Long Tail'.[2]

Importantly, those market structures allow businesses operating under such conditions to achieve significant revenues, even if they are selling only small numbers of certain items. The accumulation of many of those revenues though, may lead to profits that easily outnumber those of the market leaders. Thus, this structure fundamentally affects the way companies interact in market places that are affected or developed by the Internet. As described, this competitive structure may allow for the heterogeneous preferences of a global set of consumers with ubiquity of those goods wherever internet access is granted. As a result, cost considerations – a key constraint in current competition – may significantly lose importance.

Similarly, the diffusion of the Internet accounts for the emergence of weblogs – short blogs – that as well lead to new forms of competition. Basically blogs are simple websites, which allow editors to post information (including pictures, audio and video files or links to other sites) in a chronological order, the so called blogposts, mostly referred to as posts. In addition to the basic structuring of content in terms of general subjects, the newest posts appear on top of the page. The users then may read and evaluate this information and – if they want – add their opinions in form of comments. From a technological point of view, there is nothing more to it. But obviously it is enough to allow the ascent of 'blogging'. So there seems to be no doubt, that the "most powerful thing about blogging isn't the technology; it's this massive community driving the 'blogosphere'[3] (Wright 2006). Blogs wouldn't be such a powerful channel, if they weren't so easy to set up and operate.

Currently there is about one new blog created every second, which means more than 80 000 each day, containing 900 000 new posts every 24 hours (Perlmutter and McDaniel 2005). Though the majority of them are insignificant or having no relevance to the business, there is a potential that in the depths of the blogosphere there are some widely-read blogs talking about your company or products. Even if they are initially relatively unknown, their content might play a crucial role in the formation of public opinion in a matter of days, or even hours, on the one hand, because other blogs might be referring to them, creating rapidly growing publicity within the blogosphere and, on the other hand, because the traditional media might be picking up certain stories and then spreading them through the traditional channels.

A good example of such a development is Kryptonite, a company that produces premium priced bicycle locks. In 2004 a San Francisco cyclist found out that it is possible to hack the Kryptonite Evolution U-Lock that offers 'toughest bicycle protection in moderate to high crime areas' with just a simple ballpoint pen. He wrote a post on BikeForums.net containing videos proving this trick. Shortly afterwards, the story was being spread through different blogs (e.g., engadget.com, metafilter.com) and comments and videos from other users followed, verifying the story. But Kryptonite made no response. From the time of the first post, it took only five days until the story that 'infuriates bicyclists' made it into the *New York Times* and the *Boston Globe*, reporting that about 300 000 had read just two of the most popular posts, 'starting a full-fledged panic' (Polgreen 2004). This happened even though editors of different blogs contacted Kryptonite on this subject and never received a response.

In the end, Kryptonite not only had to bear the lock-exchange program costs of US$10 Million, but they also lost an estimated US$6 Million in sales and made it to the top of the Business 2.0's 2004 list of the '101 Dumbest Moments in Business' (Horowitz *et al.* 2005). Those numbers only suggest the damage Kryptonite's reputation and brand equity took. The key learning point of this story refers to the power and unpredictability of Internet-based consumer-generated content, of which blogs may be the most important representation. Out of the sheer numberless voices of consumers throughout the net and around the globe, only a small number achieve a high level of awareness, which may under certain circumstances – as the case of Kryptonite indicates – almost destroy a company. The challenge for researchers in the future is to analyze the underlying effects and processes and explain why certain content experiences a rapid and widespread diffusion and the resulting impact that it has.

Thus, the most important implication for managers is that this new consumer power must never be dismissed. One disappointed consumer, one spurious statement concerning important issues or just the disregard of consumers' grumbling on the Internet may, under certain circumstances, lead to severe consequences for a business. This basically goes along with a general trend about changing consumer structures. Altogether, consumers are getting more demanding and – not least because of the above-described evolution of communication – more powerful. Another consumer-based facet pertains to demographics in global markets, as for example 2.4 billion of the world's 6 billion inhabitants live in Asia. That this is going to change significantly in the decades to come is shown by the following relation: India's population under the age of 35 is almost equivalent to the combined population of the USA and Europe.

Naturally, global competition is likely to develop two foci: the first will have to emphasize older and aging consumers in Europe and Northern America. The second focus will need to concentrate on much younger consumers in India, China, Singapore, Vietnam or Indonesia. Obviously, covering these two different age groups will pose a formidable challenge to competing products. This adds a new competitive dimension unique to global competition and the winners will be those firms that find ways to master this stretch.

Naturally, businesses that establish an appropriate and sophisticated understanding and handling of the issues discussed above should obtain significant and sustainable competitive advantages in the future.

Humor, design and heritage as new dimensions of competitive conduct

In many markets, even though they provide most dynamic facets, products and markets have matured. As a result, competitive foci seemingly move to augmentations including design, heritage, and even humor. Interestingly, competing for and winning on the humor side has proven very successful for the German electronics retailer Media Markt. That company is neither the cheapest nor the one with the best stores or locations. However, it is viewed as the 'funniest' and consumers arrive in hordes. Thus, 'soft issues' such as humor may amount to an important source for competitive advantages in the future – a stark contrast to advantages like low costs or high quality described later in more detail.

Similarly, marketing competition has seemingly evolved from the old product life cycle (PLC) to a new structure. Previously, the focus rested on the traditional 4Ps and the associated aspects of price elasticity, competitive entry, exit, etc. Recently, however, a new sequence appears frequently. In this sequence quality and price competition are followed by competitive foci such as design, heritage and even previously unheard of dimensions such as humor, as described above. Examples for such trends include notebooks and mobile phones for design and Maserati or Louis Vuitton for heritage.

Global competitor intelligence

Modern businesses face the huge substantial challenge to successfully compete in increasingly globalized markets, which often change along various dimensions and at different speeds. Mainly, today's environments are changing so rapidly that it is almost imperative to be no longer reactive, but to be at least proactive, or even to anticipate competitors' actions as well as global trends. Competing around the globe, thus, requires constant monitoring of the most important markets. In addition to keeping up with ever-changing consumer demands, companies need to understand their competitors' ever-changing activities. Looking at it from a warlike position, competitors are enemies fighting over market shares, limited resources, customer satisfaction and retention and do so around the globe.

Therefore, it is necessary to precisely analyze and anticipate what their competitors' new capabilities, foci and strategies are, how these rivals are planning to realize them, where their strengths and weaknesses are developing toward and where attacks are most likely to be carried out by the opponents. To meet these challenges, a systematic global competitive intelligence (GCI) is needed. By GCI we mean the worldwide gathering of information about competitors and their relevant environments and applying this information in the firm's own strategy development, aiming for the improvement of competitive advantages around the globe and 24/7. The process includes the collection and combination of different information units and their interrelation into future developments and trends. Notably, this does not mean that GCI uses illegal or immoral practices. Instead it collects publicly available information that may have its origin in such diverse sources as business reports, research data, interviews, patent applications, job offers and so on. In short, competitive intelligence is not about generating data, it is about observing and interpreting signals that are found throughout the marketplace but mostly not very distinct. Concerning the actual focus or outcome of competitive intelligence actions, the manager faces a variety of options. Primarily – as competitor intelligence is mostly understood and applied – the present and future activities of the competitor are to be monitored and anticipated. But, besides that, other sectors or entities may serve as units of analysis.

Let us illustrate all this using the Coors Brewery, situated in the Rocky Mountains. When Anheuser Bush, a competitor several times Coors' size, announced plans to enter Coors' traditional market, management faced a daunting task. If the Goliath indeed entered exploiting its large scale, price pressure and even price wars needed to be anticipated. A good weapon to fight such wars could be to cut prices immediately and significantly, signaling Anheuser's willingness to fight and making the entry less attractive or even unattractive. If however, Anheuser's entry would probably end up being a small one, such 'warlike' acting would be undesirable, as it would hurt margins, consumer equity and profits for a long time to come. What to do?

Competitor intelligence was sufficiently in place to provide an answer. Publicly available documents from the utilities suggested that Anheuser had applied for a small provision of water only. As a result, Coors' management concluded that the entry would be rather small-scale. In short, simple, albeit creative, competitor intelligence allowed Coors to maintain margins and profits.

It is at such an instance that globalization comes into the equation, because, increasingly, globalized markets are all about dynamics. So, forecasting the evolving structures of markets may itself develop to become a strong competitive advantage. This is because those companies that achieve this may today plan the products that the world wants tomorrow.

While the importance and benefits of global competitor intelligence, it is surprising that only a small percentage of companies conduct GCI in a systematic way. While many companies collect some kind of information about the rivals, very few go all the way. By that we mean that a company that conducts GCI needs to:

- continuously collect competitor information along pre-specified dimensions;
- systematically track that information (and add new dimensions if necessary);
- analyze the information obtained;
- make the results available to the departments involved or impacted around the globe;
- explicity ask for feedback and conduct cross-references;
- condense the results in managerially meaningful and actionable terms, and
- act on it!

It is seemingly hard to believe but fewer than 10 per cent of the companies operating globally have institutionalized even part of the sequence or list above. Most companies argue though that they conduct some CI but rarely do they exploit this instrument to their potential. As a result, they render themselves more vulnerable to other global competitors that do go 'all the way'. Additionally, as indicated above, competition may evolve from previously non-relevant countries. For example, the origin for the satisfaction of consumers' needs may suddenly be fulfilled better or more cheaply in some other country. Similarly, anticipating global economic, political, sociological and technological environmental conditions may develop to be a most crucial skill for global players.

However, it is important to note that taking competitive intelligence to a global level is not just about taking it to another aggregation level. Global competitive intelligence is doubtless of multiple complexity compared with CI at country level. But surely there is no option of choosing. Globally operating businesses in the twenty-first century must engage in GCI if they want to avoid sudden surprises of totally new market and environmental conditions.

Another aspect pertains to growth in globalized markets. As many companies can no longer afford to grow organically and slowly, they need to do so through mergers and acquisitions. Especially for larger enterprises, chances are reasonable to find interesting shopping opportunities while monitoring the competitive environments. In particular, this seems to hold potential for new market entries, as businesses aiming to do so are generally well advised to take a very close look at the relevant markets. Naturally, this includes a precise investigation of enterprises operating in the field of business. Further, potential competitors that are in possession of one or more competitive advantages may as well become strong partners or even divisions if the 'war chest' allows for it.

In short, CI deals with the focused and coordinated monitoring of the competitors in a specific marketplace – who they are, where and how they (co)operate to gain competitive advantage and what their next steps will be.

Knowing the right answer for those questions brings every business a significant and sometimes even vital gain. For global markets this still holds true except for one distinction: global marketplaces are no longer specific, as they undergo most dynamic developments on different dimensions and a totally different scale. Obviously, this takes the challenge of CI to a dramatically new level. On the one hand competitive threats may arise from all sorts of countries, businesses and developments. At the same time the diversity of the global marketplace is overcrowded with a multitude of different signals that need to be interpreted and converted into strategy adjustments.

Criticism of globalization and global competition

While most citizens around the globe support globalization, a minority of about 13 per cent opposes this development. The positions, which more or less reject globalization and want to reduce the global interdependence, tend to correlate with rather extreme views on other issues. Research suggests that opponents of globalization tend to be rather leftist, right-wing or environmentalists or supporters of the idea of a global crisis.

Sometimes this takes obscure forms, significantly depreciating the deeper meaning of anti-globalization attitudes and representing only vandalism and terrorism. For example, a group of so-called environmentalists or persons engaging in saving the globe recently set several villas in Seattle ablaze to protest against the housing of the well-heeled. The Earth Liberation Front is known for using 'economic sabotage and guerrilla warfare to stop the exploitation and destruction of the natural environment', according to a press announcement. Their common targets are luxury cars, housing and other objects representing the consumption culture. A couple of years ago, the group was categorized as a serious terrorist threat by the FBI. Interestingly, the damages of the recent raid amounted to about US$ 10 million for those who had purchased the luxury housing. However, damage to the environment, arising from the huge fires and the actions taken to extinguish them, are estimated to have exceeded the aforementioned dimensions by far.

In general, many benefits around the world in terms of increased income, jobs *per se*, increased freedom and better lives in general are discounted. It also has been argued that the critique of various anti-globalization groups such as the Peoples' Global Action (PGA), WEED, World Social Forum (WSF), BUKO, ATTAC, focuses more on forms of capitalism and the free market economy itself. Overall, one can attest that, while many of the points raised have some merit, the anti-globalization groups weigh the benefits provided by globalization much lower than they do the associated costs. Additionally, and maybe more importantly, the critics fail to outline clear-cut alternatives as the market system is the best system we have to coordinate economic activities among rather free players – albeit imperfectly. However, it also needs to be stated that some of the criticism could actually enhance global competition. Some of the long list of demands posed may serve to illustrate the aforementioned and include the following:

- The financial system should be subjected to much tougher and stricter regulation. This includes more supervision of the stock market and the banking sector, even with much higher taxes on financial transactions.
- Developing countries should gain free access to the protected agricultural markets of developed countries. This demand should certainly enhance global competition as prices for many fruits and vegetables in the States and Europe are a multiple of what they should or need to be.
- The introduction of social, environmental and democratic standards in international trade agreements appears to be a two-sided sword for global competition. Continuation of the Kyoto process for the world's climate protection, even though being desirable in terms of environmental outcome, is again likely to end up much more complicated than it seems at first glance. As discussed earlier in this chapter, industrialization goes hand-in-hand with negative externalities such as pollution – although current technologies allow industrialization at much smaller rates of pollution than in previous centuries.

As a result, European and United States globalization critics need to decide to which degree the industrialized world can afford and should be 'allowed' to refuse and reject quests for economic development by less developed countries. If Europe and the USA want a global conciseness with emancipated partners and perspectives, this must generally include others' rights to develop their countries as they want. However, this also includes pollution when circumstances make it necessary and the export of low-priced goods to the USA and Europe.

Product piracy

One of the more serious threats for business operating in global markets pertains to product piracy. The returns to the counterfeiter's investments are extremely high and, in fact, high enough that some even call product piracy 'the crime of the twenty-first century'. In a sense, the phenomenon can only be discussed on the surface as no consistent definition of such practices exists. However, the relatively broad range of activities that are subsumed under product piracy do have one aspect in common; the violation of trade mark rights resulting in financial damages estimated to be worth billions of dollars. Obviously, this will affect a company's conduct in the market place, its interaction with competitors and its willingness to invest into protection against certain actual and potential competitors.

Generally, product piracy refers to the intentional copying of the name, shape, content or appearance of another product with the goal of obtaining product sales that would have gone to the original item otherwise. One automatically thinks of the millions of luxury watch copies produced in Asia and sold via different channels all over the world. This does not imply that every case of product piracy implies a '100% copy'[4] of the original product carrying the same – copied – brand. So-called 'near brands' are very similar in appearance to the original but show slight differences in their brands or logos. Instead of 'Colgate' the consumer in confronted with 'Coldgate' toothpaste, 'Cola Coca' rather than 'Coca Cola' and 'Channel' rather than 'Chanel' (Jacobs *et al.* 2001).

One form of piracy that is omnipresent pertains to digital product piracy. As discussed in the Internet section of this chapter, the digital industry exhibits market laws that are rather new. One such law entails that this industry is characterized through variable costs being close to zero, while the so-called 'first copy costs' (the cost to develop the content allowing for the production of the 'first copy') often amount to many millions of US dollars.

Concerning the variable cost this is also true for the plagiarism encountered in this sector, as copies of software, music or films require not much more than just a click and one blank CD – making the marginal costs truly close to zero. The big difference here is that the counterfeiters also have no fixed or developing costs (besides insignificant costs for appropriate hardware). Because of this principle product piracy in the digital industry is highly profitable und widely spread. The rate for products that are copies amounts to more than 95 per cent in some Asian countries, including China and Thailand. For completeness, we ignore the potential benefits arising from the so-called 'shadow diffusion'.

Examples from the car industry show that Chinese manufacturers copy cars mainly in respect to the exterior looks but put their own brand mark on the products. The Sceo build by ShuangHuan is often reported to amount to a copy of the BMW X5 and this is only one example of barefaced copies that can be found all over the Chinese motor shows. Most audaciously, the press information of

ShuangHuan states that the company has invested millions in the research and development for engineering and international design. But even if the copied cars found in China show some superficial commonalities with the original product, one thing is obvious: they do not even closely reach the quality standard of the genuine original product. This may at best be annoying – at worst in can cost your life as the chassis, brakes, impact protection and other highly relevant safety features fail to comply with the safety standards of the original. BMW recently contemplated a law suit that may amount to hundreds of millions of dollars to offset piracy-related damages. Additionally, signals in the form of 'don't do that type of stuff' to companies contemplating similar copycat behavior should make such a law suit even more beneficial.

Another dangerous form of product piracy is related to the pharmaceutical sector. While, for example, European and US markets seem to be sufficiently protected, developing markets often appear to be overcrowded with fake medicaments and prescription drugs. Offerings include antibiotics, birth control pills, or Viagra – virtually every common drug can be found in these markets. Packages look painfully similar. But, if consumers are lucky, the pills are 'only' placebos. What also happens often is that the medicaments contain other, potentially harmful substances.

Other cases that are sometimes labeled as piracy are even less obvious. Different industries face problems with re-imports or gray market goods. These are goods that are legitimately put on the market in one country and then exported by a third party into another country, for which the exporter has no license to market this product. While the exporting business sees this as a rightful action, the producers often refer to it as piracy with the 'illegitimate' distributor benefiting from marketing efforts accomplished and paid for by others.

This means that no matter how the exact definition or specification about product piracy starts and ends, the consequences are severe. Roughly 10 per cent of the world trade volume relates to some sort of plagiarism through product piracy, illegal overproduction and gray market imports. Estimates amount to €200–300 billions international economic damage. 300 000 jobs are approximately lost by product piracy in Europe.

The negative effect of the sales loss that businesses experience through product piracy is in many cases exceeded by the damage the brand, and thus the company's, reputation suffers. Not only are inferior products available on the market, but also individuals of totally different target groups consume those copies. As one can easily imagine, consumers of luxury brands such as Gucci, Prada or Louis Vuitton feel quite annoyed and see their status endangered if there are people appearing with 10$ copies of their 3,000$ bags. Even though those copies may look alike only to the inexperienced observer, plagiarism does affect actual and future brand equity massively.

Accordingly, many actions have been taken by companies and countries to defend their intellectual property against the aggressive product pirates that have their origin mostly in Asian countries. Some of the hosting countries themselves, such as Singapore, have taken certain actions against counterfeiters, while others seem to show no serious interest to fight plagiarism, as, in a sense, China. Maybe this is accounted for by the fact that central parts of the economy build on product piracy. Maybe a non-existent understanding that intellectual property may not be violated is responsible.

However, companies capable of successfully competing around the globe may be too smart to wait for others to act on their behalf. That is, affected companies started to take actions by themselves. Concerning the digital industry, sophisticated mechanisms and techniques have recently been developed that are subsumed under the concept of Digital Rights Management (DRM). Thus, producers may control the use and distribution of music, software or films. With physical products, labeling represents one form of protecting intellectual property. For example holograms are used for products such as software or music CDs and Credit Cards. However, the labeling solution is rather costly and sophisticated counterfeiters are likely to sooner or (hopefully) later also copy the copy protection of honest companies.

Governments also play an important role in the prevention of product piracy as they establish the legal infrastructure to prohibit and pursue such actions, as, for example, with patent protection. However, there is another side to the coin, which should also be closely monitored. Regulations that aim for the protection of domestic producers may also affect markets in an undesirable fashion if they harm and restrict the ingenious competition. Thus, governmental protection from product piracy is always a tightrope walk.

COMPETITIVE ADVANTAGE

One of the most fundamental issues in competitive marketing strategy pertains to competitive advantage and its sustainability – no matter if the focus is on local, national, international or global markets. Generally, to succeed in a market, a business needs to be in possession of at least one of those advantages. A business gains such a competitive advantage when it is able to offer a greater value or utility than the competitors. To understand the nature of competitive advantages it is important to note that their specific origin matter less than the degree of the advantage.

It may be that the competitive advantage results from cost-based production advantages that allow the business to sell the product at a lower price, thus leading to higher margins. On the contrary, such margins may also result from a strong brand that offers prestige to its users. Similarly, leading edge production standards and top materials may amount for the best quality on the market and translate into higher margins.

In short, competitive advantages simply position a business ahead of their competitors, in part due to their correlation higher margins. Thereby, the original base may test cost advantages, brand advantages or quality advantages. The gaining, maintaing and renewing of such competitive advantages in dynamic markets, however, amount most likely to the toughest challenge for each company engaged in market competition over time and will, most likely force companies to pay special attention to the new attributes of global competition.

Competitive advantages of countries and regions

Countries and regions possess certain advantages that play a vital role in the 'game' of global competitiveness. For example, it is generally accepted that China offers a much lower cost structure than any Western country. Combined with the ability to copy successful ideas and products, China gains massive competitive advantages when it comes to labor-intensive production. Thus, most companies assessing China regard the cost aspect as the biggest competitive advantage of businesses operating in China, as a recent survey found out (Fig. 13.1). An overwhelming 69 per cent of the respondents stated that lower cost structures and, thus, lower prices, is the basis of Chinese firms' competitive advantages. A remarkable 15 per cent

judged that no stringent patent and copyright regulations account for competitive advantages of Chinese competitors – as copying ideas and products can hardly be prevented.

However, the following example shows that the issues in the arena of global competition and competitive advantage are most often not easy to judge. The German company Heidelberger Druckmaschinen produces complex, high-end printing machines, which are used for professional offprint purposes. With a market-share of 40 per cent, they are the world market leader. One single machine consists of up to 100 000 parts and production is highly labor-intensive with bounded potential for automation. At first glance, this supports the idea of shifting production to low-wage countries. Like many producing businesses from Germany and other Western countries, Heidelberger Druckmaschinen went to China to produce low-cost printing machines. However, the company from old Europe shifted only their production of entry-level machines. This is for two vastly important reasons:

1. Inadequate protection of intellectual property interdicts the shifting of cutting edge technology – as many market entrants have painfully experienced (see also Figure 13.1);
2. Maybe even more importantly, poorly educated employees don't allow the same quality level as can be achieved in Germany with expensive but highly qualified engineers. The numbers shown in Figure 13.2 underline this second aspect.

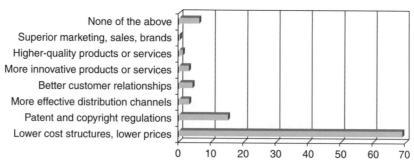

Figure 13.1 Basis of competition faced from companies based in China
Source: Mckinsey (2007): Quarterly survey of executives in Asia
Note: % of respondents (n = 197)

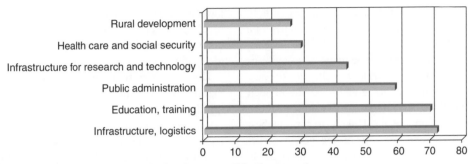

Figure 13.2   Investments needed to increase China's attractiveness
Source: January 2007 McKinsey quarterly survey of executives in Asia

More than two-thirds of the polled executives stated that education and training in China needs further investment in order to increase the country's attractiveness. In many industries this seems to be one of China's biggest competitive disadvantage, leading to two direct implications for businesses operating in other countries. On the one hand the 'old' economies may have strong competitive advantages concerning the availability of highly qualified employees – as the case of Heidelberger Druckmaschinen shows. On the other hand this brings business opportunities concerning education and training in the huge Chinese market. For example, China has shown distinct interest in establishing the highly sophisticated German system of vocational training, a combination of theoretical and practical non-academic education, qualifying in two to three years for a specific vocation/profession. Obviously, this discussion also shows that one of the most promising avenues for countries such as France, Germany or the United States appears to be building a most attractive, competent, versatile and not too expansive work force. Notably, Switzerland seems to have already mastered this challenge to a certain degree, as we will see also in this chapter.

This example of Heidelberger Druckmaschinen has interesting and important implications for strategic marketing and global competitiveness. At first glance, the case sounds just like the normal story of production shifting to low-cost countries as

happens every day. But additionally, there is one important implication this story has with a high relevance for strategic marketing. Its entry into the budget printing machines market in China has meant that Heidelberger Druckmaschinen actually develops a demand for high-end machines in China that are produced in Germany. That is due to the fact that Chinese customers buy and use the entry-level machines with all their advantages, one being the low price. At the same time, the experience of the German market leader ensures a high quality, which significantly boosts the likelihood of re-purchasing Heidelberger Druckmaschinen when the Chinese client expands and develops the need for more sophisticated machines – made in Germany. In 2007 alone the company invested another €40 million in production facilities in Germany to answer this demand. In short, this illustration shows that caution needs to be applied when judging seemingly straightforward situations concerning the sometimes 'obvious' advantages or disadvantages of regions and countries.

Next, we discuss several important issues based on the competitiveness of certain countries, as described in the Global Competitive Report 2007/08 published by the World Economic Forum. For completeness we refer to the comprehensive report as depicted in Table 13.1. In total, the report's ranking fits the perceptions and expectations that many people have about a large number of countries. For example, it is not surprising that the

Table 13.1 Global competitive index

Country/ Economy	GCI 2007–2008 Rank	GCI 2007–2008 Score	GCI 2007–2008 rank (among countries)*	GCI 2006–2007 rank	Country/ Economy	GCI 2007–2008 Rank	GCI 2007–2008 Score	GCI 2007–2008 rank (among countries)*	GCI 2006–2007 rank
United States	1	5.67	1	1	Mexico	52	4.26	49	52
Switzerland	2	5.62	2	4	Turkey	53	4.25	50	58
Denmark	3	5.55	3	3	Indonesia	54	4.24	51	54
Sweden	4	5.54	4	9	Cyprus	55	4.23	52	49
Germany	5	5.51	5	7	Malta	56	4.21	53	51
Finland	6	5.49	6	6	Croatia	57	4.20	54	56
Singapore	7	5.45	7	8	Russia	58	4.19	55	59
Japan	8	5.43	8	5	Panama	59	4.18	56	60
United Kingdom	9	5.41	9	2	Mauritius	60	4.16	57	55
Netherlands	10	5.40	10	11	Kazakhstan	61	4.14	58	50
Korea	11	5.40	11	23	Uzbekistan	62	4.13	n/a	n/a
Hong Kong SAR	12	5.37	12	10	Costa Rica	63	4.11	59	68
Canada	13	5.34	13	12	Morocco	64	4.08	60	65
Taiwan, China	14	5.25	14	13	Greece	65	4.08	61	61
Austria	15	5.23	15	18	Azerbaijan	66	4.07	62	62
Norway	16	5.20	16	17	El Salvador	67	4.05	63	53
Israel	17	5.20	17	14	Vietnam	68	4.04	64	64
France	18	5.18	18	15	Colombia	69	4.04	65	63
Australia	19	5.17	19	16	Sri Lanka	70	3.99	66	81
Belgium	20	5.10	20	24	Philippines	71	3.99	67	75
Malaysia	21	5.10	21	19	Brazil	72	3.99	68	66
Ireland	22	5.03	22	22	Ukraine	73	3.98	69	69
Iceland	23	5.02	23	20	Romania	74	3.97	70	73
New Zealand	24	4.98	24	21	Uruguay	75	3.97	71	79
Luxembourg	25	4.88	25	25	Botswana	76	3.96	72	57
Chile	26	4.77	26	27	Egypt	77	3.96	73	71
Estonia	27	4.74	27	26	Jamaica	78	3.95	74	67
Thailand	28	4.70	28	28	Bulgaria	79	3.93	75	74
Spain	29	4.66	29	29	Syria	80	3.91	n/a	n/a
Kuwait	30	4.66	30	30	Algeria	81	3.91	76	77
Qatar	31	4.63	31	32	Montenegro	82	3.91	n/a	n/a
Tunisia	32	4.59	32	33	Honduras	83	3.89	77	90
Czech Republic	33	4.58	33	31	Trinidad and Tobago	84	3.88	78	76
China	34	4.57	34	35					
Saudi Arabia	35	4.55	n/a	n/a	Argentina	85	3.87	79	70
Puerto Rico	36	4.50	n/a	n/a	Peru	86	3.87	80	78
United Arab Emirates	37	4.50	35	34	Guatemala	87	3.86	81	91
					Libya	88	3.85	n/a	n/a
Lithuania	38	4.49	36	39	Namibia	89	3.85	82	72
Slovenia	39	4.48	37	40	Georgia	90	3.83	83	87
Portugal	40	4.48	38	43	Serbia	91	3.78	n/a	n/a
Slovak Republic	41	4.45	39		Pakistan	92	3.77	84	83
Oman	42	4.43	n/a	n/a	Armenia	93	3.76	85	80
Bahrain	43	4.42	40	48	Macedonia, FYR	94	3.73	86	84
South Africa	44	4.42	41	36	Nigeria	95	3.69	87	95
Latvia	45	4.41	42	44	Dominican Republic	96	3.65	88	93
Italy	46	4.36	43	47	Moldova	97	3.64	89	86
Hungary	47	4.35	44	38	Venezuela	98	3.63	90	85
India	48	4.33	45	42	Kenya	99	3.61	91	88
Jordan	49	4.32	46	46	Senegal	100	3.61	n/a	n/a
Barbados	50	4.32	47	41	Mongolia	101	3.60	92	89
Poland	51	4.28	48	45	Gambia, The	102	3.59	93	103

continued

Table 13.1   Cont'd

Country/ Economy	GCI 2007–2008 Rank	GCI 2007–2008 Score	GCI 2007–2008 rank (among countries)*	GCI 2006–2007 rank	Country/ Economy	GCI 2007–2008 Rank	GCI 2007–2008 Score	GCI 2007–2008 rank (among countries)*	GCI 2006–2007 rank
Ecuador	103	3.57	94	94	Tajikistan	117	3.37	108	96
Tanzania	104	3.56	95	97	Madagascar	118	3.36	109	111
Bolivia	105	3.55	96	100	Kyrgyz Republic	119	3.34	110	109
Bosnia and Herzegovina	106	3.55	97	82	Uganda	120	3.33	111	110
					Paraguay	121	3.30	112	108
Bangladesh	107	3.55	98	92	Zambia	122	3.29	113	118
Benin	108	3.49	99	107	Ethiopia	123	3.28	114	116
Albania	109	3.48	100	98	Lesotho	124	3.27	115	102
Cambodia	110	3.48	101	106	Mauritania	125	3.26	116	117
Nicaragua	111	3.45	102	101	Guyana	126	3.25	117	113
Burkina Faso	112	3.43	103	114	Timor-Leste	127	3.20	118	120
Suriname	113	3.40	104	104	Mozambique	128	3.02	119	119
Nepal	114	3.38	105	105	Zimbabwe	129	2.88	120	112
Mali	115	3.37	106	115	Burundi	130	2.84	121	122
Cameroon	116	3.37	107	99	Chad	131	2.78	122	121

*Two countries that were covered in last year's *Report* but are not included in the present *Report* for lack of survey data are excluded from the comparison [Angola and Malawi]. Serbia and Montenegro, treated as one country last year, are now treated as two individual countries. We therefore do not show data for Serbia and Montenegro for last year.

Source: Global Competitive Report 2007/08, World Economic Forum.

United States occupies a top spot and, in fact, leads the list of the most competitive economies. This is due to a combination of innovative business excellence, a university system that belongs to the best in the world, featuring a close connection to the business sector. Also, the US citizens possess a general openness that facilitates the diffusion of new products as well as the movement of labor to locations where it is needed most. Other items on a list of bases for the competitiveness of the United States should include that about two thirds of the world's most valuable brands are US ones.

For Switzerland, ranked second, several comparable factors seem to exist, but there are also factors that should be considered a surprise. Again, the business culture, an excellent education system with high spendings in R&D and their conjunction are worth mentioning. However, Switzerland is a classic high-wage country, which may contradict global competitiveness at first sight. The explanation rests in the quality of Swiss products, for which reason Swiss businesses may charge the highest prices for their products and consumers around the globe will

pay for it. An illustrative example is the gallon of Swiss milk shipped to Hong Kong via airfreight and sold for a price of around US$20. Concerning the wage level, it is interesting to note that the next four places in the list of the most competitive economies are again taken by European countries (Denmark, Sweden, Germany, Finland), which are also known for their rather high wage-levels in connection with expensive, highly-developed social systems. In short, it is of utmost importance to note that high-quality strategies seem to exist for those countries that face high wages for the years to come.

China ranks 34th, with its huge markets allowing businesses to benefit from significant economies of scale. For example, every two weeks a new coal-fired power station is built in China, being on the one hand responsible for the fact that this industry has developed to be the most environmentally harming in the world, even worse than the American car industry, as some have said. On the other hand, it opens up huge markets for sophisticated environmental technologies, enabling higher efficiency and fewer

CO_2-emissions. Weaknesses of the Chinese economy are the standards and structures of the financial system, the higher education system and public and private institutions. However, China has repeatedly proved that it can change fundamentally and do so at a high speed. As a result, no manager, company or country should rest comfortably on the expectation that these weaknesses may prevail.

Other countries benefiting from their large market size are India (48th) and Russia (58th). While India is developing strongly from a third world country towards an economy with much innovative potential, Russia struggles with its institutional environment and somewhat unpredictable business standards. There seems to be a large degree of reminiscence of communism or a lack of market orientation that hinders and limits the eruption and evolution of value-creating competition.

It is estimates of the world's largest economies in the year 2050 that unveil the most dramatic changes. These changes will, most likely, lead to a fundamental repositioning of economic power and, thus, competitive advantages, as shown in Figure 13.3. Asian economies seem to be on an unstoppable rise, with the former leading economies being overtaken by rearguard actions. The numbers indicate that China's economy is estimated to be several times the size of all of the European economies combined. China may, at that point in time, account for one-third of the volume of the top ten economies – besides replacing the continent-like economy of the United States as the world's number one. Notably, the three Asian economies China, India and Japan are expected to account for 57 per cent of the Top Ten global economies.

The ongoing ascent of Asia as an economic powerhouse and even worldcenter is also evidenced by a look at the level of currency reserves (see Figure 13.4). The top four spots are occupied by Asian nations. Notably, none of the European countries makes the top five and Europe as a whole accounts for only about 10 per cent of China's and Japan's reserves. Importantly, the world's most powerful country, the United States of America, possesses very little financial reserves and is listed only as 21st and even trails behind countries such as Poland. Along with this realignment of economic structures, a massive growth of energy demand is anticipated. This shift clearly entails that the Western countries differ even more from newly developing countries, where in the future more and more energy-intensive production will occur. The anticipation of Asia's future energy consumption, combined with low production costs, also means that different types of competitive advantages and different types of competitive conduct are likely to be observed.

It has been argued that economic activity occurs at three levels: consumption, production

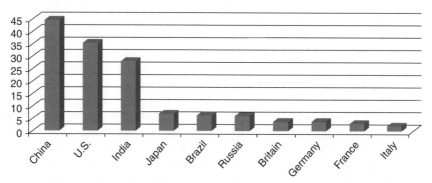

Figure 13.3   Estimates of the world's largest economies by 2050 (trillions of US$)
Source: Goldman Sachs (2003).

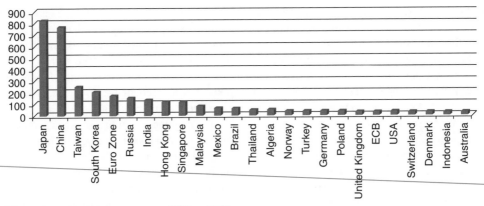

Figure 13.4   Monetary reserves (billion US$)
Source: Bloomberg 2005

and innovation. This framework suggests that during the decades to come, the economic focus of the Western countries may differ more and more from the focus of developing countries. More precisely, the framework suggests that Western countries may focus more on innovation while other countries optimize production. Obviously, this is not exactly what, for example, the emerging focus of Chinese economic policies entails – as Chinese leaders want their country to participate more and more in industries characterized by innovation. However, as the recent case of Brilliance cars indicates, this aspiration may entail a truly long march. Brilliance, one of the Chinese cars that exhibits a surprisingly similar look to cars made by other manufacturers – called a coincidence – was able to reproduce some of the surface characteristics that Western firms offer. Once tested for less obvious variables, such as stability of brakes, crash-safety or reliability, the product was shown to be still significantly behind compared with what innovative European firms such as Renault, BMW or Fiat are able to offer at this point in time.

For long-term international marketing strategy, these and other developments indicate the status quo: these are major threats from developing countries and their companies but numerous segments and

niches are unlikely to be served – some even for many years – by the new players in the game of global competition.

Global regulation for labor and products as a constraint for a global competitive strategy

Countries differ greatly as to the degree in which they pass legislation to protect their employees and regulate their markets. Figure 13.5 depicts this wide range of legislation and market regulation for a large number of countries. Naturally, a firm's global competitive strategy needs to account for such issues. If the resource labor cannot move around freely or is not allowed to move around with a degree of freedom, certain production processes may not be feasible. For example, night shifts are a necessity to produce steel and glass, since steel production and glass production require equipment to maintain extremely high temperatures 24/7 and around the year.

Similarly, if product markets are regulated in a certain country, a company's competitive advantage, albeit existent, may not be allowed to come to fruition. For example, Germany has several regulations preventing prices from being set freely, suggesting that an entrant with superior pricing competence

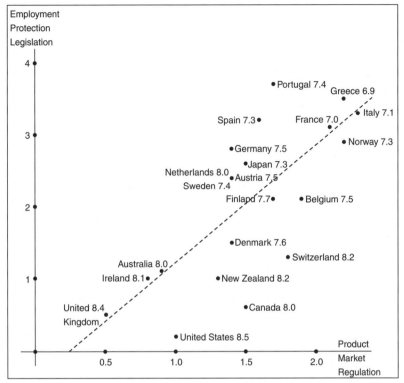

Figure 13.5.   Employment Protection and Product Market Regulation
Source: Martin (2004)

may find this market less attractive. Similarly, restricted opening hours in some parts of Europe will nullify a company's advantage in terms of being able to provide special services during late hours, such as hot soups and hot sandwiches during winter and refrigerated drinks and cold cuts in summer. The same holds true for firms that can organize deliveries around the clock or repairs and maintenance at weekends.

Figure 13.5 depicts most Western countries in terms of regulations preventing labor from moving freely and products from satisfying consumers' needs as much as possible. The large cluster of continental European countries such as Italy, France and Germany in the upper right corner may, to a degree, be viewed as alarming. It appears painfully obvious that such regulation is very likely to amount to a competitive disadvantage for certain countries and their firms.

Global competitive advantage of firms

The classical perspective in marketing strategy is to look at competitive advantage at the firm level. Below we are discussing selected aspects relating to those competitive advantages such as advantages based on cost, cooperation, branding, competitive intelligence.

Cost-based competitive advantage When discussing globalization, cost-based production advantages are among the first aspects that are usually mentioned. The case of Heidelberger Druckmaschinen outlined above seems to amount to a rather atypical story of globalization and global competitive conduct. Generally, there is a fundamental trend towards shifting labor-intensive production or production steps to low-wage countries. If highly qualified workers are not mandatory, this step seems only rational from an entrepreneurial perspective. However, such a strong focus on cost-based competitive advantages has led to one of the most troublesome faces of global competition – child labor. Even though it has been declared highly illegal, the practice of child labor persists, often being surrounded by a wall of silence and deception. In this section, we will discuss competitive cost advantages that are based on the exploitation of labor provided by children and illegal immigrants. Unfortunately, the conclusion that we arrive at entails that global competition is unlikely to stop such practices as long as consumers fail to stop buying the resulting products that entail rather high quality at very low prices.

An estimated 218 million children aged 5–17 years are engaged in child labor, excluding child domestic labor. About 126 million of these children are believed to be working in hazardous situations or conditions, such as mines, working with chemicals and pesticides or dangerous machinery. Millions of girls who work as domestic servants are especially vulnerable to exploitation and abuse. An estimated 1.2 million children are trafficked, forced into different forms of slavery (5.7 million), into prostitution and pornography (1.8 million), into participating in armed conflict (0.3 million) or other illicit activities (0.6 million). However, the vast majority (some 70 per cent) of child labor occurs in agriculture.[5]

Figure 13.6 indicates the percentage of children who have to work in different parts of the world, revealing that this amounts to a widespread phenomenon. Even if the Asian rate of children who work amounts to 'only' 16 per cent (compared with above 25 per cent in Sub-Saharan Africa), half of all child workers are found in Asia. But no matter where it happens, or to what extent, there is no doubt that child labor *per se* is unacceptable, leading to sub-optimal results – no matter if judged from a normative or a more pragmatic 'economic' perspective. Normatively, a good education and a work-free childhood are obligatory, leaving no room for further discussion. On the other hand, for more pragmatic reasons, child labor is also depreciative as it accounts for a lower wage-level in general, firing up a spiral of growing poverty. Additionally, child workers miss education, which again has a significant impact on their future careers and incomes, in turn negativley influencing the economy in total. Undoubtedly, child labor amounts to the most offensive facet of global competition. Under these circumstances child labor grabs the attention of the Western world quite easily. Activists use drastic stories and pictures of little girls and boys working in extremely hazardous conditions, earning next to nothing in wages. Frequent press coverage with high degrees of public attention has focused on this topic. Accordingly, consumers all around the globe condemn this

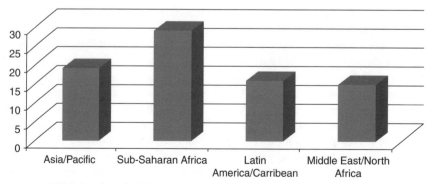

Figure 13.6   Child labor (% of children under 15 that work)
Source: UNICEF www.unicef.org/protection

abject facet of capitalism. Thus, the discussion of child labor is almost always charged with much emotional content.

Concerning the roots of child labor, a frequently occurring and rather ignorant Western explanation for this issue is the myth that parents in third world countries send their children to work because of exploitative and perverse preferences. Widespread poverty and difficult social conditions in those parts of the world tend to be responsible for the existence of child labor to a much higher extent (López-Calva 2001). But, no matter why child labor exists, such business practices should lead consumers to absolutely reject products that appear in any way related to those exploitative companies that allegedly employ children in such production facilities, often called sweatshops. Indeed, consumers around the world seem to be appalled about such conduct when they hear, read or talk about it. However, most remarkably, the vast majority seems to forget the moment they face the cash register. At least that is what market shares and revenues of those companies that have evidently been benefiting from child labor tell us. Naturally, excuses are found and spread by PR departments, why this happened and why the company couldn't have unveiled the reportedly nebulous structures of their contractors. For example, the US clothing retailer GAP has recently – and not for the first time – been accused of operating sweatshops in countries like Cambodia and India where little children had to work up to 16 hours on products carrying GAP labels. After the British Sunday *Observer* newspaper published a report, Indian Officials raided a New Delhi factory of a GAP supplier. According to CNN coverage, some child workers were not allowed to even leave the sweatshops as they were still considered to be 'trainees' and thus paid even less money.

An internal investigation that followed soon afterwards unveiled that the work had been sub-contracted to an 'unauthorized facility' without the firm's knowledge or agreement. The president of GAP North America, Marka Hansen, stated that this incident was 'all the more disappointing' as the company is 'incredibly proud of the real progress we have made over the past decade to improve working conditions in factories that make our products'. As a response GAP announced that they were about to donate US$200 000 to improve factory conditions in India as well as to optimize their own structures. In 2006 the company achieved net sales of 16 billion US$ and net earnings of 778 million US$ – that is about 80, 000 respectively 4,000 times the amount of the donation made.

Interestingly, as the above example indicates, practices of child labor don't seem to be controllable by the major companies that produce in Asia striving for cost advantages. Most remarkably, however, they all seem to manage successfully the highest standards as far as they relate to quality of the products. The answer to this aggravating issue is quite simple: companies fail to totally eliminate child labor because consumers don't care that much about it. To exaggerate a little: global competition may not need to stop exploiting children since consumers around the globe fail to care enough. If one imagines 'less-forgiving' consumers establishing capacious segments that insist on buying only those products that are guaranteed to be child-labor free – and making this their first claim – this market opportunity would quickly be served by '100% child-labor free' offers. Again, the markets are all about supply and demand. That is what those who point their finger at the multinationals that are responsible for child labor and the next day go bargain hunting themselves for the cheapest products made in China need to keep in mind. For completeness, we point to a recent publication using mathematical economics to verify that child labor is likely to be rather persistent. The authors challenge the idea that even under complete information labeling of adult-labor products, child labor will not be drive out even though it may be diminishing it (Davies 2005).

Child labor, however, represents only one form of illegally obtained labor. In December 2007, Italy witnessed a great scandal involving sweatshops using illegally immigrated Chinese workers. Even though working in Europe, these workers have no rights, insurance, or protection while putting in 80+ hours weekly for very low wages. Interestingly, they were producing fashion products for several of Italy's most prestigious and famous designer labels, which were not known for producing under lowest-cost conditions before this discovery.

In short, abusive and exploitative labor practices do not exist only in Asia – as is reported stereotypically. They can be found in the most affluent and 'advanced' countries in Europe and elsewhere in the world. The causes for such practices are also, to a large degree, rooted in countries other than those being accused of hosting child labor. Massive price competition means that many companies produce in those countries where costs are the lowest – often this goes along with work that is illegally obtained or at least morally reprehensible.

Competitive advantage due to cooperation   As described above, cost-based factors play an important role in the process of global competition. However, achieving competitive advantages due to the minimization of production costs is by far not the only avenue to compete successfully in the world's markets. Especially cooperation or collaboration may develop a potential for getting ahead of the competitors.

Just like the heterogeneity of the demand side of global markets, suppliers of one and the same product category appear rather heterogeneous in terms of their competitive advantages. Thus, the road to success lies in finding the best match between the own capabilities, the target markets needs and demands, and – if shortcomings emerge in the further development of markets – the right cooperation partner. For example, Toyota and General Motors established a joint venture in Fremont, California over 20 years ago. This happened during a time when automobile markets were truly shifting, the demand for smaller cars developed along with an intensification of the competitive interplay. New United Motor Manufacturing, Inc. (NUMMI) was established in 1983 to meet this challenge. Through the cooperation both sides benefited. Toyota gained from GM's strong market position in the United States and its production expertise, while GM benefited through the introduction of the teamwork-based working environment and production know-how for compact cars.

Today NUMMI is employing more than 5.000 people and producing close to 400.000 cars and trucks annually. Interestingly, this cooperation was established between two companies that today are the strongest competitors. Toyota announced in December of 2007 that it has replaced GM – which had held the title since 1931 – as the world's largest car manufacturer, producing over 9.5 million vehicles. No matter if in 2008 Toyota or GM is ahead, it surely will be a neck and neck race. The approach to global business both companies showed when NUMMI was established in 1983 is best expressed with the words of the former Chairman, Eiji Toyoda: 'the foundations of the development of the world economy rest on a spirit of "cooperation and competition"' – a statement which still expresses Toyota's way and may even bear more meaning today than over 25 years ago.

The above example from the 1980s represents a very up-to-date paradigm of global competitive marketing strategies in the twenty-first century. Particularly in respect to the management of innovation, the network character has outdated traditional egocentric approaches. The latter are based on the assumption that the development of new ideas can best be achieved in centralized and sealed-off structures. In this new model, the innovation value chain is broken up and certain parts are sourced from partners that operate under lower costs, offer better skills or have access to knowledge that provides differentiation. Please note that it is important that collaboration in this context does not refer to the classical outsourcing approach – a fact that is often misunderstood, as MacCormack *et al.* (2007) point out in their empirical study. The aforementioned development is enforced by four major trends of our times (MacCormack *et al.* 2007):

1 The complexity of products is increasing, mainly because of the number of technologies they include;
2 A decrease of labor costs in developing countries leads to a shifting of labor-intensive production;
3 Certain countries and regions around the globe possess unique skills that allow for a non cost-based differentiation;
4 The capabilities of modern IT allow for a cost-efficient, fast and decentralized way of working, meeting highest standards.

Please note that this concept goes beyond this idea of cheap production and includes the true sharing of knowledge and risk between global partners. Thus, it is important to see the strategic component of collaboration and not to concentrate solely on the aspect of short-term cost reduction. In short, the above-described facets of collaboration seem to develop towards a most vital source of competitive advantage in global business. Nowadays, engaging in sophisticated collaboration efforts seems to be a competitive necessity for many businesses.

Competitive advantage due to global branding
According to research conducted by Steencamp, Batra and Alden (2003), global brands positively affect consumer's willingness to buy a product. Thus, the globalness seems to create additional value in the mind of the consumers, indicating a clear competitive advantage. Mostly, this is due to the fact that products that are global are in general attributed good quality. Additionally, in consumers' perception global brands are mostly accompanied by prestige. However, this facet seems to be of significantly lower importance than perceived quality as well as being

unstable over the product life cycle (prestige is correlated to novelty). Also, prestige is a phenomenon, which seems to affect mainly certain segments, such as young people, but may be less significant for the vast market. It is important to note, however, that global brands are not *per se* of higher quality. Rather, their globalness implies certain traits, such as quality or prestige. Contrary to those perceptions are the beliefs of the ethnocentric globalization critics who basically oppose global products, just because they are globally available.

Interestingly, quality products seem to be able to diminish those attitudes to a certain extent. An example of this is the common attitude of many French people who don't feel comfortable with the global McDonald's brand. This became manifest in 1999 when a group of French farmers completely tore down a McDonald's restaurant, solely because of the strong association the company has with global consumption culture. What actually triggered the incident was the fact that the US government imposed import duties for French cheese. In the perception of the public, the gang leader became something of a folk hero when he went to jail for three months. For completeness one should add that the so-called 'violent' French farmers are reported to account for only a handful of percentage points of all French farmers – but those face higher barriers to make the headlines.

Notably, McDonald's sales in France remained strong after the incident, especially compared to other countries. Thus, at the end of the day, quality seems to be much more important than globalization attitudes, or to put it in simple words 'the French hate McDonald's, but they eat there anyway'. Holt *et al.* (2004) achieved comparable results when they revealed that consumers all over the world associate global brands with three characteristics and evaluate them along those dimensions: quality, myth and social responsibility. Again, quality gained above-average results, with 44 per cent of the brand preference being explained by this dimension (vs. 12 per cent global myth and 8 per cent social responsibility). Again – as with the above-mentioned aspects of illegally obtained labor – the vast majority of the consumers seem to get very excited over certain issues of globalization, until they approach their own consumption decisions.

If, on the other hand, many consumers have a disturbed perception of the brand, this is not going to benefit the company – even if the actual disadvantages are smaller than they first seem. Thus, the global management of the 'dark side' possessed by almost all multinationals, as Holt and colleagues (2004) have put it, is highly important. In the 1990s IBM had a strong global image of producing the highest quality. However, at the same time the brand was judged as bureaucratic and in some way arrogant – most probably due to its very successful history in upscale business, leading the company to the position it held at that time. But the impression persisted that IBM was struggling, having difficulties adapting to the dynamics of markets where IT was becoming more and more an issue for everyday people. As a response to the public perception IBM launched the campaign 'Solutions for a Small Planet' which managed to focus more on their consumers. A diversity of blue- and white-collar people, shown in a variety of business and non-business surroundings, communicated a much higher level of a consumer-orientated company. Interestingly, the campaign focussed hardly at all on the IBM products. This helped to establish a much more consumer-orientated perception of the company. In the following years IBM went even one step further and added a humoristic aspect to their campaign.

However, this does not imply that only those brands succeed that inhere a globe-spanning, well-managed, but standardized brand image. Local brands can still compete if they manage to anchor their identity within the local culture. The case of the destroyed McDonald's restaurant in France is only one of many indicating that global brands are not

necessarily liked – even if sales numbers tell another story. The global super-brands such as McDonald's, Coca-Cola or Nike have become 'lighting rods for antiglobalization protest'.[6] But even if consumers often don't like those brands, the global operating businesses certainly do. As with many other issues also, global branding is about economies of scale. So it's not so much about what the market wants, but what the producer is capable of pushing in.

On the other hand, brand perception is very complex and individually different, as the brand image is created in the mind of the consumer. Everyone picks up a different set of stimuli to form his or her image of a certain brand. Additionally, even two individuals from the same peer group may interpret one and the same stimulus rather differently. Applying this thought to the heterogeneity of globalized markets and different cultures, it becomes obvious that total standardization of a global brand must lead to only sub-optimal results.

However, many companies make a poor job of developing an understanding of the particular cultures. They enter markets without learning about the local characteristics and intricacies. But if a company does not know about the true needs of the market, it will always be merely meandering around in its search for true competitive advantage. Hence, the road to success may lie in the strategy of glocal branding, aiming for the integration of global and local claims. As Tom Long, CEO of Miller Brewing Company and former president of Coca-Cola UK, argues, the only way to successfully build brands nowadays is from the bottom up, individual by individual. The brand has to address what personally matters to the consumers – and that is obviously very different across the heterogeneity of cultures. To achieve this, those consumers have to be grouped to show commonalities in regard to the relevant characteristics. When building brands, thus, commonalities have to be identified to be able to address the necessities of specific segments. At the same time, though, brands need to be managed as global symbols, because that is how global consumers perceive them.

Even if brands are globally known, they don't necessarily have the stature of a real global brand. A recent study categorized brands using dimensions such as myth, origin, universal and category. The resulting types of brands were labeled 'master brands', 'prestige brands', 'super brands' and 'glocal brands'. For example, master brands have universal appeal, are, to a degree, mythical and entail much prestige at a price many can afford. Coca Cola soft drinks and Levis jeans provide illustrations.

Strong myth and origin are associated with prestige brands. Illustrations of such brands provide upmarket names like Luis Vuitton, Rolex, or the upper crust of American Express cards. Each of the four categories contains brands that we all know and respect – for a more detailed discussion we refer the reader to Holt *et al.* (2004). Naturally, each type of the global brand requires a tailored strategy and management should make sure that a company's brands are properly classified. Improper classification could have disastrous effects. For example, classifying a prestige brand as a master brand would cause a fundamental misspecification of the marketing mix. Especially the channel and the pricing variables would suffer from fundamental problems as the channel would be too much 'mass' and the price would be too low.

It needs to be noted that most of the companies with the biggest increases in recent brand value rankings operate as single brands globally. Today's leading global brands work hard to arrive at one distinct global identity. Obviously, this is most of the time associated with a marketing mix that is configured in a consistent fashion. Such global competition based on a consistent and stable global branding has allowed a number of brands to maintain ranking in leading positions, such as Rolex, Porsche, HSBC, Crest, Persil. As it

has been put succinctly, consistency and impact are key.

Competitive advantage due to employer branding Another important facet of global competition is a company's ability to globally brand itself as a unique employer so the company has a chance to win the global war for talent. For example, Deutsche Bank is reported to have as main foci consumer banking, corporate banking, investment banking and the global search for top talent.

To win the war for talent, so-called employer branding needs to be executed on a global scale. By employer branding we mean the transfer of branding principles to HR management. A primary goal is the increase of HR efficiency, i.e., to lower recruiting costs or to speed up the recruiting process. Ideally, the business positions itself as the employer of choice resulting in applications of the high potentials. Looking at the leading international job markets, this aspect becomes even more important, as the highest-qualified employees can usually choose between a set of different appealing job offers. Thereby, earnings only represent one of the relevant decision criteria. For many job seekers, the employer brand gets more and more important as related factors determine the potential for future development. If, for example, a European company is perceived as a company in which non-natives also may achieve good careers, potential employees from other countries are much more willing to accept a job offer because chances of advancement are not restricted by origin or mother tongue.

As discussed above, competitive advantage refers to the ability of a business to get ahead of its competitors. This is achieved through certain assets – which usually have physical character – and/or certain capabilities, which can be understood as a knowledge set that enables a company to utilize the assets in a way that competitive advantages result. This knowledge set consists of several dimensions (Day 1997; Leonard-Barton 1992) including

(1) the knowledge and skills of the employees that are embedded in (2) technical systems. The process of knowledge-generation and -control is thereby fundamentally guided through (3) management systems and the (4) values and norms that are generally associated with knowledge and its retrieval. Importantly, a holistic understanding and applied employer branding – and that means loosening it from the narrow recruiting perspective – carries the potential to influence all four of the above named dimensions globally. Knowledge and skills are obviously directly influenced through the recruitment of the best employees.

Indirectly, knowledge and skills are also affected by the encouragement of the development of such capacities with existing employees and the applied structuring and codification of knowledge and its establishment in technical systems. Obviously, the formal and informal regulations and mechanisms of knowledge generation are highly important in this context. In other words, management systems that leave room, and allow for, continuous education and personal development almost appear as the guarantor for the successful future generation of knowledge and skills. Finally, all these aspects are determined by the values and norms that a business applies to knowledge in general. In short, the establishment of a sophisticated employer brand appears as a necessity in certain industries that are affected by the global war for talent, as only those companies attract employees from the diverse target groups that have a truly global employer brand.

global strategy. It seems obvious that companies that aim to be successful on a global scale need to pay attention to new facets of competition such as humor or heritage. Similarly, for most businesses establishing some kind of a department or business unit devoted to global intelligence seems imperative. Obviously, markets around the globe develop differently and do so at different speeds. Naturally, observing, analyzing, anticipating and acting on competitive conjectures become more essential, as in the global battlefield.

Importantly, it seems obvious that firms have no choice whether they want to compete in the global marketplace or not. As we have arrived in the globalization age, it is imperative that firms consider one main market – the global market – for their strategic development. If a firm fails to do so, an important source for competition may be ignored.

The development of a global competitive strategy should start within the firm in an effort to try to identify or develop a competitive advantage – based on new and traditional determinants – that is sustainable around the globe. The resulting brands, for example, should have a rather consistent and stable world-spanning positioning, while bearing in mind that differences between markets exist.

Naturally, a firm needs to watch the evolution of markets and, especially, competition as regulations and deregulations pose fundamental opportunities and threats. Obviously, establishing a globally active system of competitor intelligence is imperative. If a firm follows the basic guidelines and pays attention to the issues raised in this chapter, its competitive vulnerability should decline significantly.

SUMMARY

In this chapter we have presented and discussed different pillars and facets of global competition and competitive global strategy. We have outlined a number of new and emerging determinants for global competition and

NOTES

1 Obviously, the aforementioned does not mean that competition is 'perfect' in the sense that the competitive process will (always) lead to results that are considered 'optimal' by consumers, producers,

unions, governments, etc. We refer to the economic literature for issues related to market imperfection.

2 In statistics this term has long been used in relation to distribution aspects. Concerning market structures Chris Anderson promoted this term in 2004 in a *Wired Magazine* article (Anderson 2004).

3 This term is commonly used to describe the network of blogs.

4 It is important to note that the vast majority of copied products intend to resemble the original accurately but often fail to do so. Mostly quality aspects are mentionable, which may in some cases result in rather unattractive, and in others, even fatal, flaws. So the term 'intended 100% copy' or 'intended onto to one copy' may be more appropriate.

5 All numbers are UNICEF estimates.

6 It is worth noting, that the general attitude toward US foreign politics and global US brands – which account for close to two-thirds of the Top 100 global brands – was not favorable at all in 2002 when the study was conducted. Notably though, the study revealed that it simply didn't matter to consumers whether the global brand they bought was a US one (Holt *et al.* 2004). Consistent with Steencamp *et al.* (2003), a discrepancy seems to exist between the beliefs of critical consumers and their actions.

ACKNOWLEDGMENT

Table 13.1: The Global Competitiveness Report 2007–2008 edited by Michael E. Porter, Professor Klaus Schwab and Professor Xavier Sala-i-Martin, The World Economic Forum published by Palgrave Macmillan reproduced with permission of Palgrave Macmillan

REFERENCES

Davies, R. B. (2005) 'Abstinence from child labor and profit seeking', *Journal of Development Economics*, 76(1): 251–263.

Day, G. S. (1997) 'Maintaining the competitive edge: creating and sustaining advantages in dynamic competitive environments' in G. S. Day, D. J. Reibstein and R. E. Gunther (eds). *Wharton on Dynamic Competitive Strategy*. New York: John Wiley & Sons, pp. 48–75.

Goldman Sachs & Co. (2003) 'Dreaming With BRICs: The Path to 2050', global Economics Paper No: 99.

Holt, D. B., Quelch, J. A., Taylor, E. L. (2004) 'How global brands compete', *Harvard Business Review*, 82(9): 68–75.

Horowitz, A., Athitakis, M., Laswell, M., and Thomas, O. (2005), '101 Dumbest Moments in Business,' in *Business 2.0*, 6. San Francisco.

Jacobs, L., Samli, A. C., and Jedlik, T. (2001) 'The Nightmare of International product Piracy: Exploring defensive Strategies', *Industrial Marketing Management*, 30(6): 499–509.

Leonard-Barton, D. (1992) 'Core capabilities and core rigidities: a paradox in managing new product development', *Strategic Management Journal*, 13(S1), 111–125.

López-Calva, L. F. (2001) 'Child labor: myths, theories, and facts', *The Journal of International Affairs*, 55(1): 59–73.

MacCormack, A., Forbath, T., Brooks, P., and Kalaher, P. (2007) *Innovation through Global Collaboration: A New Source of Competitive Advantage*. Harvard Business School, *Working Paper*, August.

Martin, S. (2004) 'Globalization and the natural limits to competition' in M. Neumann and J. Weigand (eds), *The International Handbook of Competition*. Cheltenham: Edward Elgar Publishing Limited.

Perlmutter, D. D. and McDaniel, M. (2005) 'The ascent of blogging,' *Nieman Reports*, 59(3): 60–64.

Polgreen, L. (2004) 'A ballpoint trick infuriates bicyclists,' *The New York Times*. Late Edition (East Coast), Sep. 17, p. B 1.

Steenkamp, J.-B., Batra, R., and Alden, D. L. (2003) 'How perceived brand globalness creates brand value', *Journal of International Business Studies*, 34(1): 53–65.

Wright, J. (2006) *Blog Marketing: The Revolutionary New Way to Increase Sales, Build Your Brand, and Get Exceptional Results*. New York: McGraw-Hill.

14

Global Sourcing Strategy

Masaaki Kotabe, Michael J. Mol,
and Janet Y. Murray

INTRODUCTION

As global competition suggests a drastically shortened life cycle for most products, companies can no longer survive simply by adopting a polycentric, country-by-country approach to international business. If companies that have developed a new product do follow a country-by-country approacjh to foreign market entry over time, a globally oriented competitor will likely overcome their initial competitive advantages by blanketing the world markets with similar products in a shorter period of time. Indeed, it is imperative for companies to continuously create and acquire capabilities that would help generate a sustainable competitive advantage over their rivals. Increasingly, how to source globally has become a critical strategic decision that is influenced by the capabilities needed to compete.

What we are seeing today is a gradual 'power shift' in sources of competitive advantage from proprietary technology to manufacturing and marketing competences, and now to design capability. Proprietary technology is essentially a raw muscle power to obtain initial competitive advantage, and it is easy to imitate by inventing around, by reverse engineering, or even by industrial espionage. Manufacturing and marketing competences revolve around the 'sweat and tears' of skilled human inputs, which take years to accomplish by continual improvement after improvement and, as a result, are much harder to copy, due primarily to their tacit nature.

Today, quick technological diffusion has virtually become a fact of life. Without established sourcing plans, distribution, and service networks, it is extremely difficult to exploit both emerging technology and potential markets around the world simultaneously. The increased pace of new product introduction and reduction in innovational lead time calls for more proactive management of locational and corporate resources on a global basis. In this chapter, we emphasize the choices companies make to perform activities either inside the firm or have those activities performed by others, anywhere in the world – which we call global sourcing strategy. Global sourcing strategy requires close coordination between R&D, manufacturing, and marketing activities across national boundaries (Kotabe 1992).

GLOBAL SOURCING PHENOMENON

Due to an ever more competitive and uncertain global business environment as well as a more even distribution of supply capabilities across the globe, an increasing number of large and small firms either produce in lower-cost locations or outsource goods and services from lower-cost producers. Firms realize that, in order to generate a sustainable competitive advantage over their rivals, it is imperative to continuously create and acquire capabilities. In addition to securing lower costs from global suppliers, firms increasingly outsource in order to gain access to suppliers' capabilities (Barney 1999). Thus, the core driver of the latest form of global (i.e., both onshore and offshore) outsourcing is the heightened organizational and technological capacity of firms in decoupling and coordinating a network of remotely located external suppliers performing an intricate set of activities (Levy 2005). Hence, how to source globally has become a critical strategic decision that is influenced by the capabilities needed to compete and to help sustain a firm's competitive advantage.

Although firms have embraced global sourcing of goods and services to an overwhelming extent, their experience has been mixed (Hsieh, Lazzarini and Nickerson 2002; Lacity, Willcocks and Feeny 1995). Gottfredson, Puryear and Phillips (2005) found that about 50 per cent of firms in their sample reported that their outsourcing programs fell short of expectations. Only 10 per cent were highly satisfied with the cost savings, and 6 per cent were highly satisfied with their offshore outsourcing overall. Similarly, Booz Allen Hamilton recently found that the success rate of outsourcing deals from the customer's perspective was only 12 per cent (*Fortune*, April 3, 2006). Other researchers have even suggested that outsourcing (Leiblein, Reuer and Dalsace 2002) and global outsourcing (Mol, van Tulder and Beije 2005) may have no relationship to performance. Due to the inconclusive

performance outcomes, practitioners have started to question whether universally prescribing global outsourcing is the right way to go (Doig, Ritter, Speckhals and Woolson 2001).

One plausible argument is that, based on a 'balance' perspective, there is an optimal degree of outsourcing. The outsourcing–performance relationship takes on an inverted-U shape (Kotabe and Mol 2004, 2006), implying that, as firms deviate further from their optimal degree of outsourcing, by either outsourcing (or insourcing) and offshoring (or onshoring) too much, their performance will suffer disproportionately. So, the key question for sourcing firms is how much global sourcing they should engage in order to achieve desirable performance.

Another plausible argument for the inconclusive sourcing performance findings is that desirable sourcing performance necessitates the sourcing strategy to achieve a strategic 'fit' with the environment. Indeed, researchers have theorized that the appropriateness of a particular strategy is based on its 'coalignment' or 'fit' with environmental contingencies (Drazin and Van de Ven 1985). Using contingency theory to examine the environment-strategy coalignment effect on performance (e.g., Hambrick and Lei 1985), the environment and strategy are theorized to interact in a dynamic coalignment process, and a match between them would exert a positive impact on performance (Venkatraman and Prescott 1990). Thus, firms that can adapt their strategic actions effectively to both internal and external factors are likely to achieve better performance (Atuahene-Gima and Murray 2004; Zeithaml, Varadarajan, and Zeithaml 1988).

We focus on global sourcing as it adds many more complexities that do not apply to domestic sourcing strategy. In developing viable global sourcing strategies, firms must consider not only manufacturing and delivery costs, the costs of various resources, and exchange rate fluctuations, but also availability of infrastructure (including transportation, communications, and energy), industrial and cultural environments, the ease of working with foreign host governments, and so on. Furthermore, the complex nature of global sourcing strategy spawns many barriers to its successful execution. In particular, logistics, inventory management, distance, nationalism, and lack of working knowledge about foreign business practices, among others, are major operational problems identified by both US and foreign multinational companies engaging in global sourcing.

In this chapter, we start our discussion with managerial intuition. Managerial intuition often is an important part of actual decision-making (Dane and Pratt 2007). Intuitive arguments, like 'focusing on the core' and 'strategic sourcing', have been key to legitimizing the trends toward more global outsourcing. We first discuss the recent trends in global sourcing strategy. Then, we highlight the advantages and disadvantages of global sourcing by providing a list of intuitive arguments for each. We then attempt to explain global sourcing levels and how these relate to performance based on the two complementary perspectives of 'balance' and 'fit'. By synthesizing these two perspectives, we introduce existing theories of sourcing in our chapter. In doing so, we confront managerial intuition with a scholarly approach. Through this process, we develop critical questions and issues for both academic and managerial audiences.

Trends in global sourcing

Global sourcing strategy generally refers to the management of (1) logistics identifying which production units will serve which particular markets and how components will be supplied for production, and (2) the interfaces among R&D, manufacturing, and marketing on a global basis. The primary objective of global sourcing strategy is for the firm to exploit both its own and its suppliers' competitive advantages and the comparative locational advantages of various countries in global competition. From a contractual point of view, the global sourcing of intermediate products such as components and services by firms takes place in two ways: (1) from the parents or their foreign subsidiaries on an 'intra-firm' basis (i.e., insourcing), and (2) from independent suppliers on a 'contractual' basis (i.e., outsourcing). Similarly, from a locational point of view, multinational firms can procure goods and services either (1) domestically (i.e., onshoring) or (2) from abroad (i.e., offshoring). This leads to the simple matrix of possible choices presented in Table 14.1.

Global sourcing has been around for centuries. However, the type of international trade in the times of Adam Smith was qualitatively different from what we observe in modern times, primarily for two reasons, one technical and one social. First, trade used to be mostly conducted in raw materials or final products, and seldom in intermediate products such as components or services. Trade in intermediate products started to take off as the global economy evolved and products became more complicated. Second, unlike today, buyer–supplier coordination and cooperation was not crucial, and communications were normally limited to ordering processes. Thus, we focus our discussions on recent trends of global sourcing only.

In the last 15 to 20 years we have observed three waves of global sourcing. The first wave, starting in the mid-1980s, was primarily

Table 14.1   Different sourcing strategies

Locational Aspect	Domestic	Foreign
Ownership Aspect		
Internal Sourcing	Onshore Insourcing	Offshore Insourcing
External Sourcing	Onshore Outsourcing	Offshore Outsourcing

focused on global sourcing of manufacturing activities. Research, therefore, focused primarily on manufacturing firms, with Kotabe and Omura's (1989) study as one of the first to examine global sourcing. Large manufacturing firms increasingly set up their operations globally and began to use suppliers from many countries to exploit best-in-world sources (Quinn and Hilmer 1994). As a consequence, supply chains became more global and complex, with manufacturing firms sourcing from suppliers in many countries for raw materials, intermediate and final products (Hult 1997; Trent and Monczka 2005).

A second wave began to occur in the early 1990s, when firms started eliminating their information technology (IT) departments that had grown substantially (Cross 1995; Lacity and Hirshheim 1993; Loh and Venkatraman 1992). As IT itself had become commoditized and many firms had little interest in developing new information systems in-house, this IT outsourcing wave spawned the growth of specialist providers, such as EDS and Accenture. Global sourcing mostly involved labor-intensive and standardized programming activities, which could be easily sourced from locations like India. The rise of commercial applications for a wide range of firm activities, epitomized in Enterprise Resource Planning systems, also implied that a marketplace had developed where independent suppliers could make competitive offerings.

A third wave, characterized as the offshoring movement, began in recent years. We have witnessed the rise of business process outsourcing that extends beyond IT services to a range of other services related to accounting, human resources management, finance, sales and after-sales such as call centers. India is still a primary source country, and has now produced a range of strong local business process providers such as Infosys and Wipro, but competition from elsewhere is also on the rise. It is this third wave of business process outsourcing that is now generating so much publicity. Many are concerned that foreign business processes suppliers may be moving up the knowledge chain more rapidly than expected by sourcing firms. Such knowledge transfer could in the long run undermine sourcing firms' ability to differentiate themselves from their foreign suppliers. Indeed, such hollowing-out concerns have previously been raised about outsourcing of manufacturing activities before (Bettis, Bradley and Hamel 1992; Markides and Berg 1988; Kotabe 1998). We summarize our argument on these recent waves of global sourcing in Table 14.2.

GLOBAL SOURCING STRATEGY AND PERFORMANCE

It is widely suggested that global sourcing occurs in order to improve performance, particularly cost-effectiveness (e.g., Trent and Monczka 2003). Firms located in OECD countries often find that labor costs are excessive, compared with the value that is added to their products. While emerging

Table 14.2 Recent waves in global sourcing

Time period	First wave (since 1980s)	Second wave (since early 1990s)	Third wave (since early 2000s)
Type of activity	Manufacturing	Information Technology	Business processes
Destinations	China, Central and Eastern Europe, Mexico and others	India, Ireland and others	India, Pakistan, South Africa and others
Type of firms	Manufacturing	Manufacturing, banks and others	Financial services, services more generally
Primary motives	Reduction in labor costs	Obtaining enough skilled programmers and cost reduction	Reduction in labor costs and round-the-clock service provision

countries such as China lag behind in productivity, they compensate for this lower productivity by providing much lower labor costs, sometimes even culminating in de-automation of tasks when they are transferred to these locations. Indeed, in some cases, such as a range of bicycle components, the production cost differences are so large that it is not economically viable to use domestic sourcing, especially when the labor costs represent a substantial part of overall production costs. At the other extreme, some global sourcing may be driven by knowledge concerns. Some inputs, such as aircraft parts and technical expertise, may be available only in other OECD countries, thus making global sourcing not a choice but an imperative. As for the sourcing of many raw materials, domestic sourcing is not an option since many raw materials are unavailable domestically. Certain intermediate products tend to be sourced from locations near the source of raw materials. Another argument in favor of global sourcing is that it enables a firm to produce goods closer to its customer markets, thereby increasing access to its customers and obtaining critical market knowledge for product development. For instance, Japanese manufacturing firms have, over time, replicated supply chains in North America and Europe to operate closer to these markets. Production and sourcing experience in these regions has also allowed them to improve their product offerings. Another reason to opt for global sourcing is that demand from various regions can be pooled, thus achieving maximum scale and bargaining power through single sourcing from a foreign supplier.

On the other hand, there are disadvantages associated with global sourcing. A major problem is 'cultural differences' between buyers and their foreign suppliers. Indeed, differences such as institutional and language problems may affect a relationship negatively. Cultural misunderstandings and other communication problems can lead to quality problems, in addition to those caused by differences in technical standards or expectations. Another concern related to global sourcing is its long lead times and supply chain uncertainty, and its feasibility is often determined by international trade rules (Swamidass and Kotabe 1993). Finally, foreign suppliers may be able to integrate forward into the buyer's market by inventing around patents or ignoring them altogether.

This raises another layer of issues related to the long-term sustainability of firms' core competencies, particularly when firms begin to increase reliance on independent suppliers through outsourcing (for a more extensive discussion of outsourcing and core competencies, see Mol 2007). There are two opposing views of the long-term implications of outsourcing. One school of thought argues that many successful companies have developed a dynamic organizational network through increasing cross-border joint ventures, subcontracting and licensing activities (Miles and Snow 1986). This flexible network system, also known as supply-chain alliances, allows each participant to pursue its particular competence. Each network participant is complementing rather than competing against the other participants for the common goals. Such alliances are often formed by competing companies in pursuit of complementary abilities (e.g., new technologies or skills) from one another, thus helping the sourcing firm to acquire a competitive advantage by sourcing major components that involve high asset specificity from its alliance partners (Murray 2001). The other school of thought argues that while a firm may gain short-term advantages, there could also be negative long-term consequences. As the firm becomes more reliant on its independent suppliers, it may not be able to keep abreast of constantly evolving design and engineering technologies without engaging in those developmental activities (Kotabe 1998). Consequently, the firm encounters the inherent difficulty in sustaining its long-term competitive advantages. In other words, over time, a firm's technical expertise and capability surplus vis-à-vis its foreign suppliers may diminish to the point that its value added is limited, and it may become more like a trading company.

An example of this is the development of Emerson Radio, which turned from an electronics producer into a trading company and then into nothing more than a brand that changed owners several times (see Kotabe, Mol and Ketkar 2008).

These conflicting predictions have arisen over its performance implications with varying attention for the benefits and drawbacks of outsourcing. Practitioners are now beginning to doubt whether universally prescribing outsourcing is the right way to go (Doig, Ritter, Speckhals and Woolson 2001) while academics suggest outsourcing may not be related to performance (Leiblein, Reuer and Dalsace 2002). Thus, we may have to redefine our thinking on outsourcing and performance. In this chapter, we synthesize arguments both in favor of and against outsourcing. We will first address these arguments; then, we will combine them in uncovering a new and alternative explanation. Our focus is not on any single outsourcing decision, but rather on the overall extent of outsourcing of a business unit. We empirically verify our explanation, thus making an interesting conceptual improvement with solid empirical underpinnings. This leads to a series of managerial and academic implications.

The case for outsourcing

Various arguments have been supplied to make the case for outsourcing. We briefly outline these arguments to explain why firms would want to outsource:

- Strategic Focus / Reduction of Assets
  Through outsourcing activities a firm can reduce its level of asset investment in manufacturing and related areas. Therefore, stock markets usually react favorably to outsourcing since more or less similar absolute profit levels can be obtained with lower fixed investments (Domberger 1998). Furthermore, outsourcing can help the management of a firm redirect its attention to its core competencies, instead of having to possess and update a wide range of competencies.

- Complementary Capabilities / Lower Production Costs
  External suppliers are often highly specialized in the production of components or products, allowing them to produce at lower costs than the outsourcing firm could due to scale economies. Therefore, a firm can improve production cost levels by outsourcing non-core activities (Quinn 1999; Hendry 1995).

- Strategic Flexibility
  Outsourcing may increase the firm's strategic flexibility. By using outside sources, it is much easier to switch from one supplier to another (Nooteboom 1999). If an external shock occurs, firms are able to react quickly by simply increasing or decreasing the volumes obtained from an external supplier. If the same item were produced in-house, the firm would not only incur high restructuring costs but also a much longer response time to external events.

- Avoiding Bureaucratic Costs
  Rising production costs are associated with internal production (D'Aveni and Ravenscraft 1994), due to a lack of a price mechanism and economic incentives inside a firm (Domberger 1998). As a consequence, firm efficiency will suffer.

- Relational Rent
  In recent years, many researchers have argued that certain relationships with external suppliers can deliver competitive advantage (Dyer and Singh 1998). By outsourcing items based on idiosyncratic and valuable relationships with suppliers, firms may be able to innovate, learn and reduce transaction costs.

The case against outsourcing

Extant literature on outsourcing strategy has also highlighted the disadvantages of outsourcing strategy.

- Interfaces / Economies of Scope
  Firms may benefit from internalizing production through scope economies (D'Aveni and Ravenscraft 1994). Kotabe (1998) has suggested that manufacturing firms, in their outsourcing decisions, ought to reflect on the interfaces between R&D, manufacturing, and marketing. If there are important interfaces between activities, decoupling them into separate activities performed

by different suppliers will generate less than optimal results.

- Hollowing Out
  Firms that outsource activities excessively are hollowing out their competitive base (Kotabe 1998). Once activities have been outsourced, it tends to become difficult to differentiate a firm's products on the basis of these activities. Furthermore, a firm could lose bargaining power vis-à-vis its suppliers because its suppliers' capabilities may increase relative to those of the firm.
- Opportunistic Behavior
  External suppliers may behave opportunistically (Williamson 1985) as their incentive structure varies widely from that of the outsourcing firm. Opportunistic behavior allows a supplier to extract more rents from the relationship than it would normally do, for example, by supplying a lower than agreed-on product quality or withholding information on changes in production costs.
- Rising Transaction and Coordination Costs
  Hendry (1995) has cautioned that excessive outsourcing may lead to high coordination costs. Firms are limited in their capacity to work with outside suppliers as partners and therefore have to prioritize outside partners. If they simultaneously invested time and attention to all outside suppliers, this would induce very high coordination costs indeed.
- Limited Learning and Innovation
  A form of learning that is deemed especially important for attaining tacit knowledge is learning-by-doing. The supplier may acquire tacit knowledge by performing the activity; consequently, the outsourcing firm cannot appropriate all benefits. Appropriation of innovation and rents is always a problem in buyer–supplier relationships (Nooteboom 1999) because both parties will try to obtain as many private benefits as possible. Furthermore, it may become more difficult to innovate, due to the different incentives available and the subsequent lack of interfaces between firms.

A 'balance' perspective

A 'balance' perspective can offer insights on the sourcing strategy–performance relationship. In proposing a 'balance' perspective, Kotabe and Mol (2004, 2006) examined the relationship between the degree of a firm's

outsourcing across all activities and its performance. Their underlying argument is that firms that outsource all of their activities run into a multitude of problems, such as a lack of innovation and bargaining power, and an inability to be distinct in the eyes of the customer. However, firms that only insource fail to use the powerful incentives supplied by markets, thus becoming bureaucratic and inefficient. Therefore, outsourcing some, but not all, activities provides the best solution overall, and there is an optimal degree of outsourcing. Deviations from that optimum are costly; the larger the deviations, the more severe the performance penalty will be. Hence, there is a negative curvilinear (inverted U-shaped) relationship between the degree of outsourcing and firm performance. Likewise, Leiblein, Reuer, and Dalsace (2002) empirically found that deviations from the optimal form of sourcing, as dictated by transactional attributes associated with various contracting hazards, may have a detrimental effect on performance.

We believe a similar line of reasoning can apply to the degree of internationalization of sourcing (i.e., onshoring and offshoring) and how that affects performance. More specifically, there are advantages and disadvantages associated with global sourcing, as we highlighted above. As a firm engages in more offshoring (particularly, offshore outsourcing), the disadvantages become larger to the point where they severely impede performance. If firms do not use offshoring at all, they cannot enjoy any of the advantages of offshoring, such as having a wider supply base from which to choose. This line of reasoning is consistent with research in international business, it is for instance indirectly suggested by Dunning's (1993) treatment of international sourcing, and neo-institutional economics traditions, particularly the transaction costs framework (Williamson 1985).

Williamson (1985) distinguishes between production and transaction costs. Production costs refer to the costs of producing a commodity or service, and transaction costs represent all the costs incurred as the product moves from one supply chain partner to the next. When firms use offshore outsourcing by procuring from foreign suppliers, it may help reduce their production costs. In some instances, a local supplier's production costs may be lower than those of foreign suppliers, but this is often the exception and not the rule. Transaction costs, on the other hand, tend to be higher for such offshoring, as there are many types of institutional, cultural and language barriers that must be overcome. Rangan (2000) has discussed this in terms of the costs of 'search and evaluation'. Searching for supply sources abroad, whether internal or external sources, is somewhat more expensive than searching for local supply sources. Evaluating those foreign supply sources is much more expensive, as the evaluation costs are strongly related to the familiarity that decision-makers have with the other party. Since firms are likely to be less familiar with foreign supply sources and decision-makers may not be able to draw on their networks in helping them evaluate these sources, this induces substantial evaluation costs. Rangan (2000) uses this argument to explain why buying firms are much more likely to choose a domestic than a foreign supplier, even when the physical distance between the buyer and each of these suppliers is the same.

We argue that offshoring is a balancing act between production and transaction costs. Firms need to find the proper balance between domestic and foreign supply sources (using onshoring and offshoring) if they wish to locate on the top of the curve and obtain the highest possible performance. They can achieve this by using foreign sources for part, but not all, of their sourcing. Sourcing everything from abroad produces poor performance results because the disadvantages of offshoring, like the hollowing-out argument, become too large. Focusing all efforts on onshoring, however, is a serious form of myopia, with equally disastrous effects for firm performance, primarily because the firm is not capitalizing on

important opportunities to improve competitiveness. A graphic illustration of our argument is presented in Figure 14.1.

The balance perspective can therefore best be summarized as in the box below.

> Some activities are best outsourced globally while others ought to be integrated (from a performance perspective). A firm can enjoy optimal performance when it correctly outsources and/or integrates all activities. Deviations from the optimum are costly in that the farther from the optimum, the more costly these deviations become. This produces a pattern of a negatively curvilinear (an inverted U-shaped) relationship between outsourcing and performance, with the top of the curve presenting the performance optimum.

A 'fit' perspective

Despite the heightened publicity of global sourcing, many firms have been highly dissatisfied with their sourcing performance. The problem may be due to the fact that many researchers and practitioners have adopted a deterministic view in evaluating the global sourcing strategy–performance relationship, without exercising caution that such a view tends to over-generalize the sourcing benefits. Strategic management scholars have conceptualized environment as one of the key constructs for understanding organizational behavior and performance in that 'the appropriateness of different strategies depends on the competitive settings of

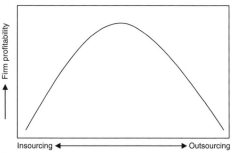

Figure 14.1   A curvilinear relationship between the degree of outsourcing and firm performance

businesses' (Prescott 1986, p. 765). Thus, failure to include environmental factors in examining the sourcing strategy–performance relationship may neglect the effects of different environments on optimal sourcing strategies.

Researchers often adopt the contingency approach in representing a 'fit' perspective of the environment–strategy–performance relationship. Extant research has confirmed that some environmental factors indeed exerted moderating effects on the sourcing strategy–performance relationship. In the manufacturing context, Murray, Kotabe and Wildt (1995) concluded that the financial performance advantage of global insourcing over global outsourcing of non-standardized (i.e., major) components strengthened with increased product innovations, process innovations, and asset specificity.

Using foreign firms manufacturing in China as subjects of their study, Murray, Kotabe, and Zhou (2005) found that global outsourcing of major components (in the form of strategic alliance-based sourcing) did not have an effect on market performance. Instead, product innovativeness and technological uncertainty moderated such a relationship. Specifically, at low levels of product innovativeness/technological uncertainty, the use of strategic alliance-based sourcing of major components by the sourcing firm is positively related to market performance. However, at higher levels of product innovativeness/technological uncertainty, the sourcing–performance relationships become a negative one.

Similarly, Leiblein, Reuer and Dalsace's (2002) findings in the manufacturing context concur with the above conclusions. In refuting the popular arguments that insourcing or outsourcing will lead to superior technological performance, they found that sourcing strategy *per se* did not significantly affect technological performance. Instead, the sourcing strategy–performance relationship was driven by factors underlying sourcing strategy choice. They further cautioned against the universalistic normative implications for firms deciding on whether or not to insource or outsource their value-chain activities and stressed the value of contingency-based theoretical approaches.

As discussed earlier, global sourcing of services did not take place until the second wave of global sourcing; therefore, extant literature on global sourcing of services is limited when compared to that in global sourcing of manufactured goods. Murray and Kotabe (1999) found that similar to components and finished goods sourcing, supplementary services were sourced globally, either by insourcing or outsourcing. In addition, the relationship between asset specificity and insourcing of supplementary services was moderated by the level of inseparability[1] and transaction frequency. Their empirical findings showed that firms tended to rely more on global insourcing for inseparable supplementary services with high asset specificity. Furthermore, the higher the asset specificity and the lower the transaction frequency of the supplementary services, the higher global insourcing is used. Finally, insourcing and off-shoring of supplementary services were negatively related to a service's market performance.

The fit perspective can therefore best be summarized as in the box below.

> There is a range of contingency factors (i.e., capital intensity, degree of service inseparability, market uncertainty, transaction frequency) at the transaction-, firm-, and context-levels. These factors determine how much global outsourcing ought to take place from a performance perspective. To an extent the contingency factors also explain how much global outsourcing actually takes place in practice. Fit is achieved when the actual global outsourcing level is in accordance with the level predicted based on the contingency factors. If a company matches an outsourcing decision to the relevant contingency factors, the resulting strategic fit helps achieve superior performance.

A 'BALANCED FIT' PERSPECTIVE

The previous discussion raises two related questions. First, are these contradictory or rather complementary perspectives; if they

are complementary, how do they complement each other? Second, how can we, taking
into account these perspectives, explain
the large increases in offshore and global
outsourcing? We now seek to answer these
two questions based on the extant literature,
specifically by drawing upon possible conceptual angles on global outsourcing.

To describe how the balance and fit
perspectives complement each other, and to
explain why over the past two decades or so
we have witnessed the degree of global sourcing shifting toward more offshoring, we need
to draw more directly upon key academic perspectives on global sourcing. We summarize
eleven such perspectives in Table 14.3.

It would go too far to describe each perspective in detail or show how different
perspectives are useful in predicting global
outsourcing (for a more detailed description,
see Mol 2007). However, it is important to
note that these perspectives operate at three
different levels: the transaction, the firm, and
the industry and institutional context. Taken
together, they represent almost all the contingency factors that the academic literature has
produced to date. Which of these perspectives
matters most is to an extent determined by
the empirical context in which outsourcing is
investigated. Some of the perspectives have
been more prominent than others in recent
academic studies of outsourcing. Transaction
cost economics and the resource-based view
come to mind as examples, which may
reflect their actual importance in practice, the
scholarly knowledge production process or
other factors. But all of them have some
bearing on global outsourcing.

This takes us back to the two questions.
The first question can be answered by stating

that *exactly where the optimal point of
outsourcing (balance) lies is determined by
the scores on the contingency factors (fit).* In
terms of the second question, the optimal
point in terms of how much a firm should
engage in offshoring will shift over time.
Over the past two decades or so we have
witnessed that the degree of global sourcing
has shifted to the right in Figure 14.1, i.e.,
toward more offshoring. This implies that
*changes in both the level of the contingency
factors as well as their constitution (i.e.,
which variables matter and to what extent)
have caused the increase in offshoring levels.*

Taken together, the implication is that the
balance in global outsourcing has shifted
toward higher levels of outsourcing because of
the need to fit global outsourcing levels to a set
of changed circumstances. We suggest two
major drivers of this change. First, information
technology, including the Internet, has greatly
facilitated cross-border business-to-business
transactions. Second, institutional changes,
which lie at the heart of the rise of both China
and India as supply destinations, have also
facilitated cross-border trade and investment,
both of which in turn lead to more global outsourcing. These conclusions provide different
implications for academic researchers and
managers. We start by discussing the former.

RESEARCH IMPLICATIONS

While outsourcing was mostly used for specialized, repetitive tasks such as facilities
management or logistics, it has now penetrated
to more visible and sensitive functions such
as customer service, R&D, and manufacturing

Table 14.3   Perspectives on global outsourcing

	Firm	Context	Transaction
Past	Resource-based view	Social networks	
Present	Costly contracting	Industrial organization	Transaction cost economics
	Micro-economics	Institutional voids	Agency
	Core competences		
Future	Real options		
	Relations and learning		

(Leiblein, Reuer and Dalsace 2002). Many firms have recently rushed to changing their sourcing practice to include more outsourcing and offshoring for a variety of activities, without making careful analysis regarding their short- and long-term performance implications. Kotabe and Mol (2006) have termed this type of behavior 'bandwagoning', implying a leader-follower behavior in offshore outsourcing decisions. Bandwagoning is not necessarily undesirable, but there is also no reason to believe that bandwagoning leads to the best performance. In fact, bandwagoning may easily induce firms to engage in an excess of outsourcing or offshoring.

Combining both a 'fit' and a 'balance' perspective on the performance implications of global sourcing, we caution managers that there are limits to both outsourcing and offshoring, in that their relationship to performance is an inverted U-shape. In other words, too much outsourcing or offshoring may affect a firm's performance negatively. Furthermore, the increased pace of technological change and the geographic and organizational dispersion of knowledge have exacerbated the complexity involved in global sourcing (Leiblein, Reuer and Dalsace 2002). Thus, to realistically evaluate the performance implications of a particular sourcing strategy, a 'fit' perspective should be adopted. The contingency approach helps build a theory of global sourcing by examining the moderating effects of environmental factors on the sourcing strategy-performance. As Baumol (1957) recommended, providing theoretical generalizations that predict what will happen under given conditions is necessary for theory development. Thus, using a contingency approach, it helps managers to evaluate critically the viability of a particular sourcing strategy. It also helps make theoretical generalizations about global sourcing.

We propose a number of interesting research questions that academics can tackle:

1 Which drivers of increased global outsourcing matter the most, and how can these be related to some of the theories mentioned earlier and perhaps other theories as well? In our academic research we have often focused on the factors that explain global outsourcing levels at any given moment in time, and often through cross-sectional research, at the expense of research that tells us why changes in these levels are taking place. This places us at a risk of becoming outdated in our thinking.

2 What factors will slow the pace of global outsourcing and offshoring, and when should such a deceleration be expected? We have witnessed big increases in recent years, but it does not necessarily mean that this trend will continue endlessly. The past is often a reasonable, but never a great, indicator for the future. Major geopolitical changes may halt the process of globalization or perhaps even reverse it. In any case, there will be some natural adjustments as well, since there is an absolute limit to the quantity of activities that can be outsourced globally.

3 Which areas of global outsourcing are driven by efficiency considerations, and which are pushed by various types of bandwagons? We mentioned the presence of bandwagoning earlier. It was a prominent feature of the IT outsourcing trend of the early 1990s. But recent research (Lewin and Peeters 2006) suggests that it is not a good explanation for the current business process outsourcing movement. Perhaps more mature forms of global outsourcing are more prone to bandwagoning. It may be the nature of the activity itself that matters. Alternatively, the structure of the supplier and buyer industries may explain some of the variance in bandwagoning levels.

MANAGERIAL IMPLICATIONS

Based on our discussions, managers should rethink and redesign their global outsourcing activities. Many managers have a strong general sense for what constitutes a sound outsourcing and offshoring policy. They realize that outsourcing and offshoring every activity may lead to disasters, just as much as they recognize that not all activities should be insourced. However, we suggest managers can improve their decision-making in various respects.

There is currently a tendency in practice to describe (performance) problems related to outsourcing or offshoring as 'implementation issues'. Managers often assume that outsourcing or offshoring is the proper design choice, so they attribute the unsatisfactory performance to implementation problems that occur when dealing with independent and overseas suppliers. We suggest that there are much more fundamental objections against outsourcing or offshoring that are unrelated to implementation problems. Rather, there are limits to outsourcing and offshoring, and many inputs of a firm should not be outsourced or offshored. Kotabe and Mol's (2005) study confirms managerial intuitions that there is an optimal level, as argued similarly by Leiblein, Reuer and Dalsace (2002). Thus, we help lower the uncertainty surrounding managerial decision-making on outsourcing or offshoring and also improve its quality.

Managers are often not conscious of the fact that there is an optimal degree of outsourcing across their entire portfolio. Instead of using this portfolio level, they tend to see the good or the evil of outsourcing or offshoring particular items or activities in that '[o]utsourcing is more than a bidding process. Companies don't do enough analysis before they jump into it' (*Fortune*, April 3, 2006, p. S4). This helps explain why in practice outsourcing or offshoring often looks like a bandwagoning process. Likewise, many academic approaches have centered on analyzing individual make-or-buy decisions. To some extent this is appropriate, since outsourcing or offshoring decisions are made on an irregular basis. However, the performance advantages of outsourcing or offshoring will only materialize when a firm has the organizational capacity to integrate outsourced and/or offshored items/activities into its operations. Furthermore, many companies make outsourcing or offshoring decisions by evaluating only a few options on the basis of their previous experience and by what their competitors are doing (Farrell 2006). For example, in June 2006, Apple Computer pulled the plug on a call center in India due to the high cost of operating there

(Kripalani 2006), although many managers still perceive India as a low-cost location for call centers.

Managers are in need of guidelines as to where the optimal point lies for their particular business at a particular time. Based on the contingency approach using a 'fit' perspective, we can suggest several indicators to help answer that question, including asset specificity, uncertainty, firm competences, industry trends, and firm nationality and location. These moderating factors may help determine what is optimal for a particular firm at a particular time. Timing is crucial, as the optimal point will shift due to changes internal and external to the firm.

From a managerial perspective, developing a model that helps determine a firm's optimal degree of outsourcing or offshoring would be very useful. Based on the model, managers could prioritize their set of activities and outsource or offshore until they more or less reach optimality. Such a model provides the next challenge for the academic community. As global sourcing is a dynamic process, competing firms may not accurately grasp the full benefit (and cost) of outsourcing or offshoring activities due to causal ambiguity. Simply bandwagoning on the first-mover's current outsourcing or offshoring strategy offers no guarantee for improved performance. We suggest that tackling that challenge involves a broader behavioral understanding of how firms' outsourcing or offshoring trajectories change over time and within industries.

NOTE

1 One of the salient characteristics of services is that a service may not be separated from the service provider. Inseparability forces the buyer into intimate contact with the production process and requires close buyer–seller interactions (Erramilli and Rao, 1993). The close buyer–seller interaction due to service inseparability has two significant implications. First, it demands the tight coordination of the demand and supply of the service activity. Second, it necessitates close interaction between (employees of) the supplier and (employees of) the buyer. Both of these are attained more effectively by performing the activity internally.

REFERENCES

Atuahene-Gima, K. and Murray, J. Y. (2004) 'Antecedents and outcomes of marketing strategy comprehensiveness', *Journal of Marketing*, 68 (4): 33–46.

Barney, J. B. (1999) 'How a firm's capabilities affect boundary decisions', *Sloan Management Review*: 137–145.

Baumol, W. J. (1957) 'On the role of marketing theory', *Journal of Marketing*, April: 413–418.

Bettis, R., Bradley, S. and Hamel, G. (1992) 'Outsourcing and industrial decline', *Academy of Management Executive*, 6(1): 7–16.

Cross, J. (1995) 'IT outsourcing: British Petrol', *Harvard Business Review*, 73(3): 94–102.

Dane, E. and Pratt, M. G. (2007) 'Exploring intuition and its role in managerial decision making', *Academy of Management Review*, 32(1): 33–54.

D'Aveni, R. A. and Ravenscraft, D. J. (1994). 'Economies of integration versus bureaucracy costs: does vertical integration improve performance?', *Academy of Management Journal,* 37(5): 1167–1206.

Doig, S. J., Ritter, R. C., Speckhals, K. and Woolson, D. (2001) 'Has outsourcing gone too far?', *McKinsey Quarterly*, 26(4): 26–37.

Domberger, S. (1998). *The Contracting Organization: A Strategic Guide to Outsourcing*. Oxford: Oxford University Press.

Drazin, R. and Van de Ven, A. H. (1985) 'Alternative forms of fit in contingency theory', *Administrative Science Quarterly*, 30(4): 514–539.

Dunning, J. H. (1993) *Multinational Enterprises and the Global Economy*. Wokingham: Addison-Wesley.

Dyer, J. H. and Singh, H. (1998) 'The relational view: Cooperative strategy and sources of interorgnaizational competitive advantage', *Academy of Management Review*, 23(4): 660–679.

Erramilli, M. K. and Rao, C. P. (1993) 'Service firms' international entry-mode choice: a modified transaction-cost analysis approach', *Journal of Marketing*, 57(3): 19–38.

Farrell, D. (2006) 'Smarter offshoring', *Harvard Business Review*, 84 (June): 85–92.

Fortune (2006) 'The global outsourcing 100', April 3: S2–S17.

Gottfredson, M., Puryear, R. and Phillips, S. (2005) 'Strategic sourcing – From periphery to the core', *Harvard Business Review*, 83(2): 132–139.

Hambrick, D. C. and Lei, D. (1985) 'Toward an empirical prioritization of contingency variables for business strategy', *Academy of Management Journal*, 28: 763–788.

Hendry, J. (1995). 'Culture, community and networks: the hidden cost of outsourcing', *European Management Journal*, 13(2): 218–229.

Hsieh, C. M., Lazzarini, S. G. and Nickerson, J. A. (2002) 'Outsourcing and the variability of product performance: Data from international courier services', *Academy of Management Proceedings*: G1–G6.

Hult, G. T. M. (1997) 'A global learning organization structure and market information processing', *Journal of Business Research*, 40 (October): 155–166.

Kotabe, M. (1992) Global Sourcing Strategy: R&D, Manufacturing, and Marketing Interfaces, New York: Quorum Books.

Kotabe, M. (1998) 'Efficiency vs. effectiveness orientation of global sourcing strategy: a comparison of U.S. and Japanese multinational companies', *Academy of Management Executive*, 12(4): 107–119.

Kotabe, M. and Mol, M. J. (2004) 'A new perspective on outsourcing and the performance of the firm', in M. Trick (ed.), *Global Corporate Evolution: Looking Inward or Looking Outward*. International Management Series, Vol. 4. Pittsburgh, PA: Carnegie Mellon University Press, pp. 331–340.

Kotabe, M. and Mol, M. J. (2005) 'Outsourcing and firm profitability: a negative curvilinear relationship'. London: London Business School Working Paper.

Kotabe, M. and Mol, M. J. (2006) 'International sourcing: redressing the balance', in J. T. Mentzer, M. B. Myers and T. P. Stank (eds), *Handbook of Global Supply Chain Management*. London: Sage Publications. pp. 393–406.

Kotabe, M., Mol, M. J, and Ketkar, S. (2008) 'An evolutionary stage model of outsourcing and competence destruction: a triad comparison of the consumer electronics industry', *Management International Review*, 48(1):65–93.

Kotabe, M. and Omura, G. S. (1989) 'Sourcing strategies of European and Japanese multinationals: A comparison', *Journal of International Business Studies*, 20(1): 113–130.

Kripalani, M. (2006) 'Call center? That's so 2004: outsourcing shops are moving fast into higher-paying businesses', *Business Week*, August 7: 40–41.

Lacity, M. C. and Hirschheim, R. (1993) *Information Systems Outsourcing: Myths, Metaphors and Realities.* Chichester: Wiley.

Lacity, M. C., Willcocks, L. P. and Feeny, D. F. (1995) 'IT outsourcing: maximize flexibility and control', *Harvard Business Review*, 73 (May-June): 84–93.

Leiblein, M. J., Reuer, J. J. and Dalsace, F. (2002) 'Do make or buy decisions matter? The influence of organizational governance on technological performance', *Strategic Management Journal*, 23(9): 817–833.

Levy, D. L. (2005) 'Offshoring in the new global political economy', *Journal of Management Studies*, 42(3): 687–693.

Lewin A. Y. and Peeters, C. (2006) 'Offshoring work: Business hype or the onset of fundamental transformation?', *Long Range Planning*, 39(3): 221–239.

Loh, L. and Venkatraman, N. (1992) 'Determinants of information technology outsourcing: a cross-sectional analysis', *Journal of Management Information Systems*, 9(1): 7–24.

Markides, C. C., and Berg, N. (1988) 'Manufacturing offshore is bad business', *Harvard Business Review*, 66(5): 113–120.

Miles, R. E. and Snow, C. C. (1986) 'Organizations: new concepts for new firms', *California Management Review*, 28 (Spring): 62–73.

Mol, M. J. (2007) *Outsourcing: Design, Process, and Performance.* Cambridge: Cambridge University Press.

Mol, M. J., van Tulder, R. J. M. and Beije, P. R. (2005) 'Antecedents and performance consequences of international outsourcing', *International Business Review*, 14(5): 599–617.

Murray, J. Y. (2001) 'Strategic alliance-based global sourcing strategy for competitive advantage: a conceptual framework and research propositions', *Journal of International Marketing*, 9(4): 30–58.

Murray, J. Y. and Kotabe, M. (1999) 'Sourcing strategies of U.S. service companies: a modified transaction-cost analysis', *Strategic Management Journal*, 20(September): 791–809.

Murray, J. Y., Kotabe, M. and Wildt, A. R. (1995) 'Strategic and financial implications of global sourcing strategy: A contingency analysis', *Journal of International Business Studies*, 26(1): 181–202.

Murray, J. Y., Kotabe, M. and Zhou, J. N. (2005) 'Strategic alliance-based sourcing and market performance: evidence from foreign firms operating in China', *Journal of International Business Studies*, 36(2): 187–208.

Nooteboom, B. (1999) *Inter-firm Alliances: Analysis and Design.* London: Routledge.

Prescott, J. E. (1986) 'Environments as moderators of the relationship between strategy and performance', *Academy of Management Journal*, 29(2): 329–346.

Quinn, J. B. (1999) 'Strategic outsourcing: leveraging knowledge capabilities', *Sloan Management Review*, 40(3): 9–21.

Quinn, J. B. and Hilmer, F. G. (1994) 'Strategic outsourcing', *Sloan Management Review*, 35(4): 43–55.

Rangan, S. (2000) 'The problem of search and deliberation in international exchange: Microfoundations to some macro patterns', *Journal of International Business Studies*, 31(2): 205–222.

Swamidass, P. M. and Kotabe, M. (1993) 'Component sourcing strategies of multinationals: an empirical study of European and Japanese multinationals', *Journal of International Business Studies*, 24(1): 81–99.

Trent, R. J. and Monczka, R. M. (2003) 'International purchasing and global sourcing – What are the differences?', *Journal of Supply Chain Management*, 39(4): 26–37.

Trent, R. J. and Monczka, R. M. (2005) 'Achieving excellence in global sourcing', *Sloan Management Review*, 47 (Fall): 24–32.

Venkatraman, N. and Prescott, J. E. (1990) 'Environment-strategy coalignment: An ecpirical test of its performance implications', *Strategic Management Journal*, 11(1): 1–23.

Venkatraman, N. and Camillus, J. C. (1984) 'Exploring the concept of 'fit' in strategic management', *Academy of Management Review*, 9(3): 513–525.

Williamson, O. E. (1985) *The Economic Institutions of Capitalism*. New York: Free Press.

Zeithaml, V. A., Varadarajan, P. R. and Zeithaml, C. P. (1988) 'The contingency approach: its foundations and relevance to theory building and research in marketing', *European Journal of Marketing*, 22(7): 37–64.

15

Uniformity versus Conformity: The Standardization Issue in International Marketing Strategy

Saeed Samiee, Constantine S. Katsikeas,
and Marios Theodosiou

INTRODUCTION

Few topics in international marketing have attracted as much attention from academicians and business practitioners as international marketing standardization. As a result, a large body of literature has evolved with hundreds of conceptual, empirical, and managerial publications. A move toward globalization by firms since the 1980s and the emergence of global strategy as a field of inquiry have further fueled interest and controversy in appropriateness and the optimal extent of international marketing strategy standardization. The deployment of standardized marketing plans offers substantial benefits, which are derived from synergies across markets that can facilitate the attainment of firms' goals (e.g., uniformity in branding, shorter time to market, and a reduction of costs on global scale). The critical importance of international marketing strategy standardization to managers and academicians alike is reflected in its coverage in virtually every comprehensive international

marketing resource (e.g., international marketing textbooks). The central issue is whether firms should pursue a uniform strategy across diverse international markets (i.e., standardization of marketing strategy) or conform to the distinct host market characteristics (adaptation or customization of marketing strategy). This chapter explores the merits of global uniformity versus host-market conformity by examining the evolution, underlying theory, critical antecedents, and managerial aspects of international marketing strategy.

THE EVOLUTION OF STANDARDIZATION IN MARKETING

Anecdotal evidence suggests that standardized international marketing strategies was often the result of firms' practice of extending domestic marketing strategies to markets abroad as they expanded internationally (see, for example, Keegan 1969). The use of standardized international marketing strategies was likely motivated by the internationalization of US firms and the subsequent rapid growth of multinational corporations (MNCs) in the post-WWII era. Domestic success with marketing plans, coupled with limited or lack of familiarity with environments abroad, favor the pursuit of standardization by default, a practice that appears to be common among smaller and sporadic exporters. The drive toward standardization was also likely fueled by advertising agencies which, client interests notwithstanding, sought to utilize their international network of operations and benefit from capturing their clients' larger international advertising budgets (Ryans 1969). Also, the economies of scale associated with, and resulting from, marketing standardization further promoted the use of a standardized approach in markets abroad. Thus, the practice of standardization in international marketing preceded academic interest and debate on the topic.

The development of international marketing standardization as an academic field of inquiry has followed the three stages of identification, conceptualization, and assimilation articulated by Bartels (1968). By most counts, Elinder (1961) was the first to formally introduce and propose standardization as a viable strategy in international marketing. The initial focus on international standardization was on the advertising function and, in addition to Elinder (1961), other authors also contributed to the dialogue on advertising standardization (e.g., Roostal 1963; Fatt 1964). Early contributions helped identify standardization as an important area for investigation while contributing to its conceptualization.

As interest in this area intensified in the ensuing years, more comprehensive and richer conceptualizations encompassing all functions of marketing strategy appeared in the literature. Several early contributors helped in building the initial platform for approaching the issue. Terpstra (1967) explored international marketing approaches of US MNCs in the Common Market countries through 25 personal interviews conducted in 1963. The implementation of similar marketing programs was one of the issues explored by Terpstra. Two other key early contributions were by Bartels (1968), followed shortly by another study by Buzzell (1968). In this seminal piece, Bartels' (1968) conceptualization was aimed at comparing domestic to international marketing. He accomplished this by distinguishing between marketing processes in various countries and by highlighting their specific environmental contexts within which processes are implemented. Though not specifically concerned about international marketing standardization, Bartels (1968) highlights an important issue about marketing processes in a given country as a function of that country's environment. He contends that marketing 'technology' (sic) has universal validity and applicability. It thus follows that when a particular marketing process is applied to similar environmental contexts, it offers the basis for international marketing standardization. An important related observation by Bartels (1968) is that perceptions of environmental similarities (or differences) by management lead to marketing decisions that correspond to these perceptions. Thus, if a manager considers the UK environment to be similar to that in the US, s/he will be likely to extend US marketing plans to the UK market; that is, to implement a standardized marketing strategy across both markets (and vice versa). Indeed, the many marketing blunders committed in the 1960s by the likes of General Foods (Jello and Betty Crocker cake mix), Campbell's Soup, and others were largely results of such managerial perceptions (cf., Keegan 1969).

Buzzell (1968), on the other hand, was sharply focused on managerial and pragmatic aspects of marketing standardization. This author's central concern in his seminal contribution focused on the marketing elements that are candidates for standardization and the extent to which these functions should be uniform across markets. The question raised by Buzzell (1968) is as pertinent today as it was four decades ago: 'Which *elements* of the marketing strategy should be standardized, and to what degree?' This issue has been repeatedly visited by scholars in a variety of settings (e.g., Sorenson and Wiechmann 1975; Killough 1978). However, Levitt's (1983) publication stressed the presence of convergent and increasingly homogenized world markets (thereby highlighting the appropriateness of much higher levels of standardization) which, in turn, polarized the issue and further fueled the standardization–customization controversy in international marketing. Subsequently, a series of conceptual (e.g., Douglas and Wind 1987; Jain 1989) and empirical studies (e.g., Boddewyn, Soehl and Picard 1986), aimed at supporting or refuting the appropriateness of standardization, were published. Much of the scholarly effort during the first three decades following Elinder's (1961) article consisted of conceptual or descriptive studies of international marketing standardization (e.g., Ryans 1969; Keegan 1969). The majority of empirical studies focused on relatively narrow aspects of international marketing, especially the advertising function (e.g., Green, Cunningham and Cunningham 1975; Peebles, Ryans and Vernon 1977; Onkvisit and Shaw 1987).

However, with the publication of Jain's (1989) conceptual framework, performance considerations resulting from a standardized strategy took the spotlight. Until then, the empirical research on the standardization–adaptation issue had neglected to incorporate performance as an outcome of marketing strategy. Subsequently, Samiee and Roth (1992) investigated this critical issue within the context of global industries. Since then a variety of empirical approaches and contexts have been used, with a common goal of establishing which strategic approach would yield superior performance. The results of these studies vary considerably. To date, only one study (i.e., Katsikeas, Samiee and Theodosiou 2006) appears to have addressed the issue in a holistic fashion.

THEORY UNDERLYING INTERNATIONAL MARKETING STANDARDIZATION

The examination of the international marketing standardization issue demands an appropriate theoretical framing, in the absence of which meaningful results are unlikely. Two approaches appear to offer a defensible basis for examining standardization. First, market segmentation is central to marketing strategy development and is the basis upon which intermarket segments can be profitably identified and cultivated. Second, to be effective, marketing strategy for host markets must incorporate environmental context. As such, strategy fit or coalignment is also a relevant basis for examining marketing standardization. It is noteworthy that the vast majority of studies published on standardization/adaptation do not make any explicit attempt to relate the concept to a broader, overarching theoretical framework like market segmentation or the contingency theory. Instead, there has been a tendency to leverage off previous conceptual and empirical work on standardization to derive appropriate hypotheses.

Market segmentation

Inasmuch as international standardization is a marketing decision, it is appropriately treated within the established contexts in the field. Conceptually, validation of international marketing standardization requires an examination of the marketing management process (Onkvisit and Shaw 1987; Jain 1989). In much of the international marketing literature, standardization is discussed without reference to a firm's relevant market segments in host markets, thus leaving the impression that the strategy is aimed at cultivating mass markets. It is further assumed that the firm pursuing international marketing standardization does so in every market, for all of its products and services, and that this strategy is successfully implemented in dozens of markets in which the MNC operates.

The central consideration in pursuing international marketing standardization is the presence of clearly identifiable intermarket segments.[1] Market segmentation is a necessary and critical component of the marketing plan and intermarket segments are those that transcend national boundaries. Adapted from the micro-economic theory of price discrimination, market segmentation essentially accomplishes one important goal. Using the relevant criteria, customers are grouped into homogeneous subsets, thereby allowing the firm to cultivate particular market niches in which fewer or no competitors are present with differentiated offerings, thus affording the firm the opportunity to gain a competitive advantage. The theory is normative with the ultimate goal of profit maximization (Frank and Massy 1965; Claycamp and Massy 1968; Engel, Fiorillo and Cayley 1972).[2] This conceptualization is shown in Figure 15.1. Note that, as per Jain's (1989) conceptualization of performance, international marketing strategy choice is shown to be a function of performance (note the direction of the path in Figure 15.1).

A critical consideration in this process is the development of separate marketing plans for various segments the firm targets to cultivate. In an international context, market segments targeted across national boundaries must be similar if they are to be cultivated with a standardized approach. Two avenues are available for achieving cross-national equivalence of segments. The first approach involves a country-by-country segment identification task in which the firm applies an identical segmentation scheme in its various country markets, with the expectation of identifying [near-] identical segments in various host markets. The resultant clusters of customers are known as intermarket segments. A second scheme consists of viewing the entire world as a single market; that is, ignoring the national boundaries from the outset. The firm then sets out to uncover clusters of homogeneous customers that are consistent with its marketing plan. The lack of large global data banks that include detailed customer information makes the first segmentation scheme more appropriate for projects that require substantial primary data. The alternative approach, on the other hand, may be deployed in situations where a particular segmentation approach relies on globally available secondary data (e.g., demographic and economic statistics). Both approaches should ideally yield similar clusters or segments across national boundaries. However, current segmentation methods tend to rely heavily on primary customer-level data which favors a country-by-country analysis of markets. If the presence of intermarket segments cannot be established to the firm's satisfaction, standardization of the marketing plan across countries becomes a moot issue from a marketing theory perspective.

The intermarket segment concept of developing international marketing programs has been repeatedly stressed in the literature and is central to Levitt's (1983) globalization of markets proposition (e.g., Simmonds 1985; Sheth 1986; Douglas and Wind 1987; Kale and Sudharshan 1987; Onkvisit and Shaw 1987; Jain 1989; Samiee and Roth 1992; Samiee, Jeong, Pae and Tai 2003).

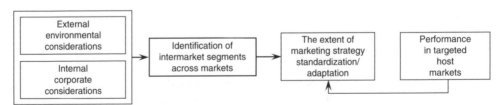

Figure 15.1   A conceptualization of intermarket segment as the basis for international marketing strategy standardization

From a theoretical perspective, the pursuit of intermarket segments by the MNC explicitly assumes the maximization of financial performance (see, for example, Claycamp and Massy 1968). It follows that, as firms intensify market segmentation in the latter parts of the product life cycle and as differentiation proliferates, the identification of profitable intermarket segments will become increasingly more challenging.

As with any marketing decision, the appropriateness of international marketing standardization within intermarket segments depends on whether it leads to superior financial performance vis-à-vis other strategy alternatives. The importance of profitability in assessing the suitability of standardization was recognized and emphasized by Buzzell (1968) but was subsequently largely ignored in empirical studies on the subject. Samiee and Roth (1992) were the first to empirically examine the standardization–performance relationship. In that study, the authors nested marketing standardization and performance within global industries as an intermarket segment and, thus, were also the first to use segmentation as the theoretical framework. Other conceptual contributions have pointed to the importance of economic payoff in decisions concerning standardizing global marketing practices (Keegan 1969; Wind 1986; Jain 1989). Increasingly financial performance outcomes are included in studies of international marketing strategy (e.g., Shoham 1996; O'Donnell and Jeong 2000; Hewett and Bearden 2001; Katsikeas *et al.* 2006). Thus, long-term economic payoff is considered to be a critical element on which the decision to standardize should be based. Inasmuch as lower costs may lead to increased profitability, a number of authors have also emphasized the scale effects associated with standardization (Sorenson and Wiechmann 1975; Hout, Porter and Rudden 1982; Rutenberg 1982; Levitt 1983; Henzler and Rall 1986; Jain 1989). However, to date, no attempt has been made to empirically validate the enhanced financial payoff presumed to be associated with lower costs

resulting from standardization of marketing strategies.

Contingency theory perspective

Dominant largely within the broader field of management, contingency theories have been used to examine a variety of areas including strategic planning and performance. The core proposition involving the contingency approach is that an organizational outcome is the result of fit or coalignment between two or more factors. As such, the concept of fit plays a pivotal role for any firm. Strategic fit has been used as the basis for theory development in several areas of strategy research since the 1960s. The critical importance of strategy fit or coalignment between the environment (i.e., external environment and internal organization factors) and strategy has long been recognized in the strategic management literature (e.g., Miles and Snow 1978; Venkatraman and Camillus 1984).

The concept of fit considers the relationship between business-level strategy and the environment. It asserts the necessity for maintaining a close and consistent linkage between the firm's strategy and the context (environment) in which it is implemented. Furthermore, a strategy needs to be internally consistent, its elements should be compatible, and it must fit across different levels of the firm's structure (Smith, Venkatraman and Wortzel 1995; Venkatraman and Camillus 1984). If the strategic plan has a good fit with its environmental context, it should lead to superior performance for the firm.

The application of the strategy fit concept in international marketing is relatively recent. As with the firm's strategic plan, a good fit between the firm's international marketing strategy (irrespective of whether or not it is standardized) and the environment in which it is applied is expected to yield superior performance. Katsikeas *et al.* (2006) were the first to apply this theoretical framework, along with its corresponding testing methods as proposed and applied in the strategy coalignment literature, in assessing the performance consequences of international marketing strategy. Using international product ventures at the subsidiary level as the unit of analysis, their results indicated that superior performance is significantly related to the coalignment of international marketing strategies, whether standardized or adapted, with host market environments. Two other articles (i.e., Dow 2006; Xu, Cavusgil and White 2006) have also leveraged off contingency theory to examine the performance impact of standardization. This conceptualization is shown in Figure 15.2.

The core proposition offered by contingency theory of strategic fit is consistent with the marketing process–environment relationship proposed by Bartels (1968), even though performance issues of [international] marketing programs were not addressed in his seminal work. Since then other scholars have also embraced the influence of environmental factors on the suitability of marketing programs. For example, internal and external environmental influences play a central role in Jain's (1989) conceptual work for standardization. Jain makes a distinction between marketing and non-marketing environments and proposes the possibility of a higher degree of standardization with greater similarity of marketing and non-marketing

environments (propositions 10 and 11). Recognition is also given to performance issues by Jain (1989), but not within the explicit context of strategic fit. Although strategic fit has been incorporated in some international marketing research, the concept as a distinct theoretical framework has received nominal attention in the broader international marketing strategy or global marketing standardization literature.

Like segmentation, the concept of strategic fit is closely linked to performance. Lemak and Arunthanes (1997) have noted that higher levels of performance in global markets depend largely on the firm's selection of a global strategy that is appropriate for its unique set of circumstances. Within the context of standardized international marketing strategy, coalignment or fit between strategy and its environmental context has positive implications for business performance (cf., Ginsberg and Venkatraman 1985; Venkatraman and Prescott 1990).

ANTECEDENTS OF INTERNATIONAL MARKETING STANDARDIZATION

The standardization literature highlights a large number of factors that serve as antecedents

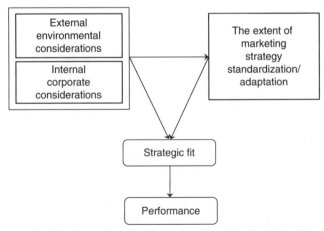

Figure 15.2   A conceptualization of contingency theory as the basis for international marketing strategy standardization–adaptation

of the marketing strategy standardization–adaptation decision. Antecedent measures have been fully discussed in a variety of publications. Jain's (1989) review of the literature, for example, highlights five groups of antecedents to standardization: target market (geographic area and economic factors), market position (market development, market conditions, and competition), nature of product (type of product and product positioning), environmental factors (physical environment, legal environment, political environment, and marketing infrastructure), and organization factors (corporate orientation, headquarter–subsidiary relationship, delegation of authority). In their review of the standardization literature, Theodosiou and Leonidou (2003) identify 25 studies that have explored the role of factors driving international marketing standardization, 15 of which established a direct link. However, only a few environmental factors have exhibited a systematic significant impact on standardization (Theodosiou and Leonidou 2003). The literature contains several review articles that provide an excellent coverage of contributions that have enriched our understanding of international marketing standardization. Rather than offering a redundant coverage of the topic, in the sections that follow we shall focus on providing greater depth along several key determinants of international marketing strategy choice.

The nature of the product

The character of a product has a profound impact on the extent to which its international marketing strategy can be standardized. Goods and services destined for consumer markets are much more susceptible to differences in lifestyle, customs and traditions, and other social and cultural factors. Additionally, regulatory systems are more likely to address issues concerning consumer products before attempting to extend such protection to business markets (for example, personal privacy issues, consumer product safety regulations, and laws governing advertising to children and the elderly) (Johnson and Arunthanes 1995; Katsikeas *et al.* 2006). As such, marketing strategy adaptation is often a matter of necessity in consumer markets. In contrast, the need for and the usage of industrial products are more likely to be cross-culturally similar than is the case for consumer products. In addition, purchase processes and decisions for business products are rational, policy-driven, and much less susceptible to emotional influences. This propensity should not be construed as the basis for a purely standardized international marketing strategy for business markets. Significant worldwide differences across consumer and business goods and services make this dimension a critical aspect of decisions regarding global marketing strategy standardization.

In general, business products tend to meet universal requirements and, thus, are said to be more suitable for standardization (Boddewyn *et al.* 1986; Levitt 1983; Jain 1989). Greater similarity across business markets worldwide only implies that standardized marketing programs for these markets are more likely. It is a foregone conclusion that all programs have to be extended to some degree, even if only minimally, to each local market. In the case of marketing of business products, for example, there is greater reliance on push strategies (e.g., personal selling) (Gegenheimer 1998). In the case of consumer markets, on the other hand, advertising tends to play a more prominent role in their marketing strategies (*Advertising Age,* 1998). Given the presence of considerable consumer differences across national boundaries, the decision to standardize advertising for consumer goods and services is much more challenging. In particular, the environment and customer characteristics in Asian markets are markedly different from those in the United States and Europe (cf., Mueller 1992) where the majority of MNCs are headquartered.

It is noteworthy that firms' choice of a standardized or adapted global marketing strategy is largely a function of the management's view of the extent of similarity of marketing environments in the home and host markets. Samiee and Roth's (1992) examination of global industries producing products for B2B markets, for example, found that, although all industries included in the sample were global and subject to similar global competitive forces, only 47 per cent of responding SBUs felt that industry conditions were globally similar and, subsequently, pursued a more standardized marketing strategy. It is likely that for these firms technical, cosmetic, service, and other adaptations are seen as necessary for successful penetration of international markets. Differences in purchasing processes and policies may also require that marketing plans be adapted to match local market conditions for industrial products.

High-technology business markets offer an excellent context to demonstrate the propensity to standardize marketing strategies in business markets (Samiee and Roth 1992; Katsikeas *et al.* 2006). New products in high technology markets tend to be capital-intensive, short-lived, and highly competitive. Such a combination demands that globally standardized marketing strategies be devised from the inception, and products be rapidly distributed worldwide to swiftly reduce per unit overhead. Each generation integrated circuits, for example, requires significant investments in clean rooms, retooling, retraining, as well as switch-over time. When technology is short-lived, as is the case in much of the electronics industry, and each new cycle represents a major change, firms concentrate their global manufacturing to one or few facilities, because with every change the factory(ies) has to be redesigned from the ground up (Samiee and Roth 1992). These conditions make the deployment of globally standardized marketing strategies imperative. It is easy to misinterpret the extent to which technological change exerts pressure upon firms to use a standardized marketing strategy, particularly when functions performed by the final

product remain largely the same. Consider, for example, surface-mount technology in the electronics industry which, on the one hand, required a complete retooling of equipment as well as systems and procedures for manufacturing and, on the other hand, required that both suppliers and customers retool their manufacturing systems. For example, manufacturers of IC ceramic casings, such as Kyocera, had to make significant investments in the design and manufacture of equipment capable of complying with the specifications of surface mount technology. Concurrently, the entire supply chain had to continue to supply replacement parts for the older generation of manufacturing systems for an extended period; that is, the introduction and the adoption of new technologies by firms are not always concurrent. These conditions explain the periodic volatility in prices of memory chips. In order to at least partially recover their overheads, firms slash prices to stimulate demand. During such periods manufacturers lose money, but it becomes necessary to retain their competitive positions and, importantly, to at least partially recover their very high overheads.

As noted earlier, consumer markets are substantially influenced by local sociocultural elements, customs and traditions, and lifestyles. These and other forces prompt consumer firms to modify their strategies in markets abroad to match local market conditions. Reassured by success in their home markets, coupled with the promise of significant cost savings, there is a tendency among many firms to extend local strategies to markets abroad (Agins 2007, Lyons 2007). The use of this approach by Home Depot and Wal-Mart, for example, led to significant problems for these giant retailers in vastly different markets of Asia, Europe, and Latin America (Bianchi and Arnold 2004; Lyons 2007). Local market conditions eventually forced both firms to leave markets in which relatively standardized strategies were imposed. Both firms amassed substantial losses in the process. In contrast, when Hilfiger decided to enter the European market in 2003, it did so with an entirely new approach and marketing strategy developed to cater to European consumers (Agins 2007). As a result, Hilfiger Denim stores, as they are called in Germany, are designed from ground up to be local. With 34 stores in Europe, the product lines, as well as other critical components of the marketing program are made to match local tastes and preferences. Hilfiger Denim stores do not share any products with their counterparts in North America, the firm's home market. Among Hilfiger's various customization measures is the establishment of a design center in Amsterdam dedicated to meeting the tastes of European markets. The objective of the center's 37 employees is to create collections that adapt the Hilfiger look for more sophisticated, upscale European audiences. Ultimately, Hilfiger's design center gives recognition to local differences in market segments to which the firm is trying to appeal: more luxury products for the Italian market (e.g., leather jackets and cashmere sweaters); more conservative and higher-quality, higher-priced clothing for the German market; and so on (Agins 2007). To compete with European premium jeans brands (e.g., Diesel, Replay, and G-Star), Hilfiger features slim-fitting jeans hanging on butcher's meat hooks and are priced three times higher than their men's jeans for the US market. Even the stores' presentation and decor are adapted to European tastes. Hilfiger stores in Europe have dark-stained wood floors and mink-gray walls in contrast to white walls and brightly lit interiors in the US stores. The European distribution network includes 4,500 small retailers, a segment to which the firm does not serve in the USA. To cater for these small shops, they opened 21 regional showrooms featuring sample lines of merchandise. This is unlike the centralized distribution method used by many American firms in Europe.

Similar examples come from a range of durable and non-durable consumer goods around the world. LG Electronics has been extremely successful in adapting its products to the needs and tastes of local markets, capturing significant market shares in host countries and, importantly, winning the hearts of consumers. LG attempts to develop a good understanding of local markets through research, manufacturing, and marketing. The introduction of the 'kimchi' refrigerator in its home market provides a good example of LG's sensitivity to local market tastes and preferences. LG's kimchi refrigerators are specifically designed to prevent the pungent odor associated with various kimchi (which permeate other foods stored in the refrigerator). The product has become a staple fixture in 65 per cent of Korean homes while forcing competitors such as Samsung to offer similar models. LG's local adaptation strategy has made it the leader in virtually every product they offer in India, a surprising accomplishment given that the firm entered the market in 1997 (Esfahani 2005). As is the case for Hilfiger in Europe, LG set up local research and design facilities, manufacturing plants, and a network of service centers for India. To meet the requirements of Indian consumers, LG developed refrigerators with larger vegetable and water storage compartments, surge-resistant power supplies, and brightly colored finishes that reflect local preferences (e.g., red in the south, green in Kashmir). LG also markets a line of Indian microwaves with dark interiors designed to mask food stains. LG also introduced a television for cricket fans that came with a built-in cricket video game. Its Ballad television was offered with extra loud sound after research showed that many Indians use their TVs to listen to music as well. Over time, these efforts have paid off. In some categories (e.g., washing machines) LG's market share is over twice as large as its nearest competitor.

Reassured by its success in Korea and India, LG has expanded its adaptation strategy to an increasing number of markets. In Iran, where the firm commands a 40 per cent share of the microwave oven market, it has incorporated a skewer rack in its ovens for preparing and a pre-set button for reheating kebabs, a favorite local cuisine. In Saudi Arabia

LG's Primian refrigerator features a special compartment for storing dates, a fruit that spoils easily. In Russia the company offers a karaoke phone, which can store and replay 100 songs and lyrics and serves as a portable entertainment device. Finally, catering to an opulent Middle Eastern audience, LG has developed and markets an $80,000 gold-plated flat-screen TV (Esfahani 2005). The marketing strategy adaptation strategy pursued by LG Electronics has won the support of local consumers across an array of developed and emerging markets.

The wide-ranging differences demonstrated by these examples may suggest the absence of or the difficulties associated with identifying consumer intermarket segments. Product categories that have similar use and appeal across national boundaries are ideal candidates for marketing standardization. Soft drinks, luxury items (e.g., fine watches and jewelry), perfumes, and distilled liquor, for example, tend to have universal appeals, uses, and market positions. Therefore, the deployment of standardized international marketing strategies appears to be more appropriate for such products.

Organization factors

Two organization factors are influential upon a preference for a standardized strategy: management's international orientation and centralization of decision-making. In general, both ethnocentric tendencies and a global orientation may lead to a standardized marketing strategy. Ethnocentric firms, confident with their 'proven' domestic strategy, simply extend home marketing practices to international markets as they enter them, thus standardizing their marketing strategies by default. These firms are also characterized by a relatively tight control by the headquarters. Exporters, particularly smaller ones, generally use a similar approach in international markets. Adaptations to marketing strategies are made only to the extent demanded by customers or import laws of host markets

(e.g., technical or safety standards). Dow (2006), for example, found that exporters, by following a status quo approach, tend to sub-optimally adapt to local markets. However, centralization of command and control is a characteristic of such firms; Özsomer, Bodur and Cavusgil (1991) reported a significant relationship between centralization and the use of standardized marketing strategies in smaller subsidiaries.

MNCs with global mindsets, on the other hand, attempt to strike a balance between standardized strategy prerequisites and their global intermarket segment conditions. These firms develop and market global products, using uniform branding and corresponding marketing strategies in relevant markets in a highly coordinated fashion. IBM, for example, is a global firm that has been organized around the industries it serves. The firm's industry groups are headquartered in different locations around the globe: banking and finance in Austria, retail and distribution in the UK, manufacturing in the US, and so on. In addition, IBM's multinational customers, e.g., ExxonMobil, are assigned to dedicated global account management teams that provide global solutions for clients' global problems. Such firms are rationally organized to provide centrally coordinated marketing programs, but with sufficient local, industry-centered, and customer-related latitude to address market needs. The relationship between international marketing standardization and globalization is depicted in Figure 15.3.

Unlike IBM which is exclusively focused on business markets, consumer-based globally minded firms must adjust to local customs, traditions, culture, and economic conditions. Yet they standardize as much of their products and processes as possible. P&G represents an excellent example of a firm vying to become as global as possible. The firm is cognizant that success in local markets hinges upon meeting local economic conditions, tastes and preferences, and hygiene practices. Oftentimes, the only part of a product that can be extended is the

Figure 15.3   The relationship between international marketing strategy standardization and globalization.
Source: Adated with modification from Yip (2003)

brand name. P&G's Crest toothpaste for the Chinese market, for example, has little other than its brand in common with Crest toothpastes marketed elsewhere. Product constituents, positioning, advertising message, and distribution are different in China. To a casual observer, however, P&G has globally standardized the marketing of Crest, whereas in reality only the brand name is internationally standardized.

Environment

These measures include a broad spectrum of economic, sociocultural, political, legal, and physical forces which have an influence, either direct or indirect, on international business operations. The importance of environmental factors lies in the belief that the greater the similarity between home and host environments the greater the likelihood of successful implementation of a standardized international marketing strategy (Jain 1989). Although intuitively it appears evident that these are important drivers of standardization, the empirical results have been mixed. In some cases, such environmental factors as regulations severely restrict the firm's ability to deploy a standardized strategy (Johnson and Arunthanes 1995; Katsikeas *et al.* 2006). The literature has addressed legal and economic considerations to a much higher degree than others, whereas sociocultural and physical aspects have been largely ignored (Theodosiou and Leonidou 2003). Fewer than half of the relationships between

environmental factors and strategy standardization (18 out of 43) examined in the literature resulted in significant results. These findings seemingly contradict the traditional view that environment is the driving force behind marketing strategy standardization.

THE MNC HEADQUARTERS VS. THE SUBSIDIARY PERSPECTIVE

The extant literature addressing international marketing standardization had a virtual focus on MNC headquarters as the source of information and indisputable knowledge regarding how international marketing strategies are formulated and implemented. For much of the time since the publication of Elinder's article, no effort was made to either gather information at the local level or validate data gathered at the headquarters by involving subsidiary management. This narrow focus led some authors (e.g., Dunn 1976; Onkvisit and Shaw 1987) to lament the reliability of data gathered from the headquarters of multinational, multi-divisional, and multi-product/brand firms. In retrospect an exclusive focus on the MNC headquarters is scientifically indefensible. Although the MNC home office plays a predominant role in charting the firm's strategic posture, studies focusing on the headquarters implicitly assume successful communication and implementation of strategic plans at the subsidiary level, in addition to complete executive knowledge of matters pertaining to dozens of subsidiaries subjected to different environmental conditions.

During the past decade, an increasing number of contributions have used data gathered at the subsidiary level which have provided significant insights regarding subsidiary perceptions, activities, and roles in international marketing standardization. Standardization decisions typically incorporate local conditions (Özsomer *et al.* 1991) and organizational imperatives which are not effectively articulated at the headquarters within the context of typical data collection effort. Key studies of marketing standardization that have attempted to unfold the subsidiary perspective include Özsomer *et al.* (1991), Hewett and Bearden (2001), Samiee *et al.* (2003), and Katsikeas *et al.* (2006). It is noteworthy that early attempts to query the subsidiary perspective (e.g., Özsomer *et al.* 1991) were motivated by calls for studies involving firms outside of North America and Europe rather than being justified on the basis of validating headquarters' points of view. Although dyadic studies of standardization (simultaneous contrasting of headquarters–subsidiary perspective) are yet to be conducted, subsidiary-level data suggest that information gathered from the headquarters is not always accurate or complete.

Greater attention to subsidiary-level strategy is of critical importance because subsidiaries must necessarily respond to local target markets and competition which are often difficult to address at the MNCs headquarters. As a result, MNCs tend to offer a mix of global, regional, and local brands. Additionally, local affiliates, particularly those catering to consumers, are better informed regarding local market opportunities for market expansion, for example, by acquiring successful local brands as an avenue for deeper penetration of local or regional markets. Nestlé is a prime example of an MNC in pursuit of successful local brands. The firm offers a staggering 8,000 brands, many of which were acquired in various markets around the world. In the United States, for example, Nestlé markets Stouffer's frozen foods, a firm

that it acquired three decades ago and which remains exclusively North American. Likewise, even though the Colgate brand of toothpaste is globally standardized (some variations exist in certain markets), its advanced Gum Protection Formula is marketed in only a handful of nations. Further, despite the global success of its Colgate brand, the firm acquired the Hong Kong-based Hawley & Hazel, the manufacturer of the regionally successful toothpaste, Darkie (renamed Darlie). After over two decades of owning the brand, it still is only a regional brand for Colgate. MNCs maintain a range of marketing approaches and strategies in local markets. Informants at the headquarters are useful sources of data in the broader context of global standardization decisions; however, accurate information regarding the full range of subsidiary activities at the headquarters is unlikely.

UNIT OF ANALYSIS AND MARKETING STANDARDIZATION

The preceding discussion highlights the critical importance of the unit of analysis in exploring international marketing standardization. Given the complexity of MNCs' scope of global operations and the involved nature of international marketing plans, the possibility of encountering a partial, non-representative view of the firm's international strategic thrust, depending on the unit of analysis employed in the investigation, can be high. To be viable, an assessment of international marketing strategy should be ecologically correct. Firms tend to offer different product mixes in various markets. In addition, a firm's product mix in a given market may include a number of local brands. It is a foregone conclusion that a standardized marketing strategy precludes local products/brands. However, a more serious consideration is that a firm may pursue a standardized strategy for some products in some markets, but simultaneously use an adaptation strategy in other markets. Thus, a fully rationalized and ecologically correct unit of analysis should be of prime concern in standardization research.

To date, a large proportion of studies on standardization has focused on export ventures (i.e., respondents are asked to focus on an export market(s)), MNCs, or host-market subsidiaries as the unit of analysis. An explicit assumption behind collecting firm-level data (i.e., the firm as the unit of analysis) is that firms pursue a single or a predominant strategy in all markets in which they compete. In reality, however, this practice applies to only a very small proportion of firms.

Some studies of standardization have focused on export transactions (e.g., the latest transaction, the largest transaction or customer, or a combination thereof incorporating the firm's most important export market). Although transaction as the unit of analysis offers clear conceptual advantages over firm-level data, it too has some restrictions. First, an assessment of marketing strategies implemented at the local level implies that the firm is able to coordinate and control marketing activities at the local level. A high level of coordination and control is unlikely without a market presence. Although MNCs supply some markets through exporting, they tend to have a presence in their key markets and, hence, know their markets well. Marketing strategy standardization is more relevant in markets where the firm has market presence. Since local market presence is not an issue for many exporters (that is, market entry via exporting tends to make local presence unnecessary), there is a high potential for information asymmetry between the host market and the exporter. Thus, the accuracy of information provided by respondents regarding exactly what is being done in host markets is open to question. Second, given the diversity of host markets and the range of products that are likely exported, validity and reliability of the information provided are open to question. Third, exporting often involves a longer distribution channel and limited control in

and knowledge of what exactly is happening in host markets. Thus, exporters may not be fully aware of host market environments or the strategies being implemented there. Finally, an active exporter may have dozens of customers and adapt its products for some (e.g., for their single largest market or importing customer), but generally standardize marketing activities for other markets or customers.

Given the range of products, brands, and strategies in place around the world, the MNC, the SBU (strategic business unit), and export transactions as units of analysis is less likely to yield accurate information regarding international standardization practices. As such, a product-level analysis is likely to best reflect the extent to which an MNC is pursuing an internationally standardized marketing strategy. Studies focusing on a single MNC product or line as the unit of analysis have been relatively recent and rare (e.g., Katsikeas *et al.* 2006). Although product-level analyses of MNCs' marketing strategies can best describe the extent of standardized strategies being implemented, they tend to shield the broader global marketing activities of MNCs. For example, the global brand and standardized strategy of a firm may constitute only a small proportion of its international activities. Thus, studies that use an internationally marketed product as their unit of analysis and concurrently provide a macro-profile of the MNC's scope of international marketing activities, are needed to provide more complete pictures of firms' international marketing strategies.

THE INFLUENCE OF MNC'S COUNTRY OF ORIGIN

There is evidence of national tendencies to pursue particular strategic approaches in markets abroad (Davidson 1989). Evidence in the international business literature further demonstrates that MNCs based in different countries manage their global networks and subsidiaries differently, for example with regard to the autonomy of local management teams, marketing practices, shared vision, operational methods, and foreign direct investment (e.g., Samiee 1987; Hennart and Larimo 1998; Johansson and Nonaka 1996; Murray, Wildt and Kotabe 1995). The international business literature hints at the greater independence of the subsidiaries of European and Japanese MNCs vis-à-vis the subsidiaries of US MNCs. Hill and James (1991), for example, found that US MNCs more aggressively pursued the transfer of their home market advertisements to markets abroad.

Greater perceived or real differences prompt MNCs from some countries to generally afford more decision making latitude in host market affiliates. This in part may be a function of the tendency to globalize as well as perceived or real differences between home and host markets (Bartlett and Ghoshal 1989; Johansson and Yip 1994; Yip 2003). A relatively high degree of international marketing standardization is essential in global strategies, even though the reverse does not necessarily follow. In general, one may expect that the variability in home-country environments may result in some degree of cross-national differences in global strategy. Japanese firms, for example, have been shown to behave differently than US companies insofar as pursuing a global strategy is concerned (Johansson and Yip 1994). Similarly, after comparing the effects of nationality on global strategy among European, Japanese, and US MNCs, Yip, Johansson and Roos (1997) conclude that firm nationality can have a significant influence in adopting various aspects of global strategy.

Despite the evidence hinting at strategic and operational differences based on MNCs' countries of origin, the issue has received scant attention with respect to international marketing standardization. One study exploring advertising standardization demonstrated that propensity to pursue standardization varies significantly across US, European, and Japanese MNCs (Samiee et al. 2003). The extent to which such national origin differences are linked to policy and operational patterns, for example, greater centralization of authority, has yet to be explored.

PERFORMANCE CONSIDERATIONS

The appropriateness of any international marketing strategy, whether standardized or adapted, ultimately depends on how well it will realize corporate goals and objectives. Within the context of marketing strategy standardization, MNC objectives are often financial in nature. The literature has persistently acknowledged the importance of performance in choosing a particular strategy, whether standardized or adapted (e.g., Buzzell 1968; Keegan 1969). However, the issue was first explicitly stressed as a pivotal issue in the strategy choice process by Jain (1989). It appears that potential cost savings associated with standardization were thought to address the financial performance considerations, even though there is no empirical evidence linking strategy standardization to lower costs or improved performance. An important contribution of Jain (1989) is his conceptualization of strategy standardization (dependent variable) as a function of performance (independent variable).

The primary motivation behind the pursuit of a standardized strategy across markets is greater efficiency and, ultimately, lower costs. Cost savings may include economies of scale in: (1) research and development (Buzzell 1968; Keegan 1969), (2) purchasing (Douglas and Wind 1987), (3) production (Keegan 1969; Douglas and Wind 1987), (4) marketing (Buzzell 1968; Keegan 1969; Green et al. 1975; Onkvisit and Shaw 1987), (5) the possibility of rationalizing international production and sourcing (Carapellotti and Samiee 1984), and (6) operating via exports (Keegan 1969). Also, implicit in many economies and advantages favoring a standardized program is easier implementation and management of a single (or a group of related) program(s). In addition, standardization offers more control over marketing programs (Green *et al.* 1975; Walters 1986). Presumably the greater ease of implementation, coordination, and control of globally standardized marketing programs leads to more efficient management and, hence, improved financial performance. Arguments stressing greater efficiency and lower costs (e.g., Levitt 1983), however, miss a key point. Lower costs are not the primary objective of MNCs; instead, firms seek increased profitability. Lower costs result in higher profits only under the assumption of relatively fixed global, industry-wide prices. According to economic theory underlying market segmentation, greater profitability in global markets for MNCs is achieved through relative pricing freedom through the identification and cultivation of intermarket segments.

Samiee and Roth's (1992) groundbreaking investigation on the performance consideration of marketing standardization filled a critical gap in the marketing standardization literature. Their investigation was conducted within the context of global industries, which are governed by similar conditions worldwide. In their conceptualization, global industries constituted an intermarket segment which is conceptually appropriate for standardization. However, given the nature of global industries, no difference in performance should be expected regardless of whether MNCs view their intermarket segments as conducive to standardization or adaptation strategies.[3] Samiee and Roth's (1992) empirical results supported this position. Eighteen empirical studies have been published since 1992 (Theodosiou and Leonidou 2003). Another five studies have been published since 2003. The majority of these studies deal with standardization within the context of exporting strategies or transactions. A few focus on MNC activities with three studies examining the issue at the subsidiary level (Hewett and Bearden 2001; Özsomer and Simonin 2004; Katsikeas *et al.* 2006). In particular, Katsikeas *et al.* (2006), using strategy

coalignment as their theoretical base, demonstrated for the first time that arguments for or against a particular international marketing strategy (whether standardization or adaptation) are moot because it is how well the strategy fits the host market environmental context that yields superior performance. An important contribution of Katsikeas *et al.* (2006) is that their conceptual framework only indirectly links performance to strategy. Despite recommendations in the literature (e.g., Jain 1989), the majority of studies conceptualize performance as the dependent variable rather then an independent variable (that is, performance is viewed as a function of standardization strategy; whereas the choice of standardization should ideally be viewed as a function performance). Direct links between the international marketing strategy construct and performance have yielded divergent results, which is the basis for the standardization–adaptation controversy.

CONCLUDING REMARKS

Strategy standardization is one of the most debated and researched topics in international marketing. The numerous studies published on this topic since the early 1960s have certainly enhanced our understanding of the environmental, organizational, and other contingency factors that determine the appropriateness of international marketing standardization. Moreover, in recent years an increasing number of methodologically sound empirical studies have investigated the crucial relationship between standardization and performance. However, few conclusive framework(s) about marketing standardization have emerged. The contribution by Katsikeas *et al.* (2006) applies the strategy coalignment concept to marketing standardization (or adaptation) and offers a sound theoretical and practical approach for viewing its appropriateness.

International marketing strategy, or marketing strategy for that matter, is generally investigated in isolation and without regard to the firm's global scope of operations, capabilities, or strategy. A decision regarding an internationally standardized or adapted strategy impacts other key policy areas within the firm (Samiee and Roth 1992). Marketing activities are dependent on other functions in the firm (e.g., manufacturing) which are managed and controlled elsewhere in the organization. For instance, to achieve economies of scale from standardization, MNCs centralize their production in large manufacturing plants which are situated in only one or a few locations. Such plants are relatively inflexible and make it difficult for a company to respond when there is change in market demand or important shifts in competition. Moreover, in such globally rationalized systems, power and control over marketing strategies are concentrated at corporate headquarters. Consequently, local entrepreneurship is eliminated and local managers are unable to respond effectively to changes in local market conditions. Thus, MNCs need to develop appropriate mechanisms for intelligence gathering at the local market level and for information and knowledge transfer between headquarters and host market operations, irrespective of whether or not the firm is represented by a subsidiary. The effective coordination and control of business operations conducted in dispersed geographical areas across the globe, either internally (e.g., a subsidiary) or by external partners (e.g., importer, channel intermediaries), is a critically important issue that requires closer attention by researchers and international marketing managers.

It is also worthwhile to revisit aspects of Levitt's (1983) propositions regarding the globalization of markets. There is little question that people are more globally in touch than ever before. International travel, the Internet, cheaper and greater ease of communications, as well as greater international reach of products all contribute to a larger global segment in the world population than ever before. The dialogue and point of contention resulting from the publication of

Levitt's (1983) contribution was largely centered on the extent to which worldwide customers and, therefore, markets are uniform and ripe for standardization. Ideally, the diametrically opposing positions regarding either the dominance of globalization (or homogenizers) or localization forces (or heterogenizers) should converge on the notion of 'glocalization' in which globalization drivers and local conditions create complex cultural settings (Robertson 1995; Singh, Nijssen and Holzmüller 2004). Glocalization, however, should be of no comfort to the international marketing manager because it implies a chaotic mix of preferences and traits. The glocalization hypothesis implies that, while customers share some characteristics, they are also independent along potentially critical marketing measures about which the firm cannot have a priori knowledge. In the end, an appropriate strategy for a given market has to incorporate local market imperatives, a notion that is consistent with the results reported by Katsikeas et al. (2006) that suggest a significant relationship between performance and strategic fit.

The ultimate yardstick for the appropriateness of any international marketing strategy is performance. Standardization is thus appropriate only to the extent to which it directly contributes to achieving optimum performance. However, this results-oriented view can be misleading because the strategy devised, whether standardized or adapted, itself must fit a very dynamic international environmental context in which it is implemented. This suggests that the homogeneity of a given intermarket segment which makes it ripe for a standardized marketing approach can and will shift across markets to varying degrees, thus necessitating more rapid international strategy planning cycles than would be expected in a domestic setting. International marketing managers and academic researchers should keep abreast of environmental changes across countries and regions so that the extent of homogeneity within its intermarket segments does not fall below the acceptable baseline.

NOTES

1 An intermarket segment is defined as the presence of a well-defined homogeneous cluster of customers across national boundaries that exhibit similar characteristics and which are identified by using similar criteria.

2 Market segmentation leverages off the theory of monopolistic competition whereby firms can gain relative pricing freedom and, thereby, become a quasi-monopolist (see Claycamp and Massy 1968). The competitive advantage offered to the firm using market segmentation can be significant in its targeted segments, as it enables firms to price their products with relative freedom from their competitors. Such pricing freedom should lead to higher margins and, in theory, optimize financial performance. A focus on narrower markets also permits firms to anticipate and react to market changes more effectively, leading to a higher level of customer loyalty.

3 Given the competitive intensity and the relatively homogeneous customer requirements of intermarket segments in which global industry SBUs compete, standardization offers the advantage of lower costs, whereas adaptation provides higher costs but improved offer attractiveness which should lead to somewhat higher volume and/or margins. As a result, margins for either standardized or adapted strategies are likely to remain about the same. Samiee and Roth (1992) offer empirical evidence for this. O'Donnell and Jeong (2000), on the other hand, reported a positive relationship between standardization and performance for firms emphasizing high-technology industrial products within global industries.

REFERENCES

Agins, T. (2007) 'Costume change: for US fashion firms, a global makeover', *The Wall Street Journal*, 2 February, A1.

Advertising Age (1998) '100 Leaders by US advertising spending', 28 September, 69 (39): S4.

Bartels, R. (1968) 'Are domestic and international marketing dissimilar?', *Journal of Marketing*, 32 (July): 56–61.

Bartlett C. A. and Ghoshal S. (1989) *Managing Across Borders: The Transnational Solution*. Cambridge, MA: Harvard Business School Press.

Bianchi, C. C. and Arnold, S. J. (2004) 'An institutional perspective on retail internationalization success: Home Depot in Chile', *The International Review of Retail, Distribution and Consumer Research*, 14(2): 149–169.

Boddewyn, J. J., Soehl, R. and Picard, J. (1986) 'Standardization in international marketing: is Ted Levitt in fact right?', *Business Horizons*, 29 (November–December): 69–75.

Buzzell, R. (1968) 'Can you standardize multinational marketing?', *Harvard Business Review*, 46 (November–December): 102–113.

Carapellotti, L. and Samiee, S. (1984) 'The use of portfolio models for production rationalization in multinational firms', *International Marketing Review*, 1(3): 5–13.

Claycamp, H. J. and Massy, W. F. (1968) 'A theory of market segmentation', *Journal of Marketing Research*, November, 5(4): 388–394.

Davidson, W. H. (1989) 'Impact of trade policies on multinational operations', in T. Agmon and C. R. Hekman (eds.), *Trade Policy and Corporate Business Decisions*. New York: Oxford University Press.

Douglas, S. P. and Wind, Y. (1987) 'The myth of globalization', *Columbia Journal of World Business*, 12 (Winter): 19–29.

Dow, D. (2006) 'Adaptation and performance in foreign markets: evidence of systematic under-adaptation', *Journal of International Business Studies*, March, 37(2): 212–226.

Dunn, S. W. (1976) 'Effect of national identity on multinational promotional strategy in Europe', *Journal of Marketing*, 40 (October): 50–57.

Elinder, E. (1961) 'How international can advertising be?', *International Advertiser* (December), 12–16.

Engel, J. F., Fiorillo, H. F. and Cayley, M. A. (1972). *Market Segmentation: Conceptions and Application*. New York: Holt, Rinehart and Winston, Inc.

Esfahani, E. (2005) 'Thinking locally, succeeding globally', Business 2.0, December. http://money. cnn.com/magazines/business2/business2_archive/2005/12/01/8364622/index.htm

Fatt, A. C. (1964) 'A multinational approach to international advertising', *International Advertiser* (September): 17–20.

Frank, R. E. and Massy, W. P. (1965) 'Market segmentation and the effectiveness of a brand's price and dealing policies', *Journal of Business*, April, 38(2): 186–200.

Gegenheimer, C. L. (1998) 'Total B-to-B Ad Spending Hits $3.49 Billion', *Business Marketing*, September, 83(9): 19–20.

Ginsberg, A. and Venkantraman, N. (1985) 'Contingency perspectives of organizational strategy: a critical review of the empirical research', *Academy of Management Review*, 10, 421–434.

Green, R. T., Cunningham, W. H. and Cunningham, I. C. (1975) 'The effectiveness of standardized global advertising', *Journal of Advertising*, 4 (Summer): 25–30.

Hennart, J.-F. and Larimo, J. (1998) 'The impact of culture on the strategy of multinational enterprises: does national origin affect ownership decisions?', *Journal of International Business Studies*, 29(3): 515–538.

Henzler, H. and Rall, W. (1986) 'Facing up to the globalization challenge', *McKinsey Quarterly*, (Winter): 52–68.

Hewett, K. and Bearden, W. O. (2001) 'Dependence, trust and relational behavior on the part of foreign subsidiary marketing operations: implications for managing global marketing operations', *Journal of Marketing*, 65 (October): 51–60.

Hill, J. S. and James, W. L. (1991) 'Product and promotion transfers in consumer goods multinationals', *International Marketing Review*, 8(2): 6–17.

Hout, T., Porter, M. E. and Rudden, E. (1982) 'How Global Companies Win Out', *Harvard Business Review*, 60 (September–October), 98–105.

Jain, S. (1989) 'Standardization of international marketing strategy: some research hypotheses', *Journal of Marketing*, (January): 70–79.

Johansson, J. K. and Nonaka, I. (1996) *Relentless: The Japanese Way of Marketing*. New York: Harper Business.

Johansson, J. K. and Yip, G. S. (1994) 'Exploiting globalization potential: US and Japanese strategies', *Strategic Management Journal*, October: 579–601.

Johnson, J. L. and Arunthanes, W. (1995) 'Ideal and actual product adaptation in US exporting firms: market related determinants and impact on performance', *International Marketing Review*, 12(3): 31–46.

Kale, S. H. and Sudharshan, D. (1987) 'A strategic approach to international segmentation', *International Marketing Review*, 4 (Summer): 60–71.

Katsikeas, C. S., Samiee, S. and Theodosiou, M. (2006) 'Strategy fit and performance consequences of international marketing standardization', *Strategic Management Journal*, 27, 867–890.

Keegan, W. J. (1969) 'Multinational product planning: strategic alternatives', *Journal of Marketing*, 33 (January): 58–62.

Killough, J. (1982) 'Improved payoffs from transnational advertising', *Harvard Business Review*, (July–August), 102–110.

Lemak, D. J. and Arunthanes, W. (1997) 'Global Business Strategy: A Contingency Approach', *Multinational Business Review*, 1, 26–38.

Levitt, T. (1983) 'The Globalization of Markets', *Harvard Business Review*, 61 (May–June): 92–102.

Lyons, J. (2007) 'Southern hospitality: in Mexico, Wal-Mart is defying its critics', *The Wall Street Journal*, March 5, A1.

Miles, R. E. and Snow, C. C. (1978) *Organization Strategy, Structure and Process*. New York: McGraw-Hill.

Mueller, B. (1992) 'Standardization vs. specialization: an examination of Westernization in Japanese advertising', *Journal of Advertising Research*, 32(1): 15–24.

Murray, J. Y., Wildt, A. R. and Kotabe, M. (1995) 'Global sourcing strategies of US subsidiaries of foreign multinationals', *Management International Review*, 35(4): October, 307–324.

O'Donnell, S. and Jeong, I. (2000) 'Marketing standardization within global industries: an empirical study of performance implications', *International Marketing Review*, 17(1): 19–33.

Onkvisit, S. and Shaw, J. J. (1987) 'Standardized international advertising: a review and critical evaluation of the theoretical and empirical evidence', *Columbia Journal of World Business*, (Fall): 43–55.

Özsomer, A. and Simonin, B. L. (2004) 'Marketing program standardization: a cross-country exploration', *International Journal of Research in Marketing*, 21(4): 397–419.

Özsomer, A., Bodur, M. and Cavusgil, S. T. (1991) 'Marketing standardisation by multinationals in an emerging market', *European Journal of Marketing*, 25(12): 50–64.

Peebles, D. M., Ryans, J. K. and Vernon, I. R. (1977) 'A new perspective on advertising standardization', *European Journal of Marketing*, 11(8): 569–576.

Robertson, R. (1995) 'Globalization: time-space and homogeneity-heterogeneity', in M. Featherstone, S. Lash, and R. Robertson (eds.), *Global Modernities*. London: Sage Publications, pp. 19–44.

Roostal, I. (1963) 'Standardization of advertising for Western Europe', *Journal of Marketing*, 27 (October): 15–20.

Rutenberg, D. P. (1982). *Multinational Management*. Boston: Little Brown & Company.

Ryans, J. K. (1969) 'Is it too soon to put a tiger in every tank?', *Columbia Journal of World Business*, 4 (March–April): 69–75.

Samiee, S., Jeong, I., Pae, J. H. and Tai, S. (2003) 'Advertising standardization in multinational corporations: the subsidiary perspective', *Journal of Business Research*, 56: 613–626.

Samiee, S. and Kendall Roth (1992) 'The influence of global marketing standardization on performance', *Journal of Marketing*, (April): 1–17.

Samiee, S. (1987) 'Pricing in marketing strategies of US and foreign-based companies', *Journal of Business Research*, 15, 17–30.

Sheth, J. N. (1986) 'Global markets or global competition?', *Journal of Consumer Marketing*, 3 (Spring): 9–11.

Shoham, A. (1996) 'Marketing-mix standardization: determinants of export performance', *Journal of Global Marketing*, 10(2): 53–73.

Simmonds, K. (1985) 'Global strategy: achieving the geocentric ideal', *International Marketing Review*, 2 (Spring): 8–17.

Singh, J. Nijssen, E. and Holzmüller, H. (2004) 'On cross-cultural research in international marketing: fundamental issues and new directions', Working Paper. Cleveland, Ohio: Case Western Reserve University.

Smith G. E., Venkatraman, M. P. and Wortzel, L. H. (1995) 'Strategic marketing fit in manufacturer–retailer relationships: price leaders versus merchandise differentiators', *Journal of Retailing*, 71(3): 297–315.

Sorenson, R. Z. and Wiechmann, U. E. (1975) 'How multinationals view marketing standardization', *Harvard Business Review*, 53 (May–June): 38.

Terpstra, V. (1967) *American Marketing in the Common Market*. New York: Praeger.

Theodosiou, M. and Leonidou, L. C. (2003) 'Standardization versus adaptation of international marketing strategy: an integrative assessment of the empirical research', *International Business Review*, 12, 141–171

Venkatraman, N. and Camillus, J. C. (1984) 'Exploring the concept of "fit" in strategic management', *The Academy of Management Review*, 9(3): 513–525.

Venkatraman, N. and Prescott, J. E. (1990) 'Environment-strategy coalignment: an empirical test of its performance implications', *Strategic Management Journal*, 11, 1–23.

Walters, P. G. P. (1986) 'International marketing policy: a discussion of the standardization construct and its relevance for corporate policy', *Journal of International Business Studies*, 17 (Summer): 55–69.

Wind, Y. (1986) 'The myth of globalization', *Journal of Consumer Marketing*, 3 (Spring): 23–26.

Xu, S., Cavusgil, S. T. and White, J. C. (2006) 'The impact of strategic fit among strategy, structure, and processes on multinational corporation performance: a multimethod assessment', *Journal of International Marketing*, 14(2): 1–31.

Yip, G. S., Johansson, J. K. and Roos, J. (1997) 'Effects of nationality on global strategy', *Management International Review*, 37(4): 365–385.

Yip, G. S. (2003) *Total Global Strategy II*. NJ: Prentice-Hall.

Developing Marketing Strategy

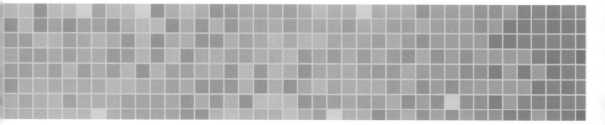

16

International Diffusion of
New Products

Trichy V. Krishnan and Suman Ann Thomas

INTRODUCTION

Our objective in this chapter is to highlight the academic research carried out in the area of new product diffusion in an international[1] context, discuss the key articles published in this area and suggest pointers for future research. We first provide a snapshot of the current level of the research activity, and then argue why it is important to do research in this area. Following that, we discuss the key published articles and record their findings. A collective analysis of those findings reveals that the extant research has not produced so far any strikingly intuitive or counter-intuitive insights that might challenge a product manager's traditional wisdom. We discuss reasons for the same and conclude the chapter, suggesting possible avenues for future research.

STATUS OF ACADEMIC RESEARCH ON INTERNATIONAL DIFFUSION

Although researchers have been talking about the adoption and diffusion of new products in the international context from the 1980s, the field gained tangible momentum in marketing with the article by Gatignon, Eliashberg and Robertson (1989)[2] article, where the authors analyzed the actual sales data of six products in 12 European countries and showed that countries with different socioeconomic factors did have different diffusion patterns for a given new product. This research article spurred a good amount of research in this area, as can be seen in Table 16.1.[3] After a slow start (1989–1995), it seems to be picking up speed in recent years, true to the diffusion phenomenon!

Now we will look at what makes analysis of international diffusion interesting and worthwhile to do.

WHY ANALYZE INTERNATIONAL DIFFUSION PATTERNS?

Adoption of a new consumer durable, especially a breakthrough product such as microwave oven and cellular phone, is a complex process. On the one hand, it depends on how convincingly the firm marketing the new product could convey the product's usefulness and value to the market. On the other hand, it depends on how quickly the

Table 16.1   Publications in international diffusion analysis

Year	Publications	Year	Publications	Year	Publications
1989	1	1995	1	2001	
1990		1996	2	2002	2
1991	1	1997	2	2003	2
1992		1998	2	2004	4
1993	1	1999	2	2005	4
1994	1	2000	3	2006,07	1

potential consumers could learn about it and evaluate its worth for their lifestyle. Further, and more importantly perhaps, because the product is not yet proven in the market place the potential consumers would like to clear their doubts regarding the product's actual performance and any potential side effects. However, they would not immediately strive to get their doubts cleared, unless of course the product is extremely essential to them. For many consumers, this uncertainty is likely to get resolved as they see the product in actual use with other consumers and/or get information from them on specific points of concern. This implies that the uncertainty will get cleared over time through word of mouth[4] and other socio-contagion processes. Note that a consumer's concern about uncertainty and the need for clearing it depends on how important the product is to him/her and whether s/he is capable of acquiring it. Since the degree of (or the concern for) such uncertainty varies from one potential consumer to another for a given new product, the eventual adoption process at the aggregate market level takes a unique pattern, which we call the diffusion pattern.

Thus, one can conclude that the diffusion of a new product in a given society is affected by the strategies used by the firm that markets the product, the nature of the product, the competitive situation in the market, and how the specific target consumers are predisposed to evaluating its usefulness and resolving their doubts through the socio-contagion processes such as word of mouth. The last-mentioned two factors imply that the diffusion of a new product is affected by the socioeconomic and cultural aspects of the society it is introduced in. Since countries differ from one another on

many dimensions, including social structure, cultural aspects and economic conditions, it is only natural to expect that a new product will experience different diffusion patterns in different countries. This is the first topic we will consider in this chapter. There are around ten research papers written on this topic.

It is important to recognize the subtle difference between 'adoption' and 'diffusion' in an international diffusion context. Consider a new product introduced in country A in year 2000. As it starts diffusing inside country A, it might be introduced into other countries B, C, D, etc. in subsequent years 2001, 2003, 2006 etc. After adoption takes place in a country, the product may take a few more years to diffuse fully within that country. Ignoring the diffusion process within each country, one can focus on the adoption timings alone (i.e., the years when the product was introduced in those countries) and analyze whether the socioeconomic and cultural aspects systematically affect those adoption timings.[5]

Similarly, some researchers look at the take-off period in the diffusion. This is the initial period in which the product is in some sort of incubation (i.e., with no major growth in sales). Here, researchers are interested in exploring when the product would eventually start growing rapidly, and how this take-off period is affected by the various social, economic and cultural factors of a country. Thus, we consider a second topic that concerns the adoption timing and take-off duration. There are around three research papers written on this second topic.

As will be shown later in detail, an important finding from the studies under the above-mentioned two topics is that countries where the new product is introduced later (than in the lead countries) have a higher diffusion speed. One possible reason for this could be that people learn about the new product from its performance in other countries and when it comes to their own country there is less uncertainty about the performance. So, they are more ready to accept it. This could also be due to the facts that multinational companies operating with their brand names and products in many countries spread the information across countries, consumers are very well aware of events happening in other countries through TV, internet, and sports events such as Euro Cup, World Cup and Olympics, and consumers frequently travel across countries and get to know about new products and brands in other countries. In other words, the world has been changing from being a conglomerate of multiple market places to one of a global market place. Thus there seems to be ample theoretical and empirical evidence to support the hypothesis that consumers in a country get influenced by a new product that is diffusing in another country, especially if the other country is a neighbor and/or culturally and economically closer. Some researchers attempt to capture this inter-country impact on the diffusion through building a systematic model and testing with actual sales data. This is the third topic we will see in this chapter. There are nine research papers that deal with this aspect of international diffusion.

Apart from the studies that come under these three topics, there are a few that we would like to classify as 'Miscellaneous'. These include meta-analyses, studies done in other areas but have some relevance to marketing, etc. Thus we have four topics to discuss. They are:

1 Does the *diffusion process*[6] differ across countries? Are these differences attributable to the cultural and other socioeconomic differences between the countries?[7]
2 Are the differences in *adoption timings* (by different countries) of a new product attributable to the cultural and other socioeconomic differences between the countries? (2a) Are the differences

in *take-off periods* (in different countries) of a new product attributable to the cultural and other socioeconomic differences between the countries?
3 How can we model and study the *inter-country diffusion impact*, i.e., the impact a new product diffusion process in one country has on the diffusion process in other countries?
4 Miscellaneous.

The managerial relevance of these topics is rather obvious and hence not elaborated here. The results from the various papers that are discussed here is consolidated and provided in the Appendix. Before we go further, however, we need to briefly explain the Bass (1969) model because it is the basic framework used in many studies and hence a clearer understanding of the Bass model would help the reader to easily comprehend the implications of various findings.

BASS MODEL (1969)

In his 1969 seminal paper, Bass synthesized the Roger's theory of innovation diffusion (Rogers 1961) with the following mathematical expression,

$$\frac{f(t)}{1 - F(t)} = p + qF(t), \tag{1}$$

which says that the probability that an individual would adopt a new product at time t given that he has not adopted until t depends on the cumulative number of adopters until t (i.e., $qF(t)$) and a constant term (i.e., p) that does not depend on the cumulative adoption. Bass labeled p and q as coefficients of innovation and imitation respectively. Later, people recognized p as also representing external communications such as advertising media that directly affect a consumer, and q as also representing internal communications such as word of mouth, network externalities and viral marketing. However, in this review paper, we are going to refer to them as simply p and q to avoid any misinterpretation.

Equation (1) can be written in other ways too.

$$S(t) = [M - Y(t-1)]\left[p + q\frac{Y(t-1)}{M}\right], \quad (2)$$

where $S(t)$ annual sales of a new product in a given market (or society), $Y(t-1)$ is the cumulative sales up to $t-1$, and M is the market potential for that product. Noting that $Y(t)/M$ is the penetration of the new product, and that $S(t) = Y(t) - Y(t-1)$, Equation (2) is rewritten as:

$$Y(t) - Y(t-1) = [M - Y(t-1)]\left[p + q\frac{Y(t-1)}{M}\right]. \quad (3)$$

Equation (3) allows researchers to normalize sales across countries of different sizes (say US and Belgium) because M, the market potential of a product, would naturally differ across countries as a direct function of the respective population sizes. The normalized version is given by Equation (4) below:

$$\frac{Y(t) - Y(t-1)}{M} = \left[1 - \frac{Y(t-1)}{M}\right]\left[p + q\frac{Y(t-1)}{M}\right]. \quad (4)$$

Here only p and q parameters will be estimated and M will be supplied by the researcher exogenously. Denoting $Y(t)/M$ by $X(t)$ and calling it penetration, Equation (4) becomes:

$$X'(t) = [1 - X(t)]\left[p + qX(t)\right]. \quad (5)$$

To get the penetration data, researchers divide the sales numbers by M, an exogenously estimated number, or simply the population size[8] of the country-concerned. Some market research companies such as Data Quest supply only these penetration figures (i.e., sales as a fraction of the population size) as data points, and hence Equation (5) comes handy in those situations. However, researchers sometimes explicitly use the population size of the respective countries to normalize the sales figures. Rewriting Equation (4) in a different way, we get:

$$\frac{Y(t) - Y(t-1)}{M_{pop}} = \left[\alpha - \frac{Y(t-1)}{M_{pop}}\right]\left[p + Q\frac{Y(t-1)}{M_{pop}}\right], \quad (6)$$

where M_{pop} is the population of the country under study, $\alpha = M/M_{pop}$ is the penetration ceiling that is achievable by the new product-under-study in the country, $Q = q\,M_{pop}/M$. If two countries were identical in all aspects except for the population size, then they both would experience the same diffusion pattern explained by Equation (6) for a given new product.

It is interesting to note that although researchers use different forms of the Bass model to achieve their results, only a few papers have used its closed-form expression. Not using the closed-form model could cause trouble because the multi-period forecasting ability is seriously hindered in the cumulative sales domain model.

REVIEW OF RESEARCH IN INTERNATIONAL DIFFUSION/ADOPTION

We will now discuss the research papers and their findings under each of the four topics explained earlier, namely, differences in diffusion process in various countries, differences in adoption time and take-off periods in different countries, inter-country diffusion impact, and miscellaneous.

Does the diffusion process differ across countries? Are these differences attributable to the cultural and other socioeconomic differences between the countries? *[10 studies]*

Researchers have been using two methods to answer this question. In the first method, which is the basic type, researchers collect sales data of a new category in multiple countries, fit a diffusion model on each country's data series separately and arrive at a set of parameters (namely, p and q) for each country. They then use t-test or a simple regression to analyze if those estimates statistically differ across the countries. They repeat this procedure with more products to find out whether the observed differences are directionally consistent (i.e., with respect to their sign) across the products tested.

In the second method, researchers explicitly model the country-specific factors (i.e., social, economic and cultural factors) to affect the diffusion process in their chosen models[9] and analyze their statistical significance and signs to infer their role on the diffusion. Under the second method, the role of country-specific factors is estimated simultaneously with the parameters of the diffusion model.

Method 1: The basic type   (4 out of the total 10 studies in Topic 1)

[1]   Takada and Jain (1991), using Equation (2), found that the USA systematically had a lower q than Japan, S. Korea and Taiwan when tested on 8 product categories. They also found that the lag countries[10] had a higher q (i.e., faster diffusion) than the lead countries.

[2]   Helsen, Jedidi and De Sarbo (1993) pooled penetration data across 11 countries (Japan, USA and some European countries).[11] They analyzed the data in two methods. In the first method, using Equation (5) and latent class segmentation approach (on p and q), they identified significantly differentiated clusters, i.e., differentiated on the diffusion parameters. They separately carried out a parallel segmentation among those countries using their social and economic factors as the clustering factors. On comparing the two segmentation results, the researchers could *not* find any similarities between the diffusion based segments and the socioeconomic factors based segments. They repeated this procedure with three consumer durable

products, but the results were the same. This made the researchers question the wisdom of using socioeconomic variables to choose countries with respect to analyzing new product diffusion.

In their second method, the researchers took countries pair wise and for each pair evaluated the differences in the p and q, and the differences in the socioeconomic factors. This enlarged the data set giving more degrees of freedom to test some hypotheses. Running the linear regression of estimates' differences on the factors' differences, the researchers report generally poor and directionally inconsistent results i.e., estimates had different signs in different products.

[3]   By using an almost similar methodology, Sundqvist, Frank and Puumalainen (2005), however, came up with different findings. They used data on annual wireless subscriptions in 25 countries[12] from 1981–2000 and estimated p, q and M for each country using the closed-form equivalent of the Bass model Equation (2). They used cultural distance of each lag country (Euclidean measure using Hofstede's four dimensions)[13] to form 4 clusters of countries. They evaluated the average p, q and M for each cluster and used ANOVA to check whether these significantly differ across the four clusters. They found that q and M did differ across the clusters! The researchers further regressed p, q, M and adoption year on per capita GDP and cultural distance (of lag country from the lead country). They found that countries that entered late had higher p (which somewhat supports a related finding in [1]), countries with higher uncertainty avoidance had higher q, and wealthy countries had higher m. Noting that this research used one product only and that is different from the products used by Helsen *et al.* (1993), it is difficult to say that the findings in these two research pieces contradict each other. One can however surely say that we don't have a result that can be generalized across various products. In other words, the net result is inconclusive.

[4]   Dwyer, Mesak and Hu (2005) followed the Helsen *et al.* (1993)'s second method

when they analyzed data on seven technology innovations from 13 European countries. They use Mansfield model, which is like a logistic model (i.e., Equation (1) without the p parameter)[14] to estimate q for each product-country combination. Averaging q's of the seven products for each country, and making pair-wise comparison (as in Helsen *et al.* 1993) they generate more data points that talk about the differences between countries pair-wise. Simultaneously, they use cultural dimensions (Hofstede 1991) to create the pair-wise distances between the countries. The resulting regression of diffusion estimates' differences on the cultural distances show that, while Individuality and Long-term Orientation reduces the diffusion rate, the Masculinity and Power Distance dimensions increase it. They also find that the per capita GDP increases the diffusion speed. Note that the results do not challenge the Helsen *et al.* (1993) results because these researchers use cultural factors while Helsen *et al.* use socioeconomic factors as explanatory variables. In other words, one could say that, while socioeconomic factors do not cause the differences in diffusion speed in two countries, the cultural factors seem to have some influence.[15]

Summarizing the findings from the four studies, we can say that the culturally different countries have different diffusion patterns, and that lag countries and wealthy countries (i.e., countries with a higher per capita GDP) have a faster diffusion speed. While it is insightful to analyze whether the cultural (and socioeconomic) differences between two countries run parallel to the differences in diffusion patterns, it would be more reliable to go one step ahead in establishing the causal connection between them. The following papers address that issue.

Method 2: Explicitly modeling the social, economic and cultural factors to affect the diffusion process (6 out of the total 10 studies in Topic 1)

[5] Gatignon *et al.* (1989) pooled a new product's sales data across 14 European countries and modeled the parameters p and q of each country as linear functions of the country's three socioeconomic factors (cosmopolitanism, mobility and women-in-labor-force). They then estimated Equation (4) where they fixed M exogenously by first estimating Equation (2) for each country separately. They repeated the procedure for five more products. In all the six product cases, the socioeconomic factors were found to be statistically significant, implying that these factors do affect the diffusion processes in a country. However, only the effect of cosmopolitanism factor on parameter p was found to be consistently positive across the six products. The rest of the effects did not have directional consistency (i.e., they were positive for some products and negative for others), and hence it would be difficult for a manger to draw any conclusion on how a particular socioeconomic factor would affect new product diffusion in a given country.

[6] Dekimpe, Parker and Sarvary (1998) pooled data from 184 countries but they used only one product (cellular phone). Since sufficient data were not available for many countries, the authors estimated Equation (2) in a staged manner. First they took M to mean αM_{pop}, and evaluated this for each country exogenously using their judgment on what factors affect α. Next, recognizing that pM is the first year sales, they regressed the first year sales of each country on the corresponding socioeconomic factors, and obtained separate estimates on those factors. Finally, they pooled data and, after making q a function of socioeconomic factors, obtained the estimates of impact of those factors. They found that, while population growth and number of competing firms positively affected the diffusion of cell phones in a country, the number of ethnic groups (i.e., population heterogeneity) negatively affected it. However, since only one product was involved in the study, it is difficult to generalize the findings. It is important to note that this study elaborates nicely the matching issues one has to consider in mixing data from different data sets.

[7] With a rather comprehensive data set, Talukdar, Sudhir and Ainslie (2002) pooled

sales data on six consumer durables from 31 countries (that included countries from four continents and covered developing countries like India and China). They used Equation (6) where the parameters p, Q and α were expressed as functions of both the product specific and the country specific (mainly socioeconomic) factors. They report that the socioeconomic factors do *not* seem to explain significantly the variation in p or q, but they do so with respect to α! The estimates pointed out that countries with higher purchasing power, urbanization and international trade had higher penetration (i.e., developed countries had higher α), countries with larger TV and newspaper reach had larger p and the more homogenous countries (i.e., those with less number of ethnic groups) had higher q. They also found that the countries that adopted late had a smaller p and higher q (which somewhat supports a related finding in [1]) to result eventually in a later peaking of sales.

[8] Stremersch and Tellis (2004) analyze data of 10 product categories from 16 European countries[16] and looked at the period past the take-off. Instead of looking at the diffusion as a continuous function, the researchers focus on two variables: growth duration and growth rate. The former is time between take-off and sales slow-down. They defined rules to mark the take-off and the time at which the growth of a new product ends. The growth rate, which can actually be equated to the diffusion speed, is defined as the annual percentage change in sales averaged over the growth duration. The researchers modeled the growth duration using the parametric hazard framework with a Weibull baseline[17] where the country factors (i.e., social, economic and cultural) and product-specific factors are modeled to affect one of the parameters of the baseline hazard. They model the growth rate as a simple linear regression on those factors. They find that white goods have longer growth duration than the entertainment and information goods but grow at a slower rate (thus offsetting the other effect), and the countries with higher economic wealth have longer duration and

higher growth rate (which supports a related finding in [4] and [6]). Interestingly, the cultural factors seemed to have no impact!

[9] Desiraju, Nair and Chintagunta (2004) analyzed the sales growth patterns of a new category of antidepressant drug in 15 countries (Canada, US and some countries in Europe, South America and Africa) using the discrete version of logistic model,[18] which can be obtained from Equation (3) by removing p and dividing both sides of the equation by $Y(t-1)$ and simplifying:

$$\frac{Y(t)-Y(t-1)}{Y(t-1)} = \theta + \gamma \frac{Y(t-1)}{M} \qquad (7)$$

where θ and γ respectively represent the penetration level and the q factor in the Bass model framework. These two parameters were made country specific by making them functions of the health-related social and economic factors of the corresponding countries. The researchers found that the q factor was significant,[19] the per capita healthcare expenditure was having a positive effect on diffusion, the lag countries had a higher diffusion speed if they are developed countries (which supports a related finding in [1] and [7]), and the developing countries had a lower diffusion speed (which supports a related finding in [4], [6] and [8]) and a lower penetration ceiling than the developed countries (which supports a related finding in [7]).

[10] Instead of looking at the diffusion as a continuous function, Kauffman and Techatassanasoontorn (2005)[20] looked at it as a series of discrete stages. They classified diffusion into three or four stages. First is the adoption stage when the country introduces the product, second is the early diffusion stage, third is the partial diffusion stage and the fourth is the maturity stage or full diffusion. The transition hazards for these stages are called as r_1 (stage 1 to 2), r_2 (stage 2 to 3) and r_3 (stage 3 to 4). Actually, these stages were derived from the Rogers' (1962) pioneering work on innovations. The objective was to study how the social, economic and cultural factors affect the transition from one stage to the next. The researchers used a proportional

hazard model (with a Weibull baseline) approach to model the transition hazard processes (i.e., r_1, r_2 and r_3) with the social and economic factors acting as covariates.[21] They pooled data on digital cellular phone adoption in 35 countries and applying the proportional hazard model found that the baseline hazard rates are different for r_1 and r_2, and that digital penetration and number of digital operators positively affected the transitions, while the analog penetration and number of analog operators negatively affected the transitions. They also found that per capita GNP positively influenced the transition r_1 (which supports a related finding in [4], [6], [8] and [9]) while the price of analog phone negatively influenced the transition r_2. This finding shows clearly the impact of economic factors on the diffusion but except for GNP there are no social or cultural factors considered. Further, since only one product was involved in the study, it is difficult to generalize the findings.

Summarizing the six research papers [5] through [10], we can say with sufficient confidence that per capita GNP positively influences both the diffusion speed and the penetration ceiling. Note that higher per capita GNP usually pertains to a developed (or wealthy) country. Most of the social factors had either inconclusive influence (as in [5]) or minimum impact (as in [10]). Interestingly, although the cultural factors are shown to have some influence, they don't stand out convincingly![22]

Having analyzed the papers that address the impact of social and cultural factors on diffusion in various countries, we will now focus on Topic 2.

Are the differences in adoption timings (by different countries) of a new product attributable to the cultural and other socioeconomic differences between the countries?

[2 studies]

[11] Dekimpe *et al.* (2000a) used the same data set described in [6] i.e., cellular phone data in 184 countries and analyzed if the adoption time – not the diffusion within each country, but the first instant of adoption by a country – of a country is affected by the social and economic factors. Using a flexible split hazard model[23] they estimated the parameters. Their findings show that there is a strong demonstration effect (i.e., a country's likelihood to adopt increases when more 'similar' countries had adopted the product, which conclusion somewhat supports a related finding in [1], [7] and [9]), and that countries that are homogenous (i.e., fewer ethnic groups), have concentrated population (i.e., number of thickly populated cities) and have high economic development are likely to be early adopters. Although they use a split hazard model to accommodate certain countries never adopting the product, the researchers found that eventually all countries would adopt. The cultural factors did not seem to make any impact here. Since only one product was involved in the study, it is difficult to generalize the findings.

[12] Dekimpe, Parker and Sarvary (2000b) yet again used the cellular data set explained in [6] and [11] to integrate the two models and study the impact of social and economic factors as a country moves through three stages of diffusion, namely, no-adoption, partial adoption (implementation) and full adoption (confirmation). The transition hazard rates are given by r_1 (time between introduction in the lead country and the adoption by the country-under-focus), r_2 (time between initial adoption to 100 per cent adoption in the country)[24] and r_3 (when a country decides to adopt the new technology fully on the initial adoption stage itself). The researchers use a proportional hazard approach to model the transition hazard rates and incorporate the influence of the factors as covariates therein. Their findings show that per capita GNP positively influences all the three transition hazards (which supports a related finding in [4], [6], [9] and [10]), installed base of the old technology and population heterogeneity slows the transition rates r_2 and r_3 (which supports a related finding in [9]),

while the late adopting countries become full adopters directly (i.e., high r_3), and the experience gained after initial adoption positively affects the transition to full adoption. The last two conclusions support the finding in [1], [7], [9] and [11].

Are the differences in take-off periods (in different countries) of a new product attributable to the cultural and other socioeconomic differences between the countries? [1 study] [13]   Using a data set that covered 10 categories from 16 European countries,[25] Tellis *et al.* (2003) looked at how the social, economic and cultural factors of different countries affect the take-off times of these products. The researchers used a parametric hazard model where one of the parameters of the baseline hazard was made a function of various country-specific and product-specific factors. The model is:

$$f(t_w) = h(t_w \mid X_{tw}) S(t_w \mid X_{tw})$$

$$= \exp \left(-\sum_{j=1}^{w} \int_{t_{j-1}}^{t_j} h(S \mid X_{t(j-1)}) \right) \qquad (8)$$

where $f(t_w)$ is the probability that the product would take off in week w, X_{tw} is the explanatory variables (of product specific and country specific factors), $S(t_w)$ is the survival function up to week w and h is the base hazard function. The hazard function takes a parametric form $\dfrac{\lambda \kappa (\lambda t)^{\kappa - 1}}{[1 + (\lambda t)^\kappa]}$, where the parameter λ is expressed as $\exp(-\beta' X_j)$. Estimating the model on the pooled data set, the authors found that Scandinavian countries always take off early and entertainment and information products (as opposed to white goods) take off early. Interestingly, the economic factors of a country such as per capita GNP were found to have no major impact on the take-off. The Hofstede cultural dimensions, especially the 'Uncertainty Avoidance' and 'Need for Achievement' partially explained the inter-country differences in take-off. The countries that were low on the former and high on the latter enjoyed a quicker take-off. Finally, the researchers found the probability

of take-off increases with prior take-offs in other countries, a result that provides further support for the finding reported in [1], [7], [9], [11] and [12]. This finding led the researchers to suggest that firms would be better off using the waterfall strategy when introducing a new product in multiple countries.[26]

Summarizing the studies [11], [12] and [13], we can say that per capita GNP is influential in the adoption stage and in shortening the take-off period, homogenously populated and developed countries adopt early, and lag countries move to full adoption quickly, i.e., without any take-off period. The late entrant seems to have a quicker adoption and a quicker take-off as well. The role of market factors (such as installed base of older technology) are found to be dominating in adoption stage but given that one and the same product was involved in all the studies concerned (i.e., [10], [11] and [12]), it is not clear if these findings could be accepted with a high confidence level in other product categories. The cultural factors seem to have no impact at adoption stage but do influence the take-off period.[27]

How can we model and study the inter-country diffusion impact, *i.e.*, the impact a new product diffusion process in one country has on the diffusion process in the other countries? *[7 studies]*

[14]   Ganesh and Kumar (1996) is the first paper that tests empirically the inter-country diffusion impact using a simple extension of the Bass model. They looked at a lag country whose sales were affected by the diffusion in the lead country. The model proposed for the lag country is:

$$S(t) = \left[M - Y(t-1) \right]$$

$$\times \left[p + q \frac{Y(t-1)}{M} + c \frac{Y_1(t-1)}{M_1} \right] \qquad (9)$$

where $S(t)$ describes the sales in the lag country, $Y_1(t-1)$ is cumulative sales in the lead country up to $t-1$, c is the learning effect parameter, and other parameters are as described by the Bass model. For the lead country diffusion process they used Equation (3). Note that equation (9) does not have a closed-form solution. The data on bar-code scanner sales in ten countries were used to test the model with the USA being the lead country. In the estimation that was done for each lag country (nine of them) separately, c was found to be significant and positive for each of the lag countries. They also found that in the lag countries diffusion was faster, giving further support for the finding reported in [1], [7], [9], [11], [12] and [13].

[15] In extending the model in [14], Ganesh, Kumar and Subramaniam (1997) modified Equation (9) to make c, the learning effect parameter, a linear function of the differences (measured on geographical factors,

Hofstede's cultural dimensions, economic factors and time-lag) between the lag country and the lead country. They took for analysis four consumer durables from 16 European countries. The data were pooled across the countries for each product. All the parameters (i.e., diffusion, learning and cultural-economic parameters) were estimated together in an integral fashion. The researchers found that geographical distance was not significant while the cultural and economic similarities between the lead and a lag country positively affected the learning happening in the lag country from the diffusion in the lead country. This finding demonstrates the diffusion effect happening between culturally and economically similar countries. The time-lag was also found to be positively affecting the diffusion in the lag country, thus supporting the finding in [1], [7], [9], [11], [12], [13] and [14].

[16] Putsis et al. (1997) introduced a mixing model as follows.

$$\frac{Y_1(t) - Y_1(t-1)}{M_1(t) - Y_1(t-1)} = \alpha_1(t) + c_1 \left[\phi_1 \frac{Y_1}{M_1} + (1 - \phi_1) \frac{Y_1(1 - \phi_1) + Y_2(1 - \phi_2) + Y_3(1 - \phi_3)}{M_1 + M_2 + M_3} \right], \qquad (11)$$

where the subscripts 1, 2, 3, ... refer to countries, variables on the right-hand-side are values for period $t-1$, ϕ is the parameter showing the mixing tendency among the populations. Equation (11) is for country 1 and can be replicated for every country. If $\phi = 1$ then there is no mixing happening among the countries while $\phi = 0$ shows the random mixing. The researchers used data on 4 consumer durables from 10 European countries. In estimation, they pooled data across countries for a given product, and assumed M for each country to be the country's population size. They made α_i depend on the number of televisions in use in country i at time t and the parameter c_i depend on the per capita GDP of the country. However, they used these economic factors exogenously to provide a tighter fit to the model and so did

not produce any estimate of the impact of those factors. Further, there is no closed-form solution for the model. The results showed that ϕ parameters are the same i.e., there was no uneven mixing among countries for a given product, and that its estimated values ranged from 0.538 for microwave ovens to 0.718 for PCs. The presence of mixing among population of different countries is clearly demonstrated. However, the roles of social, cultural or economic variables were not explored.

[17] In order to explore if learning happens from lag country to the lead country and between two countries that introduced the product simultaneously, Kumar and Krishnan (2002) introduced a different variation of the Bass model Equation (1) as follows.

$$\frac{f_i(t)}{1-F_i(t)} = \left[p + qF_i(t) \right]\left[1 + \sum_{j \neq i} \beta_{ji} \frac{dF_j(t)}{dt} \right],$$
$$i = 1, 2, \ldots \quad (10)$$

where each country's diffusion at time t is affected by the changes in the other countries' diffusion forces at time t. An advantage of this model is that it has a closed form expression. Applying their model on three products (microwave ovens, CD players and cell phones) across many European countries they showed that there were lead-lag, lag-lead and simultaneous effects. Subsequently, the researchers took the estimated β_{ij}'s and ran a linear regression on the cultural- and economic similarities between the two countries concerned, and found that the cultural and economic similarities between two countries positively influenced the learning effect between them. The results support the findings in [14] and [15] for the lead-lag effect, and [16] for the simultaneous effect between countries.

[18] Elberse and Eliashberg (2003) analyzed how the movie screenings and their ticket revenues in the lead country (i.e., where it was first introduced) affected the subsequent screenings and revenues of the movie in the lag countries where it was later released. The lead country was the USA and the lag countries were European countries. The researchers analyzed empirically both supply (i.e., screenings) and demand (i.e., revenues) simultaneously. They used a multiplicative (or log-log) model for both, where the independent variables for the demand side included number of screenings, word of mouth (i.e., previous week's revenues), season, competition, movie attributes and reviews, performance of the movie in the USA, i.e., revenues (this is not included in the demand equation in the USA), and the independent variables for the supply side included expected revenue (obtained by double smoothing procedure from previous weeks), word of mouth, competition, movie attributes and reviews and budget, performance in the US (this is not included in the demand equation in the USA). For our

review, we focus on the roles of word of mouth and the impact of US box-office performance on the supply and demand in the lag countries. The researchers split the model into two, one for first week and the other for the rest of the period. The lead country impact was on the first week's supply and demand of lag countries. The results showed clearly the presence of word of mouth (within each country), and the impact of lead country performance on the lag country's demand and supply. This is a very interesting finding because the lead-lag effect comes out to be significant even after including many other possible variables in the model. Note that although only the first week's revenue was modeled to be affected by lead country, the following weeks' performances are affected by the first week's performance through word of mouth variable. Further, the researchers found that the lead country's impact diminished if the lag countries delayed the movie release.

[19] Extending the mixing model in [16], van Everdingen, Aghiva and Fok (2005) introduced time-varying parameters in the mixing behavior. They used data from one product (internet access and mobile telephony) that were collected from 15 European countries through a survey done in 1999 (but covered periods 1990–99). By carefully following the procedures explained by Dekimpe *et al.* (1998) regarding sample matching issues, and estimating their model on the resultant data, the researchers showed that mixing did in fact take place among the population of different countries, diffusion speed varied among countries and in general Scandinavian countries adopted the product faster.

Summarizing the studies [14] through [19] we can say that diffusion in one country clearly affects diffusion in other countries and this impact is moderated by the cultural and economic similarities between the countries and the time-lag of introduction.

[20] A natural question that would then arise is 'can a company then use this information to optimally plan their new product

introduction time in the lag countries?' Interestingly, this is the question researchers tried to answer in 1995, i.e., even before the empirical facts started emerging! Kalish, Mahajan and Muller (1995) developed a theoretical duopoly model, where both the firms have to decide on the optimal introduction time for their new products in a lag country whose diffusion is affected positively by the diffusion happening in the lead country. The researchers used a game theory framework coupled with the cross-country diffusion impact. They could not get a closed-form expression for the optimal time. However, through numerical analysis they were able to conjecture that the sprinkler strategy is preferable in general, and that the waterfall strategy is suggested if product has a very long life cycle, size of market in the lag country is small or has low diffusion force.[28]

Miscellaneous [6 studies]

The first two papers in this topic used meta-analysis on prior research to find out any systematic cross-country impact due to country-specific factors. The rest of the papers are either theoretical or from a different discipline that shed some light on the international diffusion.

[21] Tellefsen and Takada (1999) analyzed 47 sets of p and q estimates from previous research studies that covered fourteen European and two Asian countries to find if mass media (TV, newspaper, radio, etc.) could explain the differences observed among those reported estimates. A linear regression model was used. The researchers found that some countries and products *per se* affected those estimates (e.g., diffusion in Japan had a lower p while diffusion in Sweden had a higher q) and that the TV penetration in a country positively influenced the p estimate and negatively influenced the q estimate.

[22] In a more elaborate study, van den Bulte and Stremersch (2004) carried out a meta-analysis on 293 sets of estimates of p and q reported in previous research articles that covered 52 consumer durables in 28 countries. The dependent variable of interest was the speed of diffusion, i.e., q/p. As explanatory variables they picked Hofstede's (2001) four cultural dimensions, income inequality, presence of competing standards and other socioeconomic variables. They ran a linear regression treating $Ln(q/p)$ as the dependent variable and the corresponding country's factors as independent variables. The findings show that social-contagion process (i.e., the q factor in the Bass model) is present, cultural factors explain partly the contagion process (a high Collectivism and a high Power Distance and high Masculinity results in a higher q/p and a higher Uncertainty Avoidance results in a lower q/p), income inequality also describes the diffusion, and the presence of competing standards results in a higher q/p. The results however have to be taken with a little caution because some of the studies considered in the meta-analysis had already had some of these country-specific factors built into the p and q estimates. Nevertheless, the results are in line with the findings reported in previous studies.

[23] Mahajan and Muller (1994) theoretically showed that under the assumption of a Bass-model type of diffusion, the complete European unification would lead to faster (slower) market penetration in a member country if the diffusion processes before unification in the member countries were different (same). They estimated the diffusion of VCRs in 16 European countries individually and found that the p and q estimates were statistically not the same across the different countries. They also found that lag countries had a higher q, thus supporting the finding in [1], [3] and [7]. This enabled them to conjecture that the diffusion of a new product in a member country would be faster after complete European unification.

[24] Mishra, Kim and Lee (1996) compared new product success factors in three countries, namely, Canada, South Korea and China, where Canada is a developed country and China is a developing country, while

S. Korea is in between the two on the economic development dimension. The researchers collected data on a wide variety of instruments through a survey among the companies operating in the three countries. These instruments measured product-specific factors such as innovativeness, firm-specific factors such as launch efforts and market research, and country-specific factors such as market competitiveness and stability. The results showed that these factors varied across the three countries in their impact on the overall new product success in those countries. In many instances, China and S. Korea behaved similar to each other but differently from Canada. This finding tells us that new product success and diffusion in a country could be affected by various product specific and country specific factors. However, the researchers did not go into cultural or other socioeconomic dimensions typically tested by marketing researchers.

[25] Bin Xu (2000) analyzed how the MNEs (Multinational Enterprises) facilitate technology transfer from the US to the developing countries. Analyzing five waves of survey data spanning 40 host countries (that covered both developing and less-developed countries), they found that the growth in total factor productivity of a developing host country is affected negatively by the technology, gap between that country and the United States, but the MNEs' active role in their host countries enabled faster transfer of technology, resulting in higher growth in the host country's productivity.[29] Although this study is not directly related to diffusion, it brings out an important fact that the MNEs' deliberate act of technology transfer and other international activities enable the diffusion of technology in the home country to affect the diffusion of that technology in the host countries. This finding will add importance to the modeling of inter-country impact on diffusion of a new product.

[26] Gielens and Steenkamp (2007) analyzed the success factors of new CPGs (Consumer Packaged Goods) in Europe by modeling how a European panel of 16 000 households accept or reject 301 new CPGs. The data is spread over four countries – the UK, France, Germany and Spain. The researchers used a latent purchase rate (Poisson) model and found that product-specific and competition-specific factors affected the success while the consumer factors (such as age, family size, etc.) had less impact. However, the objective of this research is not to test if there are differences across countries or explore whether they are affected by country-specific factors. Hence we consider this study to be not directly in line with the main focus of this chapter. Nevertheless, since it involves sales in more than one country we have included it.

CONCLUSIONS AND DIRECTIONS FOR FUTURE RESEARCH

Research in international diffusion started off in the 1980s and has picked up momentum only in the past 10 years. The earlier research works primarily aimed at demonstrating the differences in diffusion patterns across countries for a given product and showing how these differences could be attributed to the inter-country differences on social, economic and cultural dimensions. The later years' research is directed to find the actual presence of any inter-country impact (i.e., learning) between the diffusion processes of a product among two or more countries. By building models and testing them with empirical data from multiple countries and multiple new products, the researchers have established the presence of not only the differences in diffusion patterns but also the impact the diffusion processes exert upon one another across the countries. Research articles in other disciplines, mainly business policy, that look into the business practices across the globe also demonstrate the presence of cross-country effects in new product sales growth. Although one could say that research on international diffusion has unearthed some good and interesting findings, surprisingly the results are not overwhelming.[30]

Firstly, it is important to note that the findings reported in the extant literature *fail* to consistently point to any particular set of social, cultural or economic factors (barring two) that account for the diffusion pattern differences/influences across countries. The first factor that came out to be significantly relevant in almost every study is the per capita GNP (can also be called wealth, state of the economy, etc.). This factor is found to have influence on initial adoption, diffusion speed and penetration ceiling, but not on the take-off phenomenon. The other result that has been statistically established in many studies is that lag countries have quicker take-off and faster diffusion. Although these two results are strongly established they are unlikely to create any 'awe!' factor in a typical international product manager because the former (i.e., the impact of wealth) sounds somewhat obvious, while the latter effect (i.e., diffusion being faster in lag countries) is so strong that in many cases it can be inferred by simply looking at a graphical representation of the diffusion patterns in different countries (see Takada and Jain 1991 for a good self-explanatory graph). Clearly, the manger may be wondering how to make use of these findings in product launches, for which the research has not yet offered any prescription.

Secondly, the cultural factors represented by Hofstede's dimensions were found to have only minimum influence! This is interesting to note because a major element of the diffusion process is the word of mouth effect, which in turn is generally perceived to be related to the cultural factors. However, while modeling explicitly the impact of diffusion process in one country on the diffusion process in another country, researchers found that two culturally similar countries influence each other more actively than two culturally dissimilar countries.

Thirdly, the other social and economic factors seem to have some influence (e.g., social-system heterogeneity negatively affecting the diffusion, as found by Dekimpe 2000a) but their influences are yet to be established broadly (i.e., in many products) and/or unambiguously.

Thus, taken as a whole the findings are not earthshaking. Why were we unable to establish more consistent results? As very nicely elaborated in Dekimpe (2000a) article, one could point to the 'biases' that researchers exhibit in their selection of countries, products, the various social, cultural and economic factors or their sub-factors. These biases might be playing a role in many results being different across studies. Although researchers seem to take extreme care in building up their data base and offering justification to their using of a particular set of variables[31] the fact remains that a majority of the results are not consistent across countries and products. One way to avoid this problem is to set up a standardized data base for researchers to tap into and work on. Also, hopefully in the future researchers will go beyond the standard diffusion categories like cell phones and analyze grocery goods, services, industrial goods, etc. more readily. Otherwise, the generalizability of the findings is always questionable.

While looking at the scores of factors that researchers have been using (see Appendix for a full list) it appears that researchers are going into too many details and in the process getting bogged down by the nuances. Since many of the factors are highly macro-level, i.e., country-level, their direct connection with the product-level sales could turn out to be rather nebulous. That is, compared with pricing, advertising and distribution that have a direct bearing on a given product sales, these country-level factors are somewhat distanced from the product-level happenings. It is interesting to note that the extant research had not considered these marketing mix instruments at all with the exception of Desiraju *et al.* (2004), who consider price in their OTC drug sales analysis.[32] The media effect that researchers considered are all at country-level (e.g., number of TVs in use in a country) and not tied to the products under study. So, one cannot help wondering if the differences in diffusion patterns we observe across countries could simply be due to the different marketing strategies (i.e., with respect to positioning, pricing, and other marketing mix variables) firms employ in those countries.[33] If that is so, what would become of the effects of social, cultural and economic impact? For example, if we take Sanex, a new liquid soap, which was introduced in the 1980s in various European countries in a waterfall type of operation, we can see that what mattered most in its huge success was the clear product positioning (which was left unchanged across the countries) and not any of these cultural or social factors (Krishnan and Borucki 1994).

Another managerially important issue to analyze is the role of competition across international borders. If a new product is successful in one country, would a competitor take this product to another country more readily than the pioneer company?[34] In the case of pharmaceutical industry, many developing countries seem to be waging a war with the multinational companies on the patent length and generics-related issues, and hence how far these issues are affecting the international diffusion of new drugs would be another useful direction to look into.

Further, unlike price and advertising variables, most of the variables considered in these studies are hard to build up and measure or obtain from reliable secondary sources. For example, the cultural factors always find only one source to tap from – Hofstede. How far do those dimensions apply to marketing processes? Perhaps we need to take a step back and ask a different set of questions. We need to look into the cross-country differences in diffusion patterns from a managerially controllable perspective.

NOTES

1 Some researchers make a distinction between using the term 'international' and using 'global' or 'multinational'. In this chapter we treat them all the same.

2 A few other researchers had discussed international marketing of new products prior to 1990 but

a mathematical approach to analyzing the new product adoption process in an international context can be said to have started from here.

3 Our collection of articles was done through subject searches in various databases such as *ABI Inform; Business Source Premier* and *ScienceDirect*. Journals include *Marketing Science; Management Science; Journal of Marketing; Journal of Marketing Research; International Journal of Research in Marketing; Journal of International Marketing; Journal of Academy of Marketing Science; Journal of Business Research; Journal of Product Innovation Management; Technological Forecasting and Social Change,* etc.

4 As Muller and Peres (2007) note, 'word of mouth' here refers to all sorts of processes that signal to the consumer that the new product is worth adopting. These include network externalities, any signals, positive and negative feedbacks on the product, etc.

5 Dekimpe *et al.* (2000a) call the adoption vs. diffusion as breadth and depth respectively.

6 Hereinafter we use the term 'diffusion' to refer to 'new product diffusion'.

7 Note that it is difficult to establish if a factor has to be classified as cultural or otherwise. To be consistent, in this chapter we refer to Hofstede's cultural dimensions as cultural factors.

8 Depending upon the product category, the population would be the number of households (e.g., color TV), the number of households that own a pc (e.g., internet, e-commerce), the number of companies (e.g., professional MS-Office suite), etc. This will typically be left to the researcher's choice.

9 Typically, they model one or more of p, q and M parameters to be functions of the country-specific factors.

10 The lead countries are the countries where the product was introduced *prior* to the lag countries.

11 Penetration data were obtained by dividing sales data by M which was separately estimated using the Bass model on each country's sales data.

12 Initially they had 64 countries but considered only 25 whose estimates were found to be significant.

13 Almost every study that wished to study the impact of culture used the Hofstede's dimensions to characterize the cultural identity of a country. These are Individuality, Uncertainty Avoidance, Power Distance and Masculinity. For details see Hofstede (2001).

14 The resulting differential equation on solving will yield an integral constant in addition to q. But the model focuses on only one parameter, i.e., q.

15 However, the methodology used, i.e., averaging the $\{p, q\}$'s of different products in different time zones and creating additional data points with pairwise comparisons could make some question the real thrust of the findings.

16 This study is actually a sequel to Study [13] that is described later in this chapter.

17 For details see the paper or the brief description we provide later under Study [13].

18 Logistic model can be considered a special case of Bass model where p factor is absent.

19 This is interesting because the authors did not use prescription data but used the sales data which are likely to contain a significant number of replacement sales. Although other researchers also use sales data, since the products concerned in those studies are consumer durables the replacement sales would not be a major factor in those data sets.

20 There is a precursor to this approach. See [12] that comes up later.

21 Although the proportional hazard model looks different from the customarily used Bass model at first sight, Bass et al. (2000) show that these two are more or less similar. See Bass et al. (2000) for further details.

22 Note that some researchers did not even consider them.

23 Please refer to the paper for the mathematical development and other estimation details.

24 Full adoption here refers to the time when the country stops using the older technology.

25 Since the data in the take-off period was very difficult to obtain (compared to the regular diffusion data), the authors took a lot of time and effort to collect the data used in this study. The researchers report that the average take-off period is six years, which implies that each data series has, on average, 6 data points.

26 Waterfall strategy refers to introducing a new product sequentially, i.e., one country after another. The opposite is the sprinkler strategy where the product is introduced simultaneously in all countries of interest.

27 Take-off time is a growing area of research interest. In a recent paper, Wiorkowski and Gylys (2006) develop a new method to define the take-off point and measure it on the cellular phone adoption pattern in 40 different countries. However, they don't study why the take-off times differ or if any systematic differences exist.

28 Libai et al. (2005), while deriving an optimal policy for allocating marketing budget among a given set of markets where the new product is introduced, find that including the influence of inter-market influence in their proposed model does not have any major impact on the optimal budget allocation.

29 This result was not found with the less-developed countries because, as per the authors, these countries did not have the minimum human capital to benefit from technology transfer.

30 Dekimpe (2000a) come to more or less a similar conclusion. They further provide an excellent treatment on possible reasons from the 'data collection' perspective. For example, one issue of concern is that data used in testing various theories pertain mostly to European countries and the USA. This is understandable from the data availability point of view but the fact that a few researchers did collect and successfully use data from other countries (including some developing countries!) shows that with a little more effort more could be done in this direction.

31 For example, Tellis and Stremersch (2002) report that they took almost four years to build up their database.

32 A key limitation here is the availability of data but as time progresses this is likely to change just as it did with 'single' country diffusion research.

33 In fact, a couple of studies show that the differences in the competitive structures in two countries and product-related factors do play a significant role in the diffusion pattern differences.

34 We are of course not allowing for patent issues here.

REFERENCES

Bass, F. M. (1969) 'A new product growth for model consumer durables', *Management Science*, 15(5): 215–227.

Bass, F. M., Jain, D., Krishnan, T. (2000) 'Modeling the marketing-mix influence in new-product diffusion', in V. Mahajan, E. Muller and Y. Wind (eds), *New-Product Diffusion Models*. MA: Kluwer Academic Publishers, pp. 99–122.

Bin Xu (2000) 'Multinational enterprises, technology diffusion, and host country productivity growth', *Journal of Development Economics*, 62(2): 477–492.

Dekimpe, M. G., Parker, Ph. M., Sarvary, M. (1998) 'Staged estimation of international diffusion models: An application to global cellular telephone adoption', *Technological Forecasting and Social Change*, 57(1–2): 105–132.

Dekimpe, M. G., Parker, P. M. and Sarvary, M. (2000a) 'Globalization: modeling technology adoption timing across countries', *Technological Forecasting and Social Change*, 63: 25–42.

Dekimpe, M. G., Parker, P. M. and Sarvary, M. (2000b) 'Global diffusion of technological innovations: a coupled-hazard approach', *Journal of Marketing Research*, 37(1): 47–59.

Desiraju, R., Nair, H. and Chintagunta, P. (2004) 'Diffusion of new pharmaceutical drugs in developing and developed nations', *International Journal of Research in Marketing*, 21(4): 341–357.

Dwyer, S., Mesak, H. and Hsu, M. (2005) 'An exploratory examination of the influence of national culture on cross-national product diffusion', *Journal of International Marketing*, 13(2): 1–27.

Elberse, A. and Eliashberg, J. (2003) 'Demand and supply dynamics for sequentially released products in international markets: the case of motion pictures', *Marketing Science*, 22(3): 329–354.

Ganesh, J. and Kumar, V. (1996) 'Capturing the cross-national learning effect: an analysis of an industrial technology diffusion', *Journal of the Academy of Marketing Science*, 24(4): 328–337.

Ganesh, J., Kumar, V. and Subramaniam, V. (1997) 'Learning effect in multinational diffusion of consumer durables: an exploratory investigation', *Journal of the Academy of Marketing Science*, 25(3): 214–228.

Gatignon, H., Eliashberg, J. and Robertson, T. S. (1989) 'Modeling multinational diffusion patterns: an efficient methodology', *Marketing Science*, 8(3): 231–247.

Gielens, K. and Steenkamp, J.-B. E. M. (2007) 'Drivers of consumer acceptance of new packaged goods: an investigation across products and countries', *International Journal of Research in Marketing*, 24(2): 97–111.

Helsen, K., Jedidi, K. and DeSarbo, W. S. (1993) 'A new approach to country segmentation utilizing multinational diffusion patterns', *Journal of Marketing*, 57(4): 60–71.

Hofstede, G. (1991) *Cultures and Organizations: Software of the Mind: Intercultural Cooperation and its Importance for Survival*. Cambridge: McGraw-Hill.

Hofstede, G. (2001) *Culture's Consequences: Comparing Values, Behaviors, Institutions and Organizations Across Nations*, 2nd Edn. Thousand Oaks, CA: Sage Publications.

Kalish, S., Mahajan, V. and Muller, E. (1995) 'Waterfall and sprinkler new-product strategies in competitive global markets', *International Journal of Research in Marketing*, 12(2): 105–119.

Kauffman, R. J. and Techatassanasoontorn, A. A. (2005) 'International diffusion of digital mobile technology: a coupled-hazard state-based approach', *Information Technology and Management*, 6(2–3): 253.

Krishnan, T. V. and Borucki, C. (1994) 'Tilting windmills: Sanex tries to conquer Europe'. Case published and distributed by *European Case Clearing House*.

Kumar, V. and Krishnan, T. V. (2002) 'Multinational diffusion models: an alternative framework', *Marketing Science*, 21(3): 318–330.

Libai, B., Muller, E. and Peres, R. (2005) 'The role of seeding in multi-market entry', *International Journal of Research in Marketing*, 22, 375–393.

Mahajan, V. and Muller, E. (1994) 'Innovation diffusion in a borderless global market: will the 1992 unification of the European Community accelerate diffusion of new ideas, products, and technologies?', *Technological Forecasting and Social Change*, 45: 221–235.

Mishra, S., Kim, D. and Lee, Dae Hoon (1996) 'Factors affecting new product success: cross-country comparisons', *Journal of Product Innovation Management*, 13(6): 530–550.

Muller, E. and Peres, R. (2007) 'Information diffusion and new product growth: beyond a theory of communication', Working Paper presented at *Marketing Science* Conference, Singapore.

Putsis Jr., W. P., Balasubramanian, S., Kaplan, E. H. and Sen, S. K. (1997) 'Mixing behavior in cross-country diffusion', *Marketing Science*, 16(4): 354–369.

Rogers, E. M. (1962) *Diffusion of Innovations*. New York: The Free Press.

Stremersch, S. and Tellis, G. J. (2004) 'Understanding and managing international growth of new products', *International Journal of Research in Marketing*, 21(4): 421–438.

Sundqvist, S., Frank, L. and Puumalainen, K. (2005) 'The effects of country characteristics, cultural similarity and adoption timing on the diffusion of wireless communications', *Journal of Business Research*, 58(1): 107–110.

Takada, H. and Jain, D. (1991) 'Cross-national analysis of diffusion of consumer durable goods in Pacific Rim countries', *Journal of Marketing*, 55(2): 48–54.

Talukdar, D., Sudhir, K. and Ainslie, A. (2002) 'Investigating new product diffusion across products and countries', *Marketing Science*, 21(1): 97–114.

Tellefsen, T. and Takada, H. (1999) 'The relationship between mass media availability and the multicountry diffusion of consumer products', *Journal of International Marketing*, 7(1): 77–96.

Tellis, G. J., Stremersch, S. and Yin, E. (2003) 'The international takeoff of new products: the role of economics, culture, and country innovativeness', *Marketing Science*, 22(2): 188–208.

Van den Bulte, C. and Stremersch, S. (2004) 'Social contagion and income heterogeneity in new product diffusion: a meta-analytic test', *Marketing Science*, 23(4): 530–544.

Van Everdingen, Y. M., Aghina, W. B. and Fok, D. (2005) 'Forecasting cross-population innovation diffusion: a Bayesian approach', *International Journal of Research in Marketing*, 22(3): 293–308.

Wiorkowski, J. J. and Gylys, V. A. (2006) 'An empirical real-time test for takeoff with applications to cellular telephony', *Review of Marketing Science*, Vol. 4, Article 1.

Appendix

Classification	Factors	Effect	Studies
Economic Factors	Per capita wealth of a country (GNP/GDP/PPP adjusted/scale of reciprocal of inverse Gamma Distributed income/health expenditure)	+ve effect on early transition rates and mixed effect on second stage transition rates	Dekimpe et al. (2000b), Kauffman and Techatassanasoontorn (2005)
		+ve effect on time to adoption	Dekimpe et al. (2000a)
		+ve effect on rate of technological diffusion	Dwyer et al. (2005)
		+ve effect on growth rate; –ve effect on growth duration	Stremersch and Tellis (2004)
		+ve effect on m	Sundqvist et al. (2005)
		–ve effect on time to takeoff	Tellis et al. (2003)
		+ve effect on diffusion speed	Desiraju et al. (2004), Sundqvist et al. (2005)
		+ve effect on penetration level	Talukdar et al. (2002)
		+ve effect on q/p	van den Bulte and Stremersch (2004)
	Economic similarity	+ve effect on learning between lead and lag countries	Ganesh et al. (1997)
	% of women in labor force	Mixed effect on both p and q depending on the product	Gatignon et al. (1989)
		No effect on q	Talukdar et al. (2002)
	Health situation of the country	+ve effect on p; –ve effect on q	Helsen et al. (1993)
	International trade	–ve effect on p; +ve effect on q	Helsen et al. (1993)
		+ve effect on penetration potential	Talukdar et al. (2002)
		–ve effect on time to takeoff	Tellis et al. (2003)
	Standard of living of the country	+ve effect on p; –ve effect on q	Helsen et al. (1993)
	No. of major population centres	+ve effect on time to adoption	Dekimpe et al. (2000a)
		–ve effect on external influences and +ve effect on internal influences	Dekimpe et al. (1998)
	Avg. annual population growth rate	+ve effect on external influences	Dekimpe et al. (1998)
	Crude death rate	–ve effect on both external and internal influences	Dekimpe et al. (1998)
		No effect on growth duration or rate of growth	Stremersch and Tellis (2004)
	Income inequality (GINI Index)	No effect on penetration potential or q	Talukdar et al. (2002)
		+ve effect on q/p	van den Bulte and Stremersch (2004)
	Dependent : working people ratio	No effect on penetration potential	Talukdar et al. (2002)
	Urbanization	+ve effect on penetration potential	Talukdar et al. (2002)
	Illiteracy	–ve effect on p	Talukdar et al. (2002)
		–ve effect on time to take off	Tellis et al. (2003)
Social Factors	Age of consumer	–ve effect on level and +ve effect on trend of first year purchases	Gielens and Steenkamp (2007)
	Size of household	+ve effect on both level and trend of first year purchases	Gielens and Steenkamp (2007)
	Heterogeneity of social system (No. of ethnic groups in the country)	–ve effect on transition rates	Dekimpe et al. (2000b)
		–ve effect on q	Talukdar et al. (2002)
		–ve effect on time to adoption	Dekimpe et al. (2000a)

Continued

Appendix—cont'd

Classification	Factors	Effect	Studies
	Geographical proximity	−ve effect on external and internal influences	Dekimpe et al. (1998)
		+ve effect on time to adoption	Dekimpe et al. (2000a)
	Cosmopolitanism	+ve effect on p; −ve effect on q	Gatignon et al. (1989)
	Mobility	Mixed effect on both p and q depending on the product	Helsen et al. (1993)
		+ve effect on q	Gatignon et al. (1989)
		Mixed effect on both p and q depending on the product	Helsen et al. (1993)
		−ve effect on time to take off	Tellis et al. (2003)
Cultural factors	Uncertainty avoidance	+ve effect on q	Sundqvist et al. (2005)
		+ve effect on time to take off	Tellis et al. (2003)
		−ve effect on q/p	van den Bulte and Stremersch (2004)
	Individualism	−ve effect on rate of technological diffusion	Dwyer et al. (2005)
		−ve effect on q/p	van den Bulte and Stremersch (2004)
	Masculinity	+ve effect on rate of technological diffusion	Dwyer et al. (2005)
		+ve effect on q/p	van den Bulte and Stremersch (2004)
	Power Distance	+ve effect on rate of technological diffusion	Dwyer et al. (2005)
		+ve effect on q/p	van den Bulte and Stremersch (2004)
	Long-term orientation	−ve effect on rate of technological diffusion	Dwyer et al. (2005)
	Cultural similarity	+ve effect on learning between lead and lag countries	Ganesh et al. (1997)
	High context culture	+ve effect on p	Takada and Jain (1991)
	Cultural Distance	−ve effect on q	Sundqvist et al. (2005)
	Need for achievement	−ve effect on time to take off	Tellis et al. (2003)
	Industriousness	−ve effect on time to take off	Tellis et al. (2003)
Product related factors	Dispositional innovativeness	+ve effect on level and −ve effect on trend of first year purchases	Gielens and Steenkamp (2007)
	Size of installed base of old technology	−ve effect on transition rates	Dekimpe et al. (2000b)
	Cumulative international experience with technology (number of countries adopting new technology)	+ve effect on transition rates	Dekimpe et al. (2000b)
		+ve effect on time to adoption	Dekimpe et al. (2000a)
	Own experience with technology	+ve effect on transition rates	Dekimpe et al. (2000b)
	Performance in US	+ve effect on the supply of screens −ve effect on the revenues	Elberse and Eliashberg (2003)
	Word of mouth	+ve effect on supply of screens and revenues for movies in all countries	Elberse and Eliashberg (2003)
	Diffusion in lead countries	+ve effect on diffusion in lag countries, influenced by q in lag countries and c (learning effect) in lag countries	Ganesh and Kumar (1996)
	Time lag in introduction	+ve effect on learning between lead and lag countries	Ganesh et al. (1997)
		+ve effect on p; −ve effect on p	Helsen et al. (1993) and Sundqvist et al. (2005); Talukdar et al. (2002)

Category	Factor	Effect	Reference
		+ve effect on q; –ve effect on q	Takada and Jain (1991), Talukdar et al. (2002) and Sundqvist et al. (2005); Helsen et al. (1993)
		+ve effect on time to adoption	Dekimpe et al. (2000a)
		No effect in diffusion speed for developing countries but ++ve effect for developed contries	Desiraju et al. (2004)
Product related factors (cont.)	Lagged market penetration	+ve effect on rate of adoption	Takada and Jain (1991)
	Type of innovation	–ve effect on time to take off	Tellis et al. (2003)
	Existence of tehnical standard	+ve effect on learning between lead and lag countries	Ganesh et al. (1997)
	Number of prior take-offs	+ve effect on learning between lead and lag countries	Ganesh et al. (1997)
		–ve effect on time to take off	Tellis et al. (2003)
	Brown goods	–ve effect on time to take off; faster growth rate and shorter growth duration	Tellis et al. (2003); Stremersch and Tellis (2004)
	Price of the product	–ve effect on diffusion speed	Desiraju et al. (2004)
	Brand reputation	+ve effect on level and trend of first year purchases	Gielens and Steenkamp (2007)
	Newness of the product	U-shaped effect on level and trend of first year purchases	Gielens and Steenkamp (2007)
	Brand power	+ve effect on level and trend of first year purchases	Gielens and Steenkamp (2007)
	Firm power	+ve effect on level and trend of first year purchases	Gielens and Steenkamp (2007)
	Market concentration	Mixed effect on both level and trend of purchases depending on the country	Gielens and Steenkamp (2007)
	Price promotion	–ve effect on trend but mixed effect on level of first year pruchases	Gielens and Steenkamp (2007)
	New product activity in the market	–ve effect on trend but +ve effect on level of first year purchases	Gielens and Steenkamp (2007)
	Ad intensity	Mixed effect in level and +ve effect in trend of first year purchases	Gielens and Steenkamp (2007)
	Products with competing standard/systems	+ve effect on q/p	van den Bulte and Stremersch (2004)
Effect of media		+ve effect on external influences	Dekimpe et al. (1998)
	Media intensity	–ve effect on time to take off	Tellis et al. (2003)
	TV penetration	+ve effect on p	Tellefsen and Takada (1999)
	Digital mobile penetration	+ve effect on early diffusion rate and transition rate to partial diffusion	Kauffman and Techatassanasoontorn (2005)
	No. of digital mobile phone standards	–ve effect on early diffusion rate and transition rate to partial diffusion	Kauffman and Techatassanasoontorn (2005)
	No of digitial mobile operators	+ve effect on transition rate to partial diffusion	Kauffman and Techatassanasoontorn (2005)
	Digital mobile prices	–ve effect on transition rate to partial diffusion	Kauffman and Techatassanasoontorn (2005)
	Analog phone penetration	+ve effect on early diffusion rate	Kauffman and Techatassanasoontorn (2005)
	No. of analog phone operators	–ve effect on transition rate to partial diffusion	Kauffman and Techatassanasoontorn (2005)
	Analog phone prices	+ve effect on transition rate to partial diffusion	Kauffman and Techatassanasoontorn (2005)
	Licensing policy	Significant effect on transition rates to partial diffusion state	Kauffman and Techatassanasoontorn (2005)
	Newspaper	+ve effect on p	Talukdar et al. (2002)
		–ve effect on q	Tellefsen and Takada (1999)
	Homophilous communication	+ve effect on p	Takada and Jain (1991)

17

Global Branding

John Roberts and Julien Cayla

INTRODUCTION

Global brands and other intangible assets are increasingly important for corporations (Srivastava, Shervani and Fahey 1998; Luehrman 1997). The brand Coca Cola is estimated to be worth more than sixty billion US dollars (Interbrand 2007). Brands such as Coke, Intel or Microsoft now represent the majority of the market value of the companies that own these brands. Brands that span world markets have come to stand for quality, reliability and even glamour (Steenkamp, Batra and Alden 2003), allowing the companies that own them to extract a significant premium from these positive perceptions.

The rise of global brands can be explained, at least partly, by the desire of Western companies to expand beyond their borders and to do so in an efficient way. Since the second world war, global trade has expanded more than 14-fold (World Trade Organization 1998), fuelled in large part by the success of multinational corporations seeking new markets. This rapid expansion has partially fulfilled Levitt's prophecy (1983) about the inevitability of globalization.

However, Levitt's thesis of a homogenized world consuming the same brands is far from being fulfilled. As several researchers note

(Ger and Belk 1996; Douglas and Wind 1987; Kotler 1986) major differences in the perceptions, preferences and behavior of consumers in different cultural contexts are bound to greatly constrain the emergence of homogenized consumer tastes. Marketing scholars recognize that these differences demand a combination of customization and consistency dictated by context (Keller 2003; Quelch and Hoff 1986).

Global brands are the symbols of a rapidly globalizing world. The greater penetration of electronic media, growth in travel, migration, labor mobility and an altered political landscape facilitating greater free trade, have all led to an increased importance for transnational structures and their symbolic forms, such as global brands. These trends are well documented in marketing and other social sciences (see, for example, Appadurai 1996; Hofstede, Steenkamp and Wedel 1999; Quelch 2003; Keller 2003; Ries and Ries 2002; Yip 2003; and Holt, Quelch and Taylor 2004). Global brands are playing an increasingly important role in consumer lives. These brands enable consumers to feel connected to consumers in other nations (Holt, Quelch and Taylor 2004), thereby partially fulfilling the prophesy of a 'global village' (McLuhan 1964). Global brands also increasingly frame the way we view a globalizing world and its contradictions (Thompson and Arsel 2004; Holt 2002; Ritzer 1993). Like other symbols (Levi-Strauss 1975), brands have come to provide a means for us to make sense of the world. Protests against global brands such as Nike or McDonald's have become vehicles to express the fears and anxieties created by a globalizing marketplace and a new international division of labor (Klein 1999).

In this chapter, we examine two facets of this marketing equation: drivers of brand globalization coming from the supply side, such as economies of scale, learning, innovation and growth objectives; and the demand side, such as the desire of consumers to feel connected to a larger sphere than their immediate community, their increasing sophistication and their desire for premium products. By situating global brands within these two streams of research – managerial and consumer-centric – we hope to shed light on the marketer–consumer interface in the development of global brands. Importantly, our research agenda calls for a combination of these two perspectives to shed light on global branding issues, to focus transnational branding activity where it can add most value to the consumers at whom it is targeted and to generate the greatest rewards for those organizations that undertake it.

WHAT IS GLOBAL BRANDING?

When approached from a managerial perspective, global branding refers to brands that are marketed globally. For example, AC Nielsen identifies 43 global brands (Branch 2001). It defines those brands to have sales of over $US 1 billion and at least 5 per cent of their sales derived from outside the home region. Brandchannel, the internet news site of the brand valuation service, Interbrand (2007), uses a criterion of one third of a brand's sales coming from outside the home country and imposes a condition that in each country it must have 'a common goal and

similar identity' for a brand to be global. Two observations emerge from these definitions. First, globalization is clearly a relative (and subjective) concept. Secondly, these definitions are very market- and sales-based. They say nothing about what manufacturers see as a global brand, nor consumers. To understand that better, let us clarify what we mean by a brand and what we mean by global.

What is branding?

The American Marketing Association defines a brand by 'A brand is a name, term, sign, symbol or design, or combination of them, intended to identify the goods or services of one seller or group of sellers and to differentiate them from competitors' (e.g., Keller 1993, p. 3). For our purposes, we find it useful to think of a brand as a signal. That way, we can investigate it from the manufacturer's perspective (what does the manufacturer want the consumer to understand when they see the brand?) and from the demand side (what do consumers believe about a product based on the presence of a brand name?). We consider these two perspectives (that of the manufacturer and consumer), particularly with respect to the purpose or benefit derived; we are interested in what the brand does for the company (which we term the brand role) and what the brand aims to do for the consumer (which we call the value proposition or brand identity). It may also be useful to distinguish between what the company wants the brand to do for consumers (the brand identity) and what customers actually see it as doing (the brand image). We will examine global brands according to their ability to meet the objectives of their manufacturers (brand roles) and to meet the need of their target consumers (value propositions). Global brands cannot be deemed managerially successful if they do not fulfill both supply and demand sides of the marketing exchange equation. We regard this duality as fundamental to the understanding of global (and indeed all) brands' performance in the marketplace.

Supply side: The role of brands in meeting company objectives   We define the supply side objective of the brand to be the 'brand role'. Keller (1993, p. 683 and 685) suggests that brand globalization allows companies to capture economies of scale in production and distribution, lower marketing costs, increase power and scope, afford consistent brand image, enable the leveraging of good ideas quickly and efficiently, and implement uniform marketing practices.

Cost and economies of scale issues appear high on the agendas of practicing managers. To quote Harish Manwani, President Home and Personal Care of Unilever (Raman *et al.* 2003)

> A vibrant brand requires a regular stream of exciting new features and continuous updating. But the costs of innovation are so high that it makes financial sense only in the largest markets or, preferably, when resources can be pooled regionally or globally. In fact, the pooling of such resources is necessary for companies to compete effectively.

Sources of growth are also a major motive for firms, with the Ansoff matrix suggesting that growth in new markets is one of the two major sources of growth (e.g., Aaker 2005). Similarly, there are many examples where multinationals use their global brands as vehicles by which to transport innovations from one country to their worldwide network, or some part of it. For example, P&G's Pantene Shampoo is now the largest selling shampoo brand in the world. Procter and Gamble initially launched it in the United States, Taiwan, France and the United Kingdom, before progressively rolling it out to over 78 countries (Advertising Educational Foundation 2007). Finally, market defense and resisting competition may be a major reason to create a global position for brands. To quote Charles Hughes, CEO of Land Rover North America, 'You can't be a major player if you don't compete in the world's largest auto market' (Fournier 1996).

What is global?

Alden, Steenkamp and Batra (2002) find support for the existence of a global consumer cultural positioning from a supply side analysis. They make a useful classification of firms' positioning and communications strategies as local, foreign or global. Local positions appeal to the brand's pedigree in the country in which it is marketed, while foreign brands are associated with coming from overseas and usually from one particular country. Finally, global positions are more transcendental, stemming from 'the crystallization of the world as a single place' (p. 77). Not only do Alden, Steenkamp and Batra find evidence of these three distinct types of communication, they also find their usage varies by category and geography. For example, global positioning is least prevalent in the United States and most prevalent in Thailand. Local positioning is relatively more prevalent in food categories than others. Finally, the authors discuss migration paths between the three types of positioning. As an economy evolves or a brand gains acceptance, a firm may decide to shift emphasis from a local basis to a global one.

Local positioning   We see many multinational firms trying to gain the advantages of being local, using 'glocalization,' that is the adaptation of global positionings to local preferences (Thompson and Arsel 2004; Robertson 1995). For example, Unilever uses the same imagery for its ice cream worldwide, but different brand names (e.g., Streets, Walls, Kibon). HSBC, a large bank present in many countries, positions itself as 'The world's local bank' attempting to gain the benefits of both positions. Coca Cola has tried to achieve similar results with its 'Think local, act local' campaign, moving away from what was a very American GI-based pedigree. It is worth noting that the sustainability of different strategies depends considerably on the market position and objectives of the firm. For example, if Coca Cola wishes to have a greater than 60 per cent share of a hypothetical country's carbonated beverage market and 50 per cent of consumers avoid American products where possible, a US foreign position is not going to be viable.

Localization, globalization, or a hybrid strategy is needed. Coca Cola pursued such a hybrid strategy in India where initially it withdrew a local brand it took over (Thums Up), but then decided to use the brand for market coverage of Coke rejecters.

The more parochial a society, the higher the need will be to establish local acceptance. As Toyota moves to being the world's largest auto manufacturer, in a large part due to its success in the US market, it worries about this. To quote Toyota CEO, Katsuaki Watanabe, 'We constantly need to think about the potential for backlash against us. It is very important for our company and products to earn citizenship in the US. We need to make sure that we are accepted' (Welch 2007). Toyota is taking out full page ads proclaiming its US heritage (e.g., in *Business Week* January 15, 2007 'While Utah has some lovely skiing trails, we go there for the airbags').

Foreign positioning The positioning of a brand as coming from or belonging to a specific foreign country obviously highlights the characteristics of that country. That will be advantageous when inferences about that country are positively valenced in the product category. Thus, for example, BMW emphasizes its German engineering to leverage country-of-origin effects related to the perceived technical capabilities of Germany. Heineken beer, even though it is from Holland, is perceived to have a German-sounding name and Germany is seen as a country that should be able to make good beer. Heineken had beer mats made with 'Printed in Germany' on them, leveraging those associations. Ries and Ries (2002) advocate this strategy on the grounds that a firm 'can't escape [its] foreign pedigree', so it may as well make the most of it. The bottom line with foreign positionings is that if the brand is a signal (as we have argued), we need to understand the (positive and credible) signal that we want consumers to take from our foreign pedigree. If that is sufficiently valued by a large enough proportion of the target market to enable a company to meet its objectives, a foreign positioning may be advisable.

Global positioning Global positioning is becoming increasingly popular. With many global products the country of origin is not clear and, by its very positioning, it is not meant to be important. For example, the energy drink, Red Bull, originated in Thailand, but was extensively modified in Austria, before being successfully marketed in the United States. While Coca Cola has tried local and hybrid strategies to move from its American heritage, it has also attempted global ones, encapsulated in the tag line, 'I'd like to buy the world a Coke'. Such campaigns have emphasized the links between consumers in diverse places, from various backgrounds, sharing the experience of drinking the famous beverage. An important point to explore though, is whether such global claims render obsolete country-of-origin claims. In other words, should global brands abandon their national heritage in order to appeal across national boundaries? Holt, Quelch and Taylor (2004) finish their article on global brands with a word of caution; 'Our view of Global branding should be not interpreted as a call to rid transnational brands of their national heritage, for two reasons'. The first of these is that they can lose valuable country-of-origin effects and the second is that many brands need what they call a myth (or a story) and that story must have a setting. Keller (2003, p. 707) lists the conditions in which globalization of brands is likely to present a successful strategy. They include common customer needs, global customers and channels, favorable regulatory and trade environments, and compatible technical and marketing skills. Day and Reibstein (2004) also provide a good analysis of factors favoring global brands.

The global brand in summary

We can summarize global branding from a supply-side perspective, as shown in Figure 17.1. The firm must decide on its

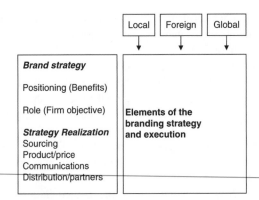

Figure 17.1   Elements of international branding from a manufacturer's perspective

strategy and the path by which it realizes that strategy. Both of these elements may be addressed by some combination of global, foreign and local elements. These choices will be predicated on how well each option realizes the company's objectives. That, in turn, will depend on consumer evaluations and behavior, as well as environmental conditions such as economic, regulatory and competitive climate.

FROM A MANAGERIAL TO A CONSUMER-CENTRIC VIEW OF GLOBAL BRANDS

Global brands have often been defined, managed and viewed internally, from the perspective of a firm trying to harmonize its offerings across markets. As Schuiling and Kapferer (2003, p. 99) argue: 'the push toward development of international and global brands has been driven more by supply-driven considerations linked to costs than by market considerations'. For example, moves by Procter and Gamble or Unilever to streamline the number of brands they promote worldwide are mostly motivated by cost savings and communication synergies. Because much of the writing and thinking on global brands has taken an internal approach,

we still have a restricted understanding of the relationship between consumers and global brands.

Definitions of global brands are mostly supply side. Brands have been defined as global based on where the firm does most of its business, its size, and the extent to which its products share similar technical specifications. A case in point is the definition of global brands in industry rankings. In their rankings of global brands, AC Nielsen and Interbrand (Branch 2001; Interbrand's Best Global Brands 2006, p. 22) look at size, geographic reach and the proportion of revenues from outside a company's home country. Interestingly though, Interbrand's ranking regularly excludes Wal-Mart because 'it is not consistently branded as Wal-Mart around the globe' (Interbrand 2007, p. 22). Note that there is an ironic circularity here that has Interbrand excluding brands that are not consistent enough, and then, based on the ranking, advising marketers that consistency will help them achieve better valuations for their brands: 'best brands achieve a high degree of consistency in visual, verbal, auditory, and tactile identity across geographies'. Definitions and conceptualizations of global brands are still developed from the company's perspective, without paying much attention to how consumers perceive global brands.

Consistency and global branding: from replication to flexible adaptation

'Consistency is the last refuge of the unimaginative.'
Oscar Wilde

Marketing textbooks suggest that brand managers should keep their brands consistent across cultural boundaries because consumers travel more and more, and thus might be confused by inconsistent branding. For example, Keller (1998, p. 555) writes that consistency 'becomes particularly important in those markets where there is much customer mobility or where media exposure transmits images across national boundaries'. Reibstein (2005, p. 176) states: 'for a global brand to be a true global brand, it must also be consistent, not just in name, but in position and what it offers'. The problem with these recommendations is that there is very little research evidence suggesting that (in) consistency is actually affecting consumer attitudes and perceptions. Managers and marketing scholars assume that people are negatively influenced by brands displaying a different logo, message or value proposition in different countries' but there is little empirical research to support this position or the degree to which it holds.

We can justify the consistency of global brands with operational arguments (cost savings; efficiencies; synergies across markets). The importance of consistency also makes sense from an information processing perspective. Social psychologists have amply demonstrated that people value consistency, especially when it is their own that is questioned or examined (Festinger 1957). Psychologists argue that people value coherence and order in the presentation of information as a way to reduce the effort of processing that information. Pepitone (1966, p. 270) argues that people like consistent structures because they 'are simpler to maintain than distinctions, discrepancies and contradictions'. The question then becomes how we define consistency. A troubling issue in the global branding literature is we have tended to define consistency purely from a supply-side perspective, without exploring the perceptions of other stakeholders such as consumers, investors, business partners or suppliers. Indeed, is consistency a meaningful construct when different consumers have different mental models of the market?

Furthermore, the practices of some major global brands are not as consistent as they first appear. Think of a brand such as McDonald's, which is regularly taken as the example of a typical global brand. McDonald's does offer a consistent face, in terms of its logo and it does stand for affordable and convenient fast-food restaurants across markets. But it undertakes very different activities with different target consumers in different markets. In Korea, McDonald's targets women who want to hold club meetings, study groups or chat over coffee. In Hong Kong, McDonald's caters mostly to kids and teenagers wanting study space away from cramped households (Watson 2003). In India, McDonald's mostly caters to middle-class and upper middle-class households and their desires to experiment with new food options. McDonald's looks, means and tastes very differently across markets. Furthermore, the company is pursuing different avenues of brand rejuvenation across markets. In Europe, McDonald's has tried to reposition itself as a trendy place with iPod stations and designer armchairs where people get 'good food fast' rather than fast-food. The look and feel of its European restaurants is now quite different from other parts of the world (Wiggins 2007).

Similarly, while Nike has a consistent logo and slogan, it has pursued very different kinds of cultural and business opportunities: from the release of compilation CDs to theme park retailing or entering new (and potentially unfashionable) sports such as golf (Grant 2006). Finally, Italian car company Fiat usually positions its vehicles as reliable and sturdy cars for middle-class consumers. In many developing countries such as Brazil, this promise was successful. In India though, Fiat had to market itself as a premium, aspirational car company. It picked cricketer Sachin Tendulkar as its endorser, to promote

Fiat as a car for cosmopolitan Indians. Overall, for all the talk of consistency in global branding, many companies seem to manage a lot of highly successful executional and positioning variations that do not appear mutually consistent.

Rather than a blueprint to be replicated across markets, it might be useful to think of global brands as stories. A small but influential stream of theoretical and managerial texts have analyzed brands as stories (Holt 2002, 2003, 2004; Randazzo 1993). Holt (2004) in particular argues that iconic brands reach their iconic status because they develop stories resolving cultural contradictions. For example, Holt mentions the disconnect between the American ideals of extraordinary athletes and entrepreneurial 'warriors', and the reality of disaffected youth working low-paid jobs. Holt attributes the success of Mountain Dew to the brand's ability to offer an alternative identity path assuaging male anxieties. Holt's work focuses squarely on national contradictions and he does not explore how brands might be managed globally to become and remain iconic. Building upon Holt's insights about brands' mythical qualities, it may be fruitful to explore global brands and global branding as a cluster of different cultural ideas (Grant 2006), archetypal heroes, and other characteristics of powerful narratives (see Polkinghorne 1988).

What do we gain from looking at global brands as stories? This metaphor helps us move away from sequential and linear models of branding based on the delivery of symbolic resources to consumers (see, for example, Erdem and Swait 1998; Keller and Lehmann 2003). Building upon Vargo and Lusch's (2004) seminal article on the dominant logic of marketing, we argue that such linear approaches find their origin in marketing's emphasis on product management, which can help understand the equity companies can derive from their branding exercises, but cannot fully capture the dynamics of brand meaning. More specifically, looking at brands through the lens of narrative helps us move away from treating the consumer as a malleable individual who can be bent to the will of a firm's brand, but instead as a co-creator of brand meaning. Examining brands as stories is a way of thinking about brands that can help us view differently the process by which brands are created and circulated, as well as the incredible symbolic power of brands in the global marketplace. In the next section, we examine the symbolic, quasi-mythical quality of global brands.

The value of global brands for consumers

There is an emerging stream of literature examining the relationship between global brands and consumers (Askegaard 2006; Holt 2002; Steenkamp et al. 2003; Thompson and Arsel 2004), but there is still little research investigating how consumers come to think of certain brands as global. Steenkamp and his colleagues (2003, p. 54) hypothesize that consumers come to perceive brands as global in two main ways: (1) by learning of a brand's global geographic reach, through travel, media exposure or other sources of information; and (2) by recognizing the 'globalness' of the brand, as evoked by a 'modern, urban lifestyle'. But these hypotheses remain to be explored and tested. We still know very little about the formation of perceptions when it comes to global brands.

What we do know is that consumers value global brands and that there are certain characteristics of global brands that they specifically value (Steenkamp et al. 2003). First, consumers associate the wide geographic reach of global brands with better quality. Steenkamp and his colleagues find that the extent to which a consumer will perceive brands as global (what they call 'perceived brand globalness') is positively related to brand quality. In the words of a Russian consumer 'the more people who buy a brand… the better quality it is'. (Holt et al. 2004).

In other words, wide market acceptance acts as a signal of quality. Alden *et al.* (1999) stress that many global brands, such as Vodafone or Ariel, feature in their advertisements a wide variety of consumers from different countries to promote this wide acceptability.

Second, consumers associate global brands with glamour, prestige and high status (Steenkamp *et al.* 2003; Kapferer 1992). Global brands convey status, power and success because they are associated with a powerful global elite of people (Holt *et al.* 2004). Studies reveal that that the degree to which a brand is perceived as global positively influences the regard in which the brand is held (Johansson *et al.* 2005). The aspirational dimensions of global brands particularly hold in certain product categories: Global brands that are from countries with a particular expertise (such as German cars or Italian clothing brands) are especially valued (Holt *et al.* 2004).

Third, global brands offer consumers a sense of connecting with other consumers in distant places. They help create transnational connections between consumers who feel like they belong to a larger, global community (Holt *et al.* 2004). Consumer researchers have amply demonstrated that consumers use brands to construct social relations. One of the emerging drivers of value for brands is their linking value (Cova 1997), that is the capacity of brands to enable the formation of communities such as the Harley Davidson or Macintosh enthusiasts (Schouten and McAlexander 1995). Similarly, global brands seem to foster a sense of belonging to a larger, transnational community. This ability for global brands to provide connections for people who have never met each other seems to be a key driver for the value of global brands. Finally, global brands have become part of the language and the prism that people use to make sense of the world. Global brands have come to embody many of the excesses of late capitalism such as exploitative labor conditions (Klein 1999). Because of their omnipresence in public debates and discussions, global brands such as Nike and McDonald's have come to symbolize capitalism in its transnational form. Global brands have become part of a certain lingua franca to talk about markets. For many consumers, global brands signal the kind of community they do not want to belong to. For example, Thompson and Arsel (2004) find consumers patronizing local coffee shops to resist the hegemony of Starbucks and assuage the feelings of cynicism and disempowerment that the global chain of coffee shop generates. The hegemony of global brands creates new spaces for companies building upon anti-corporate sentiments. The strategy of Snapple, Ben and Jerry's (before it was acquired by Unilever), or Mecca Cola, all illustrate emerging forms of resistance against global brands (Holt 2002).

GLOBAL BRANDING IN PRACTICE: REALIZING THE GLOBAL BRAND

Armed with an understanding of global brands and the consumer environments in which they operate, we are equipped to consider the implementation of a global branding strategy. Keller (2003, p. 696) provides a series of admonitions for managers attempting to build global customer-based brand equity. These start with a warning that it is necessary to understand differences and similarities between different markets, and a caution not to cut corners. From there, he addresses logistics (establish an infrastructure and build brand partnerships), localization trade-offs (balance standardization and customization and global and local control), and operations (embrace integrated communications and establish operable guidelines). Lastly, on an on-going basis, Keller suggests leveraging brand elements and implementing a brand equity monitoring system.

In moving from these guidelines to a set of actions, we propose the following framework:

- establish the brand architecture, outlining the role of each brand in each market;

- for each brand establish the value proposition with some view as to how that will be translated in different ways in various markets;
- consider a migration path to establish that brand identity in each market;
- elaborate and support the brand identity with appropriate mix elements; and finally have a diagnostic monitoring and control system.

Brand architecture decisions are critical because they dictate how much of the market a global brand must appeal to. Coca Cola can afford Coke to be perceived much more as a foreign or global brand if it has Thums Up in its portfolio of Indian brands, than if it does not. The greater the breadth of the market a brand must cover, the less depth will be possible in any given segment. Proliferation of positions, designs and communications is a danger in this environment because incremental variations for localization made at the margin can add up to very diffused branding viewed from a global perspective. For example, at one stage Palmolive soap had 22 fragrances, 17 packages, 9 shapes, and numerous positions across its different markets (Keller 2003, p. 710).

Developing the promise or value proposition consists of deciding how to gain awareness in the target market, and gaining brand associations consistent with the brand identity. Barwise and Robertson (1992) suggest that the different migration paths of (a) starting off with exports, (b) acquisition of overseas brands, and (c) brand alliances all have advantages, depending on the situation. After initial entry, Douglas (2001) proposes local market expansion and global rationalization as logical steps. That is, the degree of globalization is likely to increase with the product's maturity (and hence legitimacy) in the market. These observations apply to diffusion *within* markets. In terms of the diffusion of global brands *between* markets, Kalish, Mahajan and Muller (1995) use a game theoretic model to argue for waterfall as opposed to sprinkler entry strategies (sequential rather than simultaneous release) when fixed costs are high, competition is low, life cycles are long, markets are small, word of mouth is significant, and growth

is slow. For waterfall strategies, Hofstede, Wedel and Steenkamp (2002) note that their contiguity research suggests that roll out can be accelerated by harnessing the contagion effects of adjacent markets.

The launch that follows entry decisions must be accompanied by a detailed elaboration of the brand identity and the brand essence on which it is based. Chapter 2 of Aaker and Joachimsthaler's (2002) book provides excellent guidelines on how to undertake this exercise. The brand elaboration stage, with its rich understanding of what the firm wants the brand to mean to consumers (and how that might vary by market) leads naturally to design of the marketing mix to support the brand identity, particularly a communications strategy. At all stages of preparing for the global brand launch and its ongoing management post-launch, the need for brand equity measurement is greater than it is for single market brands. The greater the social and cultural distance between the locus of the decision makers and the target at whom their projects and services are targeted, the greater the opportunity for a lack of correspondence. Detailed consumer feedback is one way to avoid such disconnects.

FUTURE RESEARCH DIRECTIONS

Global marketing is a fast-changing field as we learn more about this fascinating area and as turbulent market and inter-market dynamics create new challenges (see, for example, Kalish *et al.* 1995). We close by looking at what we think are some of the important issues in global branding that we need to address.

Measuring brands on a global basis

As Lusch and Harvey (1994) rightly note, little research has investigated the true asset base of the corporation in the global marketplace (exceptions include Srivastava *et al.* 1998).

Some methods to measure brand differences across countries and the results from implementing them are available from the Winning Brands service of AC Nielsen (Gordon 2003). However, the conceptual challenges of calibrating brands across markets still pertain; how can we gain a comparable metric when different consumers in different markets are using different criteria? Clearly some flexible or multidimensional rules are necessary.

The perceptions of globalness

We need to better understand the relationships between consumers and global brands. A starting point may be to investigate how consumers come to categorize brands as global. Steenkamp and his colleagues (2003) suggest that consumers may either become exposed to the same brands in different countries through travel; or elaborate perceptions of firms as global because of their brand communications emphasizing globalness may apply. But to our knowledge, there is no empirical research looking into these processes.

Furthermore, we need to better distinguish between various global brands. There are many kinds of globalness and global positionings: some brands such as Armani or Chanel are heavily built on the notion of heritage and culture of origin. Part of the appeal of such brands resides in consumers' desires to demonstrate competence with regard to foreign cultures to communicate cosmopolitan tastes and build their cultural capital (Hannerz 1990). Other brands such as Coke or Nokia build a large part of their appeal on the basis of their transnationality. By transnationality, we refer to the ability of these brands to create an imagined community of consumers. In his influential work on nationalism, political scientist Benedict Anderson (1983) explains that newspapers enabled people who had never come into contact with each other to care about each other. Print-capitalism, in the form of newspapers and novels, enabled the construction of national connections and identities. Similarly, brand managers are increasingly trying to create communities of consumers at the local (McAlexander, Schouten and Koenig 2002) or transnational level (Cayla and Eckhardt 2008). Companies' future research on global brand identity should investigate how consumers relate to transnational brands and their claims of connecting people.

The paths to globalness

Global branding researchers may want to look at critiques of methodological nationalism (Beck 2000; Taylor 1996) and think of global branding research as the study of brands in the global marketplace, rather than the study of international brands. The gist of this critique is that in the wake of the Second World War, the nation became the favored and almost exclusive unit of analysis for the analysis of problems in geography, economics and other social sciences. With this focus on nations, social sciences replicated the advent of new institutions such as the United Nations, the WTO or the IMF. The focus on the nation became natural. International marketing further increased the focus on the nation by defining itself as business between nations. Drawing from its roots in international trade, the discipline of international marketing has developed a similar focus on nations. Global brands are then often evaluated on the basis of their geographic reach in many nations (Interbrand 2007). This focus on the nation as the unit of analysis becomes also evident in the literature on the standardization of marketing activities. A main stream of research analyzes the extent to which global brands might adapt their strategies to national characteristics (Roth 1995).

There are different dimensions in the globalization of the marketplace that call into question this focus on nations in international branding research. First, there is the phenomenon of 'born global' firms (Knight and Cavusgil 2004) whereby firms achieve a rapid geographic reach within a short period of time. Born global firms often expand rapidly, without any long-term domestic experience. The process of developing global brand strategy is thus likely to be quite different for these brands. Particularly relevant for research on global branding is the case of internet brands which can reach millions of people rapidly. Studies of such brands might uncover novel types of relationships between consumers and global brands. Second, migration patterns and the use of brands by immigrant communities to build connections with other members of the same Diaspora (Gillespie 2002) highlight the emergence of what we could call diasporic brands, that is brands that tend to focus on certain ethnic communities as they migrate throughout the globe. An example is OCBC, a large Singaporean bank that caters to ethnic Chinese in Singapore, Malaysia, and Indonesia. Third, there is the phenomenon of online brands such as social networking websites, which escape the boundaries of geography or the neat categorizations of international marketing. Research on such brands promises to fill an important gap in our understanding of the relationship between brands and globalization. But to conduct such research, we must re-conceptualize culture and the relationship of global brands to it. Geographic location can be far less critical and at times more misleading in defining culture and cultural particularity.

These examples also illustrate the necessity to go beyond narrow definitions of global brands. Rather than solely focusing on ubiquitous brands with deep geographic reach, we need to study a larger repertoire of brands and their relationship with globalization processes. There is no question that certain brands occupy a remarkable place in the collective imagination and the public sphere. The omnipresence of US brands such as McDonald's, Starbucks or Nike and the strong negative feelings they evoke needs to

be further researched. But studying less prominent brands might also help us better understand the different paths to globalness. The increasing number of 'born global' firms (Knight and Cavusgil 2004) suggests that smaller firms will increasingly develop a global positioning. Comparing such firms to iconic global brands such as Nike will help us understand how firms approach the global marketplace differently.

Combining managerial and consumer-centric approaches

Finally, we need to combine a managerial and consumer-based approach to researching global brands. This may involve the collaboration of academics from these two traditions or the combination of several, complementary methodologies. The managerial literature and the consumer research literatures on global brands have evolved separately. On the managerial side, the debate has centered on the opportunities for the standardization of marketing activities (e.g., Yip 1999). In terms of consumer research on brands, researchers have mostly had a psychological focus on the relationship between consumers and brands and the use of brands for personal identity projects. While managerial research has often disregarded how consumers might respond to organizational strategies of standardization, consumer research has provided a limited understanding of the relationship between brands and globalization, and the managerial actions these should guide.

Rather than treating consumer and managerial concerns as separate research domains, we encourage researchers to combine managerial insights with consumer research on global brands. A fruitful direction would be to understand and explain the disjunctures between managerial strategies and consumer perceptions. For example, researchers may investigate how successful companies are in communicating their globalness. Given the proclaimed advantages of appearing as global, many managers want to claim that positioning for their brands. Managers of Singapore-based company OSIM, a manufacturer of massage chairs and other technological devices, want their company to appear as global to reap the benefits of that positioning. For these managers, a global positioning helps build their brand as a modern brand. Yet many consumers of OSIM chairs may not value such propositions. Combining case studies of companies trying to become global with research on how consumers perceive such brands may help us to understand how consumers come to think of certain brands as global and what obstacles these brands must overcome.

We argue that the metaphor of global brands as stories is especially useful for the study of global brands and the combination of these two perspectives. We have argued that global brands can be conceived as stories with multiple parts and audiences. Companies have already been urged to develop their brands as forms of corporate narrative (Dowling 2006). Conversely, there is some evidence that consumers process brand information in the form of narratives (Adaval and Wyer 1998; Wyer 2004). Weick (1995, p. 127) argues that 'people think narratively rather than argumentatively or paradigmatically'. Building upon this insight that people commonly think in story-like form, Escalas (2004) shows how consumers interpret information about brands by fitting them into a story. When conceived as an evolving story, the construction of brands becomes a multipartite process involving a host of authors who all add their own associations: consumers, managers, but also popular culture and influencers in different cultural contexts (Holt 2003). A company may try to engineer some of these associations but, eventually, the brand's meanings are bound to remain the diverse and fragmented parts of a co-created brand story incorporating heterodox threads. Future research should examine the new role of companies in telling global brand stories, especially as we move to an environment of

value and meaning co-creation (see Vargo and Lusch 2004).

The metaphor of global brands as stories also opens new methodological avenues. For example, the study of global brands seems especially suited for the kind of multi-sited research for which anthropologists have been calling (Marcus 1986). If brands are really 'brand cultures' (Schroeder and Salzer-Morling 2006), then they might also be conceived as traveling brand cultures, picking different associations and evolving as they are introduced to different markets. It would seem to be especially fruitful to start with the kind of detailed cultural branding analysis carried out by Holt (2004), and to apply the same approach to global brands, as they are designed and marketed in different markets.

REFERENCES

Aaker, D. A. (2005) *Strategic Market Management*, 7th Edn. Hoboken, NJ: John Wiley.

Aaker, D. A. and Joachimsthaler, E. (2002) *Brand Leadership*. London: Simon Schuster.

Adaval, R. and Wyer, R. S. (1998) 'The role of narratives in social information processing', *Journal of Consumer Psychology*, 7: 207–245.

Advertising Educational Foundation (2007) 'PANTENE – the evolving approach to a global brand', http://www.aef.com/on_campus/classroom/speaker_pres/data/4001 [accessed 1 March 2008].

Alden, D. L., Steenkamp, J.-B. and Batra, R. (1999) 'Brand positioning through advertising in Asia, North America and Europe: the role of global consumer culture', *Journal of Marketing*, 63(1): 75–87.

Anderson, B. (1983) *Imagined Communities: Reflections on the Origins and Spread of Nationalism*. London and New York: Verso.

Askegaard, S. (2006) 'Brands as a global ideoscape', in J. Schroeder and M. Salzer-Mörling (eds.), *Brand Culture*. London: Routledge, pp. 91–102.

Barwise, P. and Robertson, T. (1992) 'Brand portfolios', *European Journal of Management*, 10(3): 277–285.

Beck, U. (2000) 'The cosmopolitan perspective: sociology of the second age of modernity', *British Journal of Sociology*, 51: 79–105.

Branch, S. (2001) 'AC Nielsen gives 43 brands global status', *Wall Street Journal*, 31 October: B8.

Cayla, J. and Eckhardt, G. (2008) 'Asian brands and the shaping of a transnational imagined community', *Journal of Consumer Research* (August): 216–230.

Cova, B. (1997) 'Community and consumption: towards a theory of the linking value of products and services', *European Journal of Marketing*, 31(3/4): 297–316.

Day, G. S. and Reibstein, D. J. (2004) 'Managing brands in global markets' in H. Gatignon and J. R. Kimberley (eds), *Strategies for Building Successful Global Businesses*. Cambridge: Cambridge University Press, pp. 184–206.

Douglas, S. (2001) 'Exploring new worlds: the challenge of global marketing', *Journal of Marketing*, 64 (January): 103–107.

Douglas, S. and Wind, Y. (1987) 'The myth of globalization', *Columbia Journal of World Business*, 22(4): 19–31.

Dowling, G. R. (2006) 'Corporate reputation stories', *California Management Review*, 49(1): 82–100.

Drucker, P. (1954) *The Practice of Management*. New York: Harper and Row.

Erdem, T., Swait, J. and Ana Valenzuela (2006) 'Brands as signals: a cross-country validation study', 70(1): 34–49.

Erdem, T. and Swait, J. (1998) 'Brand equity as a signaling phenomenon', *Journal of Consumer Psychology,* 7(2): 131–157.

Escalas, J. E. (2004) 'Narrative processing: building consumer connections to brands', *Journal of Consumer Psychology*, 14(1): 168–179.

Festinger, L. (1957) *A Theory of Cognitive Dissonance*. Stanford: Stanford University Press.

Fournier, S. (1996) 'Land Rover North America, Inc.' Harvard Business School Case 596-036, Soldiers Field: Harvard Business Publishing Service.

Ger, G. and Belk, R. W. (1996) 'I'd like to buy the world a Coke: consumptionscapes of the "Less Affluent World", *Journal of Consumer Policy*, 19(3): 271–304.

Gillespie, M. (2002) 'Dynamics of diasporas: South Asian media and transnational cultural politics', in G. Stald, and T. Tufte (eds.), *Global Encounters: Media and Cultural Transformations*. Luton: University of Luton Press: 151–173.

Gordon, A. (2003) 'How consumers identify good brands: what market research tells us about building strong brands in Asia-Pacific', in *Proceedings of the ESOMAR Asia Pacific conference*, Singapore, December 2002, Amsterdam. 1–15.

Helsen, K., Jedidi, K. and DeSarbo, W. S. (1993) 'A new approach to country segmentation utilizing multinational diffusion patterns', *Journal of Marketing*, 57(4): 60–71.

Hofstede, F. T., Steenkamp, J.-B. and Wedel, M. (1999) 'International market segmentation based on consumer-product relationships', *Journal of Marketing Research*, 36 (February): 1–17.

Hofstede, F. T., Wedel, M. and Steenkamp J.-B. (2002) 'Identifying spatial segments in international markets', *Marketing Science,* 21(2): 160–177.

Holt, D. (2002) 'Why Do Brands Cause Trouble? A Dialectical Theory of Consumer Culture and Branding', *Journal of Consumer Research*, 29 (June): 70–90.

Holt, D. (2003) *Brand and Branding. Research Note*. Harvard Business School.

Holt, D. (2004) *How Brands Become Icons: The Principles of Cultural Branding*. Harvard Business School Press.

Holt D., Quelch, J. and Taylor, E. (2004a) 'How global brands compete', *Harvard Business Review*, (September): 68–75.

Holt, D., Quelch, J. and Taylor, E. (2004b) 'Managing the global brand: a typology of consumer perceptions', in J. Quelch and R. Deshpande, Rohit (eds), *The Global Market*. Jossey-Bass, pp. 180–201.

Interbrand (2007) 'Lessons learned from global brands', www.brandchannel.com; [accessed 02/03/2007].

Kalish, S., Mahajan, V. and Muller, E. (1995) 'Waterfall and sprinkler new-product strategies in competitive global markets', *International Journal of Research in Marketing* (July): 105–119.

Kapferer, J.-N. (2002) 'Is there really no hope for local brands?' *Journal of Brand Management*, 9(3): 163–170.

Kapferer, J.-N. (1992) 'How global are global brands?' in *ESOMAR Conference Proceedings: The Challenge of Branding Today and in the Future*. Brussels, Belgium: ESOMAR, pp. 199–215.

Keller, K. L. (2003) *Strategic Brand Management: Building, Measuring and Managing Brand Equity*, 2nd edn. Upper Saddle River, NJ: Prentice Hall.

Keller, K. L. and Lehmann, D. R. (2002) 'The brand value chain: optimizing strategic and financial brand performance', *Marketing Management*, (May/June): 26–31.

Klein, N. (1999) *No Logo: Taking Aim at the Brand Bullies*. New York: Picador.

Knight, G. A., and Cavusgil, S. T. (2004) 'Innovation, organizational capabilities, and the born-global firm', *Journal of International Business Studies,* 35(2): 124–141.

Kotler, P. (1986) 'Global standardization – courting disaster', *Journal of Consumer Marketing*, 3(2): 13–15.

Lee, C. and Green, R. (1991) 'Cross-cultural examination of the Fishbein Behavioral Intentions Model', *Journal of International Business Studies,* 22(2): 289–305.

Levi-Strauss, C. (1975) *La Voie Des Masques*. Geneva, Switzerland: Skira.

Luehrman, T. A. (1997) 'What's it worth?' *Harvard Business Review* (May–June): 132–142.

Lusch, R. F. and Harvey, M. (1994) 'The case for an off-balance-sheet controller', *Sloan Management Review*, 35 (Winter): 101–105.

Marcus, G. E. (1986) 'Contemporary problems of ethnography in the modern world system', in J. Clifford, and G. E. Marcus (eds), *Writing Culture: The Poetics and Politics of Ethnography*, Berkeley, CA: University of California Press.

McAlexander, J. H., Schouten, J. W. and Koenig, H. (2002) 'Building brand community', *Journal of Marketing*, (January): 38–54.

Pepitone, A. (1966) 'Some conceptual and empirical problems of consistency models' in S. Feldman (ed.), *Cognitive Consistency: Motivational Antecedents and Behavior Consequents*. New York: Academic Press, pp. 257–297.

Polkinghorne, D. E. (1988) *Narrative Knowing and the Human Sciences*. Albany: State University of New York Press.

Quelch, J. (2003) 'The return of the global brand', *Harvard Business Review*, (August) Reprint F0308D.

Quelch, J. and Hoff, E. (1986) 'Customizing global marketing' *Harvard Business Review*, (May–June), Reprint 86312.

Raman, A., Thompson, P., Aaker, J., Manwani, H., Clift, S. and Kotabe, M. (2003) 'The global brand face-off', *Harvard Business Review*, 81(6): 35–37

Randazzo, S. (1993) *Mythmaking on Madison Avenue*: Chicago Probus.

Reibstein, D. (2005) 'House of brands versus branded house', *Global Agenda*, 3 (January): 175–177.

Ries, A. and Ries, L. (2002) *The 22 Immutable Laws of Branding*. New York: Harper Business.

Robertson, R. (1995) 'Glocalization: time–space and homogeneity–heterogeneity', in S. Lash and R. Robertson (eds), *Global Modernities*. London: Sage, pp. 25–44.

Roth, M. S. (1995) 'The effects of culture and socioeconomics on the performance', *Journal of Marketing Research*, 32(2): 163–175.

Schouten, J. W. and McAlexander, J. (1995) 'Subcultures of consumption: an ethnography of the new bikers', *Journal of Consumer Research*, 22(1): 43–61.

Schroeder, J. and Salzer-Morling, M. (eds). (2006) *Brand Culture*. London: Routledge.

Schuiling, I. and Kapferer, J.-N. (2004) 'Real differences between local and international brands: strategic implications for international marketers', *Journal of International Marketing*, 12(4): 97–112.

Srivastava, R. K., Shervani, T. and Fahey, L. (1998) 'Market-based assets and shareholder value: a framework for analysis', *Journal of Marketing*, 62(1): 2–19.

Steenkamp, J.-B. (2001) 'The role of national culture in international marketing research', *International Marketing Review*, 18(1): 30–40.

Steenkamp, J.-B., Batra, R. and Alden, D. (2003) 'How perceived brand globalness creates brand value', *Journal of International Business Studies*, 34(1): 53–65.

Taylor, P. J. (1996) 'Embedded Statism and the Social Sciences: Opening up to new spaces', *Environment and Planning*, 28(19): 17–28.

Thompson, C. and Arsel, Z. (2004) 'The Starbucks brandscape and consumer's (anti-corporate) experiences of glocalization',

Journal of Consumer Research, 31(3): 631–642.

van Gelder, S. (2003) *Global Brand Strategy*. London: Kogan Page.

Vargo, S. L. and Lusch, R. F. (2004) 'Evolving to a new dominant logic for marketing', *Journal of Marketing*, 68 (January): 1–17.

Vincent, L. (2002) *Legendary Brands: Unleashing the Power of Storytelling to Create a Winning Marketing Strategy*. Dearborn Trade Publishing.

Watson, J. L. (1997) 'Transnationalism, localization and fast foods in East Asia', in J. L. Waston (ed), *Golden Arches East: McDonald's in East Asia*. Stanford, CA: Stanford University Press, pp. 1–38.

Welch, D. (2007) 'Why Toyota is afraid of being number one', *Business Week,* 5 March: 42–50.

Wiggins, J. (2007) 'Burger, Fries and a Shake-up', *Financial Times*, 27 February: 7.

World Trade Organization (1998) *The Multilateral Trading System: 50 Years of Achievement*.

Wyer, R. S. (2004) *Social Comprehension and Judgment: The Role of Situation Models, Narratives and Implicit Theories*. Mahwah, NJ: Erlbaum.

Yip, G. S. (1997) 'Patterns and determinants of global marketing', *Journal of Global Marketing*, 13(1–3): 153–164.

Yip, G. S. (2003) *Total Global Strategy II*. Upper Saddle River, NJ: Prentice Hall.

18

Pricing in the Global Marketplace

Kristiaan Helsen

INTRODUCTION

Pricing is generally described as one of the most critical issues that managers face (e.g., Simon 1989). One 1995 survey of US and European managers polled from a broad range of industries found that pricing was rated as the marketing issue with the highest problem pressure (Dolan and Simon 1996, pp. 4–5). The role of price in the firm's marketing mix is twofold. First, price is the only marketing mix instrument that creates revenues for the firm. Pricing decisions will have an immediate impact on the company's sales revenues and bottom line. Second, price also signals to the market the company's intended value positioning for the product or service being sold (Kotler and Keller 2006, p. 399). At the same time, some scholars suggest that the significance of pricing has most likely increased over the years due to a multitude of factors, including inflation, intensified competition, market saturation, and rising consumerism (Simon 1989, pp. 3–4). For multinational companies (MNCs) the complexities of the global environment render price-setting policies an even more bewildering endeavor. Yet, in spite of its

claimed managerial relevance, international pricing has received remarkably little research interest relative to other marketing mix instruments. One review of international marketing research covering the 1980s found that merely 14 (1.5%) out of the 893 studies reviewed dealt with pricing (Aulakh and Kotabe 1993). Most of these international pricing studies related to transfer pricing issues. Not surprisingly, the difficulty in obtaining company information on pricing decisions is seen as a major hurdle for doing empirical research in the area (Aulakh and Kotabe 1993).

This chapter gives an overview of the current state of affairs of research on global pricing. At the end of the chapter we map out a research agenda on global pricing. We first review academic research on the international prices setting process. One very potent force is the market environment. We consider how culture affects consumers' processing of price-related information. Another crucial market force is the local competitive environment. We explore how differences in the competitive environment (e.g., between local companies and multinational companies) affect price-setting decisions. A third critical driver that we look at is currency exchange rate fluctuations and – coupled to this – exchange rate pass-through practices (Clark, Kotabe and Rajaratnam 1999). Just as with other marketing mix instruments, global marketers face two countervailing forces when setting international prices (Dolan and Simon, p. 146): price customization drivers and price harmonization drivers. Basic economics doctrine dictates that companies should maximize their profits through price discrimination. For many products one can indeed observe huge price differentials across countries (see Table 18.1). The main challenge, however, triggered by cross-country price gaps, is that price differentials often create arbitrage opportunities that possibly lead to gray market (parallel imports) situations. The final section of this chapter highlights research insights on coping with gray market challenges.

INTERNATIONAL PRICE-SETTING PROCESS

The topic of global pricing has not been entirely neglected in international marketing. Most of research, however, has focused on the drivers that influence international (primarily export) pricing decisions and different pricing practices of multinational companies. That prices do vary a great deal across countries is a well-known fact, as is illustrated in Table 18.1. This table shows the spread of retail prices (after sales taxes) in major cities around the world for a wide variety of consumer goods.

Several studies on international pricing have looked at which drivers determine such price differentials. A typical example is Cavusgil (1996) who lists five key factors that affect global pricing decisions: (1) the nature of the product or industry; (2) the location of

Table 18.1 Retail price indices for various items. (Index = Recorded price/Lowest price × 100)

Item	New York	Hong Kong	Bangkok	Tokyo	Paris	London	Sydney
Jack Daniel's Whiskey (700 ml.)	109.5	150.7	**100.0**	130.1	103.2	145.9	NA
iMac (24-inch)	110.0	**100.0**	116.8	107.5	NA	NA	116.5
Ben & Jerry's ice cream (500 ml.)	**100.0**	148.0	184.4	NA	181.0	133.8	NA
Rolex	139.5	**100.0**	124.4	107.7	NA	NA	129.4
Alfred Dunhill Bulldog cufflinks	137.0	**100.0**	132.7	139.3	138.1	130.0	116.3
Grande Coffee Frappucino at Starbucks	112.1	104.5	**100.0**	101.3	159.5	135.5	110.8
Microsoft Xbox 360 game console	125.1	110.1	NA	**100.0**	148.3	152.3	139.6
Big Bertha Titanium 454 Driver	**100.0**	138.9	175.5	NA	177.8	140.3	147.7
Crabtree & Evelyn Gardeners Hand Therapy (100 ml.)	**100.0**	114.8	NA	NA	130.7	113.9	104.5
Samsonite Thrill III suitcase	NA	103.1	100.4	NA	**100.0**	113.5	103.1
Swiss Army knife	NA	**100.0**	NA	148.2	134.8	NA	125.0
4-gig Apple iPod nano	NA	103.4	137.5	**100.0**	141.3	134.2	113.9
Tod's Decoupage handbag	NA	**100.0**	NA	181.1	165.6	165.7	NA
CD by Madonna	157.0	124.0	**100.0**	153.8	206.0	177.0	213.5
Canon digital IXUS 750 camera	NA	**100.0**	129.3	NA	151.6	173.1	NA
Clinique Happy perfume spray	**100.0**	110.4	137.8	NA	156.5	137.2	152.4
Boxed DVD set of season 1 of 'Lost'	161.1	141.0	176.3	440.9	162.0	167.2	**100.0**
Kids Cayman Crocs shoes	120.4	104.0	159.1	**100.0**	195.5	171.0	145.6
Oakley's Monster Dog sunglasses	**100.0**	110.0	173.3	126.2	162.9	169.3	157.2

Source: Based on various issues of the Weekend Journal of the *Wall Street Journal* ('Arbitrage')

the production facility; (3) the distribution system; (4) the foreign market environment; and (5) currency differentials. These studies are largely exploratory or descriptive in nature, based on surveys or executive interviews. The process of international price decision-making has been a popular research topic among research scholars in the field both for the setting of intra-company transfer prices and export prices.

Setting transfer prices

A transfer price is the price that one country subsidiary within an MNC charges to another subsidiary for tangible or intangible goods delivered to that particular unit. To maximize global after-tax profits an MNC has an incentive to shift revenues to low-tax regime countries and deductions to high-tax countries. Tinkering transfer prices is often viewed as a crucial tool in achieving such cross-border profit movements. Apart from differences in foreign tax codes many other factors could influence the transfer pricing decision process, including (Burns 1980): market conditions in the foreign market, competition, and various market imperfections (e.g., price controls, customs duties, currency controls). Given the fiscal complexities of transfer pricing, most of the empirical studies on transfer pricing are situated in the accounting literature (e.g., Harris 1993; Jacob 1996; Stevenson and Cabell 2002). Not surprisingly, these studies indicate that high tax regimes lead to aggressive transfer pricing tactics. Research has also been done on the impact of transfer pricing penalties on the market valuation of MNCs (Eden, Juarez Valdez and Li 2005). In marketing, most research on transfer pricing has been conceptual in nature. Fraedrich and Bateman (1996) spell out guidelines and different methods on how to set transfer prices. Adler (1996) discusses the major strategic dimensions of transfer pricing.

Setting export prices

The literature suggests three basic options for setting export prices (e.g., Cavusgil 1988): (1) rigid cost-plus pricing; (2) flexible cost-plus pricing; and (3) dynamic incremental pricing. With rigid cost-plus pricing, the foreign list price is set by adding all costs accrued in international sales and a gross margin to domestic manufacturing costs. The second strategy, flexible cost-plus pricing, sets foreign list prices in the same manner as the first strategy but adjusts prices to local market conditions (e.g., strength of local competition) when necessary. The final method, dynamic incremental pricing, is based on the premise that fixed costs are sunk costs. Under this option the firm seeks to recover only variable and international marketing costs. Cavusgil (1996) observes that most companies use dynamic incremental pricing only under special circumstances. An example is the launch of a new product in a market when the MNC wants to use penetration pricing to gain market share. Stöttinger (2001), in a conceptual paper, links a firm's export price setting approach to its export experience and strategic price positioning. Her exploratory analysis based on a series of 45 qualitative interviews suggests that firms with limited export experience tend to use rigid cost-plus pricing. As firms gather experience, they often switch to the flexible cost-plus pricing method. The same study also indicates that firms in a premium price segment use flexible cost-plus pricing. However, this observation is probably a bit biased as most of the firms in her small sample classified themselves as belonging to this segment. Raymond, Tanner, and Kim (2001) used a survey to compare the pricing decisions of South Korean and US export firms. Their results show that the Korean exporters price more competitively in foreign markets than in their home market. US firms exhibit a more complex pricing behavior than their Korean counterparts by using more sophisticated costing systems.

CONSUMERS AND GLOBAL PRICING DECISIONS

Traditionally marketers have encouraged companies to practice value-based pricing. To assess value, managers need to grasp a solid understanding of consumers' buying decision-making processes and the factors that will impact these processes. In global marketing, the role of cultural values and norms in consumer behavior is well recognized. Recent research has shed some light on how culture impacts consumers' price responsiveness. Researchers in marketing have also looked at psychological biases that affect how consumers evaluate prices and make purchase decisions. Recent work in this area also spans the global marketplace. This section focuses on some of the key contributions and insights at the individual consumer level of global pricing research.

Cultural effects

The role of culture on consumer behavior has been widely studied in marketing. When consumer behavior is very culture-bound, marketing strategies require customization to local market conditions. Several aspects of the relationship between price and cultural orientation have been examined. Dawar and Parker (1994) tested for so-called 'marketing universals', which they define as consumer behaviors, within a segment and for a given product category, that are invariant across cultures. Their study centered around four quality signals, including price. Their key finding is a null result: there are few managerially meaningful differences in the use of these quality signals across cultures (at least for the demographic segment and product category studied). McGowan and Sternquist (1998) is a related study that explores whether marketing universals exist for price cues among Japanese and American consumers. In particular, the authors focused on two positive price cues – price as a signal of quality and as a sign of prestige – and one negative cue – value consciousness.

Their findings found evidence of market universal behavior for all three price cues for the US and Japanese student samples.

Ackerman and Tellis (2001) compared shopping patterns of ethnic Chinese and American consumers in the United States. They found sharp differences in the shopping behaviors of these two segments. Customers in the ethnic Chinese sample inspected many more items and took much more time to shop. The authors argued that these cultural differences lead to cross-store price variations: prices were observed to be significantly lower in Chinese supermarkets than in mainstream supermarkets. Note though that the study was conducted within the United States. Whether and how such shopping behaviors also differ for other cultures and markets outside the United States remains an open question.

Researchers have also investigated the role of cultural superstitions on pricing decisions and price responsiveness. In Western economies, retail prices (especially promotional prices) often end with the digit 9. Various explanations have been suggested for this phenomenon (e.g., Schindler and Kirby 1997): consumers are believed to 'round down' or ignore one or more of the digits to the right of a price's leftmost digit. However, different patterns can be observed in Chinese culture. This is most likely due to the role of cultural superstitions: the digit 8 (ba) is associated with 'prosperity' whereas the digit 4 (si) has a negative connotation and is associated with death. A survey of price-endings in Chinese print advertising showed that the digit 8 is indeed over-represented while the digit 4 is under-represented (Simmons and Schindler 2003).

Psychological biases

Experimental research in marketing has amply demonstrated that consumer perceptions are often driven by certain heuristics. One well-known mechanism is Kahneman and Tversky's (1979) anchoring and adjustment process. According to this rule, a consumer forms an initial judgment by anchoring on an easy-to-use attribute and then adjusts that initial judgment to reflect other attributes. Recently, insights from this literature have also been used to assess how consumers treat foreign currencies and the impact of such a heuristic on people's spending behavior when using foreign currency. Raghubir and Srivastava (2002) explored how consumers value products in an unfamiliar currency setting. Their key finding is a manifestation of the anchoring-and-adjustment heuristic: consumers tend to use a foreign currency anchor on the nominal (or face) value of the unknown currency and adjust it for the exchange rate to determine the real value. However, the adjustment is typically inadequate. This focus on the face value rather than the real value of money is the well-known 'money illusion' phenomenon. As a result, when the nominal value of the foreign currency is a multiple of the home currency (e.g., for a US consumer considering a purchase in Hong Kong dollars; US$1 = HK$7.8), consumers tend to spend less in real terms when buying in the foreign currency than in the home currency. Conversely, when the nominal value of the foreign currency is a fraction of the home currency (e.g., for a US consumer contemplating a purchase in British pounds; US$1 = UK£0.5), they are likely to spend more. Via various lab experiments, the authors offer ample evidence that corroborate this money illusion phenomenon. Wertenbroch, Soman and Chattopadhyay (2007) further examined how consumers evaluate transactions in foreign currencies and reversed some of the findings of previous studies. Their results suggest that consumers anchor on the numerosity of the nominal difference between prices and salient references (e.g., budget constraints) when evaluating purchase transactions in foreign currencies. In one of the studies, subjects were asked to imagine living on a post-tax budget of HK$ 9,000 per month and to estimate how much they would pay for non-essential items like eating out, entertainment, shopping. With the 'low numerosity' condition, subjects were

then asked to imagine living on 500 'Tristania' dollars, a fictional currency worth HK$ 18 (T$1 = HK$18). When drawing up budgets, the subjects scrimped and saved their Tristania dollars but spent their Hong Kong dollars much more lavishly. This effect reverses under the 'high numerosity' condition when the foreign currency becomes the less valuable currency (T$1 = HK$1/18). In other words, feeling like a millionaire (in terms of the foreign currency) encourages people to spend like one. According to the study, consumers focus on the difference rather than the ratio of budget and price to make their purchase decisions.

The money illusion effect has also been used to explain the potential effects of the switch to the euro in 2002. Desmet (2002), for instance, contrasted the effects of the euro conversion in Germany ('small' conversion rate) and Spain ('large' conversion rate). The study found a money illusion effect with an increased purchase intention when prices are expressed in euros for Germany. However, no such effects were observed for the Spanish sample. Gaston-Breton (2006) focused on the impact of the euro launch in France on consumer reactions and price perceptions. The currency changeover had a significant effect on the perceived transaction value for the national brand but not for the private label. The study also looked at the potential impact of several moderators but only familiarity with the euro seemed to matter.

One shortcoming of this research stream is that most studies were run under experimental conditions in a lab setting. This limits the external validity of the insights of this kind of research. It might be useful to examine these effects using real-world datasets such as market- or household-level scanner data for different countries.

COMPETITIVE LANDSCAPE

The competitive landscape is another crucial dimension in making pricing decisions.

Multinational firms have to consider the likely response of other multinationals and local competitors when setting prices in their different country markets. In particular, companies have to reflect on the kind of competitive reactions that can be triggered by price moves under different scenarios. Price also has an impact by defining the brand's competitive position vis-à-vis the competing brands in the foreign market (Dolan and Simon 1996, pp. 83–84).

In spite of the critical role of price competition, very little research has been done in marketing in the global arena. Solberg (1997) proposed a taxonomy of pricing strategy approaches using two criteria: preparedness for internationalization and industry globality. This framework was applied by Solberg, Stöttinger and Yaprak (2006) to study the pricing behavior of 24 exporters from three countries (Austria, Norway, and the United States). Chintagunta and Desiraju (2005) empirically examined competitive pricing interactions of the antidepressant drugs Prozac, Zoloft, and Paxil within and across markets (the United States, the United Kingdom, Germany, France and Italy). The authors used market-level quarterly data to estimate market response and strategic interaction parameters. Not surprisingly, they found that the effects of within- and across-market interactions vary across markets and across brands within a market. Further, firms tended to behave more aggressively toward their competitors in their home market than in their overseas markets.

One special form of price competition is the price war phenomenon. The prevailing philosophy is that price warfare creates turmoil in the industry with disastrous consequences for all companies involved (e.g., Heil and Helsen 2001). Zhang and Zhou (2006), however, argue that Chinese firms have a different perspective and often view a price war as a legitimate and effective business strategy. The authors analyzed two fierce price wars (color television and microwave) that occurred in China during the 1990s. Using what they call an 'Incremental Breakeven Analysis' (IBEA),

they present a framework that sheds insights on how Chinese firms identify opportunities for a price war and decide whether and when to trigger one.

Apart from the paper by Chintagunta and Desiraju (2005) cited earlier, very little empirical or analytical research exists on competitive pricing behavior in the global arena. Within a given market, multinational companies and local domestic firms often use different rules and/or mindsets to compete, as suggested by Zhang and Zhou's (2006) paper. Multinationals may also operate differently in foreign markets than in their home market. One paradigm that looks promising here is the theory of multimarket competition. Multimarket contact relates to competitive situations where the same firms compete against one another in multiple markets – be it geographic or product-related segments. One of the key tenets of the theory of multimarket competition is the so-called mutual forbearance hypothesis, which states that firms tend to avoid competitive attacks against rivals they meet in multiple markets. As Jayachandran, Gimeno and Varadarajan (1999) observe in a review paper of the multimarket literature: 'The dearth of empirical research examining multimarket competition in the global marketing context provides opportunities for additional research in this area' (p. 63).

GLOBAL PRICING AND FOREIGN EXCHANGE RATES

Unlike purely local marketing, global marketing transactions often involve two or even more currencies. While some countries or territories (e.g., Saudi Arabia, Hong Kong) maintain a currency peg against a focal currency such as the US dollar, most currencies move freely (and occasionally with very wild volatility). Therefore, currency exchange rate movements are a major challenge for global marketers. A firm doing business in the global marketplace faces two key exchange-related managerial issues: (1) what currency should we choose to set our prices? and (2) how much of an exchange rate gain (or loss) should we pass through to our customers?

Currency choice

One major concern arising from floating exchange rates centers around the choice of the currency unit to be used in international business transactions. Motivations for currency choice vary but the most common driver is risk avoidance of exchange rate exposure. Other factors may include market position and conditions, preferences of the parties involved in the transaction, competitive conditions, administrative ease, government restrictions. Research on currency choice in the marketing area has been very limited; most of the work has been done in the international trade area. One notable exception is a study by Samiee and Anckar (1998) that looks into the correlates of currency choice with export transactions based on a survey of US, Swedish, and Finnish firms. Their results suggest that exporters who address their customers' currency requests benefit from larger sales volumes and are more likely to sustain long-term relationships with their clients. However, export profit margins tended to be smaller. One major shortcoming of the study is that it focused on the seller. In reality, the transaction currency is often negotiated between the buyer (importer) and the seller (exporter). Further research could focus on the role of negotiations through surveys or simulations. Another potential avenue is the interrelationship between currency choice and price settlement.

Exchange rate pass-through

A second important issue coupled to currency exchange rate movements is the pass-through issue. Consider the predicament of a US firm selling products in Japan. Suppose that the US exporter's manufacturing costs are incurred in US dollars whereas its revenues are accrued in Japanese yen. When the US dollar weakens against the Japanese yen, the per-unit dollar contribution for the US exporter will increase. In principle, a weaker US dollar offers the US firm an opening to lower the yen price for its goods in Japan. That way, the US firm can steal market share away from its Japanese and other strong currency competitors. When the US dollar strengthens against the yen, we have the mirror picture of the previous scenario. If the yen price remains unchanged, the US firm's unit contribution will drop. If the firm wants to sustain its profit margin, it will be forced to increase its yen price. So the firm would face a trade-off between sustaining its profit margin versus market share. Exchange rate pass-through refers to the extent to which companies pass on the gains or losses of currency swings by adjusting their prices in the export market.

Research on foreign exchange rate pass-through has been abundant in the international economics literature. Goldberg and Knetter (1997) offer an excellent overview of the key insights from that research stream. A central concept in this literature is the notion of 'pricing-to-market' (PTM). PTM is a form of price discrimination that refers to the phenomenon of firms adjusting the magnitude of their markups, triggered by currency movements based on the nature of the foreign market (e.g., price sensitivity, competition). Gagnon and Knetter's (1995) study of export price adjustments for the US automobile market contrasted the pricing decision of Japanese and German car manufacturers during a period with high currency volatilities for both the yen and German mark. They found evidence that Japanese exporters use markup adjustments much more intensively than their German counterparts: Japanese firms offset about 70 per cent of the effect of exchange rate changes on buyer's prices through markup adjustments.

While a substantial amount of work on exchange rate pass-through has been done in the international economics and industrial organization fields, very little research has been done in marketing. Desiraju and

Shrikhande (1996) developed an analytical model to study the impact of the international distribution channel on pass-through. They found that the size of the pass-through depends on the presence of an incentive problem in the channel. When the dealer needs to be buffered against adverse demand conditions in her market, the exporting manufacturer cannot allow his wholesale price to reflect all of the currency swing. The resulting reduction in pass-through will depend on the effectiveness of the dealer. Other factors that affect the magnitude of the pass-through include the demand conditions in the foreign markets and the cost parameter of the exporter. Clark and colleagues (1999) offer a conceptual framework that links the extent of pass-through to six marketing related variables, namely: exchange rate uncertainty, distribution policy, brand equity, competitive symmetry, sourcing strategy, and the firm's performance orientation (e.g., market share versus finance-based measures). The authors derive a set of a dozen propositions based on their framework; however, most of these have not been empirically tested so far.

INTERNATIONAL PRICE COORDINATION

In developing a global pricing strategy, one awkward problem multinational firms often face is how much alignment there should be between the prices set in the different countries. This challenge arises especially for global (or pan-regional) brands that can be easily shipped across borders with no or very few alterations. Lack of price coordination often creates arbitrage opportunities, thereby fostering so-called parallel imports with products being shipped from high-price to low-price countries. To buffer the company against such situations some form of price coordination is usually called for. Coupled to this challenge is the question of how much price centralization is appropriate and where the locus of price decision-making should be.

Parallel imports

In an ideal world, a multinational company would like to price discriminate between countries by charging a high price in price-insensitive countries and a low price in price-sensitive ones. Unfortunately, substantial price gaps between countries often create parallel imports ('gray markets') situations. This parallel importation channel is an unauthorized channel (usually perfectly legal) that competes with the manufacturer's authorized distributors. Parallel imports create havoc for companies as they cannibalize the sales of the authorized dealer and thereby risk undermining the channel–manufacturer relationship. Given the sensitive nature of the phenomenon, it is perhaps not surprising that empirical research on parallel imports is very scarce. The few studies that exist in marketing on gray markets are either purely analytical in nature or conceptual. On the analytical front, Dutta, Bergen and John (1994) used a transaction cost (TCA) modeling approach to examine a manufacturer's policy towards exclusive dealers who sell across their assigned territories ('bootleg'). Their main finding is that optimal enforcement policies should tolerate some level of bootlegging. Like every institution, an exclusive territory dealership (ETD) is imperfect. When deploying ETD, the firm should settle for a compromise and practice a policy of selective enforcement with some tolerance of bootlegging. The level of tolerance necessary is driven by factors such as (1) the importance of reseller services; (2) the amount of margin erosion on bootlegged sales; and (3) the reseller's beliefs on the manufacturer's long-term commitments.

Yang, Ahmadi and Monroe (1998) assess the effectiveness of four pricing strategies used by multinational manufacturers, namely: (1) 'local' (i.e., highest feasible price in each country based on the market's willingness-to-pay); (2) 'uniform' (same price across countries); (3) 'friction' (set price differences between countries equal to costs of redistributing products across countries); and (4) 'global'. The global pricing option is the one they advocate. With this option, the manufacturer first decides whether or not to fight parallel imports. Unfortunately, the paper only sketches a general picture without going into specific details. Ahmadi and Yang (2000) is a follow-up paper. It recasts parallel imports as a Stackelberg leader-follower game of price discrimination in international markets. On the one hand, the gray market undermines the manufacturer's ability to price discriminate between separate country markets. On the other hand, parallel imports effectively add another product version into the high-priced market for consumers to choose from, thereby creating a vehicle for vertical product differentiation and price discrimination. Depending on the trade-off between these two forces, the manufacturer may decide to fight or tolerate parallel imports if his goal is to maximize global profits.

Apart from the analytical research discussed above, several authors have also proposed conceptual frameworks to address the gray market quandary. Assmus and Wiese (1995) suggest four mechanisms that can be used to implement price coordination: (1) economic measures; (2) formal coordination through centralization; (3) formal coordination through formalized decision-making processes; and (4) informal coordination (e.g., information flows). To select which approach is most appropriate, the authors focus on two factors: the level of local resources and the level of environmental complexity.

However, no rigorous testing is provided to validate the proposed schema.

Another notable framework for price coordination is Simon and Kucher's (1995) price corridor. The background for their framework came from two recent developments, namely (1) the launch of the euro, which would make Europe-wide price comparisons more transparent for consumers and distributors, and (2) global sourcing by large mega-retailers (e.g., Carrefour, Tesco, Walmart). Both of these trends would lead to downward price pressure, making it more challenging for companies to maintain huge price differentials between countries. Simon and Kucher suggested a three-step procedure to cope with these challenges:

1 determine the optimal price in each country;
2 find out whether parallel imports occur at these prices;
3 if parallel imports are to be expected, set a price corridor.

The price corridor basically implies a narrowing of the cross-country price differentials by raising the price in the lowest-price countries and lowering the price in the highest-price countries (see Figure 18.1). The procedure can be seen as a practical implementation of the analytical prescriptions derived by Ahmadi and Yang (2000) for coping with parallel imports.

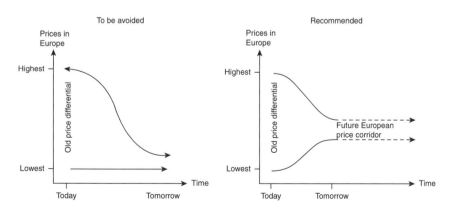

Figure 18.1 Setting a price corridor
Source: Simon and Kucher (1995), 'Pricing in the New Europe – a time bomb?', *Pricing Strategy & Practice*, p. 6. Published with permission from Emerald Group Publishing.

Pricing control

Pricing control occurs when the exporting firm influences distributor behavior in order to set 'desirable' (from the manufacturer's angle) prices in the foreign markets or when the exporter sets those prices directly. A related issue is the question of how centralized pricing decisions should be. This question is the well-known standardization versus adaptation debate that also arises for other marketing mix variables in global marketing (e.g., pricing, advertising). Several scholars have looked at possible antecedents that can be linked with the centralization question. Stöttinger (2001), for instance, argues that larger companies are more likely to centralize pricing decisions. However, in her interviews with company executives, no clear pattern emerged that led companies to standardize or differentiate their prices. Assmus and Wiese (1995) suggest that price centralization is called for when both levels of environmental complexity and local resources are low. No evidence is provided though to support their claim.

Cavusgil (1996) offers a list of reasons to support centralized (e.g., global branding, same competitors) and decentralized (e.g., quick response, local cost factors) pricing. Myers and Harvey (2001) address the antecedents and performance outcomes associated with the degree of price control by manufacturers when they use foreign distributors. To test their hypotheses, data were collected from US-based exporters. Their results suggest that a higher degree of price control the greater the international experience, the larger the firm size, the smaller the degree of asset specificity in the channel relationship, and the smaller the degree of channel dependence. The degree of price control is higher also the greater the cost-leadership orientation of the export manufacturer's strategy. The results for the performance variables were mixed. Pricing control negatively influences the exporters' strategic performance (e.g., maintaining distributor relationships, responding to competitive pressures) and

positively the economic performance. Further, the positive relationship between pricing control in the export channel and economic performance is found to be stronger when economic volatility increases and competitors become more aggressive.

CONCLUSIONS

A *leitmotiv* in many of the papers surveyed in this chapter is the observation of sheer paucity research on global pricing: 'the area of international pricing lacks large-scale empirical research' (Stöttinger 2001, p. 59); 'the lack of literature on pricing in international markets, …, the lack of a formal export pricing theory' (Raymond et al. 2001, p. 20); 'pricing remains one of the most persistently under-studied areas in international marketing' (Clark et al. 1999, p. 250); 'pricing remains an understudied dimension' (Solberg et al. 2004, p. 23). This lack of empirical research has been attributed to the difficulty in getting datasets. Most of the empirical research that has been done was based on lab experiments (e.g., Wertenbroch et al. 2007; Raghubir and Srivastava 2002) or survey data (e.g., Solberg et al. 2006; Stöttinger 2001). Survey-based research has been largely exploratory based on fairly small sample sizes. Obviously, companies' reluctance to share price and price-decision making information (Aulakh and Kotabe 1993) is a major factor behind the difficulty in getting good-quality research datasets. This is particularly the case for topics in sensitive areas such as parallel imports and transfer pricing. The Internet opens up new channels for gathering price-related datasets. Another valuable resource are the scanner datasets that are available (unfortunately often at a price) in scores of countries, including emerging markets such as China. A caveat is that these datasets typically only span a limited range of consumer goods categories.

The paucity of solid research on international pricing opens up a wide smorgasbord of research opportunities. While there is no shortage of conceptual frameworks there is clearly a lack of thorough empirical and analytical research. In particular, the following topics deserve attention:

- *Culture and Sales Promotions.* Consumer behavior scholars have studied how consumers respond to prices in different settings. Various research has also looked at the mechanisms consumers use to evaluate purchase transactions and possible biases associated with these processes. Marketers use a wide variety of sales promotion tools to induce consumers to buy their products (e.g., consumer rebates, buy-*x*-get-one-free). What is not clear is to what extent the effectiveness of such price promotions differ across cultures and why. Related questions are issues such as: To what extent is the money illusion effect a universal phenomenon? What other psychological biases enter in consumers' decision processes when evaluating price information?

- *Exchange Rate Pass-Through.* Currency pass-through is a crucial issue to marketers. There are several important questions that can be tackled: How much should be passed through? What should be the timing of pass-through? What mechanisms are used to implement pass-through and why? What is the impact of distribution channels and competition? Both analytical and empirical work is called for in this area. Apart from exchange rate fluctuations there are other areas where the pass-through issue arises in international marketing (e.g., import duties).

- *Pricing under High Inflation Regimes.* High inflation makes pricing in many countries a major headache. Often inflation leads to government-imposed price ceilings (*The Economist* 2008). Issues of interest in this domain include tools to predict the incidence and length of price controls, the competitive ramifications of such controls, and optimal mechanisms to cope with government-imposed price regulations.

- *Pricing Strategies for Emerging Markets.* One critique that can be leveled against past international pricing research is that most studies focused on developed markets. Very little research has been done on pricing strategies for emerging markets. Yet, as scholars such as Prahalad (2005) amply showed, many growth opportunities for MNCs are situated in this part of the world, including the 4 billion bottom-of-the-pyramid (BOP) consumers. Mahajan and Banga (2006, Chapter 6)

offer several strategic pricing approaches to sell to consumers with low budgets. Our understanding on the effectiveness of pricing strategies in emerging markets and BOP consumers' price responsiveness is very limited. Clearly, plenty of research opportunities exist in this area.

- *Pricing and Competition.* The role of competition in setting international prices is poorly understood. As mentioned earlier, theoretical paradigms such as multi-market competition can be fruitfully employed here both for analytical and empirical research. In many countries, companies also need to cope with a special form of competition: product piracy. One way to combat piracy is through price competition. For instance, in the DVD industry companies such as Twentieth Century Fox and Warner Brothers cut prices of their DVDs sold in China to fight against rampant piracy there (*Wall Street Journal* 2006). Little is known on how effective such pricing decisions can be to woo consumers away from counterfeits. Other areas that deserve attention here are the rivalry of store brands, price warfare phenomena.

- *Price Coordination.* The issue of standardization versus customization is to some extent a bogus issue especially in the pricing arena. Yet international pricing often demands some form of coordination. Several scholars have proposed different schemes and frameworks to pursue global price coordination but much more research is clearly needed here, both analytical and empirical.

REFERENCES

Ackerman, D. and Tellis, G. (2001) 'Can culture affect prices? A cross-cultural study of shopping and retail prices', *Journal of Retailing*, 77, 57–82.

Adler, R. W. (1996) 'Transfer pricing for world-class manufacturing', *Long Range Planning*, 29(1): 69–75.

Ahmadi, R. and Yang, B. R. (2000) 'Parallel imports: challenges from unauthorized distribution channels', *Marketing Science*, 19(3): 279–294.

Assmus, G. and Wiese, C. (1995) 'How to address the gray market threat using price coordination', *Sloan Management Review*, (36)3: 31–41.

Aulakh, P. S. and Kotabe, M. (1993) 'An assessment of theoretical and methodological development in international marketing: 1980–1990', *Journal of International Marketing*, 1(2): 5–28.

Burns, J. (1980) 'Transfer pricing decisions in U.S. multinational corporations', *Journal of International Business Studies*, 11(2): 23–39.

Cavusgil, S. T. (1988) 'Unraveling the mystique of export pricing', *Business Horizons*, 31(3): 54–63.

Cavusgil, S. T. (1996) 'Pricing for global markets', *The Columbia Journal of World Business*, 31(4): 66–78.

Chintagunta, P. K. and Desiraju, R. (2005) 'Strategic pricing and detailing: behavior in international markets', *Marketing Science*, 24(1): 67–80.

Clark, T., Kotabe, M. and Rajaratnam, D. (1999) 'Exchange rate pass-through and international pricing strategy: a conceptual framework and research propositions', *Journal of International Business Studies*, 30(2): 249–268.

Dawar, N. and Parker, P. (1994) 'Marketing universals: consumers' use of brand name, price, physical appearance, and retailer reputation as signals of product quality', *Journal of Marketing*, 58(2): 81–95.

Desmet, P. (2002) 'A study of the potential effects of the conversion to euro', *Journal of Product & Brand Management*, 11(3): 134–146.

Desiraju, R. and Shrikhande, M. (1996) 'Exchange rate pass-through and the role of international distribution channels', Working Paper 96-22, Federal Reserve Bank of Atlanta.

Dolan, R. J. and Hermann Simon (1996) *Power Pricing*. New York: The Free Press.

Dutta, S., Bergen, M. and John, G. (1994) 'The governance of exclusive territories when dealers can bootleg', *Marketing Science*, 13(1): 83–99.

Eden, L., Juarez Valdez, L. F. and Li, D. (2005) 'Talk softly but carry a big stick: transfer pricing penalties and the market valuation of Japanese multinationals in the United States', *Journal of International Business Studies*, 36: 398–414.

Fraedrich, J. P. and Bateman, C. R. (1996) 'Transfer pricing by multinational marketers: risky business', *Business Horizons*, Jan.–Feb., 17–22.

Gagnon, J. A. and Knetter, M. M. (1995) 'Markup adjustment and exchange rate fluctuations: evidence from panel data on automobile exports', *Journal of International Money and Finance*, 14(2): 289–310.

Gaston-Breton, C. (2006) 'The impact of the euro on the consumer decision process: theoretical explanation and empirical evidence', *Journal of Product & Brand Management*, 15(4): 272–279.

Goldberg, P. K. and Knetter, M. M. (1997) 'Goods prices and exchange rates: what have we learned?' *Journal of Economic Literature*, 35 (Sept.): 1243–1272.

Harris, D. G. (1993) 'The impact of U.S. tax law revision on multinational corporations' capital location and income shifting decisions', *Journal of Accounting Research*, 31(Suppl.): 111–140.

Heil, O. P. and Helsen, K. (2001) 'Toward an understanding of price wars: their nature and how they erupt', *International Journal of Research in Marketing*, 18(1 & 2): 83–98.

Jacob, J. (1996) 'Taxes and transfer pricing: income shifting and volume of intrafirm transfers', *Journal of Accounting Research*, 34(2): 301–312.

Jayachandran, S., Gimeno, J. and Varadarajan, P. R. (1999) 'The theory of multimarket competition: a synthesis and implications for marketing strategy', *Journal of Marketing*, 63 (July): 49–66.

Kahneman, D. and Tversky, A. (1979) 'Prospect theory: an analysis of decision under risk', *Econometrica*, 47 (March): 263–291.

Kotler, P. and Keller, K. L. (2006) *Marketing Management*. Upper Saddle River, NJ: Prentice Hall.

Mahajan, V. and Banga, K. with Gunther, R. (2006) *The 86 Percent Solution. How to Succeed in the Biggest Market Opportunity of the Next 50 Years*. Upper Saddle River, NJ: Wharton School Publishing.

McGowan, K. M. and Sternquist, B. J. (1998) 'Dimensions of price as a marketing universal: a comparison of Japanese and U.S. consumers', *Journal of International Marketing*, 6(4): 49–65.

Myers, M. B. and Harvey, M. (2001) 'The value of pricing control in export channels: a governance perspective', *Journal of International Marketing*, 9(4): 1–29.

Prahalad, C. K. (2005), *The Fortune at the Bottom of the Pyramid*. Upper Saddle River, NJ: Wharton School Publishing.

Raghubir, P. and Srivastava, J. (2002) 'Effect of face value on product valuation in foreign currencies', *Journal of Consumer Research*, 29 (Dec.): 335–347.

Raymond, M. A., Tanner Jr., J. F. and Kim, J. (2001) 'Cost complexity of pricing decisions for exporters in developing and emerging markets', *Journal of International Marketing*, 9(3): 19–40.

Samiee, S. and Anckar, P. (1998) 'Currency choice in industrial pricing: a cross-national evaluation', *Journal of Marketing*, 62 (July): 112–127.

Schindler, R. M. and Kirby, P. N. (1997) 'Patterns of rightmost digits used in advertised prices: implications for nine-ending effects', *Journal of Consumer Research*, 24 (Sept.): 192–201.

Simmons, L. C. and Schindler, R. M. (2003) 'Cultural superstitions and the price endings used in Chinese advertising', *Journal of International Marketing*, 11(2): 101–111.

Simon, H. (1989) *Price Management*. Amsterdam: North-Holland.

Simon, H. and Kucher, E. (1995) 'Pricing in the New Europe – a time bomb?' *Pricing Strategy & Practice*, 3(1): 4–13.

Solberg, C. A. (1997) 'A framework for strategy analysis in globalizing markets', *Journal of International Marketing*, 5(1): 9–30.

Solberg, C. A., Stöttinger, B. and Yaprak, A. (2006) 'A taxonomy of the pricing practices of exporting firms: evidence from Austria, Norway, and the United States', *Journal of International Marketing*, 14(1), 23–48.

Stevenson, T. H. and Cabell, D. W. E. (2002) 'Integrating transfer pricing policy and activity-based costing', *Journal of International Marketing*, 10(4): 77–88.

Stöttinger, B. (2001) 'Strategic export pricing: a long and winding road', *Journal of International Marketing*, 9(1): 40–63.

The Economist (2008) 'In a Fix', (23 Feb., 2008), pp. 79–80.

Wall Street Journal (2006) 'New Tactic in Piracy Fight', (13 Sept., 2006), p. 28.

Wertenbroch, K., Soman, D. and Chattopadhyay, A. (2007) 'On the perceived value of money: the reference dependence of currency numerosity effects', *Journal of Consumer Research*, 34 (June): 1–10.

Yang, B. R., Ahmadi, R. H. and Monroe, K. B. (1998) 'Pricing in separable channels: the case of parallel imports', *Journal of Product & Brand Management*, 7(5): 433–440.

Zhang, Z. J. and Zhou, D. (2006) 'The art of price war: a perspective from China', Working Paper, The Wharton School, University of Pennsylvania.

19

Global Communications

Gary J. Bamossy and Johny K. Johansson

INTRODUCTION

With the technological advances in global communications, marketing communications have taken on a much greater strategic role than before. Even the smallest firm is able to connect with customers around the globe on an instantaneous and virtually cost-free basis. By the same token, single individuals around the world can easily access a vast amount of information about any one company, and quickly transmit the information to a large number of other like-minded individuals. Google, the blogosphere and the Internet in general may or may not offer the most reliable and trustworthy information about a company or individual – but it is free, readily available and rapidly diffused to virtually anyone with a modem. The information explosion has forced global communications to the forefront of company strategy formulation and implementation.

This chapter will deal with these issues in more detail below. But first the chapter needs to establish the basic context in terms of traditional and non-traditional media as used in integrated marketing communications. IMC involve the following promotional activities, all part of the global communications of the firm:

- Global media advertising
- Global sales promotion
- Global public relations and publicity
- International trade fairs
- Internet-based marketing
- Personal selling.

Global advertising includes traditional media spending in broadcast and print, but also extends to certain Internet advertising spending, including the pop-up and banner ads so common on the Web. Sales promotion is more wide-ranging and also the faster-growing promotional activity in global communications. It includes point-of-sales and point-of-purchase (POS and P-o-p) actions, usually very localized as in-store activities. More significant to a global perspective, sales promotion involves sponsorships, event marketing and product placement,

Global public relations and publicity may seem quite insignificant as marketing tools at home, but they do take on a much more important role in the global arena, where anti-globalizers, unfavorable media coverage, and damage control in outsourcing and sweatshop practices requires constant vigilance. International trade fairs are also less visible at home, but in global communications, these occasions for parading new products and tying up new distributors take on strategic relevance. This is where industry publications and other media are instrumental in putting a positive spin on Apple and a negative face on General Motors.

The most striking new development in global communications is in the Internet world, the e-commerce and the direct marketing efforts. Web-based communications have made it possible – and necessary – to deal much more interactively, not only with the customers but also with middlemen, suppliers, bloggers, anti-globalists and diverse stakeholders. The mindset required to navigate this dynamic and disruptive terrain is quite different from the basically one-way and transactional relationships in the traditional promotional strategies. The global communicator has to engage in dialogue, not top-down promotion. We will get back to this so-called 'Web2.0' phenomenon and its implications towards the end of the chapter.

Personal Selling is treated in a separate chapter on Sales Management. The present chapter will focus on the other elements and deal with each in the order listed. But first it is important to describe the three major players in global communications – the media, the ad agencies, and the advertisers – and the massive worldwide consolidation that has taken place among these players.

The global media giants

One of the driving forces behind the growth of global communications is the emergence of giant media conglomerates. Often starting from relatively minor countrywide operations in publishing or broadcasting, these conglomerates have been assembled by strong entrepreneurs who have used mergers and acquisitions to expand their operations beyond the home country, into regional strength and

ultimately global reach. Although several are US-based, the media giants also come from Europe and Australia. Because of the M&A activity, these units do not stay the same for very long. Here is a listing of the top 6 from 2007:

1 Time-Warner (US, 2006 Global Revenues: $31.8 Billion)
2 Disney (US, 2006 Global Revenues: $23.4 Billion)
3 Bertelsmann (Germany, 2006 Global Revenues: $16.3 Billion)
4 News Corp. (Australia, 2006 Global Revenues: $13.5 Billion)
5 Viacom (US, 2006 Global Revenues: $12.86 Billion)
6 Vivendi Universal (France, 2006 Global Revenues not available).

In the media world, competition is intense. With deregulation and privatization of airwaves and media, the trend is towards ever more dominance from a few giant conglomerates able to generate scale returns and synergies by combining content and media control across borders. These six entities control vast portions of the world's film production, TV show production, cable channel ownership, cable and satellite system ownership, book publishing, magazine publishing and music production.[1] If the trend continues, national differences in news, programming, entertainment, and media coverage are gradually likely to be dominated by globally streamlined coverage.

To understand how this consolidation of control affects global communications in marketing, it is important to remember that historically in most countries media control has been independent of advertisers and advertising agencies. What the giant conglomerates control is the access to the broadcast stations and the published media. This means that the programming you may see on Star TV in China might well be similar to what you see on the Fox Network in the United States. Individual stations in both countries can sometimes opt out of sensitive programming (as routinely happens when

Tiananmen Square programming is scheduled in China, and sexually ambiguous programming is scheduled in the American Bible-belt). But the stations doing so run a risk of antagonizing their owner – both entities are owned by Murdoch's News Corp. Since in most cases the programming is underwritten by advertisers who have been promised a certain amount of geographical coverage, stations opting out of the program undermine the contract between News Corp. and the advertiser. The economic foundation for the large conglomerates is the ability to leverage their geographical reach and audience size to attract advertisers – if the stations do not program the shows, they can lose their affiliation with the network to a local competitor.

This control is one reason government officials and many independent observers in different countries are worried about these organizations' undue influence over national culture and public opinion. Media control is of course quite different from control over advertising content and commercial rates. It is unlikely that the big media organizations directly get involved in offering discounts to large advertisers or reserving programming for certain sponsors. But if Disney owns ABC and General Electric owns NBC, one would expect at least some preferential treatment for these advertisers from the networks – and similarly for other tie-ups. The fact that the buyers of commercial time in the media are usually the ad agencies, not the advertisers, is only of some consolation. With the consolidation of the agency networks (see below) they will also find it useful to negotiate directly with the media giants. With the increasing role of advertisers and ad agencies in programming, including the increasing role for product placements, one would not be surprised to find the traditional independence between media owners, ad agencies, and advertisers gradually eroded.

Of course not all media have gone private. Public broadcasting is alive and well in many countries, even in the United States where media are traditionally private and commercial. But in most countries new commercial media options have emerged, some eclipsing the traditional public stations. Of particular interest in this regard is perhaps the British Broadcasting Corporation (BBC) whose public World Service has successfully survived the challenge from commercial units, including the international arm of CNN, Cable News Network. Although BBC internationally has a much longer history, CNN pioneered the idea of around the clock and around the globe news coverage. Boosted by the continuous coverage of major international conflicts (Tiananmen, Persian Gulf War I, Kosovo, the Iraq war), CNN became the model for a new global newscast. Despite several imitators, its first-mover advantages have been largely sustained, only challenged by the BBC, which has been able to leverage its long-standing global network with former British colonies to a standoff with CNN.

The global ad agencies

The advertising agency industry has gone through a consolidation similar to that of the media industry, but actually pre-dating it. The globalization of agencies occurred primarily in the 1980s. Agencies such as McCann Erickson and J. Walter Thompson have a longer international history, having developed their global network of affiliates in response to the international expansion of the large American multinationals after World War II. But the globalization fervor, stimulated by a 1983 *Harvard Business Review* article by Ted Levitt and the concomitant Saatchi & Saatchi launch of their British Airways global campaign, led to a much broader consolidation of the industry (Levitt, 1983). Holding companies with multiple subsidiaries were created by merging previously independent agencies, many with their own already established global networks. The largest firms in 2007 are the following:

1 Omnicom Group (US, 2006 Holdings of $11.4 Billion)
2 WPP Group (UK, 2006 Holdings of $10.82 Billion)
3 Interpublic (US, 2006 Holdings of $6.1 Billion)

4 Publicis (France, 2006 Holdings of $5.87 Billion)
5 Dentsu (Japan, 2006 Holdings of $2.95 Billion)
6 Havas (France, 2006 Holdings of $1.8 Billion).

(Compiled from: The Ad Age Group, Crain Communications, Inc., 2007.)

The Omnicom group includes three world-wide agencies, BBD&O, DDB, and TBWA. BBD&O alone operates nearly 300 agency affiliates in 76 countries from its headquarters in New York. The WPP group includes J. Walter Thompson and Young & Rubicam, worldwide agencies that at one time or another were on their own the number one or two global agency in total billings. The Interpublic group's core member is the McCann Erickson Worldwide agency, for many years the leading agency internationally. Dentsu from Japan is an exception to the holding company pattern, a traditional ad agency but very dominant in its huge home market. The Publicis group is the largest in Europe, headquartered in Paris but has acquired Saatchi & Saatchi from the UK and has a strong presence also in the USA. Havas is a leading pan-European agency, but its 300 subsidiaries are also represented outside of Europe. Its lead agency is Euro RSCG Worldwide.

The main advantage of these new mega-agencies is in their economies of scale, especially in media buying, which can be done on an unprecedented large scale. They also have some economies of scope, by expanding into new businesses – into direct marketing, for example, or into public relations – and possibly acquiring a stronger presence in a newly opened country such as China. But, by and large, the day-to-day advertising business is still run through the independent agencies, and, especially the creative part of the job, rarely gains from large scale. In many cases the best creative work is done by small boutiques, and the acquisition of successful creative talent shops by large multinational agencies has historically not been very successful. The standard argument that large global agencies are needed to serve large global multinational advertisers is still valid. But again, many of these individual agencies

have served – and still serve – these very large advertisers through their existing global networks. The media buying power of a large agency group, demanding and receiving discounts for commercial time and placement of advertisements, is by far the most compelling rationale for the consolidations.

The giant advertisers

A third major player in global communications is the global advertisers, the firms whose products and services are promoted by the ad agencies through the commercial media. These companies have also consolidated their global positions over time, as their early international expansion has led to multinational reach and, especially in the period after 1980, to coordinated promotional strategies for their global brands.

The advertising spending by the large advertisers is considerable. The following listing of the top 10 global advertisers and their worldwide spending is from 2006:

1	Procter & Gamble (US)	$8.52 billion
2	Unilever (The Netherlands–UK)	$4.54 billion
3	General Motors (US)	$3.35 billion
4	L'Oreal (France)	$3.12 billion
5	Toyota (Japan)	$3.10 billion
6	Ford (US)	$2.87 billion
7	Time-Warner (US)	$2.14 billion
8	Nestlé (Switzerland)	$2.11 billion
9	Johnson & Johnson (US)	$2.03 billion
10	Daimler-Chrysler (Germany)	$2.0 billion.

Compiled from: *Global Marketers: Advertising Age's 21st Annual Report*, (November 19, 2007) Crain Communications Inc.

It is particularly interesting to note the large advertising spending by Time-Warner, a communications company. Other large communications companies that are also large advertisers include Rupert Murdoch's News Corporation (Fox network) and Disney (ABC). These advertisers are able to use their own media networks to promote their own shows.

They use their various vehicles – network TV, magazines, cable channels, Web-sites etc. – to promote their new movie, TV, and recording stars. Advertising is only the most obvious example of such cross-marketing. More insidious is the blending of content and promotion. Thus, a *Time* magazine article may feature an in-depth interview with movie star George Clooney about a forthcoming movie sequel to *Ocean's 12* from Warner Brothers, offer a very positive review of the latest music CD from Iceland's Bjork on Atlantic Records, and a favorable review of a new book by Malcolm Gladwell published by Little Brown and Company. As many readers are unlikely to realize, all three enterprises are part of the Time-Warner group.[2] To expect unbiased coverage and reviews might be asking too much of the cultural critics who write for this group.

These cross-marketing possibilities provide a not so incidental economic rationale for the consolidation into larger units. But it is hardly a very ethical use of the media power, and is easily misleading the audience. Not surprisingly, media critics in many nations are very suspicious of the large media units, and governments are occasionally attempting to rein in their power.

TRADITIONAL MARKETING COMMUNICATIONS

Media advertising

Media advertising is still the mainstay of global marketing communications. Media advertising does play a different role in different countries, dependent on matters such as availability of broadcast media, level of literacy, and Internet access. In general, the advanced economies show much greater figures for advertising per capita. However, as the emerging markets develop, they are likely to show a more intensive use of advertising, since advertising spending tends to track GDP closely. Also, emerging countries are fast closing the gap in media availability, with especially television penetration, Internet availability and cell phone usage increasing very quickly.

Media planning   The most immediate advertising impact from the expanded global communication possibilities has been on media planning. Not only have alternative global media – in particular the Internet – emerged, but the control of the media is now unified under a few global players. This means advertisers need to allocate budgets between a greater variety of different media types and vehicles than before. It also means that the advertisers and their agencies have to consider the pros and cons of globally standardized promotions across the globe, and whether staying with one global media group is preferable because of cost savings and favorable treatment.

Coordinated global strategies require media plans to be carefully calibrated and synchronized across countries. This is not an easy job, even with the unified control over any one media group. The basic data required to develop a media plan include audience size for the various vehicles (Reach) and the frequency with which the audience will attend to the medium (Frequency). In the past such data has been assumed unavailable or unreliable for many media vehicles and countries. Even when data are available, the massive and complex calculations to arrive at an optimal media schedule for even a nationwide campaign of 13 weeks has been quite a challenge for many ad agencies.

With the recent emergence of true global media networks, however, the data collection agencies and the market research firms have acted on the opportunity and developed services that help to provide reliable data on audience measurement for various vehicles. In addition, with their highly advanced professional staff, some of these firms have also dedicated expertise to such areas as computerized media scheduling across countries and regions. Thus, the AC Nielsen agency in Chicago, one of the largest market research firms in the world, has affiliated companies such as Interactive Market Systems (IMS) and NetRatings which provide consulting and analytical media planning tools for ad agencies and advertisers. Of course, implementing a media schedule in a foreign location still needs a considerable amount of local input and local know-how.

Creative localization The negative reaction in local markets has slowed down the trend towards increased globalization. Not only has global brand promotions become increasingly localized, but global expansion has largely been accomplished by the large multinationals buying up local brands and keeping them local. Thus, Belgian-based Interbrew has mainly expanded by buying up Labatt's Blue in Canada, Dos Equis in Mexico and other local brands. After the acquisitions, the local brand is typically invigorated in their home markets by the large multinationals' promotional muscle – and without any specific reference to the global parent.

Thus, while some of the large advertisers have only a few brands advertised, the packaged goods companies typically maintain a large portfolio of global and local brands, some home-grown, others acquired. For example, P&G has long had a number of leading brands – including Pampers, Head & Shoulders and Crest – but with increased globalization has also acquired other brands such as Vicks and Oil of Olay. Unilever similarly have several strong traditional brands – Dove, Lux, Knorr, Pantene – but has also acquired Lipton, Carnation, Ben & Jerry and others. Swiss giant Nestlé features not only Nescafé, Nestea and its variants, but also Perrier, Purina, and Poland spring. Thus, media spending is high, both because global brands need strong support to maintain their customer base, and also because local brands in many product categories have received new infusion of promotional funding from multinational parents.

The typical advertising campaign no longer involves a completely standardized campaign, as in the famous British Air 'Manhattan Landing' commercials. Advertising by these large advertisers is now more localized and only partially uniform across countries. The standardization of brand names is still a very important issue, and local agencies are typically asked to rely on very strict guidelines for how to portray the name and the logo. Sony wants its name to have the well-recognized slightly flattened font, IKEA should always be written in capital letters, and Coca Cola is always in cursive and so on. But there is more creative freedom at the local level, as prototype advertising has given way to pattern standardization, with quite wide margins for creative re-interpretation. The brand name, the logo, and perhaps the basic slogan are repeated – but the spokespersons, the models, the visualization are tweaked locally to what is culturally acceptable. This creative freedom helps raise local motivation in the subsidiaries and their agencies – but also ensures that local cultural differences are accounted for. As multinationals are learning from hard-earned experience, when a country develops economically, it does not simply get closer to the advanced countries' manners, but develops quickly its own idiosyncratic version of the new affluence. Chinese commercials are not simply watered-down versions of Japanese commercials from five years ago, just as Chinese consumers are not simply following the Japanese styles.

But the increased creative localization is not necessarily associated with the use of different ad agencies in the different countries. The increased consolidation of media groups, ad agencies and multinational brand owners, has naturally led to a centralization and concentration of the global advertising accounts with one or two agencies.

Recent trends While worldwide advertising spending has shown robust growth in the last few years, in the USA, the largest market, the trend is different. In recent years the advertising spending of the large US multinationals has increased relatively slowly (a modest 3.1 per cent in 2006). More importantly, the growth has been concentrated to what is usually called 'unmeasured' and non-traditional media. Measured ad media such as TV, print, and certain Internet advertising, where audiences are easier to track, accounted for only 58.2 per cent of the ad spending in 2006. The rest came from unmeasured activities such as sales promotion, direct marketing, and most forms of digital communications (including Internet media such as paid search; Bradley 2007).

This shift to unmeasured spending is exemplified by P&G, the largest advertiser, whose 3.9 per cent increase in traditional media was low compared of the 15 per cent increase in unmeasured media. By contrast, forecasts are that worldwide spending on Internet advertising will grow 28.2 per cent in 2007. The UK is ahead of other countries in the share of advertising spending now going online, with an estimated 18 per cent of UK spending directed at the Internet in 2007 (Williams 2007).

Global advertising research The thrust towards creative localization of the advertising is mirrored to some extent in the academic advertising research, where cultural differences continue to show up as significant factors that block uniform global advertising. For example, cross-cultural consumer research on advertising response has demonstrated how cultural factors make utilitarian appeals more effective than emotional appeals in a masculine culture such as the USA, but not so in a more androgynous culture, such as Taiwan (Chang 2006). Similarly, building on the American notion that advertising to African-Americans and to Hispanic immigrants should be adapted to their respective cultures, Elias and Greenspan (2007) show that Israeli ads targeting Russian immigrants need to accommodate their specific language and circumstances. In one striking application of Hofstede's cultural taxonomy to anti-smoking advertising messages, Reardon *et al.* (2006) found that 'uncertainty avoidance' moderated the effect negative advertising on packages, leading to a recommendation that even though negative ads were more common, 'positive advertisements may be more effective in low uncertainty-avoidance European countries' (p. 130).

There is also evidence in the academic research literature that the notion of a more homogeneous globe is not yet to be dismissed. For example, in a study of comparative advertising effects in Germany (where such advertising has recently been allowed) shows results very similar to those in the United States. It works best where the comparison is very focused on a relevant and non-image attribute such as price (Schwaiger *et al.* 2007). Similarly, in a comparative study of celebrity endorsements in the USA and Japan, the authors find that negative self-oriented information about a celebrity works the same way in both cultures, and can even have a positive impact on the brand advertised (Money, Shimp and Sakano 2006).

Finally, in a study of the universality of values across cultures, Chow and Amir (2006), in a large cross-national study for the German-based global market research firm GfK, found that they could identify six basic values which they empirically found to be common across 30 cultures. These six basic factors (Strivers/Fun Seekers/Creative/Devout/Intimate/Altruistic) have a high degree of similarity to the motivational domains found in the early work on cross-cultural value structures (Achievement/Enjoyment/Self Direction/Restriction/Conformity/Security/ProSocial) by Schwartz (1992) and Schwartz and Bilsky (1990) – a finding which suggests that to some extent, global consumers distinguish values according to some common or similar framework. Of course, this doesn't make the researcher's task less challenging – the key focus on global communications research when it comes to studying content and execution continues to be the tensions of dichotomy and synergy found along the 'emic/etic' continuum. The etic theme of accounting for and describing behaviors that are culturally neutral and can be applied across cultures must always be tempered by the emic perspective of accounting for behaviors and norms that are meaningful in a cultural-specific context. All communication may be global, but identifying main themes, and then teasing out key nuances along the standardization vs.

localization framework, continues to be the fundamental issue driving research in global marketing communications. As an example, the Chow and Amir (2006) study found that both brands and channels tended to be distributed along two dimensions: a 'Self-Direction vs. Conformity Dimension', and a 'ProSocial vs. Hedonism Dimension', and conclude that one application of this finding is that by recognizing the value orientation and content preferences of a brand's customer could assist in optimizing the choice of media used in communication. For academics, the research challenge is accounting for the emic behaviors along this empirical etic framework. The rise of the middle classes and increasing consumption behaviors and desires for the 'better life' in the BRIC countries (Brazil, Russia, India and China) may well indeed share similarities along the conceptual domains of Self-Direction/Confirmity and ProSocial/Hedonism, but they will certainly play out differently in terms of values and expressions of behaviors when compared to messages and media scheduling needed to optimize communication goals for consumers in other stages of materialism and economic developments, such as Europe (West, not East), and North America.

Some generalizations about media effects can be made on the basis of this and other published research. Media effectiveness varies across countries, with magazines and newspapers considerably more effective in highly developed and literate countries. Television is a very effective medium in many cultures, in particular for awareness, but is also powerful for attitudes in third-world countries because of their aspirational sentiments. While one-to-one media, including the Internet, can be useful in the highly differentiated and fragmented Western markets, traditional mass marketing is still powerful in many emerging societies.

Global sales promotion

The majority of sales promotion activities involve trade promotions through channel intermediaries (coop promotions with retail chains, in-store merchandising efforts such as p-o-p materials, coupons and rebates, etc.) and therefore are intrinsically less global in nature. But some of the other activities in sales promotion have an international reach, and become necessarily more global. This includes sponsorship of sporting events, product placement in movies, cause marketing such as supporting AIDS research, and sponsorship of touring (rock) music groups.

In many advanced markets in-store sales promotion has attracted increasing shares of the promotional budgets because in saturated markets consumers tend to be more cynical and ignore pre-selling through advertising media. This is not the case yet in most emerging markets, where brand names and image are important and in-store price deals are less effective. Thus, the main sales promotion activities effective across countries tend to be image-building sponsorships, celebrity endorsements – whether directly in paid advertisements or indirectly through product placements – and cause-related marketing.

Global sponsorships With the increase in worldwide broadcasting of sporting events, many companies have seen the opportunity to sponsor not only a participating athlete or team, but the event itself. Thus, American beer producer Budweiser, looking to establish a better foothold in the international market, became the sole sponsor of the World Cup 2006, paying FIFA (the world soccer federation) about $45 million for the rights to be the 'official beer'. The contract included a proviso that Budweiser would be the only beer for sale at all the matches. As one might have expected, with the World Cup taking place in the top beer-producing country, Germany, there was an outcry from beer-loving German soccer fans. In the end, Budweiser prevailed, but German beer producers instituted a small 'ambush' campaign by selling their beer as close to the stadiums as allowed, and the fans lining up to make sure they had had their fill before the matches got under way.

These sponsorships are very attractive to the advertisers, and with major tournaments (World Cup, the Olympics) only happening every four or so years, the fees have risen dramatically. In 2007 Visa wrestled the World Cup 2010 and 2014 credit card sponsorships from long-time sponsor Mastercard. Mastercard had offered an undisclosed amount estimated at about $180 million for the two events, but Visa offered a stronger bid. Mastercard sued FIFA for breach of contract, and the two parties settled out of court for $90 million to be paid to Mastercard in damages (Graybow 2007).

Product placement Product placement involves inserting actual branded products into the action in movies and television programs. The advertiser might pay for the product to be used, or may simply offer it free of charge (in the case of more expensive products). It is typically done surreptitiously, but might also be part of the dialogue. The idea is that if the audience sees a movie star using or talking about the brand, its image will gain and sales will soar. Especially effective for young and impressionable segments (particularly in emerging market economies) product placement has been used in a number of settings. Table 19.1 shows a list of selected product placements in films in 2006, showing the globally distributed film, the (global) star, the releasing Studio, and the Studio's Parent Media Company.

Product placement has become more important because of the success and notoriety of these and other placements. The effort has moved into more editorial control over programming – to avoid negative impressions and image-damaging dialogue – and even the co-creation between advertisers and writers of television programs and films. The movement has its critics because of the threat it poses to creative freedom. Next time Austin Powers gulps his Heineken, remember that he is paid to do it.

Cause marketing Sponsorship of worthwhile causes has become a more prominent component of global marketing communications strategies as companies have strived to establish corporate legitimacy in various countries. The typical strategy is for the corporation to select causes that have a logical relationship to the company products. Thus, for example, pharmaceutical companies often help underwrite events raising money for medical research in cancer, AIDS, diabetes etc. Soft drink companies support sporting events and charity runs. Automobile companies sponsor research which aims to cut down on pollution – and so on. A typical example is Land Rover's 2007 sponsorship of Earthwatch, the international environmental charity.

Land Rover will assist Earthwatch's activities in working to conserve endangered species and their habitats by engaging people worldwide in scientific field research and education. The first act in support of Earthwatch was to supply a Defender for work in the Samburu, Kenya, protecting zebras. Nigel Winser, Executive Director of Earthwatch (Europe) said: 'The vehicles that Land Rover provides will support the programs where off-road capabilities are required'.[3]

Land Rover has pioneered responsible off-roading through its 'Fragile Earth' policy for many years. Its sponsorship programs form part of an integrated approach towards sustainability. Land Rover engineers are at the forefront of Ford's £1bn program to develop technologies that will reduce emissions and improve fuel economy. Land Rover has also introduced the world's biggest consumer carbon dioxide offset program which offsets all of the CO_2 generated by Land Rover's manufacturing operations and the first 45 000 miles of vehicle use by its UK customers.

Defensive self-interest? Absolutely. These sponsorships still beat not doing anything, but one can also sympathize with cynical observers who also see Ford's lobbying efforts against more stringent fuel efficiency standards in the United States.

Table 19.1 A listing of brands used in product placement in select globally released films, 2006–07

Film	Studio	Brands used in product placement
The Pursuit of Happyness (starring Will Smith)	Sony	American Express, Budweiser, Campbell's, Chevrolet, Clark, Converse, Coppertone, dressbarn, Ferrari, Good & Plenty, LifeSavers, Los Angeles Lakers, MasterCard, Members Only, Mercedes, Pepsi, Rubik's Cube, San Francisco 49ers, Sesame Street, Skippy, Sony, Toyota, Utz, Visa, Volkswagen Beetle, Wonder Bread
Borat: Cultural Learnings of America for Make Benefit Glorious Nation of Kazakhstan (starring Sacha Baron Cohen)	Fox (Murdoch)	ABC, Apple, ASICS, Bank of America, Budweiser, Charlotte Russe, Chevrolet, Coca-Cola, Corvette, Dr. Pepper, FedEx, Fleetwood, Ford, General Motors, Hummer, Jeep, Kroger, Lay's, Mercedes, Panasonic, Playboy, Polo Ralph Lauren, Quicksilver, Verizon, Victoria's Secret, Virgin, Volkswagen, Volvo, Washington Mutual
The Departed (starring Jack Nicolson and Leonardo Dicaprio)	Warner Bros. (Time Warner)	adidas, Bayer, Beck's, Belstaff, Boston City Hospital, Boston Red Sox, Budget, Budweiser, Buick, Carhartt, Caterpillar, Chevrolet, Citizens Bank, Coca-Cola, Coors, Dell, Ford, Ford Mustang, GMC, Gradall, Halls, Harpoon, Harvard University, Heineken, Heinz, LifeSavers, McIntosh, Motorola, Mountain Dew, NASA, New York Yankees, North, Red Line, Samsung, Sennheiser, Sharpie, Sprint, Sprite, Suffolk University, Sun-Maid, TAG Heuer, The Boston Phoenix, Triton, Triumph, Twizzlers, University of Massachusetts, University of Notre Dame, WB, Wonder Bread, Zagat Survey
The Da Vinci Code (starring Tom Hanks)	Sony	Belstaff, BMW, BOSCH, Citroën, Cross, Ford, Gillette, Harvard University, Havoline, Heinz, Land Rover, Louvre, Mercedes, Mickey Mouse, Oxford University, Peugeot, Renault, Ritz, Rolex, Sama, Smart, Sony, Sony Ericsson, Sony Vaio, Volkswagen
Mission: Impossible III (starring Tom Cruise)	Paramount (Sony)	7-Eleven, Acura, Baby Ruth, Belstaff, BMW, Budweiser, Casio, Chips Ahoy, Chris Craft, Cisco, Coca-Cola, Dell, DHL, Dodge, Ford, Heckler & Koch, Heinz, Kodak, Lamborghini, Land Rover, Lay's, Lincoln Navigator, L'Oreal, Mazda, Mercedes, Miller, Motorola, Nokia, Oreo, Oxford University, PayDay, Philips, Prada, Ritz, Safariland, Sama, Sharpie, Snapple, Sprite, Star Magazine, Triumph, Volkswagen Beetle, Volvo
Spider Man 3 (starring Tobey Maguire, Kirsten Dunst)	Sony	Absolut, ASICS, Bombay Sapphire, Borough of Manhattan Community College, Bose, Burger King, Chevrolet, Cisco, Daily News, Foot Locker, Ford, Glamour, Hilton, Honda, Jennifer Meyers Jewelry, Lincoln, Loews, Maker's Mark, Miro Cafe, New York Magazine, New York Post, New York Times, Nikon, Planet Hollywood, Realistic, Reuters, Sabrett, Sony, Sony VAIO, Spalding, Swatch, Tisserie, Tuscan Dairy Farms, UPS, Vanity Fair, Wachovia
The Bourne Ultimatum (starring Matt Dillon)	Universal	Apple, Audi, Avis, Belstaff, BMW, BT, Canon, Carphone Warehouse, Champion, Chevrolet, Chrysler, CNN, Comanav, CRI Communication Resources, Dali, Dasani, Duane Reade, Fiat, Ford, Foster's, Google, HP, Jansport, Lincoln, Lincoln Navigator, London Underground, Mercedes, MINI, Motorola, Movistar, MTA, Nokia, North Forth Bank, Panasonic, Peugeot, Plymouth, Poland Spring, Port Authority of New York & New Jersey, Red Bull, Saab, Samsung, SIG Sauer, Société Nationale des Chemins de Fer Français, South West Trains, Staples, TAG Heuer, The Body Shop, The Guardian, The North Face, Timberland, Verizon, Vespa, Volkswagen, Volkswagen Beetle, Washington Mutual

Compiled from: http://www.brandchannel.com/brandcameo_films.asp?movie_year= 2007#movie_list

Global public relations and publicity

Global communications do not only involve paid advertising and other promotional tools but also other efforts by corporations to influence their various stakeholders. Included are the traditional public relations function and also publicity, the effort to have media publish newsworthy stories about the company and its products. One could also include the efforts to influence government policy in various countries (popularly known as 'lobbying'), but this is an area beyond the discussion here.

There should be little doubt about the increased importance of corporate communications in the new interconnected world. Multinational corporations are disparaged for offshoring production to developing world countries, with a powerful impact on local economies and labor forces in many poor countries. Whether this effect is on balance positive or negative depends on many issues, all debated in the media by analysts, anti-globalizers, academicians, and others. Companies cannot stay out of these discussions, but a credible defense often requires considerable investments in improvements and communication skills in execution, as a company like Nike has learned the hard way.

Other issues involve the increased concern about unsafe and unhealthy products sold to unsuspecting consumers. While a 'buyer beware' mindset might have been acceptable in the past, companies today face increasing demands for a 'seller beware' attitude. Companies have to be proactive in disseminating warning instructions and assurance of quality integrity and also have to be quick to acknowledge and defuse concerns about misleading labeling, quality slips, and unforeseen side effects. Companies from Coca Cola to McDonalds to Disney all have had to rely on global communications as a vehicle for 'damage control'. The fact that effective response to a crisis can sometimes generate its own goodwill towards the company only puts more pressure on the global communications skills of the top executives and others involved.

There is also a great surge in the demand for corporate responsibility and ethical decision-making by companies as members of the larger society. Early on, the demand centered on the issue of the social contract for the firm and many firms developed ethical guidelines setting explicit limits for any unfettered pursuit of profits. Gradually the discussion has moved towards the issues of large paychecks for top executives and, perhaps more emphatically, towards global warming and environmental concerns in general. There are few large companies who can today claim ignorance of their larger role in whichever country they operate.

In these and related issues, global corporations are often cast as villains. For better or for worse, their actions and reactions, and, in particular, their communications to the various stakeholders around the world, therefore become instrumental in the defense strategy of the firm. Thus, by necessity, global corporate communications, including public relations, are now part and parcel of the overall global strategy of the firm.

International trade fairs

The international trade fairs function pretty much as the traditional core of global communications. Although in our connected and distance-dead virtual world these industry gatherings can seem quaint and old-fashioned, they are in fact more vibrant than ever. The reason is that when it comes to introducing new products, establish trust and confidence in a partner, or simply keeping track of what competition is up to, there is no better way than walking around the worldwide industry fairs. Participating in a trade fair can cost a considerable amount of money, including upfront participation fees, charges for a booth, and expenses for the travel and lodging. But the best fairs give participants a first-hand look at state-of-the-art technology, cutting edge products, and new competitors to watch out for – as well as reinforcing the bond with customers, suppliers, and distributors.

This is a list of some of the traditionally most important international fairs:

- The Consumer Electronics Show (CES), Las Vegas, USA, in January
- Hannover Messe's Industrial Fair, Germany, in April
- North American International Auto Show, Detroit, USA, in January.
- Paris Airshow, Paris, France, in June (every other year)
- CeBIT Trade Fair, Hanover, Germany, in March (largest IT trade fair)
- The IFA electronics exhibition, Berlin, Germany, in August–September.
- Frankfurt Book Fair, Germany, in October
- Hong Kong Jewelry and Watch Fair, Hong Kong, in September.

Because of the boost to the local economy and even more because of the international exposure and enhanced global image, many cities now actively compete for the hosting of trade fairs. Relative newcomers include China's Shanghai, Russia's St Petersburg, Bangalore (now Bengaluru) in India, and Dubai of the United Arab Emirates.

INTERNET-BASED MARKETING

As has been repeatedly emphasized in this chapter, the most significant new development in global communications, and the media that has attracted most of the increased promotional spending, is the Internet-related marketing efforts.

This section of the chapter deals with what has become known in the popular and business press as the 'New Media', a broad term that refers to new technologies and communication methods, and the effects that these approaches have on established media such as television, radio, direct marketing and personal selling – domains of the 'traditional media'. These technologically driven new communications methods tend to be almost always Internet-related, and the digital information communicated can be uniquely individualized, economically and instantaneously delivered to people, target audiences, closely knitted communities, or special interest groups. Importantly, all the players involved in the communication process (the content creators, content distributors, and consumers) have some degree of control over the message content and further discourse about the topic.

Internet-based global communications

Because of the Internet, the new media are inherently global in reach. Of course, the so-called 'digital divide' between advanced and third-world countries makes access to the Internet less than global. The most recent statistics about Internet penetration are given in Table 19.2.

Table 19.2 World Internet usage and population statistics

World region	Population % of world	% Population of Internet users (region penetration)	Internet usage as % of world usage	Usage growth 2000–2007 (%)
Africa	14.2	4.7	3.4	882
Asia	56.5	13.7	38.7	347
Europe	12.1	43.4	26.4	231
Middle East	2.9	17.4	2.5	920
North America	5.1	71.1	18	120
Latin America and Caribbean	8.6	22.2	9.6	598
Oceania and Australia	0.5	57.1	1.5	152
World total	100	20	100	266

Accessed at: http://www.internetworldstats.com/stats.htm. Figures are as of 31 December, 2007.

Internet penetration is clearly not yet uniform across the world. As Table 19.2 shows, less than one in five people in the world have access to the internet, and this digital divide is most clearly seen in the differences between mature market economies, and emerging market economies.

While it seems legitimate to ponder the question 'has the internet become indispensible?' in mature markets (Hoffman, Novak and Venkatesh 2004; see also Shih and Venkatesh 2004), the often-used expression of 'consumers with global reach' really only applies to a small segment of the global population. Much of the debate on the homogenization of tastes and local 'culture tweaking' of global brands rests on the view that there are segments of elite/affluent consumers in emerging markets who closely align and identify with modernity and global trends (Wilk 2005). The New Media plays an active role in interpreting and localizing these symbols of consumption. Within this context, the postmodern emphasis on seeing segmentation going as far as fragmentation is a bit flawed. It can be argued that there is in fact greater polarization (and not fragmentation) based on social, cultural and economic capital. These distinctions are important, in that polarization is closely associated with our understanding of structural inequality, while the postmodern concept of fragmentation glosses over this systemic problem (Varman and Belk 2007; Mattsson and Rendtorff 2006). Having said this, there is no question that the Internet does speed up the processes of consumer participation. With the rapid economic growth of the emerging markets, one would expect the Internet to become a gradually more important communications medium. One estimate suggests that there are roughly one billion online global consumers who regularly create, participate in, and monitor the content of Web2.0 (Marketing Science Institute 2007). And as we have seen in the data for advanced markets, many firms are already shifting promotional spending from the traditional to the new media.

The New Media opportunity

The New Media are often seen as a key component of the 'new' Internet, or 'Web2.0'. Web2.0 refers to a second generation of web based communities and hosted services which facilitate collaboration and sharing between users. Although the term suggests a new generation or technical version of the World Wide Web, it is more accurately used to describe the context by which web developers and web users interact on the web. Coined by the O'Reilly Media Group in 2003, Web2.0 has been defined as

> the business revolution in the computer industry caused by the move to the Internet as platform, and an attempt to understand the rules for success on that new platform. Chief among those rules is this: Build applications that harness network effects to get better the more people use them' (O'Reilly 2006).

Examples of New Media would include interactive television, podcasts, blogs, social bookmarking, social networks, wikis, and video games. They also include chat rooms, bulletin boards, play space dungeons, MMOGs – (Massively Multiplayer Online Games, such as *Second Life*, Ankama Studio's *Dofus*, and Sony's *Everquest*), and interlinked web pages. All of these venues provide new opportunities for marketers to advertise and interact in new ways with customers and other stakeholders. Box 19.1 offers a modest start of an agenda for research of how the global marketplace formed by New Media provides a global setting in which researchers can explore new and novel research questions, as well as revisit established research streams.

Web2.0 has attracted a great deal of attention and speculation in the business and advertising press regarding its impact on promotional mixes, advertising strategies and tactics, and the re-allocation of advertising budgets between 'traditional media' and 'new media'. Marketing managers continue to shift larger portions of their budgets to on-line media sites (Bughin and Manyika 2007), and all forms of on-line advertising expenditures

---

Box 19.1 New Media and Global Communication Research Topics: New and Revisited Inquiries within the New Media Marketplace[4]

I. **Global Settings and Global Spokesperson in the New Media Space of Computer Mediated Environments**

1. How will the explosion in consumer-generated marketing communications now being posted in Consumer Mediated Environments (CMEs) (including YouTube, Second Life and elsewhere) influence the process of attitude change and strategic communications decisions across cultures?
2. How effective/credible are corporate avatars as spokespersons in global on-line marketing communications?
3. What physical dimensions influence the consumer decision-making process when shoppers encounter stimuli that represent Real Life (RL) organizations? Should a company's 'spokes-avatar' be modeled after a real person (perhaps the viewer herself)? A celebrity? A fantasy figure?
4. How important is it for visitors to be able to customize the avatars they encounter in both global and local advertising so that they control the image that speaks to them about its products?
5. What does the consumer's choice of his or her own avatar tell us about self-concept and role identity – especially since visitors often create multiple avatars to 'experiment' with different identities? What do these avatar choices suggest about local cultures, and local vs. global segmentation tactics?
6. How does the phenomenon of 'presence' (the term communications researchers use to refer to the level of immersion in a virtual social environment) relate to flow states and high involvement situations documented in consumer research?

II. **Virtual Influence and Decision-Making**

7. What are the implications for information diffusion as consumers increasingly turn to CMEs for information about new products or to read other consumers' reviews of these products? Do these reviews matter more, or less, in the global context, given that consumers have global access to information and products?
8. Can consumer researchers construct and populate virtual laboratories that will allow them to simulate RL decision-making contexts and better understand how heuristics, contextual cues, information displays and other variables will impact consumer behavior both off-line and on-line?
9. Can avatars' conversations with one another, either in pairs or in groups, be a valuable starting point for global, regional and local buzz-building and word of mouth marketing campaigns?
10. What are the public policy implications for adolescent socialization, or for the ability of children to distinguish reality-based cues from fantasy? Do these differ across global markets in ways that are important to firms who strive for 'standardized' messages?
11. What are the ethical implications of the increasingly common practice of misrepresentation whereby companies pay individuals to promote their products on websites while masquerading as 'ordinary' surfers?

III. **Virtual Culture and Global Markets**

12. What is the potential of online prediction markets (such as The Hollywood Stock Exchange) to improve researchers' and practitioners' ability to forecast global consumer trends?
13. What are the implications for cross-cultural consumer behavior as CME residents increasingly are able to interact with fellow avatars (and companies) from around the world?
14. How will the integration of avatars on other internet platforms influence consumer behavior on global e-commerce websites?

---

are expected to increase from $19.5 Billion in 2007 to $36.5 Billion in 2011, a 122 per cent increase (Digital Marketing Media and Factpack 2007). This is still a relatively small percentage of total advertising expenditures for all media – in 2007 the Top 100 advertising firms spent over $100 Billion globally – but, as was seen earlier in this chapter, this is the growth area in advertising.

In a recent large-scale global survey of companies' intentions to further invest in Web2.0 platforms, technology executives felt that Web2.0's offerings of Collective Intelligence (systems to tap the expertise of a group rather than an individual for gathering information and making decisions), *P2P* (Peer to Peer Networking to efficiently share files of any format), Social Networking (systems that allow member of a specific site to learn about other members' expertise, skills, talents, knowledge and preferences), Podcasts (audio or video recordings, typically posted in a multimedia blog), and Mashups (an aggregation of content from different online sources to create a new message, or service) were all important investments. What all these technologies have in common is the ability to communicate in new, economically efficient, engaging, and meaningful ways with customers and business partners everywhere, and to encourage collaboration within a company (Bughin and Manyika 2007). Here again, the relative ease to tracking the impact and responses of digital messages delivered via interactive digital media allows for tightly focused research efforts on message effectiveness.

New media and disintermediation

Practically since its inception, the Internet has offered consumers and businesses a strong 'disintermediation' function, serving to reduce the transaction costs between buyers and sellers. Disintermediation is intimately tied to the interactive capabilities of on-line communications. It is a term loosely used to indicate that the sender does not have complete control over a message, but the receiver is able to create and recreate the message – individualize it – and pass it on elsewhere. Much of this can be positive for both sender and receiver. For example, Dell computers can sell directly from the factory to consumers, consumers can pick and choose the features and colors of their new laptop, which is then custom-produced for them. Disintermediation pre-dates the Internet, but its impact and reach in making markets more efficient has grown dramatically since the inception of the WWW.

However, disintermediation can also pose problems for the global communicator. Consider the following example of how Web2.0 brings a new social and economic dimension, that of 'consumer agency', to the marketplace. After having his many complaints about a defective Dell laptop computer ignored, a blogger launched his 'Dell Hell' blog site, portraying Dell as an arrogant giant.

This blog struck a chord with many Dell users, and the blog went 'viral' (was read by tens of thousands, and had thousands of links-in to the blogger's URL). This rapid consumer networking spurred other on-line consumers to produce over 50 videos, lampooning Dell on *You Tube, Meta Café* and other social networking sites. In short order, the movement got picked up and became a mainstream story on traditional news media which broadcast the amateur-produced but highly satirical consumer-generated video footage in their reports.

Recognizing the power, reach, and passion of the on-line community behind this issue, Dell's response was to develop their own open access website as a forum for the airing of grievances and the sharing of product ideas (*Ideastorm*, http://www.ideastorm.com/about). As of mid-2007, Dell's open access *Ideastorm* website had over 6,000 ideas posted, and over 500 000 consumer comments in response to those ideas, with popular initiatives receiving financial support from Dell. This new website has generated widespread positive public relations for Dell in the blogosphere, as well as in traditional media (Creamer 2007). Here, the negative economic transaction costs of dealing with Dell were aired in a social network of consumers.

In the era of Web2.0, social networks can be quickly developed on a global scale, disrupting the normal flow of corporate communication programs via blogs, emails, chat rooms, fan communities, and video sites. A difficult lesson for 'traditional media' managers to understand (and trust) is that brands that do well are brands whose customers tell positive stories to each other about those brands, even to the point of forming on-line brand communities (Muñoz and Schau 2005). This is in marked contrast to the long standing (and more controllable) communication strategy in which corporations develop messages, and tell stories about their brands to their customers. Disintermediation isn't just about market transactions, it is now also about the fluid, interactive, and independent flows of a company's *and* consumers' communications in and about the market. A good example is the success of a toy helicopter from Hong Kong (see Box 19.2).

Virtual games

Another emerging development of New Media which impacts managerial thinking about global promotion is the role of Web2.0 as a Gameplaying Platform. This is not about faster/more efficient market transactions but about a fundamental change in our terms of self-reference and self-representation.

Consumers are using *MMORPGs* (Massively Multiplayer Online Role Playing Games) to create, maintain, and negotiate their virtual identities as avatars (virtual players). A user designs his or her avatar by choosing facial features, body types, clothing styles – and even non-human forms. These digital representations are socializing with one another in real time, taking virtual university courses, participating in corporate training programs, sharing reactions to new products, and of course shopping (Hemp 2006; Holzwarth, Janiszewski and Neumann 2006; Wood, Solomon and Englis 2005; Hoffman and Novak 1996).

The largest virtual networking site, *Second Life*, currently has over 6 million registered users worldwide, and commerce of $1.5 million (real dollars) in mostly branded (real brands) goods and services daily (Cannizzaro *et. al.* 2007). *Second Life* may also be the precursor of a more visual 3-dimensional Internet. Imagine dropping by a 3-D virtual store to try branded goods on your 3-D avatar-self. In *Second Life*, this is already routine. In the global world of on-line gaming, *World of Warcraft* has close to 9 million users worldwide, while more than 7 million consumers have created their own avatar on Yahoo (Hemp 2006; Castronova 2005). To date more than 40 RL (real life) companies, including GM, Dell, Sony, IBM and Wells Fargo are staking their claim to online real estate in computer-mediated environments (CMEs) such as *Second Life*, *There.com* and *Entropia Universe*.

Corporations' participation in the virtual world is an attempt to reach and entice the growing flood of consumers occupying these virtual worlds. This expanding space will be pivotal in fueling new consumer trends over the next decade. In addition, the parallel growth in spending on 'advergaming' continues to transfigure the online C2C (Consumer-to-Consumer) world. Forecasts suggest that sales of branded messages embedded in videogames will reach $733 million by 2010 (Digital Marketing and Media Factpack 2007). Eventually, these

---

Box 19.2   Off to a Flying Start

Try 'Googling' the *Picco Z helicopter*, a $30 toy helicopter manufactured in Hong Kong by *Silverlit Toys* (http://silverlit.com/).[5] In March 2007 the Google search results for the Picco produced over 109 000 URL's, while the URL's for *Silverlit Toys* was over 597 000, with many of those links pointing to major on-line global gift retailers, such as Hammacher-Schlemmer, and Toys-R-Us. Think this wide spread promotion and distribution must be the results of fabulous media planning and execution on the part of *Silverlit*? Not really. By most accounts, Ryan Miller, a 28-year-old tech worker in Chicago gets credit for starting the Picco Z Buzz. Miller bought his Picco Z in June of 2006 after reading about it on a hobbyist message board. A few months later he uploaded his homemade video of the toy on *YouTube*, and within two weeks, 15 of Miller's friends had purchased the toy, and pumped up the Picco buzz by uploading home produced videos into their own website, and pointing viewers to Miller's *YouTube* upload. Internet retailers who troll on-line conversations for fresh and exciting buzz identified the toy, and started adding their own links to the clips, and started posting their own Picco Z videos (see Warren and Jurgensen 2007 for a discussion on how businesses' track the 'buzz' of social networks). As of March 2007, there are over 190 Picco Z videos on hundreds of websites, and viewings of this consumer-generated content are well over one million.[6]

CME forums may rival traditional, marketer-sponsored E-commerce sites in terms of their influence on consumer decision-making and product adoption.

Small sites and the long tail

The large Web sites – big point-of-entry sites such as Yahoo, Google, and MSN – influence what consumers do on-line and how they find their way to information on the Web. Firms that advertise on these portal sites spend a great deal of money to get prominent positions on the portal (especially the home page), and in the results listings of search engines. The layout of portal sites, and the ways in which consumers are directed from one site to another influence strongly what type of content and information people find and view online (Hargittai, in press). The underlying premise is that a tiny minority of sites gets a large number of links, and the vast majority gets few or no links, making it difficult to be seen unless you are on the highly visible site. In 2006, the Top Ten on-line properties took in 99 per cent of Gross Ad Revenues in the United States market (Digital Marketing Media and Factpack 2007).

In the world of Web2.0 and the Blogosphere, however, this picture is incomplete. While it remains true that a small number of websites are read by many, clusters of smaller sites provide platforms for vastly greater numbers of speakers (consumers) than were heard in the mass-media environment. This so-called 'Long Tail' phenomenon allows small producers to find small cultural niches of consumers that can be profitably served (Anderson 2004; Goldstein and Goldstein 2006). The name comes from the fact that the number of Web visitors has a skewed distribution, with high numbers for a few sites, but also a 'long tail' rather than a rapid drop, representing the niche visitors to smaller sites. Graphically, the traditional curve with a lot of readers for

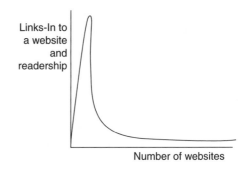

Figure 19.1

a few sites has a longer and fatter tail (see Figure 19.1).

The strategic importance of the long tail comes from the fact that the more narrow the interest group (market niche), the more dedicated and involved are the members. In the case of marketing, these loyal and motivated interest groups are variously described as User Groups, Brand Communities, or Tribes (Kozinets 2006a; Muñoz and Schau 2005). 'Long Tail' businesses can treat consumers more as individuals, providing product information and individualized customization as an alternative to mass-market fare. Likewise, on sites with consumer generated content, the long tail markets emerge and give consumers on the long end of the tail at the low end of the distribution a meeting place where there is a high degree of influence, interest, and involvement (Giesler 2006; Shirkey 2003; Anderson 2004). Filtering, synthesis, salience and trustworthiness are created through a system of peer review, where participants typically have a strong affinity for a specific topic or interest. This long tail phenomenon also provides a structure on the web which allows many small firms to be 'born global' (Oviatt and McDougall 1994). In summary, when it comes to share of visitors and links-in (and on-line ad revenues), the web has a big, prominent head, but also a potent, highly involved niched readership along its very long tail.

Mass versus niche

While economies of scale will continue to be an important consideration in global communications, the dynamics of Web2.0 require marketers and advertisers to think more carefully about the economics of aggregation. In addition to mega-budgets designed to reach millions of global consumers with the same promotional message/theme via mass broadcast media, marketers are also actively exploring how to tap into the process that allows them to build meaningful relationships by communicating with tens of thousands of consumers directly (Lee and Daugherty 2006).

Web2.0 gives consumers an unprecedented level of choice and marketers an increasingly complex range of approaches for reaching them. For marketing and advertising practitioners, managing the process of reaching multiple small segments requires a mind-set shift in thinking about what is efficient and effective. The media planning activities (rollups) for multiple niche interests require more work for an advertising department or outside agency – more media sales relationships to manage, more schedules and deadlines to keep follow than used to be the case. A Web buy requires much more effort, with maintenance work (optimization, technical support, reporting) at every step along the way while the media activity is running.

This begs the question: what tools exist to help managers manage conversations in many different places at once? Many of the tools available are based on search and search feeds, such that marketers can identify conversations of importance as they occur, monitor them and participate in them if it makes sense. Subscribing to custom searches via *RSS* (RSS was initially referred to as 'Rich Site Summary', but in the Web2.0 context, is most often referred to as 'Really Simple Syndication') is becoming a common approach to get specific conversations of importance to show up on a marketing-oriented firm's radar. A good *RSS* reader categorizes feeds, keeping tabs on subjects, brands and people that are important to the firm and its clients. Given the global reach of the Internet, *RSS* feeds can also provide key feedback from multiple global segments. In addition to automated monitoring via *RSS* feeds, the marketing research industry has seen a growth in the past three to five years of 'online analysts', professional web surfers who scour the Internet for mentions of company brands. These online analysts help managers and ad agencies achieve greater notice of the firm's products in the virtual world. Within the stream of academic marketing research, it would have been difficult to anticipate these real-time on-line analytical tools. Research using a consumer-information-processing paradigm, examining such issues as perceptions of web trustworthiness/security (Pavlou and Dimoka 2006; Schlosser, White and Lloyd, 2006; Steenkamp and Geyskens 2006), visual primes (Schlosser 2003; Mandel and Johnson 2002), and decision-making (Jap 2003; Spann and Tellis 2006;) all offer relatively unambiguous findings of reductionist/incremental value, but (in hindsight) have been overshadowed by the analytics of on-line tools which examine the issues in real time, and allow for action-oriented, instant adjustments to web offerings.

One of the more proactive (but also invasive) efforts is to join online conversations and steer them in the direction that the clients seek (Hart 2007). At the time of this writing, the dominant discourse in the popular business press is on debating and exploring the approaches by which marketers and advertisers can more effectively embrace the two-way interaction and global reach provided by Web2.0 tools. At the same time, managers continue to struggle with a mindset which trades off traditional media efficiencies of scope and scale against the new realities and challenges of the economics of re-aggregation provided by the New Media's web structure, and the dynamics and opportunities presented by its long tail.

New media marketing research

Just as marketing and advertising practitioners are searching for business models and approaches that capture the complexities and dynamics of global media fragmentation in Web2.0 space, so too are academics working with new and fresh approaches to develop scholarly knowledge (Kozinets 2002, 2006a, 2006b; Langer and Beckman 2005; Beltramini, Evans and Kleine 2005).

As technology increasingly enables fine target marketing and interaction between marketers and consumers, the roles of marketing research and promotional efforts become more intertwined. In traditional media, primary research conducted by marketing and advertising managers has been dominated by consumer surveys (however, this is now accomplished with more sampling and presentational efficiency using on-line technologies – see Neslin *et al.* 2006 for a review), warranty registration, 800-number feedback, and focus groups. Other sorts of research, from economic and trade statistics to media coverage and word of mouth, have been viewed as 'secondary' data. In the New Media environment of Web2.0, it is much of this 'secondary' data that should count the most, because of its external validity and insights into the interactive market place.

As the web has grown and changed, so too have the search engines for undertaking consumer and marketing research. The large search engines now offer group search options, allowing one to search for newsgroups and blog (web log) archives. A growing number of high quality blog search engines are designed specifically for that space (see Feedster.com, Bloglines.com, and Technorati.com as examples). These forums have not only web-surfers (or 'minglers') as readers, but typically contain a respectable concentration of insiders and devotees. Anywhere on-line consumer activity and interactions (whether opining, playing, or searching for information) are found, interesting sources of data for consumer and marketing researchers and the potential for

'netnography' to reveal insights about on-line communal consumer culture, practices, and meanings are also present. Experienced ethnographers are inevitably '*bricoleurs*', employing a number of research approaches to the rich lived worlds of cultural experience that people share and experience on-line.

Both Holt (Holt 2005; Holt, Quelch and Taylor 2004) and Keller (2003) have persuasively argued that the multiple and complex meanings of brands goes well beyond the approaches which are typically revealed using conventional psychological theories. People, places, things, and other brands are contextual inputs that often reveal brand symbolism, and deliver customer value through multiple media venues, even those which offer up globally critical perspectives of a brand (Thompson and Arsel 2004). The highly accessible, fluid, and transparent virtual world offers a rich field for ethnographic research – immersion, internationalization, awareness of cultural differences, and engagement – all lend themselves well to an on-line world, and translate into good marketing research.

THE FUTURE OF GLOBAL COMMUNICATIONS

When Apple introduced its new i-phone in 2007 the setting is the Las Vegas electronic show, the event was carefully choreographed and televised and the presenter is its intrepid leader, Steve Jobs. When Microsoft is in the news – for whatever reason, positive or negative – Bill Gates shows up. In fact, when founder Bill Gates realized that he no longer could be both chief executive and spokesperson for his firm, he chose the latter role. When Nike's sales slump, they call back founder Phil Knight. Virgin's Richard Branson is indefatigable promoting his company creations. When the Body Shop went public and the late Anita Roddick stepped down, the stores' performance suffered. Sony's performance has been uncertain ever since its charismatic leader Akio Morita passed away.

Firms can succeed even without a celebrity leader. Faceless Toyota is now the world's leading automobile maker. Nokia manages to be cool without a CEO in jeans and mock turtleneck sweater. Walmart has continued strong even after the death of its inspirational founder Sam Walton who once did the hula down Wall Street. And charismatic leaders do not ensure success. Dieter Zetsche, whose showmanship flair helped turn Chrysler around, has not had the same success at the Daimler headquarters. C. Michael Armstrong did not have much success in running AT&T despite his aura of machismo, riding a Harley-Davidson to work. Most emblematic is perhaps Enron's Kenneth Lay, whose charm and close relationship with the President of the United States hardly mattered when the cash flow did not materialize.

The point is not that the way a company leader communicates always matters. The point is that it can be made to matter positively. That is, global communications is one activity which, when done well, can be strategically very important. Traditionally, global communications has been seen as incidental to the overall strategy, part of strategy implementation rather than strategy formulation, and mainly a matter of effective dissemination of policy decisions taken. This is much too limited a view in today's globally over-saturated communications environment. In addition to ensuring successful implementation, skillful and accomplished communicators make it possible to craft strategies otherwise unavailable. To cite just one simple example, in the new era of interactive marketing and customer participation, the consumers need to be motivated to actively participate. How do you accomplish that without spending a bundle? With a charismatic leader consumers want to join up. The motivational hurdle is much lower and the need to reward consumers much less. Leaders who are adept at communications attract not only attention but also allegiance.

The fact is that today, in most companies, marketing communications are no longer the prerogative of the marketing department or the advertising manager. Neither is corporate communications solely the responsibility of public relations staff. As integrated marketing communications proponents long have preached, 'all company employees are marketers'. Some even argue that in today's wired world the firm's customers are its best marketers. In any event, top executives have to get active in the communications arena, if for no other reason that there are so many potentially negative news items about companies. In the globally connected world, no company can avoid scrutiny, bad news travels fast, and company 'damage control' needs to involve everybody from top to bottom.

That is the management perspective. For many people around the world, however, the big corporations' communications efforts represent nothing short of imperial overstretch, the desire to crush local entrepreneurs, and to marshal legal and financial resources in denial and rejection of negative news. Even if the intentions of the large firms might be misread, the evidence, judging from their activities in the local markets, often suggest that the anti-globalizers have a valid point. The new media, such as the Internet and blogosphere, might well empower the little person in any corner of the world – but the chat-rooms and the bloggers are soon joined by company representatives, operating under the guise of genuine participation. The local brands might be still available in competition with the large global brands – but they are now owned by the multinationals. And even if local community 'give-backs' are a common strategy by large firms with offshored production sites, the opening of new and even lower cost production locations show any loyalty to be short-lived.

This is the context of the integrated marketing communication activities of today's typical large firm. The task is to leverage global brand strength locally without antagonizing the host country. The job is also to support the acquired local brands without upsetting the existing brand loyal consumers. It also needs to handle potential mishaps in the off-shored production sites, including anti-foreign, anti-global sentiment among policy-makers and government officials. At home, many companies have to deal with increasingly petulant and self-centered consumers, whose latent needs have long since been satisfied and where demand increasingly comes from secondary and incidental benefits which are emotional more than functional. Balancing the experiential and sensory desires of consumers in advanced economies against the more basic and functional requirements in emerging countries is a challenge for most companies, who can no longer treat the world as a set of differentiated national markets. The new consumers in Russia want the emotional gratification of the California teenager they see on television – but they also need a product that works under very different conditions.

As we have seen, two interrelated communications developments have helped create this new context. One is the technological advance in global communications and targeted interactive media. No longer does global communication mean simply everybody watching the same TV programs, listening to the same music or getting the same news. With the 'death of distance' global communication has become personal. Cell phones, e-mail and text messaging make you connected at any time and any place. You are at the center of your own world, even controlling the kind of blogs you trust for the news. With the new global communication we no longer see a drive towards homogeneity – but a drive towards an individual universe. Your world is your own.

NOTES

1 For an overview of the vast media holdings of these six firms, see: http://adage.com/datacenter/article?article_id=116341

2 There seems to be some limit to the viability of the consolidations, however. In March 2006 the Little Brown and Company unit was sold to Hachette Livres, a large French bookseller.

3 'Land Rover Announces Earthwatch as Fifth Global Sponsorship Partner,' *Press Release*, Gaydon, Warwickshire, May 1, 2007.

4 Adapted from: Solomon, M. R. and Wood, N. T., CFP of the 27th Annual Advertising and Consumer Psychology Conference, Society for Consumer Psychology, May 1–2, 2008.

5 Adapted from multiple sources, but primarily Jennifer Alsever, Flying off the Shelves *Business2.0*, December 2006, 47–49.

6 Has the number of URL's (or 'hits') gone down since publication of this Chapter? If so, consider this a real-time example of the dynamics of Web2.0's collaborative readership platform!

REFERENCES

Anderson, C. (2004) 'The Long Tail', *Wired*, October (12): 10.

Barbási, A.-L. (2003), *Linked, How Everything Is Connected to Everything Else and What It Means for Business, Science, and Everyday Life*. New York: Penguin.

Beltramini, R., Evans, K. R. and Kleine III, R. E. (2005) 'Future directions for digital business management' *International Journal of Internet Marketing and Advertising*, 2, 1/2.

Benkler, Y. (2006) *The Wealth of Nations: How Social Production Transforms Markets and Freedom*. New Haven, CT: Yale University Press.

Bradley, J. (2007) 'Top 100 Spending Up 3.1% to $105 billion', *Advertising Age*, June 25, 2007, p. 4.

Bughin, J. and Manyika, J. (2007) 'How businesses are using Web2.0: a McKinsey global survey' March 2007, *McKinsey Quarterly: The Online Journal of McKinsey & Co.*

Calder, B. J. and Malthouse, E. C. (2005) 'Managing media and advertising change with integrated marketing', *Journal of Advertising Research*, 45: 356–361.

Cannizzaro, M. (2007) 'The 50 who matter now', *Business2.0*, Time, Inc. July, vol. 8, nr. 8, p. 61.

Carlin, I. (2005) 'A vision of media planning in 2010' *Journal of Advertising Research*, 45 (March): 2–4.

Castronova, E. (2005) *Synthetic Worlds: The Business and Culture of On-Line Games*. University of Chicago Press, Chicago, IL.

Chang, C. (2006) 'Cultural masculinity/femininity influences on advertising appeals', *Journal of Advertising Research*, 46 (September): 315–323.

Chow, S. and Amir, S. (2006) 'The universality of values: implications for global advertising strategy' *Journal of Advertising Research*, 46 (September): 301–314.

Creamer, M. (2007) 'Dell quells critics with Web2.0 tack', June 11, http://adage.com/article?article_id=117248. New York: Crain Communications, Inc.

Digital and Marketing Media Factpack (2007) Crain Communications, Inc., New York. p. 3.

Elias, N. and Greenspan, L. (2007) 'The honey, the bear, and the violin: the Russian voices of Israeli advertising', *Journal of Advertising Research*, 47 (March): 113–122.

Endicott, R. C. (2006) *Advertising Age's 20th Annual Global Marketers*. New York: Crain Communications, p. 3.

Geyskens, I., Gielens, K. and Dekimpe, M. (2002) 'The market valuation of Internet channel additions', *Journal of Marketing*, 66 (April): 102–119.

Gielser, M. (2006) 'Consumer gift systems', *Journal of Consumer Research*, 33 (Sept): 283–290.

Global Marketers: Advertising Age's 20th Annual Report (2006) Crain communications Inc., and The Ad Age Group (November).

Goldstein, D. G. and Goldstein, D. C. (2006) 'Profiting from the Long Tail', *Harvard Business Review*, 84 (June): 24–28.

Graybow, M. (2007), 'MasterCard and FIFA settle World Cup sponsor fight,' *Reuters*, June 22.

Hargittai, E. (in press), 'The changing online landscape: from free-for-all to commercial gatekeeping', in P. Day and D. Schuler (eds), *Community Practice in the Network Society: Local Actions/Global Integration*. New York: Routledge. Available on line at: http://www.eszter.com/research/pubs/hargittai-online landscape.pdf

Hart, K. (2007) 'Tracking who's saying what about whom', *Washington Post*, 29 January, D1.

Hemp, P. (2006) 'Avatar-based marketing', *Harvard Business Review*, 46(6): 48–51.

Hoffman, D. and Novak, T. P. (1996) 'Marketing in hypermedia computer-mediated environments: conceptual foundations', *Journal of Marketing*, 60 (July): 50–68.

Hoffman, D., Novak, T. P. and Venkatesh, A. (2004) 'Has the Internet become indispensable?' *Communications of the ACM*, July (7), 37–42.

Holt, D. B. (2005) 'How societies desire brands: using cultural theory to explain brand symbolism', in S. Ratheshwar and D. G. Mick (eds), *Inside Consumption: Consumer Motives, Goals, and Desires*. London: Routledge, pp. 273–291.

Holt, D. B., Quelch, J. A., and Taylor, E. L. (2004) 'How global brands compete', *Harvard Business Review*, September, pp. 68–75.

Holzwarth, M. Janiszewski, C. and Neumann, M. M. (2006) 'The influence of avatars on online consumer shopping behavior', *Journal of Marketing*, 70 (October): 19–36.

Internet World Stats: *Usage and Population Statistics*, accessed 15 June, 2007 at: http://www.internetworldstats.com/stats.htm,.

Jap, S. D. (2003) 'An exploratory study of the introduction of online reverse auctions', *Journal of Marketing*, 67 (July): 96–107.

Keller, K. (2003) 'Brand synthesis: the multidimensionality of brand knowledge', *Journal of Consumer Research*, March (29), 4, 595–600.

Kozinets, R. V. (2002) 'The field behind the screen: using netnography for marketing research in online communities', *Journal of Marketing Research*, 39 (February): 61–72.

Kozinets, R. V. (2006a) 'Click to connect: netnography and tribal advertising' *Journal of Advertising Research*, 46 (September): 279–288.

Kozinets, R. V. (2006b), 'Netnography 2.0,' in R. W. Belk (ed.), *Handbook of Qualitative Research Methods in Marketing*. Cheltenham: Edward Elgar, pp. 129–142.

Langer R. and Beckman, S. C. (2005) 'Sensitive research topics: netnography revisited', *Qualitative Market Research*, 8(2): 189–203.

Lee, W. N. and Daugherty, T. (2006) 'Cross-cultural e-Advertising', *International Journal of Internet Marketing and Advertising*, 3, 2.

Levitt, T. (1983) 'The globalization of markets', *Harvard Business Review*, May–June, pp. 92–102.

Lin, C. A. (2006) 'Predicting webcasting adoption via personal innovativeness and perceived utilities', *Journal of Advertising Research*, 46 (June): 228–238.

Mandel, N. and Johnson, E. J. (2002) 'When Web pages influence choice: effects of visual primes on experts and novices', *Journal of Consumer Research*, 29 (September): 235–245.

Marketing Science Institute, 'Creating and Cultivating Brand Connections', Carlson School of Management, University of Minnesota, June 6–8, 2007. Accessed March 31, 2007 at: http://www.msi.org/.

Mattsson, J. and Rendtorff, J. D. (2006) 'Ethical issues in electronic marketing and advertising' *International Journal of Internet Marketing and Advertising*, 3, 1.

McPhail, T. (2005) *Global Communications: Theories, Stakeholders, and Trends*, 2nd edn. London: Blackwell.

Money, R. B., Shimp, T. A. and Sakano, T. (2006) 'Celebrity endorsements in Japan and the United States: is negative information all that harmful?' *Journal of Advertising Research*, 46 (March): 113–123.

Muñoz, A. M. and Schau, H. P. (2005) 'Religiosity in the Abandoned apple Newton brand community', *Journal of Consumer Research*, 31 (March): 737–747.

Neslin, S., Novak, T., Baker, K. and Hoffman, D. (2006), 'An Optimal Contact Model for Optimizing Panel Response Rates' Working Paper, accessed 31 March, 2007 at: http://sloan.ucr.edu/

Novak, T. P., Hoffman, D. L. and Yung, Y. F. (2000), 'Measuring the customer experience in online environments: a structural modeling approach', *Marketing Science*, 19(1): 22–44.

Oviatt, B. and McDougall, P. (1994) 'Toward a theory of international new ventures' *Journal of International Business Studies*, 25(1): 45–64.

O'Reilly, T. (2006) 'Web2.0 compact definition: trying again', at: http://radar.oreilly.com/archives/2006/12/web_20_compact.html

Passariello, C., Johnson, K. and Vranica, S. (2007) 'A new force in advertising – protest by Email', *Wall Street Journal*, 22 March, p. B1, accessed 22 March, 2007 at: http://online.wsj.com/article/SB1174525313 96344892.html.

Pavlou, P. A. and Dimoka, A. (2006) 'The nature and role of feedback text comments in online marketplaces: implications for trust building and price premiums' U.C. Riverside *Working Paper*, accessed at: http://sloan.ucr.edu/2006/03/01/working-paper-pavlou-and-dimoka/

Plummer, J. (2005) 'Editorial: why look into media planning?', *Journal of Advertising Research*, 45 (March): 1.

Reardon, J., Miller, C., Foubert, B., Vida, I. and Rybina, L. (2006) 'Antismoking messages for the international teenage segment: the effectiveness of message valence and intensity across different cultures', *Journal of International Marketing*, 14(3): 115–138.

Schlosser, A. E. (2003) 'Experiencing products in the virtual world: the role of goal and imagery in influencing attitudes versus purchase intentions' *Journal of Consumer Research*, 30 (September): 184–198.

Schlosser, A. E., White, T. B. and Lloyd, S. M. (2006) 'Converting web site visitors into buyers: how web site investment increases consumer trusting beliefs and online purchase intentions', *Journal of Marketing*, 70 (April): 133–148.

Schwaiger, M., Rennhak, C., Taylor, C. R. and Cannon, H. M. (2007) 'Can comparative advertising be effective in Germany? A tale of two campaigns,' *Journal of Advertising Research*, 47 (March): 2–13.

Schwartz, S. H. (1992) 'Universals in the content and structure of values: theoretical advances and empirical test in 20 countries', in M. Zanna (ed.), *Advances in Experimental Social Psychology*. New York: Academic Press.

Schwartz, S. H. and Bilsky, W. (1990) 'Toward a theory of the universal content and structure of values', *Journal of Personality and Social Psychology*, 58(5): 878–891.

Shih, C.-F. and Venkatesh, A. (2004) 'Beyond adoption: development and application of a use-diffusion model, *Journal of Marketing*, 68(1): 59–72.

Shirky, C. (2003) 'Power laws, Weblogs, and inequality' accessed March 28, 2007 from http://shirky.com/writings/powerlaw_weblog.html

Spann, M., and Tellis, G. J. (2006) 'Does the Internet promote better consumer decisions? The case of name-your-own-price auctions', *Journal of Marketing*, 70 (January): 65–78.

Steenkamp, J.-B. and Geyskens, I. (2006) 'How country characteristics affect the perceived value of Web services', *Journal of Marketing*, 70 (July): 136–150.

Thompson, C. J., and Arsel, Z. (2004) 'The Starbucks brandscape and consumers' (anticorporate) experiences of glocalization,' *Journal of Consumer Research*, 31(3): 631–642.

Varman, R. and Belk, R. W. (2007) *Weaving a Web: Subaltern Consumers, Rising Consumer Culture, and Media, Working paper.* Department of Industrial and Management Engineering Indian Institute of Technology, Kanpur, India.

Venkatesh, A. (2006) 'Introduction to the Special Issue on "ICT" in everyday life: home and personal environments', *The Information Society*, 22:1–4.

Warren, J. and Jurgensen, J. (2007) 'The Wizards of Buzz: a new kind of website is turning ordinary people into hidden influencers, shaping what we read, watch, and buy', *The Wall Street Journal*, February 10, P1.

Wilk, R. (1995) 'Learning to be local in Belize: global systems of common difference', in D. Miller (eds.), *Worlds Apart: Modernity through the Prism of the Local.* London: Routledge, pp. 110–131.

Williams, I. (2007) 'UK online ad spending to top 4.5bn English pounds in 2011', *vnunet.com*, July 2.

Wood, N., Solomon, M. R. and Englis, B. (2005) 'Personalization of online avatars: is the messenger as important as the message', *International Journal of Internet Marketing and Advertising*, 2(1/2): 143–161.

20

Global Channels of Distribution

Daniel C. Bello and Forrest Briggs

INTRODUCTION

Global distribution systems consist of interdependent organizations involved in the process of making a product or service available for use in markets around the world (Coughlan *et al.* 2006). The structure of global distribution channels varies widely, consisting of a variety of organizational participants (foreign agents, distributors, sales subsidiaries, etc.) engaged in various functional activities (operating warehouses, managing a salesforce, etc.). As a critical aspect of marketing strategy, the methods or modes of entry into foreign markets not only determine how a multinational enterprise (MNE) goes to market internationally but also establish the extent of its participation in global distribution activities (Bello and Zhu 2006). Institutional design theorists (Carson *et al.* 1999) recognize that organizations participating in a global channel system subdivide and otherwise allocate the many activities necessary to provide valuable distribution services to end-users.

A key purpose of global distribution is to provide end-users in foreign target markets with competitive levels of demanded distributions services such as locational convenience, in-stock product availability and

variety, information, after-sales services among others (Coughlan *et al.* 2006). To deliver end-user services, organizations constituting the international channel must efficiently and effectively perform a variety of necessary logistical, marketing, and other distribution and business activities. However, these activities can be performed within a variety of organizational configurations, ranging from a single, fully integrated firm to a loose network of many individual firms, each specializing in particular tasks (Bello and Zhu 2007). Regardless of organizational form, distribution activities are conducted through exchange transactions between a principal (focal manufacturer or brand owner) and agent (personnel conducting tasks in foreign market). An agent, defined as any actor performing a distribution task in a foreign market, may be employed by an independent firm or by the principal, and may perform any number and combination of logistic, marketing, or other distribution activities. When a principal organizes and manages activities such as local selling or delivery through a foreign subsidiary, the exchange transaction between the principal and a salaried, employee-agent occurs within a corporate hierarchy (Anderson and Gatignon 1987). When the principal goes to market through a foreign distributor, the transaction for local marketing and logistics occurs within a market since the agent in this case is an independent merchant intermediary. The principal–agent transaction for distribution activities can occur within various organizational configurations, each providing the principal with a different degree of risk and control. For example, Anderson and Gatignon (1986) identify and classify 17 alternative modes of foreign-market entry, based on the level of control a principal has over its agent (high-control subsidiary to low-control, nonexclusive contracting).

As Table 20.1 illustrates, analysis of the governance or organizational design of channel activities has coalesced around a variety of theoretical perspectives, most notably transaction cost analysis (Williamson 1996), resource-based view (Barney 2007), and institutional theory (North 1990) among others. Each perspective examines the problem of

designing international channels through a specific theoretical lens that highlights certain aspects of the principal–agent relationship and distribution activities. Transaction cost analysis (TCA) views the channel strategist as rationally applying an 'economic efficiency' criterion by aligning the attributes of exchange with the governance abilities of alternative modes of entry. Based on TCA logic, the efficient organizational configuration will minimize transaction costs associated with protecting the principal's interests in exchanges with agents for global distribution activities. Unlike TCA's preoccupation with opportunism, the resource-based view (RBV) considers the channel strategist as striving to obtain the resources necessary for a sustainable competitive advantage in a foreign market. RBV suggests a principal engages in exchange with an agent possessing valuable, immobile capabilities because it is too difficult or costly to obtain such strategic

Table 20.1   Theoretical frameworks for global channels of distribution: basic logic and example research applications

	Transaction Cost Analysis	*Resource-Based View*	*Institutional Perspective*
Theoretical logic	Exchange characteristics (asset specificity, uncertainty) yield governance problems of safeguarding, adapting, and evaluating. Transaction costs incurred in overcoming governance problems are minimized by efficiently aligning exchange characteristics with governance mechanisms (market-entry modes).	Resource characteristics (inimitable, non-substitutable) yield strategic capabilities for distribution that are heterogeneous and immobile across firms. Resource deficiencies motivate nonhierarchical modes of entry.	Institutional pressures legitimize certain modes of entry due to isomorphic pressures (those constraining regulative, normative, and cognitive pressures that lead to similar entry mode choices based on a motivation to imitate others facing similar conditions).
Research examples of theory applications	Anderson and Coughlan (1987): Higher human asset specificity in foreign selling, greater likelihood of hierarchical entry rather than market-based modes.	Ekeledo and Sivakumar (2004): Higher firm-specific resources associated with subsidiary form of market entry.	Davis, Desai, and Francis (2000): Internal isomorphism yields mimetic pressures for business units to resemble others.
	Klein, Frazier and Roth (1990): Higher environmental uncertainty (unpredictability), greater likelihood of hierarchical mode of foreign market entry.	Peng and York (2001): Export intermediaries with greater resources experience higher performance.	Lu (2002): External mimetic behaviors influence entry mode for Japanese subsidiaries.
	Houston and Johnson (2000): Higher behavioral uncertainty (performance ambiguity), greater likelihood of joint venture than contractual market-based entry mode.	Dhanaraj and Beamish (2003): Exporter resources and capabilities predict strategy and firm performance.	Yiu and Makino (2002): Firms conform to regulative and normative isomorphic pressures of host countries.

resources in alternative ways. In overcoming its poor resource endowments, a principal views any threat of opportunism stemming from its global channel relationships as simply another cost of gaining access to needed capabilities. According to institutional theory, channel strategists strive to design global distribution systems to accommodate powerful regulative, normative, and cognitive forces in the foreign market (Bello, Lohtia and Sangtani 2004). Rather than focusing on economic efficiency or strategic capabilities, principals tend to conform to pressures in the host country environment that prescribe the mode of entry required to obtain social legitimacy for the foreign channel.

Because of the considerable differences in perspectives among leading theories, some analysts are pessimistic regarding the state of knowledge of global distribution. For example, Lu (2002) observes that 'after more than 25 years of relatively intensive research and investigation, there is still a lack of consensus on the antecedents and outcomes of the entry mode choice' (p. 20). While a certain theoretical tension exists among the extant channel frameworks, we believe the theories offer perspectives that are more complementary than competing on what is admittedly one of the most complex and dynamic aspects of international marketing. In organizing this chapter on global channels, we first discuss the particular constructs and conceptual logic associated with each theory, and then report on the way empirical researchers have applied and operationalized the perspective to investigate international distribution.

TRANSACTION COST ANALYSIS

As the dominant paradigm for analyzing foreign mode of entry, TCA posits efficient global distribution systems are based on the organizational configuration that minimizes transaction costs associated with organizing and managing activities in international distribution (Zhao, Luo and Suh 2004;

Williamson 1996). Transaction costs are the costs of running the global channel system and 'include such ex ante costs as drafting and negotiating contracts and such ex post costs as monitoring and enforcing agreements' (Rindfleisch and Heide 1997, p. 31). Transaction costs occur because exchange partners are characterized by bounded rationality and opportunistic tendencies, and international exchange transactions for distribution activities may be characterized by asset specificity and uncertainty (Bello and Zhu 2006). TCA logic focuses on the characteristics of exchanges involving distribution activities because, given the potential for partner opportunism, exchange attributes may give rise to the governance problems of safeguarding specific investments, adapting to change, and evaluating performance.

Importantly, the transaction costs incurred in overcoming these exchange problems are assumed to be minimized within a firm due to hierarchy's superior ability to dampen opportunism because a principal can use powerful internal control and surveillance systems over its employee-agents (Williamson 1975). In contrast, market-based exchanges provide independent parties with high-powered individual incentives, but possess much weaker capabilities for safeguarding at-risk assets, adjusting to unanticipated change, and monitoring processes and outcomes. In global distribution situations where few governance problems exist for an exchange, the lack of transaction problems and costs makes market governance the efficient mode choice, but when substantial governance problems occur, transaction costs are minimized by bringing the exchange within the boundary of the firm. Thus, the TCA approach to foreign-market entry assesses the alignment between the attributes of distribution exchanges that create transaction difficulties, and the governance mechanisms used to address the resulting governance problems.

Global distribution activities involve substantial transaction costs to the extent they employ specific, rather than general, assets and must contend with environmental and behavioral uncertainty (Bello and Zhu 2006). Specific assets are human, physical, or other types of investments dedicated or customized to a foreign transaction and have little value outside of the particular exchange relationship. An agent investing specific assets to sell a foreign brand in its local market faces a safeguarding problem, since it is at risk that its principal may exploit the assets opportunistically. For example, a foreign sales agency may invest in human and brand name specific assets when it pioneers its local market for an exporting manufacturer's complex, technical product. Specialized training for agency salespeople and the time and effort dedicated to convincing customers of the brand's benefits are at risk of loss should the manufacturer act unscrupulously and serve its self-interest through deceit, cheating, or otherwise violating the agreement. For once the agent successfully develops the foreign market, an opportunistic manufacturer could, for example, unfairly reduce sales commissions, add additional agents, or terminate the agent entirely and establish a sales subsidiary. Because, in the absence of safeguards, a rational agent would refuse to enter into such a risky arrangement, the manufacturer might utilize such risk-reducing governance mechanisms as a multi-year contract, geographic exclusivity, guaranteed commission rates, and other safeguards to protect, and thereby motivate the agent to represent its products.

Governance mechanisms capable of addressing governance problems have been conceptualized in a variety of ways. While Williamson (1975) originally considered governance as a discrete choice between market exchange and internal organization, a variety of alternative intermediate or hybrid mechanisms have now been identified (Williamson 1996). Researchers in international distribution operationalize mode-of-entry choices across many types of governance structures ranging from market, intermediate and hierarchy. For example, in their empirical study of channel integration in global distribution, Klein, Frazier and Roth (1990) specify governance form as ranging from merchant distributor (i.e., market), joint venture (i.e., hybrid), to foreign sales subsidiary (i.e., hierarchy). They find support for the TCA logic that the greater a principal's need to safeguard specific assets in a foreign exchange relationship, the greater the degree of channel integration the firm will employ to minimize transaction costs. Likewise, in this research on Canadian firms, the authors support the TCA prediction of a positive relationship between environmental volatility (creating an adaptation problem) and the principal's use of a foreign subsidiary to minimize the costs of coordinating change with its local agent. While the extant literature on applying TCA to international distribution is extensive, several recent meta-analytical reviews (Zhao, Luo and Suh 2004; Geyskens, Steenkamp and Kumar 2006) are helpful in understanding relationships among the attributes of distribution transactions and the mode of foreign-market entry. We organize our discussion around each transaction attribute and governance problem.

Asset specificity and the safeguarding problem

Despite inconsistencies in definitions, measures and sampling across studies, meta-analytical findings generally support the TCA prediction that as asset specificity increases, principals increasingly employ hierarchical modes of foreign entry compared to market-based entry methods (Zhao, Luo and Suh 2004; Geyskens, Steenkamp and Kumar 2006). A principal using an integrated, high-control entry mode (e.g., foreign subsidiary) incurs significant internal organizational overhead and bureaucratic costs, including investments in legal, administrative and operating infrastructure (Bello and Zhu 2007). Since TCA logic assumes high control is costly in terms of resource commitments, 'firms integrate when asset specificity is high, because the higher costs of vertical integration are more than offset by the benefits (of control) … when specificity is low, firms refrain from integration because the benefits of control fall short of the costs of attaining it' (Erramilli and Rao 1993, p. 21). The cost-control trade-off prescribes hierarchical entry under high asset specificity because integrated modes incur low safeguarding costs due to the principal's legitimate authority to command and control an employee-agent. However, under low asset specificity conditions, a principal has no at-risk assets to safeguard and, consequently, selects a transaction cost-efficient, low-control market entry mode.

In terms of empirical research into foreign market entry decisions, many studies find that asset specificity is positively related to higher levels of principal control in foreign host markets (Gatignon and Anderson 1988; Klein 1989; Klein and Roth 1990; Kim and Hwang 1992). Typical of the studies that test the safeguarding reasoning of TCA is Anderson and Coughlan's (1987) research on the distribution channel choice of US semiconductor companies in foreign markets. The researchers examine 94 overseas distribution arrangements by 36 firms and operationalize asset specificity as transaction-specific learning required by a salesperson to sell effectively in a foreign market. The findings are consistent with TCA logic since the higher the human specificity involved in the foreign selling task, the greater the likelihood the semiconductors are marketed by hierarchical modes (corporate sales force or distribution division) rather than by market-based modes (independent foreign distributor or sales agent).

Interestingly, Erramilli and Rao (1993) suggest the cost-control logic of TCA linking specificity to hierarchy becomes weaker when principals face three situations: (1) cost of integration is low; (2) non-TCA benefits of control are considered; and (3) ability to integrate is high. First, while focusing on entry-mode choice of service firms, Erramilli and Rao note integration costs can be low for principals considering service-based activities such as selling, advertising, and other low capital-intensive marketing tasks.

Unlike manufacturing and other tasks requiring expensive facilities and equipment, low-capital activities can be integrated and conducted by employee-agents at low cost. Second, while TCA's integration benefits are minimal safeguarding costs derived from efficiently controlling employees, integration also yields important non-TCA benefits. An internationalizing principal benefits from vertical integration because 'control facilitates global integration and coordination of strategies in multinational corporations' (p. 22) as well as extends market power and avoids conflicts with outside partners. Third, large principals with slack resources possess the financial ability to integrate and easily acquire control over foreign distribution activities. Thus, Erramilli and Rao (1993) posit that even low asset-specific principals facing these three conditions will prefer high-control, integrated modes of foreign-market entry, in contrast to TCA's prescription of market modes. Their empirical study of 381 foreign-market entry decisions by service firms largely confirms the role these three factors play in altering a principal's cost-control calculus, leading the authors to conclude 'the transaction-cost framework can be broadened to develop a more comprehensive model for understanding entry-mode choice' (Erramilli and Rao 1993, p. 19).

Environmental uncertainty and the adaptation problem

As the exchange attribute giving rise to adaptation costs, environmental uncertainty refers to unanticipated changes in circumstances surrounding an exchange involving global distribution activities (Rindfleisch and Heide 1997). Since unexpected situations cannot be contracted for in advance, an exchange subject to future volatility, unpredictability, and/or complexity requires a governance form that facilitates non-opportunistic adjustments to the terms of trade (Bello and Zhu 2006). TCA logic prescribes high-control, integrated governance, since hierarchical structures permit sequential adaptations with minimal transaction costs because re-negotiations occur with employee-agents. In contrast, market-based exchanges that require future adaptations are not recommended, since high transactions costs of haggling and bargaining would be incurred as independent partners re-negotiate details of their trading agreement. A principal faces possible loss at each adaptation occasion since its market-based, autonomous agent may opportunistically exploit re-negotiations. Meta-analysis largely supports the notion that exchanges subject to environmental uncertainty tend to be governed through high-control modes (Geyskens, Steenkamp and Kumar 2006).

Empirical studies in global distribution operationalize environmental uncertainty in a variety of ways, reflecting the various facets of exchange that may be a source of volatility. Uncertainty is operationalized as a two-dimensional concept (unpredictability and changeability) by Klein *et al.* (1990) with each dimension differentially affecting the incentives for hierarchical governance of global channels. The authors posit that unpredictability motivates integrated modes in an effort to obtain control while changeability leads to low-control, market-based modes due to the desire for flexibility. Similarly, Klein (1989) distinguishes between complexity and dynamism as facets of environmental uncertainty in a foreign market. Complexity, referring to the number of possible sources of uncertainty, is 'the degree to which the respondent perceived the environment as simple or complex' and dynamism is 'the rate at which changes in the environment occur' (p. 257). In an analysis of 338 Canadian exporters, Klein finds environmental complexity increases, but dynamism decreases, the degree of vertical control (i.e., principal's centralized and formalized control over foreign partner's distribution activities).

Several studies examine country risk as a key facet of external uncertainty in a foreign host country. In fact, in their meta-analysis of 38 empirical studies on ownership-based entry (OBE) modes (e.g., joint ventures,

cooperative alliances, and wholly owned subsidiaries), Zhao, Luo and Suh (2004) conclude that 'country risk turns out to be the most influential determinant of OBE choice' (p. 530). Collectively across these empirical studies, country risk is negatively related to high-control, integrated entry modes (OBE). Thus, this research suggests that volatility in the host country leads principals to value flexibility by selecting non-integrated modes – a finding opposite to TCA's prescription for high control modes. Anderson and Gatignon (1986) suggest that unpredictable country environments motivate principals to seek flexible entry since the low switching costs inherent in non-integrated modes permit ongoing adjustments. However, Erramilli and Rao (1993) note the impact of country risk on the structure of global channels depends upon the level of asset specificity present in the exchange involving distribution activities. These authors suggest that high-specificity principals will employ full-control entry modes regardless of country risk, noting that 'TCA argues that these firms will find control even more desirable in high-risk situations … the resultant costs of haggling and maladaptation will further enhance the attractiveness of full-control modes in volatile environments' (p. 25).

In an in-depth study of the impact of country risk in China, Luo (2005) examines how environmental volatility impacts entry mode governance in terms of designing contracts for international joint ventures (IJV). To analyze volatility's impact within the specific IJV entry mode, he conceptualizes contractual governance as a three-dimensional construct in order to capture 'functions of contractual design, such as reducing opportunism without losing adaptation' (p. 210). First, term specificity refers to the extent all relevant terms and clauses are specified. Environmental volatility is posited to increase term specificity since details enhance control by specifying managerial duties while also reducing opportunities for exploitation. Second, contingency adaptability refers to the extent a contract accounts for contingencies and delineates relevant guidelines for adjusting to them. Volatility is thought to increase adaptability because greater contingency coverage provides greater situational flexibility. Third, contractual obligatoriness involves the extent the parties are legally bound (i.e., binding force of penalties against breaching party). Volatility is hypothesized to increase obligatoriness since it constrains opportunism. In Luo's (2005) study of 110 Chinese IJVs, environmental volatility increases contractual adaptability and obligatoriness but, unexpectedly, decreases term specificity. He suggests environmental complexity may co-vary with volatility in China, making it difficult for firms to delineate explicit terms and clauses. Overall, the research demonstrates that volatility is an important determinant of contractual governance for this hybrid mode of foreign-market entry. Firms that embrace strong contractual governance over international channel partners in uncertain environments may be able to enhance adaptation while restricting opportunism.

The relationship between environmental uncertainty and opportunism by global partners is further investigated by Luo (2007) in a study of 188 IJVs in China. Consistent with the notion that opportunism is endogenous and not a pre-fixed aspect of global distribution, Luo tests the opportunistic response of foreign and domestic Chinese partners to various facets of volatility. He posits partners attempt to minimize their financial exposure to country turbulence by behaving opportunistically. Both perceived law unenforceability (poor legal enforcement due to a corrupt judiciary and other political dysfunctions) as well as information unverifiability (difficulty verifying the truthfulness of business and public information) are shown to increase opportunistic acts. Firms are thought to adapt to country volatility by behaving selfishly as a way to cope with the consequential transaction uncertainties and information-processing difficulties. Along this line Zhao, Luo and Suh (2004) recommend that future research on the impact of

uncertainty on global distribution incorporates the logic of institutional economics (North 1990) and further investigates constructs such as enforcement indeterminacy and other country-level institutional factors.

Internal uncertainty and the measurement problem

Internal uncertainty or performance ambiguity refers to difficulty in assessing partner outcomes due to information asymmetry regarding the conduct and performance of distribution tasks (Rindfleisch and Heide 1997). As an attribute of exchange, internal uncertainty gives rise to measurement problems, making it difficult and costly for a principal to evaluate whether a trading partner's task conduct is in compliance with contractual agreements (Bello and Zhu 2006). Compared with principals engaged in domestic exchanges, the literature suggests that principals involved in international distribution relationships face greater opportunistic hazards due to verification problems inherent in evaluating the performance of foreign-based partners (Anderson and Gatignon 1986). Buvik and Andersen (2002) suggest that 'The higher measurement complexity in international settings has been explained by the lack of international experience or experiential knowledge and by sociocultural differences between home and host cultures' (p. 3). As a consequence, such principals incur high transaction costs both in screening and selecting partners (*ex ante*) as well as in measuring performance (*ex post*). Due to the surveillance and control advantages of hierarchy, TCA prescribes high-control integrated foreign market operations as the governance structure most capable of minimizing measurement-related costs.

Individual studies of entry mode for foreign distribution have examined the role of internal uncertainty on governance choice. For example, Houston and Johnson (2000) find a positive relationship between a principal's performance ambiguity and the likelihood of the formation of an international joint venture rather than a contractual entry mode. Opportunism in the face of measurement difficulties is suppressed in a JV because, unlike in contractual modes, each firms' pay-off is contingent on the venture's performance instead of on fulfillment of contractual terms. In forming a JV, partners align their incentives in a way that reduces opportunistic risks. In a study of international service firms, Brouthers and Brouthers (2003) find that service firms perceiving high levels of behavioral uncertainty tend to prefer joint venture modes of entry compared with wholly owned subsidiaries. The authors reason that people-intensive service firms incur such high internal organizational costs that such in-house, bureaucratic costs exceed the transaction cost savings of hierarchy, resulting in service firms avoiding integrated modes as performance ambiguity increases (also see Erramilli and Rao 1993). They suggest that service firms prefer JVs as a way to reduce internal costs while benefiting from the notion that potential partner opportunism is held in check by the aligned JV incentive structure.

Meta-analytical research generally supports TCA's prescription for the efficient alignment of difficult to verify exchanges with integrated organizational configurations. In their evaluation of 200 empirical studies involving a mix of domestic or foreign exchanges, Geyskens, Steenkamp and Kumar (2006) report that behavioral uncertainty significantly leads to a choice of hierarchical governance over market governance, consistent with TCA predictions. In international research, the two most commonly used proxy variables for internal uncertainty are a deficient international experience (IE) and great cultural distance (CD). Across 38 international studies, Zhao, Luo and Suh (2004) find foreign experience of the principal's management is positively related to ownership-based entry modes while cultural distance between home and host countries is negatively related. Oddly, these results are in opposition to TCA since high experience and low

cultural distance minimize internal uncertainty, reducing expectations of ownership-based entry. Both performance ambiguity and measurement difficulties decline for exchanges characterized by high international experience and cultural similarities, enabling principals to exploit the efficiency advantages of market-based entry. In commenting on their meta-analytical findings, the authors note conclusions are problematic regarding main effects of IE and CD on entry mode due to moderating factors (industry type, principal's country of origin, etc.) and poor operationalizations of IE and CD as TCA-related constructs. Further, measurement inequivalence is noted to cause serious estimation and other problems across studies: 'This inequivalence not only creates considerable conceptual confusion, leading to lax interpretation of TCE determinants, but it also casts doubt on the adequacy of both CD and IE as measures for internal uncertainty' (Zhao, Luo and Suh 2004, p. 538).

Given the variety of limitations and problems associated with the transaction cost line of research, Zhao, Luo and Suh (2004) suggest that TCA be integrated with other theoretical perspectives such as the resource-based view: 'the firm boundary decision is a capability-related decision, and the choice of governance is not one of cost minimization, as proposed by TCE, but rather of the benefits … of a firm's capabilities' (p. 540).

RESOURCE-BASED VIEW

RBV theorists posit the institutional structure of international distribution channels is based upon organizational configurations that yield a sustainable competitive advantage (Barney 2007). Employing the logic that strategic resources and capabilities needed to conduct global distribution are heterogeneous across firms and immobile among firms, RBV suggests inter-organizational distribution arrangements occur as firms seek the support required to obtain a competitive advantage in a foreign market. For example, an exporter requiring a combination of transportation and warehousing capabilities favorably located in a foreign country might contract with a local distributor possessing these crucial resources as a way to access them cost effectively. Non-hierarchical governance is employed because these logistical resources are endowments of the distributor and are too difficult or costly for the exporter to bring within its own organizational boundaries. Central to RBV reasoning are key attributes of resources (valuable, rare, non-substitutable, and inimitable) that yield the strategically relevant features of heterogeneity and immobility (Barney 1991). Of particular importance is the notion resources are imperfectly imitable when they cannot be created or obtained easily by firms that do not possess them. Inimitability occurs when the possession of distribution capabilities is due to historical conditions (circumstances favoring their development have passed), path dependence (unique development sequence is required), causal ambiguity (cause-and-effect poorly understood), and social complexity (not directly manageable; evolves through informal, personal relations).

The foreign-market transportation and warehousing capabilities noted above may be so difficult to duplicate that an exporter would find it prohibitively costly to gain access to such inimitable resources by developing or purchasing them. These strategic capabilities may be too costly to create (greenfield foreign direct investment) due to historical path dependence (no new building permits and zoning waivers available, etc.) and social complexity (inability of foreigner to obtain favorable union work rules, etc.). Likewise, an acquisition or merger may be unattractive or prohibitive due to legal constraints, uncertain long-term requirements, and severe cultural or operational difficulties in integrating separate organizations. When the cost of using hierarchical governance to gain access to capabilities is high, RBV recommends non-hierarchical governance for access. In contrast to TCA, RBV recommends

non-hierarchical modes even if there are significant transaction specific investments – and thus threats of opportunism – associated with the exchange. As Barney (1999) observes, 'Opportunism stemming from transaction-specific investments is simply part of the cost of gaining access to capabilities that are too costly to obtain in alternative ways' (p. 140).

With RBV logic, opportunism is not the main driver of governance decisions because the theory focuses on the attributes of capabilities, in contrast with TCA's focus on attributes of transactions. In analyzing an organization's resource endowment, RBV is less concerned with market failure and more concerned with resource failure in the sense that outside access must be obtained if the capabilities necessary to support distribution activities are lacking and are too costly to bring in-house. Given resource heterogeneity and immobility, a firm with resources poorly suited to global activities may have little choice but to enter into various channel arrangements, with organizations specializing in needed logistics and marketing capabilities. For example, a firm seeking to distribute a complex product – one requiring highly specific technical and sales training – in a distant, unfamiliar market may contract with a foreign-based, commissioned agent for local sales representation. Despite human asset specificity, market governance in the form of an indirect sales channel is established because the agent may possess intimate, high-trust contacts with local buyers that were developed over the years.

Importantly, the RBV recognizes that the unique selling capabilities of the local agent are immobile to the extent they can not be duplicated effectively, transferred easily, or even purchased by the principal. Even if financially feasible, attempting to hire away key salespeople or vertically integrate by acquiring the foreign sales agency might greatly dissipate the very selling capability it seeks, as formerly loyal buyers become suspicious and mistrustful of the new foreign employer or owner. Immobility of a local agent's selling capability reflects a resource failure by the would-be acquirer due to its inability to replicate the agent's historical path, causal understanding, and social immersion in the local marketplace. Such a resource failure is overcome through an exchange transaction between the local partner (provides access to selling capability) and the principal (provides sales commission). In this way, RBV reasoning considers potential partner opportunism a cost of doing business when market or intermediate governance forms are the only cost-effective way to access needed resources and capabilities.

Empirical research in international marketing has relied upon the concepts and logic of the RBV to frame investigations of key issues in global distribution channels. While the number of empirical studies guided by the RBV is fewer than the number employing TCA, results generally support RBV logic in the context of global distribution. This group of studies posits various aspects of the strategic role played by resources and capabilities in the structure and performance of international distribution channels. Unfortunately, researchers seldom directly invoke RBV mechanisms such as inimitability or non-substitutability in their conceptualizations, relying instead on the general notion that possessing or acquiring superior resources improves performance outcomes. In terms of measurement, RBV constructs are seldom operationalized directly, but tend to be assessed indirectly through proxy and related variables. A representative sample of studies from the RBV stream of research on global distribution channels follows.

Ekeledo and Sivakumar (2004) developed and tested a model of a firm's entry strategy based on the RBV. They note 'systematic empirical research on entry mode choice, using the resource-based perspective, is lacking despite recognition that firm-specific resources drive successful business strategy' (p. 69). Recognizing the sole ownership mode (operationalized as wholly-owned subsidiary) is the default entry mode in the RBV, the authors posit that full-control ownership is motivated by strategic advantages of protecting resources in a foreign market. Based on a sample of 130 US manufacturing and servicing firms, firm-specific resource endowments of proprietary technology and business experience are associated with the subsidiary form of foreign market entry. Further, the need to protect specialized assets and a superior reputation are also linked to sole ownership, while a need for complementary resources is associated with shared-control modes (joint venture). The authors conclude the RBV has good explanatory abilities regarding entry mode decisions, particularly for manufacturers.

Research integrating RBV with transaction cost and agency theory is conducted by Peng and York (2001) who test hypotheses regarding the performance antecedents of US-based export intermediaries. The researchers note 'export intermediaries' performance depends on their possession of valuable, unique, and hard-to-imitate resources which help minimize their clients' transaction and agency costs' (p. 327). In the context of the indirect export channel, intermediary success is thought to be based on employing strategic resources to reduce *ex ante* agency costs and *ex post* transaction costs for the manufacturer principal. In a sample of 166 intermediaries, search cost minimizing (operationalized as foreign-market knowledge possessed by the intermediary), and monitoring/enforcement cost minimizing (intermediary taking title to goods and handling commodity products) are positively related to intermediary performance. Consistent with RBV reasoning, the findings suggest intermediary success is based on their knowledge-based resource endowments (too costly for clients to imitate) and on the transaction cost-reduction signals they send to their manufacturer clients.

Export performance research has also examined firm resources and capabilities as driving the profitability of exporters in the non-equity, market governance mode of global distribution. Representative of this research stream is an empirical study of export performance by Dhanaraj and Beamish (2003) which is grounded in the RBV and examines US and Canadian exporters. In their model of export behavior, the resource domain of an exporter is assessed by three constructs: organizational resources (firm size is proxy for slack financial and physical resources), entrepreneurial resources (scale assessing managerial drive), and technological resources (R&D intensity is proxy). Positing this unique bundle of resources sustains competitive advantage, these authors test the connection of resources to export strategy (assessed as degree of internationalization), employing a data set of 157 firms. Consistent with RBV logic, the findings reveal firm resources and capabilities to be good predictors of export strategy and firm performance.

Overall, research applying RBV reasoning to the structure and performance of global distribution is in an early stage of development (Peng 2001). Clearly, many opportunities exist to test directly the constructs and tenants of RBV in the context of international channels of distribution. For example, to what extent are the resources and capabilities necessary for global distribution heterogeneous and immobile? Which logistic and marketing resources employed by global firms are subject to path dependence, causal ambiguity, and social complexity to the extent they become inimitable? As for partner opportunism, do global firms follow TCA logic and organize to minimize *ex post* transaction costs, or do they follow RBV reasoning by accepting opportunism as a cost of business and organize to obtain access to needed resources?

INSTITUTIONAL THEORY

Institutional theorists (North 1990; DiMaggio and Powell 1983) propose the structures and processes of global channels result from, and conform to, institutional pressures that legitimize particular configurations of organizations and trading relationships (Bello, Lohtia and Sangtani 2004).

Institutions are the 'rules of the game' and are shaped by historical factors that limit the range of options open to decision-makers (North 1993). To achieve legitimacy, organizations conform to societal norms through isomorphism, 'the constraining process that forces one unit in a population to resemble other units that face the same set of environmental conditions' (DiMaggio and Powell 1983, p. 149). In contrast to TCA's economic calculus and RBV's competitive advantage logic, institutional reasoning suggests governance form 'can be viewed as the consequence of organizational responses to isomorphic pressures arising from both a firm's external environment and its internal organizational practices and routines' (Yiu and Makino 2002, p. 667). Scott (2001) identifies three institutional pillars or domains that give rise to isomorphic pressures (i.e., forces leading to similar structures through a process of convergence): regulative, normative and cognitive.

Regulative institutions refer to the demands of governments and regulatory agencies to comply with legal, bureaucratic, and other requirements. Global channels are influenced by regulatory elements through the two basic mechanisms of imposition and inducement (Grewal and Dharwadkar 2002). Imposition refers to coercive powers to impose restrictions directly through laws and rules while inducements are incentives such as subsidies, tax, tariff or other concessions designed to influence distribution behaviors. Normative forces are the shared understandings or the 'logic of appropriateness' embodied in the culture, beliefs and values of a country. When entering a foreign market with different normative characteristics, 'multinational enterprises must accommodate institutional expectations and conform to social expectations ... to build social legitimacy in host countries' (Yiu and Makino 2002, p. 671). Cognitive elements refer to socially constructed, common frameworks of meaning that achieve compliance by providing actors with 'prefabricated organizing models and scripts' (Scott 2001, p. 51) making other types of behavior inconceivable. A principal entering a foreign market can acquire cognitive legitimacy through external or internal mimicry (Yiu and Makino 2002). Externally, a principal can mimic the behaviors of other firms that are deemed legitimate; a prevalent entry mode may be institutionalized as firms repeatedly imitate it and adopt it as the legitimate practice. Internally, a multinational may be characterized by habitualized behavior patterns in relations between headquarters and subsidiaries or other distribution organizations. Internal organizational structures and processes can become institutionalized to such an extent that they elude the conscious awareness of managers.

In terms of empirical research in global channels, few studies have been conducted to test the validity of isomorphism in an international distribution setting. In fact, according to Davis, Desai and Francis (2000), 'no empirical studies confirm the nature of a relationship between institutional factors, in particular isomorphism, and firms' entry modes' (p. 240). In their own research, these authors make a contribution by examining 129 strategic business units (SBU) and the role various isomorphic forces play in choice of foreign-market modes of entry. They predict that entry mode is dependent on two distinct sets of isomorphic pressures: internal or parent isomorphism, the mimetic pressures to resemble other sub-units of the multinational, and external or host country isomorphism, the pressures to conform to local norms to be accepted as legitimate in the foreign market. Overall, internal isomorphism is found to be relatively more important than host country factors in determining entry-mode choice. This tendency is particularly pronounced for MNEs exclusively employing wholly-owned subsidiary forms of entry, suggesting cooperative sharing among standardized sister units permits combined efficiencies. In contrast, business units using exporting modes of entry stress external isomorphism more than do SBUs using other modes of entry. Apparently, such business units are less constrained by existing parent-normative

institutional practices as they enter disparate host country environments. They appear to possess the 'strategic flexibility to choose those modes of entry that best allow them to respond to exogenous factors in the environment' (Davis, Desai and Francis 2000, p. 245).

In her study of 1194 Japanese firms, Lu (2002) finds institutional theory has considerable explanatory power, beyond that of TCA, to explain the entry-mode choice of the foreign subsidiaries of these firms. The research views institutional theory as a complementary approach to TCA, which critics consider to have an under-socialized view of organizational activities. Her results confirm the incremental explanatory power of institutions, finding support for internal isomorphism through imprinting where firms persist in using a previously used entry mode. This demonstrates that frequency of mode adoption yields a 'taken for granted' approach, leading to internal replication. To examine external mimetic behaviors, she examines three types of external isomorphism: frequency-based refers to imitating the most popular governance forms (mode with most number of users), trait-based refers to imitating firms identifiable as successful (mode most frequently used by successful firms), and outcome-based refers to imitating practices generating successful outcomes (mode with best history of success). Empirical support is found for the main effects where all three forms of inter-organizational imitative behaviors influence choice of entry mode for the Japanese subsidiaries.

In another institutions-based study, Yiu and Makino (2002) also suggest that research on global distribution channels informed only by TCA is inherently underspecified. Rather than focusing solely on efficiency, principals entering a foreign market 'tend to conform to the regulative settings of the host country environment, the normative pressures imposed by local people, and the cognitive mindsets as bounded by counterparts' entry pattern in the industry as well as past foreign entry pattern within the multinational' (p. 681). In their study of 364 Japanese overseas subsidiaries, the authors find that principals are subject to conflicting conformity pressures since regulative and normative institutional pressures account for cross-national differences in entry mode choice while cognitive forces account for cross-firm variations in governance form. That is, principals largely conform to the regulative and normative isomorphic pressures of individual host countries, but also tend to conform to cognitive mimicry across sibling subsidiary units. Overall, the isomorphic pull of contextual factors provides incremental explanation of entry mode choice beyond economic-based efficiency considerations.

CONCLUSION

To explain structural and behavioral characteristics of global distribution channels, some researchers and theorists narrowly rely either on attributes of exchange transactions (TCA), firm capabilities (RBV), or exchange environments (institutional theory). However, others rely on a broader and more eclectic set of factors to analyze and explain the conduct of global distribution activities. For example, Dunning's eclectic OLI framework (Dunning 1993) has been applied to the choice of entry mode by examining the impact of three sets of variables: (1) ownership advantages (issues regarding costs, risks, and control); (2) location advantages (issues regarding resource availability and commitment); and (3) internalization advantages (issues regarding contractual, coordination, and transaction costs).

From an OLI perspective, a principal's decision to govern global distribution activities through a particular entry mode 'represents a tradeoff between its desire to control and manage these activities and that of minimizing resource commitment to achieve its objectives' (Dunning 1993, p. 235). Ownership advantage implies that a firm possessing superior asset power and skills (as reflected by its size, multinational experience and ability to develop differentiated products)

will earn economic rents that offset the costs of servicing a foreign market (Argarwal and Ramaswami 1992). However, an entry decision must also consider location-specific advantages which include a country's market potential (growth and size) and investment risk (uncertainty over the current economic and political conditions and government policies). In turn, internalization advantages (contractual and transaction risks) must be considered because opportunism and bounded rationality influence the costs of monitoring and controlling the behavior of agents conducting distribution activities.

A principal is thought to seek congruency between its OLI advantages and entry mode attributes, generally preferring more integrated, hierarchical modes of entry as its OLI advantages increase (Brouthers, Brouthers and Werner 1999). Empirical research tends to support this view, as illustrated by Tse, Pan and Au's (1997) study of the impact of ownership, locational, and internalization factors on entry mode selection in China. In examining almost 3,000 foreign business activities in China by US, European and other firms, the authors find that more wholly-owned forms of entry are utilized as the foreign entrant's OLI advantages increase. Brouthers, Brouthers and Werner (1999) conclude that Dunning's eclectic framework 'is superior to a transaction cost approach (alone or in tandem with other unrelated theories) because it incorporates multiple influential factors including internalization (transaction cost), ownership specific, and locational specific variables' (p. 839).

Whether research in global distribution invokes a narrow set of factors or a broader eclectic mix, some observers note 'that existing frameworks are ambiguous and could offer contradictory explanations for the patterns of entry-mode choices' (Davis, Desai and Francis 2000, p. 241). For example, TCA prescribes hierarchical entry for channel activities characterized by asset specificity and uncertainty, while RBV reasoning suggests non-hierarchical modes may be necessary to secure such strategic resources and capabilities.

Likewise, a phenomenon such as cultural distance between a principal and its foreign-based agent may be considered a measure of TCA's internal uncertainty construct (Zhao, Luo and Suh 2004) as well as a measure of a host country's normative institutional forces (Yiu and Makino 2002). Clearly, future conceptual and empirical research must achieve greater precision and clarity if our understanding of global distribution is to advance. While the field of international channels has a rich and diversified literature, future progress requires programmatic research that continues to probe fundamental issues and provides meaningful insights for theorists and managers.

REFERENCES

Agarwal, S. and Ramaswami, S. (1992) 'Choice of foreign market entry mode: impact of ownership, location and internationalization factors', *Journal of International Business Studies*, 23(1): 1–27.

Anderson, E. and Coughlan, A. T. (1987) 'International market entry and expansion via independent or integrated channels of distribution,' *Journal of Marketing*, 57 (January): 71–82.

Anderson, E. and Gatignon, H. (1986) 'Models of foreign entry: A transaction cost analysis and propositions,' *Journal of International Business Studies*, 17(3): 1–26.

Barney, J. (1991) 'Firm resources and sustained competitive advantage,' *Journal of Management*, 17(1): 99–120.

Barney, J. B. (1999) 'How a firm's capabilities affect boundary decisions,' *MIT Sloan Management Review*, 40(3): 137–145.

Barney, J. (2007) *Gaining and sustaining a competitive advantage*. New York: Prentice Hall.

Bello, D. C. and Zhu, M. (2006) 'Global marketing and procurement of industrial products: institutional design of interfirm functional tasks,' *Industrial Marketing Management*, 35(5): 545–555.

Bello, D. C. and Zhu, M. (2007) 'Global supply chain control,' in T. Mentzer, M. Myers,

and S. Stank (eds), *The Handbook of Global Supply Chain Management*. Thousand Oaks, CA: Sage Publications, Inc, pp. 455–472.

Bello, D. C., Lohtia, R. and Sangtani, V. (2004) 'An institutional analysis of supply chain innovations in global marketing channels,' *Industrial Marketing Management*, 33(1): 57–64.

Brouthers, K. D. and Brouthers, L. E. (2003) 'Why service and manufacturing entry mode choices differ: The influence of transaction cost factors, risk and trust,' *Journal of Management Studies*, 40(5), 1179–1204.

Brouthers, L. E., Brouthers, K. D. and Werner, S. (1999) 'Is Dunning's eclectic framework descriptive or normative?,' *Journal of International Business Studies*, 30(4): 831–844.

Buvik, A. and Andersen, O. (2002) 'The impact of vertical coordination on ex post transaction costs in domestic and international buyer-seller relationships,' *Journal of International Marketing*, 10(1): 1–24.

Carson, S., Devinney, T., Dowling, G. and John, G. (1999) 'Understanding institutional designs within marketing value systems,' *Journal of Marketing*, 63 (special issue): 115–130.

Coughlan, A., Anderson, E. Stern, L. and El-Ansary, A. (2006) *Marketing Channels*. New Jersey: Pearson Education Inc.

Davis, P., Desai, A. and Francis, J. (2000) 'Mode of international entry: An isomorphism perspective,' *Journal of International Business Studies*, 31(2): 239–258.

Dhanaraj, C. and Beamish, P. W. (2003) 'A resource-based approach to the study of export performance,' *Journal of Small Business Management*, 41(3): 242–261.

DiMaggio, P. and Powell, W. (1983) 'The iron cage revisited: institutional isomorphism and collective rationality in organizational fields,' *American Sociological Review*, 48(2), 147–160.

Dunning, J. H. (1993) *Multinational Enterprises and the Global Economy*. Wokingham: Addison-Wesley.

Ekeledo, I. and Sivakumar, K. (2004) 'International market entry mode strategies of manufacturing firms and service firms: A resource-based perspective,' *International Marketing Review*, 21(1): 68–101.

Erramilli, K. and Rao, C. (1993) 'Service firm's international entry-mode choice: A modified transaction cost analysis approach,' *Journal of Marketing* 57(3): 19–38.

Gatignon, H. and Anderson, E. (1988) 'The multinational corporation's degree of control over foreign subsidiaries: An empirical test of a transaction cost explanation,' *Journal of Law, Economics, and Organization*, 4(2): 305–336.

Geyskens, I., Steenkamp, J.-B. E. M. and Kumar, N. (2006) 'Make, Buy or Ally: A transaction cost theory meta-analysis,' *Academy of Management Journal*, 49(3): 519–543.

Grewal, R., Dharwadkar, R. (2002) 'The role of the institutional environment in marketing channels,' *Journal of Marketing*, 66(3): 82–97.

Houston, M. B. and Johnson, S. A. (2000) 'Buyer–supplier contracts versus joint ventures: Determinants and consequences of transaction structure,' *Journal of Marketing Research*, 37(1): 1–15.

Kim, W. C. and Hwang, P. (1992) 'Global strategy and multinationals' entry mode choice,' *Journal of International Business* Studies, 23(1): 29–53.

Klein, S. (1989) 'A transaction cost explanation of vertical control in international markets,' *Journal of the Academy of Marketing Science*, 17(3): 253–260.

Klein, S. Frazier, G.L. and Roth, V. J. (1990) 'A transaction cost analysis model of channel integration in international markets,' *Journal of Marketing Research*, 27(2): 196–209.

Klein, S. and Roth, V. (1990) 'Determinants of export channel structure: The effects of experience and psychic distance reconsidered,' *International Marketing Review*, 7(5/6): 27–38.

Lu, J. (2002) 'Intra- and Inter-organizational imitative behavior: Institutional influences on Japanese firms' entry mode choice,' *Journal of International Business Studies*, 33(1): 19–37.

Luo, Y. (2005) 'Transactional characteristics, institutional environment and joint venture contracts,' *Journal of International Business Studies*, 36(2): 209–230.

Luo, Y. (2007) 'Are joint venture partners more opportunistic in a more volatile environment?,' *Strategic Management Journal*, 28(1): 39–60.

North, D. (1990) *Institutions, Institutional Change, and Economic Performance*. Cambridge, MA: Harvard University Press.

Peng, M. W. (2001) 'The resource-based view and international business,' *Journal of Management*, 27(6): 803–829.

Peng, M. W. and York, A. S. (2001) 'Behind intermediary performance in export trade: transactions, agents, and resources,' *Journal of International Business Studies*, 32(2): 327–346.

Rindfleisch, A. and Heide, J. B. (1997) 'Transaction cost analysis: Past, present and future applications,' *Journal of Marketing*, 61(4): 30–54.

Scott, R. W. (2001) *Institutions and Organizations*. Thousands Oaks, CA: Sage Publications, Inc.

Tse, D., Pan, Y. and Au, K. (1997) 'How MNCs choose entry modes and form alliances: The China experience,' *Journal of International Business Studies*, 28(4): 779–805.

Williamson, O. E. (1975) *Markets and Hierarchies: Analysis and Antitrust Implications*. NY: Collier-Macmillan.

Williamson, O. E. (1996) *The Mechanisms of Governance*. New York: The Free Press.

Yiu, D. and Makino, S. (2002) 'The choice between joint venture and wholly owned subsidiary: An institutional perspective,' *Organization Science*, 13(6): 667–683.

Zhao, H., Luo, Y. and Suh, T. (2004) 'Transaction cost determinants and ownership-based entry mode choice: A meta-analytic review,' *Journal of International Business Studies*, 35(6): 524–544.

21

Global Trends in Grocery Retailing

Katrijn Gielens and Marnik G. Dekimpe

INTRODUCTION

These days, almost every corner of the globe has been affected by modern grocery retailing.[1] From Kazakhstan to Guam, Togo to Greenland, modern grocers are relentlessly increasing their presence around the world, and this trend shows little signs of getting reversed any time soon. For a long time, the retail industry was one of the least internationalized sectors (Girod and Rugman 2005). However, over the last two decades, more and more retailers have engaged in cross-border initiatives (Mulhern 1997). The current internationalization of retailing seems to cross geographical boundaries, political systems, languages and cultures. For example, even though the news that France's Carrefour may enter Iran (www.planetretail.net) is likely to have raised some eyebrows, the Iranian market seems to fit the criteria for market entry in terms of its demographics, fragmented retail sector, and (future) market potential. However, the risks of the market also illustrate just how far and wide global grocers are casting their gaze in their urge to find new, untouched markets.

This search for new markets has been brought on by the continuing need of grocers to grow in terms of size and scale. With opportunities for expansion in the more developed markets becoming ever more limited, a move into more fragmented and less developed markets became increasingly attractive (Bell, Davies and Howard 1997; Gielens and Dekimpe 2001). Moreover, as the leading international grocery retailers continued to get bigger, market power became increasingly concentrated in the hands of a few, resulting in the emergence of global power players. In this chapter, we elaborate on this growing concentration in the grocery retail industry and document in more detail the increasing internationalization of many grocery retailers. In so doing, we consider both the underlying drivers (antecedents) of their internationalization decisions, as well as the performance consequences of these decisions.

In search of new opportunities, retailers have not only diversified across market boundaries, but also across product boundaries. First, most leading retailers have developed their own private-label program.

Retailers are therefore no longer just customers of the leading national-brand manufacturers, they have also become one of their strongest competitors (Kumar and Steenkamp 2007; Steenkamp and Dekimpe 1997). Even though private-label share is growing in almost every country, there are important cross-country differences in private-label success, which we will discuss in more detail in this chapter. Second, retailers have increasingly ventured into new formats. One of the formats that have witnessed considerable growth across many markets is the discount format. Around the world, more and more consumers are getting used to their streamlined no-frills concept, and regard it as a very normal kind of store at which to shop. In this chapter, we discuss recent research insights on this international success of discount formats. We also consider another important new store format, the virtual store, whereby we focus on international differences in website evaluations. These evaluation differences are particularly relevant to the grocery retailing industry. Indeed, most leading retailers have become multi-channel operators, in that they have added an Internet channel to their portfolio. Unlike other industries, however, these websites still have an important local connotation, making insights on how these websites are evaluated very relevant.

For each of the five previously mentioned phenomena that we discuss in more detail in the remainder of the chapter, we first depict the overall trend, as observed in many countries, after which we discuss recent research findings on cross-country differences along that dimension.

CHANGES IN THE GLOBAL RETAIL LANDSCAPE

Several facets shape the attractiveness and limitations of a retail market, among which (1) the size and growth of the market (reflected in the evolution of the combined retail sales in that market); (2) the extent of retail concentration (or the degree to which retail sales are in the hands of a few retailers); and (3) the presence of international retailers (this is the extent to which retailers active in that country also have operations in other countries). In the last decade, all three facets have gone through drastic changes. One of the most salient trends is the emergence of large American, European, and Japanese retailers, which are increasingly operating on an international, and even global, scale. By using a right portfolio of countries, these conglomerates are likely to expand even further.

Table 21.1 looks at these three facets, which characterize to a large extent the attractiveness of countries and regions for expanding retailers. Whereas North America and Asia are still the largest retail markets in terms of retail sales, Europe and North America remain by far the most important geographic regions to multinational retail conglomerates. In 2006, about 83 per cent of the sales of the 10 largest chains was generated in Europe and North America (www.planetretail.net). Thanks to the growth in the emerging Central and Eastern European markets, Europe remains an important growth engine as well.

Not surprisingly, North America and the European Union have emerged as the regions with the most internationalized retail markets, with, on average, 20 per cent of the top 50 companies operating foreign ventures there. Countries such as France, Spain and the USA have been widely exploited by international retailers for a long time. More recently, CEE markets such as Poland, Hungary and Russia are witnessing a massive influx of foreign retail investments (see Gielens and Dekimpe 2007).

In Latin America and Asia Pacific, retail markets are increasingly more attractive, thanks to relatively long periods of economic growth and increasing middle classes. As a result, Brazil, Argentina and Mexico already rank among the 25 most internationalized markets (www.planetretail.net). Further large-scale influxes of international retailers can be witnessed in countries such as China (see Goldman 2001), and are expected in India, which has recently emerged as one of

Table 21.1   The retail landscape

Regions	Countries	Retail banner sales		International	C5	
		2000 (USD mn)	2007 (USD mn)	players	2000	2007
Worldwide		**3,754,514**	**6,721,820**		**11.2**	**12.5**
North America		**1,333,119**	**1,998,084**		**24.1**	**29.9**
	Canada	62,023	140,379	8	60.4	54.9
	USA	1,271,096	1,857,705	11	25.5	30,5
Asia		**1,090,266**	**1,923,880**		**8.7**	**10.2**
	China	105,036	628.125	12	3.0	4.1
	India	33,985	75.571	4	0.4	5.4
	Japan	729,038	778.512	2	17.6	20.2
	Korea, South	58,224	155.761	3	18.9	28.2
	Taiwan	31,834	38.442	4	16.1	26.9
Western Europe		**844,666**	**1,694,027**		**20.9**	**22.5**
	France	166,632	313.733	10	72.7	66.0
	Germany	179,597	298.520	4	62.2	66.4
	Italy	74,026	151.300	11	36.7	35.7
	Spain	51,245	135.199	15	62.0	64.5
	UK	187,293	423.080	7	50.4	48.5
Central and		**98,137**	**404,644**		**10.7**	**13.7**
Eastern Europe	Czech Rep.	8,286	22.735	14	32.4	43.0
	Hungary	7,098	27.481	10	45.6	45.9
	Poland	23,522	70.406	18	17.2	24.8
	Romania	6,154	30.828	9	6.5	25.2
	Russia	7,925	172.674	8	3.3	11.7
Latin America		**256,686**	**364,387**		**13.4**	**20.5**
	Argentina	37,910	20,332	4	25.4	39.0
	Brazil	76,128	108,312	4	16.6	27.5
	Chile	8,378	19,617	0	46.6	74.4
	Columbia	9,443	18,425	3	30.5	37.3
	Mexico	72,404	124,472	4	23.5	31.3
Oceania		**51,361**	**128,712**		**63.9**	**78.1**
	Australia	42,816	109.555	3	68.5	82.9
	New Zealand	6,864	16.937	2	54.2	79.2
Africa		**53,617**	**85.194**		**22.5**	**27.9**
	Egypt	11,716	13.105	1	0.8	2.2
	Morocco	3,507	6.269	4	6.6	22.8
	South Africa	13,333	26.728	0	77.4	81.6
	Nigeria	2,521	7.960	0	0.0	0.2
Middle East		**46,271**	**70.218**		**10.3**	**13.8**
	Israel	12,148	18.315	0	28.4	29.2
	Kuwait	3,020	4.836	1	10.4	13.7
	Lebanon	2,717	3.543	1	12.3	23.4
	Saudi Arabia	12,790	16.755	2	10.6	24.2
	UAE	5,927	14.235	2	27.0	25.4

Source: www.planetretail.net; C5 refers to the combined market share of the 5 largest players.

the hottest retail markets. We refer the reader to Gregory (2007) for a more in-depth discussion on recent developments in Asia.

Africa, in contrast, remains relatively unattractive, as retail sales pick up very slowly, except for some notable exceptions such as South Africa. In most African countries, 'mom and pop stores' continue to dom-

inate. In the more lucrative markets of the Middle East, and especially in the Gulf countries (for example, Kuwait, UAE), international firms are entering rapidly, resulting in an increasingly more sophisticated retail environment and higher levels of concentration. While not as fast as in the Gulf countries, similar developments are expected in other regions (we refer the reader to Heins 2007 for more detail).

Combined with these overall increasing levels of globalization, the historically fragmented retail market is rapidly moving toward a more consolidated one, with a few key players holding most of the stakes. In 2007, the five largest retailers already accounted for 12.5 per cent of the worldwide sales, compared with 11.2 per cent in 2000. This growing concentration is found across all continents, even though the rate of change differs across regions. In Oceania, for example, the top five players gained close to 15 per cent between 2000 and 2007, while Asia showed a more modest increase of 1.5 per cent. In major Western European countries such as France (66.0), Germany (66.4) and Spain (64.5), the five largest retailers now account for over 60 per cent of the market. This is also the case in Australia (82.9), New Zealand (79.2) and South Africa (81). In the world's largest market, the United States, the concentration is somewhat lower (30.5). Still, in many individual states of the USA, the concentration level is comparable to that of the individual European Union Countries (Steenkamp *et al.* 2005). Differences in concentration level are not only found across continents. Also within a given region, notable differences are observed. The concentration in some key Latin American countries, for example, ranged from 31.3 (Mexico) to almost 75 per cent (Chile) in 2007.

The more concentrated the retail market, the greater the power and size of the retailers operating in those markets. Supermarket companies are combining to create new entities on a larger scale than ever before, primarily as a defensive move against intensifying competitive pressures. As a result, as shown in Table 21.2, the largest retailers have vastly outgrown their main suppliers. The world's largest retailer, Wal-Mart, is already five times as large as the largest CPG supplier (Nestlé). Apart from Wal-Mart, also five other retailers have larger banner sales than Nestlé. Looking at another major CPG producer, Procter & Gamble, all top ten retailers have sales in excess of its revenues.

Not surprisingly, CPG suppliers have become heavily dependent on these begamoth retailers. Companies such as Del Monte (26 per cent), Mattel (20 per cent), Kellogg's (17 per cent), Kimberly Clark (13 per cent), and Sara Lee (13 per cent) rely increasingly on Wal-Mart as primary retail outlet (Gielens *et al.* 2008). In a recent survey by Planet Retail among US-listed service providers, nearly 120 businesses were identified where Wal-Mart accounted for more than five per cent of their sales, with a range from six to 74 per cent (Roberts 2007). This growing dependence of many manufacturers on a limited number of retail accounts has fuelled the academic discussion on the extent of the power shift (if any) between suppliers and retailers (see Ailawadi 2001 for a review).

Table 21.2   The relative power of retailers vis-à-vis their grocery suppliers

Rank	Retail company	Country of origin	Retail banner sales (USD bn)	Rank	CPG suppliers	Country of origin	Revenues (USD bn)
1	Wal-Mart	USA	376.4	1	Nestlé	Switzerland	74.7
2	Carrefour	France	122.2	2	Altria	USA	69.1
3	Metro Group	Germany	87.4	3	P&G	USA	56.7
4	Tesco	UK	86.8	4	Unilever	UK/Netherlands	49.6
5	Seven & I	Japan	79.1	5	Pepsico	USA	32.6
6	Ahold	Netherlands	77.5	6	Tyson Foods	Japan	26.4
7	Kroger	USA	69.5	7	Coca Cola	USA	23.1
8	Sears	USA	64.8	8	Sara Lee	USA	19.7
9	Costco	USA	64.7	9	L'Oréal	France	18.1
10	Target	USA	62.6	10	Japan Tobacco	Japan	17.7

Source: www.planetretail.net, Fortune 2006.

This global retail consolidation poses numerous challenges to national-brand manufacturers. First, global retailers may well demand uniform worldwide prices. Kumar (2005), for example, discusses the financial implications if Carrefour (the world's second largest retailer) would demand the lowest price in any country to become the global price on any SKU (stock-keeping unit). Second, manufacturers may have to reconsider their logistics to move towards cross-border (or even global) supply chains. Third, during negotiations, retailers may threaten to ban a manufacturer not only from the local shelves in a given country, but from all stores in its international portfolio, as Unilever recently experienced when negotiations with the leading Dutch retailer Albert Heijn (which has operations in eight countries) turned sour. Fourth, as there are fewer accounts which increasingly emphasize their private-label products (discussed in more detail later in this chapter), manufacturers may be forced to rationalize their assortment, and eliminate brands and/or SKUs from their assortment. We refer the reader to Kumar (2005) for an in-depth discussion of these implications.

THE INTERNATIONALIZATION OF GROCERY RETAILING

As indicated before, the number of cross-border initiatives by grocery retailers has increased dramatically over the last two decades. The world's 100 largest retailers grow much faster abroad than domestically, and many enter at least one new market every year (Mulhern 1997). Table 21.3 depicts the number of countries some of the leading retailers have operations in. Moreover, retailers are no longer limiting their internationalization moves to their neighboring countries (as done primarily during the 1970s and early 1980s), nor to countries in their own continent (as popular in the late 1980s and 1990s), but increasingly consider cross-continental moves as well. Examples of the latter include the British group, Tesco, with operations in North America and South East Asia, France's Carrefour, with operations in Chile and Indonesia (among others), and Wal-Mart with operations in the United Kingdom. Moreover, while earlier internationalization activities mostly involved entries into developed Western economies, one has recently seen an increasing number of entries into developing countries as well (see Goldman 2001; Reuling 1998). Nevertheless, entry decisions are still relatively infrequent events for most retailers and are, especially in emerging markets, difficult. Managers have limited own experience with such decisions, and therefore turn to prevailing practices in the industry to learn which decisions are good, or even best. As such, it becomes important to inventorize how retailers make decisions in their internationalization process, and how these decisions have impacted their future success in their new host markets.

Table 21.3 International operations of top 10 retail players

Rank	Retail company	Country of origin	Retail banner sales	Foreign sales (%)	Number of foreign markets
1	Wal-Mart	USA	376.4	22	14
2	Carrefour	France	122.2	53	37
3	Metro Group	Germany	87.4	55	32
4	Tesco	UK	86.8	25	13
5	Seven & I	Japan	79.1	34	8
6	Ahold	Netherlands	77.5	82	8
7	Kroger	USA	69.5	0	0
8	Sears	USA	64.8	12	2
9	Costco	USA	64.7	20	8
10	Target	USA	62.6	0	0

Source: www.planetretail.net, Fortune 2006.

Recent research has looked at both the antecedents and consequences of internationalization decisions. Goldman (2001) studied the transfer of retail formats into developing countries. Focusing on the example of China, he considered whether or not retailers change their format (or certain elements of it). Traditionally, distinctions are made between an 'as is' transfer and adaptation. However, based on extensive interviews with executives from over 25 retailers that had entered China, Goldman identified six distinct transfer strategies. Moreover, the extent of transfer change was found to be related to both the differences in economic conditions between China and the retailers' home market, and the market segments that were targeted in China.

Gielens and Dekimpe (2007) studied the entry decisions of the top 75 European grocery retailers in the transition economies of Central and Eastern Europe, and considered what could explain differences in (i) entry timing and (ii) entry size (number of outlets opened in the first year). They found that firms pay considerable attention to their competitors' prior decisions when deciding on their own entry timing and size. Prior entries first serve as legitimation (which makes sense, as there is considerably uncertainty involved when entering a transition economy), but eventually become a deterrent factor (as the best locations have become preempted). Moreover, rather than just imitating the most popular (or modal) decision of the other players, grocery retailers are found to pay closer attention to the decisions of their home competitors, and to react differently to prior entries from same-format competitors than from different-format competitors. As such, retailers augment their own experience with the experience of their close competitors when making hard-to-revert investments in uncertain conditions.

The questions remains, however, whether it pays to learn from one's competitors, and whether these initial entry decisions have indeed a long term impact on the retailer's foreign ventures. Gielens and Dekimpe (2007) showed that retailers are justified in

taking the prior actions of their competitors into account. Deviations from the prevailing industry practices, in terms of both timing and size, were found to hurt post-entry performance. Moreover, corrective actions were found to be easier to implement along the size than along the time dimension. The negative effects of entering at a different time than the industry norm would prescribe were found to persist (and even become amplified) over time, whereas the negative impact from size deviations was just temporary. Interestingly, a heavy reliance on private labels in the home country had a negative impact on both entry timing and entry size.

In an earlier paper, Gielens and Dekimpe (2001) showed that initial entry decisions may have a long-lasting impact on the performance of foreign operations. They linked the retailer's post-entry performance (operationalized as the asymptotic performance level derived from an S-shaped growth model) to five strategic entry decisions: the scale of entry, the mode of entry (greenfield expansion versus acquisitions or joint ventures), the order (timing) of entry, the adaptation of the retail format to local market conditions, and the familiarity of the store format used to the parent company. Based on 169 entry decisions by Western European retailers towards other Western and Eastern European markets, these entry decisions were all found to have a significant effect. Their relative importance is reflected in Table 21.4, which gives the elasticities evaluated at the mean of the respective drivers.

In the case of greenfield expansion, the order of entry was found to be of crucial importance. Faced with a trade-off between an early entry on a more limited scale or a later entry on a larger scale, retailers tend to be better off when they already pre-empt the locations they can. When dealing with acquisitions and joint ventures, being early is not as crucial. Indeed, with this mode of entry, one maintains the option to acquire or join forces with earlier entrants that occupy the better locations, irrespective of one's own entry timing. Put differently, the disadvantages

Table 21.4   Long-run elasticities of entry decisions

	Sales		Efficiency
	Greenfield operations	Joint ventures and acquisitions	
Scale of entry	0.35	0.35	0.08
Order of entry	−0.70	−0.39	−0.24
Format adaptation	−0.23	−0.23	−0.06
Format familiarity	0.29	0.13	0.07

of being late are harder to reverse in case of greenfield expansions. In terms of the relative importance of supply (familiarity to the parent company) and demand (newness to the market) considerations in the choice-of-format decision, we see that the former are less important in case of joint ventures and acquisitions. Indeed, the expertise and knowledge of the local partner may then be more important than of the parent company.

Interestingly, the private-label share in the home market (which was included as control variable) had a negative impact on the efficiency of the foreign subsidiary. This consistent negative impact of one's private-label focus in the home market can be motivated as follows. First, retailers that rely on their own label must convince customers in the new market to not only switch stores, but to also switch brands. Moreover, investments in one's private-label program may be seen as a sign of commitment to the home market, and limit the resources available to support the foreign entry. Third, in terms of the branded products retailers may want to carry in their foreign stores, they may not have as comfortable a position in their negotiations with their suppliers as other retailers (Kumar 1997).

The aforementioned studies looked at the performance implications for the foreign entrant himself. Gielens and colleagues (2008), in contrast, considered the performance implications for the local incumbents when a major new retailer enters the market. Using the entry of Wal-Mart in the UK (through the acquisition of Asda in 1999) as case study, they showed that (1) the impact on incumbents does not have to be negative, but turned out to be positive for some incumbents; (2) that not only incumbents in the focal market (in this case, the UK) are affected, but

also incumbents in surrounding countries; and (3) that the size of the impact depends on two key dimensions: the seriousness of the threat posed by the new entry (which is determined by the extent of overlap in assortment, positioning, and geographic location), and the incumbent's capacity to withstand that threat. Incumbents can proactively increase this capacity, either by getting experience operating in difficult markets (which will sharpen their competitive skills), or by gaining first-hand experience on how to deal with the new entrant by meeting him in other markets (which will teach them what works and what does not work by the time their home market is 'invaded').

Finally, an area which has received less attention, but which could be interpreted as the ultimate performance metric for foreign entries, is the exit of grocery retailers from foreign markets. For example, after disappointing results, Wal-Mart recently sold its operations in both Germany and Korea, while Carrefour exited from countries such as Chile and the Czech Republic. What are the main reasons to abandon these markets? Were these operation doomed from the start, or were wrong decisions made along the way? Gielens and colleagues (2008) attribute the limited success of Wal-Mart in Germany to two factors: a lack of sensitivity to the German culture, and the fact that Wal-Mart had to compete with the very efficient hard discounter Aldi, whose costs of goods sold are much lower than those of Wal-Mart (Kumar and Steenkamp 2007). More research is needed, however, on the relative impact of demand and supply side factors as drivers of foreign-market exit. An interesting tool in this respect is the framework proposed by Goldman, Ramaswami and Krider

(2002) on the limitations to market-share growth of certain retail formats, based on their diffusion across consumer segments and across product categories.

GROWTH AND REGIONAL DIFFERENCES IN PRIVATE-LABEL SUCCESS

Another important outcome of the increased pressure to pursue growth and power is the growing success of store brands (also called private labels). Not only do private labels promise greater independence from suppliers, they also allow the retailer to truly differentiate himself from his competitors. Private labels have been around for a long time, but were often seen as 'the poor cousins to the manufacturer brands' (Kumar and Steenkamp 2007, p. 4). However, in the past decades, private labels have seen a continued share increase around the globe. In Germany, for example, private-label share increased over the last three decades from 12 per cent to over 30 per cent. Worldwide, the share of private labels is currently around 18 per cent, and expected to grow to 22 per cent by 2010 (Table 21.5) The private-label markets in Europe (26 per cent), North America (22 per cent) and Australasia (19) are expected to show further growth by 2010, albeit with a smaller growth rate than in less developed private-label markets as Japan or the emerging economies in Central and Eastern Europe and Latin America. In those countries, the

private-label market is expected to grow with close to 50 per cent in the coming three to five years, albeit from a lower baseline. In many emerging economies, consumers already have a fairly positive attitude towards private labels, but since these countries experience higher economic growth, the growth in private-label sales in those countries is expected to be in double digits (Kumar and Steenkamp 2007).

Different reasons have been advanced as to why private labels have grown, including the growing concentration of the retailer scene (indeed, mom-and-pop stores will not have the size needed to develop a private-label program), the improved quality of the private labels being offered, or a shift from brand advertising to price promotions (see Kumar and Steenkamp 2007 for an in-depth discussion). Another important cause is found in the general economic climate. Lamey *et al.* (2007) found a strong and consistent dependence on economic contractions and expansions across four countries. Specifically, they showed how consumers are more prone to buy private labels during economic downturns, and how some of them keep buying these private labels even when bad economic times are long over, causing permanent scars on the performance level of national brands. Other research has focused on the profit-implications for retailers of carrying private labels (Ailawadi and Harlam 2004), the profile of private-label shoppers (Ailawadi, Neslin and Gedenk 2001), or drivers of cross-category differences in private-label success (Steenkamp and Dekimpe 1997). Much less attention has been devoted as to why private-label success varies across countries. Still, important differences are present, as shown in Table 21.5.

Steenkamp *et al.* (2005) explore differences in private-label share across 31 countries, covering several Western European (for example, Belgium, France, Germany, Spain, Portugal, Spain, Denmark, …), Central & Eastern European (for example, Romania, Czech Republic, Hungary), Asian (Hong Kong, Japan, …), and South American

Table 21.5   Private label shares

(% sales)	2000	2005	2010
Worldwide	14	18	22
Western Europe	20	26	30
Central and Eastern Europe	1	4	7
North America	20	22	27
Latin America	3	6	9
Australasia	15	19	22
Japan	2	7	10
China	0.1	0.5	3
South Africa	6	10	14

Source: www.planetretail.net

(for example, Argentina, Brazil) countries, as well as the United States. Differences in private-label success were found in terms of the countries' national cultural environment, economic-institutional environment and retail environment.

First, private labels were found to be less successful in societies that score high on (i) cultural power distance and (ii) cultural uncertainty avoidance. Cultures characterized by high power distance tend to emphasize social class. Social consciousness is high in such countries, and consumers are motivated by the need to signal the class to which they belong or to which they aspire. Buying well-known national brands is a means through which customers can express class differences and social aspirations (McCracken 1986). Uncertainty avoidance refers to the degree to which societies tend to feel threatened by uncertain, risky, ambiguous or undefined situations, and the extent to which its members try to avoid such situations by adopting strict codes of behavior (Hofstede 2001). In such societies, buying well-known manufacturer brands is an often-used way of reducing the risks involved when buying a product, making it harder for store brands to gain sizable sales.

Second, private labels success is affected positively by the competitiveness and socio-economic modernity of countries. Both measures reflect that for private labels to prosper, a certain economic infrastructure (in terms of government efficiency, business efficiency, technological and human resources) should be present.

Finally, private-label shares are found to be higher when the retail concentration is higher, when more international retailers are active in a country, and when hard discounters are present. International retailers are important as they can 'leverage their private label skills across multiple countries' (Steenkamp *et al.* 2005, p. 58), while discounters, one of the fastest-growing retail formats, are known to sell almost exclusively private-label brands.

In combination, the aforementioned national-cultural, economic-institutional and retail-environment characteristics explained 77 per cent of the variation in private-label share across the 31 countries in the sample. As such, they allow one to predict how conducive (open) a given country will be to private-label success, and to identify gaps between current private-label share and the level to be expected on the basis of the aforementioned characteristics. These findings were largely confirmed by Baszun (2005) in a study involving eight countries from Central and Eastern Europe.

Erdem, Zhao and Valenzuela (2004) linked the differential success of store brands in the United States, the United Kingdom and Spain to differences in (1) the level of uncertainty associated with store brands and national brands in those countries, (2) in their consistency in product positioning (quality) over time, (3) in the relative quality level of national brands and store brands, and (4) on in their consumers' sensitivity to price, quality and risk.

Even when countries have a similar aggregate private-label share, there are noticeable differences in how private labels are positioned in different countries. Private-label growth in Germany, for example, is largely driven by the success of the hard-discount format, as implemented by chains such as Aldi, Lidl and Penny. Aldi, for example, sells almost no national brands (less than five per cent), yet captures almost 20 per cent of the German grocery market. In the United Kingdom, in contrast, private-label growth is primarily driven by the elaborate multi-tier private-label offering of most retailers, including budget, standard and premium private labels (Geyskens, Gielens and Gijsbrechts 2007). This allows better targeting of the potentially diverse needs of different private-label buyers. In still other countries, such as Belgium and the USA, the growth in private-label sales can be attributed to both the increasing success of discount operations and to the improvement in the overall quality of the private-label offering by mainstream retailers (Lamey *et al.* 2007).

In sum, while there are several cross-country similarities, in casu private labels are growing across almost all regions in the world and seem to have a comparable sensitivity to economic fluctuations, systematic differences exist in terms of both their level and growth rate. These differences are systematically and predictably related to the cultural, economic and structural characteristics of the different countries, allowing one to make predictions beyond the specific countries considered in the aforementioned studies.

FORMAT DIVERSIFICATION

Part of many retailers' growth strategy is their adoption of multiple formats. This trend is especially noticeable with many of the larger Western retailers. Auchan, for example, launched its Atak supermarket format to complement its network of hypermarkets, while Metro Group, which operated cash and carry stores for many years, launched its first Real hypermarket in the summer of 2005. With regards to its international expansion strategy, Carrefour's approach has even revolved around all four major food retail formats: hypermarkets, supermarkets, discount stores and convenience stores (the latter only in Europe so far). As a general trend, we notice that more and more retailers complement their traditional supermarkets with newer concepts such as city-oriented convenience-store concepts, price-oriented discount stores, and virtual stores.

In many mature urban markets, the opening of city-center formats has become a widespread phenomenon, where one targets affluent shoppers who are pressed for time, offering focused convenience ranges in high-traffic locations. Retailers such as Kesko, Casino and Tesco have all introduced such concepts. After years of focusing on out-of-town superstores and hypermarkets, high street locations have regained many retailers' interest. This suggests that retailers are reacting to changing socioeconomic conditions

which dictate that, for a substantial group of customers, convenience may be a more important factor than price.

However, the price-oriented discount format in particular has proven to be very successful. In 2002, for example, all regular German grocery retailers witnessed a drop in sales, but leading discount chains such as Aldi and Lidl grew by close to 15 per cent (IGD Research 2002). Discount chains distinguish themselves from more traditional retailers by their unrelenting focus on very competitive prices, a heavy reliance on own brands, and by offering a smaller number of SKUs per category.

Discounters now occupy a prominent position in most European countries. In Belgium (10.9), Denmark (15.8) and Austria (18.9), for example, their share of the grocery market already exceeds 10 per cent, and an even higher number is obtained in Germany (26.9 per cent). Comparable stores in the USA are price-aggressive grocery discounters such as Dollar General and Family Dollar Stores, which are also witnessing a very rapid growth. In 2006, over 20 000 such stores were already operating in the USA, an increase of more than 50 per cent compared with 2001. In other markets such as the UK and Italy, however, the retail format appears to have a much harder time to take off. This difference has been attributed to a different reaction strategy of incumbent retailers to the growth of the discount format. In most countries, retailers have reacted by reducing their price and limiting their own service. However, as they could not obtain the operational efficiency of the discounters, they basically emphasized an attribute on which they could not outperform these discounters. In the UK, in contrast, retailers tend to emphasize the service dimension. In addition, they have expanded (rather than reduced) their range of product; among others with premium private labels.

The success of hard discounters is a major source of concern to both conventional supermarkets and national brand manufacturers. First, discounters are in direct market-share competition with conventional supermarkets, and put a lot of pressure on the latter to increase their operational efficiency and decrease their prices. As such, the success of the discounters has been called a major trigger for the 2003 price war among conventional retailers in the Netherlands (van Heerde, Gijsbrechts and Pauwels 2007). For manufacturers, the growing success of discounters contributes to a further, quasi-unobstructed, private-label growth. Indeed, discounters sell predominantly own brands, and de-emphasize national brand offerings in their assortment. Aldi, which already accounts for close to 20 per cent of the German grocery market, even relies almost exclusively on its own store brands (Bahl 2003). Moreover, conventional retailers, facing market-share losses because of these discounters, put increasing pressure on their suppliers to get better deals in order to compensate for the corresponding revenue losses. Not surprisingly, national brand manufacturers complain about worsening relationships with their traditional clients, and attribute this development (in part) to the growth of the discounter segment.

Conventional retailers seem to take two routes to fight back. First, some opt to also become involved in the discount format. Carrefour, Casino and Rewe, for example, have already established discount chains of their own (*in casu* ED, Leader Price and Penny), while other retailers such as Auchan, Système U and Tesco are experimenting along the same lines. In so doing, they hope to capitalize on the growth of the discount-prone segment, and to limit the further growth of competitors such as Aldi and Lidl, who only operate through the discount format. Other retailers emphasize the intrinsic strengths of their conventional formats, such as the higher service level and the much more extensive choice offered to maximally differentiate themselves from the no-frills, limited-choice, discounters. We refer the reader to Cleeren *et al.* (2007) for a discussion on the relative merits of both strategies, and to Planet Retail (2006a, 2006b, 2006c)

Table 21.6 Presence of discounters

Regions	Countries	Market share retail banner sales	Stores
North America	Canada	1.7	20,883
	USA	0.1	8
Asia	China	0.1	800
	India	0	0
	Japan	0.3	1,183
	Korea, South	0	0
	Taiwan	0	0
Western Europe	France	7.2	4,309
	Germany	27.3	15,541
	Italy	5.7	2,093
	Spain	7.5	3,783
	UK	2.0	1,210
Central and Eastern Europe	Czech Rep.	11.8	619
	Hungary	8.1	571
	Poland	6.9	1,598
	Romania	3.5	146
	Russia	0.1	12
Latin America	Argentina	2.3	452
	Brazil	0.5	290
	Chile	0.2	25
	Columbia	0.2	13
	Mexico	0.1	155
Oceania	Australia	0.7	170
	New Zealand	0	0
Africa	Egypt	0.1	12
	Morocco	0.0	1
	South Africa	0.7	120
	Nigeria	7.4	36
Middle East	Israel	4.5	66
	Kuwait	0	0
	Lebanon	0	0
	Saudi Arabia	0	0
	UAE	0	0

Source: www.planetretail.net

for in-depth descriptions on the outlook of the discounter scene in both Europe and the US.

A recent development is that national-brand manufacturers and discounters are starting to cooperate. First, manufacturers deplore that they are largely excluded from this increasingly popular format, and are eager to develop trade relationships with discounters. The latter, in turn, try to add some national-brand (NB) offerings to their assortment to differentiate themselves from other discounters. Moreover, national brands are known to often act as traffic builders. Deleersnyder, Dekimpe, Steenkamp and Koll (2004), using data from three large European countries

(Germany, Spain and the UK), considered conditions under which this cooperation could become a win-win situation for the discounter as well as for the national-brand manufacturer. The following dimensions were identified as particularly relevant in this respect: the price differential between the NB brand and the discounter's private-label brand, the between-store price differential for the NB between the discounter and conventional retailers, the attractiveness of the outer cases (as products are sold on the store floor out of these outer cases, they become an important communication element in the otherwise dull store environment characteristic of many discounters); and the innovativeness of the national brand. However, this cooperation between discounters and national brand manufacturers has potential pitfalls for the national brand manufacturers. Not only may brand manufacturers end up cannibalizing their own sales (and sell them at a lower price), they may also thereby create channel friction with the other retailers in their channel portfolio.'

We are not aware of any research that systematically explains cross-country differences in the success of discount stores, which offers an interesting area for future research. Still, there seems to be a consensus that, in the long run, many countries will converge to the German situation (Koll 2007), even though it is as yet unclear how fast this convergence will be. As Germany currently has a much higher store density than most other countries (a recent AC Nielsen study estimates this density at 1 per 9,900 inhabitants in Germany, compared to 1 per 24 000 in the Netherlands, and 1 per 83 000 in the UK), a large number of additional store openings of the discount type can be expected in the years to come. It will also be interesting to see what the addition of more and more national brands will do the operational efficiency of discount stores. In this respect, a distinction is already made between hard discounters (with no or very limited national brands in their assortment, as is the case with Aldi) and soft discounters (with more national brands, which are also prominently featured in the discounters' advertising campaigns, as for example Lidl).

Another way to become a multi-format retailer is to add an Internet store to one's channel portfolio. Because of the global reach of the Internet, consumers across the world can access websites, and most (if not all) leading retailers have added the Internet channel to their channel portfolio. In recent years, numerous studies have looked at the drivers of online success (see Bucklin and Sismeiro 2003; Danaher, Mullarkey and Essegaier 2006; Moe and Fader 2004), a new journal on the issue has emerged (*Journal of Interactive Marketing*), and also in this volume, a special chapter is devoted to the role of the Internet in global marketing (Shankar 2007).

However, one may question to what extent the Internet has really extended the global reach of grocery retailers. Despite current trends toward globalization, grocery retailing continues to have an important local component (Gielens *et al.* 2008), and retailers' web sites are often aimed more at expanding the sales volume within their home country (or countries they are already operating in), than to attract new customers from other countries where they don't have any brick-and-mortar operations. Moreover, depending on the countries the web site is primarily oriented to, different design characteristics become more relevant. As shown in Steenkamp and Geyskens (2006), country characteristics tend to systematically and predictably moderate the effect of individual-level drivers of the perceived value consumers derive from a web site. Based on a large-scale data set involving 8,500 visitors from 23 countries across three continents (Australasia, Europe, and North America), Steenkamp and Geyskens (2006) conclude that the effect of privacy/security protection on perceived value is stronger for people from countries with a weak rule of law, while people from countries that are high on national identity give more weight to whether there is cultural congruity between the site and themselves. Further, people from individualistic countries are found to give more weight to pleasure, to privacy/security protection, and to customization in their perceived value judgments than people from more collectivistic countries. As a consequence, grocery retailers may want to locally adapt their sites to the characteristics of their target population. This is especially important given the predominant local reach of their web operations.

The Internet offers numerous possibilities to implement such local adaptations, even when using a globally standardized platform that allows for certain cost efficiencies. As such, the Internet offers grocery retailers the opportunity to both globalize and localize (Steenkamp and Geyskens 2006). For example, they may use a common portal to give consumers access to various local or country sites. These sites may then have the same look and feel, but vary on other key dimension to reflect the aforementioned differences.

In spite of these possibilities for local adaptation, the online grocery business in most countries is still 'at an embryonic state'. Even in the USA, where over 170 million people have access to the Internet, only six per cent of shoppers had purchased groceries online in the past year, compared with 80 per cent who had bought other items (www.planetretail.net). While the Internet may give promising opportunities to grocery retailers, considerable threats could emerge as well. For example, a totally new set of players may enter the market. These may include not only other grocery retailers which use the Internet to extend their geographic reach, but also non-grocery players that use the Internet to enter the grocery business. The E-commerce giant Amazon, for example, has recently announced that it will be piloting a fresh grocery delivery program. Following the success of its earlier gourmet food offerings (as of 2003) and non-fresh grocery deliveries (for some 14 000 items as of 2006), Amazon now ventures into the domain of fresh groceries. When successful, grocery retailers may be faced with a powerful new competitor. This could legitimize similar attempts by other giant non-grocery on-line stores.

CONCLUSION

In this chapter, we discussed five recent trends in grocery retailing: (1) the increasing concentration in the industry; (2) the urge of many retailers to internationalize; (3) the growing success of private labels; (4) the increasing popularity of the discount format; and (5) the transition of many retailers into multi-channel operators through the addition of an Internet channel to their portfolio.

As indicated before, these developments are not independent of one another. Private labels are more successful in countries where the retail concentration rate is higher, and is largely facilitated by the rise of the discount format, as discount stores sell almost exclusively store brands. Private-label share in one's home market, in turn, was found to be a key moderator for the entry timing and entry size into foreign markets, and to also have an impact on post-entry performance. The Internet channel, in turn, can be seen as an alternative (and often, cheaper, way) to extend the geographic reach of one's operations.

These developments seem to occur across all continents, and thus can be seen as global trends. However, in each domain, important cross-country and cross-region differences were found. In many instances, these differences were found to be systematically and predictably related to key underlying drivers, such as the country's cultural and economic characteristics (in case of private-label success) and/or differences (in case of foreign entries).

Interestingly, many of these developments have been documented across both developed and developing countries. For example, Gielens and Dekimpe (2001) considered entries into both Western European countries and into the emerging economies of

Central and Eastern Europe. Similarly, Steenkamp and colleagues (2005) included countries from all over the world in their study on cross-country differences in private-label success. As such, the bias towards developed countries (and more specifically the USA and Western Europe) often encountered in international marketing research (Dekimpe and Lehmann 2004; Burgess and Steenkamp 2006) seems to be less of an issue in the international grocery retailing research.

While we have focused on some of the key trends in the industry, others could be identified as well, such as advances in information technology which give retailers a competitive edge relative to manufacturers, the shift towards more in-store promotions, changes in the use of slotting allowances, legal developments (as the harmonization imposed by the European union in terms of promotional practices) – to name just a few. While these developments are important as well, we are not aware of research that documents any regional or cross-country differences along these dimensions. Such research could, however, result in interesting new insights to complement the ones discussed in this chapter.

ACKNOWLEDGMENT

The authors gratefully acknowledge financial support from the Flemish Science Foundation (F.W.O.) under grant nr. G.0116.04.

NOTES

1 Groceries include virtually everything one would find in a standard supermarket, comprising food, beverages, tobacco products and drugstore items (such as health and beauty products, OTC drugs, household papers or household cleaners), as well as small everyday household non-foods (such as standard kitchen tools, candles, etc). Excluded from the groceries category are product groups such as clothing, electrical goods, books and music, furniture, etc. (www.planetretail.com).

REFERENCES

Ailawadi, K. L. (2001) 'The retail power-performance conundrum: what have we learned?' *Journal of Retailing*, 77(3), 299–318.

Ailawadi, K. L. and Harlam, B. (2004) 'An empirical analysis of the determinants of retail margins: the role of store brand share', *Journal of Marketing*, 68(1), 147–166.

Ailawadi, K. L., Neslin, S. and Gedenk, K. (2001) 'Pursuing the value-conscious consumer: Store brands versus National Brand Promotions', *Journal of Marketing*, 65 (January), 71–89.

Bahl, T. (2003) The hard discounter menace: Examples from Germany. Presentation given at the GfK/Europanel seminar, Kronberg, Germany.

Baszun, R. (2005) 'Private labels: A comparison in Central and Eastern Europe'. Paper presented at the ESOMAR retail conference, Budapest.

Bell, R., Davies, R. and Howard, E. (1997) 'The changing structure of food retailing in Europe: The implications for strategy', *Long Range Planning*, 30(6), 853–861.

Bucklin, R. E. and Sismeiro, C. (2003) 'A model of website browsing behavior estimated on clickstream data', *Journal of Marketing Research*, 40 (August), 249–267.

Burgess, S. M. and Steenkamp, J.-B. E. M. (2006) 'Marketing renaissance: How research in emerging markets advances marketing science and practice', *International Journal of Research in Marketing*, 23(4), 337–356.

Cleeren, K., Verboven, F., Dekimpe, M. G. and Gielens, K. (2007) *Intra and inter-format competition among discounters and supermarkets*. Working paper, University of Maastricht.

Danaher, P. J., Mullarkey, G. and Essegaier, S. (2006) 'Factors affecting web site visit duration: A cross-domain analysis', *Journal of Marketing Research*, 43 (May), 182–194.

Dekimpe, M. G. and Lehmann, D. R. (2004) 'Editorial: Introduction to the special issue on global marketing', *International Journal of Research in Marketing*, 21(4), 321–322.

Deleersnyder, B., Dekimpe, M. G., Steenkamp, J.-B. E. M. and Koll, O. (2007) 'Win-win strategies at discount stores', *Journal of Retailing and Consumer Services*, 14(5), 309–318

Erdem, T., Zhao, Y. and Valenzuela, A. (2004) 'Performance of store brands: a cross-country analysis of consumer store-brand preferences, perceptions and risk', *Journal of Marketing Research*, 41 (February), 86–100.

Geyskens, I., Gielens, K. and Gijsbrechts, E. (2007) *Proliferating private label portfolios: how introducing economy and premium private labels influences brand choice.* Working Paper, Tilburg University.

Gielens, K. and Dekimpe, M. G. (2001) 'Do international entry decisions of retail chains matter in the long run?', *International Journal of Research in Marketing*, 18(3), 235–259.

Gielens, K. and Dekimpe, M. G. (2007) 'The entry strategy of retail firms into transition economies', *Journal of Marketing*, 71(2), 196–212.

Gielens, K., Van de Gucht, L., Steenkamp, J.-B. E. M. and Dekimpe, M. G. (2008) 'Dancing with a giant: The effect of Wal-Mart's entry into the U.K. on the performance of European retailers', *Journal of Marketing Research* (forthcoming).

Girod, S. J. G. and Rugman, A. M. (2005) 'Regional business networks and the multinational retail sector', *Long Range Planning*, 335–357.

Goldman, A. (2001) 'The transfer of retail formats into developing economies: The example of China', *Journal of Retailing*, 77(2), 221–242.

Goldman, A., Ramaswami, S. and Krider, R. E. (2002) 'Barriers to the advancements of modern food retail formats: Theory and measurement', *Journal of Retailing*, 281–295.

Gregory, R. (2007) 'Asian retailers turning the tide', *E-intelligence on Global Retailing, Planet Retail*, 201 (June 28), 33–37.

Heins, O. (2007) 'A race for opportunities: top 30 grocery retailers in Africa and the Middle East', *E-intelligence on Global Retailing, Planet Retail*, 201 (June 28), 27–32.

Hofstede, G. (2001) *Culture's Consequences: Comparing Values, Behaviors, Institutions, and Organizations across Nations.* Thousand Oaks, CA: Sage Publications.

IGD Research (2002) *European Discount Retailing, Factsheet.* Watford: Future Focus. (www.igd.com/analysis)

Koll, O. (2007) FMCG Markets: The impact of discounters and private labels. Copenhagen: Global PETS forum.

Kumar, N. (1997) 'The revolution in retailing: from market driven to market driving', *Long Range Planning*, 30 (6), 830–835.

Kumar, N. (2005) 'The global retail challenge', *Business Strategy Review*, Spring, 5–13.

Kumar, N. and Steenkamp, J.-B. (2007) *Private Label Revolution.* Harvard Business School Press.

Lamey, L., Deleersnyder, B., Dekimpe, M. G. and Steenkamp, J.-B. E. M. (2007) 'How business cycles contribute to private-label success: Evidence from the United States and Europe', *Journal of Marketing*, 71 (January), 1–15.

McCracken, G. (1986) 'Culture and Consumption: A theoretical account of the structure and movement of the cultural meaning of consumer goods', *Journal of Consumer Research*, 13(1), 71–84.

Moe, W. W. and Fader, P. S. (2004) 'Dynamic conversion behavior in E-Commerce sites', *Management Science*, 50(3), 326–335.

Mulhern, F. J. (1997) 'Retail marketing: From distribution to integration', *International Journal of Research in Marketing*, 14(2), 103–124.

Planet Retail (2006a). *The Future of Discount Retailing in Europe.* 1–54. (www.planetretail.net)

Planet Retail (2006b). *The Future of Discount Retailing in the USA.* 1–27. (www.planetretail.net)

Planet Retail (2006c). *The Retail Scene in Germany 2007.* 1–34. (www.planetretail.net)

Reuling, E. (1998) 'Global retailers conquer emerging markets', *Elsevier Food International*, 3 (May), 21–24.

Roberts, B. (2007) 'Wal-Mart: Suppliers' dependency revealed', *E-intelligence on Global Retailing, Planet Retail*, Issue 201 (June), 17–26.

Shankar, Venky (2009), 'The Internet and International Marketing' in *Sage Handbook of International Marketing*, Eds. Masaaki Kotabe and Kristaan Helsen. London: Sage Publications.

Steenkamp, Jan-Benedict E.M. and Marnik G. Dekimpe (1997), "The Power of Store Brands Intrinsic Loyalty and Conquesting Power," *Long Range Planning*, 30(6), 917–930.

Steenkamp, J.-B., Nijs, V. R. Hanssens, D. M. and Dekimpe, M. G. (2005) 'Competitive reactions to advertising and promotion attacks', *Marketing Science*, 24(1), 35–54.

Steenkamp, J.-B. E. M. and Geyskens, I. (2006) 'How country characteristics affect the perceived value of web sites', *Journal of Marketing*, 70 (July), 136–150.

Steenkamp, J.-B. E. M., Geyskens, I., Koll, O., Gielens, K. and Lewis, H. (2005) *Fighting Private Label: Growth Drivers, Brand Defense Strategies and Market Opportunities*. Business Insights in Association with AIMARK and Europanel, Business Insights Ltd.

van Heerde, H., Gijsbrechts, E. and Pauwels, K. (2007) 'Price War: What is it good for? store visit and basket size response to the price war in Dutch grocery retailing', *Marketing Science Institute Report*, 07–104.

22

International Salesforce Management

Thomas Brashear Alejandro

INTRODUCTION

Personal selling and sales management are important promotional elements of almost all marketing strategies, domestic or international. Globalization, the opening of centralized and emerging markets and the importance of relationships in marketing exchange, puts more emphasis on the development and management of a high-performing salesforce. The complexity of designing and managing a salesforce in an international setting is due in part to the international salesforce acting as cultural boundary spanner, relationship manager, and provider of marketing information at a multidomestic or global scale (Chonko, Tanner and Smith 1991). What social, cultural and legal elements constrain the management of the salesforce across different markets? How are salespeople selected and what selection criteria are used in various markets? Are there similarities in these practices? The methods of training and the content of that training are important to the success of the individual and the sales organization.

Motivation and role perceptions that lead to satisfaction and performance must be evaluated given the new setting and differences of the workforce. Developing control and compensation policies of the salesforce across markets carries much more complexity in multiple markets. Are the theories of control and compensation predictive in different market and cultural conditions? Finally, the international salesforce faces ethical challenges due to cultural, social, legal and ethical interpretations in different cultures.

Cavusgil and Nevin (1981) reported the lack of research in the complex area of international sales, but since then the area is still under-researched. The focus here is to discuss international sales management studies and findings to date, and to look at potential new areas of research that are theoretically and managerially relevant. International sales management issues are defined in a broad manner and from a US-centric view. Our review covers studies that used single-country non-US samples, comparisons of two or more markets on predicted relationships without cultural moderators, and also studies that have compared two or more markets based on cultural characteristics of the markets as rationale for distinctions in the relationships.

The chapter begins by looking at the organization and administration of the salesforce.

We look at issues related to using company-based versus hired agents and the empirical findings related to those decisions. The next section looks at the literature pertaining to salesforce recruitment and selection with studies that compare the effects of culture on the selection of the salesforce. That is followed by the research on training of international salespeople. This section contains various conceptual reviews but also various empirical results from multiple markets. The largest chapter section examines research covering various issues related to performance of the salesforce. This section is structured around the meta-analytic model of Brown and Peterson (1993) to guide the presentation of the effects of role perceptions, satisfaction, commitment, turnover and performance. This section also covers the important areas of salesforce control and compensation as they relate to the structure of these sales management functions. The importance of salesforce ethics in international markets is covered next and the chapter ends with a summary and future research issues in international sales management.

DETERMINING SALESFORCE ORGANIZATION AND ADMINISTRATION

The organization and administration of the salesforce is essential to success in international and domestic markets. Strategic decisions are made that determine the organizational structure, deployment of salespeople, and sales management policies/style. These crucial decisions are made for both international and domestic markets. Although many researchers have provided guidance on the key issues and factors that must be considered in structuring the organization and administration of the international salesforce (e.g., Hill and Still 1990), few studies have examined the international salesforce structure.

The organizational structure choice is a form of the 'make or buy' decision to determine the appropriate international intermediary to use (Anderson and Coughlan 1987; Lewin and Johnston 1997). Anderson (1985) uses Transaction Cost Economics to examine the issue of a company using its own salesforce versus using outside agents or contract salespeople. The study found that difficulty in monitoring or supervising a salesforce, and the complexity of the product, lead companies to use their own salesforce. Krafft (1995) had similar findings and supported an employed (company-based) salesforce as best when smaller in size and travel requirements are lower.

Other characteristics must also be considered in the structure of the salesforce organization decision. Albers, Krafft and Bielert (1998) examine the importance of understanding work values as a reflection of law and culture when making the decision to employ agents or company-owned salesforces. They report that legal constraints exist in many countries regarding the ability of firms to terminate a salesperson or outside agent. They also found that the costs involved in making such changes are an important consideration. Hiring and firing decisions are thus more flexible in some markets than others, and the cultural or legal issues may override the theoretical arguments. Clearly, multiple dimensions must be considered in the organization and administration of the salesforce.

Hill and Still (1990) examine environmental factors (level of market development, regions, countries and industry) and structural factors (product-mix width, sales level and salesforce size) and their relationships to the structure and organization of the MNC's sales apparatus. They found that one out of five multinational salesforces covers multiple markets according to industry type. Single salesforces cover multiple markets in developed (rather than developing) countries, and the study attributes this to similarities in market conditions.

Hill, Still and Boya (1991) looked at headquarters' influence in the areas of planning, training, administration and control designs. They found that local managers have more control in these areas, suggesting support of the conjecture that activities need to take into account local conditions, including politics, laws, culture and marketing conditions. Industry type also has an effect on the level of influence played by headquarters in the local markets. Herche and Swanson (1992) suggest productivity measurement as a means to determine where to deploy and how many salespeople to allocate. Honeycutt and Ford (1995) propose that salesforce structure is based on geographic size, sales potential, ease of customer access, customer expectations, current selling practices and language. However, Albers, Krafft and Bielert (1998) suggest that while these are important issues most are affected by culture.

A comparison of highly effective companies in the United States and Australian, conducted by Cravens *et al.* (1992), found many similarities among organizational characteristics (e.g., call rates, percentages of new customers, number of assigned accounts and growth rates). Differences included the levels of expenses and turnover (higher in Australia) as well as the span of control (Australians more controlling). US firms use more evaluative monitoring, with managers spending more time in the field observing salespeople's travel and expenses. Australian sales managers, on the other hand, tend to focus on monitoring the price quotes of their salespeople.

Although cultural differences are addressed in other sections, Albers, Krafft and Bielert (1998) suggest that work values based on culture or law play a significant role in salesforce administration decisions beyond the initial decision of salesforce structure or organization. Setting the overall objectives, feedback, compensation and reward structures have cultural underpinnings that do not allow the simple carryover or extension of administrative practices from one market or country to another. Goal setting and the overall sales objectives will be affected by various elements of the culture and the political economy of the focal market(s). Marshall, Brouthers and Lamb (1998) suggest an analysis of the client firms' tendencies, and based on the economic structure (e.g. centralized, market, etc.), determine the appropriate strategy in goal setting, investment and benefits. To fill the organizational structure, firms must find and select their salesforces, an area of research that has received attention in multiple settings.

SALESFORCE RECRUITMENT AND SELECTION

The importance of strategic recruitment and selection has received considerable attention in the determination of which employees or potential employees are best suited for international assignment. Given the heightened importance of success in international settings, understanding the criteria that lead to performance and matching that to the right managers and salespeople, in each market, makes sales management and salesforce selection an even higher potential for payoff or failure. In particular, Cron *et al.* (2005) report that, given the wide variation in individual salesperson performance, 'the potential payoff from improved selection processes may be greater in sales than in other occupations' (p. 129). Selection issues extend from the discussion of salesforce organization, as the determination of owned or external agents is important to sales management structure decisions.

Organizations that decide to use a company-based salesforce must then decide on the salesforce structure. Will the employees be home nationals sent on expatriate assignments? Will host nationals be hired as employees of the firm? Or will cosmopolitans – third-country nationals – be hired to work in non-domestic markets? These decisions are required for the selection of both salespeople and sales managers. Many firms that have entered international markets have followed varying staffing policies for their management teams. Hill (2004) categorizes the staffing policies as ethnocentric, polycentric and geocentric. Firms with a simple internationalization strategy will use more home-based or parent company managers, the ethnocentric policy (or a 'people like us' policy). A polycentric policy is more likely to be found in a firm using a multidomestic (again, 'people like all of us') strategy. The firms focusing on global or transnational strategies may be more inclined to use a geocentric staffing policy for managers (Hill 2004, p. 517). No research to date has empirically examined the use of sales managers' staffing policy and the firm's internationalization strategy.

The use of expatriate employees in management or sales is quite abundant but comes with the potential for high rates of failure as selection is more difficult (Tung 1982) and the adjustment process a challenge (Black, Mendenhall and Oddou 1991). Although the degree of failure is debatable (Littrell *et al.* 2006), the potential for cultural conflicts, language barriers, family constraints and career concerns, among others, add multiple layers of additional factors that can undermine the success of the expatriate employees. Expatriate assignments may be requested when there is a perception that international assignments mean faster promotions within the organization (Daily, Certo and Dalton 2000), although no studies have looked at international sales or sales management positions, and no link has been found in a study of US chief executives (Russ *et al.* 1989). Host-country salespeople open an additional set of issues related to work values that stem from various economic, legal and cultural aspects of the host countries (Albers, Krafft and Bielert 1998). In some countries, a sales position may not be socially desirable (Still 1981; Hill, Still and Boya 1991).

Company-based salesforces that hire host country nationals provide a level of market knowledge and cultural understanding that is difficult to copy and transfer to an expatriate salesforce. The cost of maintaining a host-nation salesperson is much less than an expatriate force, although some markets have much higher salaries for managers and salespeople (Albers, Krafft and Bielert 1998).

The limitations of hiring host-nation salespeople include the potential lack of product knowledge and company knowledge, and required extensive training and organizational socialization (Honeycutt, Ford and Kurtzman 1996).

Organizational socialization is also a factor when developing a cosmopolitan salesforce. Hiring individuals from surrounding nations or countries with similar cultural, legal or business structures allow the individual to adapt to the foreign country faster than an expatriate from the company's home nation. Cosmopolitans foster potential problems of discrimination and, even though they have some similarities to the country in which they work, they may not be accepted as equals due to ethnic, religious or social issues. In addition, organizational policies would have to adapt to match the legal and social nature of work within the particular market. One final limitation to both the host nation and cosmopolitan hires, is the perception of the sales profession and the ability to recruit top level individuals into the profession (Honeycutt, Ford and Kurtzman 1996; Lewin and Johnston 1997) which, again, may not be socially desirable (Still 1981; Hill, Still and Boya 1991).

During the salesforce selection process, various criteria and methods have been used to evaluate applicants. Cron *et al.* (2005), in a comprehensive review and summary of salesforce selection practices, point to the Churchill *et al.* (1985) meta-analysis of salesforce performance as the foundation for much of the selection criteria used over the past 20 years. The major categories of selection criteria based on these performance predictors are: job skills/knowledge assessments; cognitive ability tests; personality inventories; biographical information and special purpose sales assessments. Among the cognitive abilities, two key areas were deemed to be promising – practical intelligence and emotional intelligence. Promising personality traits that they note are integrity; optimism; social competence, and cooperativeness (Cron *et al.* 2005). The role of these personality traits has strong face validity when referring to international settings with varying sets of laws, cultures and the different degrees of cooperation involved in customer and buyer relationships.

Lewin and Johnston (1997) summarized five major cultural elements that affect recruitment and selection in non-domestic markets: ethnic composition, religious orientation, social class environment, education and gender bias. Few studies have looked at the comparisons specifically across countries. Comparing the USA and Germany, Albers, Krafft and Bielert (1998) used both secondary and primary data from three studies that found US organizations have a much higher average percentage of women in the salesforce than German firms. The US composition contains 22.8 per cent women while two findings from Germany report 3 per cent and 10.8 per cent women in the German firms. They suggest that this difference is primarily due to support for working women in the USA. They also report that German firms require higher levels of product knowledge and thus their salespeople are older on average and have much higher levels of education on average than US firms' salesforces. These findings also suggest that education is a key determinant of the selection process. Correlations between selection criteria, sales jobs, and performance evaluation are found in the Avlonitis and Boyle (1989) study of UK firms. They suggest a holistic approach linking various elements. Their findings support the need to link the key selection criteria to the sales role, the training process and the performance evaluation, all of which will be dependent upon the forces that shape these functions in the specific markets (Albers, Krafft and Bielert, 1998).

Assessment methods in the selection process

When assessing salesforce selection methods, Cron *et al.* (2005) focused on three key methods of assessment: interviews; assessment centers; and resumes, CVs and applications. There appears to be a wide disparity in the use of assessment centers. Engle (1998) wrote from an executive's perspective about the multi-step, structured interview process used by Bayer AG in their selection process of sales representatives in Russia and Eastern Europe. Their process begins by reviewing the CVs of the applicants, followed by a series of three different structured interviews: a telephone interview, a 'base-line' interview, and an interview with a panel. These multiple interview formats help the company slowly become more familiar with the characteristics of the applicant and allow the company to cover many topics in multiple settings and learn more about the applicant's competencies.

Assessment centers were reported to have a huge impact on salesperson selection and training (Cook and Herche 1992). Subsequent studies have found that the familiarity and utilization of assessment centers is quite different depending on the setting. In the USA and Scandinavia (Finland and Denmark), Cook and Herche (1994) found that US marketing personnel had an extremely low level of familiarity with and utilization of assessment centers, while they were used quite frequently in Europe. Approximately 70 per cent of the European firms in their study reported using assessment centers for sales training; 40 per cent used them for hiring and selection. In assessment centers, individual interviews were used by 90 per cent of the respondents, followed by paper and pencil tests at 54 per cent. Cook and Herche (1994) suggest that the findings are a reflection of the US managers being shielded from cultural vagaries.

Honeycutt, Ford, Lupton and Flaherty (1999) compared salesforce selection among domestic and multinational firms in China and Slovakia. Among application processes and interviews, the authors found no significant differences between global and domestic firms in either China or Slovakia. The Chinese firms required individuals to respond to job situations and also used more interview panels than Slovakian firms. Multinationals in each country seem to have tailored their selection processes to match those of domestic firms.

Decision-making in a cross-cultural environment

Beyond the criteria for selection or assessment methods, a stream of research examines the decision making of managers in the selection process (Patton and King 1992; Marshall, Mowen and Stone 1995; Marshall, Stone and Jawahar 2001). The decision-makers may look at scenarios differently and thus match or choose different recruits. Marshall, Stone and Jawahar (2001) examine the level of risk and the time horizon, two factors that may be culture dependent. Rouzies, Segalla and Weitz (2003) conducted an empirical study to look at the effects of regional culture on the decision-makers' selection and promotion of recruits. Their study included managers from three 'cultural clusters': Germanic (Austria, Germany), Anglo (UK), and Latin (France, Italy and Spain). One focus was on the extent to which international profile, team spirit, skills, and objective characteristics affected the decision to hire recruits. Similar to Marshall, Stone and Jawahar (2001), managers were compared based on how much they weighed the criteria.

Rouzies and colleagues' findings, albeit mixed, show that regional culture of the manager does in some cases predict the decision making in the hiring process of certain salespeople. Managers favoring potential wanted to hire local recruits and also wanted to promote internal candidates. When international profiles were of importance to the manager, foreign recruits were selected. Local recruiting also occurs when mangers value salespersons' skills. For example, Germanic managers tend to recruit more local salespeople than do Italian managers. There was no difference for Germany, France or Spain. Germanic managers are also more likely to promote external candidates than managers from Latin countries.

TRAINING

The initial steps of selection are essential elements of the early stages in the employee training, development (Cron 1984) and the socialization processes (Dubinsky et al. 1986; Barksdale et al. 2003). All salesforces require training to develop and maintain the level of competitiveness and competency in the sales role. Key objectives of sales training are to: motivate the salesforce; increase productivity; improve customer relationship skills; sustain the morale of the salesforce; manage time and territory; and reduce the turnover in the salesforce (Churchill et al. 2000; Attia, Honeycutt and Jantan 2006). The process to determine who needs training, what the content of the training should be, how the training will occur, and the evaluation of training effectiveness are difficult decisions for managers to make (Attia, Honeycutt and Attia 2002). Training decisions also have significant financial implications for the sales managers' and organizations' bottom line through direct costs, while the potential hazard of salesforce defection increases with more training – salespeople have a higher set of skills that are in demand (Krishnamoorthy, Misra and Prasad 2005).

Training the international salesforce with the added environmental, cultural and customer demands requires particular attention (Attia, Honeycutt and Jantan 2006; Bush and Ingram 1996). Honeycutt et al. (1999) found that in the area of training, global firms in China focused more on market-oriented training than did domestic firms. Domestic Chinese firms spent a significantly larger percentage of their time on sales procedures than did the global firms. Slovakian domestic firms focused on product information more than global firms. Evaluation practices are evaluated more by global firms in both markets. Domestic Chinese firms reportedly evaluate their salesforces more during the training periods, while the global firms spent more time measuring and evaluating the training results. China's global companies consider coaching to be important and also spend more time training their salesforce.

There is a renewed emphasis on the methods of training for international assignments as the demand for such exploded over the past 20 years (Bhawuk and Brislin 2000) and in general (Mendenhall and Stahl 2000). Comparing multinational managers and their domestic counterparts, Jantan *et al.* (2004) find that higher levels of performance from salespeople are directly related to higher levels of training in company information and policies, presentation and communication skills, understanding of sales objectives, product information, technical and customer relationship skills.

Cron *et al.* (2005) summarize content areas of knowledge, skills and attributes (KSAs) as task related KSAs (knowledge of products, markets, company, selling, territory management, etc), growth-related KSAs (skills of adaptability, goal-setting, problem-solving, etc.), and meta-KSAs (self-development, management skills, knowledge development, etc.). These task, growth and meta-KSAs reflect basic to higher order levels of learning and adaptation necessary for higher levels of self management. Jantan and Honeycutt (2002), used two dimensions – cultural and business – for sales training content. Marketing management and human resources issues were found to be high on both cultural and business implications. The meta-KSAs for the most part appear to be important for success in operating in a diverse environment such as expatriate sales positions. In such positions, the ability to understand the nuances and structure of the culture is important (Bhawuk and Brislin 2000; Bush and Ingram 1996).

Training programs must look at the way the culture views the sales training and should be cautious about any efforts to standardize an entire training program for use in every market. Transferring practices from one market to another is common practice, but policies and standards may not match with certain cultures – see Lewin and Johnston (1997). Methods of instruction may vary by culture thus sales managers may not be able to teach their standard problem-solving techniques to global salespersons.

Bush and Ingram (1996) match content and structure to the needs and typologies of the salesperson, focusing on intercultural disposition and attributional disposition. They refer to the salesperson's intercultural disposition as 'attributional confidence'. Intercultural disposition is the salesperson's disposition toward other cultures as the degree toward others of stereotyping, ethnocentrism and empathy (p. 378). Attributional confidence is the uncertainty level individuals have in their ability to predict and explain behavior. Then, depending on the salesperson's combined disposition (as sensitive, pluralistic, defiant or oblivious) the cultural training is arranged or changed as necessary.

The control of sales training in international markets was first examined by Hill, Still and Boya (1991). They found that across four industries – general consumer goods, pharmaceuticals, industrial goods, and electronic data processing – local subsidiaries maintain primary decision making on the methods and the content of the sales training. Industrial and electronic data processing have the highest level of home base (headquarters) influence but only the industrial and consumer goods were significantly different. This suggests that training development and execution is driven primarily by the local subsidiaries and that cultural or other factors will have an affect on the process and results. Attia, Honeycutt and Jantan (2006) propose culture as the mediating variable between the needs for salesforce training programs and the perceived improvement in performance of those sales programs. There have been a few studies that looked at sales training programs across countries with mixed findings when looking at the differences in content, methods and evaluations of the programs.

Erffmeyer *et al.* (1993) looked at the content used in training for managers and salespeople in their comparison of US firms and Saudi firms. They focused primarily on the task-related KSAs in their research (company policy, product, sales techniques), and also evaluated the use of personal skills. Considering budget and time allocation in the training process, they found that US firms spent more time and budget on planning, where Saudi companies spent more time on implementation. Although not significant, the Saudi sample spent nearly ten percent more of their training budget on training implementation than did the US firms. The study found that both US and Saudi firms spent most of their training hours in the first year, almost three times more as compared to a typical year. The hours of training however vary greatly between the US firms and Saudis', as the US firms spent three times the hours in the first year and more than twice the training time in other years of service.

Honeycutt *et al.* (1999) is another international study that looks primarily at task KSAs. In China and Slovakia, multinationals and domestic firms devote a similar amount of time to most of these topics. Global firms in each country spend more time on marketing information for their salespeople than do the domestic firms. Domestic firms in each country tend to focus more on product information (Slovakia) and sales procedures (China). From Northern Europe (UK, Netherlands, Finland) to Southern Europe (Spain and Portugal), the content focuses primarily on task related KSAs (company policies, sales techniques, product and market/customer knowledge) (Roman and Ruiz 2003). Cultural or sociopolitical reasons explain the slight differences between Northern and Southern groups in these content areas.

The biggest difference was in the area of teamwork training: the North spent more than twice as much time than did the South. This is pointed out as an interesting finding when one takes into consideration the global push for more teamwork and cross-functional collaboration within and among sales and buying teams. Both North and South use similar mixes of training and each use on-the-job training the most often. Overall, the North uses significantly more training per method. However, one method – long external training programs – was used by the South twice as much as the North. The percentage of sales revenue allocated to training is substantially

different, with the Northern firms allocating 17 per cent compared to the South's 3 per cent. Southern Europe subsidizes a higher degree of the training at almost 40 per ceent of the training investment compared to Northern Europe's 12 per cent.

Roman and Ruiz (2003) also evaluated the effect of training and performance in their sample of Northern and Southern European firms. On-the-job and in-house training, the most common method used by both groups, leads to higher performance in the Southern sample but not in the Northern. They suggest that multi-tasking may be affected by cultural orientations (i.e., time use – monochronic vs. polychronic) and thus, training or other sales activities must be viewed from that perspective when planning sales training content and method.

Chinese domestic firms tend to evaluate their trainees much less than global firms and also spend little time on measuring training results. However, they allow trainees to evaluate more than global firms do (Honeycutt *et al.* 1999). The opposite was true in Slovakia, where high percentages of all firms, domestic and global, have trainees doing the evaluations.

SALESFORCE ROLE PERCEPTIONS AND WORK OUTCOMES

The principal models of salesforce roles, behaviors and outcomes focus primarily on the various factors that affect the key consequence of salespeople: performance. Models of performance that have driven research and managerial practice have been developed from industrial and organizational psychology, and typically include: role perceptions; motivation through leadership; compensation or rewards; job satisfaction; performance and turnover (Churchill *et al.* 2000). Characteristics of the individual salesperson, the behaviors, policies and actions of the sales managers and organization, along with various US environmental factors, have an influence on performance indirectly through the drivers of performance or direct effects on performance. Churchill *et al.* (1985) synthesized the foundational models of salesforce performance that included a variety of predictors and outcomes of performance. Subsequently, Brown and Peterson (1993) conducted a meta-analysis on satisfaction and used those findings to test a model of role perceptions (role ambiguity and role conflict), job satisfaction, performance and commitment. That model, referred to as Brown and Peterson, is both a reflection of the core of prior performance models, and the basis of many subsequent extensions. We will look at those various constructs in the international sales research.

Role perceptions

The ability of salespeople to perform their assigned tasks is hindered in many instances by unclear, conflicting, and far too demanding expectations in their roles. These factors create role stress that has negative effects on other work outcomes. Stress may be negative or positive and thus not always detrimental as is often assumed. Leadership and organizational factors are influences, or drivers, of role. One means to reduce the levels of role stressors is through the management and leadership behaviors of the sales manager. Role ambiguity and role conflict were significantly related in a study by Dubinsky *et al.* (1992). Their model, tested in the USA, Japan and Korea, found that the USA had a significantly stronger relationship between the two role stressors than did Japan.

Agarwal (1993) linked the effects of formalization of roles to cultural dimensions of power distance in a sample of salespeople from the USA and India. He found that job codification affected role ambiguity for only the US sample. Rule observation increased both role stressors in the USA but only role conflict in India. Overall, formalization has a negative effect on role perceptions in the USA and minimal effects on Indian salespeople.

Formalization's affect on role stressors has also been studied in various settings. Michaels *et al.* (1996) found that formalization affects role ambiguity across all three samples from Korea, Japan and the USA. The United States had a much stronger relationship than Korea or Japan. In the same study, only the US sample had a strong relationship between formalization and role conflict, and this was significantly different from the Korean and Japanese samples. Lee and Mathur (1997) found a link in their work with Korean salesforces. Agarwal, Decarlo and Vyas (1999) focused on the initiation of structure and leadership consideration as behaviors that reduce role ambiguity and role conflict, and looked at the power distance effects across India and the USA. Initiation of structure in the Indian sample was not related to either role ambiguity or role stress, and no cultural effects were found. Netemeyer, Brashear-Alejandro and Boles (2004) looked at inter-domain conflict between work and family in a multi-nation study. They found that work–family–conflict and family–work–conflict increase the level of role stress in their salesforce samples from the USA, Romania and Puerto Rico.

Commitment and turnover

The level of salesperson organizational commitment is affected by various role and individual level variables and has been investigated in various US studies. In a three country study (Japan, Korea, and the USA), the job satisfaction to organizational commitment relationship was consistently positive across all three countries, with no significant cross-country differences (Dubinsky *et al.* 1992). Fairness perceptions (pay level and job latitude) were significantly related to commitment in the study by Dubinsky, Kotabe and Lim (1993). Agarwal (1993) found that elements of formalization have negative effects on organizational commitment and work alienation in the USA. Positive effects were found for variables in India, contrary to their cultural predictions. It was suggested that these contradictions are outgrowths of situational factors that allow or make a consumer do things differently or to become accustomed to an environment which contradicts the logic of another market.

Agarwal, Decarlo and Vyas (1999) found similar effects for role ambiguity and role conflict on organizational commitment in their Indian and US samples. They did not find any cultural moderating effects for the differences in power-distance. The effects of formalization were not found to be the same in their samples of US, Japanese and Korean salespeople (Michaels *et al.* 1996). The relationship is significant in Korean and Japanese salesforce, but only Korea and the US relationships are significantly different.

Lee and Mathur's (1997) findings in Korea support the negative relationship between the ambiguity and conflict measures and commitment and potential to leave the organization. Naumann, Widmie and Jackson (2000) found a variety of individual characteristics (age, experience, education, and language fluency) had positive effects on job satisfaction, commitment, and job involvement for expatriate salespeople. Role stressors as well as task, skill and autonomy related to the job, also increased the level of the outcome variables. This shows that having salespeople involved in their expatriate assignment, decisions, and increasing the training and the content of their training prior to assignment will lead to higher satisfaction, higher organizational commitment and increased levels of job involvement. In a single sample of Polish retail salespeople, Brashear, Lepkowska-White and Chelariu (2003) found strong support for the relationship between role conflict and commitment, and role ambiguity and turnover.

An abundance of literature exists with regard to turnover in general (e.g., Lucas *et al.* 1979; Griffeth and Hom 2004) and among expatriates (e.g., Naumann 1992; Birdseye and Hill 1995). In studies that looked at expatriate salespeople, only two have focused on turnover. Babakus *et al.* (1996) looked at

expatriate service salespeople in a comprehensive model with high levels of commitment and job satisfaction, both reducing the salesperson's propensity to leave their job. Naumann, Widmier and Jackson (2000) conducted a comprehensive review of the turnover literature. They focus on job satisfaction, organizational commitment and job involvement as the direct predictors, and found all three to significantly reduce the intention to leave their expatriate sales assignment. Netemeyer, Brashear-Alejandro and Boles (2004) found that work–family–conflict among salespeople increases the intention to leave. This finding was consistent across three countries (United States, Puerto Rico and Romania). However, among those three samples, satisfaction showed a consistently strong negative relationship to the intent-to-leave.

Performance

The study of performance has taken place in various settings. Dubinsky, Kotabe and Lim (1993) looked at the effect of fairness on performance and found that only the fairness of distributing tasks had a significant effect on performance among Japanese salespeople. Babakus *et al.* (1996) looked at both behavioral and outcome performance in Australia. The activities of the salesforce and the territory design were both related to both forms of performance. Territory affects both outcome and behavioral performance. Baldauf and Cravens (1999) found that the differences between high-and low-performing salesforces in Austria was related to firms use of more coaching, directing and evaluating activities, as well as acceptable territory designs. In Turkey, Menguc (1996a) found that effort mediates role stressors' effects on performance. Individual skills in selling and collaboration are among the task-related KSAs to be considered during training (Cron *et al.* 2005).

In Canada, field sales unit performance increases when there are higher levels of collaborative skills but not sales skills (Menguc and Barker 2005). Total compensation, in turn, increases as the sales unit increases its performance. Selling skills have a direct effect on compensation levels but collaborative skills, along with an interaction of two skills, are indirectly related to total compensation through unit performance.

Atuahene-Gima and Li (2002) found that performance is not always related to trust. In their Chinese and US samples, the effects of trust on performance are moderated by managerial actions and characteristics of both the sales manager and salesperson. Performance increases in the Chinese sample when control mechanisms (output control) are used by the sales manager. Interactions between manager's achievement orientation and salesperson role ambiguity also increased performance. In the US sample, interactions with trust reduced the performance of the salespeople in most instances. The findings suggest that trust is not always salient in relationships and in distinct cultural settings, trust in conjunction with other salesperson variables and sales management practices, may or may not increase performance.

Job satisfaction

In a three-country study of the United States, Japan and Korea, only Japan had a link between role conflict and satisfaction (Dubinsky *et al.* 1992). Menguc (1996) replicated Brown and Peterson's (1994) model of the moderating effects of effort on performance and satisfaction. Role stressors are found to have both direct and indirect effects on satisfaction. The replication also found that effort and performance significantly predict satisfaction. Naumann, Widmier and Jackson (2000) found a variety of individual characteristics (age, experience, education, and language fluency) had positive effects on job satisfaction for expatriate salespeople. Role stressors, as well as task, skill and autonomy related to the job, also increased job satisfaction. Participation in decision-making and the perceived value of expatriate training positively affects satisfaction. Results suggest having salespeople involved in their expatriate assignment and increasing the training and content of their training prior to assignment will have more positive satisfaction with the assignment. Brashear, Lepkowska-White and Chelariu (2003) replicated the Brown and Peterson (1993) model in Poland and found similar relationships. Role conflict and role ambiguity reduced performance and satisfaction, similar to the meta-analytic model.

Decarlo and Agarwal (1999) looked at managerial behaviors of initiation of structure, consideration, and job autonomy as predictors of job satisfaction in Australia, India and the USA. Autonomy was important in all countries, and consideration significant only in India. Interactions of the predictors with autonomy were not consistent as the consideration interaction was only significant in India; the interaction with initiation of structure was significant in Australia. Dubinksy *et al.* (1992) and Babakus *et al.* (1996) found that performance is a predictor of satisfaction.

Money and Graham (1999) look at salesperson characteristics as predictors of performance, pay, and job satisfaction in Japanese and US salesforces. At issue is the salience of each of the personal characteristics and the differences across cultures. Performance in the US data is driven by education, seniority, valence for pay, but not value congruence. For the Japanese, seniority and value congruence are predictors of performance. Only in the US sample is performance a predictor of pay. Pay drives satisfaction in both samples with the Japanese getting higher levels of job satisfaction from value congruence. Culture moderated the relationships although effects are very similar. Money appears to be more important for the United States, and closeness more important for Japan. Piercy, Low and Cravens (2004) linked behavioral control to the satisfaction of the salesforce's territory designs, and found significant effects across India, Greece and Malaysia. In the Malaysian sample, compensation control was negatively related to the satisfaction with territory design.

Control and compensation

Salesforce control and compensation are important to securing and maintaining a highly productive salesforce. The existing nuances of international markets make the structure of both control and compensation very difficult to standardize across cultures and economic conditions. Behavioral control used by field sales managers was the focus of a European study by Baldauf, Cravens and Piercy (2001). They found in two samples, from Austria and the UK, that behavioral control usage is significantly correlated with levels of performance, including the sales unit, salesperson behavioral and outcome performance, and sales person characteristics. Piercy, Low and Cravens (2004) investigated behavior- and compensation-based control effects in Greece, India and Malaysia. Primarily they found that compensation control across the countries was not a good predictor of performance. Behavior-based control had strong direct effects on behavioral performance and outcome performance, and indirect effects through territory design. Overall the models account for significant levels of group-level performance. However the findings do not support compensation control's relationship with outcome performance.

The composition of compensation packages are of particular interest in international markets. Economic conditions, market and behavioral uncertainty, all affect the decisions on how to compensate the salesforce. In a sample of German sales organizations, Krafft, Albers and Lal (2004) test a comprehensive model of theoretical issues derived from transaction cost economics and agency theory predictions of compensation decisions. Their work is both a replication and extension of previous work (e.g., John and Weitz 1989; Coughlan and Narasihman 1992; Lal and Srinivasan 1993). Their findings are quite similar. Their principal assertion is that agency theory and transaction costs may work simultaneously as complements to fill in the gaps of the other theory for both salesforce

design and compensation. Their results do not support that contention, but show that transaction cost predictions are best used for the design of the salesforce, and that agency theory predictions work to develop compensation but not TCA. Their findings give credence to the potential generalizability of the underlying theory on sales compensation derived from agency theory, although there are some differences. The argument that salary components increase with performance evaluation difficulty and the ability to get precise activity reports is supported, but in contrast, they rejected various US predictions relating to salary increases as replacement becomes more difficult and uncertain. The Albers, Krafft and Bielert (1998) study found the legal and cultural differences that affect the development and management of salespeople make various US aspects of the theoretical development insignificant. Although this study is conducted in Germany, the existing theoretical tests have been primarily US-based companies and thus the comparison of the findings is both theoretically and managerially relevant to international sales management decisions.

The equity or fairness of compensation distributions is an important research area (Ramaswami and Singh 2003), with distinctive culturally anchored implications (Fischer and Smith 2003; Giacobbe-Miller, Miller and Victorov 1998). Dubinsky, Kotabe and Lim (1993) looked at a variety of fairness components related to pay in a Japanese salesforce and their link to job satisfaction, organizational commitment, and multiple dimensions of motivation. Pay rule fairness evaluations has the most significant impact across the outcome variables, with the exception of performance. The distribution of tasks was related to motivation and performance. Organizational commitment and satisfaction and the valence for pay were positively related to the latitude dimension. Overall, fairness had limited and mixed effects on motivation.

The only study to do a multi-country test of compensation was that undertaken by

Segalla *et al.* (2006) who looked at the use of and allocation of incentive compensation. Managerial decisions regarding the level (variable vs. fixed) and allocation (equity or parity) of the incentive compensation is dependent upon their culture and their emphasis on salespeople's effort levels (motivation, effort effectiveness, social control, equality and shirking prevention) and effort direction (harmony and long term orientation). Using B2B data from six European countries in Germanic, Anglo and Latin cultural regions, Segalla *et al.* (2006) find culture does affect the level of incentive compensation and incentive distribution. They also found that the Germanic region has a lower likelihood to use incentive compensation than Anglo, while Spanish managers were more likely to use equity to allocate incentives. Managers who emphasized motivation chose incentive pay over fixed pay, but when the emphasis is on salesperson parity, a fixed structure was chosen. For the allocation decision, managers who emphasize motivation, effort effectiveness and shirking prevention, will be more likely to use an incentive system. Managers who focus on social control and parity will prefer an equity distribution.

SALESFORCE ETHICS

Cultural and legal differences across markets put international sales managers and salespeople into gray areas of decision-making. Although numerous studies have been conducted regarding salesperson ethics, relatively little work has been done to examine the consistency of ethical perceptions among salespeople in different countries. In one of the early efforts to examine salespeople's ethical perceptions across cultures, Dubinsky *et al.* (1991) conducted a cross-national investigation of industrial salespeople's ethical perceptions. They looked at samples of salespeople from the United States, Japan, and South Korea to determine the consistency

of ethical perceptions across the countries. Nationality was found to influence salespeople's beliefs about the ethicality of selling practices. US salespeople perceived fewer ethical problems in selling situations than did the Japanese or Korean sales personnel. Further, almost all US salespeople reported that their firms had guidelines to control selling behaviors, and that these policies were desired by the salespeople to help them in ambiguous situations.

Honeycutt, Siguaw and Hunt (1995) examined the cultural differences associated with ethical issues and the outcomes of ethical factors on a salesperson's performance. They linked ethical factors to the salesperson's performance, job satisfaction, and customer orientation. A direct comparison of high performing salespeople showed that US salespeople reported higher levels of ethical behavior than did the Taiwanese salespeople. From the links between ethical factors (ethics training, self-perceived ethical standards, ethical behaviors, and the perceptions of the ethical standards of significant others) ethics training was negatively related to performance and perceived levels of ethicalness. Ethics training, however, influenced customer orientation in both countries.

Lu, Rose and Blodgett (1999) examined the effects of Hofstede's cultural dimensions on ethical decision making in marketing in Taiwan and the USA. Their study found that salespeople with different cultural orientations placed different values on different ethical issues. There were no significant differences between managers across the two countries but they did find that salespeople in Taiwan are more concerned with company and fellow employee interests than are US managers. This is an interesting finding as one thinks about expatriate managers from an individualistic and masculine culture, operating in a high certainty avoidance, high power distance, collectivist culture. Expatriate managers must consider their salespeople's' cultural orientation as the development of the organizational structure, climate and motivation

Blodgett *et al.* (2001) also utilized Hofstede's typology to examine the effect of culture on ethical sensitivity toward different stakeholders (i.e., doctors and lawyers). In the two-country study, ethical sensitivity to stakeholder interests was dependent on the type of stakeholder. In Taiwan, sensitivity to colleagues' interests was found to be less important to salespeople than the interests of their company and competitors. There were also differences in work related values of sales employees across the two nationalities, with uncertainty avoidance being positively related to ethical sensitivity while cultural factors of power distance and individualism negatively related to ethical sensitivity.

Li (2002) focused on opportunism and examined its manifestations by salespeople in emerging markets using multiple case studies of British firms with channels in China. The author developed a framework and identified various drivers of opportunism, including: the number of salespeople; brand power; the amount of confidence that salespeople have in their employer; and the prevalence of gray market and fake products. Roman and Munera (2005) examined the determinants and consequences of the ethical behavior of Spanish salespeople. Four determinants of ethical sales behavior were identified: reward systems; control systems; age; and education. Salespeople with high levels of fixed salary were more likely to behave ethically than those who had a lower fixed-salary percentage. Ethical sales behavioral correlated highly with the level of behavioral control systems. Salespersons' ethical behavior reduced role conflict and increased job satisfaction.

Beekun, Stedham and Yamamura (2003) conducted a comparative study to explore the effects of national culture on ethical decision-making in Brazil and the USA. They utilized Hofstede's typology of culture and found that Brazilians and Americans evaluate ethical decisions differently when applying the utilitarian criteria. However, there was no difference when applying an egoistic criterion. Millington, Eberhardt and Wilkinson (2005) explored the intersection of gift-giving, guanxi (a Chinese system of personal connections), and corruption. The qualitative study of 49 UK manufacturers in China found that illegal gift-giving was a significant problem in UK-owned companies in China. However, the perception of illegal gifts was different for the UK companies and their employees. Chinese employees agreed that illegal gifts were problematic, however, the Chinese employees did not consider gift-giving within the *guanxi* to be illegal, but helpful for building business relationships. The same group considered gift giving outside the *guanxi* to be illegal.

CONCLUSIONS

Developing and managing an international salesforce is a difficult task due to the multiple levels of issues that need to be addressed. The individual characteristics of the recruits, the differing cultural perceptions of the job, the institutional and legal issues across markets, in addition to the complexity of cross-cultural and cross-national buyer-and-seller interactions (Kale and Barnes 1992) makes research in the area a potential bounty for theory and managerial implications. Given this, there is essentially a limited amount of research in the area of international sales and sales management.

Our review provides an overview of key studies as a guide to research issues of importance. The findings we have covered have provided a better understanding of the domain of international sales management research and many empirical findings to further build the theory of international sales management. For instance, the decision on company owned or use of external agents is not a resolved issue. The underlying theories of transaction cost and agency theory provide some generalizable guidance but the empirical work is limited to two markets essentially. Training has received a significant amount of exposure but other issues related to training of expatriate salespeople and the issues for overseas assignments and repatriation

(Black, Mendenhall and Odou 1991; Feldman and Thomas 1992) have only scratched the surface in the sales literature. A key issue for expatriate adjustment is socialization (Dubinsky *et al.* 1986) and the use of mentoring (Feldman and Thomas 1992; Brashear *et al.* 2006) but there has been little attention given to those areas in sales are. Compensation is also a key area that has been addressed in a variety of studies.

There has been work in the area of performance structured from the work of Churchill *et al.* (1985), but in this research, the coverage of topics and relationships has not been fully explored and the regions or countries of interest are limited. The findings related to cultural effects on relationships tend to be inconclusive for the most part and may be related to measurement or analytical issues (e.g., Singh 1995). The use of secondary data by Albers, Krafft and Bielert (1998) provides an interesting avenue to explore the level of sales compensation based on job characteristics, tax issues or governmental regulations. Related to that is the issue of salesforce control mechanisms. This topic has received some support but is a key area of research (Baldauf, Cravens and Piercy 2005) that needs more exposure in the international arena along with the interactions of control with issues of compensation, values and fairness (e.g., Kotabe, Dubinsky and Lim 1992; Dubinsky, *et al.* 1997; Ramaswami and Singh 2003).

Another broad area of research that has not been conducted is in the area of relationship development within firms and across exchange partners. Doney, Cannon and Mullen (1998) provided a framework of trust development across markets and Atuahene-Gima and Li (2002) has tested the model in the USA and China. Lee and Dawes (2005) explore the connection of trust and *guanxi*, but there is limited relationship research and broad studies of trust do not exist. Understanding the different forms of relationships and the meaning of relationships in different markets is important (Albers, Krafft and Bielert 1998) and the new emerging markets are culturally and institutionally quite distinct, thus requiring a better understanding of how relationships develop and are managed.

Lastly, although a wish list of research could be included, these are areas that would seem to provide a significant increase in the knowledge base and also the managerial application from the research findings. One final recommendation is to look geographically. There are limited publications on sales issues in the big emerging markets of Brazil, Russia, India and China. Of these four markets, there is work related to India (e.g., Agarwal 1993; Agarwal, Decarlo and Vyas 1999; Decarlo and Agarwal 1999) with much of that data more than 10 years old. There is limited work on China with notable exceptions (Honeycutt, Ford and Kurtzman 1996; Luk, Fullgrabe, and Yi 1999; Merrilees and Miller 1999; Atuahene-Gima and Li 2002; Lee and Dawes 2005) but with exceptions most of that work was done prior to the current economic situation. There is no doubt research is being conducted in these markets but there have been limited publications in the primary academic English language journals.

The lack of coverage of publications in non-English language journals is a limitation of this review where we are sure there is a growing body of work. However, the absence of research from many geographical regions in the principal marketing and sales journals still points to the problem that sales research in the largest emerging markets is not widespread, even though it holds incredible potential for theory testing and development, as well as for managerial practice. The importance of sales management in these markets is becoming more and more evident and the field of sales and sales management needs to do more in the area of international research, particularly in the emerging and future growth markets.

REFERENCES

Agarwal, S. (1993) 'Influence of formalization on role stress, organizational commitment, and work alienation of salespersons: a cross-national comparative Study', *Journal of*

International Business Studies, 24(4): 715–739.

Agarwal, S., Decarlo T. E. and Vyas, S. B. (1999) 'Leadership behavior and organizational commitment: A comparative study of American and Indian salespeople', *Journal of International Business Studies*, 30(4): 727–743.

Albers, S., Krafft, M. and Bielert, W. (1998) 'Global salesforce management: Comparing German and US practices', in G. J. Bauer, M. S. Baunchalk, T. N. Ingram and R. W. LaForge (eds), *Emerging Trends in Sales Thought and Practice*. Westport, CT: Quorum Books, pp. 193–211.

Anderson, E. (1985) 'The sales agent as outside or employee: A transaction cost analysis', *Marketing Science*, 4(3): 234–254.

Anderson, E. and Coughlan, A. T. (1987) 'International market entry and expansion via independent or integrated channel channels of distribution', *Journal of Marketing*, 51(1): 71–82.

Attia, A. M., Honeycutt Jr., E. D. and Attiac, M. M. (2002): 'The difficulties of evaluating sales training', *Industrial Marketing Management*, 31(3): 253–259.

Attia, A. M., Honeycutt Jr., E. D. and Jantan, M. A. (2006)'Global sales training: in search of antecedent, mediating, and consequence variables', *Industrial Marketing Management*, forthcoming.

Atuahene-Gima, K. and Li, H. (2002), 'When does trust matter? Antecedents and contingent effects of supervisee trust on performance in selling new products in China and the United States', *Journal of Marketing*, 66(3): 61–81.

Avlonitis, G. J. and Boyle, K. A. (1989) 'Linkages between sales management tools and practices: Some evidence from British companies', *Journal of the Academy of Marketing Sciences*, 17(2): 137–145.

Babakus, E., Cravens, D. W. Grant, K. Ingram, T. N. and Laforge R. W. (1996) 'Investigating the relationships among sales, management control, sales territory design, salesperson performance, and sales organization effectiveness', *International Journal of Research in Marketing*, 13(4): 345–363.

Baldauf, A., and Cravens D. W. (1999) 'Improving effectiveness of field sales organizations: A European perspective', *Industrial Marketing Management*, 28(1): 63–72.

Baldauf, A., Cravens, D. W. and Piercy, N. F. (2001) 'Examining the consequences of sales management control strategies in European field sales organizations', *International Marketing Review*, 18(5): 474–508.

Baldauf, A., Cravens D. W. and Piercy, N. F. (2005) 'Sales management control research – synthesis and an agenda for future research', *Journal of Personal Selling and Sales Management*, 25(1):7–26.

Barksdale, Jr., H. C., Bellenger, D. N. Boles, J. S. and Brashear, T. G. (2003) 'The effects of realistic job preview and perceptions of training on salesperson performance and attitudinal commitment: A longitudinal study', *Journal of Personal Selling & Sales Management,* 23(2): 125–138.

Beekun, R. I., Stedham, Y. and Yamamura, J. H. (2003) 'Business ethics in Brazil and the U.S.: A comparative investigation', *Journal of Business Ethics*, 42(3): 267–279.

Bhawuk, D. P. S. and Brislin, R. W. (2000) 'Cross-cultural training: A review', *Applied Psychology: An International Business Review*, 49(1): 162–191.

Birdseye, M. G. and Hill, J. S. (1995) 'Individual, organizational work and environmental influences on expatriate turnover tendencies: An empirical study', *Journal of International Business Studies*, 26(4): 787–813.

Black, J. S., Mendenhall, M. and Oddou, G. (1991) 'Towards a comprehensive model of international adjustments', *Academy of Management Review*, 16(2): 291–317.

Blodgett, J. G. Lu, L.-C. Rose, G. M. and Vitell, S. J. (2001) 'Ethical sensitivity to stakeholder interests: A cross-cultural comparison', *Journal of the Academy of Marketing Science*, 29(2): 190–202.

Brashear, T. G., Bellenger, D. N., Boles, J. S. and Barksdale, Jr., H. C. (2006) 'An exploratory study of the relative effectiveness of different types of salesforce mentors', *Journal of Personal Selling & Sales Management*, 26(1): 7–18.

Brashear, T. G., Lepkowska-White, E. and Chelariu, C. (2003) 'An empirical test of the Brown and Peterson model In a Polish context', *Journal of Business Research* 56(12): 971–978.

Brown, S. P. and Peterson, R. A. (1993) 'Antecedents and consequences of salesperson job satisfaction: Meta-analysis and assessment of causal effects', *Journal of Marketing Research*, 30(1): 63–77.

Brown, S. P. and Peterson, R. A. (1994) 'The effect of effort on sales performance and job satisfaction', *Journal of Marketing*, 58(2): 70–80.

Bush, V. D. and Ingram, T. (1996) 'Adapting to diverse customers: A training matrix for international marketers', *Industrial Marketing Management*, 25(5): 373–383.

Chonko, L. B., Tanner, J. F., Jr., Smith, E. R. (1991) 'Selling and Sales Management in Action: The Sales Force's Role in International Marketing Research and Marketing Information Systems', *The Journal of Personal Selling & Sales Management,* 11(1): 69–79.

Churchill, Jr., G. A., Ford, N. M. Hartley, S. W. and Walker, Jr., O. C. (1985) 'The determinants of salesperson performance: A meta-analysis', *Journal of Marketing Research*, 22(2): 103–118

Churchill, Jr., G. A., Ford, N. M., Walker, Jr., O. C., Johnston, M. W. and Tanner, J.F. (2000) *Salesforce Management*. Chicago, IL.: Irwin.

Cook, O. A and Herche, J. (1992) 'Assessment centers: An untapped resource for global salesforce management', *Journal of Personal Selling & Sales Management*, 12(3): 31–38.

Cook, O. A and Herche, J. (1994) 'Assessment centers: A contrast of usage in diverse environments', *The International Executive*, 36(5): 645–656.

Coughlan, A. T. and Chakravarthi Narasimhan (1992) 'An empirical analysis of sales-force compensation plans', *The Journal of Business*, 65(1): 93–121

Cravens, D. W., Grant, K. Ingram, T. N. LaForge, R. W. and Young, C. (1992) 'In search of excellent sales organizations', *European Journal of Marketing*, 26(1): 6–23.

Cron, W. (1984) 'Industrial salesperson development: A career stage perspective', *Journal of Marketing*, 48(3): 41–52.

Cron, W. L., Marshall, G. W. Singh, J., Spiro, R. L. and Sujan, H. (2005) 'Salesperson selection, training, and development: Trends, implications, and research opportunities', *Journal of Personal Selling and Sales Management*, 25(2): 124–136.

Daily, C. M., Certo, S. T. and Dalton, D. R. (2000) 'International experience in the executive suite: A path to prosperity', *Strategic Management Journal*, 21(4): 515–523.

Decarlo, T. E. and Agarwal, S. (1999) 'Influence of managerial behaviors and job autonomy on job satisfaction of industrial salespeople: A cross cultural study', *Industrial Marketing Management*, 28(1): 51–62.

Doney, P. M., Cannon J. P. and Mullen M. R. (1998) 'Understanding The Influence of National Culture on the Development of Trust', *The Academy of Management Review*, 23(3): 601–620.

Dubinsky, A. J. and Hanafy, A. (1996) 'Executive insights: the super salesforce – Politicians in the world market', *Journal of International Marketing*, 4(3): 73–87.

Dubinsky, A. J., Jolson, M. A., Kotabe, M. and Lim, C. U. (1991) 'A cross-national investigation of industrial salespeople's ethical perceptions', *Journal of International Business Studies*, 22(4): 651–670.

Dubinsky, A. J., Kotabe, M. Lim, C. U. and Wagner, W. (1997) 'The impact of values on salespeople's job responses: a cross-national investigation', *Journal of Business Research*, 39(3): 195–208

Dubinsky, A. J., Kotabe, M. and Lim, C. U. (1993) 'Effects of organizational fairness on Japanese sales personnel', *Journal of International Marketing*, 1(4): 5–24.

Dubinsky, A. J., Michaels, R. E., Kotabe, M., Lim, C. U. and Moon, H. -C. (1992) 'Influence of role stress on industrial salespeople's work outcomes in the United States, Japan and Korea', *Journal of International Business Studies*, 23(1): 77–99.

Dubinsky, A. J., Howell, R. D., Ingram, T. N. and Bellenger, D. N. (1986) 'Salesforce socialization', *Journal of Marketing*, 50(4): 192–207

Engle, R. (1998) 'Multi-step, structured interviews to select sales representatives in Russia and Eastern Europe', *European Management Journal*, 16(4): 476–484.

Erffmeyer, R. C., Al-Khatib, J. A., Al-Habib, M. I. and Hair, J. F. (1993) 'Sales training practices: A cross-national comparison', *International Marketing Review*, 10(1): 45–59.

Feldman, D. C. and Thomas, D. C. (1992) 'Career management issues facing expatriates', *Journal of International Business Studies*, 23(2): 271–293.

Fischer, R. and Smith, P. B. (2003) 'Reward allocation and culture: A meta-analysis', *Journal Of Cross-Cultural Psychology*, 34(3): 251–268.

Giacobbe-Miller, J. K., Miller, D. J., Victorov, V. I. (1998) 'A comparison of Russian And U.S. pay allocation decisions, distributive justice judgments, and productivity under different payment conditions', *Personnel Psychology*, 51(1): 137–163.

Griffeth, R. and Hom, P. (2004) *Innovative Theory and Empirical Research on Employee Turnover*. Charlotte, NC: Information Age Publishing.

Herche, J. and Swenson, M. J. (1992) 'The global productivity matrix: Facilitation of global salesforce deployment decisions', *Journal of Global Marketing*, 5(4): 81–95.

Hill, C. W. L. (2004). *Global Business Today*. New York, NY: McGraw Hill-Irwin.

Hill, John S., Still, R. R. and Boya U. O. (1991) 'Managing the multinational salesforce', *International Marketing Review*, 6(1): 19–31

Hill, J. S. and Still, R. R. (1990) 'Organizing the overseas salesforce: How multinationals do It', *The Journal of Personal Selling and Sales Management*, 10(2): 57–66.

Honeycutt, E. D. and Ford, J. B. (1995) 'Guidelines for managing an international salesforce', *Industrial Marketing Management*, 24(2): 135–144.

Honeycutt, E. D, Siguaw, J. A., and Hunt, T. G. (1995) 'Business ethics and job-related constructs: a cross-cultural comparison of automotive salespeople', *Journal of Business Ethics*, 14(3): 235–248

Honeycutt Jr., E. D., Karande, K. W. and Jantan, M. A. (2002) 'Sales training in Malaysia': High-vs. low-tech methods', *Industrial Marketing Management*, 31(7): 581–587.

Honeycutt, E. D., Ford, J. B. and Kurtzman, L. (1996) 'Potential problems and solutions when hiring and training a worldwide sales team', *Journal of Business & Industrial Marketing*, 11(1): 42–54.

Honeycutt, E. D., Ford, J. B., Lupton, R. A. and Flaherty, T. B. (1999) 'Selecting and training the international salesforce: Comparisons of

China and Slovakia', *Industrial Marketing Management*, 28(6): 627–635.

Jantan, M. A. and Honeycutt, Jr., E. D. (2002) 'Sales Training Practices In Malaysia', *Multinational Business Review*, 10(1): 72–78.

Jantan, M. A., Honeycutt, E. D., Thelenc, S. T. and Attia, A. M. (2004) 'Managerial perceptions of sales training and performance', *Industrial Marketing Management*, 33(7): 667–673.

John, G. and Weitz, B. (1989) 'Salesforce Compensation: An empirical investigation of factors related to use of salary versus incentive compensation', *Journal of Marketing Research*, 26(1):1–14.

Kale, S. H. and Barnes, J. W. (1992) 'Understanding the domain of cross-national buyer–seller interactions', *Journal of International Business Studies*, 23 (First Quarter): 101–132.

Kotabe, M., Dubinsky, A. J., and Lim, C. U. (1992) 'Perceptions of organizational fairness: A cross-national perspective', *International Marketing Review*, 9(2): 41–58

Krafft, M. (1995) 'New insights in to a classic choice problem? An investigation of hypotheses of the new institutional economics regarding the choice between outside agent or employed reps', *Die Betriebswirtschaft* (in German), 56(6): 759–776.

Krafft, M., Albers, S. and Lal, R. (2004) 'Relative explanatory power of agency theory and transaction cost analysis in German salesforces', *International Journal of Research in Marketing*, 21(3): 265–283.

Krishnamoorthy, A., Misra, S. and Prasad, A. (2005) 'Scheduling salesforce training: theory and evidence', *International Journal of Research in Marketing*, 22(4): 427–440.

Lal, R. and Srinivasan, V. (1993) 'Compensation plans for single- and multi-product salesforces: An application of the Holmstrom-Milgrom model', *Management Science*, 39(7): 777–793.

Lee, D. Y., and Dawes, P. L. (2005) 'Guanxi, trust, and long-term orientation in Chinese business markets', *Journal of International Marketing*, 13(2): 28–56.

Lee, K. S. and Mathur, A. (1997) 'Formalization, role stress, organizational commitment, and propensity-to-leave: A study of Korean industrial salespersons', *Journal of Global Marketing*, 11(2): 23–42.

Lewin, J. E. and Johnston, W. J. (1997) 'International salesforce management: A relationship perspective', *Journal of Business & Industrial Marketing*, 12(3/4): 236–252.

Li, L. (2002) 'Research note: Salesforce opportunism in emerging markets: An exploratory investigation', *Thunderbird International Business Review*, 44(4): 515–531

Littrell, L. N., Salas, E., Hess, K. P., Paley, M. and Riedel, S. (2006) 'Expatriate preparation: A critical analysis of 25 years of cross-cultural training research', *Human Resource Development Review*, 5(3): 355–388.

Lu, L. C., Rose, G. M. and Blodgett, J. G. (1999) 'The effects of cultural dimensions on ethical decision making in marketing: An exploratory study', *Journal of Business Ethics*, 18(1): 91–105.

Lucas Jr., G. H., Parasuraman, A., Davis, Robert A., and Enis, B. (1979) 'An empirical study of salesforce turnover', *The Journal of Marketing*, 51(3): 34–59.

Luk, S. T. K., Fullgrabe, L. and Li, S. C. Y. (1999) 'Managing direct selling activities in China: a cultural explanation', *Journal of Business Research*, 45(3): 257–266

Marshall, G. W., Mowen, J. C. and Stone, T. H. (1995) 'Risk taking in sales-force selection decisions: The impact of decision frame and time', *Psychology & Marketing*, 12(4): 265–285.

Marshall, G. W., Stone, T. H. and Jawahar, L. M. (2001) 'Selection decision making by sales managers and human resource managers: Decision impact, decision frame and time of valuation', *The Journal of Personal Selling & Sales Management*, 21(1): 19.

Marshall, G., Brouthers, L. E. and Lamb, Jr., C. W. (1998) 'A typology of political economies and strategies in international selling', *Industrial Marketing Management*, 27(1): 11–19.

Mendenhall, M. E. and Stahl, G. K. (2000) 'Expatriate training and development: where do we go from here? '*Human Resource Management*, 39(2–3): 251–265.

Menguc, B. (1996a) 'Evidence for Turkish industrial salespeople', *European Journal of Marketing*, 30(1): 33–51.

Menguc, B. (1996b): 'The influence of the market orientation of the firm on salesforce behavior and attitudes: further empirical results', *International Journal of Research in Marketing*, 13(3): 277–291.

Menguc, B. and Barker, T. (2005) 'Re-examining field sales unit performance', *European Journal of Marketing*, 39(7/8): 885–909.

Merrilees, B., and Miller, D. (1999) 'Direct selling in the west and east: the relative roles of product and relationship (Guanxi) drivers', *Journal of Business Research*, 45(3): 267–273.

Michaels, R. E., Dubinsky, A. J., Kotabe, M. and Lim, C. U. (1996) 'The effects of organizational formalization on organizational commitment and work alienation in US, Japanese, and Korean Industrial Salesforces', *European Journal of Marketing*, 30(7): 8–24.

Millington, A., Eberhardt, M. and Wilkinson, B. (2005) 'Gift giving, guanxi and illicit payments in buyer-supplier relations in China: Analysing the experience of UK companies', *Journal of Business Ethics*, 57(3): 255–268

Money, B. R. and Graham, J. L. (1999) 'Salesperson performance, pay and job satisfaction: Tests of a model using data collected in the United States and Japan', *Journal of International Business Studies*, 1 (First Quarter): 149–172.

Naumann, E. (1992) 'Conceptual model of expatriate turnover', *Journal of International Business Studies*, 23(3): 499–531.

Naumann, E., Widmier, S. M. and Jackson Jr., D. W. (2000) 'Examining the relationship between work attitudes and propensity to leave among expatriate salespeople', *The Journal of Personal Selling & Sales Management*, 20(4): 227–241.

Netemeyer, R. G., Brashear-Alejandro, T. and Boles, J. S. (2004) 'A cross-national model of job-related outcomes of work-role and family-role variables: A retail sales context', *Journal of the Academy of Marketing Science,* 32(1): 49–60.

Patton, W. E. 'Pat' and King, R. H. (1992) 'The use of human judgment models in salesforce selection decisions', *Journal of Personal Selling & Sales Management*, 12(2): 1–14.

Piercy, N. F., Low, C. S. and Cravens, D. W. (2004) 'Consequences of sales management's behavior- and compensation-based control strategies in developing countries', *Journal of International Marketing*, 12(3): 30–57.

Ramaswami, S. N. and Singh, J. (2003) 'Antecedents and consequences of merit pay fairness for industrial salespeople', *Journal of Marketing*, 67(4): 46–66.

Román, S. and Munuera, J. L. (2005) 'Determinants and consequences of ethical behaviour: an empirical study of salespeople', *European Journal of Marketing*, 39(5/6): 473–495.

Roman, S. and Ruiz, S. (2003) 'A comparative analysis of sales training in Europe', *International Marketing Review*, 20(3): 304–327.

Rouzies, D., Segalla, M. and Weitz, B. A. (2003) 'Cultural impact on European staffing decisions in sales management', *International Journal of Research in Marketing*, 20: 67–85.

Russ, K. R., Hair, J. F., Erffmeyer, R. C., Easterling, D., Boone, L. E., Kurtz, D. L. and, Milewicz, J. C. (1989) 'Is professional selling the route to the corporate hierarchy', *Journal of Personal Selling & Sales Management*, 9(1): 42–54.

Segalla, M., Rouzies, D., Besson, M. and Weitz, B. A. (2006) 'A Cross-national investigation of incentive sales compensation', *International Journal of Research in Marketing*, 23(4): 419–433.

Singh, J. (1995) 'Measurement issues in cross-national research', *Journal of International Business Studies*, 26(3): 597–619.

Steenkamp, J.-B. E. M. and Baumgartner, H. (1998) 'Assessing measurement invariance in cross-national consumer research', *The Journal of Consumer Research*, 25(1): 78–90.

Still, R. R. (1981) 'Cross-Cultural Aspects of Sales Force Management', *The Journal of Personal Selling & Sales Management*, 1,2 (Spring/Summer), 6–9.

Tung, R. L. (1982) 'Selection and training procedures of US, European, and Japanese multinationals. Find more like this', *California Management Review*, 25(1): 57–71.

Emerging Issues in Global Marketing

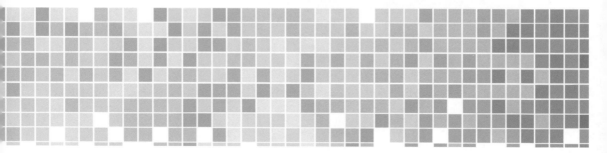

23

The Internet and International Marketing

Venkatesh Shankar and Jeffrey Meyer

INTRODUCTION

The Internet has reshaped international marketing in unprecedented ways. On the demand side, the Internet has opened doors for firms to new markets, customers, ways of doing business, and improved customer service capabilities across the globe. On the supply side, firms have been able to leverage the Internet to reduce the cost of their international marketing and sales operations and to improve the productivity of these operations. From the perspective of international marketing, however, the demand side effects of the Internet merit deeper examination than do supply side effects.

Consider the following statistics relating to the Internet in the international context. Although Internet penetration rate is highest in North America (71 per cent), about 39 per cent of all Internet users are in Asia, and Africa and the Middle East are the regions with the highest compound growth rate in Internet usage during 2000–07 (www.internet worldstats.com/stats.htm). Furthermore, more than 70 per cent of Web users are non-English speakers and US e-marketplaces derive more than 40 per cent of their revenues from abroad (Shankar and Donato 2003). These numbers suggest that the Internet has an important role to play in the international business context.

We use the term 'Internet' to broadly include the World Wide Web (or simply the Web), email, and any other public medium or vehicle of electronic communication or transaction. Despite the importance of the Internet to international marketing, there is a dearth of a systematic framework about the role of the Internet in international marketing decisions and the impact of the Internet on firm performance in international markets. The lack of a systematic framework is partly due to limited research on the role of the Internet in international marketing.

Several important questions on the Internet and international marketing remain unanswered for academics and practitioners alike. How does the Internet affect a firm's international marketing decisions? What are the direct and indirect effects of the Internet and Internet marketing strategy on firm performance in international markets? What are some emerging trends and future issues related to the Internet and international marketing? We address these questions in this chapter.

The remainder of the chapter is organized as follows. In the next section, we provide an organizing framework to study the impact of the Internet and Internet strategy on international marketing decisions and their outcomes. The subsequent four sections cover the roles of the Internet in international product development; international communication; international pricing; and international distribution. Following these four sections, we outline some emerging trends and future issues related to the Internet and international marketing. We close by summarizing the chapter.

AN ORGANIZING FRAMEWORK AND INTERNATIONAL INTERNET MARKETING STRATEGY

To better understand the role of the Internet in international marketing strategy, we first need to examine the purpose for which companies use the Internet in the international marketing context. Through a case study of six software firms, Moen, Endresen and Gavlen (2003) conclude that the two most important purposes for which firms use the Internet are information gathering and customer support or postpurchase activities. Nearly all six firms in their study reported using the Internet for obtaining information about possible customers, distributors, and partners. The international software firms also believed that the Internet is a powerful tool for strengthening bonds and increasing customer satisfaction through customer support and postpurchase activities.

In addition to the two purposes identified by Moen *et al.* (2003), the Internet may also play an important role across a gamut of international marketing decisions. It serves as a good information source and information dissemination vehicle in conducting international market research and can be used to identify common customer segments across countries. It is also a good medium for conveying a brand's value proposition or position to its target audience across countries. However, its most significant impact is perhaps on the formulation and effectiveness of international marketing mix decisions. Therefore, we focus on the role of the Internet and Internet marketing strategy in these decisions.

An organizing framework relating the Internet and international marketing decisions and firm performance is shown in Figure 23.1. The international marketing mix

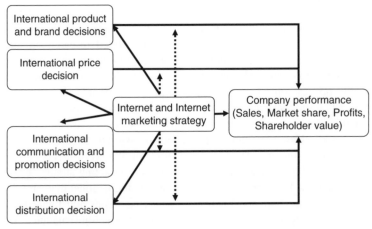

Notes: Bold lines represent direct effects. Dashed lines represent moderating effects.

Figure 23.1   An organizing framework for the Internet and international marketing

decisions include those on product, brand, price, communication, promotion and distribution. Certainly the Internet and the firm's Internet marketing strategy directly influence both the international marketing mix decisions and the firm's performance. But, in addition to having a direct effect on the firm's performance, the Internet and the Internet marketing strategy of a firm also have moderating effects on the impacts of each international marketing mix decision on firm performance. Because firm performance is critically important to firms, we mainly focus on the direct and moderating effects of the Internet and Internet marketing strategy on firm performance.

A summary of selected research on the Internet and international marketing appears in Table 23.1. The table lists the key issues studied, methodology, key findings, and important limitations of each of the selected papers. We discuss the papers in this table in the relevant sections of this chapter. Although a number of papers are summarized in this table, it must be noted that research on the Internet and international marketing is still in its infancy and the research questions we raised in the introduction section largely remain under-explored.

In formulating its international Internet marketing strategy, a firm should compare different countries on dimensions such as infrastructure, geographical distance, language, buyer behavior, buyer demographics, payment systems, currency and reputation (Guillen 2002). Guillen (2002) proposes a framework (shown in Table 23.2) for deciding on the international Internet marketing strategy based on two dimensions: global integration and local responsiveness. Depending on the combination of these dimensions, he advances four types of international Internet marketing strategies: pure local adaptation, global cost leadership, nationally differentiated, and transnational cost adaptation strategies. According to this framework, each type of strategy is appropriate for specific product categories. As an example of a nationally differentiated strategy, Guillen cites products whose features are most amenable to direct inspection, such as clothing, cars, and collectibles. These products may need high local responsiveness in Web site design, language, return policy, and customer service, but do not need a great deal of integration across countries. Guillen claims that for such product categories, an Internet strategy that is differentiated by country is most appropriate. The framework is useful to broadly categorize products, but does not offer specific guidelines on how to leverage the Internet in the international marketing context for specific products.

The success of international Internet marketing strategy may depend on several factors. Based on a survey of 123 business-to-business (B2B) companies, Eid and Trueman (2004) identify five key dimensions for perceived success in international Internet marketing. These dimensions are: marketing strategy factors; global dimension-related factors; external factors; Web site factors; and other internal factors. We briefly discuss three of these dimensions below.

Within the marketing strategy factor, Eid and Trueman (2004) identify five sub-factors. Based on these sub-factors, Eid and Trueman recommend that: (1) companies should have top management support and commitment to successfully implement international Internet marketing; (2) companies should clearly define their strategic goals for the use of the Internet in global marketing; (3) a company's Internet strategy should be part of the company's overall marketing strategy (Eid and Trueman 2004, p. 23); (4) firms should collaborate with partners, suppliers, and company employees in formulating their strategy; and (5) companies should clearly define their potential audiences.

Within the global dimension-related factor, Eid and Trueman (2004) also identify five sub-factors. These sub-factors are: (1) foreign market environments, including the legal system, political climate, trade regulations, and currency issues; (2) resources required to work globally; (3) the role of language and communication in creating and managing multilingual Web sites; (4) cultural considerations; and (5) international delivery of goods and services.

Table 23.1 Summary of selected studies on the Internet and international marketing

Paper	Key Issues Studied	Methodology	Key Findings/Insights	Key Limitations
Ancarani et al. (2005)	Investigate price levels and price dispersion across retailers across countries	Statistical analysis of data on CDs and books from retailers in European countries	- Price levels, including shipping costs, are higher online than offline in every country. - Price dispersion is persistent across countries. - Multichannel retailers have the highest price levels in every country, but they do not exhibit the highest price dispersion.	The study is restricted to CDs and books in three Western European countries.
Deshpandé (2002)	Identify global trends affecting competition; specifically, the coming together of globalization and e-commerce	Conceptual analysis	- The Internet allows information sharing among consumers in a way not seen before. - The Internet has affected pricing through knowledge transparency on the part of consumers.	The analysis is conceptual with no empirical validation.
Eid and Elbeltagi (2005)	Determine the effect of Internet usage on B2B marketing efficiency through international marketing activities	Survey of 123 B2B international companies	- There is a positive relationship between the Internet and B2B marketing activities, international marketing activities, and B2B marketing efficiency. - Results support previous research suggesting the Internet is advantageous to companies seeking to expand internationally.	The data are self-reported.
Eid and Trueman (2004)	Identify dimensions that impact the perceived success of B2B Internet international marketing	Survey of 123 B2B international companies	- Marketing strategy related factors have the highest effect on perceived success, followed closely by the global dimension factors. - External factors and internal factors are also significant dimensions.	The data are self-reported.
Javalgi et al. (2005)	Present an integrative framework to explain the role that customer behavior and CRM play in developing a profitable SCA for Internet companies	Conceptual analysis	- Because Internet firms have extensive global reach, they must have both a consistent and an effective brand image on their Web sites across countries. - The brand must be built in such a way that the brand has global appeal based on local perceptions, values, and language. - Firms can also localize Web sites, incorporating country specific displays to build a customer base, increase sales, and foster satisfaction and loyalty.	The analysis is conceptual with no empirical validation.

Table 23.1 Cont'd

Paper	Key Issues Studied	Methodology	Key Findings/Insights	Key Limitations
Luna et al. (2002)	The impact of culture on measures of Web site attitude and effectiveness	Experiments	- Congruency between graphics and brand name/brand attributes moderates language effects on attitudes towards cross-cultural Web sites. - Culturally congruent Web sites result in higher product attitudes for second language sites relative to first language sites.	- Experimental subjects were bilingual. The experiment did not consider subjects that spoke only one language. - The experiment was based on Web sites for purchases, not necessarily Web sites for informational purposes only.
Melewar and Stead (2002)	Examine the challenge facing firms using the Internet and whether the Internet enhances building and maintaining a global customer base	Conceptual analysis	- The Internet can help break down cultural barriers due to its 'placelessness' and price positioning strategies, but challenges remain such as localization versus standardization. - The Internet as a global marketing tool also creates challenges from regulatory and organizational barriers.	The analysis is conceptual with no empirical validation.
Moen et al. (2003)	Focus on how small exporting firms use the Internet in international marketing activities	Case study of six Norwegian companies	- In this industry, firms report using the Internet for information about customers, distributors, and partners, but not as the primary sales, promotion, and distribution tool. - Firms believe the Internet can aid in personal selling efforts by developing positive company image. - Firms believe the Internet may be better suited for standardized products. - Firms report the Internet is extensively used for support and postpurchase activities.	- The sample is small. - The analysis is on a single, specialized industry (B2B computer software)
Shama (2005)	Provide information about e-commerce firms' marketing and international marketing strategies	Survey of 136 e-commerce companies	- 77% of e-commerce companies have at least some sales in foreign markets. - 47% with international sales have an English only web-site, with 43% having both English and 'local language.' - 57% with international sales have customer service in the foreign country, and when they do, 72% say it is offered only in English. - Product and distribution are most often adapted (55% and 54%, respectively). - Price and promotion are each adapted to the local market 50% of the time.	The study is mainly descriptive.

Continued

Table 23.1 Cont'd

Paper	Key Issues Studied	Methodology	Key Findings/Insights	Key Limitations
Singh et al. (2003a)	Determine if local country Web sites reflect local cultural values	Content analysis across four countries	- Local country Web sites reflect the local country's culture based on classical cultural value orientation dimensions of individualism–collectivism, power distance, masculinity, and high/low contextuality.	The study does not look at global firms' local Web sites (only local firms' local web sites are examined).
Singh et al. (2003b)	Examine cultural adaptation on the Web and provide insights to Web marketers on developing culturally adapted Web sites	Content analysis across two countries	- US-based global firms with Web sites in both the US and China have culturally adapted their Chinese Web sites based on classical cultural value orientation dimensions of individualism–collectivism, uncertainty avoidance, power distance, masculinity, and high/low contextuality.	- The study compares two countries that have been established to be far apart culturally. - The study does not look at non-US based companies' Web sites. - The study analyses only one pair of countries.
Singh et al. (2004)	Explore whether foreign consumers prefer local Web content and localized messages or standardized Web content, and whether foreign consumers perceive the Web sites in terms of cultural congruency	Survey across five countries	- Web sites with high adaptation levels were generally rated higher in presentation, navigation, attitude towards site, and purchase intention than medium and low adaptation Web sites. - Local Web sites are generally preferred to adapted or standardized Web sites.	- The study does not examine non-US based companies' Web sites in a non-local environment (e.g., does not look at a German company's Web site in the USA).
Singh et al. (2006)	Explore whether foreign consumers prefer highly culturally adapted Web sites to standardized Web sites	Survey across three countries	- Web sites with high adaptation levels were generally rated higher in presentation, navigation, attitude towards site, and purchase intention than medium and low adaptation Web sites, as well as standardized Web sites.	- The study does not examine non-US based companies' Web sites in a non-local environment (e.g., does not look at a German company's Web site in the USA).

Table 23.2   International Internet marketing strategy by nature of product category

Local Responsiveness	Global Integration	
	Low	High
Low	Pure local adaptation strategy (e.g., produce, Internet access)	Global cost leadership strategy (e.g., books, DVDs, videos, industrial components)
High	Nationally differentiated strategy (e.g., clothing, cars, collectibles)	Transnational cost adaptation strategy (e.g., wine, financial products)

Source: Adapted from Guillen (2002).

Finally, Eid and Trueman (2004) propose five sub-factors within the external factor, although these sub-factors are not necessarily specific to international Internet marketing. The sub-factors are trust; security; affordable access; customer acceptance; and building deeper customer relationships. Eid and Trueman's (2004) factors help understand the broad sets of factors involved in the success of international Internet marketing strategy. However, they are somewhat general and do not offer any specific guidelines on the directional impact of the Internet on different international marketing mix decisions. Using the same sample of 123 companies, Eid and Elbeltagi (2005) find that the use of the Internet has a positive effect on B2B marketing efficiency. These findings offer useful initial insights into the impact of the Internet on firm performance in international markets. An important limitation of these studies, however, is that they use self-reported data and their results are not validated by hard data.

Although we have some idea about the direct impact of Internet marketing strategy on firm performance in the international context, we need to better understand the moderating effects of the Internet and Internet marketing strategy on the influences of international marketing mix decisions on firm performance. In the following four sections we focus on these effects.

THE INTERNET AND INTERNATIONAL PRODUCT DEVELOPMENT

The Internet is increasingly used in global product development. For example, Fleetguard,

a manufacturer of filtration and related components for diesel-powered equipment, claims that it is using Web-based design tools such as markup tools and screen sharing so that everyone can connect in an Internet room and look at the same image while communicating in real time (Costlow 2006). A driving force in using the Internet in global product development is shorter design cycles as the workday moves away from 9 am to 5 pm in a single location to 24 hours globally. In fact, the use of the Internet in global product development is becoming common enough that some software companies are creating products and platforms specifically targeted to facilitate the global product development process using the Web. For example, the Product Development Company has introduced a product that allows product development team members across the globe to share information (www.ptc.com).

Companies such as Dell and Schneider-Electric use global Web-based design platforms to develop products through collaborative teams across the world. The primary benefits of Web-based global product development are reduced product development time, ability to use ideas and inputs from design engineers around the world, and better time-leveraging of talent located at different time zones. Sethi, Pant and Sethi (2003) suggest that the effectiveness of Web-based new product development systems depends on factors such as firm strategic orientation, product-market factors, business environment, organizational factors, information technology factors, and partner factors. Of these factors, business environment and partner factors are likely to vary the most across countries, so the benefits of a Web-based global product development system will depend on differences across countries in issues such as competitiveness, regulatory issues, economic trends, and partner technology readiness. Based on the results of a survey, Lewin and Couto (2006) find that small firms are more likely than large firms to use these Web-based systems to work together across the globe with 'offshoring' partners.

The Internet also plays an important part in the diffusion of a new product within and across countries. For example, for products such as pharmaceutical drugs and movies, the Internet serves as a powerful medium to inform potential users and customers of products across countries. Consequently, firms can better leverage the Internet to accelerate the diffusion of products across countries. By the same token, the Internet can act as a detriment to the success of new products in new international markets if customers in the initial markets had adverse experiences. Negative word of mouth from poor customer experiences can travel just as fast as positive word of mouth over the Web across countries, so the Internet has made companies plan more carefully about better designing and managing product launches in the initial markets.

To summarize, the Internet can play an important role in product development across countries. Managed appropriately, the Internet can result in better new product ideas, more effective collaboration, shorter development cycle time, and better leveraging of talent across multiple time zones. The effectiveness of Web-based new product development systems, however, depends on firm strategic orientation, product-market factors, business environment, and organizational, technology and partner factors. The Internet can also play both positive and negative roles in the diffusion of new products across cultures and countries, so firms will have to more carefully plan their product introductions in the initial countries.

THE INTERNET AND INTERNATIONAL COMMUNICATION

The Internet plays a key role both in companies' communication and promotion efforts and in their effectiveness in the international arena. We discuss this role in two types of communication efforts: company-generated and user-generated. Company-generated communication efforts are typically centered on company Web sites. User-generated communication efforts relate to activities such as the creation and management of community sites, blogging, and file sharing.

Company-generated communication

Research shows that culture affects customer attitudes toward company Web sites. Therefore, it is unsurprising that culture has a strong effect on Web site effectiveness. Luna, Peracchio and de Juan (2002) argue that Web sites with low cultural congruity (equivalence of the cultural content on a Web site with the culture of the local geography) increase information processing requirements for local visitors, leading to decreased positive attitudes toward those Web sites. Language is a big part of cultural congruity. Based on experiments, Luna et al. (2002) find that congruency between graphics and brand name or brand attributes moderates language effects on attitudes toward cross-cultural Web sites, and that culturally congruent Web sites result in more positive product attitudes for second language sites than to first language sites.

Business practices appear to be consistent with the conclusion of Luna et al. (2002). For example, Procter & Gamble created regional sites during the 2006 World Cup soccer championship to promote its Gillette, Braun, Duracell and Oral B brands and to raise awareness of its status as an official sponsor. Users from several countries first selected one of four geographical regions on its Web site and then had the ability to choose the language in which the Web site appeared.

The results on the interaction of the Internet with international cultures from the study by Luna *et al.* (2002) should be viewed against the backdrop of two key limitations of the study. The experimental subjects were bilingual and the experiments were restricted to transactional Web sites.

Companies differ in the choice of language on their Web sites in different countries. Based on a survey of 136 e-commerce companies, Shama (2005) reports several findings about their international marketing strategies. About 47 per cent of the companies with international sales have their Web sites only in English, while 43 per cent have both English and 'local language' versions. In terms of customer service, 57 per cent of the companies with international sales have customer service centers in foreign countries. Of these companies, 72 per cent report that their customer service Web sites are only in English. Shama's (2005) analysis, however, is mainly descriptive without theoretical explanations for the results.

Research suggests that local language and local adaptation are keys to successful global marketing on the Internet (e.g., Luna *et al.* 2002; Singh *et al.* 2003b, 2004, 2006). Unfortunately, many barriers and challenges exist for firms wanting to use the Internet in their global marketing aspirations. According to Melewar and Stead (2002), three important barriers are cultural barriers, regulatory barriers, and organizational barriers. Culture comes into play with translations, cultural preferences, and the standardization versus localization decision. Regulatory barriers include issues related to currency, taxes and payments. While the Internet is effective in eliminating physical barriers to global commerce, it poses problems for determining the jurisdiction of countries whose laws are relevant. Organizational barriers also exist as firms struggle with scarcity of resources and channel conflicts.

An important strategic issue related to the Internet in the international context is the globalization versus localization of products and Web sites. Globalization refers to the standardization of products and sites across countries and cultures, while localization refers to the adaptation of products and sites to different countries (Shankar and Donato 2003). Adaptation occurs when a company's local Web site reflects cultural values specific to the country. How much should a company's Web site be adapted to the home country's characteristics and needs? A series of studies by Singh and colleagues (2003a; 2003b, 2004, 2006) provides the following two results. First, many companies' sites are locally adapted. Second, Web sites with high adaptation levels are generally rated high on presentation, navigation, attitude toward the site, and purchase intention. This view is supported by Javalgi *et al.* (2005), who argue that global brand building is facilitated by localized Web sites. An example of local adaptation of a global Web site is McDonald's German Web site shown in Figure 23.2. Visitors to this site are greeted by a lederhosen-clad character performing a traditional local Bavarian folk dance.

Although the studies by Singh and his colleagues offer interesting findings on the international standardization and adaptation of Web sites, they suffer from a few limitations. These studies examine neither the local Web sites of global firms nor the Web sites of non-US based companies. Furthermore, the work by Javalgi *et al.* (2005) is conceptual with no empirical validation. Therefore, a more comprehensive investigation is needed for us to generalize the findings from these studies.

User-generated communication

The Internet allows powerful information sharing among users. It allows the creation of communities that are focused on specific topics, leading to a growing number of global

Figure 23.2   McDonald's localized Internet ad campaign in Germany

brand communities. For example, before the launch of Playstation 2, a global brand community that allowed consumers to discuss and anticipate attributes of the new product emerged. However, because the Internet also allowed 'brand terrorists' (users who can control a brand in ways detrimental to the firm owning the brand), Sony decided to launch its own global brand community so that it could monitor and shape the conversations among consumers. When consumers share their ideas in global brand communities, they affect the way the products are marketed and distributed (Deshpandé 2002). Another example is Stormhoek Wines in South Africa. Through the use of various online marketing activities, including blogging, Stormhoek increased its shipments to the UK from 50 000 cases in 2005 to 350 000 cases in 2007 (*Business Day* 2007).

Other examples of global online brand communities include Nike, Microsoft, General Motors, and Google. Figures 23.3 and 23.4 shows screen shots of global user

community Web pages for Nike's NikePlus and Microsoft's Silverlight, respectively. NikePlus, designed with music collaboration from Apple, offers an array of useful tools for running enthusiasts. These tools include the ability to manage own runs, issuing running challenge to friends, socializing with other community members across the world, obtaining music through Apple, and sharing information through blogs. Silverlight is a cross-browser, cross-platform plug-in for delivering the next generation of media experiences and rich interactive applications (RIAs) for the Web. The developers for this product are located across the globe and constitute a potentially strong global brand community. The major purpose of these user-generated communication efforts is to create a superior customer experience for a worldwide user base.

In summary, the Internet has an important influence on the effect of communication and promotion on firm performance. By better understanding customer needs across different

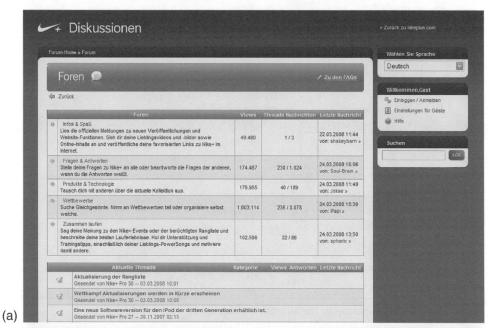

Figure 23.3 (a) Online community for Nike's NikePlus User-Generated Discussion Forum in German; (b) online community for Nike's NikePlus Spanish/Latin America community site

Figure 23.4   Online community for Microsoft Silverlight

countries and cultures, firms can develop suitable content on their Web sites in different markets. They could also facilitate the development of user-generated communication efforts that have positive effects on firm performance.

THE INTERNET AND INTERNATIONAL PRICING

The Internet affects prices and the dispersion of prices across sellers for many items. The Internet has allowed different segments to become aware of prices offered to one another, regardless of where the segments are physically located. For example, the pricing of pharmaceuticals in Europe is changing because consumers know that the price of a drug in Germany is different from that of the identical drug in Italy. Thus, the use of pricing

as a tool to discriminate among consumers or establish the global positioning of a product is changing (Deshpandé 2002). Deshpandé's (2002) analysis, however, is conceptual and not empirically validated.

Consider the case of pricing of Apple's *iTunes* in Europe (Sweeny 2008). Until 2008, the prices for downloading a song or album through *iTunes* were higher in the United Kingdom (UK) than in 16 other European countries. For example, in France and Germany, music buyers were charged €0.99 (74p) per track, while British music fans were charged 79p. Similarly, the average price of an album through *iTunes* in the UK was £7.99, while that across the rest of the continent was €9.99 (£7.48). Following consumer complaints, the European Commission investigated Apple for unfair pricing. In early 2008, Apple agreed to reduce the price it charges to UK users to buy tracks from *iTunes* by almost 10 per cent within six months to bring them in line with the rest of Europe. Although Apple finally made the decision to follow a harmonized pan-European pricing policy, its ability to do so also depends on the willingness of the major record labels to adopt a pan-European standardized view of pricing.

The *iTunes* example highlights the role of price transparency in firms' pricing strategy across international markets. Although the Internet has brought increased transparency on costs and prices, it has also allowed firms to highlight and differentiate on non-price attributes (Shankar, Rangaswamy, and Pusateri 2001). It is possible for firms to tailor their offerings to the needs of consumers in different countries or offer branded variants across countries, thereby reducing the inclination or ability to directly compare prices of the same item across countries.

There are differences among prices and the dispersion of prices among retailers across different countries. Ancarani *et al.* (2005) argue that on the one hand, retailer price levels and dispersion may be similar across countries because: (1) channel competition and the roles of channels are increasingly similar across countries; and (2) the borderless feature and transparency of the Internet can have a positive influence on the similarity of retailer pricing across countries. However, on the other hand they suggest that retailer price levels and dispersion may be different across countries because: (1) the adoption rate of the Internet is different in different countries; (2) consumer attitudes toward the Internet may be different across countries; and (3) price sensitivities and competitive landscape may differ across countries.

Ancarani *et al.* (2005) present an empirical analysis of retailer price levels and dispersion using data collected for different product categories (e.g., books, CDs) in three European countries, namely, France, Germany, and Italy. Their results show that in general, price levels, including shipping costs, are higher online than offline in each of these three countries and that price dispersion is persistent across these countries. Multichannel retailers have the highest price levels in each of these countries, but they do not exhibit the highest price dispersion. Their results suggest that the opportunities for price differentiation for a given type of retailer may be different in different countries. Their data, however, are restricted to two product categories in three group 7 (G7) countries and may not be generalizable across developing economies.

To summarize, consumer and company uses of the Internet have important influences on firm prices and on the effect of pricing on firm performance. The Internet promotes price transparency and allows customers to compare prices across countries. However, empirical analysis of price levels and price dispersion across countries suggest that price dispersion is persistent across countries, and the opportunities for price differentiation do exist and may be different across countries.

THE INTERNET AND INTERNATIONAL DISTRIBUTION

The Internet serves as a distribution channel for many firms. It often acts as a direct distribution channel for marketers of items ranging from apparel to computer hardware and software to books to CDs and DVDs to electronic equipment. In many cases, the Internet serves as a substitute channel for other distribution channels such as physical stores and catalogs. In other cases, it acts as a complementary channel. The use of the Internet as an important distribution channel in the emerging practice of multichannel marketing is growing (Kushwaha and Shankar 2007).

In the international context, the use of the Internet as a distribution channel is significant because it allows many firms to reach a wide international audience without substantially increasing the cost of channel development. However, the practice of multichannel marketing in the international context would depend on the extent of substitute or complementary effects of the Internet relative to other channels in each country. In countries where the complementarity of the Internet with other channels is high, firms will practice greater multichannel marketing than in countries where the Internet is perceived as a substitute to other channels.

The evidence for the use and success of the Internet as a distribution channel in the international context, however, is mixed. While many firms use their Web sites as store fronts to customers in multiple countries and fulfill orders that they receive through their sites, in case studies of six international software firms, Moen *et al.* (2003) find that the Internet is not used as the primary sales and distribution tool. Because of the level of investment required by the clients, the firms in the study believed that, in addition to the Internet, physical market presence and personal contact were more important for sales. However, the firms studied do believe the Internet can aid in their personal selling efforts by developing a positive company image. Information designed for and placed on the Internet can improve a firm's reputation and credibility, making personal selling easier in international markets.

The example of Stormhoek Wines in South Africa illustrates how the use of the Internet can help global distribution for some types of products. Stormhoek enlisted the help of UK bloggers in a bid to sell directly to UK consumers. Over a period of two years, it became 'the wine of the blogging world'. Stormhoek's shipments to the UK increased from 50 000 cases in 2005 to 350 000 in 2007 (*Business Day* 2007). A firm's extent of use of the Internet as a distribution channel in each country may depend on the country, customer, company, and competition factors. The country factors include regulatory issues, taxes, transportation modes, geographical proximity of the country to fulfillment center, Internet penetration level, and logistical infrastructure. Customer factors include desired delivery speed, willingness to pay, the extent of physical inspection desired,

and the influence of consumer-generated Internet media. Company factors comprise market reach goals, distribution competency, fulfillment capability, shipping costs, and the like. Competition factors include the number and intensity of competitors in that country, the distribution channels of competitors in the country, channel expertise of competitors, and anticipated channel moves of competitors. Depending on the combination of these factors, a firm may tailor the extent of the use of the Internet as a distribution channel for different countries.

It is reasonable to expect that a well-designed channel strategy involving the Web across international markets should improve firm performance. However, aside from anecdotal evidence, the effects of the Web as a distribution channel on firm performance across international markets are not well known.

In summary, there is mixed evidence on the use of the Internet as a distribution channel in international markets. The use of the Web as a channel is contingent on several country, customer, company, and competition factors. Although the use of the Web as a channel is likely to have a positive effect on firm performance in international markets, insufficient research exists on this topic for us to make a strong conclusion.

EMERGING TRENDS AND FUTURE ISSUES

As Internet penetration in different countries continues to climb, the role of the Internet in international marketing will continue to rise. The impact will be more significant and often more dramatic in countries (such as those in Africa) where Internet penetration is still low and has enormous possibilities for improvement. In some countries, the ability of the Internet as a viable new medium of communication and channel of distribution can significantly impact the economic rise of the population.

A major development related to the Internet is the spread and rise of mobile media and technology across the world. Mobile devices such as cell phones, personal digital assistants, MP3 players (e.g., iPod), and hybrid devices (e.g., iPhone) now provide more pervasive connectivity to Web sites and users through mobile Internet than ever before. Many developing countries are leapfrogging others in the use of the mobile Internet and email (through short-messaging service or SMS). For example, two emerging economic superpowers, China and India, are major beneficiaries of the surge of mobile Internet. China has the biggest user base of mobile phone subscribers while India has the fastest growing mobile subscriber base (Balasubramanian and Shankar 2008). Such rapid penetration of the mobile Internet and connectivity will accelerate the impact of Internet marketing activities on firm performance across the world.

The rise in importance of the Internet and the mobile media in the international context offers several opportunities for future research on relevant managerial issues. Important questions in this regard are: How does customer behavior with regard to the use of the Internet vary across countries? How do customers differ in mobile media usage across countries? How does the mobile Internet affect a firm's marketing mix decisions? What impact does the mobile Internet have on firm performance? What is the impact of user-generated communication among customers across diverse cultures on the diffusion of products across countries?

With regard to measures of firm performance, research on the Internet and international marketing has at best focused on company sales. Future research should examine measures such as profits and shareholder value. The availability of data on Internet marketing activities in the international context will continue to be a challenge. In particular, because company data on costs and profits by country are confidential, it would be difficult to collect such data. Nevertheless, more empirical research in these areas will offer deeper insights into Internet and international marketing.

Very little is known on the differences between goods and services with regard to the role of the Internet in international marketing. Are the effects of the Internet on international marketing mix decisions and on the relationships between these decisions and firm performance the same for goods and services? In particular, are there differences between digitizable goods and digitizable services? Digitizable products (e.g., books music, video, software) are those that can be easily distributed over the Internet to customers. In the international context, these products assume significance as they can be downloaded by customers in multiple countries any time. The *iTunes* is an example of such a digitizable product. Another digitizable product, software as service (SAS), is also growing in popularity. Future research could address these interesting questions and topics.

CONCLUSION

The advent and rapid growth of the Internet has had a substantial impact on international marketing. The Internet and Internet marketing strategy have both a direct effect and moderating effects on the impact of marketing mix decisions on firm performance. With regard to international product development, the Internet has significant influence on the effectiveness and speed of new product development and its impact on firm performance. The Internet also has an important role in the effects of both company- and user-generated communication efforts on firm performance. On the international pricing dimension, the Web allows more pricing transparency, but also permits opportunities for differentiation across countries. With regards to international distribution, the Web may serve as either a substitute or a complementary channel in different international markets, and smart management of the Internet, together with other channels, could help firms improve performance in international markets.

Going forward, continued Internet penetration and the surging growth of mobile media are expected to result in continuing changes in the way international marketing is practiced and in the impact of international marketing decisions on firm performance. More research is needed to better understand the relationships among the Internet, mobile Internet, marketing mix decisions, and firm performance in the international context.

ACKNOWLEDGMENT

Table 23.2: This figure was orginally featured in an article by Mauro F. Guillen. This article was published in *Business Horizons* (May–June), Guillen, Mauro, F., " What is the Best Global Strategy for the Internet", pp. 39–46, © Elsevier (2002).

REFERENCES

Ancarani, F., Jacob, F., Jallat, F. and Shankar, V. (2005) *Are Price Levels and Price Dispersion Among Retailer Types Similar Across Countries? A Cross-Country Empirical Analysis*, Presentation, Marketing Science Conference, Atlanta, GA.

Balasubramanian, S. and Shankar, V. (2008) *Mobile Interactive Marketing*. Working Paper. Chapel Hill, NC: University of North Carolina.

Business Day (2007) 'Blogging, MXit challenge traditional marketing', June 25, 5.

Costlow, T. (2006) 'Design goes global: Web fuels collaborative product development', *Design News*, March 20, 61.

Deshpandé, R. (2002) 'Performance companies', *International Journal of Medical Marketing*, 2(3): 225–231.

Eid, R. and Elbeltagi, I. (2005) 'The influence of the Internet on B-to-B international marketing activities: an empirical study of the UK companies', *Journal of Euromarketing*, 15(2): 51–73.

Eid, R. and Trueman, M. (2004) 'Factors affecting the success of business-to-business Internet Marketing (B-to-B IIM): an empirical study of UK companies', *Industrial Management and Data Systems*, 104(1), 16–30.

Guillen, M. F. (2002) 'What is the best global strategy for the Internet?', *Business Horizons*, (May-June), 39–46.

Javalgi, R. G., Radulovick, L. P., Pendleton, G. and Scherer, R. F. (2005) 'Sustainable competitive advantage of Internet firms: A strategic framework and implications for global marketers', *International Marketing Review*, 22(6), 658–672.

Jones, G. (2006) 'P&G launches global online brand push for world cup tie-in', *New Media Age*, June 15: 4.

Kushwaha, T., Shankar, V. (2007) *'Single Channel vs. Multichannel Customers: Determinants and Value to Retailers'*. Working Paper. College Station, TX: Texas A&M University.

Lewin, A. Y. and Couto, V. (2006) *'Next Generation Offshoring: The Globalization of Innovation'*. Offshoring Research Network, 2006 Survey Report. Executive summary available at https://offshoring.fuqua.duke.edu/ORNreport_exec_summary.pdf.

Luna, D., Peracchio, L. A. and de Juan, M. D. (2002) 'Cross-cultural and cognitive aspects of web site navigation', *Journal of the Academy of Marketing Science*, 30(4), 397–410.

Melewar, T. C. and Stead, C. (2002) 'The impact of information technology on global marketing strategies', *Journal of General Management*, 27(4): 29–40.

Moen, Ø., Endresen, I. and Gavlen, M. (2003) 'Use of the Internet in international marketing: A case study of small computer software firms', *Journal of International Marketing*, 11(4), 129–149.

Sethi, R., Pant, S. and Sethi, A. (2003) 'Web-based product development systems for integration and new product outcomes: A conceptual framework', *Journal of Product Innovation Management*, 20(1), 37–56.

Shama, A. (2005) 'An empirical study of the international marketing strategies of E-Commerce companies', *Thunderbird International Business Review*, 47(6), 695–709.

Shankar, V. and Donato, M. P. (2003) 'Personalization of Global Sales and Marketing Activities in the Digital Economy', in N. Pal and A. Rangaswamy, (eds), *Power of One*. Penn State University, University Park, PA: eBRC Press.

Shankar, V., Rangaswamy, A. and Pusateri, M. (2001) *The Online Medium and Customer Price Sensitivity*. Working Paper. University Park, PA: Penn State University.

Singh, N., Fassott, G. Zhao, H. and Boughton, P. D. (2006) 'A cross-cultural analysis of German, Chinese and Indian consumers' perception of web site adaptation', *Journal of Consumer Behavior*, 5 (February): 56–68.

Singh, N., Furrer, O. and Ostinelli, M. (2004) 'To localize or to standardize on the web: empirical evidence from Italy, India, Netherlands, Spain, and Switzerland', *The Multinational Business Review*, 12(1), 69–87.

Singh, N., Zhao, H. and Hu, X. (2003a) 'Analyzing the cultural content of web sites: A cross-national comparison of China, India, Japan, and US', *International Marketing Review*, 22(2), 129–146.

Singh, N., Zhao, H. and Hu, X. (2003b) 'Cultural adaptation on the Web: A study of American companies' domestic and Chinese web sites', *Journal of Global Information Management*, 11(3), 63–80.

Sweeny, M. (2008) 'Apple to cut UK prices for iTunes tracks', *The Guardian*, 8 January.

24

Organizational Heritage, Institutional Changes and Strategic Responses of Firms from Emerging Economics

Preet S. Aulakh and Raveendra Chittoor

INTRODUCTION

A significant aspect of the changes in the global economy in the last two decades is the economic liberalization of protected markets and the further liberalization of market economies. As part of these reforms, a number of developing countries implemented policies aimed at encouraging competition in the domestic marketplace, urging domestic firms to build international levels of competitiveness, and allowing multinational enterprises (MNEs) to enter their erstwhile protected markets. In the context of these institutional reforms, a critical question faced by local firms in developing countries is how to respond to the challenges presented by a radically changed competitive environment. The nature of local firms' strategic responses in this changed environment has strong implications for the perceived success or failure of economic reforms undertaken by developing country governments.

Since the inception of economic reforms in a number of developing economies, firms from the so called third-world countries have come a long way: 'While globalization has opened new markets to rich-world companies, it has also given birth to a fast moving, sharp-toothed new multinational that is emerging from the poor world' (*The Economist* 2007, p. 11). Similarly, a report by the Boston Consulting Group notes that 'a revolution in global business is under way. Companies based in rapidly developing economies (RDEs) ... armed with ambitious leaders, low costs, appealing products or services, and modern facilities and systems, are expanding overseas and will radically transform industries and markets around the world' (BCG 2006, p. 5). These reports are further supported by recent high-profile acquisitions of foreign companies by firms from developing economies, as well as the general upward trajectory of the increased pace of outward foreign direct investment flows from these countries, which grew from $65 billion in 1980 to $849 billion in 2002 (UNCTAD 2006).

While the anecdotal evidence and reports in the business press are hailing the 'transformative' nature of emerging economy firms to global competition, academic research on firms from developing economies is still in its infancy. According to Hoskisson *et al.* (2000) emerging markets present unique environments and challenges that require re-examination of Western theories and development of new concepts or modification of old ones. Dunning (1999) stated that the motives as well as determinants of internationalization are different for different countries or regions and hence theories of multinational activity need to be set in specific geographical context. The purpose of this chapter is to take stock of existing research on emerging economy firms in two broad areas (and the related research questions):

1 Transformation of firms within developing economies in response to institutional changes emanating from economic liberalization and globalization. (Was the response of firms primarily to protect their turf from the threat of competition by developing, acquiring and deploying critical resources or to exploit new opportunities by aggressively entering new industries? Has the strategic response of firms systematically changed over time, thereby forming distinct phases in the post-liberalization era? What kind of theoretical lenses best explain the phenomena? What are the performance implications of different types of strategic responses?)
2 Internationalization/multinationalization strategies and performance of emerging economy firms. (What were the determinant characteristics of firms that went for internationalization? What were the broad types of strategies deployed by them to succeed in developed and developing markets? What were the determinants of their entry mode choices and subsequent mode choices for doing business in foreign markets? What type

of resources and capabilities were critical for their successful internationalization? How did they acquire, develop and leverage those resources and capabilities? Do some of the unique characteristics of emerging economy firms and their internationalization processes, present opportunities for development of new theories that are very distinct from Western theories?)

We conduct a review of extant literature on the above topics. A thorough search of electronic databases such as PROQUEST, EBSCO and JSTOR was done for literature on emerging economies, as well as a separate search was conducted in major journals and books. We also examined a number of special issues related to emerging economy firms to identify the major studies related to the focus of our chapter. These include *Academy of Management Review* (2000), *Academy of Management Journal* (2000), *Journal of International Management* (2007), *Journal of International Business Studies* (2007), and *Journal of Management Studies* (2005). Particular focus was paid to the 1994–2007 period, given the fact that the topic chosen is a young field, though a few select articles of the earlier period too were reviewed. As in any review article, our purpose is not to provide an exhaustive review, but to summarize some of the key ideas that are prevalent in existing research. Furthermore, at the end of the chapter, we identify some key areas that remain under-examined and provide directions for future research. We also want to note that there are two other streams of research related to emerging economies, one dealing with macro-level studies related to the liberalization process in emerging economies (e.g., Gillespie 1984; Gillespie and Alden 1989) and the second related to foreign MNCs' opportunities, entry modes and competitive strategies in these liberalizing economies (e.g., Wright *et al.* 2005). While both these research streams have provided important insights to our understanding of emerging economies at both macro- and micro-levels, these are beyond the scope of our chapter.

INSTITUTIONAL CHANGES AND FIRM TRANSFORMATIONS IN EMERGING ECONOMIES

Firms from emerging markets face turbulent environments with rapid changes in political, economic and institutional forces. These firms not only have to cope with these turbulent changes, but also face new competition, which includes global firms entering domestic markets due to opening up of trade boundaries, liberalization and deregulation. What are the theoretical perspectives that can best explain the strategic response and choices of emerging market firms in such environments? In a context such as this, what types of research issues have attracted the attention of strategy scholars?

Organizational transformation

One of the important studies examining organizational transformation in emerging economies was a conceptual paper by Newman (2000). She argued that institutional changes in Eastern and Central Europe in the 1990s 'initiated a period of intense social, political, and economic change in the region' that 'destroyed the underlying assumptions of economic activity' (Newman 2000, p. 602). Such monumental changes required second-order organizational learning (defined as change in the core values, templates and archetypes). However, it was speculated that firms which were more embedded with the past institutional environment were less likely to accomplish second-order transformation necessitated by changed 'rules of the game'. This view finds empirical support in a study on Lithuania. Kriauciunas and Kale (2006) surveyed 67 firms to assess the factors that influence transition economy firms to change their operating know-how and knowledge sets (i.e., second-order learning defined by Newman (2000)) to compete in a changed environment. Their findings suggest firms that were formed during the socialist era (thus having a 'socialist imprinting') were less able to change their operating knowledge. In addition, firms that were able to access external sources of knowledge were better able to meet the 'demands of the new market-oriented environment' (Kriauciunas and Kale 2006, p. 659).

State-owned enterprises and privatization

One way for organizational transformation and to access outside resources (including capital, technology, and managerial know-how) is through the privatization of state-owned enterprises in a number of developing economies as part of the liberalization process. As stated by Zahra et al.:

> [b]y placing the means of production outside of state ownership and control, privatization unleashes the forces and discipline of the free market .... Privatization, therefore, has the potential to transform national economies, industries, and organizations by infusing a spirit of entrepreneurial risk taking. These changes are in process currently across the world's six major continents, making privatization an integral part of emerging, developing, and developed countries' twenty-first-century strategic agendas. Effective privatizations however, ... without creating significant unemployment and related disruptions, are difficult to achieve. (2000, pp. 509–510)

In this regard, a number of studies have examined strategic transformation through privatization of state-owned enterprises (SOEs). Ramamurti (2000) proposed a multi-level theoretical model incorporating firm-, industry- and country-level factors to explain the likelihood of a particular SOE being privatized and how they impact post-privatization performance of these firms. Johnson, Smith and Codling (2000), Cuervo and Villalonga (2000) and Dharwadkar, George and Brandes (2000) use institutional, public choice and agency theories, respectively, to address managerial level transformation in privatizing organizations through restructuring of reward and incentive structures as well as overall corporate governance aspects. Spicer, McDermott and Kogut (2000, p. 630), using the case study of privatization in Central Europe, suggest that 'entrepreneurship is better fostered through gradualist policies permitting negotiated solutions to restructuring, as opposed to market-driven reforms'. Konings, Cayseele and Warzynski (2005) use panel data of Bulgarian and Romanian manufacturing firms and suggest that creation of competitive markets and privatization go hand-in-hand.

The general approach of gradualist reforms and transformation is seen in the liberalization model followed by China, where state-owned enterprises continue to play an important role. However, organizational transformation in a market-based regime is accomplished through accessing external resources through inter-organizational collaborations and changes in intra-organizational norms and culture. Using a sample of Chinese state-owned pharmaceutical firms, White (2000) examined the impact of a set of internal and external factors on how the state-owned enterprises acquire new technology by make, buy or ally decisions. The external factors considered are suggested by transaction cost and resource dependency perspectives and the internal factors are suggested primarily by an organizational capabilities perspective. One of the key findings of the study was that these factors were primarily based on subjective managerial perceptions of the threat of opportunistic behavior by other organizations and the required marginal investment in organizational capabilities. Ralston *et al.* (2006) examine the transformation of Chinese state-owned enterprises from hierarchical and bureaucratic structures to market-oriented forms through a change in organizational cultures. Peng and Luo (2000) demonstrate that Chinese firm managers' micro personal ties with other executives and government officials helped improve organizational performance.

Hitt *et al.* (2000) study the resource acquisition and learning opportunities for emerging economy firms through international alliances. Their main contribution was that partner selection criteria are context-dependent and vary across emerging and developed economies. In particular, they find that the firms from emerging markets place greater importance on financial assets, technical capabilities, intangible assets and willingness to share expertise as criteria for partner selection. On the other hand, firms in developed markets are found to stress unique competencies, knowledge and access to local markets. In a follow-up comparative study of firms from China and Russia, Hitt *et al.*: find

> that China's more stable and supportive institutional environment has helped Chinese firms take a longer-term view of alliance partner selection, focusing more on the potential partner's intangible assets along with technological and managerial capabilities. In contrast, the less stable Russian institutional environment has influenced Russian managers to focus more on the short term, selecting partners that provide access to financial capital and complementary capabilities so as to enhance their firms' ability to weather that nation's turbulent environment. (2004, p. 173)

The institutional changes experienced in the centrally planned command economies such as China and Eastern European countries manifested through full privatization of state-owned enterprises (e.g., Eastern Europe) or partial privatization (e.g., China through the mode of equity joint ventures). This, in turn, brought about dramatic increases in inflows of foreign direct investment (FDI) and led to high rates of growth, primarily driven by inward FDI. A number of other emerging economies such as India, Brazil, and Mexico initiated liberalization through opening up their markets and general deregulation of key sectors. This resulted in stronger competition from domestic and foreign players and the issue of strategic transformation in these economies is fundamentally different. Aggarwal (2000) examined the innovation strategies of Indian firms in the pre- and post-liberalization era. She finds that 'unlike in a regulated regime where technology imports [were] viewed important for filling gaps in domestic technological capabilities, in a deregulated regime technology upgradation seems to be the major role of technology imports' (p. 1081). Similarly, Chittoor *et al.* (2008) study the transformation of the Indian pharmaceutical industry due to institutional changes brought about by liberalization and intellectual property regime change. They find dynamic effects of arm's length technology and financial imports to build capabilities to compete in both domestic and international markets.

Strategic choices for emerging market firms

Besides the focus on institutional changes and the associated organizational transformations described above, another stream of research has examined strategic choices of emerging economy firms as they face greater competition from foreign MNCs in their liberalized domestic markets. In one of the first such studies, Kim and Lim (1988) attempted to test whether some widely used strategic concepts in the West, such as Porter's generic strategies, are applicable in a context that is very different – that of high-growth electronics industry in a rapidly developing country of Korea. The authors collected data from 54 electronics firms on sets of environmental and strategic variables and, through cluster analysis, divided the firms into four distinct strategic groups in four different environmental settings. The study found that even in the same industry the environment was perceived in four distinctly different ways. Also the generic strategies identified in the study were similar to those developed in industrialized economies. The strategies of cost leadership, differentiation and focus emerged, though not as pure types but mostly as a mix of two generic strategies.

With the resurgence of firms from emerging economies, especially in the latter half of the nineties, scholars began to acknowledge that these firms can hold fort against MNCs from developed countries by leveraging on some of their unique strengths. Offering some strategic prescription to emerging

market firms, Craig and Douglas (1997) wrote that these firms need to move beyond the cost-based strategies that rely on low cost labour and other cheap resources to value-creating strategies. They recommended six generic strategies for firms from emerging markets: (1) low-cost commodity; (2) component manufacturing; (3) private-label manufacturing; (4) low-cost leader; (5) first-generation technology; and (6) specialized niche. These six strategies represent respectively an increasing value appropriation in the transnational value chain and require moving up the value chain from strategy 1 to strategy 6. The paper also discussed in depth the pros and cons of each of these strategies.

Another normative article on the strategic choices for emerging market firms was by Dawar and Frost (1999). Arguing that the intensity of the pressures of globalization vary significantly across industries, they offer a typology of strategic options for local companies in emerging markets to survive and compete with global giants. They propose that the emerging market firms have a set of unique assets or resources that offer them competitive advantages vis-à-vis global giants, some of which can also be transferred overseas to compete effectively in the global market place. The authors present four broad strategic options for emerging market firms: (1) Defender – when globalization pressures are weak and when company's unique assets are not transferable abroad, the company should concentrate on defending its turf; (2) Extender – when globalization pressures are weak and when unique assets are transferable abroad, the company can extend its success to limited markets abroad; (3) Dodger – when globalization pressures are strong and when unique assets are not transferable abroad, the company can try and dodge its global rivals by leveraging on its unique assets; and (4) Contender – when globalization pressures are strong and when company's assets are transferable, the company may actually be able to compete head on with multinationals.

Peng (2000) examined strategic choices during institutional transitions. Severe institutional transitions pose a challenge to organizations as they can cope when the new rules are not completely known. In such circumstances, organizations face two broad strategic choices – a network-based strategy emphasizing managers' inter-personal ties as well as the firm's inter-organizational relationships with other firms; and a market-based strategy that relies on the firm's unique competitive resources and capabilities. Also, during such transitions, three types of firms emerge – incumbent firms, entrepreneurial start-ups and foreign entrants. In the initial phases of transitions, all the three types of firms are likely to compete on the basis of networks and relationships rather than competitive resources and capabilities. In this phase, in order to pursue network-based strategies even foreign entrants are more likely to form joint ventures and alliances. During the later phases of transitions, except old incumbent firms that continue to compete based on relationships, all other types of firms such as new, young incumbent firms, start-ups and foreign entrants, will move towards competing based on competitive resources and capabilities through restructuring and transformation.

The role of business groups

A rich body of work has established the significance of business groups in the socio-economic landscape of emerging economies (Strachen 1976; Amsden 1989; Keister 1998; Khanna and Palepu 1997, 1999; Ghemawat and Khanna 1998). Ranging from Korean *Chaebols*, Turkish *families*, Latin American and Spanish *grupos* to Indian business *groups*, they have been defined as 'a set of firms which, though legally independent, are bound together by a constellation of formal and informal ties and are accustomed to taking coordinated action' (Khanna and Rivkin 2001, p. 47). While the focus of earlier research was to understand the rationale

behind business groups, and relate their underlying characteristics to different country contexts (e.g., Khanna and Palepu 2000a, 2000b; Guillen 2000; Kock and Guillen 2001), recent studies have been motivated by an attempt to understand their strategic responses to institutional transformations that potentially undermine the very reasons for group formation in the first place (e.g., Hoskisson *et al.* 2004, 2005; Yiu, Bruton and Lu 2005).

Business groups are a strategic response to strategic factor market imperfections in emerging economies (Khanna and Palepu 2000a; Khanna and Rivkin 2001). Due to information asymmetries, poor contract enforcement, and imperfect regulatory structures, institutional voids tend to develop in product, labor and capital markets. The absence of intermediary institutions increases transaction costs in acquiring inputs such as technology, finance and managerial talent. In response, business groups emerge. Performing the role of missing institutional intermediaries, business groups fill these voids by generating their own internal markets for financial capital and managerial talent. Member firms of a group are thus able to leverage their group's scale, scope, track record and reputation and benefit from sheer availability and lower input costs of scarce resources. In a large-sample study conducted using data from Indian firms, divided between those affiliated to and not affiliated to business groups, Khanna and Palepu (2000b) find evidence to support that large diversified business groups add value. They find that accounting and stock market performance measures initially decline with group diversification and subsequently increase once the group diversification crosses a threshold level.

Guillen (2000) offered an alternative view on the rationale for business groups. Claiming that the prevailing predominant explanations for existence of business groups in emerging economies – market imperfections, authority structures or late development – were not convincing enough, the author offers a resource-based view explanation. Guillen posits that firms and entrepreneurs create business groups when they acquire and possess resources and capabilities to enter new industries quickly and in a cost-effective manner. Also, it is argued that this capability will be inimitable only under conditions of asymmetric foreign trade and investment, which limit this capability to a select few firms. Findings of an empirical study based on cross-sectional data on business groups from nine emerging economies indicate that asymmetries in foreign trade and investment are associated with business groups after controlling for alternative explanations.

In a recent study on business groups, rejecting the established view that business groups in emerging markets exist primarily to fill institutional voids, Yiu *et al.* (2005) attempted to integrate the resource-based view with the institutional view by proposing that the value created by the business groups varied depending on the type of resources and capabilities they were able to acquire. Unlike most studies on business groups that were conducted at the member firm level, this study examined directly a sample of 224 largest business groups in China. Yiu *et al.* (2005) proposed that there were two kinds of potential resources and capabilities that a business group could possess – (1) endowed and (2) acquired/developed resources. Age of the group, government ownership, top management background, etc. were classified as endowed resources, whereas those acquired through mergers and acquisitions, development of internal capabilities, international diversification and so on were classified as acquired/developed resources. The results of the study indicated that most of the endowed resources did not help business groups to create a competitive edge. Instead, the business groups that had sought to develop new capabilities through acquisitions, internal development, or international diversification showed better group performance.

Carney and Gedajlovic (2003) studied the origin, evolution and growth of Chinese Family Business Groups (FBGs) in East and Southeast Asia. The authors adopt a historical perspective to identify and describe the environmental conditions that led to the emergence of Chinese FBGs and how their organizational forms and business practices (administrative heritage) have co-evolved with their distinct institutional environments in a path-dependent manner. As a consequence, a firm's administrative heritage may act as a stumbling block to respond to the environmental challenges of a subsequent era. The authors point out, as one of the key limitations of these FBGs, a lack of capacity for strategic innovation. Due to these reasons, they predict that the administrative heritage of the FBGs may slow down industrial reform in the East and Southeast Asian region.

In spite of their benefits, some associated costs of business groups have also been identified (Keister 1998; Khanna and Palepu 2000). While controlling families have been known to interfere in both tactical and strategic decision-making, member firms tend to suffer from conflict of interests between controlling (typically family) and minority shareholders. Bertrand, Mehta and Mullainathan (2002) found evidence that controlling shareholders of Indian business groups engage in *tunneling*, or moving profits from firms where they have low cash flow rights to those where they have high cash-flow rights. Further, due to inequity and nepotism, inefficient compensation systems tend to develop across group companies, with detrimental effects on market for talent. Coupled with the security that group affiliation offers, managers of group-affiliated firms typically have weaker incentives to run their firms efficiently (Khanna and Rivkin 2001). As the variety of the businesses within a group increases, the dominant logic of the traditional businesses may prove to be increasingly inadequate when applied to emerging initiatives, thus leading to suboptimal decisions and organizational inertia.

Recent research has queried the relevance as well as the ability of business groups to respond to disruptive institutional changes arising due to economic liberalization. As emerging economies continue to improve their economic institutions, largely as a consequence of market reforms, the performance of many large business groups, which acted as market-substitute mechanisms, has been reduced (Hoskisson *et al.* 2005). Business group affiliation, which was considered a plus during periods of under-developed capital markets and protectionist regimes that hindered the inflow of required technological know-how and other resources, is thus being questioned in a post-liberalization era. Local firms require second-order organizational changes in response to market reforms, which in turn requires greater emphasis on both exploratory and exploitative learning (Newman 2000). Firms that are embedded in past institutional frameworks are, however, less likely and slower to undertake transformations when faced with environmental changes than firms that are less so (Greenwood and Hinings 1996; Newman 2000; Kriauciunas and Kale 2006). For instance, Hoskisson, *et al.* (2004) find that, while business group affiliated firms were more responsive in restructuring their assets than non-group affiliated firms to environmental contingencies that arose from domestic opportunities, they were less responsive than independent firms to regulatory changes and new competition. Similarly, given their market power and institutional positioning, business groups are more likely to follow sustaining strategies than independent firms during periods of environmental upheaval (Hoskisson *et al.* 2005). Khanna and Palepu (2000a) examine the issues of the future of business groups, especially in the changing institutional context brought about by a wave of deregulation in the emerging economies. The paper offers evidence from Chile, which has undergone significant changes in its institutional context, through a study of changes in the value creation by business groups between the late 1980s and the mid-1990s. Contrary to the evidence from studies in the western context, the authors find support

to their hypothesis that marginal increases in group (unrelated) diversification will lead to marginal increase in firm performance, though the net benefits are found to kick in after the diversification reaches a threshold. This threshold was found to rise as market institutions evolve over time. The authors also find a non-diversification-related net positive effect of group affiliation, which however diminish over time as emerging markets evolve. The authors conclude that the value-creating potential of business groups is reduced gradually with the evolution of the institutional context.

Kim *et al.* (2004) propose an evolutionary model of the business groups by tracing the evolution and restructuring of two large business groups in Korea – the LG group and Hyundai Motors. The 30 largest *Chaebols* formed the backbone of Korean economy, but many of them suffered severe financial problems during the Asian crisis in 1997. Many of the *Chaebols* undertook restructuring measures either on government directive or on their own. The authors propose that the sources of value-creating potential of business groups change and evolve along with its institutional environment and the strategy-structure fit is a key determinant of the performance of the diversified business groups. Initially, under weak market environments, the internal market capability of *Chaebols* (mainly unrelated business groups) under the organizational structure of co-operative M-form served as a rare and valuable resource. However, with increased competition and evolution of markets, the value of the internal market capability diminished. The *Chaebols* have two restructuring options – either change their structure to competitive M-form or refocus themselves into related businesses.

To conclude this section, the research reviewed so far deals primarily with the impact of institutional changes on organizational transformations in emerging economies. These include radical transformation, such as sale of erstwhile state-owned enterprises to private hands who are often foreign multinationals, capability transformation through external acquisition of resources and internal governance mechanisms to cope with external competitors entering domestic markets, and evolution of the business group functions in market-oriented environments. Another strategic response and which resonates well with the export-led development goals of emerging economy governments, is through aggressive internationalization strategies. We now turn to the literature that examines the increased participation of developing economy firms in global markets.

INTERNATIONALIZATION OF EMERGING MARKET FIRMS

There is a growing interest in understanding the competitive strategies of firms from these economies as they respond to institutional transitions and begin to compete in global markets (Aulakh 2007; OECD 2006; *Business Week* 2006; BCG 2006). Part of this interest arises from unique business models of these firms, derived from the diverse institutional contexts as some of them transform to 'emerging multinationals', directly competing with the 'traditional MNCs' from developed economies. However, the phenomenon of internationalizing developing economy firms is not new and there was a stream of studies in the 1980s that examined the 'third world multinationals'. Heenan and Keegan (1979, p. 109) wrote that:

> [t]he multinational corporation, long regarded by its opponents as the unique instrument of capitalist oppression against the impoverished world, could prove to be the tool by which the impoverished world builds prosperity .... Third world multinationalism, only yesterday an apparent contradiction in terms, is now a serious force in the development process.

We briefly review these studies from the 1980s to identify the patterns of internationalization of these firms before turning to the contemporary phase of internationalization. Yeung (1994) provides a more detailed review of this research.

Third-world multinationals

Heenan and Keegan (1979) identified three categories of economies giving rise to MNCs in the third world – resource-rich developed economies (e.g., OPEC block); labor-rich, rapidly industrializing countries (e.g., Hong Kong, China and Korea); and market-rich, rapidly industrializing countries (e.g., Brazil, Mexico, Philippines). They also predicted that the Japanese model of internationalization, without any disruption of social and cultural values, would be the role model that the third-world multinationals would follow. The rise of the new MNCs would be strongly aided by their respective governments and were likely to emerge from a pool of state-owned enterprises, general trading companies fashioned in the image of Japanese *Zeibatsu*s and corporate alliances and joint ventures. FDI in other developing economies allowed these firms to exploit 'firm-specific advantages in product and process technologies that were appropriate to the factor costs, input characteristics, and demand conditions in the host countries in which they invested' (Lecraw 1993, p. 590).

The common thesis across these studies (e.g., Kumar and Mcleod 1981; Aggarwal 1985a, 1985b; Lall 1986a, 1986b; Lall 1983; Wells 1983) was that emerging economy firms have developed certain advantages owing to their unique home market institutional contexts, which can be extended into international markets. Emerging economy firms possess the unique advantage of dealing with institutional voids which they exploit to counter foreign multinationals, both in their local economies as well as in markets with similar institutional environments (Khanna and Palepu 2006). Thus, the main focus of this stream of research was to explain south–south internationalization and foreign direct investment flows. While the leveraging of existing advantages, either through internationalization into other developing-country markets or by positioning within an established MNCs' global network, provides opportunities for niche strategies to avoid competing with established multinationals, these do not account for the emergence of the global competitors from emerging economies competing in more developed markets and the development of capabilities associated with more advanced value-added products and services required in globally competitive products and markets (Mathews 2006). Thus, as suggested by the OECD report (2006), the existing 'literature on emerging MNCs is mostly based on a few anecdotal evidence, and deduction and inference from the history of North-South capital flows, rather than a body of systematic research'. In the following paragraphs, we examine the internationalization strategies of emerging economy firms in the post-liberalization era of globalization.

Motives of internationalization – learning and capability building

Many researchers explored whether the motives of internationalization for emerging market firms are similar or distinctly different from those of their counterparts in developed economies. For example, Sim and Pandian (2003) found in the Asian context that the main motivation to invest abroad was search for low-cost labor and market expansion and a majority of the firms' strategic advantages stemmed from cost, responsiveness, manufacturing processes and knowledge of the local market conditions.

Lee and Beamish (1995) examined the motivation issues from the viewpoint of joint venture (JV) formation in emerging economies. While a majority of studies on joint ventures focus on JVs between (a) developed country firms with other firms in developed countries and (b) developed country firms with local firms in developing countries, this study examines the joint ventures between firms from a newly industrialized country such as Korea and firms from developing countries. The authors examine the characteristics of Korean JVs in terms of ownership, stability, partner form, venture-creating

rationale, performance, ownership control and control-performance relationships. The findings on the characteristics of Korean JVs are compared with previous findings on joint ventures in developed countries and developing countries. Some of the key findings are as follows. The need for partner's knowledge was found to be a more important motivation for the JV than government regulatory requirement. Second, Korean JVs were found to be more stable than developed country JVs. Third, Korean JVs with local private partners were found to be more stable than those with public (government) partners. Fourth, Korean JVs seemed to prefer majority JVs. The satisfaction level of Korean JVs in developing countries was higher than that of developed country JVs in developing countries.

Tsang (1999) viewed internationalization as a process of transferring a firm's knowledge, which embodies a firm's advantage, whether it be the knowledge underlying technology, production, marketing or other activities. Also, transferring social technologies that involve a lot of intangible elements is much more complex than transferring physical technologies. Companies that learn efficiently are able to expand into foreign markets faster as they learn and gain experience in transferring knowledge. Hence, efficient and effective organizational learning mechanism through sharing and institutionalization of experiences hasten the internationalization process. The author made these propositions supported by empirical evidence from 19 Singapore companies and their operations in China.

Seeking to view internationalization of firms from an organizational perspective, in contrast to the predominant economic view, Guillen (2002) treats foreign expansion as an instance of organizational and strategic change shaped by not only economic variables but also inter-organizational variables, primarily structural inertia and imitation. A number of hypotheses regarding the impact of inter-organizational effects on foreign expansion are tested on a data set of decisions of listed South Korean firms to set up manufacturing plants in China during 1987–1995. Support was found for imitation effects, but the same was found to decrease in strength after the firm's first entry. This could be due to the fact that an entry would facilitate direct learning from the foreign country instead of an indirect learning from other industry players. The study however does not find a significant support for the impact of inertia on foreign expansion.

In another significant paper, Makino, Lav and Yeh (2002) examined two distinct perspectives of foreign direct investment (FDI) – asset exploitation, where FDI is viewed as the transfer of the firm's proprietary assets across national borders; and asset-seeking, where FDI is viewed as a means to acquire strategic assets such as technology, marketing and management expertise. These authors hypothesize that firms from Newly Industrialized Economies (NIE) engaging in FDI in developed countries (DCs), do so not only for asset exploitation but also to seek technology-based resources and skills and test the hypotheses using a sample of 328 manufacturing Taiwanese firms, focusing on the strategic decision of investment location. They find support for the hypotheses that NIE firms tend to invest in DCs for either strategic asset-seeking or market-seeking purposes, small LDCs (less developed countries) for labor-seeking purposes and large LDCs for both market-seeking and labor-seeking purposes. However, these investment location decisions are moderated by firm-specific capabilities that are needed to support the investments.

There is a current debate within the international business research community which revolves around the 'asset seeking' versus 'asset exploitation' motivations behind firm internationalization/multinationalization (Dunning 1988, 2006; Mathews 2006; Narula 2006). A fundamental assumption typical of Western models of international expansion is that the firm already possesses the technology and product-related knowledge it needs in order to meet the needs of the foreign

markets, and the act of internationalization is undertaken in order to exploit this stock of existing know-how, or ownership advantages (Dunning 1988). Internationalization is thus viewed as a process of transferring a firm's knowledge across borders, whether it is knowledge underlying technology, production, marketing or other activities. However, an alternative approach to internationalization suggests that, even prior to firms moving into international markets, they would need to upgrade their technological and scientific know-how so as to be able to offer products commensurate with the more advanced needs of the international markets. Many times, inward internationalization can act as a starting point to international activity (Mathews 2006). Thus, according to this view, internationalization of firms from emerging economies is also motivated by learning objectives that allow these firms to overcome the initial resource hurdles arising due to technological gaps and late mover disadvantages in international markets. A number of the studies described above, as well as some recent papers (e.g., Chittoor and Ray 2007; Klein and Wocke 2007; Li 2007), contribute to the current debate in the international business literature on whether ownership advantages or firm-specific capabilities precede or are a consequence of multinationality (see Narula 2006; Mathews 2006; Dunning 2006).

Strategies and performance of internationalizing firms

Based on the assumption that a majority of the emerging market firms would still be in the early stage of internationalization process, with exporting being the dominant mode, a number of emerging market studies focused on export strategies and export performance (with export activity characterized by manufacturing in the home country and sale of products to foreign markets). We found that the largest number of studies on the internationalization of emerging market firms were export-related studies. Given the fact that in many developing countries there exist a number of short term incentives to encourage exports and generate foreign exchange earnings, Christensen, Rocha and Gertner (1987) wanted to investigate the factors that characterized the firms that continued to export even after an initial period. A sample of 152 Brazilian export firms in 1978 was examined again in 1984 (of which 61 ceased to export) to determine a set of factors that were correlated with continuance of exports. Three types of firm profiles were defined – (1) based on firm characteristics; (2) based on export management practices; and (3) on the perceptions and attitudes of senior managers. The successful exporters had such characteristics as better quality products, larger size, more diversified, growing and having less idle capacity than exexporters. Some of the practices associated with exporters, in contrast to ex-exporters, were less reliance on government incentives, usage of market research for entry decisions, interaction with foreign trading companies and intermediaries, determination of prices taking international prices into account and so on. In terms of managerial perceptions and attitudes, the key finding of the study was that government incentives acted only as a secondary stimulus for exports and not as primary motivation, thus playing only a less important role to encourage exports.

Korea and Taiwan seem similar in terms of their export-led growth of their economies, through a study of firms in three industries – footwear, assembled personal computers (PCs) and keyboards of PCs – Levy (1988) proposed that firms from the two countries are very distinct in terms of their strategic orientation. While Korean firms focused on high-volume, high-productivity manufacture of standardized products, Taiwanese firms stressed flexibility and rapid response in market niches for nonstandardized products, which in turn gave rise to different export channels for the two sets of firms. The author also traced the origin of these distinct strategic orientations to the historical evolution of the firms from the two countries.

Although the exports of most Latin American countries consisted of traditional exports (basic commodities), there was a growing emphasis on increasing the proportion of non-traditional exports. Using a cross-national sample of firms from Central America, Dominguez and Sequeira (1993) identified three distinct patterns of export performance associated with different export marketing strategies or groups of exporters. These three groups differ in their emphasis on product-service quality, direct dealing with users, market diversification, emphasis on developed countries and use of market research for targeting markets. The three distinct groups identified by the author are, (1) low-volume, low-content exporters forming the largest Central American group; (2) high-volume, low-cost, high-growth exporters forming the second group; and (3) a group of differentiated markers relying on product-service quality improvement and formal market research studies. The last two groups are the higher-performing ones.

In another study, Aulakh, Kotabe and Teegen (2000) conduct a large sample study to examine the linkage between export strategies and performance of emerging economy firms. They tested a set of hypotheses relating the export strategies of firms from Brazil, Chile and Mexico and their performance in foreign markets – broadly divided into developing and developed economies. The study examined the effects of three broad sets of strategies – competitive strategies (differentiation, cost leadership and an integrated mix of both); segmentation (marketing standardization versus adaptation in target markets) and scope (geographic diversification). It was found that the cost leadership strategy enhanced export performance in developed as well as developing economies, but the impact was more in case of exports to developed economies. In a similar manner, the differentiation strategy worked better in case of exports to developing countries. In regard to standardization of marketing programs, the study found that standardization led to lower export performance, but the negative effect was not significant in case of exports to developing countries. Lastly, the study found that while some export market diversification improves export performance, a high level of diversification had an adverse effect on export performance, thereby displaying an inverted 'U' relationship between geographical diversification and performance.

Using a sample of privatized firms in the countries of former Soviet Union, namely Russia, Ukraine and Belarus, Filatotchev *et al.* (2001) developed and tested hypotheses based on the governance-conduct-perform-ance framework of strategic management with export intensity as the outcome. The authors developed a model for these privatized firms, whereby export-promoting strategic decisions may be affected by managerial incentives and attitudes towards risk-taking, linked to firm ownership structure and corpo-rate governance. The effects of strategy on export intensity were in turn moderated in the model by firm-specific demographics (size, experience, etc.) and environmental factors (product competition, country effects, industry factors, etc.). The authors also posited and found support for a negative rela-tionship between unrelated external acquisi-tions and export intensity suggesting that export development substitutes for external acquisitions.

Extending an earlier study conducted in a developed market context (Brouthers, Werner and Matulich 2000), Brouthers and Xu (2002) examined evidence from Chinese exporting firms which are stereotyped to follow price leadership strategies. Brouthers, Werner and Matulich (2000) had posited that the unique home-country environments of different countries resulted in distinct price/quality product strategies ('regional stereotypes') such as 'superior value' for Japan, 'economy' for US and 'premium' for EU. They found that while a majority of Chinese exporters did follow price leadership strategies, this did not always result in supe-rior profitability performance. Their results indicate that following a branding strategy helped Chinese firms attain better export performance, especially if it is targeted at Less Developed Countries (LDCs) compared with developed countries.

In a recent paper on the same theme, Brouthers, O'Donnell and Hadjimarcou (2005) theorize that by mimicking the appropriate Triad nation price/quality product (generic) strategy, emerging market firms (EMFs) can improve their export performance satisfac-tion. Going by the assumption that EU is known for 'premium' strategy, Japan for 'superior value' strategy and the US for 'economy' strategy, they hypothesize that EMFs that (1) target the EU and use a 'pre-mium' strategy; (2) target Japan and use a 'superior value' strategy; or (3) target the USA and use an 'economy' strategy will, on average, achieve higher levels of satisfaction with export performance than EMFs that enter emerging markets or EMFs that employ other product strategies in Triad nation mar-kets. In other words, they posit that imitation can (1) be used to simplify international strategic decisions and (2) lead to superior EMF export performance satisfaction. These hypotheses were tested and supported on a sample of Romanian and Chinese exporters.

Networks, internationalization and foreign entry modes

In the emerging economy context, firms are known to form networks and their strategies and performance are posited to be strongly influenced by these networks. Using three longitudinal cases from China, Peng (1997) explores whether growth of the firm in tran-sitional economies has a distinct theoretical explanation compared to the Western theories given the vast differences in the institutional environments. Top managers of three Chinese firms representing different ownership types were interviewed over the 1989–96 period. Based on these case studies, Peng (1997) posits that in a transition economy such as China, firms adopt a network-based strat-egy. This involved a process of what the author calls 'boundary blurring' through development of inter-organizational relationships with other firms. This unique strategy of growth has enabled the firms to avoid the tricky issue of ownership transfer of assets while allowing them access to complementary assets in the uncertain period of transition. This hybrid strategy, which is neither market nor hierarchy, was adopted by firms due to constraints on generic expansion or acquisitions imposed by the institutional environment. Elango and Pattnaik (2007) study the role of networks in the internationalization of Indian firms. Using a panel data of 794 firms, they find support for their hypothesis that international experience of their parental and foreign networks help these firms to build capabilities to succeed in international markets. Similarly, Garg and Delios (2007) explore the role of business group affiliation on the performance of foreign subsidiaries of emerging economy multinationals. Operationalizing performance as subsidiary survival, they find that advantages associated with business group affiliation are more transferable in other developing countries (with similar institutional environments) than in developed-country markets. Yiu, Lau and Bruton (2007) examine the internationalization strategies of Chinese enterprises and conclude that:

> the roles of business networks, for example, in sharing market information and securing control over a supply chain, constitute a weaker direct effect on international venturing, as compared with institutional networks. The findings show that institutional networks play a more important role at this stage of economic development of the country under study. This indicates that institutional networks may help firms in emerging economies such as China to cope with the transitioning institutional environment better (p. 12).

Entry mode choice had been a popular research theme in the context of entry of firms from developed countries into emerging economies. Replicating the theme, there was a study by Rajan and Pangarkar (2000) on the entry mode choice of emerging market firms. This was a quantitative study aimed at identifying the determinants of the choice of mode of foreign entry, which was proxied as

the degree of equity stakes (a continuous variable) held by Singaporean manufacturing firms in their foreign investments. Based on the conceptual framework of Hill, Hwang and Kim (1990), the authors used three categories of independent variables, namely, strategic control variables, competence variables and cost variables. Some of the key findings of the study were: (1) Singaporean multinationals were strongly influenced by their strategic motivations and their desire to exploit synergies; (2) when the investing parent perceived a risk of opportunism on the part of the host country firms, there was a strong tendency to choose higher control entry modes; (3) the sample firms were strongly influenced by the degree of previous exposure they had in that specific host country and not by their general international exposure, in their choice of high-control entry modes. In another recent study Filatotchev *et al.* (2007) examine the entry modes of Taiwanese MNCs into China. They show that:

> the ownership structure of the parent company matters with regard to its FDI decisions, and various investor constituencies may have different impacts on the firm's choice of entry mode. More specifically, share ownership by foreign financial institutions in NIE firms is associated with a high-commitment FDI strategy .... In contrast, high levels of shared ownership by the family and domestic institutional investors are associated with low levels of equity commitment (p. 14).

CONCLUSIONS AND FUTURE RESEARCH DIRECTIONS

In this chapter, we have attempted to highlight certain trends in the research on emerging economy firms. We focus the chapter on two aspects: (1) transformation of organizations in these economies as a response to the dual imperatives of economic liberalization initiated by home country governments and a global environment of economic integration partially facilitated by multilateral organizations such as GATT, World Bank and the WTO; and (2) internationalization strategies of emerging economy firms to respond to increased competition in their erstwhile protected markets and the general push from their governments to accomplish export-driven economic development. In the following paragraphs, we highlight some avenues of research that have the potential to further our understanding of firms from emerging economies.

While the research reviewed has provided important insights into the strategic transformations of firms in diverse institutional contexts, there is generally a paucity of comparative research to examine whether theoretical refinements to existing models are applicable across firms from different emerging economies. This could well be because of the nascent stage of research, or due to data limitations in comparative frameworks. However, we believe that comparative research can uncover some important aspects in the theoretical development and boundary conditions of emerging economy firms' transformation. For instance, a recent report entitled *The New Global Challengers* by the Boston Consulting Group (BCG 2006) identifies 100 top companies from developing economies and provides some descriptive data of these firms, as well as speculates on the underlying reasons for their growing success. China (44) and India (21) together represent almost two-thirds of these emerging multinationals. The report further makes an interesting comparison between Chinese and Indian companies on the list (page 9):

> Where the globalizing Chinese companies differ dramatically from the globalizing Indian companies is in their ownership structures. More than two-thirds of the Chinese companies ... are state owned and state controlled, often with publicly traded subsidiaries or with minority stakes in the hands of strategic investors .... Of the remaining companies, some have a mixed-ownership structure but only four Chinese companies on the list are privately owned. The shares of the Indian companies are usually divided among private owners, strategic investors, and the general public, with no single investor possessing a majority stake. All the Indian companies on our list are publicly traded ... and only one Indian company on the list is state controlled.

Along with this comparison, the BCG Report notes that none of the 100 firms in its sample comes from Eastern Europe, 'because the large globalizing companies in these countries are actually subsidiaries of foreign multinationals' (BCG 2006, p. 8). These observations thus suggest that there are unique models of responding to institutional changes arising from economic liberalization across the three geographical contexts, China, Eastern Europe, and India, although major liberalization efforts were initiated in the same time period. A comparative empirical analysis could shed light on the strategic transformation paths followed by firms across different institutional contexts and the effectiveness of these paths in achieving macro-national and micro-organizational goals.

Another important avenue for future comparative research could be to examine the roles played by supra-firm institutions in the strategic transformation and internationalization of domestic firms. For instance, the role played by state-owned enterprises in driving China's export-led growth and the associated direct and indirect support these firms receive from the state is well documented in both the academic and business press (BCG 2006). In the Indian context, the government has played a lesser role in promoting the internationalization of the domestic firms. However, an important feature of the Indian corporate landscape is the prevalence of business groups. Although existing research sees the role of these business groups in India mainly as response to institutional voids in the pre-liberalization era, the continuing presence and even growth (and emergence of new ones) of these business groups in the post-liberalization era could suggest facilitating role in transforming their member companies, similar to ones played by the Chinese government for the state-owned enterprises.

While the business press has heralded the 'emerging multinationals' from developing economies, there is a need to understand the sustainability of global competitiveness of these firms. This brings out issues of capability development of firms from emerging economies. Two recent conceptualizations explaining the international success of emerging economy firms highlight capability development through accessing international resources. Mathews (2006) proposes a linkage, leverage and learning (LLL) framework:

> latecomer and newcomer MNEs do not depend for their international expansion on prior possession of resources, as was the case for most traditional MNEs from Triad countries expanding abroad in past decades. Instead, these new firms utilize international expansion in order to tap into resources that would otherwise be unavailable .... [T]he LLL framework is a powerful strategic tool for accelerated international expansion in conditions of global inter-connections, that is potentially available to a very wide class of companies (pp. 22–23).

Luo and Tung (2007) propose a 'springboard' perspective whereby emerging market multinationals 'systematically use international expansion as a springboard to acquire critical resources needed to compete effectively against global rivals at home and abroad and to reduce their vulnerability to institutional and market constraints at home' (p. 4). While access to globally dispersed resources as a motivation for internationalization is a reasonable proposition, and which could also explain the internationalization of developed-country MNEs (although the nature of accessed resources may be different), it is not entirely clear how resources lead to capability development for emerging economy firms.

In fact, systematic studies on innovation in these firms are rare and future research could explore the genesis of innovative capabilities of firms from emerging economies. This is an important gap because despite the success of emerging economy firms measured in terms of growth rates, stock prices, and other financial measures, there is a concern about innovation capabilities of these firms. For instance, a recent report by China's Ministry of Science and Technology has blamed the joint ventures with foreign partners for the lack of innovative capabilities of domestic manufacturer's because of the psychological and economic dependence on foreign partners (Wang 2005). Similarly, a recent article in Business Week (2007), entitled *The Tech Dragon Stumbles*, highlights the problems faced by Chinese companies such as Lenovo and TCL as they mature to established multinationals. More fine-grained analyses of the interplay of organizational characteristics, such as absorptive capacity with experiential learning across industries and national contexts, could potentially help in understanding the transformation of resources to capabilities which are sustainable for emerging economy firms.

REFERENCES

Academy of Management Review (2000) Special issue: Privatization and entrepreneurial transformation, 25(3).

Academy of Management Journal (2000) Special issue: Strategy in emerging economies, 43(3).

Aggarwal, A. (2000) 'Deregulation, technology imports and in-house R&D efforts: An analysis of the Indian experience', *Research Policy*, 29: 1081–1093.

Aggarwal, R. (1984) 'The strategic challenge of Third world multinationals: a new stage of the product life cycle of multinationals', in R. N. Farmer (ed.), *Advances in International Comparative Management*, Vol.1. Greenwich, CT: JAI Press, pp. 103–122.

Aggarwal, R. and Weekly, J. K. (1982) 'Foreign operations of third world multinationals: a literature review and analysis of Indian companies', *Journal of Developing Areas*, 17(1): 13–30.

Amsden, A. (1989) *Asia's Next Giant: South Korea and Late Industrialization*. New York: Oxford University Press.

Aulakh, P. S. (2007) 'Emerging multinationals from developing economies: motivations, paths and performance', *Journal of International Management*, 13(3): 235–240.

Aulakh, P. S., Kotabe, M., and Teegen, H. (2000) 'Export strategies and performance of firms from emerging economies: evidence from Brazil, Chile, and Mexico', *Academy of Management Journal*, 43(3): 342–361.

Austin, J. E. (1990) *Managing in Developing Countries: Strategic Analysis and Operating Techniques*. New York: The Free Press.

BCG Report. (2006) The new global challengers: How 100 top companies from rapidly developing economies are changing the world. Boston Consulting Group research.

Bereznoi, A. V. (1990) *Third World Newcomers in International Business: Multinational Companies from Developing Countries*. Delhi: Ajanta Publications.

Bertrand, M., Mehta, P. and Mullainathan, S. (2002) 'Ferreting out tunneling: an application to Indian business groups', *Quarterly Journal of Economics*, 117, 121–148.

Brouthers, K. and Brouthers, L. E. (2001) 'Explaining the national cultural distance paradox', *Journal of International Business Studies*, 32, 177–189.

Brouthers, L. E., Werner, S. and Matulich, E. (2000) 'The influence of triad nations' environments on price-quality product strategies and MNC performance', *Journal of International Business Studies*, 31(1): 39–62.

Brouthers, L. E. and Xu, K. (2002) 'Product stereotypes, strategy and performance satisfaction: the case of Chinese exporters', *Journal of International Business Studies*, 33(4): 657–677.

Brouthers, L. E., O'Donnell, E. and Hadjimarcou, J. (2005) 'Generic product strategies for emerging market exports into triad nation markets', *Journal of Management Studies*, 42(1): 225–245.

Bruton, G. D., Ahlstrom, D. and Wan, J. C. (2003) 'Turnaround in East Asian firms: evidence from ethnic overseas Chinese communities', *Strategic Management Journal*, 24, 519–540.

Business Week (2006), Emerging giants, Business Week, Cover Story, July 31.

Carney, M. and Gedajlovic, E. (2003) 'Strategic innovation and administrative heritage of East Asian family business groups', *Asia Pacific Journal of Management*, 20: 5–26.

Chang, S. and Hong, J. (2000) 'Economic performance of group-affiliated companies in Korea: intragroup resource sharing and internal business transactions', *Academy of Management Journal*, 43: 429–48.

Chang, S. and Hong, J. (2002) 'How much does the business group matter in Korea?', *Strategic Management Journal*, 23: 265–274.

Chang, S. J. (2003) 'Ownership structure, expropriation, and performance of group-affiliated companies in Korea', *Academy of Management Journal*, 46: 238–253.

Chittoor, R., Ray, S., Aulakh, P. S., and Sarkar, M. B. (2008) 'Strategic responses to institutional changes: Indigenous growth model of the Indian pharmaceutical industry', *Journal of International Management*, forthcoming.

Chittor, R. and Ray, S. (2007) 'Internationalization paths of Indian pharmaceutical firms – a strategic group analysis', *Journal of International Management*, 13(3): 338–355.

Christensen, C. H., Rocha, A. and Gertner, R. K. (1987) 'An empirical investigation of the factors influencing exporting success of Brazilian firms', *Journal of International Business Studies*, 18: 61–77

Craig, C. S. and Douglas, S. P. (1997) 'Managing the transnational value chain: strategies for firms from emerging markets', *Journal of International Marketing*, 5(3): 71–84.

Cuervo, A. and Vilalong, B. (2000) 'Explaining the variance in the performance effects of privatization', *Academy of Management Review*, 25(3): 581–591.

Dawar, N. and Frost, T. (1999) 'Competing with giants: survival strategies for local companies in emerging markets', *Harvard Business Review*, March–April, 119–129.

Dharwadkar, R., George, G. and Brandes, P. (2000) 'Privatization in emerging economies: an agency theory perspective', *Academy of Management Review*, 25: 650–669.

Djankov, S. and Murrell, P. (2002) 'Enterprise restructuring in transition: a quantitative survey', *Journal of Economic Literature*, 40: 739–792.

Dominguez, L. V. and Brenes, E. (1997) 'The internationalization of Latin American enterprises and market liberalization in the Americas: a vital linkage', *Journal of Business Research*, 38: 3–16.

Dominguez, L. V. and Sequeira, C. G. (1993) 'Determinants of LDC exporters' performance: a cross-national study', *Journal of International Business Studies*, 24: 19–40.

Dunning, J. H. (1985) 'Research on third world multinationals', *Multinational Business*, 4 (December): 39–45.

Dunning, J. H. (1988) 'The eclectic paradigm of international production: a restatement and some possible extensions', *Journal of International Business Studies*, 19(1): 1–31.

Dunning, J. H. (1999) 'Globalization and the theory of MNE activity', in N. Hood and

S. Young, (eds), *The Globalization of Multinational Enterprises Activity.* Basingstoke: Macmillan, pp. 21–54.

Dunning, J. H. (2006) 'Comments on dragon multinationals: New players in 21st century globalization', *Asia Pacific Journal of Management*, 23: 139–141.

Elango, B. and Pattnaik, C. (2007) 'Building capabilities for international operations through networks: a study of indian firms', *Journal of International Business Studies*, 38(4): 541–555.

Filatotchev, I., Buck, T. and Zhukov, V. (2000) 'Downsizing in privatized firms in Russia, Ukraine and Belarus', *Academy of Management Journal*, 43: 286–304.

Filatotchev, I., Dyomina, N., Wright, M. and Buck, T. (2001) 'Effects of post-privatization governance and strategies on export intensity in the former Soviet Union', *Journal of International Business Studies*, 32: 853–871.

Filatotchev, I., Wright, M., Hoskisson, R., Uhlenbruck, K. and Tihanyi, L. (2003) 'Governance, organizational capabilities, and restructuring in transition economies', *Journal of World Business*, 38: 331–347.

Filatotchev, I., Strange, R., Piesse, J. and Lien, Y-C. (2007) 'FDI by firms from industrialized economies in emerging markets: corporate governance, entry mode and location', *Journal of International Business Studies*. 38(4): 556–572.

Garg, M. and Delois, A. (2007) 'Survival of foreign subsidiaries of TMNCs: the influence of business group affiliation', *Journal of International Management*, 13(3): 278–295.

Ghemawat, P. and Khanna, T. (1998) 'The nature of diversified business groups: A research design and two case studies', *Journal of Industrial Economics*, 46: 35–62.

Gillespie, K. (1984) *The Tripartite Relationship: Government, Foreign Investors, and Local Investors During Egypt's Economic Opening.* New York: Praeger Publishers.

Gillespie, K. and Alden, D. (1989) 'Consumer product export opportunities to liberalizing LDCs: a life cycle approach', *Journal of International Business Studies*, 20: 93–113.

Gomez, H. (1997) 'The globalization of business in Latin America', *International Executive*, 39(2): 225–254.

Greenwood, R. and Hinings, C. R. (1996) 'Understanding radical organizational change: bridging together the old and new institutionalism', *Academy of Management Review*, 21: 1052–1081.

Guillen, M. (2000) 'Business groups in emerging economies: a resource-based view', *Academy of Management Journal*, 43: 362–380.

Guillen, M. F. (2002) 'Structural inertia, imitation, and foreign expansion: South Korean firms and business groups in China, 1987–95', *Academy of Management Journal*, 45(3): 509–525.

Heenan, D. A. and Keegan, W. J. (1979) 'The rise of third world multinationals', *Harvard Business Review*, January–February: 101–109.

Hill, C. W. L., Hwang, P. and Kim, H. (1990) 'An eclectic theory of the choice of international entry mode', *Strategic Management Journal*, 11(2): 117–128.

Hitt, M. A., Dacin, M. T., Levitas, E., Arregle, J-L, Borza, A. (2000) 'Partner selection in emerging and developed market contexts: resource-based and organization learning perspectives', *Academy of Management Journal*, 43(3): 449–467.

Hitt, M. A., Ahlstrom, D., Dacin, M. T., Levitas, E. and Svobodina, L., (2004) 'The institutional effects on strategic alliance partner selection in transition economies', *Organization Science*, 15(2): 173–185.

Hoskisson, R. E., Johnson, R. A., Tihanyi, L. and White, R. E. (2005) 'Corporate restructuring in emerging economies: balancing institutional change, transaction and organization costs', *Journal of Management*, 31(6): 941–965.

Hoskisson, R. E., Cannella, A. A., Tihanyi, L. and Faraci, R. (2004) 'Asset restructuring and business group affiliation in French civil law countries', *Strategic Management Journal*, 25: 525–539.

Hoskisson, R. E., Johnson, R. A., Yiu, D. and Wan, W. P. (2001) 'Restructuring strategies of diversified business groups: differences associated with country institutional environments', in M. A. Hitt, R. E. Freeman and J. S. Harrison (eds), *Handbook of Strategic Management*. Oxford: Blackwell Publishers, pp. 433–463.

Hoskisson, R. E., Kim, H., White, R. E. and Tihanyi, L. (2004) 'A framework for understanding international diversification by business groups from emerging economies' in M. A. Hitt and J. L. C. Cheng (eds),

Theories of the Multinational Enterprise: Diversity, Complexity, and Relevance. Advances in International Management, Vol. 16. Oxford: Elsevier/JAI Press, pp. 137–163.

Hoskisson, R., Eden, L., Lau, C-M. and Wright, M. (2000) 'Strategy in emerging economies', *Academy of Management Journal*, 43: 249–267.

Hu, Y.-S. (1995) 'The international transferability of the firm's advantages', *California Management Review*, 37(4): 73–88.

Johnson, G., Smith, S. and Codling, B. (2000) 'Microprocesses of institutional change in the context of privatization', *Academy of Management Review*, 25(3): 572–581.

Journal of International Business Studies (2007) Focused issue: International expansion of emerging market businesses, 38(4).

Journal of International Management (2007) Special issue: Emerging multinationals from developing economies: Motivations, paths and performance, 13(3).

Journal of Management Studies (2005) Special issue: Strategy research in emerging economies: Challenging the conventional Wisdom, 42(1).

Keister, L. (1998) 'Engineering growth: business group structure and firm performance in China's transition economy', *American Journal of Sociology*, 104: 404–440.

Ketchen, D. J. *et al.* (1997) 'Organizational configurations and performance: a meta analysis', *Academy of Management Journal*, 40(1): 223–242.

Khanna, T. and Palepu, K. (1997) 'Why focused strategies may be wrong for emerging markets', *Harvard Business Review*, 75 (July–August): 3–10.

Khanna, T. and Palepu, K. (1999) 'The right way to restructure conglomorates in emerging markets', *Harvard Business Review*, 77(4).

Khanna, T. and Palepu, K. (2000a) 'The future of business groups in emerging markets: long-run evidence from Chile', *Academy of Management Journal*, 43: 268–285.

Khanna, T. and Palepu, K. (2000b) 'Is group affiliation profitable in emerging markets? An analysis of diversified Indian business groups', *Journal of Finance*, 55(2): 867–891.

Khanna, T. and Palepu, K. (2006) 'Emerging giants: building world-class companies in developing economies', *Harvard Business Review*, 84(10): 60–70.

Khanna, T. and Rivkin, J. (2001) 'Estimating the performance of business groups in emerging markets', *Strategic Management Journal*, 22: 45–74.

Kim, B. and Lee, Y. (2001) 'Global capacity expansion strategies: lessons learned from two Korean carmakers', *Long Range Planning*, 34(3): 309–333.

Kim, E. M. (2000) 'Globalization of the South Korean *chaebol*', in Samuel S. Kim (ed.), *Korea's Globalization*. Cambridge: Cambridge University Press, pp. 102–125.

Kim, H., Hoskisson, R., Tihanyi, L. and Hong, J. (2004) 'The evolution and restructuring of diversified business groups in emerging markets: the lessons from chaebols in Korea', *Asia Pacific Journal of Management*, 21: 25–48.

Kim, L. and Lim, Y. (1988) 'Environment, generic strategies, and performance in a rapidly developing country: a taxonomic approach', *Academy of Management Journal*, 31: 802–827.

Klein, S. and Wocke, A. (2007) 'Emerging global contenders: the South African experience', *Journal of International Management*, 13(3): 319–337.

Kock. C. J. and Guillen, M. F. (2001) 'Strategy and structure in developing countries: business groups as an evolutionary response to opportunities for unrelated diversification', *Industrial and Corporate Change*, 10(1): 77–113.

Konings, J., Cayseele, P. V. and Warzynski, F. (2005) 'The effects of privatization and competitive pressure on firms' price-cost margins: micro evidence from emerging economies', *The Review of Economics and Statistics*, 87(1): 124–134.

Kriauciunas, A. and Kale, P. (2006) 'The impact of socialist imprinting and search on resource change: a study of firms in Lithuania', *Strategic Management Journal*, 27: 659–679.

Kumar, K. and McLeod, M. G. (eds.) (1981) *Multinationals from Developing Countries*. Lexington: D.C. Heath.

Lall, R. B. (1986a) *Multinationals from the Third World: Indian Firms Investing Abroad*. Delhi: Oxford University Press.

Lall, R. B. (1986b) 'Third world multinationals: the characteristics of Indian firms investing abroad', *Journal of Development Economics*, 20 (March): 381–397.

Lall, S. (1983) *The New Multinationals: The Spread of Third World Enterprises.* Wiley: New York.

Lecraw, D. J. (1981) 'The internationalization of firms from LDCs: evidence from the ASEAN region', in K. Kumar and M. G. McLeod (eds), *Multinationals from Developing Countries.* Lexington: D.C. Heath, pp. 33–51.

Lecraw, D. J. (1993) 'Outward direct investment by Indonesian firms: motivation and effects', *Journal of International Business Studies,* 24(3): 589–600.

Lee, C. and Beamish, P. (1995) 'The characteristics and performance of Korean joint ventures in LDCs', *Journal of International Business Studies,* 26: 637–654.

Levy, Brian (1988) 'Korea and Taiwanese firms as international competitors: the challenges ahead', *Columbia Journal of World Business,* 23(1): 43–51.

Li, P. P. (1998) 'The evolution of multinational firms from Asia – a longitudinal study of Taiwan's Acer Group', *Journal of Organizational Change Management,* 11(4): 321–337.

Li, P. P. (2007) 'Toward an integrated theory of multinational evolution: the evidence of Chinese multinational enterprises as latecomers', *Journal of International Management,* 13(3): 296–318.

Lim, Mah-hui and Teoh, Kit-fong (1986) 'Singapore corporations go transnational', *Journal of South East Asian Studies:* 336–365.

Lin, Y. and Szenberg, M. (1998) 'Determinants of outward Taiwanese foreign direct investment, 1965–93', in J. H. Dunning (ed.) *Globalization, Trade and Foreign Direct Investment.* Oxford: Pergamon, pp. 175–193.

Luo, Y. and Tung, R. L. (2007) 'International expansion of emerging market enterprises: a springboard perspective', *Journal of International Business Studies,* 38(4): 481–498.

Lyles, M., Saxton, T. and Watson, K. (2004). 'Venture survival in a transition economy', *Journal of Management,* 30: 351–373.

Makhija, M. (2003). 'Comparing the resource-based and market-based views of the firm: empirical evidence from Czech privatization', *Strategic Management Journal,* 24: 433–452.

Makhija, M. and Stewart, A. (2002). 'The effect of national context on perceptions of risk: a comparison of planned versus free-market managers', *Journal of International Business Studies,* 33: 737–756.

Makino, S., Lau, C. M. and Yeh, R. S. (2002) 'Asset-exploitation versus asset-seeking: Implications for location choice of foreign direct investment from newly industrialized economies', *Journal of International Business Studies,* 33(3): 403–422.

Manimala, M. (1996) 'Organisational response to economic liberalization', *Social Engineering,* 1(1): 34–55.

Mathews, J. A. (2002) *Dragon Multinational: A New Model for Global Growth.* Oxford: Oxford University Press.

Mathews, J. A. (2006) 'Dragon multinationals: New players in 21st century globalization', *Asia Pacific Journal of Management,* 23: 5–27.

May, R., Stewart, W. and Sweo, R. (2000) 'Environmental scanning behavior in a transition economy: evidence from Russia', *Academy of Management Journal,* 43: 403–428.

McDermott, M. C. (1990) 'The internationalisation of the South Korean and Taiwanese electronic industries', in S. Young and J. Hamill (eds), *Europe and the Multinationals.* Aldershot: Edward Elgar.

Meyer, K. E. (2004) 'Perspectives on multinational enterprises in emerging economies', *Journal of International Business Studies,* 35: 259–276.

Nachum, L. (2004) 'Geographic and industrial diversification of developing country firms', *Journal of Management Studies,* 41: 273–294.

Narula, R. (2006) 'Globalization, new ecologies, new zoologies, and the purported death of the eclectic paradigm', *Asia Pacific Journal of Management,* 23: 143–151.

Neto, Raul de Gouvea (1995) 'Brazilian emerging multinationals: a conduit for export of technology', *The International Executive,* 37(6): 583–597.

Newman, K. (2000) 'Organizational transformation during institutional upheaval', *Academy of Management Review,* 25: 602–619.

OECD (2006) *Emerging Multinationals: Who Are They? What Do They Do? What Is At Stake?* Paris: OECD.

Oh, Donghoon, Choi, Chong Ju and Choi, Eugene (1998) 'The globalization strategy of Daewoo Motor Company', *Asia Pacific Journal of Management*, 15: 185–203.

Pananond, P. and Zeithaml, C. P. (1998) 'The international expansion process of MNEs from developing countries: A case study of Thailand's CP Group', *Asia Pacific Journal of Management*, 15: 163–184.

Pananond, P. (2001a) 'The international expansion of Thailand's Jasmine Group: built on shaky ground?', *Asia Pacific Business Review*, 8: 121–148.

Pananond, P. (2001b) 'The making of Thai multinationals: a comparative study of the growth and internationalization process of Thailand's Charoen Pokphand and Siam Cement groups', *Journal of Asian Business*, 17: 41–70.

Pangarkar, N. (1998) 'The Asian multinational corporation: strategies, performance and key challenges', *Asia Pacific Journal of Management*, 15: 109–118.

Peng, M. W. (1997) 'Firm growth in transitional economies: three longitudinal cases from China, 1989–96', *Organization Studies*, 18(3): 385–413.

Peng, M. W. (2000) *Business Strategies in Transition Economies*. Thousand Oaks, CA and London: Sage.

Peng, M. W. (2003). 'Institutional transitions and strategic choices', *Academy of Management Review*, 28: 275–296.

Peng, M. W. (2004). 'Outside directors and firm performance during institutional transitions', *Strategic Management Journal*, 25: 453–471.

Peng, M. W. and Hearth, P. S. (1996) 'The growth of firms in planned economies in transition: Institutions, organizations and strategic choice', *Academy of Management Review*, 21(2): 493–526.

Peng, M. W. and Luo, Y. (2000). 'Managerial ties and firm performance in a transition economy: the nature of a micro-macro link', *Academy of Management Journal*, 43: 486–501.

Peng, M. W., Tan, J. and Tong, T. (2004) 'Ownership types and strategic groups in an emerging economy', *Journal of Management Studies*, 41: 1105–1129.

Rajan, K. S. and Pangarkar, N. (2000) 'Mode of entry choice: an empirical study of Singaporean multinationals', *Asia Pacific Journal of Management*, 17(1): 49–66.

Ralston, D. A., Terpstra-Tong, J., Terpstra, R. H., Wang, X. and Egri, C. (2006) 'Today's state-owned enterprises of China: are they dying dinosaurs or dynamic dynamos?', *Strategic Management Journal*, 27(9): 825–843.

Ramamurti, R. (2000) 'A multilevel model of privatization in emerging economies', *Academy of Management Review*, 25(3): 525–550.

Ramamurti, R. (2004) 'Developing countries and MNEs: extending and enriching the research agenda', *Journal of International Business Studies*, 35: 277–283.

Sim, A. B. and Pandian, J. R. (2003) 'Emerging Asian MNEs and their internationalization strategies – case study evidence on Taiwanese and Singaporean firms', *Asia Pacific Journal of Management*, 20(1): 27–50.

Spicer, A., Kogut, B. and McDermott, G. (2000) 'Entrepreneurship and privatization in Central Europe: the tenuous balance between destruction and creation', *Academy of Management Review*, 25: 630–649.

Strachen, H. (1976) *Family and Other Business Groups in Economic Development: The Case of Nicaragua*. New York: Praeger.

The Economist (2007) 'Globalisation's offspring: How the new multinationals are remaking the need', April 7–13, p. 11.

Toulan, O. (2002) 'The impact of market liberalization on vertical scope: the case of Argentina', *Strategic Management Journal*, 23: 551–560.

Tsang, E. W. K. (1999) 'Internationalization as a learning process: Singapore MNCs in China', *Academy of Management Executive*, 13(1): 91–101.

Uhlenbruck, K., Meyer, K. E. and Hitt, M. A. (2003) 'Organizational transformation in transition economies: resource-based and organizational learning perspectives', *Journal of Management Studies*, 40: 257–283.

UNCTAD (2006) *World Investment Report: FDI from Developing and Transition Economies: Implications for Development*. New York/Geneva: United Nations.

Vernon-Wortzel, H. and Wortzel, L. H. (1988) 'Globalizing strategies for multinationals from developing countries', *Columbia Journal of World Business*, 23 (Spring): 27–35.

Wan, Chun-Cheong (1998) 'International diversification, industrial diversification and firm performance of Hong Kong MNCs', *Asia Pacific Journal of Management*, 15: 205–217.

Wan, W. and Hoskisson, R. (2003) 'Home country environments, corporate diversification strategies, and firm performance', *Academy of Management Journal*, 46, 27–45.

Wang, Z. (2005) *2005 Report of Transnational Corporations in China*. China Economic Publishing House.

Wells, L. T. Jr. (1977) 'The internationalization of firms from developing countries', in T. Agmon and C. P. Kindleberger (eds), *Multinationals from Small Countries*. Cambridge, MA: The MIT Press, pp. 33–56.

Wells, L. T. Jr. (1983) *Third World Multinationals: The Rise of Foreign Investment from Developing Countries*. Cambridge, MA: The MIT Press.

White, S. (2000) 'Competition, capabilities, and the make, buy, or ally decisions of Chinese state-owned firms', *Academy of Management Journal*, 43: 324–341.

White, S. and Linden, G. (2002) 'Organizational and industrial response to market liberalization: the interaction of pace, incentive, and capacity to change', *Organization Studies*, 23: 917–948.

Yeung, W.-C. H. (1994) 'Third world multinationals revisited: a research critique and future agenda', *Third World Quarterly*, 15(2): 297–317.

Yiu, D., Bruton, G. D. and Lau, Y. (2005) 'Understanding business group performance in an emerging economy: acquiring resources and capabilities in order to prosper', *Journal of Management Studies*, 42(1): 183–206.

Yiu, D. W., Lau, C. and Bruton, G. D. (2007) 'International venturing by emerging economy firms: The effects of firm capabilities, home country networks, and corporate entrepreneurship', *Journal of International Business Studies*, 38(4): 556–572.

Zahra, S. A., Ireland, D., Gutierrez, I. and Hitt, M. A. (2000) 'Privatization and entrepreneurial transformation: emerging issues and future research agenda', *Academy of Management Review*, 25(3): 509–524.

25

Small Multinational Enterprises under Globalization

Gary Knight

INTRODUCTION

Smaller firms that conduct international marketing are increasingly common around the world. Historically, in most countries, international business was the domain of large multinational enterprises (MNEs); companies with thousands of employees that established subsidiaries and affiliates in nations throughout the world. In recent years, however, various trends are facilitating the emergence of a relatively new class of international firm, the international small-and medium-sized enterprises (ISME). Such firms can be defined broadly as companies with 500 or fewer employees that derive a substantial proportion of their revenues from international business activities.

Despite the scarce financial and human resources that characterize most smaller firms, ISMEs are increasingly the norm in the landscape of international trade and investment. Perhaps the most interesting manifestation of this trend is the widespread emergence of born-global firms ('born globals'), companies that internationalize at or near their founding. Born globals sell a substantial share of their offerings in international markets from an early stage in their development. Born globals are also sometimes called 'international new ventures' or 'global start-ups' (Oviatt and McDougall 1994). The distinguishing feature of these firms is that their origins are international, as demonstrated by management's tendency to view the world as their marketplace. From an early stage, born globals commit certain types of organizational resources to international activities.

The phenomenon of ISMEs is relatively universal and has been reported in various countries (e.g., Okura-sho Insatsu Kyoku 1995; OECD 1997). Simon (1996) investigated 500 'hidden champions', successful international ISMEs that operate in global niche markets. One of the first major studies on the widespread internationalization of small- and medium-sized enterprises was by the Organisation for Economic Cooperation and Development in 1997. By the late 1990s, the number of internationally active small- and medium-sized enterprises was growing rapidly in nations worldwide. Small and medium-sized enterprises generally comprise over 90 per cent of firms and many generate much of their revenues from foreign markets (OECD 1997).

Reports on the emergence of ISMEs from various sources indicate that they are an important phenomenon and may be the result of contemporary global forces. Globalization reflects the economic integration of national economies and the growing tendency of firms to involve themselves in international investment, production, sourcing, and marketing as well as cross-border alliances for product development, distribution, and other value-chain activities. A related trend is the emergence of information and communications technologies that facilitate company internationalization.

ISMEs are emerging in large numbers worldwide, becoming substantially more numerous than traditional, large multinational firms. While MNEs and negative aspects of globalization often dominate reports in the popular press, the increasing role of ISMEs is an optimistic trend. It implies that any firm, regardless of size and resource base, can be an active participant in international marketing. The aim of this chapter is to shed light on this relatively new, important breed of international firm. Initially, we set the context within which the ISME phenomenon is taking place. Next, we review key findings on ISMEs. Key theoretical perspectives are then offered from the extant literature. Finally, conclusions and future research directions are provided.

THE CONTEXT: GLOBALIZATION

Globalization involves the widest range of firms in international investment, production, sourcing, and marketing, as well as cross-border alliances for product development and distribution. Companies source input goods from suppliers worldwide, and sell their products and services in dozens, or even hundreds, of national markets. Global companies devise extensive multi-country operations via investments aimed at production and marketing activities. The aggregate activities of these firms are giving rise to ongoing integration of national economies, the most salient macro-dimension of globalization. Cross-national trade and investment have increased dramatically since the 1980s, particularly in the wake of falling government trade barriers and the emergence of numerous regional free trade agreements. By the early 2000s, for example, the total of merchandise exports and imports amounted to more than 40 per cent of world GDP (IMF 2006).

Globalization also reflects the convergence of buyer lifestyles and needs. Products and services in both consumer and industrial markets are increasingly standardized, meaning they are similar or uniform in design. As income levels rise, demand preferences are converging for both industrial and consumer goods and services. By emphasizing a common lifestyle, movies, TV, and Internet-based global media contribute to the homogenization of world consumer preferences. Converging tastes and global production platforms facilitate sales of standardized products and services to buyers around the world.

Related to globalization are contemporary information and communications technologies (ICTs). The most critical advances are in telecommunications, satellites, wireless technology, the Internet and computers. These technologies play two important roles. First, they reduce the costs of internationalization, helping explain why so many smaller firms are venturing abroad (e.g., Aspelund and Moen 2001). Such technologies permit low-cost, worldwide communications and the acquisition of substantial market data, once largely inaccessible to most smaller firms. The microprocessor has enabled explosive growth in low-cost computing. Numerous ISMEs use electronic commerce to reduce costs and maximize effectiveness in managing their international supply chains. Staying constantly linked to suppliers and distributors helps firms manage inventory, product specifications, and purchase orders, as well as product life cycles. Internet-based procurement systems save money on transaction processing and reduce order cycle times. Until the 1990s, communications with foreign suppliers, distributors, and customers were costly or time-consuming, typically accomplished via old-style telex machines and the postal service. Today the cost of international communications has fallen to virtually zero. Scanners and electronic data interchange technologies send documents worldwide, essentially for free. ICTs and transportation technologies have substantially shrunk the geographic and cultural distances that separate nations.

The second important role of ICTs is that they facilitate internationalization. The increased ease of global communications and the widespread dissemination of information and knowledge support the rise of ISMEs. ICTs change the way information is obtained and organized, and the fundamental processes of how firms undertake international business. Search engines, databases, reference guides, and countless government and private support systems assist managers to maximize knowledge and skills for international business success. Firms of all sizes employ Internet-based communications systems such as intranets, extranets, and e-mail. The Internet is the information backbone of the global economy, facilitating cross-border business transactions. The widest range of goods and services – from bank loans to auto parts – are marketed online. ICTs facilitate networking and ability of smaller firms to find appropriate distributors and other partners abroad. ICTs connect individuals and small groups across the globe. The Internet provides a means to build networks and to collaborate online with suppliers, clients, agents, distributors, and R&D partners. Globalization and ICTs facilitate networking and ability of smaller firms to find appropriate distributors and other partners to support their international activities (e.g., Kuemmerle 2002; Loane 2006).

Thanks to the Internet, services as diverse as designing an engine, monitoring a security camera, selling insurance, or secretarial work have become easier to export than car parts or refrigerators. The Internet is stimulating economic development and a massive global migration of jobs, particularly in the services sector. Transmitting voices, data, and images is essentially costless, making Boston, Bangalore, and Beijing next-door neighbors, instantly. A teenager in Hungary or India has all the information and software available to apply knowledge in countless ways. Communications and information technology connect knowledge pools wherever they are in the world. Much of what has ever been written and recorded on paper, tape, or film is increasingly accessible online (Friedman 2005).

FINDINGS ON ISMEs

In the 1990s, significant numbers of scholars began to investigate ISMEs. There have been numerous exploratory, comparative, descriptive, and hypothesis-testing studies that employ surveys and case-based studies of actual ISMEs. Most of the studies conducted to date have attempted to describe, understand and interpret the reasons underlying the growing emergence of these firms (Rialp, Rialp and Knight 2005). Empirical research attempts to reveal the differentiating characteristics and behaviors that characterize ISMEs.

The extent to which ISMEs are different from traditional, large MNEs is a conundrum. ISMEs differ from larger firms in terms of their resource base, particularly in areas such as financial and tangible resources. Limited resources affect the ability of ISMEs to undertake substantial risks. Smaller firms are also particularly affected by the indirect effects of terrorism, such as falling consumer demand and new government security measures, which can delay shipments or raise the costs of international business (Czinkota, Knight and Liesch 2004). ISMEs also lack the economies of scale characteristic of larger MNEs, which can hinder the ability to pursue strategies based on cost leadership.

However, despite resource deficiencies, many ISMEs manage to internationalize early and succeed in world markets (Freeman, Edwards and Schroder 2006). ISMEs often compensate for inadequacies via greater flexibility, innovativeness, and a focus on niche markets too small to interest larger competitors. Smaller firms frequently internationalize faster than their larger counterparts. One survey of born globals in Finland found that such firms had internationalized much earlier than traditional MNEs. Born globals pass quickly through the internationalization stages described in the internationalization literature (e.g., Johanson and Vahlne 1977), or jump over some stages (Luostarinen and Gabrielsson 2006). My own research has uncovered thousands of ISMEs that substantially internationalized within three years of their founding (e.g., Knight and Cavusgil 2004).

Oviatt and McDougall (1994) are credited with introducing the concept of 'international new ventures' in the academic literature. They sought to present an explanatory framework of early internationalizing ISMEs. Their conceptualization integrated accepted MNE and international business theory with developments in entrepreneurship research. They noted that many smaller international firms succeed via control over unique resources, especially knowledge. In a follow-up article, McDougall, Shane and Oviatt (1994) compared five generally-accepted perspectives – Monopolistic Advantage Theory (Hymer 1976); Product Cycle Theory (Vernon 1966); Stage Theory of Internationalization (e.g., Bilkey and Tesar 1977; Cavusgil 1982); Oligopolistic Reaction Theory (Knickerbocker 1973); and Internalization Theory (Buckley and Casson 1976) – and concluded that some aspects of ISMEs are not well explained by extant international business theories.

Bell (1995) similarly concluded that the Stage Theory of Internationalization (e.g., Cavusgil 1982) could not account for the early international expansion of ISMEs, and made a call for using the Network Approach for better explaining the frequently non-linear foreign development of smaller firms. Knight and Cavusgil (2004) argued that traditional internationalization theories do not adequately account for the emergence of certain types of ISMEs. These scholars proposed factors that account for their emergence, and argued that born global firms are a particularly distinctive form of ISMEs. They pointed to several major trends that appear to be promoting the emergence of ISMEs, including the emergence of international niche markets; advances in ICTs and other technologies; inherent advantages of smaller firms, such as flexibility and adaptability; and leveraging global networks.

Subsequently, Oviatt and McDougall (1999) devised a framework to stimulate theoretical and empirical efforts that might lead to development of a contemporary dynamic theory of company internationalization involving smaller firms. These scholars also highlighted the importance of the management team in the foreign expansion of international new ventures.

Much empirical research has focused on revealing the characteristics and factors that determine the performance of ISMEs. Although ISMEs are often more concentrated in the high-technology sectors, smaller international firms in fact can be found across a wide range of industries (Madsen and Servais 1997). Scholars emphasize the role of specific organizational capabilities that engender ISME international success (e.g., Burgel and Murray 1998). For example, Knight (2000) investigated the interrelationships of entrepreneurial orientation, marketing strategy, and firm performance among ISMEs affected by globalization. Results indicated that among small firms affected by globalization, entrepreneurial orientation is associated with the development of specific types of marketing strategies that enhance international performance. ISMEs strongly affected by globalization appear to emphasize the acquisition of useful technologies, responding to internationalization and preparing to enter foreign markets.

Research also points to international marketing as significant in ISME success (e.g., Knight and Cavusgil 2004). International marketing orientation refers to a managerial mindset that emphasizes the creation of value, via key marketing elements, for foreign customers (Cavusgil and Zou 1994). Market orientation, marketing competence, and other marketing-related activities engender superior performance in internationalizing firms (e.g., Cavusgil, Zou and Naidu 1993). Within their markets, marketing-oriented firms generally attempt to offer products and services whose value buyers perceive to exceed the expected value of alternative offerings. The urge to continuously provide superior buyer value and improve performance drives the firm to create and maintain a business culture that fosters requisite business behaviors. A marketing orientation provides the foundation through which ISMEs can interact with diverse foreign markets (Knight and Cavusgil 2004).

Another approach that may be significant to ISMEs is a focus on the customer. This view is consistent with Simon's (1996) findings on 'hidden champions', international-niche specialist ISMEs. The approach of these firms is 'deep, not wide', with emphasis on core competencies and getting close to the customer. Simon found that global start-ups which focus on customers and product excellence are more successful in their markets than firms that operate more broadly.

Empirical research suggests that ISMEs are likely to be formed by entrepreneurs who proactively pursue foreign ventures. Managers often have significant international experience and extensive foreign networks. The firms leverage pre-emptive technology or marketing to achieve early international success (Knight 2000; Oviatt and McDougall 1995). International entrepreneurial orientation, differentiation strategy, quality products, and strong foreign partners appear to be particularly important to ISME international success (Knight and Cavusgil 2004).

The emergence of ISMEs has given rise to a new field of scholarly enquiry: international entrepreneurship (e.g., McDougall and Oviatt 2000; Zahra and George 2002). It investigates the tendency of some young or smaller firms to proactively pursue international business. For example, the top managers in the 500 'hidden champions' (Simon 1996) have substantial 'fearlessness' and 'single-mindedness' in pursuit of international goals. ISMEs appear to leverage an entrepreneurial drive that allows them to find and target markets around the world. Entrepreneurial firms have an organizational culture that supports active exploration and pursuit of international opportunities. Entrepreneurial orientation gives rise to certain 'processes, practices, and decision-making activities' that are associated with new entry and ultimate success in newly entered markets (Kuivalainen, Sundquist and Servais 2007; Lumpkin and Dess 1996). Having an entrepreneurial orientation might be viewed as a necessary characteristic of smaller firms, which are particularly susceptible to the 'liability of newness' typical of many international ventures (Stinchcombe 1965). Because young businesses are much more inclined to fail than established ones, aggressive posturing might be critical to their survival and success.

Given the limited resources of smaller firms, ISMEs may be unable to undertake costly foreign market entry modes, such as vertical integration of channels. The international marketing environment entails unique challenges and considerable risk, much of which are mitigated by leveraging the localized market knowledge and marketing skills of foreign intermediaries (e.g., Freeman et al. 2006). ISMEs that internationalize via joint ventures and other collaborative entry strategies tend to enjoy superior performance (Gleason and Wiggenhorn 2007). ISMEs leverage the resources of partners for increasing the likelihood of foreign entry success. Relationships and networking help smaller firms overcome 'resource poverty' (Rasmussen, Madsen and Evangelista 2001; Coviello and Munro 1995; Larimo 2001). Distribution partners carry out downstream promotion, pricing, and customer relationship activities. Intermediation by cooperating firms supports small firms because they are more likely than larger businesses to depend on external entities for attaining resource sufficiency in their operations (Steensma *et al.* 2000).

Bell and McNaughton (2000) investigated new challenges posed by ISMEs for developers of public policy. They highlighted that the current activities of most national export promotion organizations (EPOs) focus on the needs of traditional firms, as they are structured to support firms' incremental internationalization processes. The earlier and often faster internationalization of ISMEs presents a major challenge to EPOs, regarding the nature of support provided, and in terms of providing assistance in a timely manner.

KEY THEORETICAL PERSPECTIVES

While the literature on international entrepreneurship is still in its infancy, research in this area is evolving. Certain key conceptual foundations help to explain the emergence of ISMEs. Initially, compared to large, established multinational firms, many ISMEs appear to lack substantial administrative heritage. They appear to lack a long-standing strategic momentum characteristic of large, long-established businesses. Administrative heritage constrains strategic and tactical choice (e.g., Collis 1991). Well-established firms have systematized routines that are costly to change and limit the ability of the firm to innovate. The older firms' previous investments and their repertoire of organizational routines constrain their future behavior. Older firms emphasize knowledge and routines closely related to their existing knowledge and routines, but which may be sub-optimal in light of evolving or varying environmental circumstances.

By contrast, ISMEs are younger or more agile firms with fewer infrastructural and mental barriers to overcome in internationalization. Flexibility and entrepreneurial maneuverability in ISMEs may be key factors that allow them to overcome shortcomings associated with limited human and financial resources (Chaston 1997). In international activities, smaller size can confer greater flexibility, which is particularly important in evolving foreign markets. Moreover, when corporate culture is internationally oriented from an earlier stage in the firm's development, employees are likely to be more effective in their international marketing efforts (Knight and Cavusgil 2004). When management's collective outlook is attuned to operating in markets that are both geographically and psychically distant, the firm acquires internationalization advantages in terms of knowledge acquisition about international markets and how to succeed in them.

Second, learning orientation also appears to be an important factor in ISME success. Organizational learning concerns the processes involved in assimilating new knowledge into the organization's knowledge base (e.g., Senge 1990). Organizational learning theory suggests that the development of new organizational knowledge occurs best under conditions in which there are little or no existing organizational routines to unlearn (Cohen and Levinthal 1990; Nonaka and Takeuchi 1995). This implies that less-established firms may be more adept at acquiring requisite knowledge about international marketing, and more efficient and effective at developing new international activities.

Findings point to the critical role of entrepreneurial learning and foreign market knowledge on the international success of ISMEs (e.g., Weerawardena *et al.* 2007; Zhou 2007). Moreover, the set of dynamic capabilities that are built and nurtured by internationally oriented entrepreneurial founders enable these firms to develop leading-edge products and other advantages that pave the way for foreign market entry (Weerawardena *et al.* 2007). For these firms, foreign market knowledge tends to emanate from the innovative and proactive pursuit of entrepreneurial opportunities across national borders, rather than from incremental accumulation of experience in foreign markets (Zhou 2007). Internationalization gives rise to further learning opportunities that benefit the firm's performance because of the range of unique environments and competitive situations to which the ISME is exposed as it ventures increasingly into foreign markets.

International expansion promotes further organizational learning, and the development of skills and competencies that help the firm achieve competitive advantages (Cohen and Levinthal 1990). Consistent with findings by Zahra, Ireland and Hitt (2000), the diversity of the international marketing environment may enhance the ISME's knowledge stock through learning based on interactions with local knowledge bases and exposure to diverse systems of innovation. Moreover, contact and the development of relationships with various foreign intermediaries also promotes learning and innovation. The diversity of international environments offers exposure to new and diverse ideas from multiple market and cultural perspectives, and help the ISME progress rapidly up the international marketing learning curve.

Third, ISMEs appear to hold a collection of capabilities that support them in pursuing international markets and achieving performance goals abroad. Capabilities are organizational resources that bring corporate assets together and enable them to be deployed advantageously (Day 1994). They are complex bundles of skills and accumulated knowledge that are exercised through organizational processes in the coordination of the firm's rent-seeking activities. Capabilities are intangible – deeply embedded in the organization's routines and practices – and cannot be traded or imitated. The importance of capabilities is rooted in evolutionary economics (Nelson and Winter 1982), which implies that the superior ability of certain firms to create new knowledge leads to the development of organizational capabilities. These firm resources in turn lead to superior performance, particularly in highly competitive or challenging environments (Nelson and Winter 1982).

The task of management is to determine how best to improve and exploit its capabilities, and to develop new capabilities when needed (Day 1994). The firm acquires as many capabilities as needed in order to move its products and services through the value chain. Some of these capabilities must be developed and leveraged especially well to outperform competitors and achieve sustainable international marketing performance. They must be distinctive and allow the firm to obtain and support a particular market position. They must be managed with special care through the focused commitment of organizational resources, dedicated individuals and continued efforts to learn (Day 1994).

Fourth, ISMEs also appear to be characterized by innovatory capacity (Knight and Cavusgil 2004). The ability to internationalize despite limited company resources is a function of the internal capabilities of the firm (McDougall, Shane and Oviatt 1994; Zahra et al. 2000). In addition to introducing new goods and methods of production, R&D supports the opening of new markets and re-inventing the firm's operations to serve those markets optimally (Nelson and Winter 1982). Innovation is a domain of entrepreneurs, who function 'to reform or revolutionize the pattern of production by exploiting an invention or, more generally, an untried technological possibility for producing a new commodity or producing an old one in a new way, by opening up … a new outlet for products' (Schumpeter 1942, p. 132). Firms' innovative culture, combined with appropriate capabilities, engenders the development or improvement of methods for doing business (Nelson and Winter 1982; Dosi 1988). Internationalization, or new entry into markets overseas, is an innovative act (Schumpeter 1939; Simmonds and Smith 1968) and ISMEs appear to be particularly innovative in this regard. ISMEs might be characterized by a particular pattern of innovativeness that gives rise to early internationalization. Innovatory capacity might also engender management to devise new strategies and tactics that support performance as the firm expands abroad.

Fifth, ISMEs appear to possess unique resources. Resources are (tangible and intangible) assets that are tied semi-permanently to the firm (Wernerfelt 1984). Resources that lead to profitability include assets such as brand names, in-house knowledge, employment of skilled personnel, trade contacts, and efficient procedures (Hunt 2000; Wernerfelt 1984). Researchers have investigated the role of resources, especially those of an intangible character, on the path of ISMEs (Rialp and Rialp 2007). Human and organizational capital resources appear to have a significant positive influence on the success of ISMEs (Rialp and Rialp 2007). The resource-based view (RBV) (Barney 1991; Hunt 2000; Wernerfelt 1984) provides insights on how smaller firms can compete in international markets. The RBV can make a significant contribution to international marketing through its identification of specific knowledge and skills as valuable, unique, and hard-to-imitate resources that separate winners from losers in global competition, allowing small firms to differentiate themselves and succeed overseas (Peng 2001).

ISMEs typically lack substantial financial and tangible resources, and must compete via intangible knowledge and capabilities. Compared with large MNEs, the importance of 'intangible resourcefulness', that is, the ability to do more with less, should be relatively important to ISMEs (Peng 2001). Consistent with the RBV, ISMEs appear adept at leveraging unique and often scarce organizational resources. ISMEs manifest specific resources comprising orientations and competencies that are instrumental to the conception and implementation of activities in international markets. ISMEs seem to leverage a collection of fundamental resources that facilitate their international success (Knight and Cavusgil 2004; McDougall, Shane and Oviatt 1994). Much of these resources consist of the know-how, skills, and overall capabilities that reside in the managers who work at these firms.

Sixth, unique product positioning reflects the creation and marketing of a product that is perceived as unique. It is akin to differentiation strategy and involves creating customer loyalty by uniquely meeting a particular need. Differentiation strategy provides a means for reducing competition by creating entry barriers to entry of would-be rival firms (e.g., Porter 1980). Marketing scholars recognize the inherent value in providing unique offerings, so as to differentiate the firm from rivals (e.g., Day 1994). Valuable unique assets allow resource-constrained smaller firms, such as ISMEs, to more readily enter international markets. The approach is typically associated with innovative product features, excellent customer service, or patented know-how – all factors that distinguish the firm from its competitors. The differentiation that arises from marketing unique products is particularly appropriate to ISMEs that operate in niche markets. Differentiation strategy is based on product innovation and intensive marketing/image management (Miller 1988). Evidence suggests that many ISMEs differentiate via product innovation, often by leveraging new technologies.

Private knowledge provides the foundation for new technology development and is perhaps, therefore, the key resource ISMEs leverage in order to differentiate products from those of rivals and overcome the indigenous advantages enjoyed by local firms in the numerous countries where ISMEs operate (Oviatt and McDougall 1994). To the extent that the knowledge used to develop a unique product is imperfectly imitable (Barney 1991), the ISME is able to keep such knowledge proprietary. Unique knowledge can be maintained if its development is associated with processes that are socially complex or causally ambiguous in ways that prevent rivals from understanding how the knowledge emerged (Menon and Varadarajan 1992). Unique product positioning allows ISMEs to serve specific markets well, giving rise to increased market share and sales growth in the niche markets that the firm serves. In general, offering unique products, at least to the extent buyer's special needs are served and direct competitive rivalries are minimized, should support superior international performance.

Finally, network connections appear instrumental to the success of many ISMEs (e.g., Bell 1995; Coviello and Munro 1995; Rasmussen *et al.* 2001; Larimo 2001). The role of new organization forms, especially strategic partnerships and networks, is increasingly recognized in international marketing. Network relationships are replacing simple market-based transactions and traditional bureaucratic hierarchical organizations. A more recent conception of marketing emphasizes managing strategic relationships and strategically positioning the firm between suppliers and customers (e.g., Hakansson 1990; Webster 1992). An industrial network is defined as an organizational structure in which a large number of interconnected actors (firms and individuals) are involved in economic activities (production) which convert resources (inputs) to finished goods, semi-finished goods, and services for consumption by end-users (firms and other entities). Actors are the catalyst, for they own and control the resources and they carry out the activities. In practical terms, the network consists of firms from several different industries. Such relationships are seen to assist ISMEs in their internationalization efforts.

Internationally, networks assist firms in promoting long-term strategic cooperation. They are intended to accomplish important organizational goals such as risk reduction, innovation, and a division of labor and organizational functions. Joint ventures (and other forms of inter-firm cooperation) help firms create new products, keep abreast of rapidly-changing technologies, and enter foreign markets efficiently. They aid with government suasion (that is, overcoming government regulation or barriers to entry), the acquisition of needed skills, know-how, and assets (such as access to a distribution channel abroad) (Coviello and Munro, 1995; Rasmussen *et al.* 2001).

Generally, internationally entrepreneurial firms proactively seek success in foreign markets. However, owing to their smaller size, most such firms cannot compete head-to-head with larger or more established rivals. Accordingly, smaller firms typically target niche markets via the pursuit of product differentiation strategies, that is, via the creation and marketing of products that are relatively unique. Strongly marketing-oriented firms that are smaller and relatively resource-constrained undertake strategies that differentiate their offerings from rivals, thereby facilitating short-term survival and longer-term competitive advantages.

The theoretical perspectives given above help explain how small firms can succeed in global markets. Such businesses can survive and thrive in competitive foreign markets by applying a unique gestalt of approaches and by aligning key strategic variables with the demands of local markets. When combined with the strong international orientation of ISMEs and the tendency of management to view the world as a single marketplace, as well as the high degree of strategic flexibility and associated reduced administrative heritage inherent in less-established firms, the above perspectives help to explain how ISMEs are able to succeed in foreign markets.

CONCLUSIONS AND RESEARCH DIRECTIONS

Small multinational enterprises now comprise a substantial proportion of new enterprises in Europe, Asia, North America and elsewhere. Their emergence reflects the internationalization of a breed of firms heretofore not generally regarded as significant international players. Despite the immense hurdles that smaller businesses typically face, many ISMEs are faring well in their pursuit of foreign markets – environments generally more risky than those found in the firm's home market. Research evidence suggests that ISMEs make use of a particular constellation of knowledge, capabilities, and unique resources that may help them overcome the rather considerable challenges of being relatively small players in a competitive global marketplace. Despite the scarce financial and tangible resources that usually characterize small firms, ISMEs appear willing and able to tackle the considerable challenges of international marketing.

The rise of ISMEs is partially driven by globalization and advancing technologies. These companies are guided by managers who tend to view the world as their marketplace and undertake substantial international selling activities, often from the firm's earliest days, managing to achieve considerable international success. In many respects, it is possible that smaller size confers flexibility and agility, and may be best suited for serving niche markets abroad.

Findings from past research have particularly emphasized the role of international entrepreneurial orientation as an antecedent to international performance in ISMEs. Strong entrepreneurial orientation may be associated with the development of strategies and approaches that support internationalization and business success abroad. Other research findings also support a significant role for international marketing approaches in the performance of ISMEs. The proactive development of substantive marketing approaches and business strategies abroad is likely to play a role in the performance of ISMEs because the international context imposes numerous uncontrollable and often unique challenges to internationalizing firms. The significance of entrepreneurial orientation, marketing orientation, and customer focus is likely to vary by industry and target market, but their importance to ISME success appears significant.

In a world characterized by falling trade barriers, economic integration, and other globalization trends, ISMEs might be seen as relatively disadvantaged because of their small size. According to this view, such businesses cannot create the massive operations deemed necessary to leverage economies of scale and scope across an integrated global marketplace. The global environment might be seen as too harsh for many smaller firms.

But this view fails to recognize several factors. First, facilitating technologies and globalization-induced infrastructures are helping many ISMEs to do business in various countries. Globalizing trends are not a burden; they appear to be a boon to many such firms. Indeed, doing business internationally can be an important source of competitive advantage. ISMEs are exposed to various business environments abroad, which can give rise to learning that helps managers advance firms' performance goals.

Second, many ISMEs are at the forefront of new products and technologies that engender monopoly power (Hymer 1976) and give them unique advantages over rivals. Offering unique or superior products helps create customer loyalty by meeting particular needs better than rivals. While the literature specifies numerous approaches for achieving international business success, innovative processes that drive the development of superior, unique products appear particularly important to many smaller firms.

Third, the inherent flexibility enjoyed by many ISMEs confers key advantages for adapting to evolving buyer tastes and other shifting environmental conditions across myriad markets and industries that larger firms are unwilling or unable to serve. The flexibility of agile firms enhances their ability to transform product and process innovations into business activities that support superior business performance. The flexibility afforded through judicious use of foreign distributors enables entrepreneurial firms to respond rapidly to evolving customer needs, competitor actions, and shifting environmental contingencies.

Finally, the majority of ISMEs operate in niche markets that often are ignored by larger firms. Such markets allow for sufficient economies of scale and scope as well as experience curve effects. Penrose (1959) portrayed the role of small enterprises as exploiters of the 'interstices' created by large firms. In every industry, there exist niche markets that are underserved by the broad brush approaches of big business. Owing to limits on how quickly they can expand, larger companies are simply incapable of exploiting all emergent international marketing opportunities. These interstices can be exploited by smaller entrants.

Research suggests that the rise of ISMEs might challenge earlier views on the internationalization of the firm. Conventional models long have emphasized that this is a slow, almost plodding process (e.g., Cavusgil 1982; Johanson and Vahlne 1990). In part, the slowness reflects the view that management is unable to acquire relevant knowledge, experience, and market information rapidly. But ISMEs seem to be taking an approach that suggests the traditional models need to be reassessed. Small size, paucity of financial and tangible resources, and limited manpower are no longer serious barriers to substantial internationalization and success abroad. This outcome is compelling because, realistically, international marketing is no longer an option for many firms – it has become a necessity. Based on findings presented in extant literature, it is likely that ISMEs are gradually becoming much more commonplace in international business. They are undoubtedly playing a greater role in international marketing than ever before.

It is useful to explore here how improvements might be made in future research on ISME firms. First, numerous past studies were theoretical expositions in which no empirical data were collected. Future research should collect data on ISMEs in order to gain a realistic understanding of the characteristics and other relevant factors regarding these firms. In addition, future empirical studies might focus on obtaining data from various countries, in order to assess the extent and nature of the ISME phenomenon in diverse international settings. For example, evidence suggests that small- and medium-sized enterprises in the United States are less internationalized than those in several European countries (OECD, 1997). It is useful to examine ISMEs in various countries in order to assess the external validity of findings and to uncover any possible differences in ISME characteristics and other factors around the world.

Future research might investigate issues such as the following:

- What accounts for international performance in ISMEs?
- What conditions in smaller firms give rise to internationalization?
- What is the role of company characteristics, such as managerial vision, drive, and experience, as well as the invention of new products and other discoveries in the firm?
- Is the ISME phenomenon prevalent in particular types of industries or economic sectors? For example, to what extent does the ISME phenomenon occur among firms that emphasize high-technology products, versus firms that deal in mainly low-technology products? To what extent does the ISME phenomenon occur in the manufacturing sector, as opposed to the services sector?
- Are ISMEs more internationally oriented than older-style companies that expand abroad incrementally? If so, does an international orientation confer any types of advantages in company performance?
- What is the role of network relationships in the internationalization of ISMEs? How do networks advance internationalization goals and international performance? What is the nature of network relationships in high-performing ISMEs?

Ongoing research on ISMEs should aim at unifying and improving operational definitions and indicators of these firms, in order to make future research efforts more understandable and comparable. Diverse conceptual approaches on ISMEs are motivated by the lack of a generally-accepted, fully-explanatory model of this phenomenon. Better formulated and more highly integrated theoretical frameworks should aim to support the development of research propositions and hypotheses that clarify the ISME phenomenon. The best approaches combine quantitative and qualitative research methods. A methodological strategy based on a number of case-based studies of ISMEs, together with longitudinal surveys of large-scale, representative samples of firms should prove useful. Research should aim to clarify the performance antecedents, environmental characteristics, internationalization processes, and main characteristics of these firms, as well as the characteristics of the entrepreneurs and managers who run them.

These and numerous other issues can be targeted for future research. Once the nature and success factors of ISMEs are significantly understood, research might investigate which public policy initiatives can facilitate and promote the development and progress of this distinctive breed of enterprise. Given the limited financial and tangible resources that usually characterize ISMEs, public policy might aim at supporting the success of such businesses in their international endeavors. Over time many firms will flourish, some will founder, and a substantial proportion will merge or be absorbed by larger organizations. ISMEs are often drivers of national economic development and innovativeness. Accordingly, research is needed that assists policy-makers to better understand what types of public policies can best support the emergence and success of these firms.

REFERENCES

Aspelund, A., and Moen, O. (2001) 'A generation perspective on small firms' internationalization – from traditional exporters and flexible specialists to born globals', in C. Axinn and P. Matthyssens (eds), *Reassessing the Internationalization of the Firm*, (Advances in International Marketing, volume 11). Amsterdam: JAI/Elsevier, pp. 197–225.

Barney, J. (1991) 'Firm resources and sustained competitive advantage', *Journal of Management*, 17(1): 99–120.

Bell, J. (1995) 'The internationalization of small computer software firms: a further challenge to "stage" theories', *European Journal of Marketing*, 29(8): 60–75.

Bell, J. and McNaughton, R. (2000) 'Born global firms: a challenge to public policy in support of internationalization', in J. Pels and D. Stewart (eds), *Proceedings of the American Marketing Association*, pp. 176–185.

Bilkey, W. J. and Tesar, G. (1977) 'The export behavior of smaller Wisconsin manufacturing firms', *Journal of International Business Studies*, 9 (Spring/Summer): 93–98.

Buckley, P. and Casson, M. (1976) *The Future of the Multinational Enterprise*. London: MacMillan.

Burgel, O. and Murray, G. (2000) 'The international market entry choices of start-up companies in high-technology industries', *Journal of International Marketing*, 8(2): 33–62.

Cavusgil, S. T. (1982) 'Some observations on the relevance of critical variables for internationalization stages', in Michael Czinkota (ed.), *Export Management*. New York: Praeger, pp. 276–286.

Cavusgil, S. T., Zou, S. and Naidu, G. M. (1993) 'Product and promotion adaptation in export ventures: an empirical investigation', *Journal of International Business Studies*, 24 (Fall): 479–506.

Cavusgil, S. T. and Zou, S. (1994), 'Marketing strategy-performance relationship: an investigation of the empirical link in export market ventures', *Journal of Marketing*, 58 (January): 1–21.

Chaston, I. (1997) 'Small firm performance: assessing the interaction between entrepreneurial style and organizational structure', *European Journal of Marketing*, 31 (11/12): 814–831.

Cohen, W. and Levinthal, D. (1990) 'Absorbtive capacity: a new perspective on learning and innovation', *Administrative Science Quarterly*, 35: 128–152.

Collis, D. (1991) 'A resource-based analysis of global competition', *Strategic Management Journal*, 12 (Summer, Special Issue): 49–68.

Czinkota, M., Knight, G. and Liesch, P. (2004) 'Terrorism and international business: conceptual foundations', in G. Suder (ed.), *Terrorism and the International Business Environment*. Northampton, MA: Edward Elgar Publishing.

Day, G. (1994) 'The capabilities of market-driven organizations', *Journal of Marketing*, 58 (October): 37–52.

Dosi, G. (1988), 'Sources, procedures, and microeconomic effects of innovation', *Journal of Economic Literature*, 26(3): 1120–1171.

Freeman, S., Edwards, R. and Schroder, B. (2006) 'How smaller born-global firms use networks and alliances to overcome constraints to rapid internationalization', *Journal of International Marketing*, 14(3): 33–49.

Friedman, T. (2005) *The World Is Flat*. New York: Farrar, Straus, & Giroux.

Gleason, K. and Wiggenhorn, J. (2007) 'Born globals, the choice of globalization strategy, and the market's perception of performance', *Journal of World Business*, 42(3): 322–331.

Hakansson, H. (1990) 'International marketing and purchasing of industrial goods: an interaction approach', in H. Thorelli and S.T. Cavusgil (eds), *International Marketing Strategy*, 3rd edn. New York: Pergamon Press, pp. 87–101.

Hunt, S. (2000) *A General Theory of Competition*. Thousand Oaks, CA: Sage Publications.

Hymer, S. (1976) *The International Operations of National Firms*. Cambridge, MA: MIT Press.

IMF (2006) *World Economic Outlook Database*, April 2006, Washington DC: International Monetary Fund, data accessed at www.imf.org.

Johanson, J. and Vahlne, J-E. (1990) 'The mechanism of internationalization', *International Marketing Review*, 7(4): 11–24.

Knickerbocker, F. T. (1973) *Oligopolistic Reaction and the Multinational Enterprise*. Cambridge, MA: Harvard University Press.

Knight, G. (2000) 'Entrepreneurship and marketing strategy: the SME under globalization', *Journal of International Marketing* 8(2): 12–32.

Knight, G. and Cavusgil, S. T. (2004) 'Innovation, organizational capabilities, and the born-global firm', *Journal of International Business Studies*, 35(2): 124–141.

Kuivalainen, O., Sundqvist, S. and Servais, P. (2007) 'Firms' degree of born-globalness, international entrepreneurial orientation and export performance', *Journal of World Business*, 42(3): 253–259.

Kuemmerle, W. (2002) 'Home base and knowledge management in international ventures', *Journal of Business Venturing*, 17(2): 99–122.

Larimo, J. (2001) 'Internationalization of SMEs – two case studies of Finnish born global firms', in C. Axinn (ed.), *Proceedings, CIMaR Annual Conference*, Sydney, Australia. pp. 1–21.

Loane, S. (2006) 'The role of the internet in the internationalisation of small and medium sized companies', *Journal of International Entrepreneurship*, 3(4): 263–277.

Lumpkin, G. T. and Dess, G. (1996) 'Clarifying the entrepreneurial orientation construct and linking it to performance', *Academy of Management Review*, 21(1): 135–172.

Luostarinen, R. and Gabrielsson, M. (2006) 'Globalization and marketing strategies of born globals in SMOPECs', *Thunderbird International Business Review*, 48(6): 773–785.

Madsen, T. and Servais, P. (1997) 'The internationalization of born globals: an evolutionary process?', *International Business Review*, 6(6): 561–583.

McDougall, P. and Oviatt, B. (2000) 'International entrepreneurship: the intersection of two research paths', *Academy of Management Journal*, 43(5): 902–906.

McDougall, P., Shane, S. and Oviatt, B. (1994) 'Explaining the formation of international new ventures: the limits of theories from international business research', *Journal of Business Venturing*, 9(6): 469–487.

Menon, A. and Varadarajan, P. R. (1992) 'A model of marketing knowledge use within firms', *Journal of Marketing*, 56 (October): 53–71.

Miller, D. (1988) 'Relating Porter's business strategies to environment and structure: analysis and performance implications', *Academy of Management Journal*, 31(2): 280–308.

Mort, G. S. and Weerawardena, J. (2006) 'Networking capability and international entrepreneurship; how networks function in Australian born global firms', *International Marketing Review*, 23(5): 549–561.

Nelson, R. and Winter, S. (1982) '*An Evolutionary Theory of Economic Change*'. Cambridge, MA: Belknap Press.

Nonaka, I. and Takeuchi, H. (1995) *The Knowledge-Creating Company*. New York: Oxford University Press.

OECD (1997) *Globalization and Small and Medium Enterprises (SMEs)*. Paris: Organisation for Economic Cooperation and Development.

Okura-sho Insatsu Kyoku (1995) *Chuushoo Kigyoo Hakushoo* (White paper on small and medium-size enterprise). Tokyo: Okura-sho Insatsu Kyoku (Treasury Department, Government of Japan).

Oviatt, B. and McDougall, P. (1994) 'Toward a theory of international new ventures', *Journal of International Business Studies,* 25(1): 45–64.

Oviatt, B. and McDougall, P. (1995) 'Global start-ups: entrepreneurs on a worldwide stage', *Academy of Management Executive,* 9(2): 30–43.

Oviatt, B. and McDougall, P. (1999) 'A framework for understanding accelerated international entrepreneurship', in A. Rugman and R. Wright (eds), *Research in Global Strategic Management: International Entrepreneurship.* Stamford, CT: JAI Press Inc, pp. 23–40.

Peng, M. (2001) 'The resource-based view and international business', *Journal of Management,* 27: 803–829.

Penrose, E. (1959) *The Theory of the Growth of the Firm.* London: Basil Blackwell.

Porter, M. (1980) *Competitive Strategy.* New York: Free Press.

Rasmussen, E., Madsen, T. and Evangelista, F. (2001) 'The founding of the born global company in Denmark and Australia: sensemaking and networking', *Asia Pacific Journal of Marketing and Logistics,* 13(3): 75–107.

Rialp, A. and Rialp, J. (2007) 'Faster and more successful exporters: an exploratory study of born global firms from the resource-based view', *Journal of Euro–Marketing,* 16(1/2): 71–85.

Rialp, A., Rialp, J., and Knight, G. (2005) 'The phenomenon of early internationalizing firms: what do we know after a decade (1993–2003) of scientific inquiry?' *International Business Review,* 14: 147–166.

Schumpeter, J. (1942) *Capitalism, Socialism, and Democracy.* New York: Harper & Brothers Publishers.

Senge, P. (1990) *The Fifth Discipline: The Art and Practice of the Learning Organization.* New York: Doubleday.

Simon, H. (1996) *Hidden Champions: Lessons from 500 of the World's Best Unknown Companies.* Boston: Harvard Business School Press.

Simmonds, K. and Smith, H. (1968) 'The first export order: a marketing innovation', *British Journal of Marketing,* (Summer): 93–100.

Steensma, H. K., Marino, L., Weaver, K. M. and Dickson, P. (2000) 'The influence of national culture on the formation of technology alliances by entrepreneurial firms', *Academy of Management Journal,* 43(5): 951–973.

Stinchcombe, A. (1965) 'Social structure and organizations', in J. March (ed.), *Handbook of Organizations.* Chicago: Rand McNally, pp. 142–193.

Vernon, R. (1966) 'International investment and international trade in the product cycle', *Quarterly Journal of Economics,* 80: 190–207.

Webster, F. (1992) 'The changing role of marketing in the corporation', *Journal of Marketing,* 56 (October): 1–17.

Weerawardena, J., Mort, G. S. Liesch, P. W. and Knight, G. (2007) 'Conceptualizing accelerated internationalization in the born global firm: a dynamic capabilities perspective', *Journal of World Business,* 42(3): 294–303.

Wernerfelt, B. (1984) 'A resource-based view of the firm', *Strategic Management Journal,* 5(2): 171–180.

Zahra, S., Ireland, D. and Hitt, M. (2000) 'International expansion by new venture firms: International diversity, mode of market entry, technological learning, and performance', *Academy of Management Journal,* 43(5): 925–950.

Zahra, S. and George, G. (2002) 'International entrepreneurship: the current status of the field and future research agenda', in M. Hitt, R. Ireland, M. Camp and D. Sexton (eds), *Strategic Leadership: Creating A New Mindset.* London: Blackwell, pp. 255–288.

Zhou, L. (2007) 'The effects of entrepreneurial proclivity and foreign market knowledge on early internationalization', *Journal of World Business,* 42(3): 281–290.

26

Ethics and Corporate Social Responsibility for Marketing in the Global Marketplace

Georges Enderle and Patrick E. Murphy

INTRODUCTION

This chapter explores the relevance of ethics and corporate responsibility for marketing in the global marketplace. Structured into four sections, it first presents the emergence of ethics and corporate social responsibility (CSR) during the last 20 years. It then undertakes to clarify key ethical concepts of morality, ethics, responsibility and marketing ethics. Subsequently, the context of 'the global marketplace' is characterized as a field of applied ethics with its implications for marketing ethics. To conclude, evolving perspectives are delineated for marketing ethics in the global arena.

EMERGENCE OF ETHICS AND CSR IN THE GLOBAL MARKETPLACE

In the 1980s we hardly could have predicted the explosive growth and rising ethical expectations and initiatives regarding business behavior that have emerged worldwide over the past two decades. Of course, this does not mean that these expectations were consistent, nor met, and that all these initiatives were well designed and successful. Nevertheless, despite the mixed record, the emergence of ethics and corporate social responsibility as a prerequisite in the global marketplace is a recognized phenomenon. In this chapter we first explore a multitude of forms of broadly defined ethics and CSR that have emerged globally and in different countries and regions. We then explore the underlying arguments which may have driven those multiple expectations and initiatives. To conclude this section, we try to elucidate several views about ethics in general that seem to steer the assessment of those phenomena.

Multiple forms in different countries, regions and worldwide

Sustainability   In 1987 the World Commission on Environment and Development published its report *Our Common Future* (WCED 1987) and offered a fairly precise definition of 'sustainability', namely 'to meet the needs of the present without compromising the ability of future generations to meet their own needs' (p. 8). In other words, we have to think and act today in terms of intergenerational ethics so that our children and grandchildren will have at least the same conditions we enjoy, to live their own lives. This definition was also adopted by the United Nations Conference on Environment and Development in 1992 in Rio de Janeiro, Brazil, and has been playing a guiding role ever since in dealing with issues such as the depletion of the ozone layer, biodiversity, and global climate change.

In the business sector, the World Business Council on Sustainable Development (WBCSD) has taken multiple initiatives to advance environmental awareness and promote business conduct that is sustainable as defined above. This notion of sustainability, which is a goal for the society as a whole, should not be confused, as WBCSD states, with 'eco-efficiency' that denotes both economic and ecological efficiency (Schmidheiny and Zorraquin. 1996, p. 17). It also clearly differs from many other usages of the term sustainability, for example in 'sustainable profit' or 'sustainable business', which often means merely for the long haul without environmental qualifications. Rather, the commitment to sustainable development includes economic growth, ecological balance, and social equity. Over the years WBCSD has grown to be a powerful organization (see www.wbcsd.org) and documented in a number of publications how business can operate in a genuinely sustainable manner: *Changing Course. A Global Perspective on Development and the Environment* (Schmidheiny 1992); *Financing Change. The Financial Community, Eco-Efficiency, and Sustainability* (Schmidheiny and Zorraquin 1996); *Eco-Efficiency. The Business Link to Sustainable Development* (DeSimone and Popoff 2000); *Walking the Talk. The Business Case for Sustainable Development* (Holliday *et al.* 2002).

Compared with the late 1980s, it seems fair to say that the challenge of sustainability is now recognized by far more people and businesses. To illustrate this change, the worldwide dissemination of the 'Equator Principles' since 2005, an industry approach for financial institutions in determining, assessing and managing environmental and social risk in project financing (www.equator-principles.com); and the Award for Sustainable Banking (2008 in its third year) sponsored by the *Financial Times* and IFC, the private sector arm of the World Bank Group (*Financial Times*, Special Report, June 7, 2007) deserve mention. It should also be noted that the pressing need for sustainability has increased dramatically and the degree of recognition and taking action varies a great deal among countries and populations.

Corruption   Corruption is another issue that was widely underestimated in the 1980s and has then turned out to be a serious problem in developing and developed countries. While the United States, in the aftermath of the Lockheed and other scandals, enacted the Foreign Corrupt Practices Act in 1977 and amended it in 1988 (Alpern 2005), it took the OECD another decade to set up the OECD Anti-Bribery Convention (1997) that had to be incorporated into national legislation. As of February 2008, 37 countries ratified the Convention (see www.oecd.org). Because the World Bank was not ready to tackle corruption head-on in the early 1990s, in 1991 a senior officer, Dr. Peter Eigen, left the Bank and founded Transparency International (TI), a nongovernmental organization with the mission to fight corruption. It is headquartered in Berlin because corruption should be considered primarily a challenge for developed countries. TI has become a very influential NGO with more than 90 national chapters and issued numerous publications, in particular the annual Global Corruption Report, the Corruption Perceptions Index and Bribe Payers Index (see www.transparency.org). In the last few years, corruption has become a major concern for the World Bank too. (The search result for 'corruption' under the World Bank's Data & Research shows about 8860 references as of February 27, 2008.)

There is a vast literature on corruption and bribery, several features of which might be highlighted in the following. A first set of publications deals with conceptual and measurement issues: Moran (1999), D'Andrade (2005), Wilhelm (2002), and Sampford *et al.* (2006). Second, questions of understanding corruption and bribery are discussed from an economic perspective (Beets 2005; Rose-Ackerman 2006; Lambsdorff 2007), in the context of development (Nwabuzar 2005; O'Higgins 2006), and as concerns of companies (Argandona 2001, 2003, 2005). A third set of issues is addressed in global and regional studies: Vogl (2007); Husted (2002); Bolongaita and Bhargava (2003); Davis and Ruhe (2003); Black (2004); and De Maria (2007). Fourth, action proposals for combating corruption in countries or companies are developed in Nielson (2000); Ryan (2000); Bolongaita and Bhargava (2003); Berenbeim and Conference Board (2006), Richter and Burke (2007); and Vogl (2007). Finally, Getz (2006) investigates the effectiveness of global prohibition regimes with regard to corruption and the anti-bribery convention.

Human rights A third area of emerging concern relates to the responsibilities of companies with respect to human rights. Traditionally, it was up to specific countries to make sure that the human rights codified in international declarations and conventions were incorporated into national laws and enforced by national governments. However, in the process of globalization the relationships between government, business, and civil society have changed considerably. The power of multinational corporations has increased dramatically. Nongovernmental organizations have multiplied, become more vocal and applied more pressure. And governments in many countries are or have become weak. Therefore, the responsibility

of business has changed, as stated in the report of the United Nations High Commissioner for Human Rights:

> Business, like all actors in society, has to operate in a responsible manner, including through respecting human rights. Business has an enormous potential to provide an enabling environment for the enjoyment of human rights through investment, employment creation and the stimulation of economic growth. Its activities have also threatened human rights in some situations and individual companies have been complicit in human rights violations. (Quoted in Chandler 2005, p. 39)

In order to better understand the nature and scope of business responsibilities with regard to human rights, John Ruggie was appointed by Kofi Annan to reconcile the often-conflicting demands of companies, NGOs, and governments and to elaborate common standards for operationalizing the normative principles of human rights. Unfortunately, despite Ruggie's relentless and patient efforts, no compromise could be found until now (see Davis 2006; Zerk 2007; Chandler 2007). In his report of February 9, 2007 (Ruggie 2007) Ruggie takes stock of the existing international human rights standards of responsibility and accountability for corporate acts. His second report (Ruggie, 2008), presents a framework on how business should address human rights issues.

United Nations Global Compact and other initiatives These three areas of concern have been also addressed by the United Nations Global Compact based on 'shared values for the global market' and launched by Kofi Annan in 2000 (www.globalcompact.org). Businesses (and later also cities, business schools and other organizations) are invited to become signatories of the ten principles of human and labor rights, environmental protection, and anti-corruption, to shape their behavior accordingly, and to report on their performance every two years. As of February 2008, over 3,200 companies (or organizations) have joined the UN Global Compact (UNGC) and submitted a 'Communication of Progress'. The Global Reporting Initiative

(GRI), another voluntary effort, was started in 1997 and has developed 'Sustainability Guidelines' for economic, social, and environmental performance on the basis of 11 reporting principles and with a series of specific indicators (www.globalreporting.org). Since its inception, approximately 20 000 people have engaged in the GRI network (as of February 2008). The GRI complements the Global Compact, and now actually collaborates with it, by providing measurable standards to the UNGC's general principles.

Among the many initiatives undertaken in the past 20 years for setting standards of corporate 'responsible' behavior (however ill defined) we should also mention the worldwide and long-lasting activities of the International Organization for Standardization (ISO; http://isotc.iso.org). After developing the standards ISO 9000 for quality management and ISO 14000 for environment conduct, ISO is in the process of producing ISO 26000 for social responsibility by October 2008. ISO might cooperate with other international organizations, particularly with the International Labor Organization and the UN Global Compact.

While all the aforementioned initiatives unmistakably involve an ethical dimension, either implicitly or explicitly, the following declarations and statements clearly articulate the ethical nature of those expectations. In particular, the Declaration toward a Global Ethic (1993), the Interfaith Declaration of International Business Ethics (1994), the Caux Roundtable Principles for Business (1994), and the statement of the InterAction Council (1996) (all presented in Enderle 1999) are noteworthy. Whereas these documents are of global scope and promulgate universal ethical norms, a worldwide survey of business ethics in 1996 focused on the situations in different countries and continents and described various forms of emerging business ethics issues (Enderle 1997).

Interaction between law and ethics initiatives As ethical concerns have sometimes led to

laws and regulations (for example, in the case of corruption), legislation and other government initiatives have also brought about increasing ethical awareness and likely, even better business conduct. In the United States the Federal Sentencing Guidelines, enacted in 1991, accounted for the corporations' proactive compliance efforts in reducing the fines for their wrongdoing, and the revised Guidelines of 2004 explicitly require the judges to take into account the ethical effort made by the defendant organization. As a result of these regulations, now most major corporations have established positions of compliance and ethics officers (Ethikos 2003, 2004). The Sarbanes-Oxley Act (2002) is another example of the legislation's impact on corporate ethics. Although one might disagree on the appropriateness of certain provisions (for instance, its applicability to smaller companies or its treatment of foreign corporations), one can still agree that this Act, by and large, has helped to raise the awareness of the importance of ethical business conduct (Ethikos 2002).

Corporate social responsibility or CSR More than in North America, the promotion of 'corporate social responsibility' or CSR has been advanced in Europe, particularly by the European Union in the early years of the twenty-first century. In 2001 the Commission of the European Communities published a Green Paper to promote 'a European Framework for Corporate Social Responsibility' (Commission 2001), followed by a Communication (2002) that invited many stakeholders to participate in a European-wide dialogue on CSR. In 2004 the Commission published the final results of this dialogue and recommendations. Two years later it refocused its attention on 'implementing the partnership for growth and jobs' and, by doing so, hoping 'to make Europe a pole of excellence on CSR'. Unfortunately, this publication was not the product of a multi-stakeholder dialogue (as the European CSR definition would have required), but was the result of negotiations between the Commission and business leaders alone. Besides these initiatives of the EU in Brussels, as a matter of fact, there is a considerable diversity of CSR notions and practices in Europe, well documented in *Corporate Social Responsibility across Europe* (Habisch *et al.* 2006) with reports from 23 countries.

CSR expectations and initiatives have emerged in other continents as well. Numerous examples are discussed in *Responsibilidad Social Corporativa – Una Mirada Global* (Arroyo, *et al.* 2006) as well as a report on business ethics in Latin America, published by *The Ethical Corporation* (November 2005). Moreover, since 2001 and on a regular basis this magazine has reported on CSR and ethical challenges and initiatives around the world, to mention, in particular, the reports on Africa (November 2002), Asia (June 2002 and September 2003), China (March 2004), and India (April 2007).

The efforts of companies (especially multinationals) in developing more coherent CSR strategies has been documented in a number of recent sources (Porter and Kramer 2006; Engardio 2007; Savitz 2006).

Four arguments for business and marketing ethics

Given the abundance of emerging expectations and initiatives regarding ethics and CSR in the global marketplace, one may question the underlying drivers or arguments that can explain these developments. Although the circumstances vary a great deal across the countries and industries, four arguments can be identified which apply to different contexts in varying degrees.

The argument of scandals   Business scandals did not begin with the Enron and Parmalat cases. The list of scandals is long and seemingly unending: bribery in the procurement of aircraft; explosions of highly toxic substances

in the chemical industry; spectacular environmental pollution of rivers and seas; food contamination; dubious marketing practices in developing countries; car ferry disasters; illegal armament exports; insider trading; deceptive financial reporting; excessive executive compensations, etc. It is fair to say that no country is spared from such scandals. But what are their consequences for improving business practice in the long run? It is true that scandals naturally provoke outrage along with a call for new and better business conduct. Yet, in spite of the dramatic publicity they receive, the scandals argument does not seem to be very strong. One just reacts, mostly emotionally and without adequate background knowledge. Scandals can shake up, but not motivate for lasting changes in practice.

The argument of economization   This argument states that business nowadays plays an ever more important guiding role for the whole of social life, that an 'economization' of society is underway. Economic thinking and acting are penetrating and dominating more and more domains: large investments; research and development; mass media; politics; education; healthcare; culture; and the family, for example. Thus, only what counts economically and yields profit is relevant. The potentially disastrous consequences are compounded through the process of globalization. What can be said about this argument? Even if this statement appears to be exaggerated, various tendencies toward economization cannot be denied. Against them, business ethics is called to support insurmountable boundary lines imposed by laws and regulations. The remedy comes from outside business, which is necessary but certainly not sufficient for introducing and strengthening 'new practices'.

The argument of 'good business'   This is also called 'making the business case' for ethics and CSR. Now widely used, particularly in North America, it says that 'good business' and 'good ethics' go hand in hand. Ethical conduct lies in the self-enlightened interest of the companies and is seen as an important motivational and unifying force to compete in the global marketplace. Because this argument comes from within business and is not imposed from outside, it is especially attractive for business people. However, here the role of business ethics seems to be ambiguous, as will be discussed later (in the subsection on Corporate Responsibility and CSR). Is 'good ethics' only a means to achieve business ends? What happens if it does not help to meet them? Should it then be dropped? If this argument holds only in the long run, what is a company supposed to do in the short term?

The argument of challenges This reason for business ethics is forward-looking as we face the great challenges in the twenty-first century. Emotional reactions to scandals, imposed restrictions on business from outside, and trust in self-regulation and making the business case for better business conduct are considered insufficient. Merely reactive attitudes and behaviors will fail. What is imperative is an anticipatory, proactive, and 'entrepreneurial' approach. Among the great challenges, we may include: an ecologically compatible economy, which allows all human beings to live decently on the planet earth; the overcoming of worldwide poverty and unemployment; the abolition of discrimination relating to gender, nationality, race, and religion; the establishment of relatively corruption-free business environments; the shaping of just international business relations, not biased by reckless competition and extreme power imbalances, but promoting efficient and peaceful cooperation among all business partners.

While these four arguments can explain, to some extent, the emergence of ethics and CSR, they may involve very different views and attitudes about ethics in this process.

Different views and attitudes about ethics

In describing the emergence of ethics and CSR for marketing in the global marketplace we took stock of a wide array of things that business should do, either because business itself embraces those responsibilities or because other groups expect business to fulfill them. We talked about sustainability, corruption, human rights, and many other issues. These are all ethical questions in the sense that they ask the fundamental question of ethics: What should I do, what should we do? However, the more specific this question is formulated and the more closely we look at the proposed answers, the more diverse and even bewildering becomes the picture. When we attempt to reach out to a global understanding (which is an almost impossible endeavor), we may realize something of the enormous diversity and contradictions of cultural norms and values. In fact, as Christian Tyler observed some years ago, 'we live *in an age of ethical confusion* (emphasis added), and are prone to periodic outbreaks of moral panic' (Tyler 2000).

There are different ways of facing, and reacting to, this confusion, which have also affected the emergence of ethics and CSR described above. One way could be called '*ethical imperialism*', that is the attitude of people, organizations, and governments to impose their own norms and values on other people, organizations, and governments. For example, various developed countries and NGOs are accused of ethical imperialism because they require developing countries to meet their own labor and environmental standards. Or the enforcement of human rights is interpreted by certain Asian leaders as an act of Western ethical imperialism, while similar feelings arise among non-Asians (and Asians as well) at the promulgation of so-called Asian values.

The countervailing attitude to ethical imperialism is ethical relativism. Instead of imposing one's ethical views on other cultures and countries, one refuses to make ethical judgments on them. Relativism states that ethical values and judgments are ultimately dependent upon, or relative to, one's culture and society, and there is no right or wrong, moral or immoral, except in terms of a particular culture or society (DesJardins 2006: 22-6). For instance, widespread corruption in a particular country cannot be ethically criticized by foreigners. If companies want to operate there according to the relativist, they are morally obliged to play by the rules of the corrupt regime.

A third attitude, often in response to ethical confusion and particularly directed to international affairs, is ethical skepticism. It holds that we cannot reasonably assess ethical values and norms at all. Doubt and uncertainty prevent us from making any ethical judgment. Therefore, ethics has no place in the global marketplace. At best, a pragmatic approach can bring about some practical rules and standards.

Having considered the emergence of ethics with various underlying arguments on the one hand and widespread attitudes about ethics on the other hand, what can we conclude? Is there no way to overcome ethical confusion and find well-founded ethical guidance? We suggest that the discussion so far has shown that as long as we deal with human activities, organizations, and institutions, ethics or the notions of right and wrong, just and unjust are unavoidable. But it also brought to the fore that we need to clarify ethical language and ethical concepts.

CLARIFICATIONS OF ETHICAL CONCEPTS

Morality, ethics and responsibility

The fundamental question of morality and ethics is: What should I do, what should we do? If we do not ask ourselves this question, any talk about morality and ethics is in vain. This was already unambiguously clear to the Chinese philosopher and teacher of ethics

Confucius (551–479 BCE) when he admitted that 'I can do nothing for those who do not ask themselves what to do' (Analects 15:16). Hence morality and ethics are about action and essentially normative, not explicative. Their primary focus is on what we *should* do; neither on what we *can* do nor on what we can *know*.

The terms 'morality' and 'ethics' are derived from the Latin *mores* and the Greek *ethos* respectively, both words meaning the same thing, namely 'the morally appropriate conduct that conforms to what has become the norm or law in one's own home and region of life through habit, tradition, and convention' (Rich 2006, p. 11). Accordingly, to be 'moral' or 'ethical' meant to conduct oneself according to social norms and customs.

However, with the emergence of conflicting social norms and customs and the critical call of Socrates (469–399 BCE) and others to examine one's own life, the Greek word *ethos* has gained a somewhat different meaning: 'instead of habitual conduct, it came to mean that which I *should* do based on my reasoned insight and thus in accordance with my convictions' (Rich 2006, p. 11). In other words, that which I *should* do was opposed to that which *one does*, conscience to convention. 'The ethical question in its true nature is thus a question about the *good* and the *right*, which is more than morals, customs, and civic legality'. (Rich 2006, p. 12) As a consequence of this change of meaning, to be 'ethical' or 'moral' now means to be 'good' and 'right' that which stands the test of reasoned examination.

While in contemporary language the adjectives of 'moral' and 'ethical' are most often used interchangeably, the noun of 'morality' and 'ethics' are frequently (though not always) distinguished, the first term relating to practice and the second to reflection on that practice. In this way Richard De George offers the following definitions:

> Morality is a term used to cover those practices and activities that are considered importantly right and wrong; the rules that govern those activities; and the values that are embedded, fostered, and pursued by those activities and practices. (De George 2006, p. 19)

In contrast, ethics is the study of morality or:

> Ethics is a systematic attempt to make sense of our individual and social moral experiences, in such a way as to determine the rules that ought to govern human conduct, the values worth pursuing, and the character traits deserving development in life. (De George 2006, pp. 19–20)

These definitions can help clarify several key features. First, it is crucial to distinguish between the practice of individual and social moral experiences (be they positive or negative) on the one hand and the study and examination on the other hand, the terms 'morality' and 'ethics' pointing to this difference. It means that study cannot substitute for practice, but also practice needs systematic examination to scrutinize 'what is considered importantly right and wrong' in order to determine what *should* be importantly right and wrong. We may remember Socrates questioning social norms and customs in order to gain reasoned insight for our convictions. Ethics, understood in this sense, cannot put up with the aforementioned attitudes of ethical skepticism, imperialism, and relativism and would not qualify everything in our previous survey of the emergence of ethics as pertaining to 'ethics'. There, sustainability and human rights are considered importantly right and corruption importantly wrong. But to be considered as such does not make them ethically required without a systematic attempt to make sense out of them.

Second, morality and ethics are not only about practices and activities but also about rules, values, and character traits. Although the fundamental ethical question is: What should I do, what should we do?, thus focusing on practices and activities, it is important to include this wider scope of relevant aspects because practices are necessarily governed by (certain) rules, embedded and nourished by (certain) values and steered by character traits and habits (e.g., virtues or vices) of decision-makers and actors. It goes without saying that, according to these proposed definitions, morality and ethics cannot be confined to solely rules or values or character traits (i.e., virtue ethics).

Third, in order to avoid blunt and undifferentiated ethical judgments, it is advisable to distinguish three different levels of ethical obligation: minimal ethical requirements which must be met under all circumstances; positive obligations which determine 'good practices'; and the aspiration for ethical ideals which strives for ethical excellence (see De George 1993, pp. 184–188). If one falls short of being excellent, one is not necessarily unethical, and if one violates minimal ethical standards, one cannot be 'good' or 'excellent'. A corporation that contributes millions of dollars to philanthropy, supports the local ballet and cleans up neighborhood parks, claiming to be 'socially responsible', is not really ethically and socially responsible if it is cheating in their core business activities. Although the lines between the three levels are not always easy to draw, it is not too difficult to substantiate minimal ethical requirements to do no harm. They are globally applicable, supported by a wide consensus and frequently incorporated in legal standards, though more often in developed than in developing countries (for further discussion, see section 'In search of an overlapping consensus'). With regard to 'positive obligations', they go beyond the minimum, require doing good in a broader and vaguer sense, are more country- and culture-specific and dependent on the socioeconomic system. As an example, we may mention the obligation to be charitable or help the needy. Here, in contrast to the first level, each person has a certain amount of discretion in determining how to fulfill this obligation. At the third level, one has even more discretion, not only in choosing the means but also in setting the goals of ethical excellence. It is a space wide open to moral imagination and abundant diversity that cannot be determined by rules and standards. So, in a nutshell, the importance of this three-level distinction lies in cautioning against a blunt either-/or of 'ethical' versus 'unethical' and fostering a more differentiated approach to ethical evaluation, be it of persons or organizations.

Fourth, morality and ethics presuppose freedom. Thus, robots and animals cannot be ethical. The actors, be they persons or organizations, must have some space of freedom to choose. To have such space that might vary among actors and over time means to have 'real freedom' to make decisions and take actions. It also means to be subject to constraints that can be of different nature (physical, legal, economic, social, cultural and other) and lie beyond the actor's control. The actor has the ethical obligation to use his or her space of freedom in an ethical manner to the fullest extent possible. At the same time the actor should not be held ethically accountable for what he or she cannot control, based on the fundamental principle, held throughout the history of ethics, that 'ought implies can'. Does this imply that the constraints are not subject to ethical examination and change? The answer is 'no' in so far as constraints are human made. But the changes have to be made by those who are capable of making them, if not individuals, then collective bodies, perhaps organizations, governments, or international institutions.

Marketing ethics and ethical marketing
Definitions of marketing ethics and ethical marketing build upon these principles. In an earlier book, Laczniak and Murphy (1993) define marketing ethics as: the systematic study of how moral standards are applied to marketing decisions, behaviors and institutions. This definition builds upon the work of De George and others cited above. More recently, Murphy *et al.* (2005, p. xviii) define ethical marketing as: 'practices that emphasize transparent, trustworthy, and responsible personal and/or organizational marketing policies and actions that exhibit integrity as well as fairness to consumers and other stakeholders'.

The practice vs. study aspect of ethics is addressed as well as the focus on several virtues essential to becoming ethical marketers in this definition.

Freedom and responsibility Responsibility has become a key concept of contemporary morality, maybe even more important than integrity[1] and fairness[2] (for the following, see Enderle 2006). The word 'responsibility' contains the idea of responding or giving valid answers to questions asked by others, similar to the meaning of the word 'accountability'. Thus, responsibility reflects the relational structure of human existence. According to Walter Schulz (1972), who offers a very deep understanding of responsibility in his masterwork *Philosophie in der veränderten Welt* (*Philosophy in the World That Changed*) the concept of responsibility includes a polarity. On the one hand, there is the inner pole or self-commitment originating from freedom ('*Selbsteinsatz aus Freiheit*'). Responsibility thus rests on and requires an inner decision. A responsible person cannot hide him/herself behind a given role. Rather, the exercise of responsibility may demand one act above and beyond conventional morality. Think of a whistle-blower in an oppressive corporate culture or of what we said about Socrates. On the other hand, at the opposite pole, this self-commitment originating from freedom has its point both of departure and destination in a worldly relationship ('*in welthaftem Bezug*').

> In as far as the human being indispensably stands in historical situations, responsibility is always responsibility *toward* ... and responsibility *for*. This means, responsibility is a category of relationship. Consequently, in an ethics of responsibility the questions of interpersonal conduct must be to the fore, to be precise, as concretely as possible. (Schulz 1972, p. 632; translated by Enderle)

As we can see, Schulz anchors responsibility in the freedom of the human person as decision maker, stretching it to an authority toward whom one is responsible and to a very concrete matter for which one is responsible. So we may conclude that responsibility involves three components: (1) the subject of responsibility or who is responsible; (2) the content of responsibility or for what one is responsible; and (3) the authority toward whom one is responsible. This distinction may help to better sort out ambiguous and complex issues of responsibility and illuminate our investigation in corporate responsibility in the following section.

Unfortunately, the fundamental link between freedom and responsibility is often ignored or even rejected. We want more freedom without being willing to bear more responsibility. But, if liberalization, deregulation, and privatization are to be advanced, the commitment to ethical responsibility needs to march in step. As Viktor Frankl, a psychiatrist and survivor of the Auschwitz concentration camp, provocatively states in his book *Man's Search for Meaning:*

> Freedom is only part of the story and half of the truth. Freedom is but the negative aspect of the whole phenomenon whose positive aspect is responsibility. In fact, freedom is in danger of degenerating into mere arbitrariness unless it is lived in terms of responsibility. That is why *I recommend that the Statue of Liberty on the East Coast be supplemented by a Statue of Responsibility on the West Coast.* (Frankl 1984, p. 134)

Corporate responsibility and CSR

The corporation as moral actor In her remarkable book, *Value Shift*, Lynn Sharp Paine examines the legal history and the contemporary pervasive presence of the corporation and comes to the conclusion that '[I]n today's society, the doctrine of corporate amorality is no longer tenable' (Paine 2003, p. 91). Indeed, unless we recognize the status of the corporation as a moral actor, it does not make sense to speak of unethical corporate conduct, to promote the ethical corporation, to hold the corporation morally accountable for its impact, or to publish corporate responsibility reports.

So, how can we understand the corporation to be a moral actor? Does Schulz's concept of responsibility help us to find an answer? For sure, the corporation is a 'worldly' thing and is therefore an intrinsic part of responsibility. But what about the first pole of his concept, the notion of 'self-commitment originating from freedom'? At first glance, it seems hard to apply it to an organization. Can an organization really make an inner and free decision to commit itself? After all, the

organization is not a human being and hence not a moral person. Nevertheless, we uphold the 'free' enterprise as a hallmark of our economic system. Analogous to the human person, the corporation has and develops an 'identity' (which is crucial for reputation management and brand recognition). It pursues a purpose, nurtures a culture, has some space of freedom to make decisions, and impacts people, society, and nature. With all these characteristics it appears reasonable to conceive the corporation as a moral actor. In other words, it makes sense to identify the subject or bearer of corporate responsibility that can and should be held responsible. According to Schulz, it is crucial that responsibility not only consists of a set of ethical values and norms but also that it be anchored in actors. This is a very basic requirement with far-reaching consequences for any type of ethics.

In analyzing the concept of responsibility further, not only should we anchor responsibility in accountable actors but also draw a sharp distinction between the authorities toward whom the actors are responsible and the contents for which they are responsible. It is fair to say that, unfortunately, the discussion of the stakeholder theory often confuses these two aspects. Being responsible to the customers, employees, communities, and other stakeholders only determines toward whom the company is or should be responsible, while leaving the various contents of corporate responsibility completely vague. Even if we can establish a responsibility relationship between the company and a particular stakeholder in an ethically proper fashion (as, for instance, Robert Phillips [2003] does), we still have to answer the question of what this responsibility should contain. While the stakeholder theory remains silent on this, the CSR initiatives, mentioned earlier, offer a multitude of proposals to identify and measure the contents of corporate responsibility.

Purposes and responsibilities of corporations Intrinsically related to the question of contents is the question of the purpose of the business organization. The purpose sets the direction of the whole company. It inspires its mission, motivates its managers and employees, and defines the benchmarks of its achievements and failures. If the purpose is well defined and wholly embraced, the organization can overcome a great deal of difficulties and achieve lasting success. In fact, it equally holds for the organization what Friedrich Nietzsche said of the person: '[H]e who has a *why* to live for can bear with almost any *how*'. (Nietzsche cited by Frankl 1984, p. 84)

The 'why' of the business organization has been commonly defined in merely financial or economic terms: to make money; to increase stock value; to accumulate or create wealth; to use resources efficiently; or to provide goods and services, to name a few. When the purpose is limited to a single one such as these, all non-financial and non-economic aspects are thus conceived either as 'constraints' (such as legal requirements) or as 'means' to achieve this single purpose (for example, treating employees fairly in order to increase their productivity).

In our view, a better way of understanding the corporation is to conceive it as a multi-purpose organization that has an economic, social, and an environmental purpose. It is crucial to note that each purpose, having intrinsic value, is related to the others in a circular, not hierarchical, manner. In other words, the pursuit of, say, the environmental purpose is not only a means to achieve the economic purpose, but it makes sense on its own right as a move toward more sustainability (as defined, for example, in the earlier section on that topic). This recognition of the environmental purpose for its own sake can be found in an increasing number of corporate responsibility reports and recent statements of business leaders, sometimes clearly articulated and sometimes more implicitly assumed.

In this vein, for instance, Jeffrey Immelt, chairman and chief executive of GE, has recently defended a consistent policy on cleaner energy by arguing that 'we are crossing the threshold where solving energy and environmental problems is the profitable thing to do as well as the right one' (*Financial Times*, June 29, 2005, p. 13). Here Immelt clearly makes a double argument for justifying GE's recently launched research investment project 'Ecomagination' of $1.51 billion. On the one hand, the project is extolled as 'profitable' (that is achieving the economic purpose), and on the other hand, it is affirmed as 'the right thing' by contributing to improving the environment (that is the environmental purpose). We suggest that both lines of argument are indispensable and ought to be stated publicly on an equal footing. They should not be played against each other as if they were necessarily contradictory. It is noteworthy that the improvement of the environment is considered here a purpose, not just a constraint or an impact of a profit-seeking policy. Only a purpose, not a constraint or an outcome, has the power to inspire and motivate for excellence. Again, as Nietzsche said: '[H]e who has a *why* to live for can bear with almost any *how*'.

In fact, both arguments need each other and can create synergistic power. Although the profit argument, or the so-called 'business case', might be strong under certain conditions, it obviously is not overpowering given its dependence on an uncertain and thus risky future. Otherwise, if it were convincingly dominant, businesses would not hesitate to flock to the 'green road'. As for the recognition of the environmental purpose, it might be a lofty ideal and an imperative in the long run. But it cannot serve as a business purpose if it lacks economic feasibility.

In exploring the multi-purpose character of the business organization, we can develop similar thoughts with regard to its 'social' purpose. The pursuit of being a 'good corporate citizen' (as numerous corporate reports proclaim) should not be conceived and used only as a means to achieve the economic goal, but should be recognized by the organization as a value in its own right. As a result of such a principled decision and policy, the company can gain respect and trust as a genuinely social actor, shrugging off the ugly reputation of being merely a 'money machine' that behaves 'decently' for financial reasons alone.

Contrasting concepts of corporate social responsibility Having applied the concept of responsibility with its three components to the business organization and explored its multi-purpose character, we may now contrast this proposed concept with three other concepts of corporate responsibility that have become quite influential in the CSR debate: the definition of CSR by the European Union, the 'Good Company' according to *The Economist*, and a widespread notion advocated by Archie Carroll, an American business ethicist.

First, the *European Union's Green Paper on CSR* in 2001 and its subsequent communications (Commission 2002, 2004, 2006) define CSR as: 'a concept whereby companies integrate social and environmental concerns in their business operations and in their interaction with their stakeholders on a voluntary basis' (Commission 2001: no. 3).

As one can see, this definition includes several valid elements: the mention of both social and environmental concerns, the need of integrating them in the business operations and stakeholder relations, and the importance of a voluntary commitment of the companies. However, we should also point to a number of questionable aspects. It does not raise the basic ethical question about the commitment of the company that precedes the issue of mandatory versus voluntary action, and it seems to assume that CSR can only be voluntary. The qualitative difference between 'social' and 'environmental' is rather blurred and the fashionable term of integration turns out to be a kind of 'black box' ready to be filled with any content. Last but not least, the use of the letter S for 'social' is quite ambiguous and inconsistent. On the one hand, it indicates content of responsibility, namely 'social concerns' as distinct from environmental concerns and business operations. On the other hand, it relates to the authority to whom companies are responsible, namely society.

So what does it actually mean? Indeed, the term CSR is rather confusing and better replaced by 'corporate responsibility' with regard to economic, social, and environmental performance (as is actually done by an increasing number of companies).

Second, in January 2005, *The Economist* published 'a survey of corporate social responsibility'. Lamenting over the victory that the CSR movement has won in the battle of ideas, the survey rightly observes that CSR as practiced means many different things. After 22 pages it comes up with the conclusion that 'The proper business of business is business. No apology required' (*The Economist* 2005, p. 22). What can we say in a few words about this survey? Unfortunately, it is not much more than a warmed-over of Friedman's 35-year-old article and largely ignores the considerable advancements in the understanding of corporate ethics and responsibilities, which have been made in this period by an entire generation (see, for instance, Paine 2003). It is certainly true, as the survey notes, that ethics is now given an explicit and indispensable role for business behavior, namely that 'ordinary decency' and 'distributive justice' need to be understood in relation to the proper goal of the firm. 'Without these basic values, business would not be possible' (p. 20). However, the survey suggests that the firm has only one single purpose, defined as simply as seeking profit. No thoughts are given as to what genuine wealth creation of the company could mean. Moreover, it is naively assumed that 'merely by running a profitable company, [successful managers] are likely to be advancing the public good as well' (p. 6). And, lastly, while the survey establishes a supposedly close and dangerous link between the CSR movement and changes in the capitalistic system, this link is far from obvious and much more complex than the authors indicate.[3]

A third contrasting concept of corporate social responsibility has been proposed by Archie Carroll, printed in the first, but not second edition of *The Blackwell Encyclopedic*

Dictionary of Business Ethics (Werhane and Freeman 1997, pp. 593–595) and taken up by numerous scholars (for instance, Ferrell, Fraedrich and Ferrell 2005, pp. 47–48; Matten and Moon 2006, pp. 337–340). As Carroll states, 'the social responsibility of business encompasses the economic, legal, ethical and discretionary expectations that society has of organizations at a given point in time' (p. 594), the details of this view being elaborated in Carroll and Buchholz (2003, pp. 39–40). Although this four-part perspective seems to be 'practical', it reflects a serious misunderstanding of ethics, at least in the sense of responsibility as 'self-commitment out of freedom'. Despite some mitigating remarks, 'ethics' is essentially compartmentalized into one single part of social responsibility, while the 'economic', 'legal', and 'discretionary' parts appear to be 'ethics-free'. No levels of ethical obligations are distinguished, environmental concerns are conspicuously absent, and the economic purpose seems to trump any other purpose.

In short: a concise concept of corporate responsibility   To conclude, we summarize our concept of corporate responsibility in four points. First, responsibility, as *'self-commitment originating from freedom'*, is a rich and central concept of contemporary morality and can be applied to the business organization as a moral actor. By doing so, the widely and vaguely used term of responsibility, in business language and corporate reports, gains clarity and depth. As a result, the decisive challenge for business shifts. Rather than only asking whether CSR should be mandatory or voluntary, as it has been hotly debated in the European Union, the decisive challenge for business is whether or not it commits itself out of freedom. Indeed, ethical responsibility is not limited to voluntary actions as if mandatory actions were only a matter of legal responsibility. Even legal and regulatory requirements need the support of ethical responsibility, since one should pursue not only the letter but also the spirit of the law.

Second, responsibility includes three components:

(1) It needs to be anchored in a clearly defined subject or bearer of responsibility (which might be an individual, a group, an organization, a nation, or another entity). Only with such anchorage can the language of responsibility and accountability make sense and be effective.
(2) Executing responsibility means answering the questions asked by others who have legitimate authority to do so, now commonly called 'stakeholders.' This relationship comprises more than simply being 'responsive' as many business consultants have recently urged companies to become. For this relationship has an ethical quality, which means that the company is concerned about what is right and wrong, just and unjust. But this relationship is also less than numerous stakeholder theorists claim because the substantive issues of responsibility are not identified yet.
(3) Hence the third component of corporate responsibility deals with the contents that can be divided into three major groups: economic, social, and environmental.

Third, given the widespread custom of opposing corporate social responsibility against business ethics, one might assume that CSR has nothing to do with ethics. However, in our conceptual approach, we place ethics at the heart of corporate responsibility permeating the company's purposes, constraints, performances, and impacts. The company's ethical responsibility extends as much as its space of freedom. Moreover, by distinguishing three levels of ethical obligations, that is ethical minima, positive obligations, and ethical ideals, we reject the simplistic alternative to choose between either 'ethical' or 'unethical', offering instead a differentiated way of evaluating corporate ethical conduct. Indeed, simplistic alternatives make reasonable ethical evaluation impossible for companies and their critiques alike.

Fourth, the discussion about the purposes of the company brings to the fore that *'making the business case'* for CSR can be misunderstood very easily. If social and environmental concerns are merely used as means (that is, not recognized as purposes in their own right) in order to achieve a single and often simple economic purpose (for instance, to make money), the endeavor of making the business case becomes self-defeating, entailing mistrust and skepticism among those inside and outside the company, as this kind of strategy is revealed. Instead of promoting the slogan 'ethics pays', one had better follow the principle that 'ethics counts' (Paine 2003, p. 141). Having said this, one should also acknowledge the financial success that follows the pursuit of the triple purpose of the company.

In search of an overlapping consensus

The emergence of ethics and CSR we have been witnessing in the last 20 years raises the question if there is also a growing common ethical ground that could provide a firm basis for business in the global marketplace. Although the multitude of initiatives seems to point to a certain convergence, major obstacles might not give us too much cause for optimism; we may recall John Ruggie's Herculean task or think of the debates over climate change. Moreover, convergence is not only a practical matter, but also needs an ethical foundation.

The idea of an overlapping consensus (J. Rawls)
In order to avoid ethical imperialism, relativism, and skepticism, we suggest approaching this question with the help of John Rawls's 'idea of an overlapping consensus' (Rawls 1996, pp. 133–172) applied to the global context (and thus transcending Rawls's more restricted application to democratic societies). The challenge is to find a common ethical ground for a stable and just world society, given the 'fact of pluralism' (Rawls) that characterizes the permanent condition of society with their conflicting and even incommensurable religious, philosophical, and moral doctrines. Even if society is free, that is

if the basic rights and liberties of free institutions are warranted, this pluralism will not pass away; for it is part of 'the burdens of reason'. If, however, a single comprehensive doctrine should prevail, state power is necessary to impose it and to repress the others. So the fundamental problem is the following: how can we affirm the pluralism of more or less comprehensive 'conceptions of the good' and at the same time find a 'political conception of justice', which regulates the living together of humans and is supported by the various 'conceptions of the good'? This problem arises at all levels of human action (in families, companies, countries, etc.), yet more palpably and urgently at the global level.

One solution can be found in an 'overlapping consensus'. This implies that no religious, philosophical, and moral doctrine may claim that its respective moral values and norms are exclusively valid globally. Only a common minimum consensus provides an ethically sound base. However, this consensus must be 'free-standing' (Rawls) or rooted in human nature and also supported by the respective cultural and religious traditions. The 'common minimum consensus' must find maximum support. Otherwise it would be extraneous to the adherents of the respective doctrines and unstable.

Based on such an overlapping consensus, are there any principles, norms, or values that can provide well-founded ethical guidance in the global marketplace? The Golden Rule, human rights, and the conception of capabilities advanced by Amartya Sen and Martha Nussbaum all qualify.

The golden rule It is a noteworthy phenomenon in the history of humankind that the so-called 'Golden Rule' can be found in very diverse cultures and religions: in ancient Greece, in the Hebrew Bible and the New Testament, in Islam, Confucianism, Taoism, Hinduism, Buddhism, Jainism, Sikhism, and Parsism (see Dalla Costa 1998, pp. 141–142; Enderle 2008; Plaks 2005).[4] In one form or another it says negatively: 'do not do unto others what you would not have others do unto you! and positively: 'do unto others as you would have others do unto you!' Passed on over thousands of years, the Golden Rule has been often badly understood and undervalued in its importance and even criticized by renowned philosophers (such as Immanuel Kant, Bernhard Gert, and Kwame Anthony Appiah). Despite a certain vagueness, possible misinterpretations, and obvious limitations, it can provide powerful guidance and is also one of the fundamental principles of the Declaration Toward a Global Ethic (see earlier section 'United Nations Global Compact and Other Initiatives').

The Golden Rule is based on a two-person model, in which person A (the active participant) makes a decision and takes an action that affects person B (the passive participant). In fact, the Golden Rule includes four rules: (1) The rule of empathy requires a thought experiment: put yourself (A) in the position of the person (B) who will be affected by your decision and action! (2) The rule of autonomy demands that you should ask yourself (your conscience) how you in that position (B) want to be affected by such a decision and action (from A). (3) The rule of reciprocity requires returning to your original position (A) and to decide and act accordingly. (4) The rule of prudence suggests that you act in your own enlightened interest and treat your fellow now as you want to be treated by him or her in the future.

In many situations the application of the Golden Rule is straightforward. Think of the customer who does not want to be cheated or the employee who wants to be respected. More difficult is the application when the position of the affected person is not sufficiently defined. How should the child be treated by her parent, the patient by his doctor, or the criminal by the judge? Notions of a child's needs, a patient's will or a criminal's basic rights might be necessary to qualify the affected person. Even more difficult, if not impossible, is the application of the Golden Rule to situations that transcend the two-person model, particularly to institutional arrangements and intergenerational challenges. Here the principles of reciprocity and sustainability, as well as the notion of human rights, seem to be indispensable.

Human rights After the atrocities of the Second World War the establishment of human rights as a global ethical framework has progressed considerably through the Universal Declaration of 1948 and numerous international conventions as well as national and international legislation. Human rights are an important legacy of the Enlightenment, as Lynn Hunt demonstrates in her remarkable book *Inventing Human Rights* (2007). But the genesis of human rights is not an exclusively Western process. Rather, it has developed in various Western and non-Western streams greatly intermingling over time (see Sen 1999, Chapter 10). Although by now human rights are widely recognized, many controversies remain and challenges from different cultures and religions need to be addressed. This is possible in East Asia and with Confucianism, as is thoroughly discussed in a number of books: *Confucianism and Human Rights* (De Bary and Tu 1998), *Asian Values and Human Rights. A Confucian Communitarian Perspective* (De Bary 1998), *The East Asian Challenge for Human Rights* (Bauer and Bell 1999), *East Meets West: Human Rights and Democracy in Asia* (Bell 2000). With regard to questions about Islam and human rights, we refer to four international conferences on human rights held in Qom, Iran, and documented on the website of Mofid University http://chrs.mofidu.ac.ir/.

Due to substantial progress in the human rights discussion, it is fair to say that the focus of controversy has shifted from the foundation and identification of human rights to the questions of who is responsible to fulfill them and how they can best be enforced. As already mentioned above, business is expected to play an important role, particularly 'within its sphere of influence' and avoiding 'complicity' with human rights violators.

It is up to the Ruggie commission to determine what this means more specifically.

Human capabilities A third way of substantiating the contents of an overlapping consensus is the conception of human capabilities developed by Amartya Sen (1985, 1999) and somewhat differently by Martha Nussbaum (2006), who have influenced the *Human Development Reports* published annually since 1990 by the United Nations Development Program. (Its 2000 report is dedicated to human rights and human development; UNDP 2000.) This conception focuses on 'the real freedoms that people enjoy' (Sen 1999, p. 3) or the 'capabilities' of persons to lead the kind of lives they value and have reason to value. They include five types of freedoms: political freedoms, economic facilities, social opportunities, transparency guarantees, and protective security. The capability approach provides an informational basis that is truly people-centered. It goes beyond the measurement of well-being in terms of income, commodities, and primary goods (J. Rawls) and overcomes the unsolvable measurement problems of utilitarianism. For international business, the capability approach offers consistent and adaptable cross-cultural or universal standards. It can help specify the corporations' economic, social, and environmental responsibilities (see Enderle 2004) and can be easily combined with the human rights approach.

'THE GLOBAL MARKETPLACE' AS A FIELD OF APPLIED ETHICS

Globalization and the global marketplace

In recent years the debate on globalization has become widespread and highly controversial as it explores what the concept is, how it impacts the world, and what it should be (see, for example, Stiglitz 2002). Given these controversies, the often evoked image of the world as 'a global village' seems rather innocent and even misleading, although it correctly points to the increasing interconnectedness of the world, due to an immense reduction in the cost of transportation and communication. Globalization can be understood as a kind of international system in the making. It is:

> not simply a trend or a fad but is, rather, an international system ... that has now replaced the old Cold War system, and ... has its own rules and logic that today directly or indirectly influence the politics, environment, geopolitics and economics of virtually every country in the world (Friedman 2000, p. ix)

Although economic globalization is of paramount importance, it would be shortsighted to conceive of it exclusively in these terms. This system in the making is about 'global transformations' in the plural, including political, cultural and environmental globalization, migration and the expanding reach of organized violence (see Held *et al.* 1999; Held and McGrew 2000, 2002).

In order to understand and evaluate economic globalization, one has to investigate and account for not only economic activities and their impact but also the institutions and the rules (or 'the system') that govern and should govern these activities and consequences. Hence the institution and the rules of the market in particular are at stake.

It is useful to recall the strengths and weaknesses of the market in the domestic context of industrialized countries to investigate the question of what markets can and cannot provide in the international arena. Free and competitive markets, properly regulated, provide freedom to economic actors (individuals, organizations, and countries). They have an equalizing impact insofar as they are based on economic performance, expressed by the price system, as distinct from non-economic characteristics such as race, gender, religion, and nationality. At the same time, from economic theory and practical experience we know that economic growth is not necessarily sustainable. Markets by themselves cannot ensure an acceptable distribution of economic opportunities or results.

Even if they are perfect, they fail in providing public goods. Moreover, some markets, particularly in the areas of labor, basic health care and education, are inherently unreliable at maximizing aggregate output in these areas (see Turner 2001).

Given these strengths and weaknesses of the markets in the domestic realm, these same factors must be taken seriously in the shaping of economic globalization as well. Global markets need global institutions that should not only enhance freedom, efficiency, and economic growth. They should also promote sustainability and distributive justice, provide international public goods that are essential for living and collaborating in the 'global village', strengthen fairness in labor markets and ensure basic health care and education (as suggested, for instance, by the capability approach in the section 'Human Capabilities'). The lessons learned in the domestic realm should be applied to 'the international system in the making' in general and to economic globalization in particular.

However, effective, fair, and sustainable global institutions do not suffice single handedly to make economic globalization succeed. The successful 'game' depends not only on the quality of the rules but also on how 'the players play'. First and foremost, it is the moral responsibility of the 'big players', that is, powerful nation-states, unions of states, and multinational corporations, to shape globalization according to universal ethical standards. This enormous task includes two simultaneous tracks: the big players should exhibit exemplary behavior towards the goal of globalization 'with a human face', while also fairly participating in establishing the necessary global institutions.

A multi-level and two-legged approach to business and marketing ethics

In order to deal with the highly complex challenges of marketing ethics in the process of globalization, it does not suffice to focus only on institutions and rules or on the behavior of particular states and corporations alone. Rather, a more sophisticated approach to the complex field of global marketing ethics is needed, which we might call a multi-level and two-legged approach (see Enderle 2003, pp. 534–540).

In order to identify the subjects of responsibility as concretely as possible, three qualitatively different levels of acting are proposed, each of which includes actors with their respective objectives, interests, and motivations: the micro-, meso- and macro-levels. At the micro-level, the focus is on the individual, that is what he or she, as employee or employer, colleague or manager, consumer, supplier, or investor, does, can do, and ought to do in order to perceive and assume his or her ethical responsibility. Also groups, composed of small numbers of individuals and without organizational structures, making collective decisions and taking collective actions, are attributed to this level. At the meso-level, at stake is the decision making and action of economic organizations, chiefly business firms, but also trade-unions, consumer organizations, professional associations, NGOs, etc. Finally, the macro-level includes the economic system as such and the shaping of the overall economic conditions of business: the economic order with its multiple institutions, economic, financial, and social policies, and others. It goes without saying that this conception includes the broad field of marketing in society (see Gundlach et al. 2007).[5]

At each level, the actors are supposed to have more or less extended spaces of freedom for decision-making with corresponding ethical responsibilities, and to be limited by conditions (that is constraints) that they cannot change, at least for the time being. No level can substitute for another. This means that even if all problems at one level (for example, macro-level) could be satisfactorily solved, many problems at the other levels (for instance, meso- and micro-levels) still remain.

Acting responsibly at all levels can require ethical displacement, a technique of resolving a dilemma, or sometimes solving an ethical problem, by seeking a solution on a level other than the one on which the dilemma or problem appears (De George 1993, p. 97). For example, in order to prevent sexual harassment of saleswomen, an explicit corporate policy and a sustained corporate culture (at the meso-level) might be necessary if a change of attitude and behavior by individual actors (at the micro-level) is not sufficient. If such organizations and institutions at higher levels do not exist (as is the case with many international problems), it might be necessary to create them.

In order to adapt this three-level conception to the global marketplace, we propose an extended three-level model that accounts for different types of international relations at all three levels. At the micro-level special attention is paid to personal (inner-group) relations and responsibilities across national borders; for example, cross-national groups of managers and employees or cross-national families. At the meso-level the focus is on inner-organizational relations and responsibilities across national borders; for example, multinational corporations, international trade unions or consumer organizations. The macro-level includes inner-systemic relations and responsibilities across national borders, incorporated, for instance, in bilateral agreements, regional treaties or global institutions such as the World Trade Organization.

While the extended three-level conception helps to identify different types of actors, the two-legged approach suggests how to understand the relationship between ethics and marketing. As 'applied ethics' can have many different connotations, so does marketing ethics as a form of 'applied ethics'. One notion is to promulgate absolute ethical principles and impose them on marketing practices, which implies that marketing theory is irrelevant to marketing ethics. Another approach holds that marketing ethics has its own imperatives that are markedly, or even completely, distinct from high ethical requirements. Our following proposal, called a two-legged approach, offers a more sophisticated understanding: on the theoretical level,

'applying' means placing ethical theory and marketing theory in a two-way relationship that fosters productive interdisciplinary communication. With regard to practice, this combined theoretical knowledge is being 'applied' to practical issues like product safety or power in the channel which, in turn, influence this theoretical knowledge. This means that marketing ethics needs the competences of practical marketing expertise as well as the theoretical knowledge of marketing science and ethics, and should take them seriously by fostering mutual communication among these kinds of competencies (see Enderle 1998).

Empirical research in international marketing ethics has largely focused on testing the Hunt-Vitell (1986) model of marketing ethics. Scott Vitell and a number of co-authors (Vitell and Paolillo 2003) have compared Hofstede's (1983) four factors in the USA, UK, Spain and Turkey and found moral intensity and ethical judgments to be similar across these countries. A similar second study (Vitell *et al.* 2004) found that corporate culture and organizational commitment play an important role in ethical perceptions and decision making. The *Journal of Business Ethics* published special issues on marketing ethics in 1999 (Vol. 18, No. 1) and 2001 (Vol. 32, No. 1). Of the 15 articles in these two issues, eight dealt with cross-cultural comparisons of marketing ethics. A general conclusion from this research is that while cultural differences do exist, there is agreement on major ethical issues such as the importance of honesty and negative effects of bribery across societies. In addition, a recent textbook (Brenkert 2008) devotes one chapter to marketing ethics in a global society.

EVOLVING PERSPECTIVES

Increasing importance of corporate reporting in economic, social, and environmental terms

In exploring the emergence of ethics and CSR in the global marketplace (see earlier section) we have identified multiple forms, different drivers, and various underlying arguments. Compared with the 1980s, it is fair to say that today's expectations about corporate responsibilities in economic, social, and environmental terms are considerably higher; the pressures on corporations by nongovernmental organizations have substantially increased; many companies have expanded their PR efforts on CSR and some also improved their behaviors; and various legal and regulatory provisions have supported the emergence of ethics and CSR.

Thus, it comes as no surprise that reporting on and monitoring of corporate responsibilities have gained momentum, greatly facilitated by the Internet. We can find an abundance of all kinds of reports. Under a variety of titles, such as sustainability report; corporate social responsibility report; corporate citizenship report; energy report, and corporate responsibility report, they vary greatly in format, length, and substance, Increasingly, they are posted on the Internet. The numbers are in the thousands and websites such as ethicalperformance.com and www.globalreporting.org regularly publicizes these reports. However one might assess the quality of those reports, the upshot is that they are now available in the public domain. The advent of blogs and critical web analyses of many corporate actions should have the effect of 'keeping companies honest' in these reports.

The American Marketing Association Statement of Ethical Norms and Values for Marketers

In 2004, the American Marketing Association (AMA) published a new statement of norms and values. It is shown in Appendix 1. This document replaced an earlier code of ethics that the association found to be unworkable and dated. Members of the committee believed that a more aspirational statement was needed. As can be seen in the General Norms section, these three points tie in well with our discussion in the section 'Morality, Ethics and Responsibility' of this chapter.

The six ethical values of honesty; responsibility (also examined in the section cited above); fairness; respect; openness; and citizenship represent ideal characteristics for marketing practitioners. The bullet points below each of them are purposely formulated in the affirmative so that AMA members and other readers understand that these are positive duties rather than negative admonitions. The final value of citizenship says that individual marketers should approach their personal obligations in a similar manner to the CSR themes we have emphasized throughout this Chapter. Like companies, some AMA members will take their citizenship role more seriously than others. The final Implementation section encourages marketing researchers and other specialists to delineate ethical policies and guidelines for their group.

The need for a global code of marketing ethics was outlined by Rallapalli (1999) and he noted that any such code should include both normative guidelines and specific behaviors. As the American Marketing Association Statement of Norms and Values states, such a statement cannot account for many of the specific behaviors that may cause ethical transgressions in marketing. A comparative study of ethics codes in the USA and Spain (Guillen et al. 2002) found that although Spanish companies lag behind US-based ones, there is a steady movement of institutionalizing ethics policies in large Spanish companies. This study noted that codes must be supported by other ethical initiatives, such as training programs, in order to be effective in organizations. The focus on specific marketing activities within codes has generally been lacking. Murphy's (2005a) longitudinal research found selling practices to be covered by over 60 per cent of codes, while advertising and product safety ranked at the bottom of 13 items, with only 30 per cent of companies having specific guidance in these areas. Thus, it appears that marketing ethics has not received the emphasis within codes that one might expect.

Normative perspectives for ethical and socially responsible marketing

In a recent article, one of the authors and a colleague (Laczniak and Murphy 2006) outlined seven basic perspectives (BPs) for ethical and socially responsible marketing. They are:

BP 1: Ethical marketing puts people first.
BP 2: Ethical marketers must achieve a behavioral standard in excess of the law.
BP 3: Marketers are responsible for whatever they intend as a means or ends with a marketing action.
BP 4: Marketing organizations should cultivate better (that is higher) moral imagination in their managers and employees.
BP 5: Marketers should articulate and embrace a core set of ethical principles.
BP 6: Adoption of a stakeholder orientation is essential to ethical marketing decisions.
BP 7: Marketing organizations ought to delineate an ethical decision-making protocol.

Although all of the basic perspectives have some relationship to the topics discussed in this Chapter, we concentrate on two of them here – BP 1 and BP 5. The first BP focuses on the centrality of people in all ethical exchanges and relationships. The foundation in marketing is the revered marketing concept where the needs of the consumer are placed ahead of the needs of the marketer. The upshot of BP 1 is that marketing managers have an undeniable responsibility to society. When marketers treat stakeholders merely as means, they flunk the test of placing people first. The iron law of responsibility that states that when entities, such as marketing organizations, have great economic power and do not exhibit proportionate social responsibility, they will have their power proportionately

diminished (Murphy *et al.* 2005; see also sections 'Morality, Ethics and Responsibility' and 'Corporate Responsibility and CSR').

These points tie in well with our earlier discussion that identified the centrality of persons/people in all ethical relationships. If marketers are to place people as the focal point of their efforts, they will likely be successful. The discussion of the iron law of responsibility means that more is expected of the larger organizations, as we noted in the section 'Globalization and the Global Marketplace'. Consequently, Wal-Mart, Tesco, Toyota, Sony and other multinational manufacturers or retailers (MNCs) should be expected to take the lead in bringing responsible behavior to the markets where they operate.

The other BP that relates in directly to our analysis here is the fifth one. Laczniak and Murphy (2006) state: 'marketers who aspire to operate on a high ethical plane should articulate and embrace a core set of ethical principles' (p. 164). These principles should address ethical issues concerning the rightness or fairness of various marketing tactics. The first is the principle of 'nonmalfeasance' meaning that marketers should never knowingly do harm when discharging marketing duties. The area of product safety is one where much attention has been devoted over the years. American MNCs have been charged over the years for 'dumping' less safe products in lesser developed countries. More recently, imports ranging from tires to foodstuffs from China to the USA have been criticized for not meeting US safety laws.

The second principle is one of 'nondeception'. This principle states that marketers ought to never intentionally mislead or unfairly manipulate consumers. This is obviously consistent with BP 1's notion of respecting people. Deceptions such as over-selling extended warranties, channel stuffing by sales reps and promising more than any product can violate this principle.

Protecting vulnerable segments represents the third principle. Uniquely vulnerable segments include children, the elderly, mentally or physically handicapped and economically disadvantaged consumers. Marketers must always take extraordinary care when engaging in exchanges with vulnerable segments (Brenkert 1998). The rationale undergirding this particular principle stems from some of the basic tenets discussed previously on human dignity and the doctrines of major religions. Multinational marketers have been criticized over the years for exploiting consumers who lack education or sophistication in the workings of the marketplace. The new focus on the base of the pyramid as a market (Hart 2005; Prahalad 2005) will necessitate that marketers take precautions in dealing with these emerging markets.

The fourth essential moral precept for marketing is the principle of 'distributive justice'. This principle suggests that there is an obligation on the part of all marketing organizations to assess the fairness of marketplace consequences flowing from their collective marketing practices. The theoretical foundation for the principle of distributive justice is based on the work of John Rawls (1971). The difference principle argues that marketing practices are unethical if, over time, they contribute to the further disadvantage of those market segments that are the least well-off (Laczniak and Murphy 2008). A marketing manifestation of this principle is in the digital divide, where low-income consumers both domestically and internationally cannot avail themselves of products and price discounts that are only available through the Internet and e-commerce.

A fifth principle of enlightened marketing is 'stewardship' which reminds marketers of their social duties to the common good. Following this principle, marketing managers are obligated to ensure that their operations will not impose external costs on society, especially the physical environment, that result from their internal operations. Employing illegal immigrants at reduced wages to reduce costs, while knowing that incremental social costs accrue to the community (for example, additional healthcare, education and law enforcement) is an example of a violation of this principle.

The stewardship principle particularly addresses environmental/ecological responsibilities of marketers. It suggests that marketers have a moral obligation to protect the environment via a socially sustainable pattern of consumption such that damages are not imposed on the ecological system in a way that penalizes future generations. Although some marketing organizations initially looked at the environment as only a promotional opportunity and were guilty of 'greenwashing' by touting products of questionable environmental as being compatible, such as plastic trash bags, several firms such as Interface and its visionary Chairman Ray Anderson (as well as GE mentioned above) have embraced sustainable practices and changed their product and marketing efforts dramatically (Murphy 2005b).

These two normative perspectives illustrate the fact that ethical precepts such as those outlined in earlier sections of this essay are necessary for changes to occur. To implement these changes, Laczniak and Murphy (2006) offer implications for educators, practitioners, public policy-makers and academic researchers.

CONCLUSION

Although many other marketing issues such as bribery, branding, selling and product pricing in international markets have ethical and CSR implications, we believe that the concepts and principles discussed above can be applied to these decisions. Marketers now know that expectations regarding the ethical and societal dimensions of their decisions are increasing. This heightened global expectation means that greater scrutiny is given to even everyday marketing decisions. The need for transparency and knowledge that corporate ethical reputation matters are forces marketers should not resist. Thus, we advocate that ethical and CSR issues should play a prominent role in both marketing strategy development and execution in both domestic and international markets.

NOTES

1 See, for instance, 'The many faces of integrity' by R. Audi and P. E. Murphy (2006).

2 See, for instance, the discussion of fairness in 'Fairness and the Renminbi-Dollar Exchange Rate: An Integrated Market and Ethical Framework and Some Policy Recommendations' by G. Enderle and R. D. Huang. Forthcoming.

3. On January 19, 2008 *The Economist* (2008) published again a special report on corporate social responsibility. Now CSR is 'just good business', nothing else. Once again, it seems that neither an ethical motivation for CSR nor a richer concept of wealth creation beyond profit maximization deserves serious consideration.

4 Among the numerous formulations of the Golden Rule we may mention the following:

In Judaism: *When he went to Hillel, he said to him, 'What is hateful to you, do not do unto your fellow man: that is the entire Torah.'* (Talmud, Shabbat 31a)

In Christianity: *In everything do to others as you would have them do to you. For this is the law and the prophets.* (New Testament, Matthew 7:12)

In Islam: *None of you [truly] believes until he wishes for his brother what he wishes for himself.* (Forty Hadiths of Al-Nawawi, No. 13)

In Hinduism: *One should not behave towards others in a way which is disagreeable to oneself. This is the essence of morality. All other activities are due to selfish desire.* (Mahabharata 13:114:8)

In Buddhism: *Hurt not others in ways that you yourself would find hurtful.* (Udana Varga 5:18)

In Confucianism: *Tsukung asked, 'Is there a single word which can be a guide to conduct throughout one's life?' Confucius replied, 'It is perhaps the word shu – reciprocity: Do not impose on others what you yourself do not desire.'* (Confucius, Analects 15: 23) Also: *Try your best to treat others as you would wish to be treated yourself, and you will find that this is the shortest way to benevolence.* (Mencius VII.A.4)

5. This three-level conception contrasts with the common distinction between the micro- and the macro-levels in economics and sociology in two respects. The individual person is explicitly addressed as moral actor, differing from the decision maker in micro-economics and micro-sociology. Moreover, the business organization is considered a moral actor, too, though of a special nature. This emphasis of the meso-level expresses the enormous importance of organizations in modern societies. Note also the distinction between 'institutions' and 'organizations' proposed by Robert Bellah *et al.* (1992). For instance, the institution of the American corporation attributed to the macro-level includes the essential features of all American corporations (Bellah *et al.*, 1992; pp. 3–18) while an individual American corporation, characterized by those features, is an 'organization' at the meso-level, having, in addition, its particular identity, culture, and conduct.

REFERENCES

Alpern, K. D. (2005) 'Foreign Corrupt Practices Act (FCPA)' in P. H. Werhane and R. E. Freeman (eds), *The Blackwell Encyclopedia of Management. Business Ethics*, 2nd edn. Malden, MA: Blackwell, pp. 203–204.

Argandona, A. (2001) 'Corruption: The corporate perspective', *Business Ethics: A European Review*, 10(2): 163–175.

Argandona, A. (2003) 'Private-to-private corruption', *Journal of Business Ethics*, 47(3): 253–267.

Argandona, A. (2005) 'Corruption and companies: the use of facilitating payments', *Journal of Business Ethics*, 60(3): 251–264.

Arroyo S. J., Gonzalo and Suárez, A. (2006) *Responsibilidad Social Corporativa. Una Mirada Global.* Santiago de Chile: Universidad Alberto Hurtado.

Audi, R. and Murphy, P. E. (2006) 'The many faces of integrity', *Business Ethics Quarterly*, 16(1): 3–21.

Bauer, J. R. and Bell, D. A. (eds) (1999) *The East Asian Challenge for Human Rights.* Cambridge: Cambridge University Press.

Beets, S. D. (2005) 'Understanding the demand-side issues of international corruption', *Journal of Business Ethics*, 57(1): 65–81.

Bell, D. A. (2000) *East Meets West: Human Rights and Democracy in Asia.* Princeton, NJ: Princeton University Press.

Bellah, R. N., Madsen, R., Sullivan, W. M., Swidler, A. and Tipton, S. M. (1992) *The Good Society.* New York: Random House.

Berenbeim, R. E. and Conference Board (2006) *Resisting Corruption: How Company Programs Are Changing.* Washington, DC: Conference Board.

Black, W. K. (2004) 'The *Dango* tango: Why corruption blocks real reform in Japan', *Business Ethics Quarterly*, 14(4): 603–623.

Bolongaita, E. T. and Bhargava, V. K. (2003) *Challenging Corruption in Asia: Selected Case*

Studies and a Framework for Improving Anti-Corruption Effectiveness (Directions in Development). Washington, DC: World Bank.

Brenkert, G. G. (1998) 'Marketing to inner city blacks: powermaster and moral responsibility', *Business Ethics Quarterly*, 8(1): 1–18.

Brenkert, G. G. (2008) *Marketing Ethics*. Malden, MA: Blackwell.

Carroll, A. (1997) 'Social responsibility', in P. H. Werhane and R. E. Freeman (eds), *The Blackwell Encyclopedic Dictionary of Business Ethics*. Malden, MA: Blackwell, pp. 593–595.

Carroll, A. B. and Buchholz. A. K. (2003) *Business and Society: Ethics and Stakeholder Management*, 5th edn. Mason, OH: Thompson South-Western.

Chandler, Sir G. (2005) 'An important step in defining corporate human rights responsibilities', *The Ethical Corporation*, March, p. 39.

Chandler, Sir G. (2007) 'Compelling corporate action on human rights', *The Ethical Corporation*, April, p. 48.

Commission of the European Communities (2001) *Green Paper. Promoting a European Framework for Corporate Social Responsibility*. Brussels: COM(2001) 366 final.

Commission of the European Communities (2002) *Communication from the Commission Concerning Corporate Social Responsibility: A Business Contribution to Sustainable Development*. Brussels: COM(2002) 347 final.

Commission of the European Communities (2004) *European Multistakeholder Forum on CSR. Final Results and Recommendations*. Brussels: COM(2004).

Commission of the European Communities (2006) *Implementing the Partnership for Growth and Jobs: Making Europe a Pole of Excellence on CSR*. Brussels: COM(2006).

Dalla Costa, J. (1998) *The Ethical Imperative: Why Moral Leadership is Good Business*. Reading, MA: Addison-Wesley.

D'Andrade, K. (2005) 'Bribery' in P. H. Werhane and R. E. Freeman (eds), *The Blackwell Encyclopedia of Management. Business Ethics*, 2nd edn. Malden, MA: Blackwell, pp. 52–54.

Davis, J. H. and Ruhe, J. A. (2003) 'Perceptions of country corruption: antecedents and outcomes', *Journal of Business Ethics*, 43(4): 275–288.

Davis, P. (2006) 'John Ruggie – the story so far', *The Ethical Corporation*, March, pp. 37–39.

De Bary, W. T. (1998) *Asian Values and Human Rights. A Confucian Communitarian Perspective*. Cambridge, MA: Harvard University Press.

De Bary, W. T. and Tu, W. (eds) (1998) *Confucianism and Human Rights*. New York: Columbia University Press.

De George, R. T. (1993) *Competing with Integrity in International Business*. New York: Oxford University Press.

De George, R. T. (2006) *Business Ethics*, 6th edn. Upper Saddle River, NJ: Pearson Prentice Hall.

De Maria, W. (2007) 'Does African corruption exist?', *African Journal of Business Ethics*, 2(1): 1–9.

DeSimone, L. D. and Popoff, F. with the World Business Council for Sustainable Development (2000) *Eco-Efficiency. The Business Link to Sustainable Development*. Cambridge, MA: MIT Press.

DesJardins, J. (2006) *An Introduction to Business Ethics*, 2nd edn. Boston: McGraw Hill.

Enderle, G. (1997) 'A worldwide survey of business ethics in the 1990s', *Journal of Business Ethics*, Special issue: 1475–1483.

Enderle, G. (1998) 'A framework for international marketing ethics: preliminary considerations and emerging perspectives', *Journal of Human Values*, 4(1): 25–43.

Enderle, G. (ed.) (1999) *International Business Ethics. Approaches and Challenges*. Notre Dame: University of Notre Dame Press.

Enderle, G. (2003) 'Business ethics', in N. Bunnin and E. P. Tsui-James (eds), *The Blackwell Companion to Philosophy*, 2nd edn. Oxford: Blackwell, pp. 531–551.

Enderle, G. (2004) 'Global competition and corporate responsibilities of small and medium-sized enterprises', *Business Ethics: A European Review*, 13(1): 51–63.

Enderle, G. (2006) 'Corporate responsibility in the CSR debate', in Josef Wieland *et al.* (eds), *Unternehmensethik im Spannungsfeld der Kulturen und Religionen*. Stuttgart: Kohlhammer, pp. 108–124.

Enderle, G. (2008)' Rediscovering the Golden Rule for a globalizing world', in Tze-wan Kwan (ed.), *Responsibility and Commitment: Eighteen Essays in Honor of Gerhold K. Becker*. Waldkirch: Edition Gorz, pp. 1–15.

Engardio, P. (2007) 'Beyond the green corporation. Imagine a world in which eco-friendly and socially responsible practices actually help a company's bottom line. It's closer than you think', *BusinessWeek*, January 29, 50–64.

Ethikos and Corporate Conduct Quarterly. (2002) 'The corporate reform law: what does it mean for ethics programs?', 16(2): 1–3, 16.

Ethikos and Corporate Conduct Quarterly (2003) 'Proposed amendments to the Sentencing Guidelines: changes in the wind', 17(3): 1–3, 13.

Ethikos and Corporate Conduct Quarterly (2004) 'The new corporate Sentencing Guidelines', 18(1): 1–4, 16.

Ferrell, O. C., Fraedrich, J. and Ferrell, L. (2005) *Business Ethics. Ethical Decision Making and Cases*, 6th edn. Boston: Houghton Mifflin.

Frankl, V. E. (1984) *Man's Search for Meaning*. New York: Touchstone.

Friedman, T. L. (2000) *The Lexus and the Olive Tree*. New York: Anchor Books.

Getz, K. A. (2006) 'The effectiveness of global prohibition regimes, corruption and the Anti-bribery Convention', *Business and Society*, 45(3): 254–281.

Guillen, M., Mele, D. and Murphy, P. (2002) 'European vs. American approaches to insti-tutionalization of business ethics: The Spanish case', *Business Ethics: A European Review*, 11(2): 167–178.

Gundlach, G., Block, L. and Wilkie, W. (eds) (2007) *Explorations of Marketing in Society*. Cincinnati: Thomson Southwestern.

Habisch, A., Jonker, J., Wegner, M. and Schmidpeter, R. (2006) *Corporate Social Responsibility Across Europe*. Berlin: Springer.

Hart, S. L. (2005) *Capitalism at the Crossroads*. Upper Saddle River, NJ: Wharton.

Held, D. and McGrew, A. (eds) (2000) *The Global Transformations Reader*. Cambridge: Polity Press.

Held, D. and McGrew, A. (eds) (2002) *Governing Globalization. Power, Authority and Global Governance*. Cambridge: Polity Press.

Held, D., McGrew, A., Goldblatt, D. and Perraton, J. (1999) *Global Transformations. Politics, Economics and Culture*. Stanford: Stanford University Press.

Hofstede, G. (1983) 'National cultures in four dimensions: a research-based theory of cultural differences among nations', *International Studies of Management & Organizations*, 13: 46–74.

Holliday, Jr., C. O., Schmidheiny, S. and Watts P. (2002) *Walking the Talk. The Business Case for Sustainable Development*. Report by the World Business Council for Sustainable Development. Sheffield: Greenleaf.

Hunt, L. (2007) *Inventing Human Rights*. New York: Norton.

Hunt, S. and Vitell, S. (1986) 'A general theory of marketing ethics', *Journal of Macromarketing*, 8(1): 5–16.

Husted, B. W. (2002) 'Culture and interna-tional anti-corruption agreements in Latin America', *Journal of Business Ethics*, 37(4): 413–422.

Laczniak, G. R. and Murphy, P. E. (1993) *Ethical Marketing Decisions: The Higher Road*. Boston: Allyn and Bacon.

Laczniak, G. R. and Murphy, P. E. (2006) 'Normative perspectives for ethical and socially responsible marketing, *Journal of Macromarketing*, December: 154–177.

Laczniak, G. R. and Murphy, P. E. (2008) 'Distributive justice: pressing questions, emerging directions, and the promise of Rawlsian analysis', *Journal of Macromarketing*, 28(1): 5–11.

Lambsdorff, J. (2007) *The Institutional Economics of Corruption and Reform: Theory, Evidence, and Policy*. Cambridge: Cambridge University Press.

Matten, D. and Moon, J. (2006) 'A conceptual framework for understanding CSR', in A. Habisch et al., *Corporate Social Responsibility across Europe*. Berlin: Springer, pp. 335–356.

Moran, J. (1999) 'Bribery and corruption: The OECD Convention on combating bribery of foreign public officials in international business transactions', *Business Ethics: A European Review*, 8(3): 141–150.

Murphy, P. E. (2005a) 'Developing, communi-cating and promoting corporate ethics state-ments: a longitudinal analysis', *Journal of Business Ethics*, 62: 183–189.

Murphy, P. E. (2005b) 'Sustainable marketing', *Business & Professional Ethics Journal*, 24(1 & 2): 171–198.

Murphy, P. E., Laczniak, G. R., Bowie, N. E. and Klein, T. A. (2005) *Ethical Marketing*. Upper Saddle River, NJ: Pearson Prentice Hall.

Nielson, R. P. (2000) 'The politics of long-term corruption reform: a combined social move-ment and action-learning approach', *Business Ethics Quarterly*, 10(1): 305–317.

Nussbaum, M. (2006) *Frontiers of Justice. Disability, Nationality, Species Membership*. Cambridge, MA: Belknap.

Nwabuzar, A. (2005) 'Corruption and development: new initiatives in economic openness and strengthened rule of law', *Journal of Business Ethics*, 59(1–2): 121–138.

O'Higgins, E. R. E. (2006) 'Corruption, underdevelopment, and extractive resource industries: Addressing the vicious cycle', *Business Ethics Quarterly*, 16(2): 235–254.

Paine, L. S. (2003) *Value Shift. Why Companies Must Merge Social and Financial Imperatives to Achieve Superior Performance*. New York: McGraw-Hill.

Phillips, R. (2003) *Stakeholder Theory and Organizational Ethics*. San Francisco: Berrett-Koehler.

Plaks, A. H. (2005) 'Golden rule', in Lindsay Jones (editor-in-chief) (2005), *Encyclopedia of Religion*, 2nd edn. Vol. 6. Detroit: Thomson, pp. 3630–3633.

Porter, M. E. and Kramer, M. R. (2006) 'Strategy and society. The link between competitive advantage and corporate social responsibility', *Harvard Business Review*, December: 78–92.

Prahalad, C. K. (2005) *The Fortune at the Bottom of the Pyramid*. Upper Saddle River, NJ: Wharton.

Rallapalli, K. (1999) 'A paradigm for development and promulgation of a global code of marketing ethics', *Journal of Business Ethics*, 18(1): 125–137.

Rawls, J. (1971) *A Theory of Justice*. Cambridge, MA: Harvard.

Rawls, J. (1996) *Political Liberalism*. New York: Columbia University Press.

Rich, A. (2006) *Business and Economic Ethics. The Ethics of Economic Systems*. Leuven: Peeters.

Richter, W. L. and Burke, F. (2007) *Combating Corruption, Encouraging Ethics: A Practical Guide to Management Ethics*. Lanham, MD: Rowman and Littlefield.

Rose-Ackerman, S. (2006) *International Handbook on the Economics of Corruption*. Northampton, MA: Edward Elgar.

Ruggie, J. G. (2007) *Business and Human Rights: Mapping International Standards of Responsibility and Accountability for Corporate Acts*. UN Document A/HRC/4/035, 19 February.

Ruggie, J. G. (2008) *Project, Respect and Remedy*: A Framework for Business and Human Rights. UN Document A/HRC/8/5, 7 April.

Ryan C. S. V., L. V. (2000) 'Combating corruption: the twenty-first century ethical challenge', *Business Ethics Quarterly*, 10(1): 331–338.

Sampford, C. J. G., Shacklock, A., Connors, C. and Galtung, F. (2006) *Measuring Corruption (Law, Ethics and Governance)*. Aldershot: Ashgate.

Savitz, A. W. (2006) *The Triple Bottom Line*. San Francisco: Jossey-Bass.

Schmidheiny, S. with the Business Council for Sustainable Development (1992) *Changing Course. A Global Perspective on Development and the Environment*. Cambridge, MA: MIT Press.

Schmidheiny, S. and Zorraquín, F. with the World Business Council for Sustainable Development (1996) *Financing Change. The Financial Community, Eco-Efficiency, and Sustainability*. Cambridge, MA: MIT Press.

Schulz, W. (1972) *Philosophie in der veränderten Welt*. Pfullingen: Neske.

Sen, A. (1985) *Commodities and Capabilities*. Amsterdam: North-Holland.

Sen, A. (1999) *Development as Freedom*. New York: Knopf.

Stiglitz, J. E. (2002) *Globalization and Its Discontents*. New York: Norton.

The Economist (2005) 'The good company. A sceptical look at corporate social responsibility,' January 22.

The Economist (2008) 'Just good business. A special report on corporate social responsibility', January 19.

The Ethical Corporation: Report on CSR in Africa (November 2002), Asia (June 2002 and September 2003), China (March 2003), India (April 2007), and Latin America (November 2005).

Turner, A. (2001) *Just Capital. The Liberal Economy*. London: Macmillan.

Tyler, C. (2000) 'The Age of Moral Confusion', *Financial Times*, April 22.

United Nations Development Program (UNDP) (2000) *Human Development Report 2000*. New York: Oxford University Press.

Vitell, S., Bakir, A, Paolillo, J., Hidalgo, E., Al-Khatib, J. and Rawwas, M. (2003) 'Ethical judgments and intentions: a multinational study of marketing professionals', *Business Ethics: A European Review*, 12(2): 151–171.

Vitell, S. and Paolillo (2004) 'A cross-cultural study of the antecedents of the perceived role of ethics and social responsibility',

Business Ethics: A European Review, 12(2/3): 185–199.

Vogl, F. (2007) 'Global corruption: Applying experience and research to meet a mounting crisis', *Business and Society Review*, 112(2): 171–190.

Werhane, P. H. and Freeman, R. E. (eds) (1997) *The Blackwell Encyclopedic Dictionary of Business Ethics*. Malden, MA: Blackwell.

Werhane, P. H. and Freeman, R. E. (eds) (2005) *The Blackwell Encyclopedia of Management. Business Ethics*, 2nd edn. Malden, MA: Blackwell.

Wilhelm, P. G. (2002) 'International validation of the Corruption Perceptions Index: Implications for business ethics and entrepreneurship education', *Journal of Business Ethics,* 35(3): 177–89.

World Commission on Environment and Development (WCED) (1987) *Our Common Future*. New York: Oxford University Press.

Zerk, J. (2007) 'Ultimate governance: The international regulation of corporate responsibility', *The Ethical Corporation*, January, pp. 38–41.

APPENDIX 1
AMERICAN MARKETING ASSOCIATION ETHICAL NORMS AND VALUES FOR MARKETERS

Preamble

The American Marketing Association commits itself to promoting the highest standard of professional ethical norms and values for its members. Norms are established standards of conduct expected and maintained by society and/or professional organizations. Values represent the collective conception of what people find desirable, important and morally proper. Values serve as the criteria for evaluating the actions of others. Marketing practitioners must recognize that they serve not only their enterprises but also act as stewards of society in creating, facilitating and executing the efficient and effective transactions that are part of the greater economy. In this role, marketers should embrace the highest ethical *norms* of practicing professionals as well as the ethical values implied by their responsibility toward stakeholders (e.g., customers, employees, investors, channel members, regulators and the host community).

General norms

1. Marketers must first do no harm. This means doing work for which they are appropriately trained or experienced so they can actively add value to their organizations and customers. It also means adhering to all applicable laws and regulations, as well as embodying high ethical standards in the choices they make.
2. Marketers must foster trust in the marketing system. This means that the products are appropriate for their intended and promoted use. It requires that marketing communications about goods and services are not intentionally deceptive or misleading. It suggests building relationships that provide for the equitable adjustment and/or redress of customer grievances. It implies striving for good faith and fair dealing so as to contribute toward the efficacy of the exchange process.
3. Marketers should embrace, communicate and practice the fundamental ethical values that will improve consumer confidence in the integrity of the marketing exchange system. These basic values are intentionally aspirational and include: honesty, responsibility, fairness, respect, openness and citizenship.

Ethical values

Honesty – this means being truthful and forthright in our dealings with customers and stakeholders

- We will tell the truth in all situations and at all times.
- We will offer products of value that do what we claim in our communications.
- We will stand behind our brands if they fail to deliver their claimed benefits.
- We will honor our explicit and implicit commitments and promises.

Responsibility – this involves accepting the consequences of our marketing decisions and strategies.

- We will make strenuous efforts to serve the needs of our customers.
- We will avoid using coercion with all stakeholders.
- We will acknowledge the social obligations to stakeholders that come with increased marketing and economic power.
- We will recognize our special commitments to economically vulnerable segments of the market such as children, the elderly and others who may be substantially disadvantaged.

Fairness – this has to do with justly trying to balance the needs of the buyer with the interests of the seller.

- We will clearly represent our products in selling, advertising and other forms of communication; this includes the avoidance of false, misleading and deceptive promotion.
- We will reject manipulations and sales tactics that harm customer trust.
- We will not engage in price fixing, predatory pricing, price gouging or 'bait and switch' tactics.
- We will not knowingly participate in material conflicts of interest.

Respect – this addresses the basic human dignity of all stakeholders.

- We will value individual differences even as we avoid customer stereotyping or depicting demographic (e.g., gender, race, sexual) groups in a negative or dehumanizing way in our promotions.
- We will listen to the needs of our customers and make all reasonable efforts to monitor and improve their satisfaction on an on-going basis.
- We will make a special effort to understand suppliers, intermediaries and distributors from other cultures.
- We will appropriately acknowledge the contributions of others, such as consultants, employees and co-workers, to our marketing endeavors.

Openness – this focuses on creating transparency in our marketing operations.

- We will strive to communicate clearly with all our constituencies.
- We will accept constructive criticism from our customers and other stakeholders.
- We will explain significant product or service risks, component substitutions or other foreseeable eventualities affecting the customer or their perception of the purchase decision.
- We will fully disclose list prices and terms of financing as well as available price deals and adjustments.

Citizenship – this involves a strategic focus on fulfilling the economic, legal, philanthropic and societal responsibilities that serve stakeholders.

- We will strive to protect the natural environment in the execution of marketing campaigns.
- We will give back to the community through volunteerism and charitable donations.
- We will work to contribute to the overall betterment of marketing and its reputation.
- We will encourage supply chain members to ensure that trade is fair for all participants, including producers in developing countries.

Implementation

Finally, we recognize that every industry sector and marketing sub-discipline (e.g., marketing research, e-commerce, direct selling, advertising, etc.) has its own specific ethical issues that require policies and commentary. An array of such codes can be linked to via the AMA website. We encourage all such groups to develop and/or refine their industry and discipline-specific codes of ethics in order to supplement these general norms and values.

Source: AMA Ethics Committee (O.C. Ferrell–chair; M. Etzel, G. Findley, G. Laczniak, L. Lee and P. Murphy – members). Approved in 2004 by AMA board.

Index

Research Methods Books from SAGE

Basics of QUALITATIVE RESEARCH 3e

Juliet Corbin
Anselm Strauss

The Mixed Methods Reader

Vicki L. Plano Clark ▪ John W. Creswell

DOING QUALITATIVE RESEARCH USING YOUR COMPUTER

A PRACTICAL GUIDE

CHRIS HAHN

SECOND EDITION
INTERVIEWS
Learning the Craft of Qualitative Research Interviewing

Steinar Kvale
Svend Brinkmann

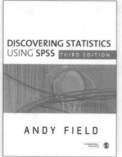

DISCOVERING STATISTICS USING SPSS THIRD EDITION

ANDY FIELD

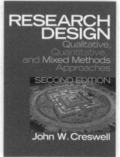

RESEARCH DESIGN
Qualitative, Quantitative, and Mixed Methods Approaches
SECOND EDITION

John W. Creswell

www.sagepub.co.uk

SAGE

Supporting researchers for more than forty years

Research methods have always been at the core of SAGE's publishing. Sara Miller McCune founded SAGE in 1965 and soon after, she published SAGE's first methods book, Public Policy Evaluation. A few years later, she launched the Quantitative Applications in the Social Sciences series – affectionately known as the "little green books".

Always at the forefront of developing and supporting new approaches in methods, SAGE published early groundbreaking texts and journals in the fields of qualitative methods and evaluation.

Today, more than forty years and two million little green books later, SAGE continues to push the boundaries with a growing list of more than 1,200 research methods books, journals, and reference works across the social, behavioral, and health sciences.

From qualitative, quantitative, mixed methods to evaluation, SAGE is the essential resource for academics and practitioners looking for the latest methods by leading scholars.

www.sagepublications.com